SETTLED 1700
A TOWN 1821
INDUSTRY
EDUCATION
PROGRESS
SACHEM'S ROCK
1649
CITY OF BROCKTON, 1881.

The My Lai Massacre and Its Cover-up:

Beyond the Reach of Law?

The My Lai Massacre and Its Cover-up:

Beyond the Reach of Law?

The Peers Commission Report
with a Supplement and Introductory
Essay on the Limits of Law

Joseph Goldstein
Burke Marshall
Jack Schwartz

Note:
The Peers Report is the work of General William R. Peers, not of a commission. The use of the word "Commission" in connection with the Report is an error.

The Editors

THE FREE PRESS
A Division of Macmillan Publishing Co., Inc.
NEW YORK

Collier Macmillan Publishers
LONDON

The Free Press
A Division of Macmillan Publishing Co., Inc.
866 Third Avenue, New York, N.Y. 10022

Collier Macmillan Canada, Ltd.

Library of Congress Catalog Card Number: 75-38298

Printed in the United States of America

printing number

1 2 3 4 5 6 7 8 9 10

Library of Congress Cataloging in Publication Data

United States. Dept. of the Army.
The My Lai massacre and its cover-up.

W. R. Peers, chairman of the inquiry.
Consists of the report first issued in 1974 under title: Report of the Department of the Army review of the preliminary investigations into the My Lai incident: volume I, The report of the investigation. Vols. 2 and 4 of the original report were not released and v. 3 was not reproduced.
Includes texts of documents from World War II and Nuremberg and from the Vietnam War.
1. My lai (4), Vietnam--Massacre, 1968. I. Peers, William R. II. Goldstein, Joseph. III. Marshall, Burke IV. Schwartz, Jack
V. Title.
DS557.8.M9U54 1976 355.1'334 75-38298
ISBN 0-02-912240-6 pbk.
ISBN 0-02-912230-9

Contents

SUPPLEMENT

From World War II and Nuremberg

From Vietnam War

Biographical Notes

WILLIAM R. PEERS is a graduate of the Army War College, 1953, and LL.D., Myongi University, Korea, 1973. He was commissioned Second Lieutenant, U.S. Army, 1938; advanced through grades to Lieutenant General, 1968; Operations Officer, OSS, Burma, 1942–43; Commander of Detachment 101, 1944–45; Deputy Director, China Theater, 1945; Intelligence Instructor, the Command and General Staff College, Fort Leavenworth, 1946–49; Director, CIA training, 1950–51; worked with Intelligence Department, Army, overseas, 1951–52; member of the Army General Staff for Operations, 1953–56; and at Headquarters, U.S. Forces, Europe, 1956–57. He was Commander, First Battle Group, Fifth Infantry, Germany, 1957–59; Executive Secretary, Weapons Systems Evaluation Group, Washington, 1959–61; Head, Liaison Group, Joint Strategic Targets, and Planning Staff, Joint Chiefs Staff, 1962–63. He served as Assistant Division Commander, Fourth Infantry Division, Fort Lewis, Washington, 1963–64; Assistant Deputy Chief of Staff of Military Operations for Special Operations, Special Assistant to Chief of Staff of Special Warfare Activities, and senior Army representative, Inter-American Defense Board, 1964–66. He was Special Assistant for Counter Insurgency and Special Activities, Joint Chiefs Staff, 1966–67; Commanding General, Fourth Infantry Division, U.S. Army, Vietnam, 1967–68; Deputy, later Commanding General, First Field Force, Nha Trang, Vietnam, 1968–69; and Chief, Office Reserve Components, Headquarters, Department of the Army, Washington, D.C., 1969–71. He headed the investigation of the My Lai incident, 1969–70, and later served as Deputy Commanding General, Eighth Army, Korea, 1971–73. He retired in 1973.

JOSEPH GOLDSTEIN is Walton Hale Hamilton Professor of Law, Science and Social Policy at Yale University Law School. A political scientist, lawyer, and psychoanalyst, he is the author of many books, including *The Government of A British Trade Union, Crime, Law and Society* (with Abraham S. Goldstein) and *Criminal Law: Theory and Process* (with Alan M. Dershowitz and Richard D. Schwartz). He served in the United States Army from 1943 to 1946. He holds degrees from Dartmouth College, The London School of Economics, and Yale Law School, and is a graduate (career research) of The Western New England Psychoanalytic Institute.

BURKE MARSHALL is Professor of Law at Yale University Law School, with undergraduate and law degrees from Yale. He served in the United States Army from 1942 to 1946, practiced law in Washington, D.C. until 1961, following law school, and was Assistant Attorney General of the United States in charge of the Civil Rights Division until 1965, and general counsel and Senior Vice-President of International Business Machines Corporation from 1965 to 1970. He was also Chairman of the National Advisory Commission on Selective Service, appointed by President Johnson in 1967 to review the selective service system, and is currently Chairman of the Boards of the Vera Institute of Justice, the Center for Community Change, and the Robert F. Kennedy Memorial.

JACK SCHWARTZ was an enlisted man in the U.S. Army for four years. In 1967 he served in Vietnam as a translator-interpreter. A graduate of the Yale Law School, he is now in government practice in Washington.

My Lai Chronology

1968

3–16 combat assault on Son My village

1969

3–29 Ridenhour's letter

4–23 case officially given to the Inspector General with instructions to make full inquiry

6–13 WO1 Thompson identifies Calley in a line-up as the lieutenant he had encountered at My Lai

8–4 Westmoreland orders the IG to turn over the investigation to the Criminal Investigation Division

9–5 charges brought against Calley—no details released

11–13 first Hersh story with rudimentary facts about My Lai published in 30 newspapers

11–14 SSG Mitchell charged with assault with intent to murder

11–20 second Hersh story with eyewitness accounts; Haeberle's black-and-white photographs published

11–24 Meadlo interviewed on CBS; Westmoreland orders Peers to conduct inquiry

12–13 Secretary of Defense Laird says in an interview that any present or former serviceman found to have had any role in the killing of civilians at My Lai would be brought to trial

1970

2–10 CPT Willingham charged with unpremeditated murder

3–10 CPT Medina charged with murder

3–14 Peers Report transmitted to Westmoreland

3–17 14 officers charged with offenses relating to cover-up, principally failure to obey regulations and dereliction of duty: Koster, Young, Henderson, Luper, Parson, Gavin, Guinn, Calhoun, McKnight, Watke, Boatman, Johnson, Medina, Willingham

6–9 all charges against Willingham dropped "for lack of evidence"

6–23 charges against Young, Parson, and McKnight dropped
11–20 Mitchell acquitted

1971

1–6 charges against Gavin, Guinn, Calhoun, and Watke dropped
1–29 charges against Koster dropped "in the interests of justice"
2–26 charges against Johnson dropped; Henderson ordered tried for dereliction of duty, failure to obey regulations, false swearing, and making false statement
3–29 Calley convicted
3–31 Calley sentenced to life
4–3 White House announces that Nixon will personally review and decide Calley case before sentence is carried out
5–19 Army disciplines Koster by reducing his rank to BG—both Koster and Young are stripped of their DSMs and given letters of censure
8–20 Calley's sentence reduced to 20 years by Third Army commander
9–22 Medina acquitted of all charges
12–17 Henderson acquitted of all charges

1972

9–2 Army completes administrative measures in connection with My Lai: Parson stripped of Legion of Merit, given letter of censure; Johnson given a letter of reprimand

1973

2–16 Court of Military Review upholds Calley conviction and 20-year sentence
4–12 Army announces retirement of Peers; Walsh, inquiry counsel, says move adds to "the impression that the Army was not really serious about punishing those responsible"
12–21 Court of Military Appeals upholds Calley conviction

1974

4–16 Secretary Callaway reduces Calley's sentence to 10 years
9–24 Calley's conviction overturned by District Judge Elliott
11–9 Calley released on bond
11–13 Peers Report released in part

1975

9–10 Calley released on parole
U.S. Court of Appeals for the fifth circuit reverses District Judge Elliot
Calley remains on parole

1975

10–10 *Calley* v. *Callaway*. In the Supreme Court of the United States: Petition for a Writ of Certiorai to the United States Court of Appeals for the Fifth Circuit

The My Lai Massacre
and Its Cover-up:

Beyond the Reach of Law?

The Limits of Law: On Establishing Civilian Responsibility for the Enforcement of Laws Against War Crimes

Joseph Goldstein, Burke Marshall, Jack Schwartz

In March, 1968:

> U.S. Army troops of the Americal Division massacred a large number of noncombatants (comprised almost exclusively of old men, women, and children) in two hamlets of Son My Village (known as My Lai), Vietnam. The precise number of Vietnamese killed was at least 175 and may exceed 400. (See Ch. 12, p. 314)
>
> A part of the crimes visited on the inhabitants [of My Lai] included individual and group acts of murder, rape, sodomy, maiming, and assault on noncombatants and the mistreatment and killing of detainees. They further included the killing of livestock, destruction of crops, closing of wells and the burning of dwellings within several subhamlets. (See Ch. 12, p. 315)
>
> At every command level within the Americal Division, actions were taken, both wittingly and unwittingly, which effectively suppressed information concerning the war crimes committed [at My Lai]. (See Ch. 12, p. 316)

These are some of the findings of Lieutenant General Peers in *The Report of the Department of the Army Review of the Preliminary Investigations Into the My Lai Incident*. The Peers inquiry was conducted more than a year and a half after the My Lai massacre, pursuant to an order issued jointly by the Secretary of the Army and the Chief of Staff on November 26, 1969. But for a letter from a civilian to the Secretary of Defense, that order to investigate the cover-up at My Lai might never have been given. In his letter of March 29, 1969, Ronald L. Ridenhour,

We wish to acknowledge the helpful criticism of Professors Joseph W. Bishop, Jr., Owen M. Fiss, Myres M. McDougal, and William Michael Reisman of the Yale Law School.

a veteran of Vietnam, presented evidence that he had gathered on his own in an effort to lay at rest or substantiate the persistent rumors of massacre at My Lai. Convinced that "something very black" had occurred, he admonished the Secretary:

> [I]f you and I do truly believe in the principles of justice and the equality of every man, however humble, before the law, that form the very backbone that this country is founded on, then we must press forward a widespread and public investigation of this matter with all our combined efforts.

General Peers conducted an investigation and forwarded a four-volume report to the Secretary of the Army and the Chief of Staff on March 14, 1970. This report of the cover-up at My Lai was kept secret for more than four years. In November 1974, the Secretary of the Army finally authorized publication of Volumes I and III.

To encourage a full-scale public examination of the implications for law and justice of both the massacre at My Lai and the efforts to suppress evidence of it, we decided to reproduce in full, for widespread distribution, Volume I of the Peers Report.* It consists of the analyses, findings, conclusions, and recommendations of the Peers inquiry. To place its findings and recommendations in context, we have supplemented the Report with materials related to the power of civil and military authorities to hold accountable those responsible for My Lai and its cover-up. The supplement, drawn from a seminar at Yale Law School, "On The Law's Capacity For Social Control," includes the instruction to the jury that led to the acquittal of Captain Medina, excerpts from the many *Calley* cases, the Moscow Declaration of 1943, the Charter of the International Military Tribunal, and case material from the war crime trials at Nuremberg and in the Pacific War Zone following World War II.

We publish the Report and Supplement to accord with that "larger obligation" which Telford Taylor addressed in his opening statement to the Nuremberg Tribunal in the case against the Nazi doctors for their crimes against humanity:

> The mere punishment of the defendants, or even of thousands of others equally guilty, can never redress the terrible injuries which the Nazis visited on these unfortunate peoples. For them it is far more important that these incredible events be established by clear and public proof, so that no one can ever doubt that they were fact and not fable; and that this Court, as the agent of the United States and as the voice of humanity, stamp these acts, and the idea which engendered them as barbarous and criminal.[1]

* For the convenience of the reader who might want to consult the original document, we have retained in Volume I cross references to materials not included in that volume but which can be found in the complete report.

And we publish for another reason: to press into active consideration a proposal that responds to the fundamental concerns posed by the Ridenhour letter and the Taylor statements. We later propose and discuss in detail the establishment of a jurisdiction, outside of the military, to investigate, prosecute and hold accountable those under our command who commit war crimes and crimes against humanity.

In releasing to the public the text of Volume I of General Peer's Report into the "My Lai Incident," Secretary of the Army Howard H. Callaway asserted that its release "concludes a dark chapter in the Army's history." "It is an incident," he continued, without revealing whether he had in mind the massacre, its cover-up, or the combination of the two, "from which the Army has learned a great deal. The lessons have been acted upon. . . . Today's soldier—today's Army—has learned from its anomalies of the past without losing sight of a better future." [2] Self-serving assurances like these are no longer credible to a citizenry informed by Watergate. Indeed, the use of the word "incident" in the title of the Report, which is pre-Watergate, and in the Secretary's announcement, which is post-Watergate, justifies asking whether the lessons of My Lai and its cover-up have even been identified, let alone learned. Common usage and most dictionary definitions emphasize the trivial, nonessential, and fortuitous quality of an occurrence called an "incident." To substitute "incident," or for that matter a phrase like "anomalies of the past," for accurate descriptions like "massacre," "murder of old men, women and children," and "destruction of war crimes evidence" is to debase the language and so destroy the ability of citizens to understand and evaluate the conduct of their government. Fraudulent word play like this is a form of institutional denial by which persons in authority habitually absolve themselves of responsibility, while righteously appearing to support a national commitment to respect for law and for man's dignity. "The first task of free men," as Judge Irving Younger observed, "is to call things by their right name." [3] Although the Peers Report often does call things by their right name, the reader is forewarned that it and its interpreters often do not.

Nor do the statistics on actions taken against individuals listed in the Peers Report buttress the Secretary's assertion about lessons learned and acted on. Instead, they evidence the Army's inability to enforce the law of war and to hold its people accountable for their part in crimes like those committed at My Lai. The Peers Report lists 30 individuals who were involved in criminal omissions and commissions, either at the massacre itself or during its cover-up. As of November 1974, when the Report was finally released, Calley was the only person among the 30 held to account through the system of military justice. Three others were brought to trial but acquitted. Charges brought against 12 of the 30 were dismissed before trial. Administrative action—presumably by demotion, or reprimand, or the like—was taken against seven of the twelve and one of the three acquitted after trial. Charges were also preferred against nine additional persons not listed in the Peers Report, but were dismissed before trial in the case of seven of the nine, the other two being acquitted on trial. We recite these facts not on the assumption that those listed are guilty, but rather to demonstrate that the Army has failed to establish who among those in command and in the field were responsible, and to hold them accountable, for what no one will deny were war crimes.[4]

Given the magnitude of the crime at My Lai and the Peers Report's plain documentation of its cover-up, this record cannot be explained by the difficulties of litigation, or the technical problems of courtroom constraints on admissible evidence, or essential weaknesses in the prosecutor's case. It must reflect underlying flaws in the system of accountability that have yet to be identified and understood inside the military or from outside. Is the problem one of process—of an incapacity of the military to sit in judgment of itself—comparable to the apparent disability of the executive branch that led to the creation of an independent special prosecutor to deal with Watergate? Is it a lack of clarity in the line between the killing that is inevitable and lawful in war and the killing that is a war crime, such that the military judges and juries sitting on the cases could not be sure that they would not have acted like the defendants, had they been there? Is the record a reflection of a lack of institutional will caused merely by the instinct of a bureaucracy to protect itself, or rather of legitimate and serious institutional concerns about the effect of aggressive enforcement of the law against war crimes on discipline in the field, and therefore on the safety as well as the efficiency of men in combat?

The *Calley* case holds that obedience to an order of a superior officer is not a defense to a war crime charge if the order was unlawful and its recipient knew that it was, or a man of ordinary sense and understanding would have known, even if the actual recipient did not.[5] This means, of course, that the duty of the soldier who receives an order is to determine whether it is unlawful, and if it is, to disobey it. If an order is disobeyed for this reason, but wrongly so, what kind of defense is permissible? Does the military recognize disobedience on good faith, or is every soldier—whose fundamental job description, career goals, and training, after all, command obedience—compelled to act at his peril, at the deadly risk of being second guessed, either formally by military judges, or informally by his superiors, for having made a mistake about the rules of warfare?

This question should not be left to the evolution of law through future court constructions if the military—if our polity—is serious about establishing disobedience to unlawful commands as a part of the practice and tradition of our armed services. The Peers Report, in detail and in its entirety, demonstrates the practice that exists in fact—to conceal and tolerate war crimes when they occur. Given this tradition of what the Peers Report beningly calls "a permissible attitude toward the treatment and safeguarding of noncombatants" (See Ch. 12, p. 314), it would take enormous courage, especially in combat, and particularly for a career soldier, to disobey even a plainly unlawful order.

If the courage of disobedience is to be recognized, justifiable disobedience to an unlawful order must become more than a technical defense to a charge. It must be rewarded in the ways that other acts of courage are rewarded in military life. Furthermore, the giver of the unlawful order, and those who countenance it, must be held accountable through a process that affords as much speed and sureness of result as is consistent with fairness. Neither the Peers Report nor other responses of the military to My Lai suggest that either part of this process of institutionalization has yet begun. And such a process cannot begin until the United States honestly faces, as the Peers Report does not, the strong and understandable resistance to holding its own men accountable for their war crimes. Only the acknowledgment of such natural resistance will allow the government to recognize the need to bring the force of law against war crimes, and to facilitate the development of an underlying consensus essential to its enforcement. The government must not either be so naive as to deny the inherent tension between the exigencies of combat and the enforcement of law or so intimidated by those realities as to be paralyzed. By engaging the harsh reality of war it will better see the need and the possibility of giving serious consideration to a proposal for the equal application of the Nuremberg principle to itself as well as to its enemies.

It is important to remember that the Nuremberg principle itself was developed by the United States and its allies not only as a response in law to the official barbaric policies of the Nazi government, which are primarily classified as crimes against humanity rather than war crimes, but also to small-unit war crimes committed in combat areas. An example appears in the following contemporaneous report of the killings at Oradour sur Glane in 1944, drawn from the evidence presented by the French prosecutor at Nuremberg:

> On Saturday, 10 June, beginning in the afternoon, a detachment of SS, belonging very likely to the "Das Reich" Division which was present in the area, burst into the village after having surrounded it entirely, and ordered the population to gather in the central square. It was then announced that a denunciation had indicated that explosives had been hidden in the village and that searches and verifications of identity were about to take place. The men were invited to group together in four or five units, each of which

was locked into a barn. The women and children were led into and locked in the church. It was about 1400 hours. A little later machine-gunning began and the whole village was set on fire, as well as the surrounding farms. The houses were set on fire one by one. The operation lasted undoubtedly several hours, in view of the extent of the locality and the town.

In the meantime the women and the children were in anguish as they heard the echoes of the fire and of the shootings. At 1700 hours, German soldiers penetrated into the church and placed upon the communion table an asphyxiating apparatus which comprised a sort of box from which lighted fuses emerged: A little time shortly thereafter the atmosphere became unbreathable. Someone was able to break the door which brought the women and children back to consciousness. The German soldiers then started to shoot through the windows of the church, and they came in to finish off the survivors with machine guns. Then they spread upon the soil inflammable material. . . .

An absolutely reliable witness was able to see the body of a woman holding her child in her arms at the entrance of the church and in front of the altar [sic] the body of a little child kneeling, and near the confessional the bodies of two children arm-in-arm. . . .

Outside the church the soil was freshly disturbed, children's garments were piled up, half burned. Where the barns had stood could be seen completely calcinated human skeletons, heaped one on the other, partially covered with various clothes. They constituted a horrible sight. . . .

Since that time an inquiry was conducted, and you will find it in the book which has been placed before you. The inquiry has shown that no member of the French Forces of the Interior was in the village. There was none within several kilometres. It is even proved that the causes of the massacre of Oradour sur Glane were distant and remote. The unit which perpetrated this crime apparently did so as an act of vengeance, because of an attempt against it about 50 kilometres away.

The German Army ordered a judicial inquiry: . . . The version given by the German authority is that: "The reprisals appear to be absolutely justified for military reasons. The German military commander who was responsible for it fell in combat in Normandy."

We recall the phrase "The reprisals appear to be justified for military reasons." Therefore, in the eyes of the German Army, the crime of Oradour sur Glane which I have described to you plainly, is a crime which is fully justified.[6]

"Justified for military reasons." Such was the mask for lawlessness and self-deception in the Americal Division after My Lai. Colonel Henderson's report of April 24, 1968, for example, concluded that "20 noncombatants were inadvertently killed when caught in the cross fire of the US and VC forces on 16 March 1968. It is further concluded that no civilians were gathered together and shot by US soldiers." (See Ch. 10, p. 286) Inadvertent civilian deaths—a justifiable, albeit regrettable, byproduct of guerrilla warfare.

Oradour sur Glane was, of course, only a fragment in the mosaic of Nazi butchery. It is true that the Peers Report is unequivocal in its condemnation of My Lai and its cover-up as a shocking betrayal of the standards of the U.S. Army. Oradour sur Glane was the straightforward execution of immoral German policy whereas My Lai, according to Peers, was the immoral flouting of clear American policy. Yet the conduct of American soldiers at My Lai is no more to be excused than that of the German soldiers depicted in the extract above, merely because it was forbidden by American law and official policy, as well as by the laws of warfare. What was done by Americans at My Lai might have been exceptional in its magnitude, but it was not unique, nor was it an isolated occurrence. The Peers Report itself finds that prior to My Lai "there had developed . . . a permissive attitude towards the treatment and safeguarding of non-combatants which was exemplified by an almost total disregard for the lives and property of the civilian population . . . on the part of commanders and key staff officers." (See Ch. 12, pp. 314–15) One need not accept every allegation in the antiwar literature to conclude that American soldiers in Vietnam committed numerous war crimes beyond those at My Lai even though there is no hard evidence of any other such crimes of comparable magnitude.[7]

The sincerity of the Peers Report is unquestionable. The sufficiency of its analysis is not. For Peers, the standards of the Army were limned in regulations. Again and again in his discussion of the actions of the Americal Division officers is the phrase, "It is difficult to understand why . . .:" why Major Watke took no effective action after receiving Warrant Officer Thompson's report, why Lieutenant Colonel Holladay took no steps to verify Thompson's allegations, why brigade and division commanders failed to inquire about the "highly unusual" tactical situation on March 16, why no officer acted upon what Peers terms "indicators of unusual events" at My Lai. His tone is of pained professionalism—how could these officers be so derelict, when their responsibility to act was clearly stated in regulations? Chapter 9 of the Report is a detailed review of all the rules, regulations, and directives that were supposed to prevent war crimes or, failing that, to ensure prompt, complete reporting and investigation.

Peer's attitude was even clearer in his conduct of the hearings. According to Seymour Hersh, Peers reacted to one witness's testimony about the pervasive practice in the Americal Division of concealing war crimes by reading excerpts from regulations forbidding such crimes.[8] To another's testimony about the burning of homes, Peers responded with a speech, the witness said later, "that sounded like it could be almost word for word from any Army manual."[9]

A regulation is not a talisman, but words only. And words are meaningless if they do not correspond to the world of the people who hear them. Men arrive at basic training with their moral autonomy intact, including the deeply rooted belief that it is wrong to kill one's fellow human beings. That belief is incompatible with warfare. So the Army's solution is "treatment for an unadjusted conscience," as a military psychology text once termed it.[10] Each soldier, trained for duty in Vietnam, heard the words of war crimes regulations in one hour of basic training amidst hundreds of hours of instruction on how to obey and how to kill. The method used to train them was simple enough: Don't think, just do what you're told. In bayonet drill when you thrust your weapon forward to impale your imaginary enemy, yell "Kill!" at the top of your lungs when your left foot hits the ground. Don't think about it, do it.

The place of the law of war in this regime of training is not surprising:

> . . . there were classes where the instructors cautioned us not to just shoot anything and to be careful. And you know, to preserve civilian lives and to treat the civilians decently. But these classes, well, there weren't many of them, and they were so short and they were so overshadowed by all of the other classes where the instructors constantly, you know, taught us "blow them away, blow them away," and I would also like to point out that the people who instructed us were noncommissioned officers, and most, if not all, were Vietnam veterans. And they would train us by the book as far as the class goes, they would tell us all of these little points the book says.
>
> Then they would turn around and tell us stories, their stories, which did not quite go along with what they taught us. They would tell us stories of blowing away civilians, of what to expect in Vietnam, and they would always refer to the Vietnamese as gooks, and slant eyes and dinks, and we got the overall picture, at least I did, and I believe most of the other guys got the impression, you know, you cannot trust anybody, and as long as nobody is watching to be hard, tough, and have no feeling, and blow them away. It was always blow them away.[11]

General Peers would decry this hypocrisy. His Report attributes to the 11th Brigade's training deficiencies a "significant part" of the reason for the massacre, and he recommends reform, although with no more specification than that "consideration be given to the modification of applicable policies, directives and training standards, in order to correct the apparent deficiencies. . . ." (See Ch. 12, p. 320) But he does not consider whether or how training in the law of war that gives authoritative voice to the obligation to disobey criminal orders, can be made meaningful consistent with the overall goal of military training—the molding of reflexively obedient killers.

The words of war crime regulations are tested anew in the world of the battlefield. The combat environment of any war precludes much ethical or legal sensitivity:

> In mortal danger, numerous soldiers enter into a dazed condition in which all sharpness of consciousness is lost. When in this state, they can be caught up into the fire of communal ecstasy and forget about death by losing their individuality, or they can function like cells in a military organism, doing what is expected of them because it has become automatic. It is astonishing how much of the business of warfare can still be carried on by men who act as automatons, behaving almost as mechanically as the machines they operate.[12]

The Vietnam war added its own vicious strains. It was a war in which all Vietnamese were regarded as a subhuman species called "gooks," in which everyone remaining in a free-fire zone after efforts to evacuate noncombatants was presumed to be an enemy, and in which military effectiveness was calculated by body counts. The enemy, when he was not simply a statistic, was little more than an element of technology, either the unseen artificer of the crude technology of his booby traps or the unseen object of the sophisticated technology of our aircraft and artillery.

War crimes regulations could mean little to the GI in the field, whose reality was an incomprehensible sequence of boredom and fatigue and terror—whose chief measure of his own lost humanity was the number of days left until he returned to "The World."

The Peers Report takes Colonel Barker to task for his "inability to make the kind of distinctions required of successful commanders in the Vietnam war." (See Ch. 8, p. 200) But the essential fact about Vietnam was that distinctions were not made—whatever the regulations purported to require—could not be made so long as military success was synonymous with killing. "The concept of a battlefield war crime did not exist in the 11th Brigade," [13] or anywhere else in Vietnam, except in the words of the regulations. Lieutenant Calley, in a single terse answer during cross-examination at his court-martial, stated a truth about Vietnam that General Peers does not engage: "I didn't discriminate between individuals in the village, sir. They were all the enemy, they were all to be destroyed, sir." [14] In other words, "justified for military reasons."

The question comes down to whether an army can effectively impose upon itself obligations of lawful conduct that would impair its right to use violence. The German military in World War II frankly ignored the law of war; military necessity knew no law. The Army in Vietnam proclaimed it in words and ignored it in practice. The Peers Report judges men's actions with a kind of noble blindness, treating law as if it were a part of each soldier's reality and as if compliance with it were compatible with the waging of counter-insurgency warfare. The section on "Omissions and Commissions by Individuals" is in substance a criminal indictment. It is the most important vindication of the law of war since Nuremberg—perhaps more important, since it lacks all taint of victor's justice. To the objection that enforcing the law against war crimes is a hopeless task in a world governed by war, Peers would insist that military honor requires no less.

Must the Peers Report be yet another victim of military necessity? Or may it serve to force into view the need and the opportunity for understanding the plight of the soldier in the heat of combat, and thus the greater responsibility of law to hold his superiors accountable for war crimes and crimes against humanity? To answer these questions, we briefly recapitulate the lessons we have learned from the Peers Report and the massacre at My Lai, in order to place in context a proposal we make for responding to such criminal disasters.

As the Peers Report explicitly finds, there was an effective block preventing investigation or any other law enforcement effort with respect to the My Lai massacre until the Ridenhour letter of March 29, 1969. (See Ch. 2, pp. 55–56) The commander of the 11th Brigade "deliberately set out to conceal" what had happened (Finding 4); investigations within the Americal Division were "superficial and misleading" (Finding 5); efforts were made "at every level of command from company to division to withhold and suppress information" (Finding 6); and these failures "served to suppress effectively information concerning the matter received from the Vietnamese." (Finding 7)

Only Ridenhour's personal decision, one year after the massacre, to break out of official channels and go public prompted action. The Peers Report, therefore, correctly starts with his letter; nothing would have happened without something like it—no effective investigation, no charges, no trials, no punishment, no publicity or official response of any kind. Even after a torrent of publicity about My Lai, the documents evidence doubt by General Peers and his superiors that a believable investigation and report would take place. Thus General Westmoreland, as well as Secretary Resor, signed all documents ordering the Peers investigation, perhaps to show that more than transitory civilian interest was involved, and to ensure cooperation by military career men. Thus, also, General Peers almost immediately responded to the need for "public recognition and acceptance of the objectivity of the inquiry and its effectiveness" by the appointment as legal counsel of "a distinguished jurist of impeccable integrity." (See Chap. 1, p. 30)

The Peers Report starts with the Ridenhour letter, but also stops with it, in accordance with the original directives to General Peers confining the inquiry to "the time period beginning March 1968 until Mr. Ronald L. Ridenhour sent his letter, dated 29 March 1969, to the Secretary of Defense and others." (See p. 34) Its primary function was not so much to establish the underlying truth about the massacre, since it expressly did not include the subject matter of criminal investigations then underway, as to establish the truth about the cover-up during that period. It is not concerned at all with the period between the Ridenhour letter and the start of the Peers inquiry itself, some seven months later. It predates, and therefore cannot take into account, the statistics showing one conviction on charges out of all those involved in the underlying crime and its cover-up. It obviously also could not take into account the fact that it was kept secret from March 1970 until November 1974. Finally, its three sentences of recommendation (See Ch. 12, p. 320) are confined to suggesting legal action limited to the My Lai events themselves, and a review of training methods; they deal not at all with either the adequacy of the military procedures in dealing with crimes such as the massacre, or the inevitable efforts at their cover-up.

Within the confines of his charter, General Peers did notable work. His report is thorough in detail and generally forthright in its findings. Yet the net institutional response to the My Lai massacre and its cover-up is to continue to rely on self-correcting mechanisms that the Peers Report itself shows do not work under stress, and that the subsequent Watergate affair shows we should not rely on in matters of great public importance.

We are convinced that the Peers Report and the events preceding and following it call for something more. As matters stand, the aftermath of My Lai is wholly unsatisfactory.[15] It reveals the military's institutional incapacity to deter, or punish, or even bring to light that kind of crime, and it therefore requires institutional changes to make the nation's commitment to the Nuremberg principle credible, even to itself.

We specifically urge that an appropriate body—either a congressional committee or a presidential commission or both—explore how best to separate from the military responsibility for the function of investigating and prosecuting crimes like the My Lai massacre (and related obstructions of justice). We propose that the inquiry begin with a detailed evaluation of the possibility of vesting jurisdiction for the trial and punishment of such crimes in the United States District Court for the District of Columbia, and responsibility for their prosecution in the Department of Justice.

Our proposal raises difficult and complex questions that must be examined with great care:

1. *Does Congress have the power to give courts in the United States jurisdiction to try and to punish persons for acts done outside the United States?*

The answer is clearly "yes," provided that there is a sufficient connection between the crimes and some identifiable interest of the United States. In the case of war crimes and crimes against humanity committed by United States personnel, the connection is plainly sufficient. Indeed, the *Yamashita* case, which we have included in these materials, upholds the assertion of power by an American tribunal over crimes committed by a foreign enemy national, not even against American troops but against Philippine civilians. There has never been any question of the validity of the exercise by the military of the authority to prohibit and to punish conduct by its own men anywhere. Congress is expressly granted power in Article I, Section 8 of the Constitution "to make Rules for the Government and Regulation of the land and naval Forces," and there seems no reason why it cannot do so by entrusting the enforcement machinery over particular military-connected crimes to an appropriate civilian tribunal instead of to the military. Moreover, crimes like My Lai are plainly in violation not only of the military law of the United States, but also of the international law of war, and Congress has the additional power to implement these international obligations explicitly and to prescribe punishments, under its authority "to define and punish . . . offenses against the Law of Nations." There are decisions holding that the United States has authority without any explicit congressional action to prosecute and punish violations of the law of war.[16] However, we believe that in the interest of fairness and orderly process, as well as national policy, Congress should itself define the offenses and prescribe the punishments that will implement the commitment of the United States to its obligations under the international law of war.

2. *Is the United States District Court for the District of Columbia an appropriate civilian tribunal for this purpose?*

One legal problem stems from the fact that this court probably is what is known as a "constitutional court" established pursuant to Article III of the Constitution to exercise the judicial power of the United States as it is defined in Article III.[17] It is thus to be contrasted with a tribunal created by Congress to exercise regulatory function under one of the specific grants of legislative (as against judicial) authority under Article I, such as a military tribunal, or special civilian tribunal, set up to implement rules for the government of the armed forces under the provision just quoted. But there seems to be no reason why Congress could not (although it has not, to date) confirm the prohibition against war crimes and crimes against humanity in the federal criminal code, thus making adjudication of such criminal cases part of the judicial business of the federal courts, and then vest exclusive jurisdiction over them in the United States District Court for the District of Columbia. Article III generally gives a person charged with a federal crime the right to be tried where the crime was committed, as well as right to trial by jury, but it goes on to say that when the crime was "not committed within any State, the Trial shall be at such a Place or Places as the Congress may by law have directed."

3. *Would it not be better to set up a special civilian tribunal to try*

such cases, rather than entrust their trial to a court of general jurisdiction with no special experience with military matters?

We think not, even though there is no question that Congress has the power to do so. For one thing, a special tribunal would have an inconstant work load, sudden peaks of activity followed by spells with no work at all. This was one of the many objections to Watergate-related proposals for the creation of a permanent Special Prosecutor independent of the Department of Justice. Agencies with no continuing functions—for example, the Subversive Activities Control Board—tend to atrophy. Second, a more significant basis for objection is the process of cooptation that takes place in special constituency agencies like the Federal Communications Commission, the Civil Aeronautics Board, and the Interstate Commerce Commission.[18] Cooptation occurs when the special agency is in effect captured by the industries or groups whose activities are to be regulated. Experience suggests that if a special prosecutorial office and court were created for war crimes alone, their limited jurisdiction might lead to overreliance on military "expertise." For these reasons we have expressly proposed vesting trial jurisdiction in a court of general jurisdiction and the prosecutorial function in the Attorney General, who need not keep an office manned solely for this function.

4. *Can the District Court in Washington really grant persons accused of war crimes a fair and speedy trial?*

The constitutional path we have proposed would unquestionably require that trial be by jury, a procedural difficulty that has simply been avoided by the use of military tribunals. However, there is no reason to think that a District of Columbia jury would not be as fair and responsible as a jury selected from some other area, or that it could be successfully challenged on constitutional grounds simply because its members had no connection with the geographic location of the crime, or the kind of local knowledge that juries were supposed to have when they were first used. A serious problem might well arise in some cases because of the absence of compulsory process over witnesses in other countries. The inability of the court to compel their attendance might constitute a denial of due process of law in a particular case if the defense were able to show that it was incapacitated in presenting its defense by the absence of the witnesses. This is a problem, however, that would arise, if at all, from the nature and location of the crime involved, and not from the location or authority of the tribunal conducting the trial. The District Court can deal with it, and other such complications, as expeditiously and fairly as could any other forum.

5. *Is it possible to define the offenses of war crimes and crimes against humanity with sufficient specificity so as to distinguish them from the ordinary crimes they include, like murder, assault, rape, pillage and arson?*

We recognize that there will be considerable technical drafting and substantive difficulty in defining war crimes and crimes against humanity in a way that is sufficiently concrete to withstand constitutional challenge on the grounds of vagueness. The definitions taken from Nuremberg, which we have included in this book, might not meet this constitutional test. Yet this is a task that ought to be amenable to resolution by lawyerly skills. Both war crimes and crimes against humanity have an historical context from which to build. Equally difficult problems of legislative writing have been overcome in giving content to complex federal crimes like those consisting of the deprivation of civil rights by official or private action.

The problem of duplication, of dual jurisdiction, is inescapable, however. Many war crimes and crimes against humanity are made up of acts that under our system would include regular military offenses like murder, rape, and pillage, as well as offenses under whatever local law is effective in the area. This will cause administrative complications of a sort familiar to American lawyers and courts because of the many instances in which the same underlying conduct is subject to concurrent federal and state prosecution. It may also lead to constitutional litigation on double jeopardy grounds in cases where the same acts are in fact the subject of prosecution both under military law and in the federal court. However, this matter, like the claim of vagueness, is the kind of legal question that the federal courts and the appellate process are best equipped to resolve. The quite extensive experience with similar problems in federal–state relationships affords no ground for a belief that such complexities are insurmountable, or that they would seriously hamper execution of a decision to make civilian prosecution of war crimes a fact of national policy.

As difficult and complex as these issues are, they must not become justifications for inaction. They must not become acceptable explanations for not establishing an authority, outside of the military, to investigate, prosecute, and hold accountable those who, under our command, commit war crimes and crimes against humanity. However those crimes come to be defined, there can be no question that they must include such massive killings of infants, women, and the aged as occurred at My Lai on March 16, 1968, as well as any efforts by those in command to suppress evidence of such criminal activity.

The law does not fail when crimes are committed, for no law against crime—not even against murder—can prevent all crimes. The law fails when it does not seek to discover and hold responsible those who commit crime.

The Peers Report is at once a powerful vindication of the law of war and an example of the military's ignoble failure to enforce that law. In its aftermath, the United States has the opportunity, as only a powerful and confident democracy could, to demonstrate that Nuremberg is law for its people and not just "law" which the strong and victorious impose upon the weak and the vanquished.

Notes

1. United States v. Karl Brandt *et al.* 1. *Tribunal of War Criminals* (Nuremberg Military Tribunals), 27–29 (1946).
2. Statement of Nov. 13, 1974, p. 4, reproduced in full infra.
3. People v. McMurty, 314 N.Y.S.2d 194, 197 (N.Y. Crim. Ct. 1970).
4. It should be noted that the Supreme Court has held that the military cannot constitutionally court-martial civilians who have been discharged from the army for acts committed while they were in the military. Toth v. Quarles, 350 U.S. 18 (1955). It is not clear from the statistics made public with the Peers report how many escaped liability for this reason, or how many of those could have been prosecuted but for delays for which the military itself was responsible, either because of the cover-up or for other reasons.
5. United States v. Calley, 22 U.S.M.C.A. 534, 48 C.M.R. 19 (1973) (reprinted infra); see also U. S. v. Keenan, 15 U.S.C.M.A. 108, 39 C.M.R. 108 (1969).
6. *The Trial of German Major War Criminals,* 331–333 (1946).
7. Reported cases: see, e.g., United States v. Keenan, 18 U.S.C.M.A. 108, 39 C.M.R. 108 (1969); United States v. Schultz, 18 U.S.C.M.A. 133, 39 C.M.R. 133 (1969); United States v. Crider, 45 C.M.R. 815 (N.C.M.R. 1972); United States v. Willey, 44 C.M.R. 390 (A.C.M.R. 1971); United States v. Bumgarner, 43 C.M.R. 559 (A.C.M.R. 1970); United States v. Griffen, 39 C.M.R. 586 (A.B.R. 1968); United States v. Potter, 39 C.M.R. 791 (N.B.R. 1968).

   Unreported courts-martial: *The New York Times,* quoting Army sources, said that of those charged with crimes in Vietnam similar to that for which First Lieut. William L. Calley, Jr. was convicted, 38 had been convicted under U.C.M.J. Art. 118 (murder), 20 had been convicted of lesser offenses, and 23 had been acquitted. *The New York Times,* April 7, 1971, 12, col. 4.

   Other war crimes: see generally Citizens Commission of Inquiry (ed.), *The Dellums Committee Hearings on War Crimes in Vietnam* (1972); Vietnam Veterans Against the War, *The Winter Soldier Investigation* (1972); Kunen, *Standard Operating Procedure* (1971); Coates, Limquero, and Weiss (eds.), *Prevent the Crime of Silence* (1971); Russell, *War Crimes in Vietnam* (1967).
8. Hersh, *Cover-Up,* 237 (1972).
9. Hersh, *My Lai 4,* 175 (1970).
10. National Research Council, *Psychology for the Armed Services,* E. G. Boring (ed.) (1945).
11. *Dellums Committee Hearings, op. cit.,* 271–272.
12. Gray, *The Warriors,* 2d Edition, 102 (1970).

13. Hersh, *Cover-Up, op. cit.,* 50 (1972).
14. Quoted in Hammer, *The Court-Martial of Lt. Calley,* 263 (1971).
15. Joseph W. Bishop, Jr. in *Justice Under Fire,* 291–292 (1974), commenting on the My Lai prosecutions said:

> Some of the acquittals were probably unjustified, and in at least one case, that of Captain Ernest Medina, the acquittal may have been based on the military judge's erroneous instruction that Medina had no responsibility for the My Lai massacre unless he had "actual knowledge" of it: as laid down by the Supreme Court in General Yamashita's case, the law is that a commander is responsible for war crimes committed by his subordinates if he knew, *or should have known,* that they were going on and failed to do what he could to prevent or punish them. It is also safe to assume that many war crimes committed by Americans have never been investigated, tried, or punished. The Pentagon has not shown much enthusiasm for investigating the possible failures of commanders at divisional and higher levels to take adequate measures to prevent and punish war crimes. Moreover, the Department of Justice seems to take the position that an honorably discharged serviceman cannot be tried for a war crime committed prior to his discharge. The Supreme Court did hold some years ago that such a discharged soldier could not be tried for an ordinary offense —*i.e.,* one that was not a war crime—committed prior to his discharge. But it had earlier held, in World War II, that a Nazi saboteur who was an American civilian could constitutionally be tried by a military commission for a war crime, and it did not overrule that decision. I am myself of the opinion (though I seem to be in the minority) that a discharged serviceman *can* be tried by a military court on a charge of violating the law of war. In any case, Congress could and should give the federal courts jurisdiction to try such cases: under the Geneva Conventions, in fact, the United States in obligated to "enact any legislation necessary to provide effective penal sanctions" for persons committing "grave breaches."
>
> The record is thus very far from perfect. All that can be said is that it is a better record than that of any other nation in the world and that it lends a degree of credibility to the Pentagon's numerous orders and regulations that aim to prevent and punish war crimes by requiring a report and an investigation of such incidents, and the training and indoctrination of the troops on the subject.

16. See *ex parte Quirin,* 317 U.S. 1 (1942); *The Paquet Habana,* 175 U.S. 677, 700 (1900).
17. Articles I and III provides in pertinent part: Art. I, Section 8:

> The Congress shall have the power . . . to constitute Tribunals inferior to the Supreme Court.

Art. III, Section 1:

> The judicial power of the United States, shall be vested in one Supreme Court, and in such inferior courts as the Congress may from time to time ordain and establish.

Art. III, Section 2:

The judicial power shall extend to . . . the trial of all Crimes.

18. See e.g., Huntington, "The Marasmus of the ICC: The Commission, The Railroads, and the Public Interest," 61, *Yale L.J.*, 467 (1952).

THE PEERS COMMISSION REPORT

Statement of Secretary of the Army
Howard H. Callaway
To Accompany Release of the Peers Report
November 13, 1974

I am today making available for release to the public the text of Volume I and all but two of the documentary exhibits contained in Volume III of the "Report of the Department of the Army Review of the Preliminary Investigations into the My Lai Incident," commonly referred to as the "Peers Report".

Volume I consists of the analyses, findings, conclusions, and recommendations that were provided to Secretary Resor and General Westmoreland in March 1970 by Lieutenant General William R. Peers, the investigating officer, and the distinguished civilians and officers who assisted him. Volume III contains all of the documentary evidence amassed by the Inquiry other than witness testimony and reports of criminal agency investigations into the My Lai incident. The testimony and investigation reports, which are contained in Volumes II and IV respectively, are not being released. The only parts of Volume I not being made available at this time are the footnotes accompanying the text which refer to material contained in Volumes II and IV of the Report. Book 1 of Volume III contains two Republic of Vietnam Armed Forces documents now classified confidential. These documents also will not be released.

Ever since submission of the Report, more than four years ago, there has been considerable public interest of the press, individual representatives of Congress, and concerned citizens, as to the information developed during the course of the Peers Inquiry. However, as noted by Secretary Resor on March 17, 1970, the Report could not then be made available to the public "because of the obvious potential for prejudice in ongoing court-martial cases." In the opinion of my lawyers, disclosure of any of the matter contained in the Report would have affected adversely both investigatory as well as judicial proceedings, and would have unduly prejudiced the rights of individuals whose conduct in the My Lai incident and its aftermath needed to be subjected to adjudication, either judicial or administrative in nature.

I note that a great deal of material regarding the My Lai incident has already been made available to the public both through the press and through various reports of Department of the Army proceedings concerned with the incident. The latter include court-martial records which contain not only the testimony of various witnesses, but also much documentary material, including Army records germane to the scope of the Peers Inquiry. I believe that the material which is already in the public domain, when coupled with that contained in Volumes I and III of the Peers Report, which I am releasing today, provides the public with a complete account of the facts and conclusions developed during the Inquiry. In addition, I note that the Congress, through its Armed Services Committees, was provided the complete report of the Peers Inquiry immediately following its completion in March, 1970. Also, full access to the entire report was given to both the attorneys for the prosecution and the defense in the course of the Calley court-martial.

The decision that I announce today was most difficult to make, and was arrived at only after a thorough review of all the interests involved. Most importantly, I have had to weigh carefully the public interest in obtaining a complete account of the events surrounding the My Lai incident and its aftermath, against the possible harm to the lives and reputations of various individuals which could result from public release of certain material contained in the Report.

The findings and conclusions contained in Volume I are based upon the voluminous evidence amassed during the Inquiry. In reconstructing the events that occurred, the Inquiry necessarily was required to judge the credibility of the various witnesses and to weigh the evidence presented. Volume I thus reflects the considered judgment of those individuals who had the opportunity to observe the demeanor of witnesses and to pose questions designed to bring the facts to light.

I am acutely aware that release of Volume I, insofar as it reflects determinations that certain named individuals failed in their duty to report the My Lai incident or suppressed evidence concerning it, may have a detrimental impact upon the lives and reputations of those individuals and their families. However, after much deliberation, I have concluded that the interests of the Army and the nation are best served by making available to the public Volume I of the Report without deletion of any names. In use of this material, I urge anyone who may read it to exercise judgment and restraint, since much of the material being released has not been challenged in open forum.

With regard to the material contained in Volumes II and IV of the Report, I have concluded that continued protection is required. The evidence contained in these volumes includes hearsay of the kind which no judicial forum could accept, as well as impressions, suppositions, and mere rumors offered by witnesses testifying before the Inquiry. All of this evidence is raw, investigatory material. Because of the manner in which the Inquiry was conducted none of the individuals against whom allegations were made had the opportunity to cross-examine in the course of the Inquiry the witnesses making these allegations. Many of these individuals, for one reason or another, such as lack of sufficient evidence, or lack of jurisdiction, were never prosecuted or subjected to adverse administrative action, and may have managed to escape public attention altogether. I am convinced that release of Volumes II and IV could result in severe and irreparable damage to the lives, careers, and reputations of those individuals against whom allegations were made, many of whom may be completely innocent of any wrong-doing. After careful consideration I have concluded that the harm to individuals that could result from release of these volumes clearly outweighs the interest of public access to whatever additional information may be contained in these volumes which has not previously been made available to the public, or which is being provided through release of Volumes I and III.

As you know, the United States Court of Appeals for the District of Columbia has held that the Freedom of Information Act does not require the Army to release the Peers Report to the public. Agencies subject to the Act are, of course, always free to disclose voluntarily any records that would otherwise be exempt from release under the law. We continue to believe that the entire Peers Report is an investigatory file of the kind afforded protection under the Freedom of Information Act. However, in the same spirit with which we invoked the protection which the

Congress and the courts offered in the Act, we now relinquish reliance upon that protection insofar as Volumes I and III are concerned. The Court of Appeals' ruling will, of course, permit us to withhold the other volumes, and, as I have noted, we continue to believe there is a legitimate purpose in doing so.

Chapter 12 of the Report contains the findings of the Inquiry. Included are findings that 28 officers and two enlisted men mentioned by name, failed to report what they knew of the My Lai incident, or suppressed such information. As a sequel to Chapter 12, there is attached to this statement a list of those persons with explanatory notes as to whether adverse action was subsequently taken against them.

The release of this report concludes a dark chapter in the Army's history. It is an incident from which the Army has learned a great deal. The lessons have been acted upon. Army training has been revised to emphasize the personal responsibility of each soldier and officer to obey the laws of land warfare and the provisions of the Geneva and the Hague Conventions. The Army of 1974 is embarked on a course marked by new challenges and a renewed sense of purpose. Today's soldier -- today's Army -- has learned from its anomolies of the past without losing sight of a better future.

Volume I will be available to you on request today at the Public Information Division of General Hill's office. Volume III will also be available for scrutiny there for a few days before it becomes a part of the Army Library's reference section.

SUMMARY OF ACTIONS TAKEN AGAINST INDIVIDUALS LISTED IN PEERS REPORT -- "OMISSIONS AND COMISSIONS"

- Number listed: 30

  -- Number against whom charges were preferred: 16

  --- Number brought to trial: (4)

  • Number acquitted: (3)
  • Number convicted: (1)

  --- Number against whom charges were dismissed: (12)

  -- Number against whom administrative action was taken 8*

  -- Number against whom no action was taken: 14

  --- Number deceased: (4)
  --- Number civilians: (7)
  --- Chaplains: (1)
  --- Others: (2)**

- Additional personnel not listed in Peers Report against whom charges were preferred: 9

  -- Number against whom charges were dismissed: (7)

  -- Number acquitted: (2)

* These 8 personnel had charges preferred; charges against 7 were dismissed and 1 was tried by court-martial and acquitted.

** The two individuals were accused primarily of "failing to report" whatever knowledge they had of the incident to higher authority. One was the supporting aviation battalion commander and the other was assigned duty as Senior Advisor, 2d ARVN Division. Neither were in the chain of command of the maneuver elements involved.

DEPARTMENT OF THE ARMY
WASHINGTON, D.C. 20310

CS (Peers Inquiry)

14 March 1970

MEMORANDUM FOR: SECRETARY OF THE ARMY

CHIEF OF STAFF, US ARMY

SUBJECT: Letter of Transmittal

1. Pursuant to your directive of 26 November 1969, I have completed the investigation of facts and circumstances surrounding the original Army investigation of incidents which occurred during the pericd 16-19 March 1968 in Son My Village, Quang Ngai Province, Republic of Vietnam.

2. Forwarded herewith is the final report of investigation.

1 Incl
as

W. R. PEERS
Lieutenant General, USA

Volume I of the Report of the Department of the Army Review of the Preliminary Investigations into the My Lai Incident has been declassified and released by the Secretary of the Army. This volume contains the body of the report. It has not been altered in any way except to delete footnotes which refer in large part to material in Volumes II and IV which will not be released.

Volume III of the report has also been declassified and released by the Secretary of the Army. Due to its volume (seven books), however, it will not be reproduced. A complete set of Volume III is available for examination in the reference section of the Army Library, Room 1A 526 in the Pentagon.

For sale by the Superintendent of Documents, U.S. Government Printing Office
Washington, D.C., 20402 - Price $6.20
Stock Number 0800-00210

14 March 1970

MEMORANDUM FOR: SECRETARY OF THE ARMY

CHIEF OF STAFF, US ARMY

SUBJECT: Final Report of Investigation

I would like to record my concurrence in the basic findings of the report and my satisfaction with the manner in which the Inquiry has been conducted by LTG Peers. I am satisfied that every reasonable effort has been made to determine the full facts surrounding the original Army investigation of the incidents and that the report fairly records what was found.

Since joining the Inquiry on December 5, 1969, Mr. Jerome K. Walsh, Jr., and I, as civilian legal counsel, have served as integral members of the Inquiry team. Our advice has been continually solicited in the course of the Inquiry and our suggestions as to issues to be examined and information to be sought have been conscientiously pursued. We fully participated in the interrogation of witnesses, the review of the evidence and the preparation of the report. While there have been many aspects essential to the Inquiry and to a complete report which go beyond a layman's sphere of knowledge, every attempt was made by LTG Peers and members of his team to provide us with the background information required to enlarge our participation.

It became clear to me in the course of the Inquiry that the resources and technical competence of the Army itself were essential to a sound, thorough and effective examination of this matter. I am convinced that it was desirable from the point of view of the public and of all concerned that this matter in the first instance be fully examined by the Army. I believe it has been well done.

Robert MacCrate

ROBERT MacCRATE
Special Counsel

Chapter 1. Introduction

A. Purpose of the Inquiry

On 26 November 1969, the Secretary of the Army and the Chief of Staff, US Army, issued a joint memorandum directing Lieutenant General William R. Peers to explore the nature and scope of the original Army investigations of what occurred on 16 March 1968 in Son My Village, Quang Ngai Province, Republic of Vietnam, and to determine:

1. The adequacy of such investigations or inquiries and subsequent reviews and reports within the chain of command; and
2. Whether any suppression or withholding of information by persons involved in the incident had taken place (Inclosure 1).

The same memorandum specified that the Inquiry would be concerned with the time period beginning March 1968 and continuing until receipt by the Secretary of Defense and others of information concerning the incident in a letter dated 29 March 1969 (Inclosure 2). It was further provided that the Inquiry would neither include nor interfere with criminal investigations in progress. Mr. Bland West, Assistant General Counsel of the Army, was named as General Peers' deputy for purposes of the Inquiry.

B. Scope of the Inquiry

The primary focus of the Inquiry has been on the subsequent reports and investigations of the Son My incident rather than on the incident itself; however, it became apparent at an early stage that the adequacy of those reports and investigations could not be evaluated intelligently without a thorough undertaking of what actually took place during Task

Force (TF) Barker's operations in the Son My area on 16–19 March 1968.* Additionally, knowledge of the operational facts, including those relating to the commission of atrocities, was essential to a determination as to whether there had been any subsequent suppression or withholding of information by persons having a duty to report.

For these reasons, the scope of the Inquiry included a complete examination into the operational situation throughout TF Barker's area of operations (AO) during the period 16–19 March 1968, together with an exploration of the facts relating to atrocities committed in the course of such operations. The latter aspect was pursued in sufficient depth to determine the substantive facts concerning such atrocities, but no direct effort was made to establish the criminal liability of particular individuals for possible violations of criminal statutes or the law of war. The Office of the Provost Marshal General of the Army assumed responsibility for investigation of these possible violations in July 1969, and certain testimony and other evidence developed in the course of that investigation have been made available and incorporated in the record of this Inquiry.

C. Organization and General Conduct of the Inquiry

General Peers informed the Chief of Staff and Secretary of the Army on 30 November 1969 that he intended to proceed by:

1. Reviewing the facts then available for background information;
2. Collecting pertinent official records of units in Vietnam;
3. Locating and interrogating all witnesses known or determined to have information bearing on the incident; and
4. Preparing a report on the results of the investigation, including appropriate findings and recommendations (Inclosure 3).

On that same date, General Peers also recommended that a distinguished lawyer be made available to the investigative team in order to promote public recognition and acceptance of the objectivity of the Inquiry and to enhance its effectiveness (Inclosure 4). In response to this request, the Secretary of the Army obtained the services of Robert Mac-

* By memorandum to the Secretary of the Army and the Chief of Staff, US Army, dated 21 January 1970 (Inclosure 6), General Peers pointed out that the name "My Lai (4)" used on some US maps was a misnomer in the sense that it is not commonly used by the Vietnamese and that the operations of TF Barker under investigation took place in several of the hamlets and subhamlets of Son My Village. On 2 February 1970, the Secretary of the Army and the Chief of Staff, US Army, confirmed to General Peers that exploration of matters throughout all of Son My Village was considered to be within the scope of the original directive for investigation (Inclosure 7).

Crate, Esq., a partner in the New York law firm of Sullivan & Cromwell and a Vice President of both the New York State Bar Association and the Association of the Bar of the City of New York, who agreed to serve as special counsel. Jerome K. Walsh, Jr., Esq., of the New York law firm of Walsh & Frisch, was appointed associate special counsel.

An investigating team of Department of the Army personnel, including field grade officers having extensive experience in battalion-size combat operations in Vietnam and administrative and support personnel, was assembled to assist General Peers. Additional personnel were added to the team as requirements became more clearly defined. Further details respecting the organization, procedures, and methods employed in the course of the Inquiry are set forth in Inclosure 3.

On 9 December 1969, the Inquiry was officially designated as "The Department of the Army Review of the Preliminary Investigations into the My Lai Incident" (Inclosure 5) and was given the short title of "The Peers Inquiry."

The first phase of the Inquiry began at the Pentagon on 2 December 1969 with the taking of testimony from witnesses and the collection and review of documentary evidence. Interrogation of witnesses proceeded on a 6-day per week basis, and by 24 December, 39 witnesses had given testimony, some of them on more than one occasion. Simultaneously, the investigative team was assembling and studying numerous directives, orders, logs, reports, maps, photographs, and other evidentiary materials bearing upon the matters under review. On 13 December, two officers departed for Vietnam to provide the team with continuing in-country representation and to complete arrangements for the Vietnam phase of the Inquiry.

On 26 December, General Peers, the civilian special counsel, and other members of the investigating team departed for Vietnam. Other members of the team, under direction of the deputy, Mr. West, continued to examine additional witnesses at the Pentagon during the period General Peers was in Vietnam.

The Vietnam phase of the Inquiry, which continued from 28 December 1969 until 8 January 1970, involved the taking of testimony from or interviews with key personnel throughout the US military chain of command, US civilian personnel, officials of the Government of Vietnam, Army Republic of Vietnam (ARVN) officers and enlisted personnel, and Vietnamese civilians residing in the Son My Village area. Documents considered relevant to the Inquiry were obtained from various headquarters, including US military Assistance Command, Vietnam (USMACV); US Army, Vietnam (USARV); III Marine Amphibious Force (III MAF); Americal Division; and the 11th Infantry Brigade. Further documentation was made available to the team by various Republic of Vietnam (RVN) officials and ARVN headquarters. General Peers, the civilian special counsel, and other members of the investigative team made an on-site inspection of certain significant areas within Son My Village, and other such areas were closely inspected by General Peers at very low altitude utilizing an OH-6, a small, observation-type helicopter. Two members of the investigating team remained in Vietnam to continue the assembling of documents and to obtain further information from in-country witnesses as developments indicated the need.

The third phase of the Inquiry began with the return of General Peers and party to Washington on 8 January 1970. During his absence, the portion of the team working under Mr. West in Washington had interrogated 41 additional witnesses. In order to enable the investigative team to interrogate every person who might reasonably be expected to have useful information without unduly delaying completion of the Inquiry, General Peers established three interrogation teams to take testimony concurrently. A fourth team was added later for a limited purpose.* This procedure made it possible for the Inquiry to interrogate a total of 399 witnesses, some of them on several different occasions, and nevertheless complete the taking of testimony by 7 March 1970.

Editing, reviewing, and summarizing of the transcripts of testimony, preparation of exhibits, analysis of the issues and evidence, and drafting of portions of the report were carried forward by other members of the investigative team concurrently with the taking of testimony. Consequently, upon the completion of hearings in early March and despite the vast volume of assembled evidence, General Peers was in a position to complete his review and analysis of the evidence and to prepare this report within a minimum of time.

* During the operation of TF Barker on 16–19 March 1968, two rifle companies were employed on offensive operations in the Son My Village area. The third rifle company, A/3–1 Inf, was employed essentially in a blocking position north of Son My. The fourth interrogation team was established to check out a lead of possible misconduct by A Company. No reliable evidence of misconduct was developed and, therefore, the activities of A Company are not given detailed treatment in the report.

DEPARTMENT OF THE ARMY
WASHINGTON, D.C. 20310

26 November 1969

MEMORANDUM FOR LIEUTENANT GENERAL WILLIAM R. PEERS
218-34-7471

SUBJECT: Directive for Investigation

Confirming oral instructions given you on 24 November 1969, you are directed to explore the nature and the scope of the original U.S. Army investigation(s) of the alleged My Lai (4) incident which occurred 16 March 1968 in Quang Ngai Province, Republic of Vietnam. Your investigation will include a determination of the adequacy of the investigation(s) or inquiries on this subject, their subsequent reviews and reports within the chain of command, and possible suppression or withholding of information by persons involved in the incident.

Your investigation will be concerned with the time period beginning March 1968 until Mr. Ronald L. Ridenhour sent his letter, dated 29 March 1969, to the Secretary of Defense and others. The scope of your investigation does not include, nor will it interfere with, ongoing criminal investigations in progress.

The procedures contained in AR 15-6 are authorized for such use as may be required.

You are authorized to select and use on a full-time basis officer and civilian members of the Army whom you deem necessary for the conduct of the investigation. Your deputy is designated as Mr. Bland West, Assistant General Counsel, Department of the Army. Should you require other assistance, please let us know.

You will inform us at an early date of the expected completion date of your report.

W. C. WESTMORELAND
General, U.S. Army
Chief of Staff

Stanley R. Resor
Secretary of the Army

Mr. Ron Ridenhour
1416 East Thomas Road #104
Phoenix, Arizona

March 29, 1969

Gentlemen:

It was late in April, 1968 that I first heard of "Pinkville" and what allegedly happened there. I received that first report with some skepticism, but in the following months I was to hear similar stories from such a wide variety of people that it became impossible for me to disbelieve that something rather dark and bloody did indeed occur sometime in March, 1968 in a village called "Pinkville" in the Republic of Viet Nam.

The circumstances that led to my having access to the reports I'm about to relate need explanation. I was inducted in March, 1967 into the U. S. Army. After receiving various training I was assigned to the 70th Infantry Detachment (LRP), 11th Light Infantry Brigade at Schofield Barracks, Hawaii, in early October, 1967. That unit, the 70th Infantry Detachment (LRP), was disbanded a week before the 11th Brigade shipped out for Viet Nam on the 5th of December, 1967. All of the men from whom I later heard reports of the "Pinkville" incident were reassigned to "C" Company, 1st Battalion, 20th Infantry, 11th Light Infantry Brigade. I was reassigned to the aviation section of Headquarters Headquarters Company 11th LIB. After we had been in Viet Nam for 3 to 4 months many of the men from the 70th Inf. Det. (LRP) began to transfer into the same unit, "E" Company, 51st Infantry (LRP).

In late April, 1968 I was awaiting orders for a transfer from HHC, 11th Brigade to Company "E," 51st Inf. (LRP), when I happened to run into Pfc "Butch" Gruver, whom I had known in Hawaii. Gruver told me he had been assigned to "C" Company 1st of the 20th until April 1st when he transferred to the unit that I was headed for. During the course of our conversation he told me the first of many reports I was to hear of "Pinkville."

"Charlie" Company 1/20 had been assigned to Task Force Barker in late February, 1968 to help conduct "search and destroy" operations on the Batangan Peninsula, Barker's area of operation. The task force was operating out of L. F. Dottie, located five or six miles north of Quang Nhai city on Viet Namese National Highway 1. Gruver said that Charlie Company had sustained casualties; primarily from mines and booby traps, almost everyday from the first day they arrived on the peninsula. One village area was particularly troublesome and seemed to be infested with booby traps and enemy soldiers. It was located about six miles northeast of Quang Nhai city at approximate coordinates B.S. 728795. It was a notorious area and the men of Task Force Barker had a special name for it: they called it "Pinkville." One morning in the latter part of March, Task Force Barker moved out from its firebase headed for "Pinkville." Its mission: destroy the trouble spot and all of its inhabitants.

When "Butch" told me this I didn't quite believe that what he was telling me was true, but he assured me that it was and went on to describe what had happened. The other two companies that made up the task force cordoned off the village so that "Charlie" Company could move through to destroy the structures and kill the inhabitants. Any villagers who ran from Charlie Company were stopped by the encircling companies. I asked "Butch" several times if all the people were killed. He said that he thought they were, men, women and children. He recalled seeing a small boy, about three or four years old, standing by the trail with a gunshot wound in one arm. The boy was clutching his wounded arm with his other hand, while blood trickled between his fingers. He was staring around himself in shock and disbelief at what he saw. "He just stood there with big eyes staring around like he didn't understand; he didn't believe what was happening. Then the captain's RTO (radio operator) put a burst of 16 (M-16 rifle) fire into him." It was so bad, Gruver said, that one of the men in his squad shot himself in the foot in order to be medivac-ed out of the area so that he would not have to participate in the slaughter. Although he had not seen it, Gruver had been told by people he considered trustworthy that one of the company's officers, 2nd Lieutenant Kally (this spelling may be incorrect) had rounded up several groups of villagers (each group consisting of a minimum of 20 persons of both sexes and all ages). According to the story, Kally then machine-gunned each group. Gruver estimated that the population of the village had been 300 to 400 people and that very few, if any, escaped.

After hearing this account I couldn't quite accept it. Somehow I just couldn't believe that not only had so many young American men participated in such an act of barbarism, but that their officers had ordered it. There were other men in the unit I was soon to be assigned to, "E" Company, 51st Infantry (LRP), who had been in Charlie Company at the time that Gruver alleged the incident at "Pinkville" had occurred. I became determined to ask them about "Pinkville" so that I might compare their accounts with Pfc Gruver's.

When I arrived at "Echo" Company, 51st Infantry (LRP) the first men I looked for were Pfc's Michael Terry, and William Doherty. Both were veterans of "Charlie" Company, 1/20 and "Pinkville." Instead of contradicting "Butch" Gruver's story they corroborated it, adding some tasty tid-bits of information of their own. Terry and Doherty had been in the same squad and their platoon was the third platoon of "C" Company to pass through the village. Most of the people they came to were already dead. Those that weren't were sought out and shot. The platoon left nothing alive, neither livestock nor people. Around noon the two soldiers' squad stopped to eat. "Billy and I started to get out our chow," Terry said, "but close to us was a bunch of Vietnamese in a heap, and some of them were moaning. Kally (2nd Lt. Kally) had been through before us and all of them had been shot, but many weren't dead. It was obvious that they weren't going to get any medical attention so Billy and I got up and went over to where they were. I guess we sort of finished them off." Terry went on to say that he and Doherty then returned to where their packs were and ate lunch. He estimated the size of the village to be 200 to 300 people. Doherty thought that the population of "Pinkville" had been 400 people.

If Terry, Doherty and Gruver could be believed, then not only had "Charlie" Company received orders to slaughter all the inhabitants of the village, but those orders had come from the commanding officer of Task Force Barker, or possibly even higher in the chain of command. Pfc Terry stated that when Captain Medina (Charlie Company's commanding officer Captain Ernest Medina) issued the order for the destruction of "Pinkville" he had been hesitant, as if it were something he didn't want to do but had to. Others I spoke to concurred with Terry on this.

It was June before I spoke to anyone who had something of significance to add to what I had already been told of the "Pinkville" incident. It was the end of June, 1968 when I ran into Sargent Larry La Croix at the USO in Chu Lai. La Croix had been in 2nd Lt. Kally's platoon on the day Task Force Barker swept through "Pinkville." What he told me verified the stories of the others, but he also had something new to add. He had been a witness to Kally's gunning down of at least three separate groups of villagers. "It was terrible. They were slaughtering the villagers like so many sheep." Kally's men were dragging people out of bunkers and hootches and putting them together in a group. The people in the group were men, women and children of all ages. As soon as he felt that the group was big enough, Kally ordered an M-60 (machine-gun) set up and the people killed. La Croix said that he bore witness to this procedure at least three times. The three groups were of different sizes, one of about twenty people, one of about thirty people, and one of about forty people. When the first group was put together Kally ordered Pfc Torres to man the machine-gun and open fire on the villagers that had been grouped together. This Torres did, but before everyone in the group was down he ceased fire and refused to fire again. After ordering Torres to recommence firing several times, Lieutenant Kally took over the M-60 and finished shooting the remaining villagers in that first group himself. Sargent La Croix told me that Kally didn't bother to order anyone to take the machine-gun when the other two groups of villagers were formed. He simply manned it himself and shot down all villagers in both groups.

This account of Sargent La Croix's confirmed the rumors that Gruver, Terry and Doherty had previously told me about Lieutenant Kally. It also convinced me that there was a very substantial amount of truth to the stories that all of these men had told. If I needed more convincing, I was to receive it.

It was in the middle of November, 1968 just a few weeks before I was to return to the United States for separation from the army that I talked to Pfc Michael Bernhardt. Bernhardt had served his entire year in Viet Nam in "Charlie" Company 1/20 and he too was about to go home. "Bernie" substantiated the tales told by the other men I had talked to in vivid, bloody detail and added this. "Bernie" had absolutely refused to take part in the massacre of the villagers of "Pinkville" that morning and he thought that it was rather strange that the officers of the company had not made an issue of it. But that evening "Medina (Captain Ernest Medina) came up to me ("Bernie") and told me not to do anything stupid like write my congressman" about what had happened that day. Bernhardt assured Captain Medina that he had no such thing in mind. He had nine months left in Viet Nam and felt that it was dangerous enough just fighting the acknowledged enemy.

Exactly what did, in fact, occur in the village of "Pinkville" in March, 1968 I do not know for <u>certain</u>, but I am convinced that it was something very black indeed. I remain irrevocably persuaded that if you and I do truly believe in the principles, of justice and the equality of every man, however humble, before the law, that form the very backbone that this country is founded on, then we must press forward a widespread and public investigation of this matter with all our combined efforts. I think that it was Winston Churchhill who once said "A country without a conscience is a country without a soul, and a country without a soul is a country that cannot survive." I feel that I must take some positive action on this matter. I hope that you will launch an investigation immediately and keep me informed of your progress. If you cannot, then I don't know what other course of action to take.

I have considered sending this to newspapers, magazines, and broadcasting companies, but I somehow feel that investigation and action by the Congress of the United States is the appropriate procedure, and as a conscientious citizen I have no desire to further besmirch the image of the American serviceman in the eyes of the world. I feel that this action, while probably it would promote attention, would not bring about the constructive actions that the direct actions of the Congress of the United States would.

Sincerely,

/s/ Ron Ridenhour

A TRUE COPY

C. D. LYNN
MAJ, AGC

30 November 1969

MEMORANDUM FOR: SECRETARY OF THE ARMY
CHIEF OF STAFF, UNITED STATES ARMY

SUBJECT: Investigation of the Adequacy of the Preliminary Inquiries into the My Lai (4) Case

REFERENCE: Memorandum, Sec/Army and CofS, subject: Directive for Investigation, 26 November 1969

1. This responds to your request in Referral Slip No. 58313, 26 November 1969, for a memorandum outlining the concept of the subject investigation, the organization of the investigative team, and an estimated completion date of the report of investigation.

2. Concept of Investigation.

The above reference assigns me the mission of determining the adequacy of the original inquiries into the My Lai (4) incident of 16 March 1968, the propriety of the command actions based thereon, and whether there was any improper suppression of information by persons in the chain of command or otherwise responsible for reporting the incident to superior authority. I have organized a team of investigative assistants and propose to accomplish the mission by reviewing the facts available to date for background purposes, collecting pertinent official records of the units in Vietnam involved in the assault on My Lai (4), locating and interrogating all witnesses known to have information bearing on the mission, and by preparing a report on the results of such investigation, including appropriate findings and recommendations.

3. Organization.

I will be assisted in the investigation by the following personnel:

Mr. Bland West, OGC (Deputy)
Colonel W. V. Wilson, OTIG
Colonel Robert E. Miller, OTJAG
Major E. F. Zychowski, OPMG
Mr. James S. Stokes IV, OGC
Major Clyde Lynn, Recorder
Four Court Reporters not yet named
Lieutenant Colonel J. H. Breen, Executive
Two or more clerk/stenos

SUBJECT: Investigation of the Adequacy of the Preliminary Inquiries into the My Lai (4) Case

Points of contact have been established with OCINFO, OCACSI, TAG and Headquarters USMC. Others will be arranged as required.

4. Tentative Schedule of Activities.

It is planned that the organization and administration will be finalized on 1 Dec 69 at which time personnel immediately associated with the investigation will be sworn in. The interrogation of witnesses will begin on 2 Dec 69. There being thirty to forty witnesses, the interrogations will probably go on for at least two weeks. Thereafter, a visit will be made to Vietnam to review records, reports, files and other pertinent documents. Upon return to the States additional testimony will be taken as required and the report drafted and finalized. The estimated date of completion is 10 Jan 70.

5. It is recommended that:

a. The investigation be given an official title to establish its separate identity and to facilitate communications.

b. Information as to its title and purpose be disseminated to appropriate military commands with instructions to provide requisite assistance.

W. R. PEERS
Lieutenant General, USA

30 November 1969

MEMORANDUM FOR: SECRETARY OF THE ARMY
CHIEF OF STAFF, UNITED STATES ARMY

SUBJECT: Appointment of Legal Counsel

REFERENCE: Memorandum, Sec/Army and CofS, subject: Directive for Investigation, 26 November 1969

1. As you are aware, intense interest has been expressed in Congressional quarters and by the public as to whether the preliminary inquiries into the My Lai (4) incident involved a "cover-up by the Army." I intend to conduct the investigation as directed by the above reference in a completely impartial manner. However, I believe that public recognition and acceptance of the objectivity of the inquiry and its effectiveness would be promoted if I had available to me a distinguished jurist of impeccable integrity. It is visualized that he would observe and appraise the investigation as it progresses and provide assistance and guidance as to the proceedings and any legal matters related thereto.

2. Accordingly, I recommend that you solicit the services of such an individual and designate him to serve as my legal counsel.

W. R. PEERS
Lieutenant General, USA

JOINT MESSAGEFORM

SECURITY CLASSIFICATION: UNCLAS EFTO FOR OFFICIAL USE ONLY

PAGE	DRAFTER OR RELEASER TIME	PRECEDENCE ACT	PRECEDENCE INFO	LMF	CLASS	CIC	FOR COMMUNICATIONS CENTER ONLY
01 OF 01		PP			EEEE		1969 DEC 9 00 04Z

BOOK — MESSAGE HANDLING INSTRUCTIONS

FROM: DA

TO: AIG 7401

UNCLAS E F T O FOUO

OCofSA

SUBJ: Investigation of Reporting of My Lai (4) Incident

General Westmoreland sends.

1. The Secretary of the Army and I have appointed Lieutenant General William R. Peers, 218-34-7471, to explore the nature and scope of the original U.S. Army investigation(s) of the incident which allegedly occurred on 16 March 1968 at My Lai (4) in Quang Ngai Province, Republic of Vietnam. Mr. Bland West, 446-01-8436, Office of the Army General Counsel, has been appointed as LTC Peers' Deputy. Selected Department of the Army personnel will assist LTG Peers.

2. LTG Peers' investigation will be referred to as "The Department of the Army Review of the Preliminary Investigations into the My Lai Incident" (Short title: "Peers' Inquiry").

3. Request you provide assistance to LTG Peers and members of his team as required.

DISTR: ADDED DISTR: OCS (PER SGT. CHANNEY, OCS) USCINCPA (...)
DCSOPS, DCSPER, TJAG, TPMG, CINFO, TIG, COPO, ACSC-E, TAG, CMH, OSA
COA, CLL, OCofSA, LTG PEERS' TEAM (LTC BREEN)
USCONARC-LO USAINTC-LO

998773 DA OUT 3773

DRAFTER TYPED NAME, TITLE, OFFICE SYMBOL AND PHONE: LTC JAMES H. BREEN, ODSGS (CAR), 50441/x295

RELEASER TYPED NAME, TITLE, OFFICE SYMBOL AND PHONE: GEN W. C. WESTMORELAND, CHIEF OF STAFF

SIGNATURE: W C Westmoreland

SPECIAL INSTRUCTIONS

UNCLAS E F T O

SECURITY CLASSIFICATION: FOR OFFICIAL USE ONLY

FOR OFFICIAL USE ONLY

DD FORM 1 JUL 68 173 REPLACES DD FORM 173, 1 NOV 63 AND DD FORM 173-1, 1 NOV 63, WHICH ARE OBSOLETE.

DEPARTMENT OF THE ARMY
WASHINGTON, D.C. 20310

CS(Peers Inquiry) 21 January 1970

MEMORANDUM FOR: SECRETARY OF THE ARMY

CHIEF OF STAFF US ARMY

SUBJECT: Scope of Investigation

1. Reference, Secretary of the Army/Chief of Staff US Army memorandum, Subject: Directive for Investigation, dated 26 Nov 69 (Tab A).

2. The above-referenced directive appoints the undersigned as the investigating officer to explore the nature and scope of the original US Army investigation(s) of the alleged My Lai (4) incident which occurred 16 March 1968 in Quang Ngai Province, Republic of Vietnam. Our recent visit to South Vietnam as well as the testimony taken to date indicate:

a. The name My Lai (4) as indicated on some US maps is a misnomer in the sense that it is not commonly used by the Vietnamese. That part so designated as My Lai (4) is referred to as Thuan Yen Sub-hamlet of Tu Cung Hamlet.

b. Activities which took place in Tu Cung Hamlet on 16 March 1968 involved at least parts of three other sub-hamlets, namely Binh Tay, Binh Dong and Trung Hoa.

c. There is evidence to show that other atrocities and/or violations of military regulations were committed in the other three hamlets of Son My Village, namely; Co Luy, My Lai and My Khe.

3. A chart showing the Vietnamese names for the hamlets and sub-hamlets in Son My Village as compared to those shown on US maps is attached at Tab B. A graphic portrayal of this information is at Tab C.

4. In light of the above, it is recommended that the geographic scope of the final report be extended to include the entire Son My Village. This would be more realistic in terms of the area and activities involved and would permit better

CS (Peers Inquiry) 21 January 1970
SUBJECT: Scope of Investigation

definition within the report of the actions which took place in some of the sub-hamlets.

5. Recommend the memorandum at Tab D be approved and signed.

W. R. PEERS
Lieutenant General, USA

4 Incl
as

DEPARTMENT OF THE ARMY
WASHINGTON, D.C. 20310

2 FEB 1970

MEMORANDUM FOR LTG WILLIAM R. PEERS

SUBJECT: Son My Investigation

The recommendation contained in your memorandum of 21 January 1970, to the effect that your inquiry in final report should cover all of Son My Village, Quang Ngai Province, Republic of Vietnam, is approved. The exploration of matters within Son My Village is considered to be within the scope of your original directive for investigation, dated 26 November 1969.

W. C. Westmoreland
General, U. S. Army
Chief of Staff

Stanley R. Resor
Secretary of the Army

Chapter 2. Summary Report

A. The Son My Village Incident

During the period 16–19 March 1968, a tactical operation was conducted into Son My Village, Son Tinh District, Quang Ngai Province, Republic of Vietnam, by Task Force (TF) Barker, a battalion-size unit of the Americal Division.

TF Barker was an interim organization of the 11th Brigade, created to fill a tactical void resulting from the withdrawal of a Republic of Korea Marine Brigade from the Quang Ngai area. The Task Force was composed of a rifle company from each of the 11th Brigade's three organic infantry battalions—A/3–1 Inf, B/4–3 Inf, C/1–20 Inf. The commander was LTC Frank A. Barker (now deceased).

The plans for the operation were never reduced to writing but it was reportedly aimed at destroying the 48th VC Local Force (LF) Battalion, thought to be located in Son My Village, which also served as a VC staging and logistical support base. On two previous operations in the area, units of TF Barker had received casualties from enemy fire, mines, and boobytraps, and had not been able to close effectively with the enemy.

On 15 March 1968, the new 11th Brigade commander, COL Oran K. Henderson, visited the TF Barker command post at Landing Zone (LZ) Dottie and talked to the assembled staff and commanders. He urged them to press forward aggressively and eliminate the 48th LF Battalion. Following these remarks, LTC Barker and his staff gave an intelligence briefing and issued an operations order. The company commanders were told that most of the population of Son My were "VC or VC sympathizers" and were advised that most of the civilian inhabitants would be away from Son My and on their way to market by 0700 hours. The operation was to commence at 0725 hours on 16 March 1968 with a short artillery preparation, following which C/1–20 Inf was to combat assault into an LZ immediately west of My Lai (4) and then sweep east through the subhamlet. Following C Company's landing, B/4–3 Inf was to reinforce

C/1–20 Inf, or to conduct a second combat assault to the east of My Lai (4) into an LZ south of the subhamlet of My Lai (1) or "Pinkville." A/3–1 Inf was to move from its field location to blocking positions north of Son My.

During or subsequent to the briefing, LTC Barker ordered the commanders of C/1–20 Inf, and possibly B/4–3 Inf, to burn the houses, kill the livestock, destroy foodstuffs and perhaps to close the wells. No instructions were issued as to the safeguarding of noncombatants found there.

During a subsequent briefing by CPT Medina to his men, LTC Barker's orders were embellished, a revenge element was added, and the men of C/1–20 Inf, were given to understand that only the enemy would be present in My Lai (4) on 16 March and that the enemy was to be destroyed. In CPT Michles' briefing to his platoon leaders, mention was also apparently made of the burning of dwellings.

On the morning of 16 March 1968, the operation began as planned. A/3–1 Inf was reported in blocking positions at 0725 hours. At about that same time the artillery preparation and fires of the supporting helicopter gunship were placed on the C/1–20 Inf LZ and a part of My Lai (4). LTC Barker controlled the artillery preparation and combat assault from his helicopter. COL Henderson and his command group also arrived overhead at approximately this time.

By 0750 hours all elements of C/1–20 Inf were on the ground. Before entering My Lai (4), they killed several Vietnamese fleeing the area in the rice paddies around the subhamlet and along Route 521 to the south of the subhamlet. No resistance was encountered at this time or later in the day.

The infantry assault on My Lai (4) began a few minutes before 0800 hours. During the 1st Platoon's movement through the southern half of the subhamlet, its members were involved in widespread killing of Vietnamese inhabitants (comprised almost exclusively of old men, women, and children) and also in property destruction. Most of the inhabitants who were not killed immediately were rounded up into two groups. The first group, consisting of about 70–80 Vietnamese, was taken to a large ditch east of My Lai (4) and later shot. A second group, consisting of 20–50 Vietnamese, was taken south of the hamlet and shot there on a trail. Similar killings of smaller groups took place within the subhamlet.

Members of the 2d Platoon killed at least 60–70 Vietnamese men, women, and children, as they swept through the northern half of My Lai (4) and through Binh Tay, a small subhamlet about 400 meters north of My Lai (4). They also committed several rapes.

The 3d Platoon, having secured the LZ, followed behind the 1st and 2d and burned and destroyed what remained of the houses in My Lai (4) and killed most of the remaining livestock. Its members also rounded up and killed a group of 7–12 women and children.

There was considerable testimony that orders to stop the killing were issued two or three times during the morning. The 2d Platoon received such an order around 0920 hours and promptly complied. The 1st Platoon continued the killings until perhaps 1030 hours, when the order was repeated. By this time the 1st Platoon had completed its sweep through the subhamlet.

By the time C/1–20 Inf departed My Lai (4) in the early afternoon, moving to the northeast for link-up with B/4–3 Inf, its members had killed at least 175–200 Vietnamese men, women, and children.* The evidence indicates that only 3 or 4 were confirmed as Viet Cong, although there were undoubtedly several unarmed VC (men, women, and children) among them and many more active supporters and sympathizers. One man from the company was reported as wounded from the accidental discharge of his weapon.

Since C Company had encountered no enemy opposition, B/4–3 Inf was air-landed in its LZ between 0815 and 0830 hours, following a short artillery preparation. Little if any resistance was encountered, although the 2d Platoon suffered 1 KIA and 7 WIA from mines and/or boobytraps. The 1st Platoon moved eastward separately from the rest of B Company to cross and secure a bridge over the Song My Khe (My Khe River). After crossing the bridge and approaching the outskirts of the subhamlet of My Khe (4), elements of the platoon opened fire on the subhamlet with an M–60 machinegun and M–16 rifles. The fire continued for approximately 5 minutes, during which time some inhabitants of My Khe (4), mostly women and children, were killed. The lead elements of the platoon then entered the subhamlet, firing into the houses and throwing demolitions into shelters. Many noncombatants apparently were killed in the process.

It is believed that only ten men in B/4–3 Inf directly participated in the killings and destruction in My Khe (4); two of these are dead and the remaining eight have either refused to testify or claim no recollection of the event. As a result, it has not been possible to reconstruct the events with certainty. It appears, however, that the number of noncombatants killed by B/4–3 Inf on 16 March 1968 may have been as high as 90. The company reported a total of 38 VC KIA on 16 March, but it is likely that few if any were Viet Cong.

On the evening of 16 March 1968, after C/1–20 Inf and B/4–3 Inf had linked up in a night defensive position, a Viet Cong suspect was apparently tortured and maimed by a US officer. He was subsequently killed along with some additional suspects by Vietnamese National Police in the presence of US personnel.

During the period 17–19 March 1968 both C/1–20 Inf and B/4–3 Inf

* Casualty figures cited for My Lai (4) were developed by this Inquiry solely on the basis of statements and testimony of US personnel. Separate estimates by the Criminal Investigation Division (CID) agency together with other evidence, indicate the number of Vietnamese killed in the overall area of Son My Village may have exceeded 400.

were involved in additional burning and destruction of dwellings, and in the mistreatment of Vietnamese detainees.

B. Reports of the Incident

1. REPORTS OF CIVILIAN CASUALTIES

Commencing early in the operation, commanders began receiving reports of civilian casualties in My Lai (4). At about 0930 hours, MG Koster was advised by COL Henderson that he had observed 6 to 8 such casualties. The figure was increased when LTC Barker reported to Henderson during the afternoon that the total was 12 to 14, and was further increased to 20 in a report Barker made that evening. This last report was relayed to MG Koster at about 1900 hours. None of these reports was entered in unit journals or reported outside the Americal Division.

2. OBSERVATIONS AND COMPLAINTS BY AVIATION PERSONNEL

One element which provided combat support to TF Barker on 16 March was an aero-scout team from Company B, 123d Aviation Battalion. A pilot of this team, WO1 (now 1LT) Hugh Thompson, had been flying at a low altitude over My Lai (4) during the morning hours and had observed the actions of C/1–20 Inf. He became greatly concerned over the "needless and unnecessary killings" he had witnessed. He landed his helicopter several times to aid the inhabitants and in an attempt to stop the killing.

Shortly before noon, WO1 Thompson returned to LZ Dottie and reported his observations to his company commander, MAJ Frederic Watke. The complaints of WO1 Thompson were confirmed by other pilots and crewmen who had also been over My Lai (4). The complaints were expressed in most serious terms; those who were present heard the terms "killing" and "murder" used freely with estimates of the dead in My Lai (4) running over 100. Upon receipt of this report, MAJ Watke went to the commander of TF Barker and advised him of the allegations. Watke stated that Barker then left for his helicopter, presumably to visit C/1–20 Inf. Watke considered the matter was "in the hands of the man who could do something about it" and took no further action at that time. Later that day, he again encountered Barker who advised him that he could find nothing to substantiate Thompson's allegations. While Watke testified that he was convinced at the time that LTC Barker was lying, he took no further action until 2200 hours that night when he reported to his battalion commander, LTC Holladay, and related for the second time the substance of what is hereafter referred to as the "Thompson Report."

3. THE ORDER TO RETURN TO MY LAI (4)

At about 1530 hours on 16 March, after receiving a second report of civilian casualties, COL Henderson stated he became suspicious and directed TF Barker to send a company back through My Lai (4) to ascertain the exact number of casualties and the cause of death. As the order was being transmitted to C/1–20 Inf by TF Barker, it was monitored by MG Koster, the commander of the Americal Division, who inquired concerning the reasons. After a brief explanation by the CO of C/1–20 Inf, during which time MG Koster was advised that 20–28 noncombatants had been killed, MG Koster countermanded the order and directed that COL Henderson be notified. There were no further efforts to make an on-site determination of the cause or extent of the civilian casualties.

4. THE THOMPSON REPORT REACHES DIVISION HEADQUARTERS

Because of the late hour at which LTC Holladay received the report from MAJ Watke, they waited until the following morning before reporting to BG Young, an Assistant Division Commander. Watke repeated his story, which both he and LTC Holladay agree contained the allegations that there had been "lots of unnecessary killing . . . mostly women, children and old men" and that a confrontation had taken place between personnel of aviation and ground units; however, there is conflict as to the number of casualties mentioned. LTC Holladay and MAJ Watke also agree that BG Young was advised that the complaints made by Thompson had been confirmed by other aviation unit personnel.

At about noon on the 17th, BG Young reported to MG Koster the information he had received from MAJ Watke and LTC Holladay. There is substantive disagreement in testimony between what BG Young testified he received from Watke and Holladay and what the latter two state they reported. BG Young stated he was not apprised of any charge of indiscriminate or unnecessary killing of noncombatants. He further stated that it was his impression the matter of major concern was that there had been a confrontation between the ground forces and an aviation unit, resulting from an incident in which noncombatants had been caught in a cross fire between US and enemy forces.

BG Young contends that it was this lesser charge he brought to MG Koster, who directed BG Young to instruct COL Henderson to conduct a thorough investigation of the incident. MG Koster has confirmed parts of BG Young's account of this conversation but in a previous statement before the Criminal Investigation Division (CID), MG Koster stated that he had been advised of some indiscriminate shooting of civilians.

The Inquiry has concluded that the two general officers received a muted version of the Thompson Report from Watke and Holladay, but one that included the allegation that noncombatants had been indiscriminately killed. Upon receipt of the report, it seems most likely that they related it to the information MG Koster had received from TF Barker the previous day, that 20–28 noncombatants had been inadvertently killed. The information concerning noncombatant casualties had not been forwarded outside of the Division, although MACV and III MAF regulations required such action, nor were the new allegations reported to higher headquarters. Adopting a "close hold" attitude concerning all information relating to this matter, MG Koster directed BG Young to have COL Henderson investigate the incident.

C. Investigation of the Incident and Review

1. COL HENDERSON'S "INVESTIGATION"

BG Young made arrangements for a meeting which was held on 18 March at 0900 hours at LZ Dottie. The meeting was attended by five officers: BG Young, COL Henderson, LTC Barker, LTC Holladay, and MAJ Watke. BG Young told the group of the Division Commander's instructions concerning the investigation and MAJ Watke repeated his account of the complaints. When the meeting terminated, COL Henderson commenced his "investigation" with an interview of WO1 Thompson and two other aviation unit personnel. (While Henderson states he talked only with Thompson and for only a few minutes, the testimony of others indicates that he talked individually with three persons for almost an hour.) These interviews, together with the information already possessed by Henderson from personal observation and conversations with TF Barker personnel, should have provided a full awareness of the nature and extent of the incident at My Lai (4). From at least this point forward, Henderson's actions appear to have been little more than a pretense of an investigation and had as their goal the suppression of the true facts concerning the events of 16 March.

Following his interview with aviation personnel, Henderson questioned CPT Medina, whose explanation concerning civilian casualties left him "suspicious." The remainder of Henderson's "investigation" was without substance; his "interview with a substantial number of C Company personnel" consisted of a discussion on the afternoon of 18 March with a group which, COL Henderson claims, numbered from 30 to 40 personnel. After complimenting them on their performance in the operation, he asked them collectively if they had witnessed any atrocities. Henderson stated that the response he received was negative. While COL Henderson claims he spoke with other individuals and responsible commanders, available evidence indicates that his so-called investigative actions ended after a brief flight which he stated he made over the area of operation on 18 March.

Commencing on 19 March, COL Henderson is said to have made a series of oral reports to BG Young and MG Koster in which he was purported to have related to them the results of his "investigation." It seems clear that in his reports Henderson deliberately misrepresented both the scope of his investigation and the information he had obtained. He reported that while 20 civilians had been killed by artillery and/or gunships, there was no basis in fact to the allegations made by WO1 Thompson. Henderson's final oral report was accepted by MG Koster as adequately responding to the charges made by WO1 Thompson. The matter appears to have rested there until about mid-April 1968, when information was received at Division Headquarters from Vietnamese sources.

2. REACTION TO INFORMATION FROM VIETNAMESE SOURCES

The initial reports from Vietnamese sources concerning the incident were apparently received by the US Advisory teams in Son Tinh District and Quang Ngai Province.

The Son My Village Chief submitted a report to the Son Tinh District Chief containing allegations of mass killings by US Forces in Son My Village. The District Chief in turn forwarded two reports of the incident to the Quang Ngai Province Chief based on the information furnished to him by the Village Chief. The first of these reports, dated 28 March 1968, contained little of substance and remained within Vietnamese channels. The second was dated 11 April 1968, and copies of it were provided to both the Province and District Advisory teams. In addition, a copy of the District Chief's 11 April letter went to COL Toan, the Commanding Officer of the 2d ARVN Division.

In his 11 April letter, the District Chief referred to an incident of 16 March in which it was alleged that a US Army unit had assembled and killed more than 400 civilian residents of Tu Cung Hamlet * of Son My Village and had killed an additional 90 people at Co Luy Hamlet.** He stated that, if true, he considered this an act of insane violence.

Also in the first half of April, VC propaganda alleging that US forces had killed 500 people in Son My Village in the middle of March came into the hands of COL Toan and LTC Khien, the Province Chief of Quang Ngai Province and, possibly somewhat later, into US hands. Both COL Henderson and MG Koster appear to have discussed the District Chief's report and the VC propaganda with COL Toan and LTC Khien, and apparently with LTC Guinn, the US Deputy Province Advisor.

MG Koster indicated that the receipt in mid-April 1968 of the VC propaganda and the information from the District Chief reopened the subject of civilian casualties in the 16 March operation. However, it did not stimulate any fresh inquiry. COL Henderson had already completed his "investigation" and had given an oral report to MG Koster. The receipt of the allegations from Vietnamese sources resulted only in MG Koster's directing COL Henderson to commit his oral report to writing.

In response to this direction, COL Henderson prepared and submitted a so-called "Report of Investigation" dated 24 April 1968 to MG Koster. The report consisted of two typewritten pages and two inclosures. The first inclosure was a typed copy of a statement dated 14 April 1968 with the signature block removed, which this Inquiry determined was prepared by the Deputy Senior Advisor, Son Tinh District, at the request of the Province Advisory Team. This statement indicated that the report of the Son My Village Chief alleging mass killings was not given much importance by the Son Tinh District Chief. The second inclosure was a translation of the VC propaganda message regarding the incident. COL Henderson's report briefly summarized the operation, listed personnel purportedly interviewed (but made no reference to WO1 Thompson or to any other member of the aero scout unit), and summarized what purported to be the District Chief's attitude toward the allegation. The conclusion stated by COL Henderson in the report was that 20 noncombatants were inadvertently killed by artillery and by cross fire between the US and VC Forces, that no civilians were gathered and shot by US Forces, and that the allegation that US Forces had shot and killed 450–500 civilians was obviously VC propaganda.

MG Koster testified that when he received the 24 April report he found it unacceptable and directed the conduct of a formal investigation through either BG Young or COL Parson, the Division Chief of Staff. Both Young and Parson denied having received or passed on any such

* Includes the subhamlet of My Lai (4).

** Includes the subhamlet of My Khe (4).

instructions. MG Koster and COL Henderson agreed that such an investigation was conducted, and a report submitted, by LTC Barker. Both described in detail the form and substance of this report, but the evidence appears conclusive that no such report was ever prepared.

D. Suppression and Withholding of Information

Within the Americal Division, at every command level from company to division, actions were taken or omitted which together effectively concealed the Son My incident. Outside the division, advisory teams at Province, District and possibly the 2d ARVN Division also contributed to this end. Some of the acts and omissions that resulted in concealment of the incident were inadvertent while others constituted deliberate suppression or withholding of information.

Efforts initiated in 1968 deliberately to withhold information continue to this day. Six officers who occupied key positions at the time of the incident exercised their right to remain silent before this Inquiry, others gave false or misleading testimony or withheld information, and key documents relating to the incident have not been found in US files.

1. AT COMPANY LEVEL

No reports of the crimes committed by C/1–20 Inf and B/4–3 Inf during the operation were made by members of the units, although there were many men in both companies who had not participated in any criminal acts. The commander of C/1–20 Inf assembled his men after the operation and advised them not to discuss the incident because an investigation was being conducted, and he advised one individual not to write to his Congressman about the incident. He also made a false report that only 20–28 noncombatants had been killed and attributed the cause of death to artillery and gunships.

The commander of B/4–3 Inf submitted false reports (possibly without knowing they were false) that 38 VC had been killed by his 1st Platoon and that none of them were women and children.

2. AT TASK FORCE AND BRIGADE LEVELS

Significant information concerning irregularities in the operation and the commission of war crimes by C/1–20 Inf was known to the commanders and staff officers of both TF Barker and the 11th Brigade on

16 March but was never transmitted to the Americal Division. Reports of VC killed by C/1–20 Inf on 16 March terminated at 0840 hours when the total reached 90, although the killing continued. In addition to withholding information, the 11th Brigade headquarters submitted false and misleading reports to Division. One instance concerned a C/1–20 Inf VC body count report of 69, which was changed to attribute the cause of death to artillery and to move the location at which the purported VC were killed from inside the hamlet of My Lai (4) to a site 600 meters away. A second false report involved an interrogation report from C/1–20 Inf that 30–40 VC had departed the hamlet immediately prior to the combat assault. The record of this interrogation report as received at the Americal Division on 16 March stated that there were many VC in the C/1–20 Inf area of operation.

A reporter and photographer attached to the 11th Brigade Information Office accompanied TF Barker on 16 March and observed many war crimes committed by C/1–20 Inf. Both individuals failed to report what they had seen, the reporter wrote a false and misleading account of the operation, and the photographer withheld and suppressed from proper authorities the photographic evidence of atrocities he had obtained.

In response to a routine division requirement, LTC Barker submitted a Combat Action Report, dated 28 March 1968, concerning his unit's operations on 16 March. The report significantly omitted any reference to noncombatant casualties and other irregularities, falsely depicted a hotly contested combat action, and appears to have been an outright effort to suppress and mislead.

Perhaps the most significant action taken to suppress the true facts of the Son My operation was the deception employed by COL Henderson to mislead his commander as to the scope and findings of his investigation of the Thompson allegations. His later submission—the so-called Report of Investigation, dated 24 April 1968, which dismissed the allegations from Vietnamese sources as baseless propaganda and restated the fiction that 20 noncombatants had been inadvertently killed—continued the original deception practiced upon his commander.

3. AT DIVISION LEVEL

A. Within Aviation Units

There is no evidence to suggest that there were deliberate attempts within the division aviation unit to conceal information concerning the Son My incident. However, there were acts and omissions by the commanders of the 123d Aviation Battalion, and of Company B of that unit, which contributed to concealment of the facts. One of the principal reasons why the full import of the Thompson Report was probably not appreciated at the division command level can be attributed to these two commanders and their failure to verify or document the serious charges made by WO1 Thompson and others. Neither took action to obtain documentary substantiation, to conduct a low-level aerial reconnaissance or otherwise to verify the allegations, or to confirm in writing what they reported orally to BG Young. The initial delay in reporting the matter through command channels needlessly prevented the report from reaching the Americal Division command group until approximately 24 hours after the incident had occurred.

A second serious charge against both of these two commanders is that they failed to take any action when they became convinced that the investigation of the incident was a "cover-up." An admonition was issued by the B Company Commander to his unit to halt further discussion of the incident while it was being investigated. This action was not taken to conceal information, but it probably had the unfortunate, although unintended, result of aiding in the suppression of the facts.

B. WITHIN HEADQUARTERS, AMERICAL DIVISION

Americal Division Headquarters was the recipient of much information concerning the Son My operation from both US and GVN sources. Except for routine operational data forwarded on 16 March, none of the reports or allegations concerning irregularities at Son My were transmitted to higher headquarters, although directives from III MAF and MACV clearly required such action. As previously indicated, the Inquiry has concluded that on 17 March, when they received a muted version of the Thompson Report, MG Koster and BG Young may have viewed the report in relation to information previously received that 20–28 noncombatant casualties had been caused by artillery and gunships. While COL Henderson's later reports were false, and the general officers were negligent in having accepted them, they probably believed they were withholding information concerning a much less serious incident than the one that had actually occurred.

Additional information from Vietnamese sources reaching the Americal Division sometime in April implied that a far more serious event had taken place at Son My. The command response to this information was so inadequate to the situation and so inconsistent with what would ordinarily be expected of officers of the ability and experience of MG Koster and BG Young that it can only be explained as a refusal or an inability to give credence to information or reports which were not consistent with their original, and erroneous, conclusions.

In summary form, the following are the significant acts done or omitted at the Americal Division headquarters which contributed to the concealment of the true facts concerning Son My:

1. There was a failure to report information concerning noncombatant casualties and allegations for war crimes known to be of particular interest to COMUSMACV and required to be reported by directives of both III MAF and MACV;
2. Having decided to withhold from higher headquarters information concerning civilian casualties, MG Koster directed that the matter be investigated by COL Henderson. However, he did not insure that a thorough investigation was conducted nor did he subject COL Henderson's reports to adequate review, thereby nullifying his efforts to determine the true facts;
3. The Division command group acted to control closely all information regarding the Son My incident. Information regarding the incident was not included in daily briefings or provided the General or Special Staff, and the investigative resources of the staff were not employed.

4. BY PERSONS OUTSIDE THE AMERICAL DIVISION

Among the Vietnamese officials who came in contact with information concerning possible war crimes in Son My during the period 16–19 March, there was a natural reluctance to confront their American counterparts with such serious allegations and to insist upon inquiry into the matter. Such information as did reach US advisory personnel was not forwarded through advisory channels, but referred only to the Americal Division and its 11th Brigade. In addition, there is evidence that at the Quang Ngai Province and Son Tinh District levels and probably at the 2d ARVN Division, the senior US military advisors aided in suppressing information concerning the incident.

E. Summary of Findings *

It is concluded that:

1. During the period of 16–19 March 1968, troops of Task Force Barker massacred a large number of Vietnamese nationals in the village of Son My.
2. Knowledge as to the extent of the incident existed at company level,

* The complete findings and recommendations are contained in Chapter 12.

at least among the key staff officers and commander at the Task Force Barker level, and at the 11th Brigade command level.

3. Efforts at the Americal Division command level to conceal information concerning what was probably believed to be the killing of 20–28 civilians actually resulted in the suppression of a war crime of far greater magnitude.
4. The commander of the 11th Brigade, upon learning that a war crime had probably been committed, deliberately set out to conceal the fact from proper authority and to deceive his commander concerning the matter.
5. Investigations concerning the incident conducted within the Americal Division were superficial and misleading and not subjected to substantive review.
6. Efforts were made at every level of command from company to division to withhold and suppress information concerning the incident at Son My.
7. Failure of Americal Division headquarters personnel to act on information received from GVN/ARVN officials served to suppress effectively information concerning the Son My incident.
8. Efforts of the Americal Division to suppress and withhold information were assisted by US officers serving in advisory positions with Vietnamese agencies.

Chapter 3. Background

A. Enemy Situation in March 1968

As a basis for evaluating the enemy situation in Quang Ngai Province, it is noted that in March 1968, enemy strength throughout South Vietnam was estimated to be approximately 263,200 men. Of this total, about 55,900 were Viet Cong (VC) combat forces, 87,400 were North Vietnamese Army (NVA) combat troops, and 69,100 were guerrillas, with the remaining 50,800 comprising administrative personnel.

The enemy maneuver battalions in South Vietnam were estimated by HQ, Military Assistance Command, Vietnam (MACV) to total 278 (158 North Vietnamese and 120 Viet Cong), distributed throughout the four corps tactical zones as follows:

I Corps—77 North Vietnamese and 18 Viet Cong
II Corps—55 North Vietnamese and 18 Viet Cong
III Corps—26 North Vietnamese and 50 Viet Cong
IV Corps—34 Viet Cong

Considering only Quang Ngai Province (sketch 3–1), enemy strength ranged between 10,000 and 20,000 men during the 4 years preceding the Son My incident. In early 1968 enemy strength was estimated to be between 10,000 and 14,000 men of which 2,000–4,000 were regular forces, 3,000–5,000 were guerrillas, and 5,000 were assigned to administrative units.

A number of VC and NVA regiments operated in Quang Ngai Province from 1964 to 1966. However, four local force battalions and eleven companies of VC were the forces primarily responsible for harassing the area under government control. The 48th Local Force (LF) Battalion became the principal enemy force in Son Tinh District, although it also operated in the Batangan area to the north as well as to the south of the Song Tra Khuc. Members of the 48th LF Battalion reportedly lived with the local villagers in order to conceal their presence, often working as farmers during the day and fighting as guerrillas at night.

While enemy main force regiments were operating primarily to the west and south of Quang Ngai City in 1967, elements of the 1st VC Regiment and the 21st NVA Regiment of the 2d NVA Division probably operated in Son Tinh District early in the year. During February and March the 1st VC Regiment moved southwest of Quang Ngai City and in April the 21st NVA Regiment was deployed to Quang Tin. After this, enemy main force/local force battalions operated in increasing numbers in Son Tinh District in 1967. The 409th Sapper Battalion began operating in the northern portion of the district in January, augmenting the 48th LF Battalion. Toward the end of 1967, these two battalions were joined by the 81st and 85th LF Battalion.

Prior to the 1968 *Tet* offensive, the VC formed two regiments in Quang Ngai Province by consolidating main and local force battalions. The 401st NVA Regiment was formed from main forces and infiltration packets, and three of the prominent LF battalions in the area, the 38th, 48th, and 81st Battalions, were consolidated to form the 328th VC Regiment. During *Tet* those two regiments, plus an independent battalion and at least 10 local force companies totaling over 3,000 men, attacked Quang Ngai City and other towns in the province. These attacks were eventually repulsed, but the VC continued to pose a threat, causing the Quang Ngai Province officials extreme concern over the possibility of a second attack on Quang Ngai City. In the *Tet* operation the 48th LF Battalion overran the Regional Force/Popular Force Training Center near Son Tinh and held it briefly until driven out by counterattacking 2d ARVN Division forces. In the ensuing fight the 48th LF Battalion reportedly suffered about 150 casualties, including the battalion commander and two company commanders, and a third company commander captured.

With the failure of the assualt of Quang Ngai City and other province towns, VC units filtered back to their home areas, mostly to the south and west. Because of its heavy losses during *Tet,* elements of the 48th LF Battalion withdrew to the mountains in western Quang Ngai to reorganize and refit, while other elements of the battalion returned to their habitual area of operation on the Batangan Peninsula. By late February, the 48th LF Battalion headquarters had reportedly returned to the peninsula, but the unit remained out of contact during the first part of March, apparently to continue recuperating from the *Tet* setback. At the time of the Son My incident, the 48th LF Battalion had an estimated strength of 200–250 and was the only major enemy unit with elements in the Son My area. However, there were two additional local force companies in the district which on occasion joined the 48th LF

Battalion in carrying out specific operations. Overall guerrilla strength in Son Tinh District was reported to be about 700 strong.

B. Son My Village

Son My Village is located approximately 9 kilometers northeast of Quang Ngai City and fronts on the South China Sea. In March 1968, the village was composed of four hamlets, Tu Cung, My Lai, My Khe, and Co Luy, each of which contained several subhamlets (sketch 3–2).* Most of the residents of Son My either farm the rich alluvial soil along the rivers and streams or engage in offshore fishing operations.

C. The People of Quang Ngai Province

Historically, the people of Quang Ngai Province have a long record of supporting rebellion. In the 19th century they had been a focal point of resistance to French control of Indochina. Later, in the 1930's, they had fomented peasant revolts against Vietnamese supporting the French. After World War II when the French sought to reestablish themselves in Indochina, Quang Ngai became a Viet Minh stronghold and by 1948 Ho Chi Minh considered it free from French rule. Duc Pho, in southern Quang Ngai, became one of the largest rest and recreation areas for the Viet Minh forces until the country was divided by the Geneva Accords in 1954.

Although most of the Viet Minh departed for the north after the settlement of the Geneva Accords, some remained behind and their influence was particularly strong in the rural areas. By the 1960's, a whole generation of young people had grown up under the control of the Viet Minh and the later National Liberation Front.

When the Government of South Vietnam launched the Strategic Hamlet Program in 1962, Quang Ngai Province became a principal objective. The government attempted to separate the villagers from the

* The Vietnamese knew many of these subhamlets by names different from those indicated on US topographic maps of the area. Where there is a difference, the American designation is shown in parentheses on the sketch map. For example, the subhamlet identified on the topographic map as My Lai (4) is actually named Thuan Yen; the subhamlet identified on the map as My Khe (4) is known to the Vietnamese as My Hoi. Except for Thuan Yen and My Lai (4), which are used interchangeably, the US Map designations for the subhamlets are used throughout this report, since those names are cited by witnesses in testimony.

National Liberation Front soldiers and organizers, usually by forcing the people to move to new fortified villages. The old villages and fields were often burned to prevent their use by the rebel elements. The program frequently aroused resentment and it was eventually superseded by the New Life Hamlet Program which emphasized aid and development for the villagers rather than being primarily security oriented. The end result of both these programs was usually less than satisfactory, for the concentration of villagers in strategic hamlets did not alter their allegiance to the National Liberation Front. Many villages remained under the domination of the Front and continued to provide recruits, taxes, food, supplies, and information to the VC and North Vietnamese units operating in their locale.

The village of Son My fell into this category. Some of its subhamlets, such as My Lai (1), had been burned to the ground by ARVN Forces well before American forces were deployed to Quang Ngai. Many of the villagers had been brought to Quang Ngai City as refugees with plans to resettle them in other areas. Life in the refugee centers was depressing; consequently, many villagers drifted back to their old home areas and to VC control. In the eyes of the Government of Vietnam (GVN) the people who continued to live in the Son My area were considered generally to be either VC or VC sympathizers.

D. Enemy Tactics and Techniques

As previously discussed, the enemy forces which operated in Quang Ngai Province and Son Tinh District included guerrillas, local and main force units and, at times, NVA units. These forces were highly skilled in hit-and-run guerrilla tactics and had the ability to survive in a counterinsurgency environment.

During the initial phases of the war, the Communists placed primary reliance on the employment of guerrilla tactics which were carried out by basic three-man VC guerrilla cells. Working covertly, these guerrilla cells performed assassinations, acts of terrorism, and conducted sabotage and limited clandestine military operations with the objective of gradually bringing more and more villages under VC control.

As the war expanded, the Communists increased their forces in South Vietnam by the organization of local and main force units up to battalion and regimental size and in late 1964, began a large-scale infiltration of NVA units. The local force units were normally recruited from a particular district and limited their operations to within the district. They lived with the people as a means of concealment and as a source of support. Main force units were organized and operated at province level, usually from secure base areas located in the mountains or jungle from where they could strike targets in the populated areas. Normally NVA units had assigned areas of operation but could be employed wherever the situation required.

Regardless of the type unit, the tactics employed by the Communist forces recognized their own shortcomings and were designed to exploit the weaknesses of the US, ARVN and other Free World Military Assistance Forces. Lacking the strength and firepower to survive an extended major battle, they relied primarily on operations which permitted them to mass, attack, and withdraw before US or GVN/ARVN forces could react. Their operations at every level were characterized by methodical planning, detailed rehearsals, and violent execution.

Prior to undertaking an operation, the VC/NVA normally would obtain very detailed information regarding their potential targets including the location of fighting positions, key installations, and the identification of security weaknesses. Using this information, which might require weeks or months to develop, they would then prepare a detailed step-by-step plan for the operation. The plan would then be rehearsed until every man in the force was thoroughly familiar with details of the target area and the functions he was to perform.

The VC had the choice of the time they wanted to fight and were willing to delay execution of an operation for as long as necessary in order to improve their chances of success. Once the decision was made to attack, the unit was moved, using clandestine techniques, to the target area. In doing this, the VC would often attempt to infiltrate demolitionist, sapper type personnel into the area to destroy key installations, and artillery and automatic weapons positions. Their final attack normally was executed only at a predetermined time or after the presence of their infiltrators had been detected. As an alternate type of attack they sometimes employed mortars, rockets, and recoilless rifles in stand-off attacks against population centers and military installations to prepare or soften the target for attack. These same basic procedures were generally followed in every type of operation, operations characterized by stealth, surprise, and shock action.

Typical operations conducted at the local force level included the ambushing of small convoys, attacking of village and district offices or security outposts, the assassination or kidnapping of local Vietnamese officials, and other acts designed to illustrate their control of the area in which they operated. The main force and NVA units assisted the local force units but primarily conducted large-scale operations against US and ARVN forces and installations.

The VC made extensive use of mines and boobytraps, especially at the hamlet and village level. In addition to the men in their combat units, children, women, and old men were used to construct homemade boobytraps and mines which they normally emplaced at night under the cover of darkness. The mines and boobytraps were used in a wide variety of ways. Some of them were employed as weapons of terror against the population; such as mines planted under or along well used roadways to blow-up buses and other vehicles; demolition devices installed in theaters and other crowded areas; or a simple grenade thrown into a group of people. In another tactic, they used them as defensive weapons to cover roads, paths, and other avenues of approach to and within their controlled areas. Some such areas were literally infested with VC mines and boobytraps and had the effect of slowing and restricting friendly offensive operations. It was this latter type of employment which tended to create hatred and frustration against the unseen enemy.

The operations of all VC/NVA forces in a particular area were closely controlled and coordinated with the local VC infrastructure's political and administrative apparatus in the attempt to achieve their objective of total domination of the people. The Communists recognized but few restraints in their operations and were often ruthless in conducting them. All operations were planned and executed keeping in mind the ultimate goal of seizing control of the Government of South Vietnam and the people.

E. Free World Military Assistance Forces (FWMAF) Objectives for 1968

In furtherance of the objective of attaining a stable and independent non-Communist government in South Vietnam, the Military Assistance Command, Vietnam (MACV), in coordination with the GVN and other FWMAF set forth three military objectives after the *Tet* offensive in January–February 1968 to: (1) Counter the enemy's *Tet* offensive and destroy and eject North Vietnamese invasion forces; (2) restore security to population centers and other vital areas and emphasize recovery from the recent pacification disruptions; and (3) resume the effort to fulfill the objectives of the 1968 Combined Campaign Plan to destroy enemy forces in the Republic of Vietnam and extend government control throughout the country.

To carry out the military objectives, MACV proposed the following military tasks to: (1) inflict maximum attrition upon the enemy; (2) abandon no territory; (3) support the Government of Vietnam in providing territorial security for pacification; (4) open and secure lines of communication; and (5) build the armed forces of the Republic of Vietnam physically and psychologically into an effective fighting force.

Operations for the remainder of the year were to be directed at searching out and destroying enemy main, local, and guerrilla forces and at identifying and eliminating the enemy's infrastructure. Particular attention was to be given to the pursuit and destruction of enemy forces in the densely populated areas and to the containment of the enemy in the border areas. Renewed efforts were also to be made to destroy base areas and to neutralize progressively the less important strongholds.

In the I Corps, north of the Hai Van Pass, MACV objectives were to restore security in Hue and other populated centers; to counter and destroy the North Vietnamese enemy forces; to destroy the enemy base complexes along the Laotian border and in and to the north of the demilitarized zone; to secure Route 1, and to open Route 9, the vital logistics artery from Dong Ha to Khe Sanh; to occupy the Ashau Valley and to destroy the infiltration complexes leading to the valley; to eliminate the threat posed by enemy forces operating from Base Areas 101 and 114; and to assist the Republic of Vietnam Armed Forces in restoring security and the pacification program in Quang Tri and Thua Thien Provinces. South of the Hai Van Pass, the main tasks were to destroy the 2d NVA Division; to neutralize the Do Xa area; and to establish a more secure situation for Da Nang, Hoi An, Tam Ky, Quang Ngai City, and other population centers in the pacification priority area.

F. Status of Pacification

The enemy *Tet* offensive had a serious impact upon the pacification effort in Quang Ngai Province. Two districts, Duc Pho and Nghia Hanh, came under virtual VC control and two others, Tu Nghia and Son Tinh, where Son My Village is located, had what was considered a heavy VC presence in the wake of the *Tet* operations. In addition, because of its large population, Son Tinh had taken the heaviest losses in Quang Ngai insofar as human lives, crops, and livestock were concerned.

There were four Regional Force (RF) companies, each with an authorized strength of 123, and 33 Popular Force (PF) platoons, each with an authorized strength of 33, to provide security for the population of over 120,000 people in Son Tinh District. Additionally, three battalions of the 2d ARVN Division supported the Rural Development Program in the province under the operational control of the Province Chief. The province also had 41 Revolutionary Development (RD) Teams of 59 men each. Of these, 25 were working in the hamlets. However, many of the RD teams removed from the area of Route 1 * did not remain

* Route 1 is the major north–south land route of communication in South Vietnam. It is correctly identified as QL 1 but is commonly referred to by US personnel as Route 1 or Highway 1.

in the hamlets overnight, as they were supposed to, but retired to protected bases until the following day.

Many of the RF and PF did not return to their pre-*Tet* positions in Son Tinh District until late February and early March due to the continuing threat of VC forces against the population centers and the lines of communication. For the greater part the RF/PF were employed in manning static defense positions, providing bridge and line of communications security, and guarding the approaches to Quang Ngai City.

They were not oriented toward village or hamlet security nor had they been trained fully as reaction forces for rapid deployment to critical areas as needed. Thus, the RF/PF were not positioned to provide protection for population centers, except for Quang Ngai City, and seldom ventured away from their defensive posts. Their preoccupation with their own fortified bases led to a lack of communication or contact with the people, thereby minimizing government influence in the district and province.

At the beginning of March 1968 security conditions in Quang Ngai did not permit a resumption of normal rural development activities. Fear still existed that a second phase of the *Tet* offensive might be launched at any time, despite strong indications that only enemy local force battalions were in the area and the fact that no strong possibility of imminent operations had been uncovered. In Son Tinh District, little effort had been made as of March to broaden government control of the countryside or to renew its pacification activities. Government officials were primarily occupied with the restoration of authority in areas lost during *Tet* and had little time to concern themselves with villages, such as Son My, which had been long under the control of the VC.

G. US Psychological Operations (PSYOPS)

The Joint United States Public Affairs Office (JUSPAO), which was formed in 1965, was responsible for the development of US psychological operations policy in Vietnam. Within the context of this guidance and published campaign plans, MACV policy specified that commanders would plan and conduct psychological operations in support of each military operation and pacification program. The JUSPAO established theme for the post-*Tet* PSYOPS campaign, which extended from 4 February to 21 March 1968, was "Chieu-Hoi" which means rally to the Government of Vietnam.

Accordingly, the Chieu Hoi program was being emphasized throughout the Americal Division AO immediately prior to the Son My incident. In addition, PSYOPS missions emphasizing the Volunteer Informant

Program and the Return to Government Control program were being conducted.

The TF Oregon SOP, which was still applicable at this point, cited the following situations as appropriate for exploitation by PSYOPS:

1. Explain the presence of American and friendly powers and show that the VC cannot match the GVN, US, and allied commitments.
2. Exploit victories by both ARVN and friendly forces to maintain a winning spirit within the ARVN forces and the civilian populace.
3. Exploit the Chieu Hoi program to encourage VC ralliers at every opportunity.
4. Take advantage of VC/NVA vulnerabilities, such as mounting casualties, alienation of population due to: increased terrorism, taxation, impressment, lowered living conditions, examples of lower morale, and increasing defections.
5. Exploit information from VC/NVA ralliers or PW's.

MAJ (now LTC) Stanley E. Holtom, Division PSYOPS Officer in March 1968, stated that while PSYOPS should support tactical operations, development of the program was left primarily to his initiative as to the time, themes, and media of dissemination which should be employed. Apparently, there was minimum coordination with G3 or other staff sections. According to Holtom, there was little or no effort to plan PSYOPS to support tactical operations prior to June 1968. In fact, there seemed to be little emphasis on PSYOPS within the Americal Division during this period. All psychological operations were conducted independently and were generally limited to the available standard prerecorded messages or leaflets which applied to any locale rather than being targeted at a specific area. Citing the Son My operation as an example, he stated that he had no knowledge of the planning of the operation. He added that he did work in close coordination with GVN officials regarding programs aimed at instilling in the people a sense of loyalty and responsibility to the government.

The 11th Brigade tactical SOP (draft) stated that commanders would plan and incorporate PSYOPS into all tactical operations and activities involving contact with the local populace. The SOP specified that all PSYOPS activities within the brigade would be directed at achieving the following objectives:

1. Convince all audiences that GVN victory is inevitable with the support of the US and FWMAF.
2. Persuade all audiences that the fastest way to end the war and achieve peace and security is to support free Vietnam and oppose the Viet Cong.

3. Convince all audiences that the US presence in Vietnam is to help the RVN and is temporary in nature.
4. Convince the Viet Cong that returnees will be sincerely welcome.

While the staff coordination at brigade level appears to have been somewhat closer than that at division, the Brigade S5 still was not completely informed or always consulted regarding PSYOPS support for tactical operations. The 11th Brigade S5 stated that most psychological operations were conducted routinely, and somewhat independently, except for multibattalion operations conducted west of Route 1 for which the S3 would direct him to prepare an annex to the operations order. According to the S5, there were no PSYOPS ever conducted in direct support of any tactical operation along the coastal plains. He stated that PSYOPS in such areas of operation consisted primarily of standard broadcasts and leaflet drops targeted at areas normally selected by him spread throughout the Duc Pho and Mo Duc areas plus the TF Barker AO. Areas in which effective results were achieved were targeted repeatedly.

H. Friendly Situation

In March 1968, FWMAF in South Vietnam totaled 576,200 of which over 515,200 were US. The Republic of Vietnam Armed Forces (RVNAF) had a strength of over 310,700. In addition, there were over 400,000 Vietnamese serving in the Regional Forces, Popular Forces, Police Forces, Self-Defense Forces, and other such organizations. At that time there were 300 friendly maneuver battalions deployed throughout South Vietnam. Of this total, 55 US, 4 Free World, and 36 RVNAF battalions were deployed in the I Corps area.

During the year prior to the Son My incident, Quang Ngai Province had been the responsibility of ARVN, ROK Marine, US Marine, and US Army forces all of which had conducted many small unit operations in the province. Those which were more significant are summarized below.

In February 1967, US Marines, ROK Marines, and the 2d ARVN Division conducted the first combined operation in the I Corps against the 21st NVA Regiment, 2d NVA Division, in western Quang Ngai, employing seven battalions, three of them ARVN airborne. As the 21st NVA Regiment pulled back under ROK Marine pressure, the airborne forces made heavy contact with the North Vietnamese units and reportedly inflicted over 800 casualties upon them.

During September, the 2d ROK Marine Brigade launched Operation Dragon Fire against enemy forces in eastern Son Tinh and Binh Son Districts. This three-battalion operation lasted until the end of October with the ROK Marines claiming over 540 enemy killed and 138 suspects captured during the campaign.

The 2d ARVN Division carried out several search and destroy missions in eastern Son Tinh District during December 1967. One such operation employed two companies in coordination with one RF company and a PF platoon in a one-day operation northwest of My Lai (4). The Vietnamese forces reported that they had killed 40 of the enemy, while suffering casualties of 11 killed and 8 wounded.

When the decision was made to deploy the 2d ROK Marine Brigade out of Quang Ngai Province into Quang Nam Province to reinforce northern I Corps, the Americal Division, in cooperation with the 2d ARVN Division, was asked to take over the ROK area of responsibility; areas of operation were changed accordingly (sketch 3–3). Elements of the 198th Infantry Brigade moved into the area in late December with the mission of locating and destroying enemy MF/LF units and extending government control over the districts. Initial contacts were light and friendly; casualties were low.

On 2 January 1968, the 3d Brigade, 4th Infantry Division, assumed operational control of most of the Muscatine AO (sketch 3–4), the 198th Brigade retaining a small sector in the north. Relief of the 2d ROK Marine Brigade continued until completion on 22 January. In the meantime, the Americal units which conducted operations in the area took a steady toll of casualties from enemy mines and boobytraps. In one heavy contact on 17 January, about 10 miles north of My Lai (4), elements of the 198th Brigade combat assaulted the village of An Thinh (1). Blocking the escape routes and using gunships effectively, the battalion sent one company to sweep the village. As the enemy tried to flee, they were engaged by gunships and the units in the blocking positions. At the end of the day, it was reported that 83 VC had been killed and 34 weapons captured, while the US forces had five men wounded.

The 198th Brigade resumed control of the entire Muscatine area on 25 January to include the operational control of the 11th Infantry Brigade's, 4th Battalion, 3d Infantry (–) and the Task Force (TF) Barker which had been formed to assist in controlling the area vacated by the ROK Marine Brigade. Subsequently, the 3d Brigade, 4th Infantry Division, moved north into Quang Ngai Province to replace the 3d Brigade, 1st Air Cavalry Division, in Operation Wheeler/Wallowa.

When the 2d ARVN Division learned that elements of the 22d NVA Regiment, 3d NVA Division, had moved into the area southwest of Quang Ngai City following the *Tet* offensive, it launched Operation Quyet Thang 22 on 24 February 1968, to seek out and destroy them. Aided by strong tactical air and artillery support during a 2-week campaign, the South

Vietnamese maintained continuous pressure against heavily dug-in enemy positions until the latter finally broke contact and withdrew on 10 March.

In the meantime, in Operation Muscatine, the ground contacts had been light. Since most of the enemy local force units had been committed to the attacks on Quang Ngai City during *Tet,* it was not surprising that the sector was inactive. Gunships, however, engaged a force of 150 VC about 8 kilometers north of My Lai (4) on 30 January and reported that they had killed over 40 of the enemy. TF Barker units made scattered contacts with small groups of VC in the Batangan Peninsula area during the *Tet* period, but none of any significance.

On 4 February, the 11th Brigade assumed control of the southern and western portions of the Muscatine AO and of its own 4th Battalion, 3d Infantry (–), and TF Barger. The 11th Brigade now had operational responsibility for both the Muscatine AO and the Duc Pho/Mo Duc District areas. The districts lying between the 11th Brigade's areas—Tu Nghia and Nghia Hanh—and the southern part of Son Tinh District, north and west of Quang Ngai City, were the responsibility of the 2d ARVN Division (sketch 3–5). In the Muscatine AO, TF Barker was responsible for the region lying east of Route 1 in Son Tinh and southern Binh Son Districts and the 4th Battalion, 3d Infantry (–) for the territory west of the road (sketch 3–6). For TF Barker the main task was to conduct operations to locate and destroy main and local force units and guerrillas and to eliminate the VC infrastructure in the area north and northeast of Quang Ngai City.

Headquarters TF Barker was at LZ Dottie, about 11 kilometers northwest of My Lai (4). Its direct support artillery, D Battery, 6th Battalion, 11th Artillery (105mm howitzer), was located at LZ Uptight, about 8 kilometers north of My Lai (4). Troop lift and gunships for the TF were provided by the 174th Assault Helicopter Company, located at LZ Bronco in Duc Pho, and aero-scout activities were carried out by Company B, 123d Aviation Battalion, whose rear base was at Chu Lai and forward base at LZ Dottie. Two "Swift Boats" from the Coastal Surveillance Force, US Navy were available for patrolling operations offshore in conjunction with the TF's ground operations.

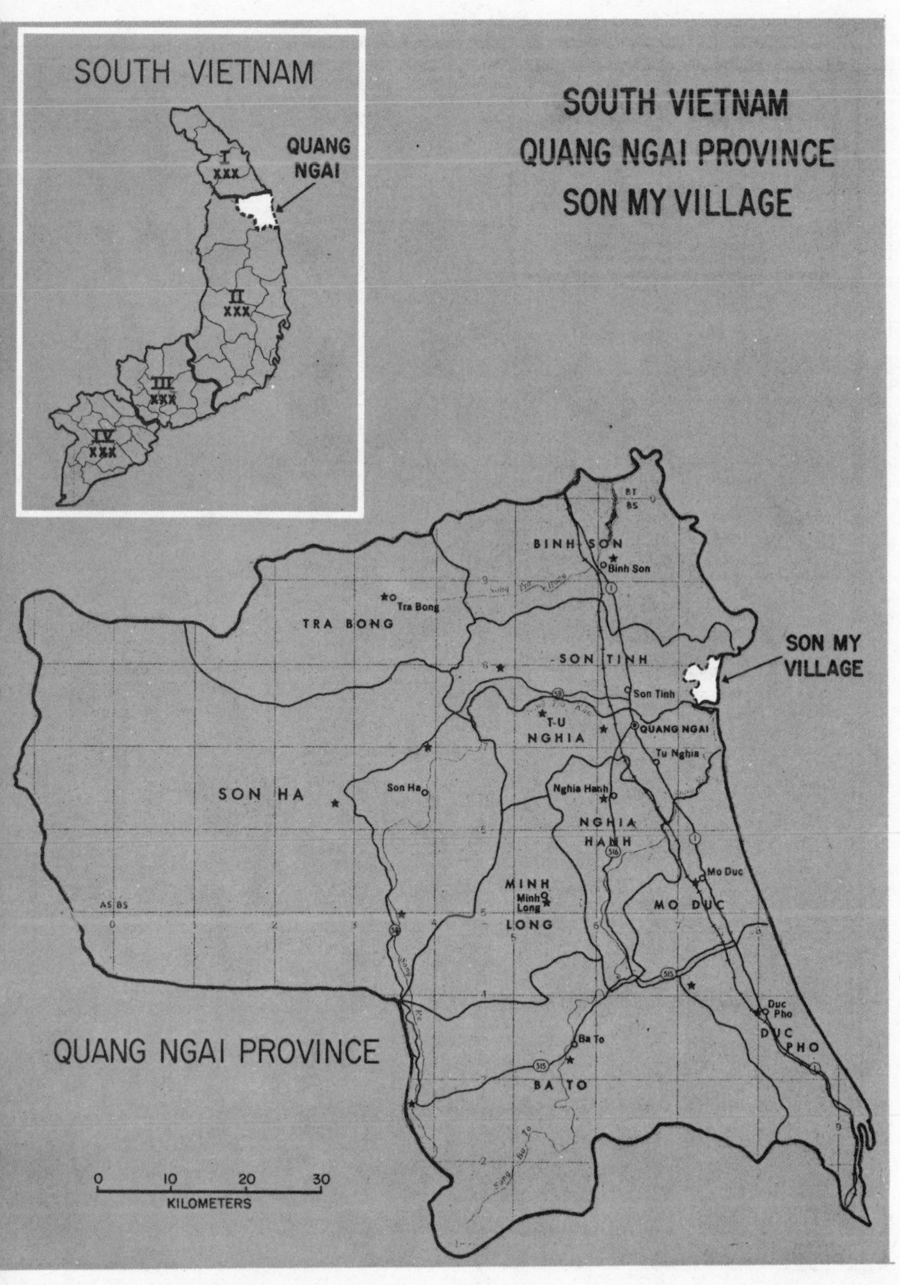
SOUTH VIETNAM
QUANG NGAI
I XXX
II XXX
III XXX
IV XXX
SOUTH VIETNAM
QUANG NGAI PROVINCE
SON MY VILLAGE
BINH SON
Binh Son
Tra Bong
TRA BONG
SON TINH
SON MY VILLAGE
Son Tinh
T-U NGHIA
QUANG NGAI
Tu Nghia
Son Ha
SON HA
Nghia Hanh
NGHIA HANH
Mo Duc
MINH LONG
Minh Long
MO DUC
Duc Pho
DUC PHO
Ba To
BA TO
QUANG NGAI PROVINCE
0 10 20 30
KILOMETERS

SKETCH 3-1

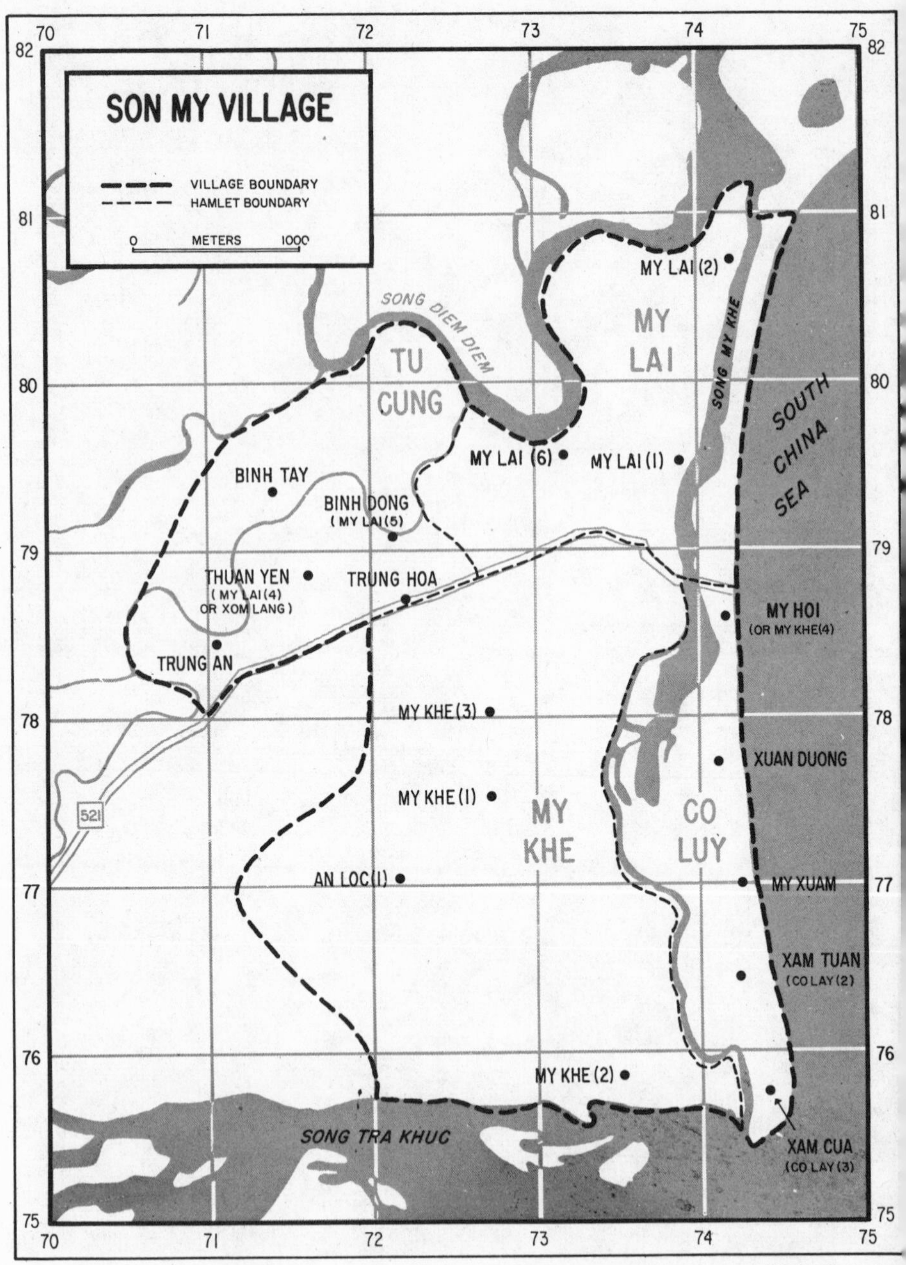
SON MY VILLAGE
VILLAGE BOUNDARY
HAMLET BOUNDARY
0 METERS 1000
SONG DIEM DIEM
TU CUNG
MY LAI
MY LAI (2)
SONG MY KHE
SOUTH CHINA SEA
MY LAI (6)
MY LAI (1)
BINH TAY
BINH DONG (MY LAI (5)
THUAN YEN (MY LAI (4) OR XOM LANG)
TRUNG HOA
TRUNG AN
MY HOI (OR MY KHE (4)
MY KHE (3)
XUAN DUONG
MY KHE (1)
521
MY KHE
CO LUY
AN LOC (1)
MY XUAM
XAM TUAN (CO LAY (2)
MY KHE (2)
SONG TRA KHUC
XAM CUA (CO LAY (3)
70
71
72
73
74
75
82
81
80
79
78
77
76
75

SKETCH 3-2

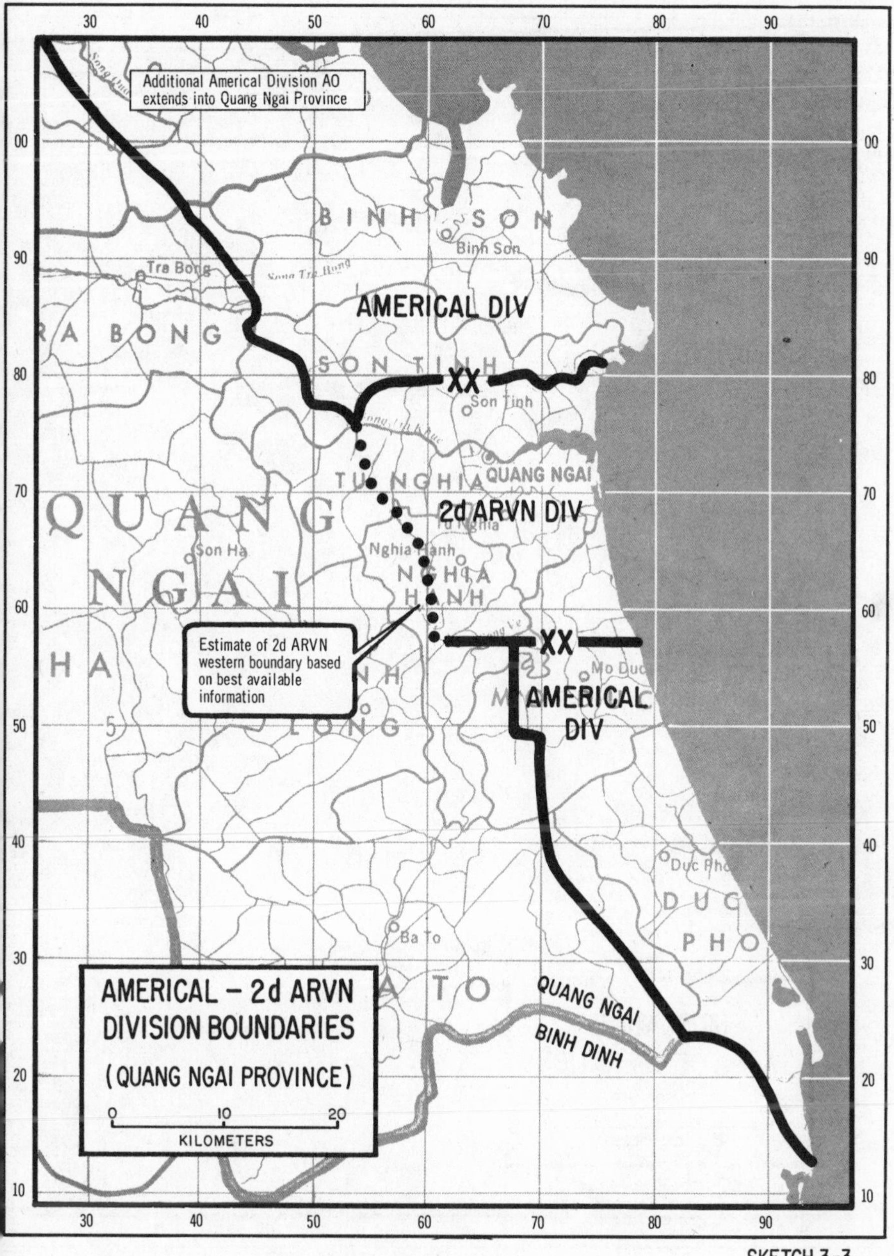
Additional Americal Division AO extends into Quang Ngai Province
BINH SON
Binh Son
Tra Bong
Song Tra Bong
AMERICAL DIV
RA BONG
SON TINH
XX
Son Tinh
QUANG NGAI
TU NGHIA
2d ARVN DIV
Tu Nghia
QUANG
NGAI
Son Ha
Nghia Hanh
NGHIA HANH
Estimate of 2d ARVN western boundary based on best available information
XX
Mo Duc
AMERICAL DIV
LONG
Duc Pho
DUC PHO
Ba To
AMERICAL – 2d ARVN DIVISION BOUNDARIES
(QUANG NGAI PROVINCE)
0
10
20
KILOMETERS
QUANG NGAI
BINH DINH

SKETCH 3-3

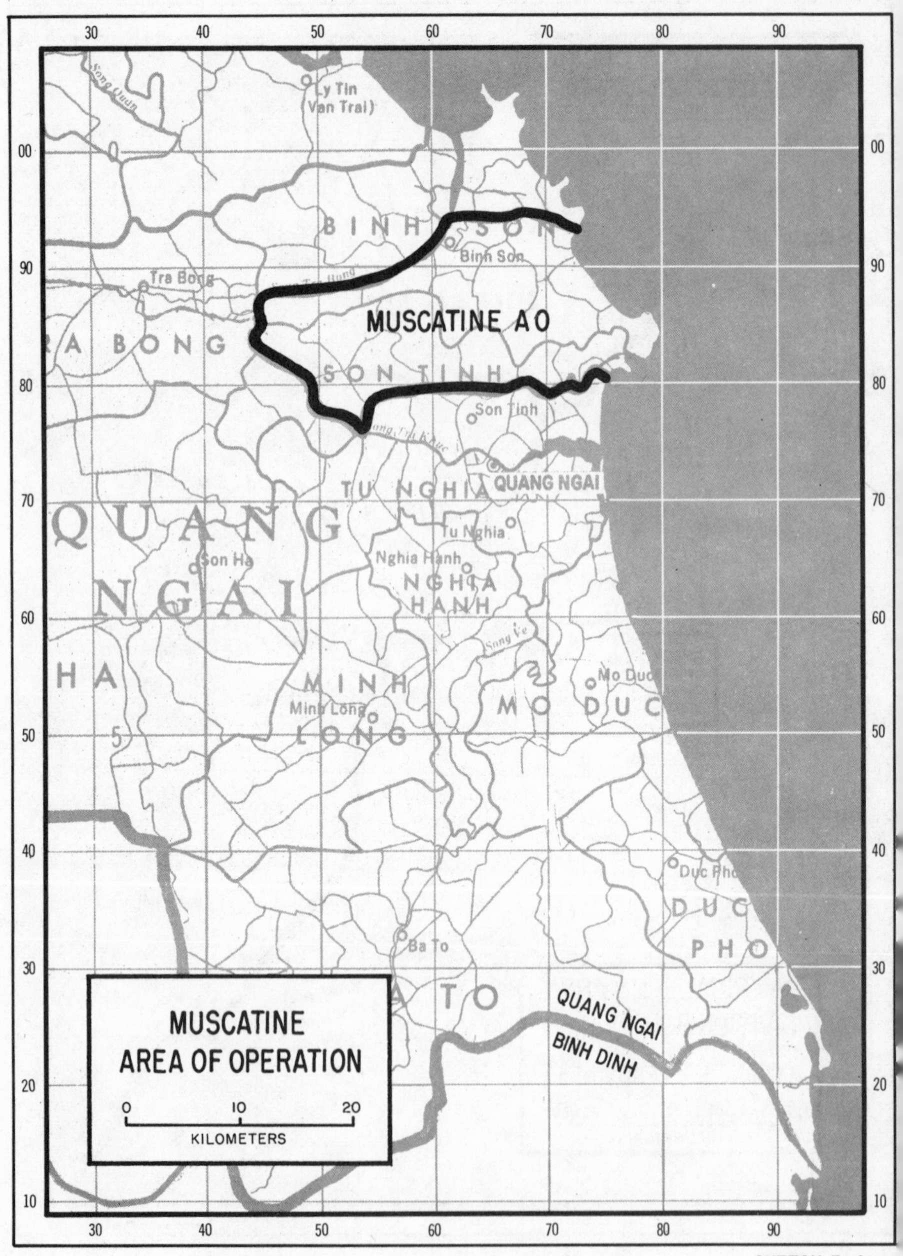
MUSCATINE AO
MUSCATINE
AREA OF OPERATION
0
10
20
KILOMETERS
Ly Tin
(Van Trai)
B I N H S O N
Binh Son
Tra Bong
R A B O N G
S O N T I N H
Son Tinh
QUANG NGAI
T U N G H I A
Tu Nghia
Q U A N G
N G A I
Son Ha
Nghia Hanh
N G H I A
H A N H
Song Ve
M I N H
Minh Long
L O N G
Mo Duc
M O D U C
H A
Duc Pho
D U C
P H O
Ba To
A T O
QUANG NGAI
BINH DINH

SKETCH 3-4

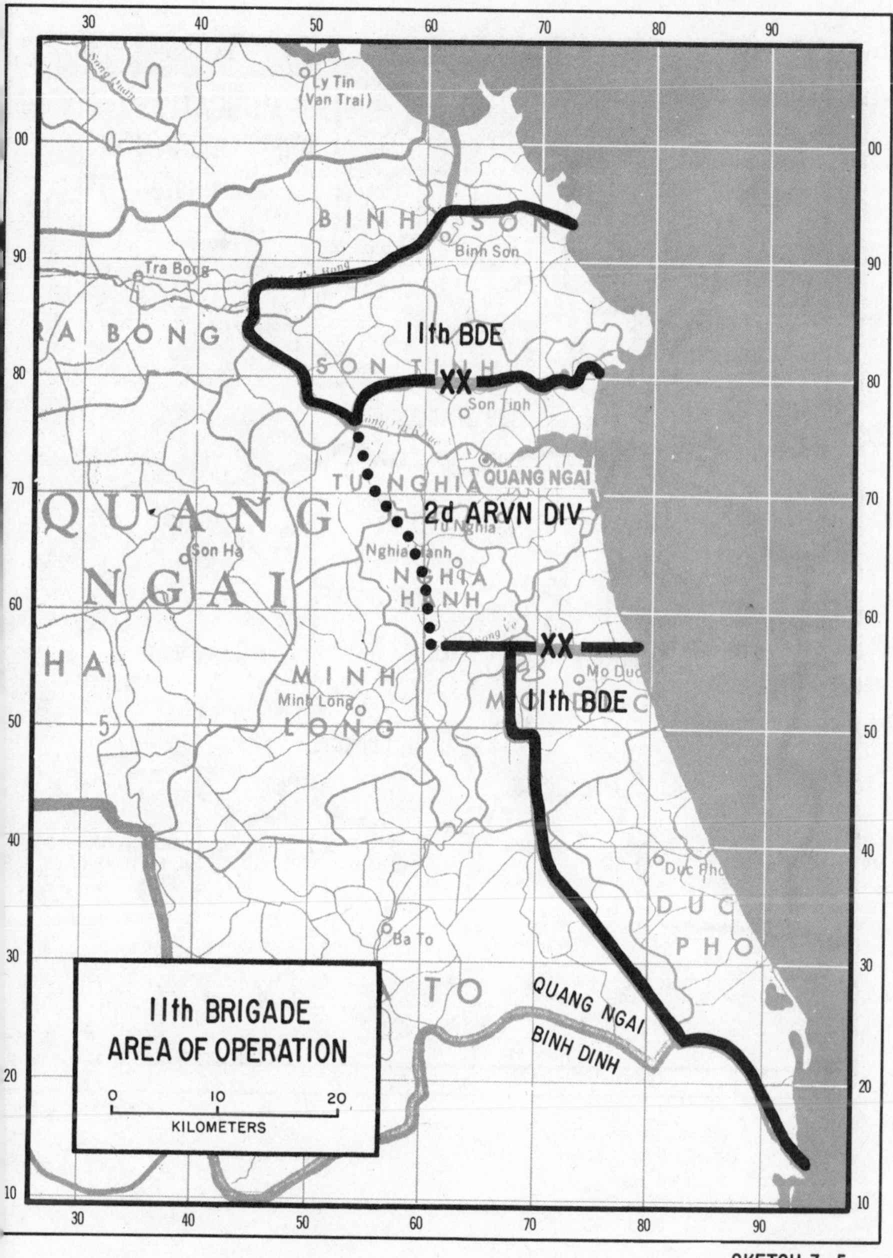

11th BRIGADE
AREA OF OPERATION
0
10
20
KILOMETERS
11th BDE
2d ARVN DIV
11th BDE
XX
XX
QUANG NGAI
BINH DINH
Ly Tin
(Van Trai)
Binh Son
Tra Bong
Son Tinh
QUANG NGAI
Tu Nghia
Son Ha
Nghia Hanh
Mo Duc
Minh Long
Duc Pho
Ba To
BINH SON
SON TINH
TU NGHIA
NGHIA HANH
MINH LONG
DUC PHO
QUANG NGAI

SKETCH 3-5

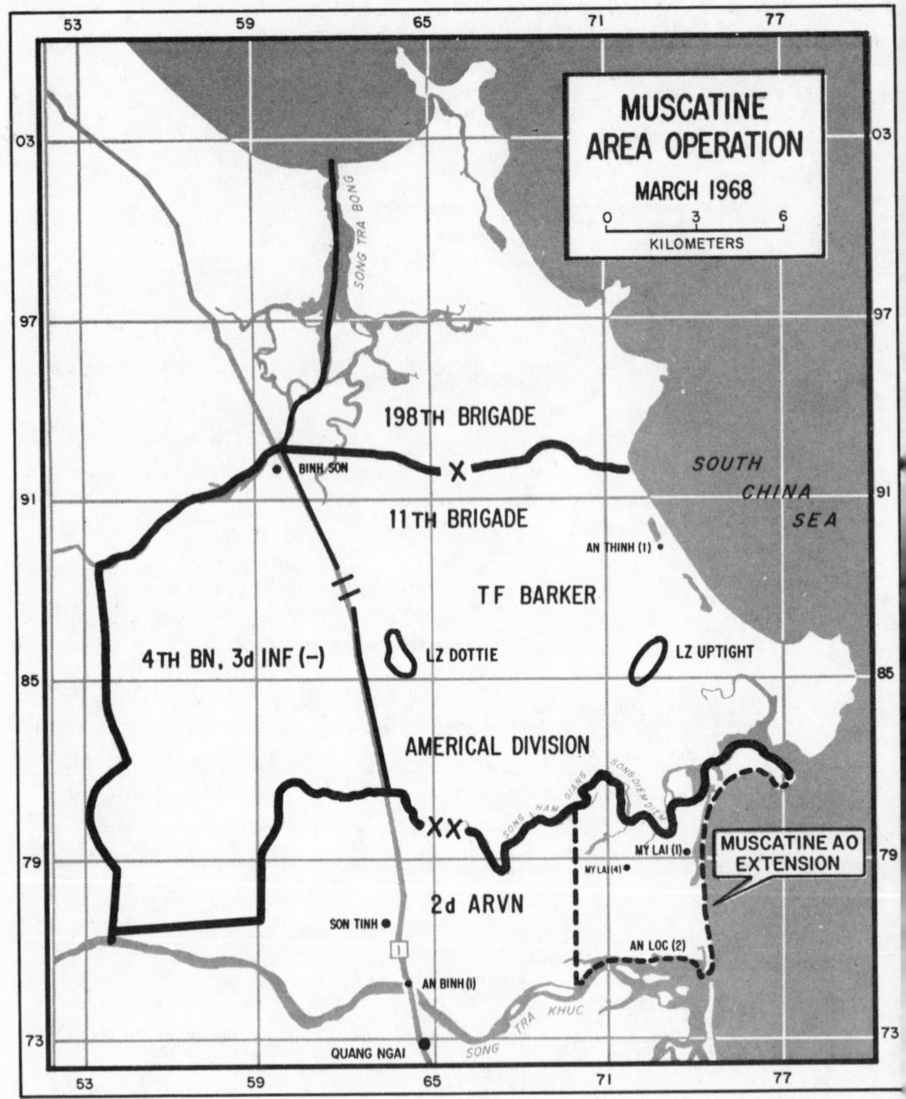
MUSCATINE
AREA OPERATION
MARCH 1968
0
3
6
KILOMETERS
53
59
65
71
77
03
97
91
85
79
73
SONG TRA BONG
198TH BRIGADE
BINH SON
11TH BRIGADE
SOUTH CHINA SEA
AN THINH (1)
TF BARKER
4TH BN, 3d INF (–)
LZ DOTTIE
LZ UPTIGHT
AMERICAL DIVISION
SONG HAM GIANG
SONG DIEM DIEM
MY LAI (1)
MY LAI (4)
MUSCATINE AO EXTENSION
2d ARVN
SON TINH
1
AN LOC (2)
AN BINH (1)
SONG TRA KHUC
QUANG NGAI

SKETCH 3-6

Chapter 4. Organization, Operations, and Training of US Units

The principal units involved in the Son My incident were B/4–3 Inf and C/1–20 Inf of the 11th Infantry Brigade which, upon its deployment to Vietnam, was attached to the Americal Division.

A. Americal (23D) Division

The Americal Division was organized in September 1967 and formally activated in October, when MG S. W. Koster was presented the division colors. Like its predecessor, Task Force (TF) Oregon, and the original Americal, the division was a patchwork organization. Only one of the three separate brigades to be attached to the division, the 196th Infantry, was in Vietnam at the time of activation. The remaining two brigades, the 198th Infantry and the 11th Infantry, were both still in training in Texas and Hawaii, respectively. In the meantime, the Americal Division assumed temporary operational control of 3d Brigade, 4th Infantry Division, and the 1st Brigade, 101st Airborne Division, plus the forces supporting TF Oregon. On 4 October, the 3d Brigade, 1st Air Cavalry Division, was also placed under the operational control of the Americal Division, to participate in Operation Wheeler/Wallowa and so remained until 25 January 1968.

In late October, the 198th Light Infantry Brigade arrived in Vietnam, and, after a month's training at Duc Pho, relieved the 196th Infantry Brigade in place at Chu Lai. The latter, in turn, relieved the 1st Brigade, 101st Airborne Division, which departed from I Corps in late November. In December, the 11th Infantry Brigade deployed from Hawaii, trained in the Duc Pho area under the sponsorship of the 3d Brigade, 4th Infantry Division, and subsequently assumed responsibility for the Duc Pho area on 2 January 1968. The 3d Brigade, 4th Infantry Division, was released from the Americal Division, was moved to II Corps, and was placed under the operational control of I Field Force on 29 February. The 3d Brigade, 82d Airborne Division, was also attached to the Americal Division (less operational control) for a short time on 16 February to 12 March 1968.

By mid-March, the Americal Division was composed of three attached brigades: 11th, 196th, and 198th, plus supporting forces. The division initially was organized with a light division base, since the necessary support elements were organic to each of the three separate brigades. These brigades were initially established as independent brigades to provide the Commander, United States Military Assistance Command Vietnam (COMUSMACV) forces which could be detached and immediately deployed to higher priority areas without disrupting one of the combat divisions or the normal administrative and logistical support system. It was not until April 1969 that the division was fully reorganized and the brigades made organic to the division. This was accomplished by attaching each of the brigade headquarters to the division and relieving the maneuver battalions from assignment to the brigades and assigning them to the division.

It was also necessary to reorganize the austere TF Oregon staff into a full division staff. This proceeded in a piecemeal fashion over a long period of time and, with the division controlling the operations of up to five brigades and about 24,000 men in its early stages, many of the division staff sections experienced difficulty. The staggered arrival of the 198th and 11th Brigades from the United States, for example, necessitated the gradual merger of the personnel services elements of all three brigades into a consolidated unit. New regulations and procedures had to be published quickly to insure uniformity and responsiveness of the personnel management system to support the once independent brigades.

The division faced major personnel problems in meeting the 12-month rotational policy, as did all units in Vietnam. Control of the rotational "hump" within the brigades was particularly acute and required the transfer of personnel between the brigades, known as the infusion program, to reduce the impact and to remain within the restrictions established as to percentage of unit strength allowed to rotate within any one month. This infusion program, plus the receipt of large numbers of replacements arriving from the United States, created considerable personnel turbulence. New arrivals had to be integrated and to become familiar with their new commanders and noncommissioned officers and the operating procedures of their new unit. For the two brigades arriving from the United States in October and December, personnel shortages and the infusion process tended to further reduce the effectiveness of their training and operational readiness.

As the 11th Infantry Brigade completed its movement to Vietnam, the Replacement Detachment of the Americal Division moved to Chu Lai and took over the Division Combat Center where the total replacements received for training each week increased from 300 to a peak of 1,000 for an average of over 500 per week. The Combat Center conducted a 6-day in-country orientation and replacement training course for all replacement personnel plus assigned and attached units. This course was climaxed by a live combat patrol-night ambush operation. Part of the first day's instruction was devoted to the handling of prisoners of war (PW's) and the provisions of the Geneva Conventions. Records of the Americal Division state that 7,700 replacements received instruction in the Geneva Conventions during the period 12 December 1967 to 29 March 1968. (The United States Army, Vietnam (USARV) Inspector General (IG) inspection report of 31 July 1968 lists as a deficiency the lack of instruction on the Geneva Conventions.) Classes were also presented in combat leadership and long-range patrol techniques. As facilities at Chu Lai were substandard in many cases, considerable time was devoted to their improvement in order to provide adequate housing and training facilities for the new replacements. Beginning in December 1967, refresher training was conducted for units to correct deficiencies noted during combat operations and was tailored specifically to the needs of the squad or platoon undergoing the course.

The combat capability of the Americal Division during the September 1967–March 1968 period is difficult to assess, since the composition of the division changed continually, with only the 196th Brigade attached to the Americal for the entire 6 months. The 196th Brigade, operating against elements of the 2d North Vietnamese Army (NVA) Division in Operation Wheeler/Wallowa in January 1968, performed well and accounted for 192 enemy killed in action (KIA) on a single day. Americal Division totals in Wheeler/Wallowa from 1 November 1967 to 31 January 1968 claimed 1,718 Viet Cong (VC) and 1,585 North Vietnamese KIA and 492 individual weapons and 115 crew-served weapons captured. Division losses over the same period in the operation were 220 killed, 713 wounded evacuated, and 342 minor wounded.

B. The 11th Infantry Brigade (LT)

The 11th Infantry Brigade was reactivated in Hawaii in 1966 and was organic to the 6th Infantry Division. Initially the brigade consisted of three infantry battalions—the 3d Battalion, 1st Infantry; the 4th Battalion, 3d Infantry; and the 1st Battalion, 20th Infantry—and had the mission of acting as the US Army Pacific reserve.

When the Secretary of Defense approved, in July 1967, General Westmoreland's request for deployment of additional US ground forces to Vietnam by February 1968, the 11th Infantry Brigade was selected as one of the units to be deployed. Since the brigade was designated for attachment to the Americal Division, it had to be reorganized as a separate light brigade to conform with its two sister brigades. The general effect was to increase the number of infantry troops, to reduce the amount of vehicles and other heavy equipment, and to provide the brigade with additional support elements.

During 1967, the brigade had conducted an active training program which began with air mobility training and was followed by tactical exercises during February and March. In April, an accelerated training program was initiated. Special emphasis was placed upon advanced individual training which included use of the Jungle Warfare Training Center (JWTC). This facility was renovated after being in a caretaker status since departure of the 25th Infantry Division. Each company used the facility for one week. Instructor personnel were sent to Hawaii from the US Continental Army Command (USCONARC) to aid in the training program and 400 fully trained infantrymen joined the brigade to assist in meeting the criteria necessary for an emergency deployment.

In late May and June, the brigade administered battalion and company Army Training Tests (ATT). After the alert was received in July, the brigade began preparation for participation in a 10-day amphibious exercise (Coral Sands II) which was conducted in August off the island of Molokai. This provided one of the limited opportunities for the brigade headquarters to practice command and control over all subordinate manuever elements during a field exercise.

Upon completion of the amphibious exercise, the brigade concentrated upon preparing personnel for deployment. Language training for men who were to be used as interpreters, individual weapons familiarization and record firing, classroom instruction and field firing for crew-served weapons personnel, and orientation lectures on the Vietnam social and tactical environment helped to prepare brigade members for their upcoming mission.

One of the more serious problems facing the brigade was the replacement of over 1,300 men who were nondeployable under existing deployability criteria. The decision in October 1967 to deploy the brigade to Vietnam in December rather than January further magnified the replacement problem. Many filler personnel were added to the brigade to meet the personnel shortfalls. Replacements continued to arrive up until the deployment date, requiring numerous adjustments in the training program. It was necessary to shorten the training schedule from the normal 8 weeks to 4, which made it difficult to provide adequate unit training. The combination of all these factors resulted in considerable confusion and caused significant turmoil in the brigade's personnel status which was detrimental to their predeployment preparation. Even with the influx of replacements, the brigade was still short over 700 men at the time of deployment.

Subordinate units were rescheduled through the JWTC for a 3-day course which all units of the brigade had to attend and complete. One of eleven stations set up for the training was a typical Southeast Asian village where the soldier was taught the proper methods of securing, searching, and clearing villages as well as how to work best with the civilian population. In addition, new M–16 rifles were issued to all personnel just 2 weeks before deployment, which required that familiarization and range firing be conducted up to the last minute.

The 4th Battalion, 21st Infantry, was assigned as the 11th Brigade's 4th Battalion in November 1967 but did not deploy with the brigade to Vietnam in December. It remained in Hawaii to complete its organization and training, and arrived in Vietnam in April 1968.

The main body of the brigade moved by sea from Hawaii to Vietnam during the period 5–22 December, debarking at Qui Nhon and moving to Duc Pho by land and air. It replaced the 3d Brigade, 4th Infantry Division, which acted as the host unit, in the Duc Pho area of operation.

To compensate for the shortened training period in Hawaii, Military Assistance Command, Vietnam (MACV) had agreed to provide the brigade with a month of additional training in-country before it was committed to operations. The 3d Brigade, 4th Infantry Division, provided 3 days of a planned 7-day orientation course (curtailed due to operational requirements) and the 174th Aviation Company instructed brigade personnel on the characteristics of helicopter gunships and troop carriers "Slicks" and conducted combat assault training for the infantry units. The 2d ARVN Division provided a Vietnamese village training course that lasted one day. Conducted in a deserted village near Duc Pho, the course gave a practical demonstration of VC methods of concealment and boobytrapping and emphasized correct search techniques. Other instruction received by the brigade in January included search procedures for locating VC bunkers and "holes," ambush techniques, and the destruction of enemy fortifications and rice caches.

As the brigade made its last-minute preparations for commitment to combat, there was one disturbing element. Additional replacements to bring the brigade up to strength plus the infusion of personnel to ease the rotational hump had produced considerable personnel turbulence. Although undersirable, this was not an uncommon occurrence for many of the units deployed to Vietnam who performed effectively despite this difficulty.

C. Task Force Barker

When the 11th Brigade assumed responsibility for the Muscatine area of operations (AO), it was necessary for the brigade commander to reorganize his forces in order to occupy the area with six rifle companies, which the division commander considered the minimum force required to control the area. BG Andy A. Lipscomb, the brigade commander, opted to establish a separate TF during the period 20–22 January to man the eastern part of the Muscatine AO and designated the 4th Battalion, 3d Infantry (–) as the unit responsible for the western section. This permitted the brigade commander to put six companies in the area.

The TF commander plus an austere staff were drawn from the staff of the 11th Brigade. This weakened and reduced the effectiveness of the brigade staff. LTC Frank A. Barker, Jr., the brigade S3, was chosen to be the TF commander. MAJ Charles C. Calhoun, the brigade S1, was designated a combination Executive Officer/S3, and CPT Eugene M. Kotouc was later assigned as the TF S2.

TF Barker (named after its commander) consisted of three companies, one from each of the brigade's battalions. These were: A/3–1 Inf, B/4–3 Inf, C/1–20 Inf. Each was considered by the brigade commander to be the best company in its battalion. Also attached to the TF were: the 3d Platoon, Troop E, 1st Cavalry (–); elements of the 2d Platoon, Company C, 26th Engineer Battalion; and a squad from the 11th MP Platoon. Battery D, 6th Battalion, 11th Artillery (a provisional battery consisting of four 105 howitzer instead of the normal six) located at Landing Zone (LZ) Uptight was in direct support.

From 22 January through 15 March 1968 the TF suffered over 100 friendly casualties, about 40 percent of which occurred during operations in the Son My area during the month of February. During the same period the TF estimated enemy casualties to be about 300 killed and wounded and 50 captured; the recorded individual weapons captured totaled about 20.

D. Company C, 1st Battalion, 20th Infantry (C/1–20 INF)

Company C had an authorized strength of six officers and 175 enlisted men until early March 1968, when the authorized enlisted strength was reduced to 158 men by an Army-wide change to the rifle company Table of Organization and Equipment (TOE). However, the operating strength of the unit was much lower. Of the 5 officers and 125 enlisted men available for duty in mid-March, approximately 20 were required to remain at the company's rear base to provide administrative and logistics backup for the company. Eleven enlisted men from other units were attached to the company, increasing field operating strength to about 120 men.

Organized as a standard rifle company, the unit had a headquarters platoon, three rifle platoons, and a weapons platoon. Because of the company understrength, some of the platoons operated with only two squads.

Since December 1966, the company had been commanded by CPT Ernest L. Medina. He had led the unit through the regular training program conducted by the 11th Infantry Brigade in Hawaii, where Company C had participated in intensive jungle training, as well as limited amphibious and air mobility training and exercises and had passed its ATT. After the brigade was alerted in mid-1967 for deployment to Vietnam at the end of the year, the company began an accelerated training program for the oversea movement.

Among the many subjects covered, according to testimony of some witnesses, was routine instruction on the handling and treatment of prisoners. This instruction was directed primarily toward the so-called 5 S's—Search, Silence, Segregate, Speed, and Safeguard. During this instruction, little emphasis was placed on the treatment of civilians and refugees or the responsibility for reporting war crimes or atrocities.

Company C was selected to deploy with the advance element of the brigade in the move to Vietnam and was consequently scheduled to leave Hawaii on 1 December 1967. The earlier departure date further compressed all training to a minimum during November as the company was heavily engaged in screening out personnel ineligible to deploy, receiving new replacements, and drawing and preparing equipment for the move. The influx of newly assigned personnel into the company (over 50 percent of the strength) during the predeployment period tended to further reduce the effectiveness of the training program.

After arriving in the Duc Pho area in early December, the company attended the brigade's in-country indoctrination training program. Indications are that instruction on the handling and treatment of civilians or refugees was not covered during this training. The company immediately began to carry out small squad-size patrols, to man the brigade perimeter at night, and to construct bunkers during the day. Orientation and training in the Duc Pho area continued until January 1968 when the company was assigned to TF Barker and moved to the Muscatine AO.

During the 7 weeks prior to the Son My operation, Company C did not engage in any major combat action. It did participate in patrolling and other offensive operations and also acted as a base security force.

Contacts with the enemy were light and confined to sniper fire. The bulk of the company's casualties from hostile action during the January to mid-March period were caused by enemy mines and boobytraps. Of the casualty total of 4 killed and 38 wounded, only 1 of the killed and 2 of the wounded resulted from direct enemy contact.

A survey of the personnel assets of Company C indicates that none of the men had had significant combat experience before the Son My operation and that this was their first major assault role. In the matter of leadership, CPT Medina was considered to be an outstanding company commander by his men and superiors, but the platoon leaders were not so regarded.

Two-thirds of the 23 noncommissioned officers in the company were enlistees and the majority were above the average in all evaluated areas. There was a higher percentage of high school graduates and men with college credits in this group than was found throughout the Army at that time with the majority being above the average in general learning and infantry ability.

The remainder of the enlisted men represented an average cross section of enlistees and inductees with about 40 percent being enlistees and slightly over 60 percent inductees. The inductees, as a group, had less education and were less trainable than the average for Army-wide accession for the period. Despite this, they were better than average in infantry aptitude. Well over 50 percent were high school graduates and almost a fourth of the enlistees had some college credits. The average age of the enlistees was just under 21 years. The inductees were above the average in practically every evaluated area. Close to 80 percent were high school graduates and about 17 percent had college credits. Average age of the inductees was 22 years.

About 8 percent of the enlisted personnel, less noncommissioned officers, fell into the Project One Hundred Thousand category and were in the lowest mental group. The percentage of this group was lower than the Army-wide accession figure of 12 percent.

Taken as a whole, the personnel composition of Company C contained no significant deviation from the average and there was little to distinguish it from other rifle companies.

E. Company B, 4th Battalion, 3D Infantry (B/4–3 INF)

Company B had an authorized strength of 6 officers and 175 enlisted men until March 1968, when the enlisted strength was reduced to 158 men.

In mid-March 1968, there were 5 officers and 134 enlisted men assigned to the company. Of these, 2 officers and 63 enlisted men had been assigned since the company's arrival in Vietnam. Because of personnel requirements for administrative and logistic backup for the company, the field operating strength was reduced to approximately 115 men. The company was organized as a standard rifle company, but because it was understrength, the first and second platoons were reduced to two rifle squads each for the Son My operation.

During 1967 the company followed the regular training program conducted by the 11th Infantry Brigade in Hawaii. After the brigade was alerted in mid-March 1967 for deployment to Vietnam, the company began, as did all other units, an intensive training program to prepare for tactical operations in Vietnam emphasizing weapons training, the Vietnam social environment, and counterinsurgency operations. Routine instruction on the handling and treatment of prisoners was also covered. Again, no special emphasis was placed on the treatment of civilians and refugees or the responsibilities for reporting war crimes or atrocities. The assignment of approximately 50 replacement personnel during the 2-month period before embarkation undoubtedly resulted in deployment of some personnel without adequate unit training.

After arriving in the Duc Pho area in mid-December, the company received the same indoctrination training as all other rifle companies of the brigade and soon began to carry out small squad-size patrols, to man the perimeter at night, and to construct bunkers during the day. Orientation and training in the Duc Pho area continued until January 1968 when the company was assigned to TF Barker and moved to the Muscatine AO.

A survey of the personnel assets of Company B indicates that few of the men had had significant combat experience. There were no Vietnam returnees in the company and only two noncommissioned officers had previous combat experience before Vietnam. However, the company was familiar with and respected the hazards of the Son My area due to its previous operations there.

In the matter of leadership, the company commander, CPT Michles, was considered an extremely conscientious, career-motivated officer. He had commanded Company B for 15 months and had demonstrated sincere interest in the welfare of his officers and men. He led his company into this operation short one commissioned platoon leader. He took to the field two lieutenants. One was considered a mature, solid officer trying to do a job. The other was described as quiet, intelligent, but basically not motivated toward a career as an Army officer. The latter officer had arrived in-country only 3 weeks before the Son My operation.

The noncommissioned officers in the company were apparently well selected with emphasis on quality. Two-thirds of the 27 noncommissioned officers were enlistees. The majority were above the average found throughout the Army in all evaluated areas. This included overall trainability, infantry aptitude, general learning ability, distribution among the four mental categories, and percentage of high school graduates or higher.

The remainder of the enlisted men ranked below the average for the Army in all areas evaluated except preinduction education. This group was composed of 29 percent enlistees and 71 percent inductees. The only significant differences within the categories of inductees and enlistees were that the enlistees were better in infantry aptitude and the inductees had a higher percentage of high school graduates and men who had attended college.

When the noncommissioned officers and other men are analyzed as a group, the enlisted personnel of the company are nearly identical to the accessions that entered the Army during the same period of time.

Taken as a whole, the personnel composition of Company B contained no significant deviation from the Army-wide average and there was little to distinguish it from other rifle companies.

F. Previous Task Force Barker Operations in the Son My Area

There were two significant operations conducted in the Son My area by TF Barker during the month of February 1968.

The first of these operations began on 13 February and was targeted against the 48th Local Force (LF) Battalion. The general concept was for C/1–20 Inf to act as a blocking force north and northwest of My Lai (4) for elements of B/4–3 Inf pushing toward that position from just north of Route 521. A/3–1 Inf was to attack east on the northside of Route 521 to My Lai (1). Elements of the 2d ARVN Division also participated in this operation but remained south of Route 521, the boundary between the units.

As B Company approached My Lai (4), heavy fire was received from the enemy occupying prepared positions in the hedgerows and tree lines. A platoon of B Company attempted to flank the enemy position and was pinned down. A platoon of armored personnel carriers (APC's) was committed and, by using heavy suppressive fires, extracted the platoon. ARVN withdrew their forces during the night and B Company was withdrawn. Company B had one man killed and five men wounded in the action. There were 78 VC reportedly killed by the end of the day.

Company A continued the attack the following day and encountered heavy resistance from My Lai (1). The third day, B Company was airlifted into the area to support A Company in a sweep of My Lai (1). However, the VC had slipped away during the night and only light resistance was encountered. A search of the hamlet revealed an intricate and deep tunnel complex with reinforced brick rooms located 12 to 20 feet underground. After securing approximately 3 tons of enemy equipment, the two companies partially destroyed the tunnel system and returned to their base area. Results of the 3-day operation were 3 US killed and 15 wounded with 80 VC reported killed; no enemy weapons were captured.

The second operation began on 23 February with the 48th LF Battalion again being the target. Two rifle companies, A/3–1 Inf and B/4–3 Inf, plus the same platoon of APC's, were the principal forces in the operation. C/1–20 Inf was located about 10 kilometers north of My Lai (4).

Company B occupied blocking positions north and northeast of My Lai (4). Company A had the mission of attacking to the east toward My Lai (1) while the platoon of APC's screened the right flank along Route 521. Heavy enemy fire was received, including mortars, recoilless rifles, rockets, and automatic weapons, as Company A and the APC's advanced toward the coast. Artillery and air strikes were quickly called in and the APC's swept toward the enemy outpost line; two APC's were hit and the platoon leader was seriously wounded. Following additional artillery and air strikes against the enemy positions, the APC's again attacked and, this time, took a heavy toll of the enemy. In the meantime, Company A continued to put pressure on the VC, but lost some of its momentum when the company commander was wounded. By late afternoon the enemy broke contact and was able to escape by intermingling with civilians evacuating the combat zone and by using the complex tunnel system honeycombing the sector.

Company B, which had only light contact throughout the operation, linked up with Company A, and, with the APC's, withdrew to the TF base. During the night and the following day Company B lost one man and had 10 men wounded from enemy grenades and boobytraps. To the north, Company C suffered five casualties from sniper fire and killed two VC.

The total casualties for the 2-day operation were three US killed and 28 wounded, plus two APC's damaged. There were 75 VC reported killed, one PW, and six individual weapons captured during the operation. This was the last major offensive action in the Son My area prior to the 16 March 1968 assault.

In addition to these tactical operations, there were some psychological operations conducted in the area during the period immediately prior to the Son My incident, although none were targeted specifically at Son

My.* The Son My area had been a frequent target of earlier psychological campaigns aimed at encouraging the people to leave the VC-controlled area and return to Government of Vietnam (GVN) control. According to the Division Psychological Operations (PSYOPS) officer, standard leaflets and broadcasts which followed the theme of "move out now and begin a new life under the GVN" were normally used for this purpose. Some leaflets apparently implied that those who elected to remain in the area would be considered as VC or VC sympathizers. Even so, there was no indication that all the noncombatants had moved out of the area.

* AERIAL BROADCASTS

Date	*Location*	*Length*	*Theme*
1 Mar	3 Kms NW of Thuan Yen (My Lai (4))	20 min	Unite with GVN to build an economical powerful Vietnam
2, 4 Mar	3 Kms N-NW of Thuan Yen	20 min	Surrender to the just cause of the GVN
13 Mar	4 Kms NW of Thuan Yen	30 min	Chieu Hoi

LEAFLET DROPS

Date	*Location*	*Number*	*Theme*
4 Mar	3 Kms N-NW of Thuan Yen	100,000	Reward for VC Weapons
13 Mar	4 Kms NW of Thuan Yen	250,000	(1) Chieu Hoi; (2) These planes will destroy you (3) Message for Infiltration Troops
13 Mar	2 Kms NE of Thuan Yen	150,000	Chieu Hoi

Chapter 5. The Son My Operation, 16-19 March 1968

The purpose of this chapter is to provide an overview of the preparations for and conduct of the Son My operation conducted by TF Barker during the period 16–19 March 1968.

A. Concept of the Operation

The Son My operation was conceived and planned by LTC Frank A. Barker, CO of Task Force (TF) Barker, and his immediate staff. Within the Americal Division, it was normal procedure for a battalion or TF commander to plan and conduct operations within his assigned area of operations (AO). It was also the policy for the division commander to approve the scheme of operation prior to its execution. Although MG Koster testified that he did not recall approving the operation, he remembers part of the plan being described to him, and it is likely that he did approve it. It is also probable that BG Lipscomb, commander of the 11th Brigade until 15 March 1968, approved the concept and timing of the operation as the basis for obtaining an extension of the brigade's normal AO from the 2d Army Republic of Vietnam (ARVN) Division (see sketch 5–1). COL Henderson, who became CO of the 11th Brigade on 15 March 1968, was also briefed on the operation and gave it his approval. It is probable, however, that none of these commanders was briefed on the details for executing the plan.

The concept of the operation was that TF Barker, employing all three of its attached rifle companies, would conduct a search and destroy operation in the Son My area beginning on 16 March 1968. Search and destroy operations were at that time officially defined by Military Assistance Command, Vietnam (MACV) directives as those operations conducted for the purpose of seeking out and destroying enemy forces, installations, resources, and base areas. These operations were oriented on enemy forces inside or outside of US units' assigned tactical areas of responsibility. In the case of TF Barker, the objective was the entrapment and elimination of the 48th Viet Cong (VC) Local Force (LF) Battalion and two separate local force companies, and the destruction of their logistical support base and staging area. The 48th had, for several years, roamed throughout Son Tinh District and, more recently, had used the Son My area as a base for its logistical support activities. During the March 1968 time frame the 48th probably received periodic resupply by enemy sea trawlers operating off the Batangan Peninsula.

At the time of the 16–19 March operation, the 48th was considered as posing a continuing and imminent threat against Quang Ngai City. A MACV intelligence assessment, issued the latter part of February 1968, indicated that the 48th had recently been furnished with additional troops from district forces and a possible North Vietnamese Army (NVA) replacement packet, and intended to combine with other local forces to initiate an offensive against Quang Ngai City. Previous operations by TF Barker elements in the Son My area had clearly established that the 48th possessed heavy weapons, including 12.7mm machineguns, rockets, and mortars. It was believed by the TF headquarters that the 48th had been instrumental in inflicting casualties on TF elements during those previous operations (see chap 4).

Since the Son My area * was not within TF Barker's normal AO, clearance for the temporary extension of the AO was obtained through Son Tinh District and Quang Ngai Province headquarters, and from the 2d ARVN Division which had primary tactical responsibility for the area.

B. Issuance of Orders and Instructions

The order for the Son My operations was issued orally by LTC Barker at Landing Zone (LZ) Dottie, site of the TF Barker command post, on the afternoon of 15 March 1968. LZ Dottie was located approximately 11 kilometers northwest of the Son My area. No written orders were issued by the 11th Brigade concerning the operation and there has been no substantial evidence developed to indicate that TF Barker issued either

* Village, hamlet, and subhamlet titles used in the reconstruction of events described in this chapter (and depicted on accompanying sketch maps) are based on US Army Topographic maps in existence at the time of the Son My operation. Refer to chapter 3 for titles currently used by Government of Vietnam (GVN) authorities for the various political subdivisions within Son My Village.

an operation overlay or a written fragmentary order to supplement the oral instructions. (One witness [CPT Gamble] testified that he received an information copy of a written operation order subsequent to the 15 March briefing, but it appears from the testimony of CPT (now Mr.) Vazquez, who was the TF Barker fire support coordinator, that CPT Gamble is referring to an artillery firing overlay prepared by Vazquez, rather than an operations overlay from TF Barker. In any event, the overlay was destroyed by Gamble soon after he received it.) Other witnesses who testified as to the possible issuance of operations overlays/orders were not able to recall specifically their content or eventual disposition.

Attending the 15 March briefing were:

LTC Frank A. Barker	CO, TF Barker
MAJ Frederic W. Watke	CO, B Company (Aero-Scout), 123d Avn Bn
MAJ Charles C. Calhoun	S3, TF Barker
CPT Eugene M. Kotouc	S2, TF Barker
CPT Stephen J. Gamble	CO, D Battery, 6–11th Arty
CPT (now Mr.) Dennis R. Vazquez	Artillery Liaison Officer
CPT (now Mr.) William C. Riggs	CO, A/3–1 Inf
CPT Earl R. Michles	CO, B/4–3 Inf
CPT Ernest L. Medina	CO, C/1–20 Inf
* 1LT (now Mr.) Donald R. Millikin	Plt Leader ("Dolphins"), 174th Avn Co
* WO1 (now 1LT) Michael O. Magno	Assistant S3, 174th Avn Co

COL Henderson had arrived at LZ Dottie at 1330 hours, and prior to issuance of the operation order addressed all or most of the assembled group. He briefly reviewed the concept of the forthcoming operation and then discussed several combat performance areas in which he and BG Lipscomb, previous commander of the 11th Brigade, felt that TF Barker elements had been deficient and, as a result, had failed to accomplish their objective. He emphasized the necessity and advantages of establishing and maintaining close and aggressive contact with the enemy. Several witnesses testified that he also alluded to the elimination of the 48th LF Battalion "once and for all." CPT Medina testified that COL Henderson's briefing also linked together the unit's past failure to aggressively prosecute enemy contacts with the low rate of enemy weapons captured in those

* Probable attendees.

operations. According to CPT Medina, COL Henderson referred to their lack of aggressiveness as permitting "men, women, or children, or other VC soldiers in the area" to pick up the weapons and get away. SPT Medina's recollection of this aspect of COL Henderson's briefing is not substantiated by the testimony of other witnesses who were in attendance at the briefing, but MAJ Calhoun, the S3, did testify concerning an earlier operation in the Son My area during which a captured enemy mortar was retrieved by two armed VC women in the midst of a firefight.

C. Intelligence Briefing

Following COL Henderson's remarks and his departure from LZ Dottie at 1415 hours, CPT Kotouc, the TF S2, gave an intelligence briefing to the assembled group. In his briefing, he indicated that the 48th VC LF Battalion was dispersed throughout the Son My area. He testified that both he and LTC Barker felt that the VC headquarters and two companies, totaling over 200 enemy, would be located in the subhamlet of My Lai (4). MAJ Calhoun and MAJ Watke testified, however, that the TF Command group deduced that the enemy headquarters was located in "Pinkville" or My Lai (1). Whatever the basis for the intelligence estimate, the testimony of CPT Medina and other members of C Company indicates clearly that they fully expected, based on the intelligence briefing, to encounter an enemy force of between 200–250 in My Lai (4) on the following morning.

During the intelligence briefing and/or LTC Barker's operational briefing (see below), the civilian population within the Son My area was categorized as "active sympathizers with the VC." Several witnesses testified that it was stated by both Barker and Kotouc that most of the civilian inhabitants would be out of the Son My hamlets and on their way to local markets by 0700 hours on the morning of 16 March 1968 (this was a Saturday morning, normally a marketing day for the Vietnamese). Some reference was also apparently made, or had been made, to previous leaflet drops and helicopter-borne loudspeaker broadcasts which had allegedly warned the civilian inhabitants of Son My to evacuate the area and move to GVN-controlled areas in order to avoid potential injury from forthcoming allied operations. The context in which the leaflet drop/loudspeaker information was briefed to TF Barker personnel on 15 March, and, in fact, whether it was actually briefed on 15 March (as opposed to an earlier or later date) is not certain from the testimony developed. Examination of pertinent records of TF Barker, the 11th Brigade, and the Americal Division, however, reveals no evidence of any leaflet drop or aerial broadcast directed at the inhabitants of My Lai (4) during the period 1 through 20 March 1968, and those drops and broadcasts which were conducted in the vicinity of the Son My area during this time did not advise the inhabitants to evacuate the area. In any case, the probable presence of civilians within the operational area on the morning of 16 March 1968 was taken into account by LTC Barker in the development of his operational plan, particularly as it pertained to the employment of artillery preparatory fires.

D. Operational Orders and Instructions

Following the intelligence briefing by CPT Kotouc, an operations briefing and implementing instructions were given by MAJ Calhoun, TF S3, and LTC Barker. MAJ Calhoun testified to the effect that he does not recall specifically what information was presented by him and what information/instructions were given by LTC Barker, but that Barker had personally selected the location for the landing zones and the artillery preparation which were to be used on the following day. MAJ Calhoun also testified that the instructions presented at the 15 March briefing pertained only to plans for the first day of the operation, 16 March.

LTC Barker's death in action on 13 June 1968 and the absence of any written instructions or operational overlays provided during the operations briefing have made it necessary to reconstruct the planned scheme of maneuver and operational instructions almost exclusively from testimony of witnesses present at the briefing and/or who habitually worked in the TF Headquarters. While the instructions described herein and the planned scheme of maneuver depicted on sketch map 5–2 are presented as a cohesive entity, the preponderance of the pertinent testimony indicates that the orders and instructions were issued to various individuals in a somewhat piecemeal fashion throughout the afternoon of 15 March, and that during MAJ Calhoun's briefing on the planned scheme of maneuver, the details were depicted only on the tactical operations center (TOC) map, which was presumably erased or discarded subsequent to the Son My operation. (As part of a Combat After-Action Report which he submitted on 28 March 1968, LTC Barker inclosed a sketch depicting the maneuver of his attached and supporting units [see exhibit R–2]. The sketch generally corroborates the testimonial reconstruction of his overall scheme of maneuver, but it is inconsistent in its depiction of the movement of C Company, with that discussed during the 15 March 1968 briefing and with the actual maneuver of C Company which occurred during the combat assault.)

LTC Barker's plan called for the operation to commence at 0725 hours on 16 March with a 3- to 5-minute artillery preparation to precede the initial airmobile combat assault by Company C into a LZ west of the subhamlet of My Lai (4) (see sketch 5–2). Planned insertion time for the first lift of Company C was 0730 hours, to be followed by a second lift as soon as possible. Insertion of the first lift, following the artillery preparation, was to be supported by suppressive fire from helicopter gunships during the touchdown and unloading of the assault troops. Following completion of the combat assault, Company C was to move generally east through My Lai (4). (The preoperational briefing apparently did not include instructions pertaining to C Company actions which occurred in the subhamlet of Binh Tay and other subhamlets east of My Lai (4) on 16 March. Those actions resulted from supplementary orders issued during the course of the operation (see chap. 6).) After completing the sweep of My Lai (4), C Company was to move northeast to link up with Company B in a nighttime defensive position approximately 1½ to 2 kilometers to the northeast of My Lai (4). The nighttime position was apparently designated as an objective area primarily to provide a basis for coordinating the movements of Company C and Company B.

Following insertion of Company C, a second combat assault was to be conducted by Company B into an LZ south of My Lai (1), unless they were required to reinforce Company C in the assault on My Lai (4). A secondary artillery preparation was also planned on the LZ south of My Lai (1) to precede insertion of B Company elements. Thereafter, B Company was to move north through My Lai (1), then west to link up with C Company.

Company A, the third attached rifle company, was assigned the mission of moving the night of 15–16 March from field positions located east of LZ Dottie into blocking positions on the northern bank of the Song Diem Diem, almost due north of the Son My area. Company A was to maintain these blocking positions throughout 16 March in order to trap enemy forces attempting to escape from the Son My area to the north.

The 174th Aviation Company was to provide five troop-carrying helicopters, LTC Barker's command and control helicopter, and accompany gunships required to support and control the combat assaults by C Company and B Company. Four additional troop lift helicopters were to be provided by the 71st Aviation Company.

An aero-scout team from B Company, 123d Aviation Battalion, which provided direct support for TF Barker, was to screen the area to the south of the My Lai (4) and My Lai (1) complex. (The aero-scout team consisted of one OH–23 observation helicopter and two accompanying UH–1B armed helicopter gunships.)

TF Barker had also arranged to have US Navy "Swift Boats" patrol the coastal waters east of the Son My area off the Batangan Cape.

A fourth rifle company, A/4–3 Inf, was also placed under the operational control of TF Barker during the period 14–18 March 1968. It played no active role in the Son My operation per se, but was employed to provide local security for LZ Dottie and LZ Uptight during the course of the operation. It was returned to control of its parent battalion at 1700 hours on 18 March.

From the evidence available, it appears that unit movements followed subsequent to 16 March were not specifically planned or discussed during the 15 March briefing. The scheme of maneuver for 17, 18, and 19 March was apparently contingent on the events of 16 March and was executed in response to supplementary oral orders issued by LTC Barker following the combat assaults on 16 March.

After the operational briefing, LTC Barker took several of his subordinates on an aerial reconnaissance of the target area.

E. Issues Concerning LTC Barker's Briefing

In view of subsequent events at Son My, the key issues which emerge concerning the 15 March briefing involve the orders and instructions issued by LTC Barker and his staff (and subsequently by his subordinates) concerning (a) the planned artillery and gunship preparatory fires, (b) the burning or destruction of houses and other structures, (c) the killing of livestock and destruction of other foodstuffs, and (d) the handling of noncombatants encountered during this operation.

The artillery preparation was to be fired by D/6–11 Arty (consisting of four 105mm howitzers) which was located at LZ Uptight. There is conflicting testimony as to whether LTC Barker planned to have the artillery preparation fired on the LZ for C Company, on the hamlet of My Lai (4), or on parts of each. CPT Vazquez, artillery liaison officer to the TF, testified that LTC Barker wanted the preparation placed on the LZ but had also specified that he wanted the tree and bunker line along the western edge of the hamlet "covered" to knock out enemy weapon positions which he expected to be set up there. CPT Gamble, CO of D/6–11 Arty, testified from memory that the general location of the planned preparation was to the west of My Lai (4) but stated that any confirmatory records which would have contained the precise map coordinates of the planned preparatory fires were destroyed (in accordance with his unit SOP) after retention in the unit's files for a period of 6 months. CPT Gamble's immediate superior, LTC (now COL) Luper, stated that he discussed the planned preparatory fires with LTC Barker on 15 March 1968 and that LTC Barker wanted the fires placed on

My Lai (4). MAJ Calhoun and CPT Kotouc both testified to the effect that LTC Barker considered the probability of noncombatants' being present in My Lai (4) at the time of the artillery preparation, and decided to fire the preparation anyway as a means of minimizing friendly casualties from the entrenched enemy which he also expected to be present at My Lai (4) on the morning of 16 March. The preponderance of the testimony thus indicates that LTC Barker's plan called for the artillery preparation to be fired onto the LZ for Company C and into the western and southwestern portions of My Lai (4) without prior warning to the inhabitants (see sketch 5–3). Testimony provided by aviation witnesses also indicates that LTC Barker's plan called for helicopter gunship suppressive fires to be placed on and around the LZ to protect the troop-carrying helicopters in the interval from the time the artillery preparation ceased until the troops were inserted on the ground.

While there is some conflict in the testimony as to whether LTC Barker ordered the destruction of houses, dwellings, livestock, and other foodstuffs in the Son My area, the preponderance of the evidence indicates that such destruction was implied, if not specifically directed, by his orders of 15 March. (CPT Medina testified that during the aerial reconnaissance of the target area, subsequent to the briefing at LZ Dottie, he received explicit instructions from LTC Barker to destroy My Lai (4). These instructions were apparently not overheard by other participants in the aerial reconnaissance, but would have been consistent with the planned objective of neutralizing or destroying the 48th VC Battalion's logistical support base in the Son My area.) Whether LTC Barker attempted to make any distinctions, during the briefing or in his subsequent instructions, between dwellings, livestock, and foodstuffs of noncombatants versus those belonging to the VC is highly doubtful since he and his staff apparently acted upon the intelligence assessment that virtually the entire Son My area was controlled and inhabited by VC and VC sympathizers. Further, CPT Kotouc testified that at some time on the 15th he was informed by LTC Barker that the village was to be destroyed, including homes, livestock, and foodstuffs.

The preponderance of the evidence also indicates that at the TF level no specific plans or arrangements were made for the handling of any noncombatants found in the Son My area. Further, the testimony of persons who were present at the 15 March briefing indicates strongly that LTC Barker did not issue any instructions pertaining to the problem of collecting and processing noncombatants who might be encountered during the planned operation. Several witnesses have testified to a vague recollection of the unit standing operating procedure (SOP) to be followed in evacuating noncombatants from operational areas, but there is no indication that such an SOP was referred to by LTC

Barker or any of his staff during the 15 March briefing. (While the evidence also indicates that TF Barker had no written SOP, it would be normal for a battalion or task force to operate on the basis of unwritten but generally understood "standing operating procedures.")

There is no substantial evidence that LTC Barker directly ordered the deliberate killing of noncombatants. However, when considered in the light of the information concerning (a) the alleged leaflet drops and loudspeaker broadcasts, (b) the generally accepted intelligence picture of Son My as being comprised almost exclusively of "VC and VC sympathizers," (c) the assumption that most of the civilians would be "gone to market" at the time of the artillery preparation and combat assault, (d) LTC Barker's decision to fire the artillery preparation on at least a portion of My Lai (4), (e) the commonly known results of previous operations by TF Barker in the Son My area, and (f) the overall concept of the operation, it seems reasonable to conclude that LTC Barker's minimal or nonexistent instructions concerning the handling of noncombatants created the potential for grave misunderstandings as to his intentions and for interpretation of his orders as authority to fire, without restriction, on all persons found in the target area.

Following the briefing, LTC Barker took all of his company commanders, CPT Vazquez, and possibly CPT Kotouc on an aerial reconnaissance of the Son My area. The reconnaissance was apparently intended to provide the company commanders and the artillery liaison officer with a final visual familiarization of the target area, to include their own landing zones and assigned objectives, and to provide CPT Gamble and CPT Michles with transportation back to LZ Uptight. As noted earlier, CPT Medina testified that during the reconnaissance LTC Barker specifically instructed him to destroy My Lai (4). There is no evidence to suggest, however, that LTC Barker embellished his original orders and instructions during the reconnaissance or at any subsequent time prior to the actual beginning of the operation.

F. Subsequent Briefings by Company Commanders

Following LTC Barker's briefing and the aerial reconnaissance, his company commanders returned to their unit areas and issued their own implementing orders. (Since the evidence developed in this Inquiry shows no positive indications of war crimes perpetrated by members of A Company during the ensuing operation, only the briefings given by the B and C Company commanders are described herein.)

CPT Michles, the B Company commander, followed his normal

procedure of issuing his orders to the platoon leaders, his artillery forward observer (FO), and selected members of his command group. Key personnel who attended his briefing were:

1LT (now CPT) Kenneth W. Boatman	Artillery FO
1LT (now CPT) Thomas K. Willingham	Platoon Leader, 1st Platoon
1LT Roy B. Cochran	Platoon Leader, 2d Platoon
SSG (now Mr.) Franklin McCloud	Acting Platoon Leader, 3d Platoon
SSG Edward O. Vann	Acting Platoon Leader, Weapons Platoon
SGT (now Mr.) Barry P. Marshall	Squad Leader, CP Security Squad
SP4 (now Mr.) Lawrence Congleton	Radio/Telephone Operator (RTO)

(CPT Michles was killed in a helicopter crash with LTC Barker on 13 June 1968. The details of the orders which he issued on 15 March 1968 have been developed from the testimony of some of the individuals listed above.)

1LT Boatman testified that CPT Michles began his briefing by quoting LTC Barker as having said, "everything down there was VC or VC sympathizers." 1LT Boatman also said Michles told them, "we've had a lot of trouble there, not just a little," and they were to "go down and clean the place out."

1LT Willingham stated that he received instructions from CPT Michles to "burn all villages." 1LT Boatman also testified that similar instructions were issued by CPT Michles. The command group and platoon leaders all understood that the operation was to be a search and destroy operation. In particular, 1LT Willingham said this was the first operation during which the company had to destroy the hamlets of the "Pinkville" area. SP4 Congleton left the briefing with the impression that the area was to be completely destroyed.

The testimony from individual members of the rifle and weapons platoon has provided conflicting information concerning the issuance of orders for the operation. The majority recalled that the briefings were conducted by their squad leaders, although the second platoon may have been briefed by 1LT Cochran. The testimony indicates that these briefings provided more details on the essentials of getting to the objective area than a thorough orientation on the methods of accomplishing the mission. Generally, the substance of the briefings was considered routine and standard procedures were to be used. They did not receive any special instructions on destruction of villages and livestock or on the handling of VC suspects and noncombatants. Because of their experience from two previous operations in the area, they expected to encounter numerous mines and boobytraps. Although the term "search and destroy" was used to describe the mission by most witnesses, they were not told, nor did they expect to get orders on destruction procedures until they were in the objective area.

There were exceptions to the above interpretation. Three men, two from the first platoon, believe they were to shoot anyone found in the objective area. One of these men recalled either CPT Michles or his platoon leader saying, "This is what you have been waiting for—'search and destroy'." Undoubtedly there is some substance to these exceptions. The testimony does not suggest that there was a special effort to prepare the company emotionally for a revenge-type mission. CPT Michles did not stress this operation (in the same manner as CPT Medina) by assembling his men and discussing it with them on 15 March. While at the pickup zone on the morning of the 16th, however, he did remind the men to be extra cautious.

CPT Medina assembled most of the officers and men of C Company to issue his orders and instructions for the planned operation. (C Company witnesses testified that CPT Medina's briefing was held following a memorial service for a former member of the company who had been killed in action a few days previously. The testimony of these witnesses is inconclusive as to whether the service was held on 15 March immediately prior to the briefing, or whether it was held prior to the 15th.)

Key personnel who attended CPT Medina's briefing were:

CPT Eugene M. Kotouc	TF S2
2LT (now Mr.) Roger L. Alaux, Jr.	Artillery FO
2LT (now 1LT) William L. Calley	Platoon Leader, 1st Plt
2LT Stephen K. Brooks	Platoon Leader, 2d Plt
2LT (now Mr.) Jeffery U. LaCross	Platoon Leader, 3d Plt
SFC Isaiah Cowan	Platoon SGT, 1st Plt
SSG David Mitchell	1st Squad Leader, 1st Plt
SSG L. G. Bacon	2d Squad Leader, 1st Plt
SFC (now 1SG) Jay A. Buchanon	Platoon SGT, 2d Plt
SGT Kenneth L. Hodges	1st Squad Leader, 2d Plt
CPL (now SGT) Kenneth Schiel	2d Squad Leader, 2d Plt
SGT Lawrence C. LaCroix	3d Squad Leader, 2d Plt
SSG (now SFC) Manuel R. Lopez	Platoon SGT, 3d Plt
SGT (now Mr.) John H. Smail	1st Squad Leader, 3d Plt
SP4 (now Mr.) Joe Grimes, Jr.	3d Squad Leader, 3d Plt
SFC Leo M. Maroney	Platoon SGT, Mortar Plt

(One witness from C Company testified that there were one or more field grade officers also in attendance at Medina's briefing. This is not substantiated by other available evidence.)

CPT Medina testified that at the time of his briefing he felt sure that the company would make heavy contact with the enemy the next morning and would probably suffer heavy casualties. He stated that he was deeply concerned about it and that he "tried to convey this same message to the people in Charlie Company" during the course of his briefing. Using a stick or some such device he sketched out the planned scheme of maneuver on the ground as he briefed his men. All of his orders and instructions were issued orally, as is the usual case with a company-size unit.

During his briefing, CPT Medina reiterated the purported intelligence concerning the 48th VC Battalion's location in My Lai (4). He told his men that they would probably be outnumbered approximately 2 to 1 and that he expected the LZ to be "hot," or under enemy fire, when the first lift touched down. He informed his men of the artillery preparation and then described his planned scheme of maneuver (see sketch 5–4). The 1st Platoon, which was to be inserted onto the LZ first, was assigned the right (or southern) sector of the hamlet with the mission of "sweeping the enemy out to the open area on the east side of the village." The 2d Platoon was assigned the left (or northern) sector of the hamlet and had the same mission as the 1st Platoon. The 3d Platoon was to be used initially as the company reserve, with the mission of providing security for the LZ and then to search and clear the hamlet in greater detail after the 1st and 2d Platoons had completed their sweeps. A mortar squad from the Weapons Platoon was to accompany the 3d Platoon into the LZ and provide mortar fire support to the company, if needed. If not required, the squad was to move with and assist the 3d Platoon. CPT Medina also issued general instructions concerning cleaning of weapons, and discussed ammunition loads to be carried the next day. He reminded his men of the need to be thorough and careful in searching and destroying the numerous tunnels and bunkers which he expected to encounter at My Lai (4). At the same time, allegedly because of COL Henderson's earlier remarks, CPT Medina reemphasized the necessity for aggressively closing with the enemy in order to prevent retrieval of enemy weapons from dead VC by "other men, women, children, or other VC soldiers in the area."

With respect to the key issues involved in his issuance of orders and instructions, the evidence is conclusive that CPT Medina ordered the men of his company to burn and destroy My Lai (4), and to kill all livestock and destroy other foodstuffs found in the area. The evidence is less explicit but equally convincing that CPT Medina's orders and instructions concerning the inhabitants of My Lai (4) left little or no doubt in the minds of a significant number of men in his company that all persons remaining in the My Lai (4) area at the time of combat assault were enemy, and that C Company's mission was to destroy the enemy. According to his own testimony, this was based on his having been told (during the TF briefing) that "there would be no civilian population in the village. Any men, any women and children would be gone to market at 0700 hours." CPT Medina's acceptance of this estimate is further evinced by his own testimony that during his remarks to his men "any reference made as to what we might find in My Lai (4) was that of the 48th VC Battalion." He explained that he was trying to prepare his men "mentally and physically to meet a VC Main Force Battalion . . . trying to build their morale up, giving them psychological bread to go in and do battle with the 48th VC Battalion." Many witnesses have testified that CPT Medina also made reference to casualties which the company had recently taken from enemy mines, booby-traps, and sniper fire, and that he alluded to the forthcoming operation as an opportunity for "revenge" or to "get even" with the enemy. In a very real sense, then, it appears that the operation took on the added aspect of a grudge match between C Company and an enemy force in My Lai (4).

There is no substantial evidence to indicate that CPT Medina discussed procedures to be followed in case any civilian inhabitants of My Lai (4) elected to stay home from the market on the morning of 16 March 1968.

Later in the evening, CPT Medina held another meeting with his platoon leaders and their platoon sergeants. Testimony concerning the substance of this meeting is conflicting, but it appears that nothing was said which altered in any way his earlier instructions concerning the next day's operation.

The testimony of key personnel is also inconclusive with regard to the conduct or content of subsequent platoon-level briefings by 2LT's Calley, Brooks, or LaCross. LT LaCross testified to the effect that any instructions issued by him related only to organizing and equipping his men for the operation. Briefings of a similar nature apparently were given by LT's Calley and Brooks.

The preponderance of the testimony from most C Company personnel is consistent in their description of the men's reaction to CPT Medina's briefing as described in the following representative examples:

> When we left the briefing we felt we were going to have a lot of resistance and we knew we were supposed to kill everyone in the village.
>
> —William Calvin Lloyd, 1st Plt, C/1–20 Inf

> . . . the attitude of all the men, the majority, I would say was a revengeful attitude, they all felt a little bad because (we) lost a number of buddies prior to My Lai (4).
>
> —SGT Gregory T. Olson, 1st Plt, C/1–20 Inf

> That evening, as we cleaned our weapons and got our gear ready, we talked about the operation. People were talking about killing everything that moved. Everyone knew what we were going to do.
>
> —Robert Wayne Pendleton, 3d Plt, C/1–20 Inf

I would describe the mood (of C Company) as a feeling that they were going to wreak some vengeance on someone—things hadn't been very good to us up until that time.

—SGT Michael A. Bernhardt, 2d Plt, C/1–20 Inf

Although CPT Medina didn't say to kill everyone in the village, I heard guys talking and were of the opinion that everyone in the village was to be killed. At this time we had had a lot of casualties from a minefield and everybody was pretty well shook up.

—James Robert Bergthold, 1st Plt, C/1–20 Inf

. . . we were all "psyched" up because we wanted revenge for some of our fallen comrades that had been killed prior to this operation in the general area of "Pinkville."

—Allen Joseph Boyce, 1st Plt, C/1–20 Inf

We expected strong VC resistance. We were really expecting trouble. We were all psyched up.

—Dennis Irving Conti, 1st Plt, C/1–20 Inf

. . . it seemed like it was a chance to get revenge or something like that for the lives we had lost.

—Tommy L. Moss, 2d Plt, 1C/1–20 Inf

The succeeding portions of this chapter provide a summary of the chronology and sequence of events which occurred throughout the Son My operation. Chapter 6 contains a more detailed account of C Company actions in and around the subhamlet of My Lai (4) on 16 March and in the hamlet of My Khe on 17 March. Chapter 7 contains a similar account of B Company actions in the hamlets of Co Luy and My Lai during the period 16–19 March.

G. Summary of Operations on 16 March

During the night of 15–16 March, the 2d Platoon of A Company moved from the company's night defensive position in the vicinity of Hill 108 (see sketch 5–5) to a blocking position along the river due south of the hill mass. At approximately 0530 hours on the morning of the 16th, the remainder of the company began its movement by foot toward designated blocking positions along the Song Diem Diem, north of the Son My area. As the company moved to the east, its lead elements received fire from an estimated squad-size enemy force located in the vicinity of Phu My (1), and one man from Company A was slightly wounded. The fire was returned, the enemy dispersed, and the 1st and 3d Platoons continued moving toward their respective blocking positions located to the east and south of Phu My (1). At 0725 hours all elements of A Company were reported to be in position.

By 0708 hours, five troop-carrying helicopters and two accompanying gunships from the 174th Aviation Company, and four troop-carrying helicopters from the 71st Aviation Company arrived at LZ Dottie. They were loaded with the 1st Platoon (consisting of approximately 28 men), with a 6–8 man command group from the company headquarters (including CPT Medina), and with 18–24 members of the 2d Platoon. The first load lifted off from LZ Dottie at approximately 0715 hours.

The initial marking round for the artillery preparation was fired from LZ Uptight at approximately 0722 hours and detonated about 1,000 meters to the north of My Lai (4). CPT Vazquez, the artillery liaison officer, stated that he observed the smoke marking round from his vantage point in LTC Barker's command and control helicopter, and relayed firing adjustment instructions to the fire direction center at LZ Uptight. He has testified that the firing adjustment instructions were coupled with his order for the entire battery to "fire for effect" immediately following the 1,000-meter shift. CPT Vazquez subsequently testified that this order was given to conserve time and "get on with the operation."

The full artillery preparation began at approximately 0724 hours and impacted both on the LZ for C Company and in the southwestern portion of My Lai (4). There is conflicting testimony as to the number and type of rounds that were fired in the preparation. Several witnesses testified that the preparation probably consisted of as few as 30 rounds and contained no white phosphorous shells. The preponderance of the evidence, however, indicates that from 60 to 120 mixed rounds of point detonating high explosive ammunition along with some white phosphorous ammunition were fired in the preparation.

Shortly before insertion of C Company's first lift, the aero-scout team from B Company, 123d Aviation Battalion arrived in the Son My area and established their aerial screen generally parallel to and south of Route 521. Several members of the aero-scout team observed the artillery preparation going into the north of their location.

The lead ship of the troop-carrying helicopters, inbound toward the LZ at about 0727 hours, contacted LTC Barker by radio and was advised by him that there were "no restrictions on door gunners" in the placing of helicopter suppressive fires on the area. Following completion of the artillery preparation at about 0729 hours, gunship suppressive fires, consisting of rockets and machinegun fire, were placed on the LZ and probably on portions of My Lai (4).

The lead elements of C Company touched down at 0730 hours, approximately 100–150 meters west of My Lai (4). The LZ was officially recorded as "cold" or free of enemy fire. C Company personnel hit the ground running and immediately took up positions from which to secure the LZ for subsequent lifts. The troops lift helicopters returned to LZ Dottie for pick up of the second lift while the two accompanying "Shark" gunships remained orbiting over the My Lai (4) area.

The second lift of C Company departed from LZ Dottie at 0738 hours. It consisted of the remaining personnel from the 2d Platoon, the entire 3d Platoon (approximately 30 men), seven to nine men from the company mortar platoon, two men from the 52d Military Intelligence detachment, and two personnel from the 11th Brigade Public Information Office (PIO).

The second and final lift of C Company was inserted at 0747 hours. As the helicopters were departing the LZ, the lead ship reported having received fire from one of the hamlets in the vicinity of My Lai (4) but apparently sustained no hits on the aircraft nor any casualties among the troop passengers.

COL Henderson's command group, on the morning of 16 March, consisted of COL Henderson, MAJ McKnight (11th Brigade S3), LTC Luper (CO 6–11th Artillery), LTC MacLachlan (Air Force Liaison Officer to the 11th Brigade), CSM Walsh (11th Brigade Sergeant Major), and SGT Adcock (COL Henderson's radio operator). COL Henderson and MAJ McKnight have testified that the command and control helicopter had reported late to the brigade headquarters that morning, and the command group consequently did not arrive over the operational area until approximately 0750 hours. However, LTC MacLachlan and SGT Adcock testified that the command group arrived over the area in time to observe the artillery preparation and first insertion by C Company (approximately 0725 hours). LTC Luper also testified that the preparation was visible from a distance as they arrived in the area and that they observed the landing of C Company's first elements. CSM Walsh remembered few of the details concerning the combat assault.

Upon arriving in the vicinity of My Lai (4), both COL Henderson and MAJ McKnight recall observing helicopter gunships orbiting to the northeast of the LZ and dropping red smoke markers on the ground. COL Henderson orbited above that point and observed two bodies dressed in uniforms with web gear and two weapons. He and MAJ McKnight testified that at about this same time, they also observed a large number of personnel (approximately 300) moving out of the operational area in "an orderly manner" along Route 521 to the southwest. At approximately 0800 hours, MAJ McKnight contacted LTC Barker by radio to advise him of the mass departure. Barker acknowledged the transmission and informed McKnight that he would send the aero-scout team over the area to "check out" the people along the road. Shortly afterwards, MAJ McKnight contacted the aero-scout team himself and informed them that COL Henderson's command and control ship was orbiting over the column of departing personnel and had observed three individuals dressed in black. The scout team subsequently notified

MAJ McKnight that two of the three individuals had been stopped and were available to be picked up. At approximately 0810 hours, the two suspects were picked up by COL Henderson's command and control helicopter. COL Henderson then observed B Company's combat assault.

After completion of the C Company combat assault, the troop lift helicopters had flown to LZ Uptight where they loaded the first lift of B Company. A second artillery preparation, which was to support the B Company landing, began at 0808 hours and was completed at approximately 0812 hours. Shortly afterwards, the first lift of B Company was inserted onto the LZ, located approximately 500 meters south of My Lai (1). The LZ was reported as being "cold." By 0830 hours, the remaining elements of B Company had been lifted from Uptight into the same LZ.

Following B Company's combat assault, COL Henderson apparently returned to the area north of My Lai (4) where he had previously observed the two bodies with weapons.

On the ground, C Company had earlier formed up with the 1st and 2d Platoons generally on line and had begun its movements to the east toward My Lai (4) (see sketch 5–6). Lead elements of the company entered its western edge at approximately 0750 hours. CPT Medina and the command group initially remained behind on the LZ as elements of the company entered the hamlet.

At approximately 0830 hours, during the course of the company's movement through the hamlet, the 2d Platoon moved out into the open area to the north of My Lai (4) to retrieve the two enemy weapons observed by COL Henderson. The location of the weapons was marked by "Shark" gunships which had returned from supporting the B Company combat assault. After retrieving the weapons, the platoon was directed by CPT Medina to move to the subhamlet of Binh Tay located 400 meters north of My Lai (4) proper.

Following his observation of the C Company elements, COL Henderson returned to LZ Dottie, arriving there at approximately 0845 hours. He released the two VC suspects to a Military Intelligence prisoner interrogation team and spoke to MG Koster who arrived later. COL Henderson denied having spoken to LTC Barker during this time or having visited the TOC where the details of the operation were being monitored, recorded, and reported to his headquarters at Duc Pho. LTC MacLachlan and MAJ Calhoun testified, however, that they observed COL Henderson talking with LTC Barker, inside the TOC, during this period of time.

MG Koster arrived at LZ Dottie at 0935 hours. He apparently spoke to COL Henderson for approximately 15–30 minutes and then departed. According to his testimony, he had spent the earlier part of the morning in the northern part of the Americal Division's zone, and is uncertain as to whether he flew over the Son My area prior to his arrival at LZ Dottie. COL Henderson testified that he was under the impression, at the time he spoke to MG Koster, that Koster had flown over the area.

LTC Barker spent most of the morning in his command and control helicopter over the operational area, controlling and coordinating the combat assaults. Evidence indicates that he returned to LZ Dottie on at least three occasions during the morning. He returned the first time at approximately 0835 hours for refueling. The evidence available indicates that he remained on the ground until approximately 0855 hours and that he took advantage of the time not only to refuel his helicopter, but also to bring the personnel in his TOC up to date on the results of the operation.

Back in the Son My area, the 2d Platoon of C Company reached the subhamlet of Binh Tay at approximately 0845 hours, and remained in and around that area for approximately one hour. Following completion of its action, the platoon returned to My Lai (4) to rejoin the rest of the company which had set up a perimeter along the eastern edge of the hamlet.

To the east, B Company had encountered no reported resistance to its movement north toward My Lai (1), but suffered one man killed (the 2d Platoon leader) and four wounded from a boobytrap detonated on the southwestern edge of the hamlet (see sketch 5–7).

At approximately 0850 hours, the aero-scout team screening to the southwest of B Company reported capturing two 60mm mortar tubes along with 60mm and 82mm mortar ammunition. This report was later amended to reflect only the 60mm mortar ammunition.

As B Company progressed toward My Lai (1), another enemy boobytrap was detonated, wounding three men. LTC Barker had returned from LZ Dottie to the My Lai (1) area and used his command and control helicopter to evacuate the three wounded men from B Company at approximately 0945 hours.

Because of the heavy concentration of mines and boobytraps in and around My Lai (1), the 3d Platoon of B Company was diverted to the northwest to search out the hamlet of My Lai (6) while the 2d Platoon and the command group remained in the area west of My Lai (1).

Following his pickup of the B Company wounded, LTC Barker had the helicopter drop him off for a second time at LZ Dottie at approximately 0950 hours, while the wounded men were taken by his helicopter to the medical facility at Chu Lai.

After leaving LZ Dottie at approximately 1000 hours, COL Henderson returned to the operational area until about 1030 hours, when he departed for a courtesy call on the 2d ARVN Division Commander at

Quang Ngai City, and a subsequent lunch break at his headquarters in Duc Pho. MG Koster apparently also departed LZ Dottie at approximately 1000 hours.

Although lead elements of the 1st Platoon of C Company had reached the eastern edge of My Lai (4) by about 0900 hours, the company continued to operate in that area until about 1330 hours before moving on to the northeast to link up with B Company.

By the time the company was ready to begin its movement to the northeast for the link-up, a total of 90 VC had been reported killed along with 3 weapons captured, and 23 VC suspects detained in the vicinity of My Lai (4). One soldier from C Company had been wounded in the foot apparently as a result of the accidental discharge of a weapon while inside My Lai (4).

B Company's 1st Platoon, which was operating along the coast to the east of My Lai (1), reported killing several groups of enemy and capturing assorted enemy equipment at the same general location beginning at 0955 hours (see sketch 5–7). The platoon reported a total of 30 enemy KIA accumulated by 1025 hours and by 1420 hours had reported killing a total of 38 enemy and capturing assorted gear. By that time, the remainder of the company had completed its sweep through My Lai (6) and the area west of My Lai (1) and had reached the night defensive position west of the hamlet. The 1st Platoon subsequently moved north from the site of the reported enemy dead and established a platoon defensive position along the coastline near My Lai (3) (see sketch 5–8).

COL Henderson testified that he returned to the operational area early in the afternoon, following his meeting at Quang Ngai City and a subsequent stopoff at the brigade headquarters at Duc Pho. During the afternoon, he stopped off at LZ Dottie on at least two occasions, during which time he discussed the operation with LTC Barker. He also testified that he overflew the Son My area, observing the operation, at least twice during the afternoon. He returned to Duc Pho in the late afternoon.

By approximately 1530 hours, C Company had completed its movement from My Lai (4) to the night defensive position and shortly thereafter linked up with B Company (see sketch 5–9). (According to the TF Journal, the 1st Platoon of C Company subsequently moved to a night defensive position located about 800 meters to the southwest of the main defensive site.) C Company brought 10 suspects to the night defensive position where they were subsequently interrogated by Vietnamese National Police elements. The National Police had been flown into the position by helicopter and were accompanied by CPT Kotouc, TF S2. CPT Kotouc also delivered instructions from LTC Barker concerning the continuation of the operation on 17 and 18 March.

During the day, A Company had suffered two boobytrap casualties within the 3d Platoon blocking position, but had failed to detect any enemy fleeing north toward their positions.

The aero-scout team from B Company, 123d Aviation Battalion had continued to support the operation in Son My and the peripheral area throughout most of the afternoon of the 16th.

Operating to the east of B Company, the Navy "Swift Boats" sighted and boarded several sampans containing Vietnamese males and children. At approximately 1700 hours, these detainees were turned over to B Company elements.

After having visited the 11th Brigade headquarters at Duc Pho (from 1510 to 1535 hours), MG Koster returned to LZ Dottie at 1645 hours, bringing with him LTG Edgar C. Doleman (Ret.) who was visiting the Americal Division in conjunction with a special study of communications systems in Southeast Asia (COMSEA). MG Koster and LTG Doleman (Ret.) were briefed on the operation by LTC Barker, and departed LZ Dottie at 1715 hours.

By the evening of 16 March 1968, TF Barker had reported a total of 128 VC killed, 3 weapons captured, assorted mines, boobytraps and equipment captured and destroyed, and friendly casualties of 2 killed and 11 wounded from the first day's action in the Son My operation. With the possible exception of one man, slightly wounded, from A Company, none of the TF Barker casualties was inflicted by direct enemy fire.

H. Summary of Operations on 17 March

At 0400 hours on the morning of the 17th, persons assumed to be VC were detected crossing the bridge south of the blocking position occupied by A Company's 1st Platoon. They were engaged by the platoon and withdrew immediately. Following this encounter, A Company remained in its designated blocking positions throughout most of the remainder of the day.

Early that morning, both C Company and B Company began moving toward the south from their night defensive position. B Company skirted the southern edge of My Lai (1) and moved to the bridge located to the southeast of the hamlet (see sketch 5–10). The company began crossing the Song My Khe at that point at about 0800 hours. At 0810 hours the company had one man wounded from a boobytrap detonated near the eastern end of the bridge and shortly thereafter reported receiving sniper fire from the vicinity of My Khe (4). The company continued moving to the south along the coastline. At 1320 hours, B Company's 2d Platoon reported killing one VC approximately 400 meters north of Co Lay (1). Subsequently, the company passed through Co Lay (2) and Co Lay (3) before returning to the north again later in the day.

C Company also moved to the south, generally parallel to B Company, and passed through the subhamlets of My Khe (3), My Khe (1), and My Khe (2) (see sketch 5–10). En route, one man was wounded by an enemy mine or boobytrap detonated in the vicinity of Hill 85 at 0930 hours. He was evacuated by helicopter at 1000 hours.

During the course of its movement to the south, C Company discovered several mines and boobytraps in and around the hamlets, and at 1410 hours reported engaging and killing two VC to the southwest of My Khe (1). At 1530 hours, while moving into My Khe (2), C Company reported apprehending three VC suspects consisting of two men and one woman.

After reaching the Song Tra Khuc, C Company turned back to the north toward a night defensive position located to the east of My Khe (1) and on the western side of the Song Kinh Giang (see sketch 5–11). While en route to this location, elements of the company were reported to have found one VC hiding in a tunnel approximately 1,000 meters north of My Khe (2). The individual was killed by the throwing of a grenade into the tunnel. C Company reached their selected night location at approximately 1800 hours.

After reaching the Song Tra Khuc, B Company also turned back to the north and moved along the coast until it reached its defensive position, located approximately halfway between Co Lay (1) and My Khe (4) (see sketch 5–11). B Company was closed into that location by 1900 hours, and reported no further action during the remainder of the 17th.

Late in the afternoon, A Company (minus the 2d Platoon) had moved from its northern blocking positions to night ambush sites located in the vicinity of Giem Dien (1), on the southern side of the Song Diem Diem (see sketch 5–12). In the meantime, the 2d Platoon had moved from its position along the Song Diem Diem, to establish a night ambush position approximately 1 to 1½ kilometers to the northwest. At 2115 hours, the company commander reported that the company (–) had received six to seven rounds of enemy 60mm mortar fire. Friendly casualties from the fire were two killed and five wounded. The casualties were subsequently determined to have been caused by hand grenades apparently hurled into the company's positions by enemy sappers. The wounded were evacuated by 2245 hours and A Company reported no further action on the 17th.

I. Summary of Operations on 18 March

By 0800 hours on the morning of 18 March, both B and C Companies had moved out from their previous night positions. C Company initially moved west back through My Khe (1) and then swung north toward the pickup zone in the vicinity of My Lai (3). B Company continued to move along the coast in the direction of the fish ponds north of My Lai (2) (see sketch 5–13).

As C Company passed to the west of My Lai (1), it suffered two more casualties from an enemy boobytrap. One platoon was left behind to secure a pickup zone for the medical evacuation helicopter and the remainder of the company continued its movement to the north.

At approximately 1300 hours, the company received word that COL Henderson was en route to its location to talk with the company commander, CPT Medina. A landing site was secured approximately 900 meters to the northwest of My Lai (1) and COL Henderson and members of his command group landed shortly thereafter. They remained on the ground 10–30 minutes, then departed, and the company continued its movement to the helicopter extraction site near My Lai (3).

After reaching the My Lai (3) area, C Company secured its own pickup zone. The extraction began at 1420 hours and was completed, with all elements back at LZ Dottie, by 1630 hours. The extraction was carried out through the use of two or three UH–1 "Slick" helicopters. The first load of C Company men to be extracted was met at LZ Dottie by COL Henderson.

Earlier that morning, A Company (–) had begun moving northwest from the Giem Dien area. The company crossed the Song Ham Giang at a fording site and by 2045 hours that night had reached a night defensive position in the vicinity of Hills 108 and 109 (see sketch 5–14). The company reported no further action that night.

By 1900 hours, B Company had reached the fish ponds in the vicinity of Ky Xuyen (1), and collected the inhabitants to facilitate a search of the area (see sketch 5–15). Subsequently, the inhabitants of Ky Xuyen (2) and An Ky were also rounded up and moved into Ky Xuyen (1) so that the two subhamlets would be clear for searches to be conducted by B Company on the following day. The 1st Platoon then established an ambush location approximately 200 meters to the north of Ky Xuyen (1). No further activity was reported by B Company on 18 March.

J. Summary of Operations on 19 March

At 0130 hours on 19 March, CPT Michles reported that B Company was receiving incoming mortar rounds. Approximately 15–16 mortar rounds and enemy small arms fire were received in the initial volley, resulting in one soldier killed and five wounded. CPT Michles requested a medical evacuation helicopter and a light fire team (two gunships) to assist him. By 0245 hours the wounded had been evacuated and the gunships were on station. They remained on station until 0300 hours and then returned to Duc Pho. At 0440 hours, CPT Michles reported receiving an additional two rounds of enemy mortar fire with no resultant friendly casualties.

After first light, the 1st Platoon searched the area to the northeast of its night defensive position in an attempt to locate the enemy mortar position and found the mortar firing position but no enemy mortar.

At 1050 hours, LTC Barker began extraction of B Company from the Son My area, using his command and control helicopter for troop lift. The 1st Platoon was extracted first and was taken to LZ Uptight. The remainder of the company was extracted to LZ Dottie and had closed at that location by 1345 hours.

B Company's return to LZ Dottie on 19 March 1968 concluded TF Barker operations in the Son My area.

K. Subsequent Operations by TF Barker (See sketch 5–16)

There is no evidence to indicate that any TF Barker elements entered the Son My area again following the 16–19 March operation.

Following the operation, the rifle companies of the TF were employed in operations which were apparently routine and of no present significance, until they left the TF to rejoin their present battalions. Until they left the TF, the companies were employed in the areas and time periods described below. During this period they were apparently broken down into platoon and squad-size elements and conducted semi-independent operations within their assigned areas.

Following its arrival in an area northeast of LZ Uptight on 19 March, A Company continued to conduct operations along the eastern coast of Binh Son District until 24 March. These operations were apparently designed to assist in protecting the rice harvest which was then in progress. No significant enemy contacts were reported during this period. The Company returned by helicopter to LZ Dottie on 24 March, remained there through the 25th, and then moved to provide local security for LZ Thunder located to the south near Duc Pho. Following its movement to LZ Thunder, A Company did not participate in any further operations by TF Barker.

On 19 March, B Company was airlifted from the Son My area to LZ Dottie, and remained at that location through 23 March, to provide local security forces for both LZ Dottie and LZ Uptight. On 24 March, the company moved by foot to the vicinity of hill mass 108–109, approximately 3 to 5 kilometers to the southwest of LZ Uptight, and continued operations in that area through 1 April. Only scattered contacts occurred during this period, with a total of five VC reported as killed by the time B Company returned to LZ Dottie and LZ Uptight on the afternoon of 2 April. B Company remained at LZ Dottie until the TF was disbanded on 8 April.

After being relieved of the local security mission by B Company, C Company moved overland on 20 March to an area approximately 5 kilometers east of LZ Dottie. Operations were conducted from that location to a distance of about 5 kilometers to the northwest during the period 20–25 March with no reported enemy contact. On 26 March, the company was airlifted back to LZ Dottie where it assumed the security mission from A Company until 2 April. On 3 April the company conducted a one-day operation approximately 6 kilometers north-northeast of LZ Dottie, and returned to Dottie by nightfall of that same day. On 4 April, the company moved by foot to an area approximately 6 kilometers north-northwest of LZ Dottie and conducted operations in that area until 8 April. On 8 April, C Company was extracted by helicopter and was moved to rejoin its parent battalion (1st Battalion, 20th Infantry) which was then engaged in Operation Norfolk Victory (I) southwest of Quang Ngai City.

TF Barker was officially disestablished at 1200 hours, 8 April 1968.

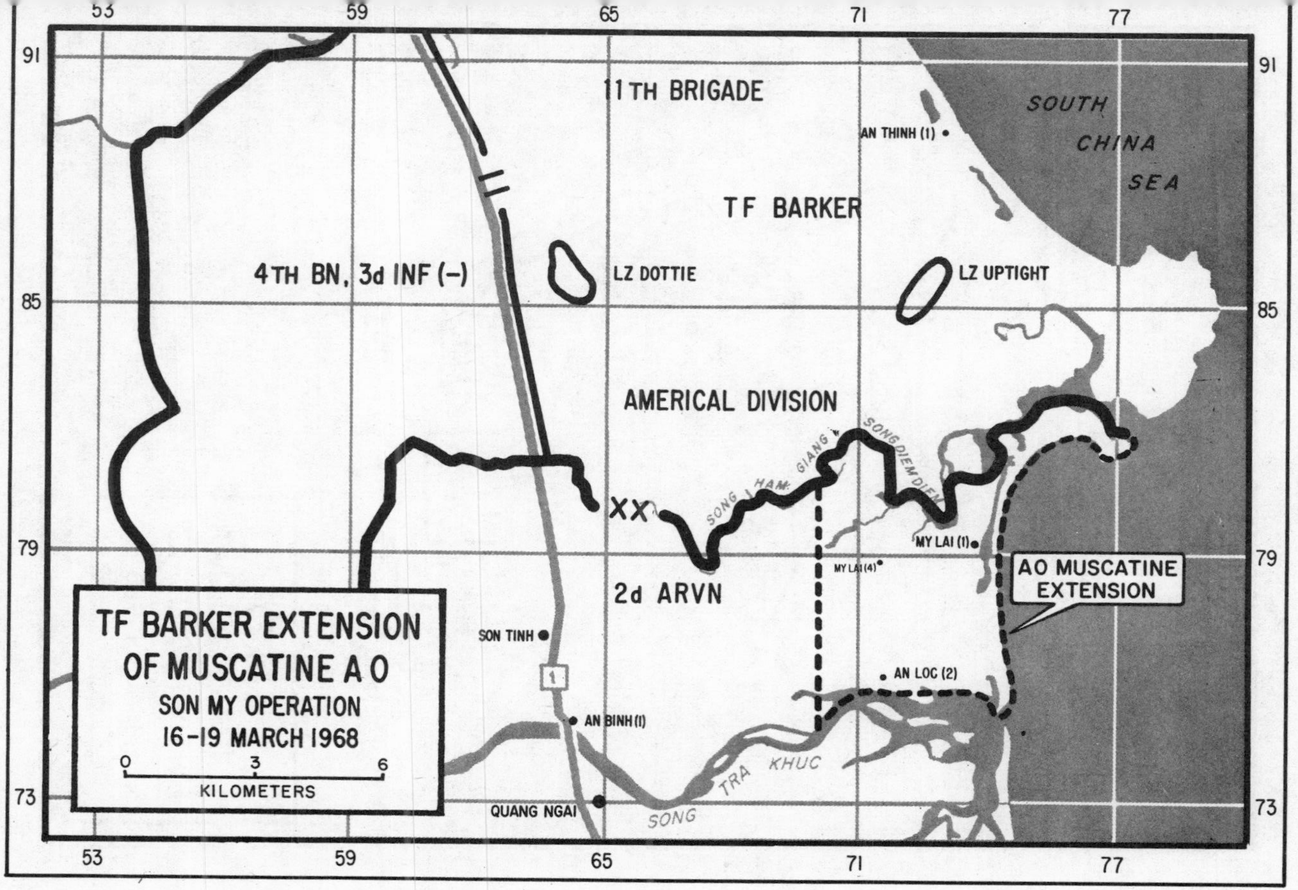

TF BARKER EXTENSION
OF MUSCATINE A O
SON MY OPERATION
16-19 MARCH 1968
0
3
6
KILOMETERS
11TH BRIGADE
TF BARKER
4TH BN, 3d INF (-)
LZ DOTTIE
LZ UPTIGHT
AMERICAL DIVISION
2d ARVN
XX
SOUTH CHINA SEA
AN THINH (1)
MY LAI (1)
MY LAI (4)
AN LOC (2)
SON TINH
AN BINH (1)
QUANG NGAI
SONG HAM GIANG
SONG DIEM DIEM
SONG TRA KHUC
AO MUSCATINE EXTENSION
1
53
59
65
71
77
91
85
79
73

SKETCH 5-1

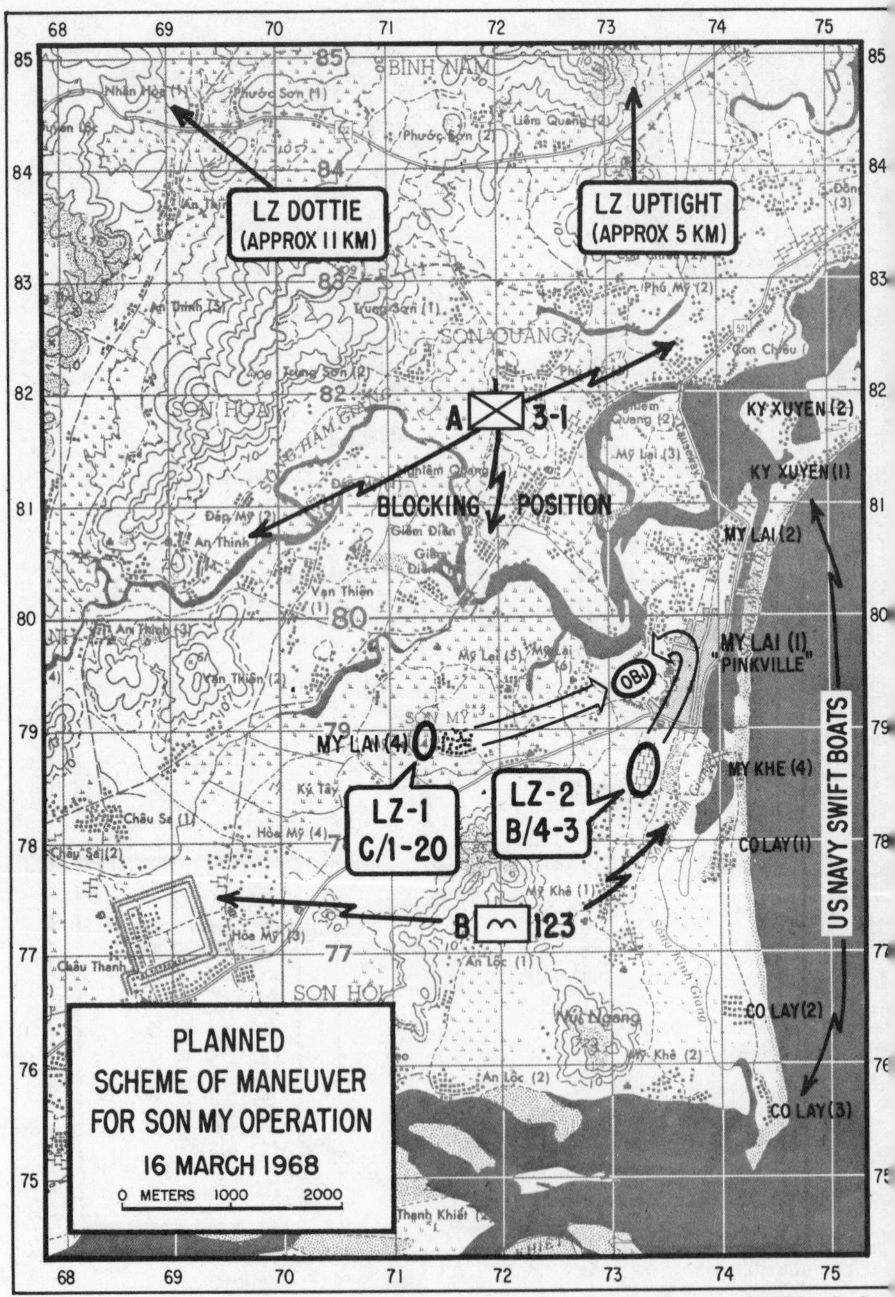
LZ DOTTIE
(APPROX 11 KM)
LZ UPTIGHT
(APPROX 5 KM)
A 3-1
BLOCKING POSITION
MY LAI (4)
OBJ
LZ-1
C/1-20
LZ-2
B/4-3
B 123
KY XUYEN (2)
KY XUYEN (1)
MY LAI (2)
MY LAI (1)
"PINKVILLE"
MY KHE (4)
CO LAY (1)
CO LAY (2)
CO LAY (3)
US NAVY SWIFT BOATS
PLANNED
SCHEME OF MANEUVER
FOR SON MY OPERATION
16 MARCH 1968
0 METERS 1000 2000

SKETCH 5-2

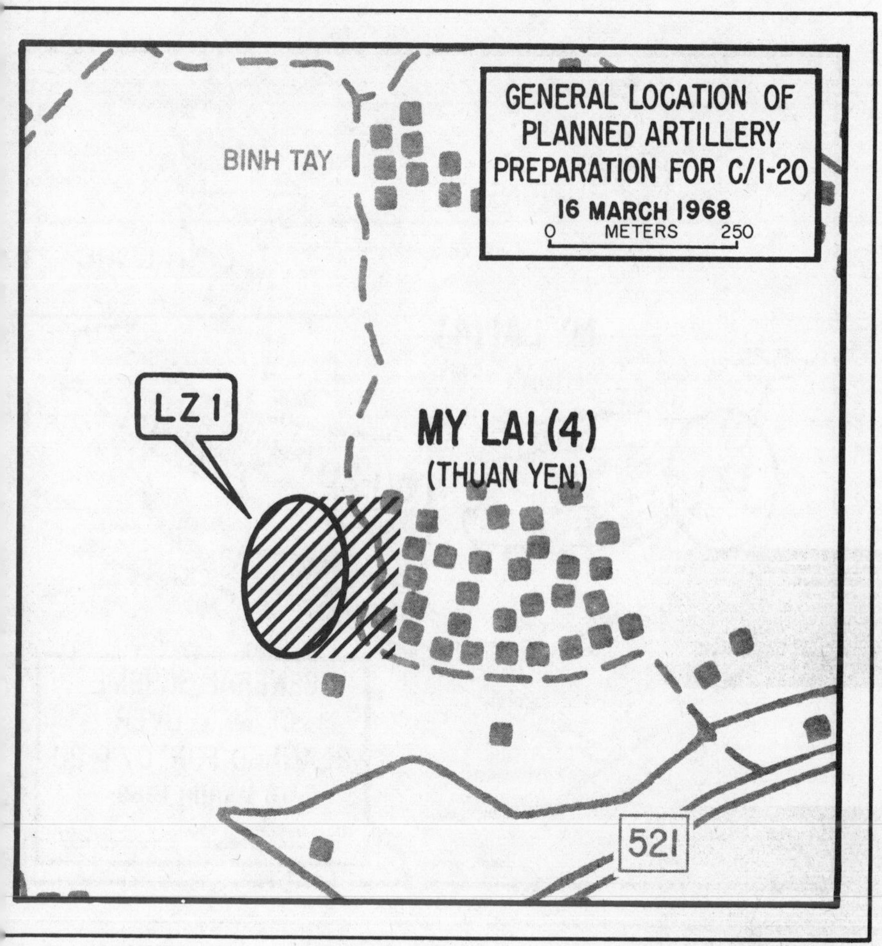
GENERAL LOCATION OF
PLANNED ARTILLERY
PREPARATION FOR C/1-20
16 MARCH 1968
0 METERS 250
BINH TAY
LZ 1
MY LAI (4)
(THUAN YEN)
521

SKETCH 5-3

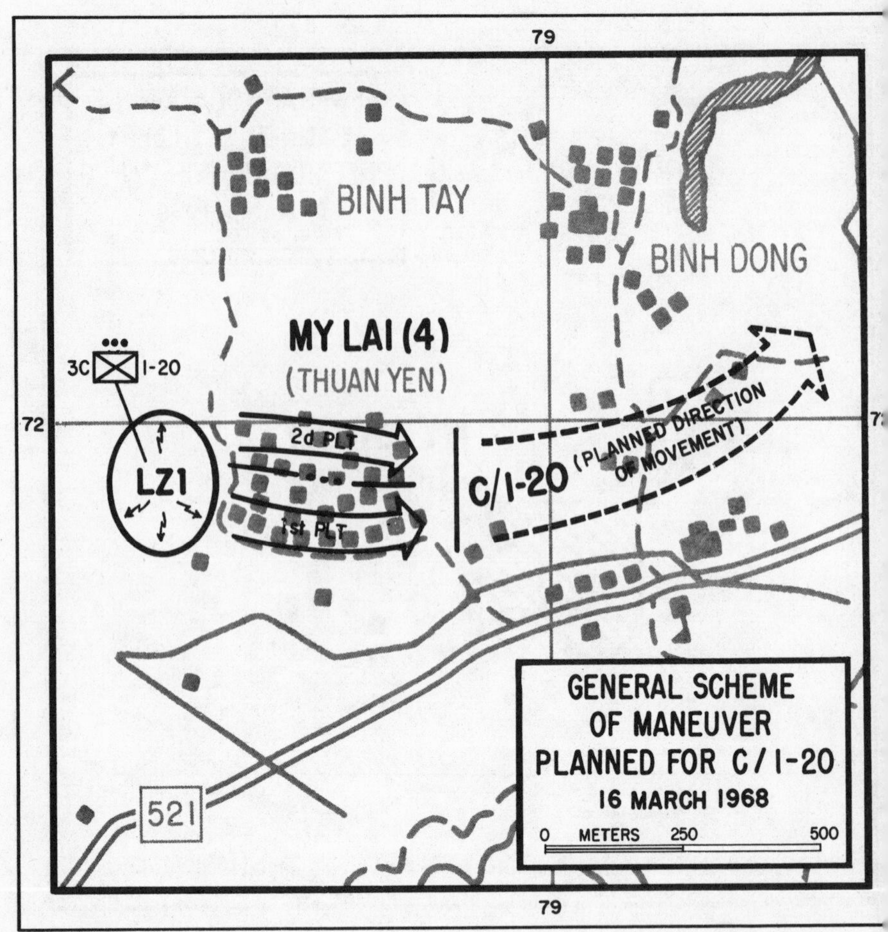

79
BINH TAY
BINH DONG
MY LAI (4)
(THUAN YEN)
3C
1-20
72
2d PLT
1st PLT
LZ1
C/1-20
(PLANNED DIRECTION OF MOVEMENT)
GENERAL SCHEME
OF MANEUVER
PLANNED FOR C/1-20
16 MARCH 1968
0 METERS 250 500
521
79

SKETCH 5-4

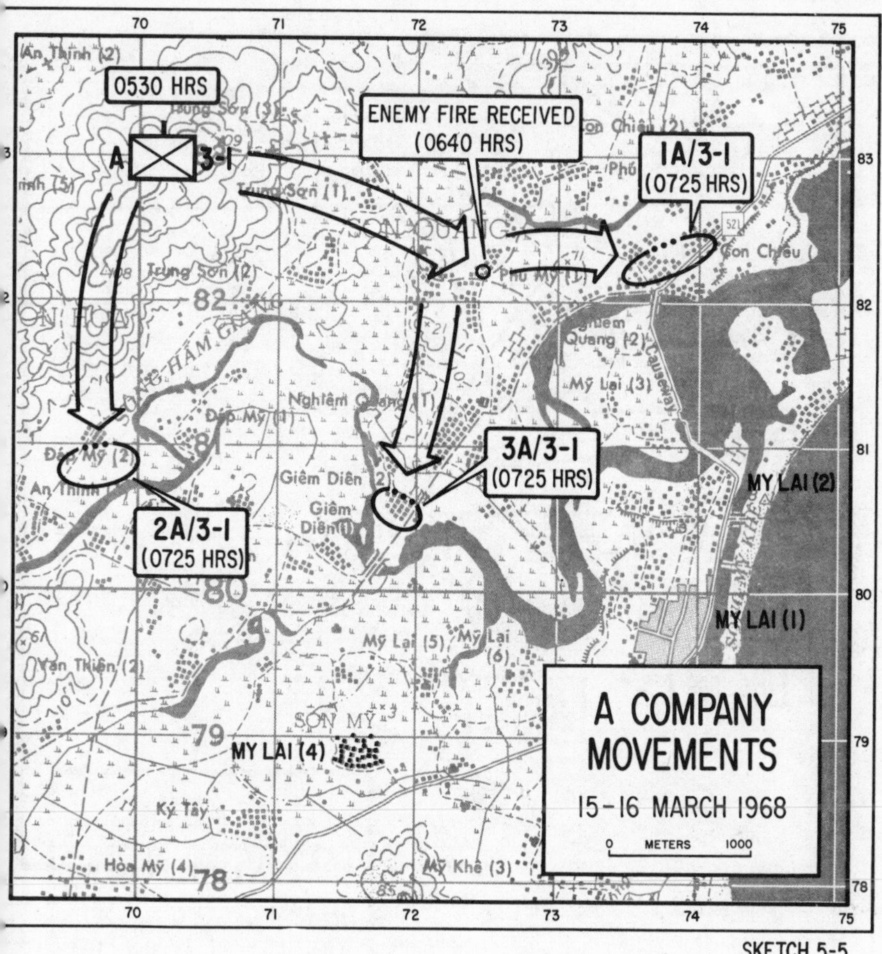
0530 HRS
A 3-1
ENEMY FIRE RECEIVED
(0640 HRS)
1A/3-1
(0725 HRS)
2A/3-1
(0725 HRS)
3A/3-1
(0725 HRS)
MY LAI (2)
MY LAI (1)
MY LAI (4)
A COMPANY
MOVEMENTS
15-16 MARCH 1968
0 METERS 1000

SKETCH 5-5

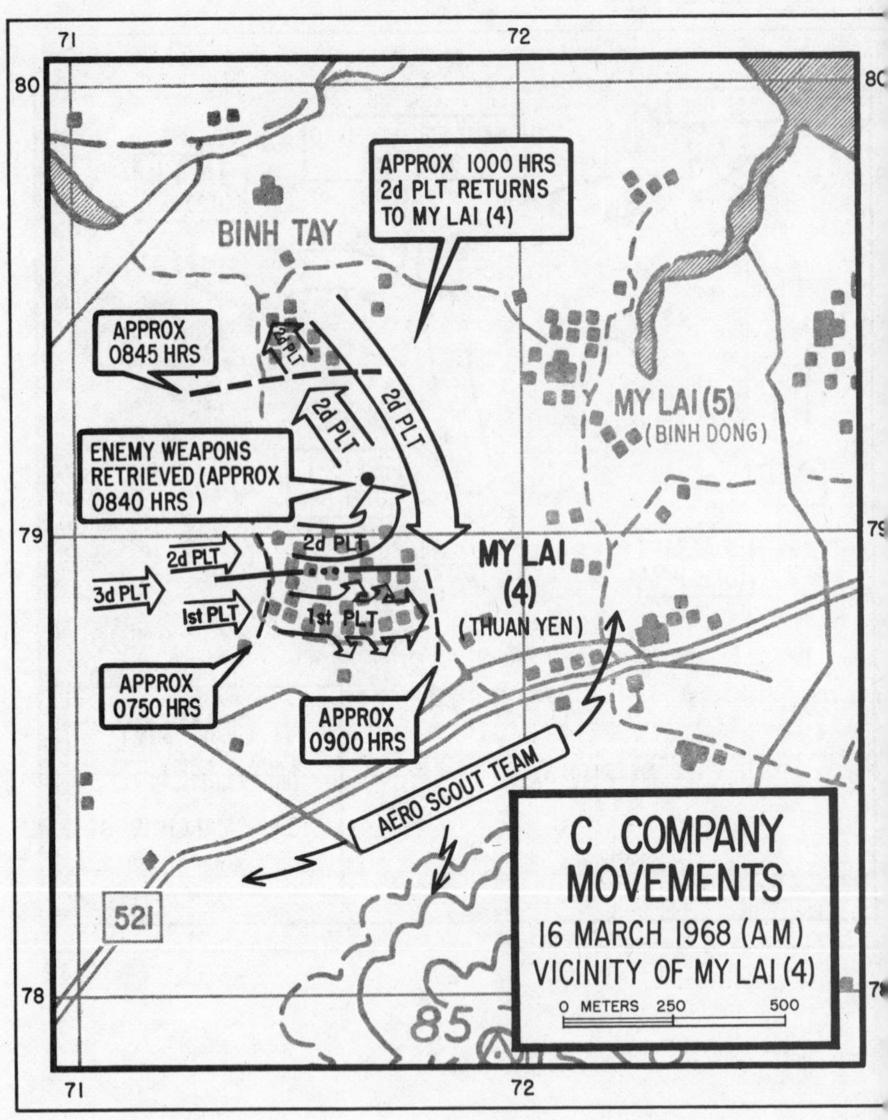
71
72
80
79
78
BINH TAY
APPROX 1000 HRS
2d PLT RETURNS
TO MY LAI (4)
APPROX
0845 HRS
2d PLT
2d PLT
2d PLT
ENEMY WEAPONS
RETRIEVED (APPROX
0840 HRS)
MY LAI (5)
(BINH DONG)
2d PLT
3d PLT
1st PLT
2d PLT
1st PLT
MY LAI
(4)
(THUAN YEN)
APPROX
0750 HRS
APPROX
0900 HRS
AERO SCOUT TEAM
521
85
C COMPANY
MOVEMENTS
16 MARCH 1968 (AM)
VICINITY OF MY LAI (4)
0 METERS 250 500

SKETCH 5-6

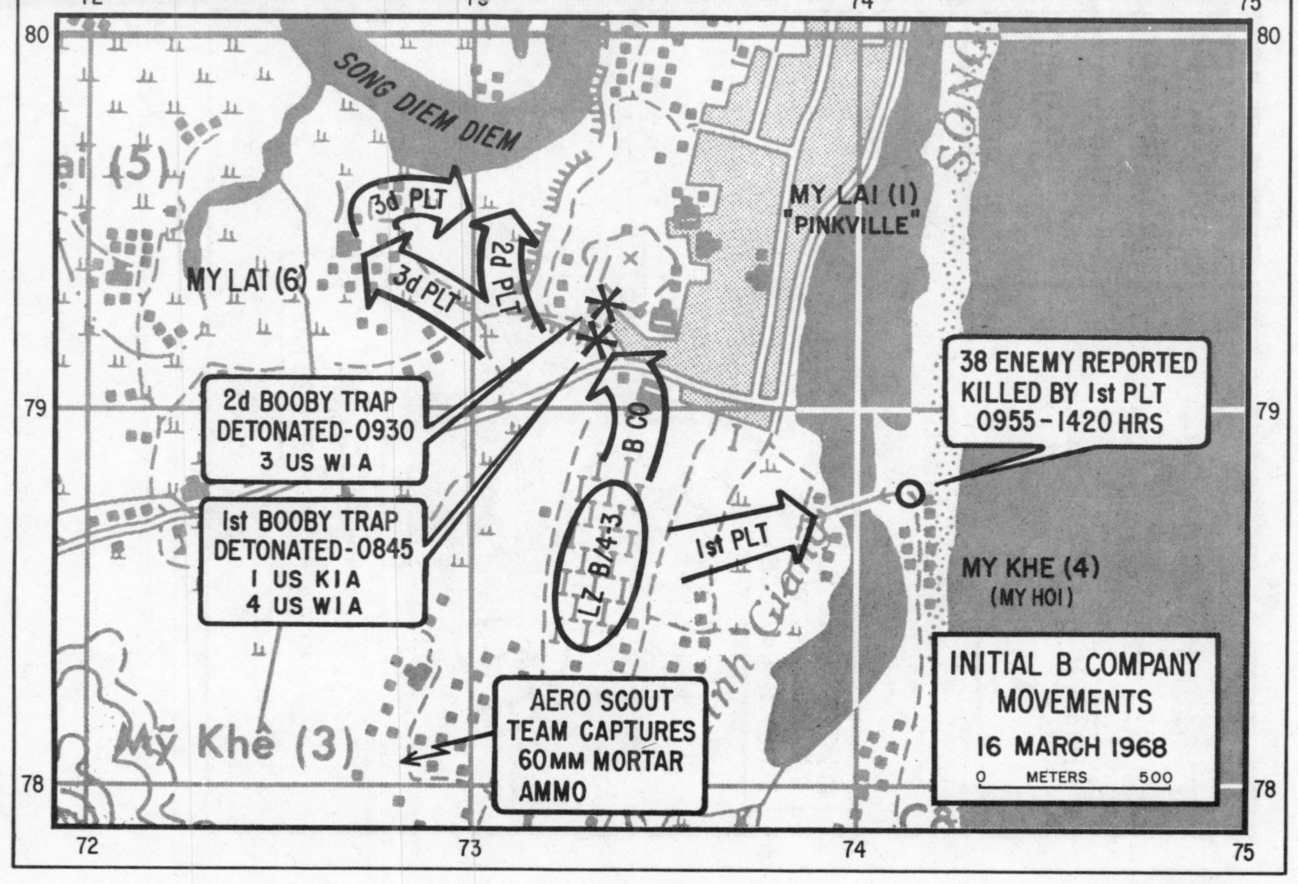

SONG DIEM DIEM
MY LAI (1)
"PINKVILLE"
3d PLT
2d PLT
3d PLT
MY LAI (6)
B CO
LZ B/4-3
1st PLT
38 ENEMY REPORTED
KILLED BY 1st PLT
0955-1420 HRS
2d BOOBY TRAP
DETONATED-0930
3 US WIA
1st BOOBY TRAP
DETONATED-0845
1 US KIA
4 US WIA
MY KHE (4)
(MY HOI)
Mỹ Khê (3)
AERO SCOUT
TEAM CAPTURES
60MM MORTAR
AMMO
INITIAL B COMPANY
MOVEMENTS
16 MARCH 1968
0 METERS 500
80
79
78
72
73
74
75

SKETCH 5-7

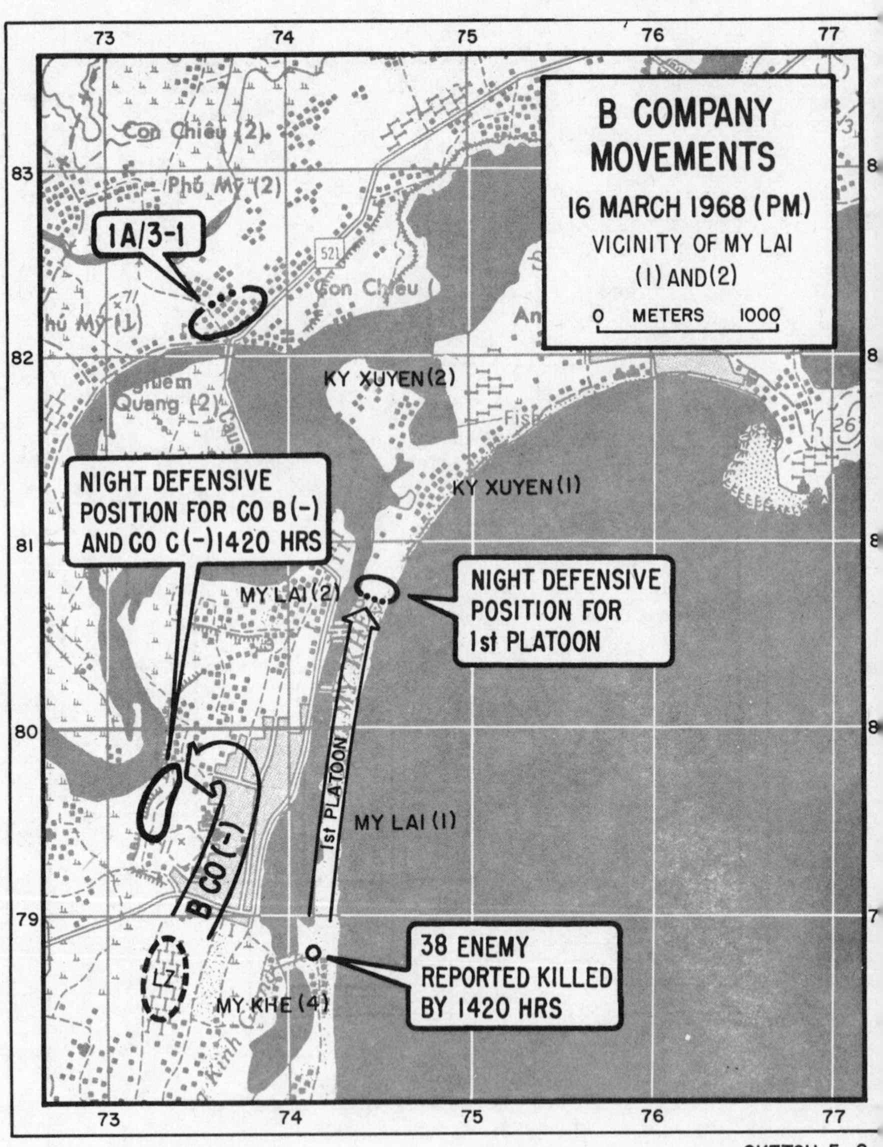
B COMPANY MOVEMENTS
16 MARCH 1968 (PM)
VICINITY OF MY LAI (1) AND (2)
0 METERS 1000
1A/3-1
NIGHT DEFENSIVE POSITION FOR CO B (-) AND CO C (-) 1420 HRS
NIGHT DEFENSIVE POSITION FOR 1st PLATOON
38 ENEMY REPORTED KILLED BY 1420 HRS
B CO (-)
1st PLATOON
LZ
KY XUYEN (2)
KY XUYEN (1)
MY LAI (2)
MY LAI (1)
MY KHE (4)
73
74
75
76
77
83
82
81
80
79

SKETCH 5-8

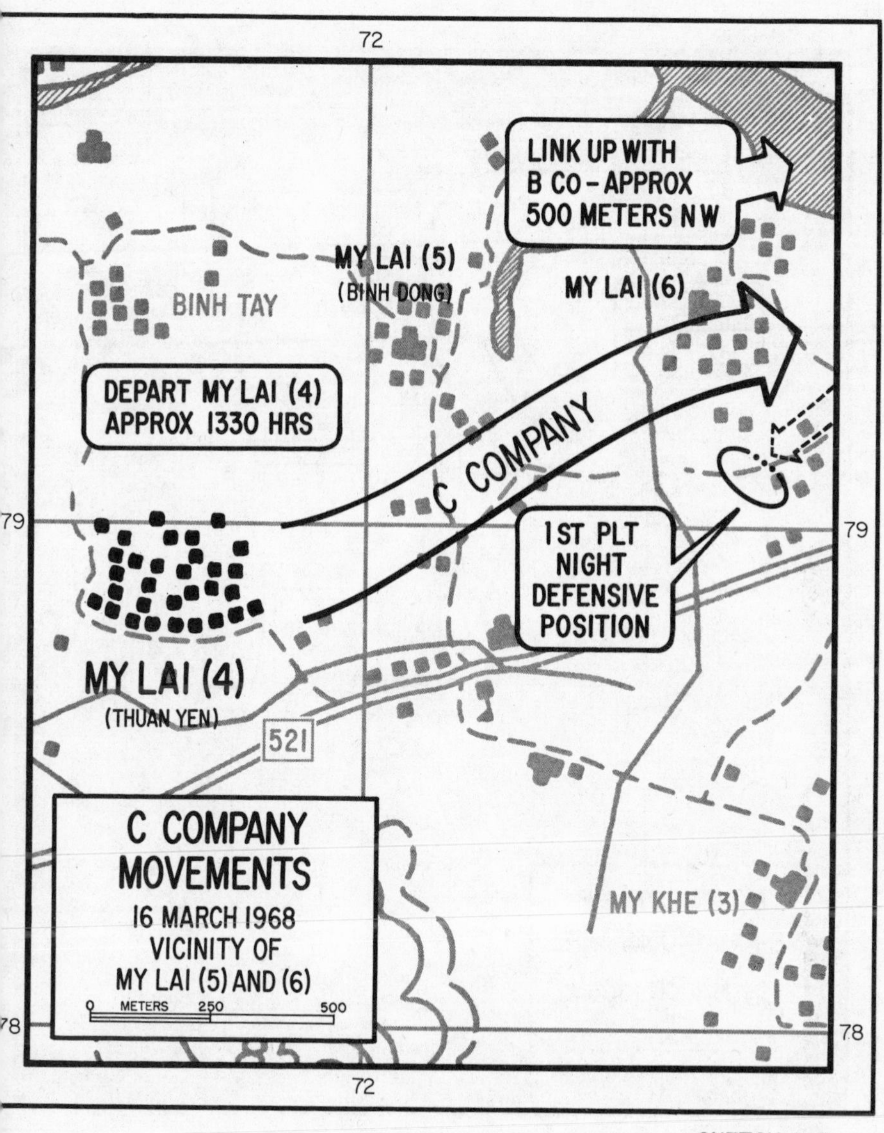
72
LINK UP WITH
B CO – APPROX
500 METERS NW
MY LAI (5)
(BINH DONG)
MY LAI (6)
BINH TAY
DEPART MY LAI (4)
APPROX 1330 HRS
C COMPANY
79
1ST PLT
NIGHT
DEFENSIVE
POSITION
MY LAI (4)
(THUAN YEN)
521
C COMPANY
MOVEMENTS
16 MARCH 1968
VICINITY OF
MY LAI (5) AND (6)
0 METERS 250 500
MY KHE (3)
78
72

SKETCH 5-9

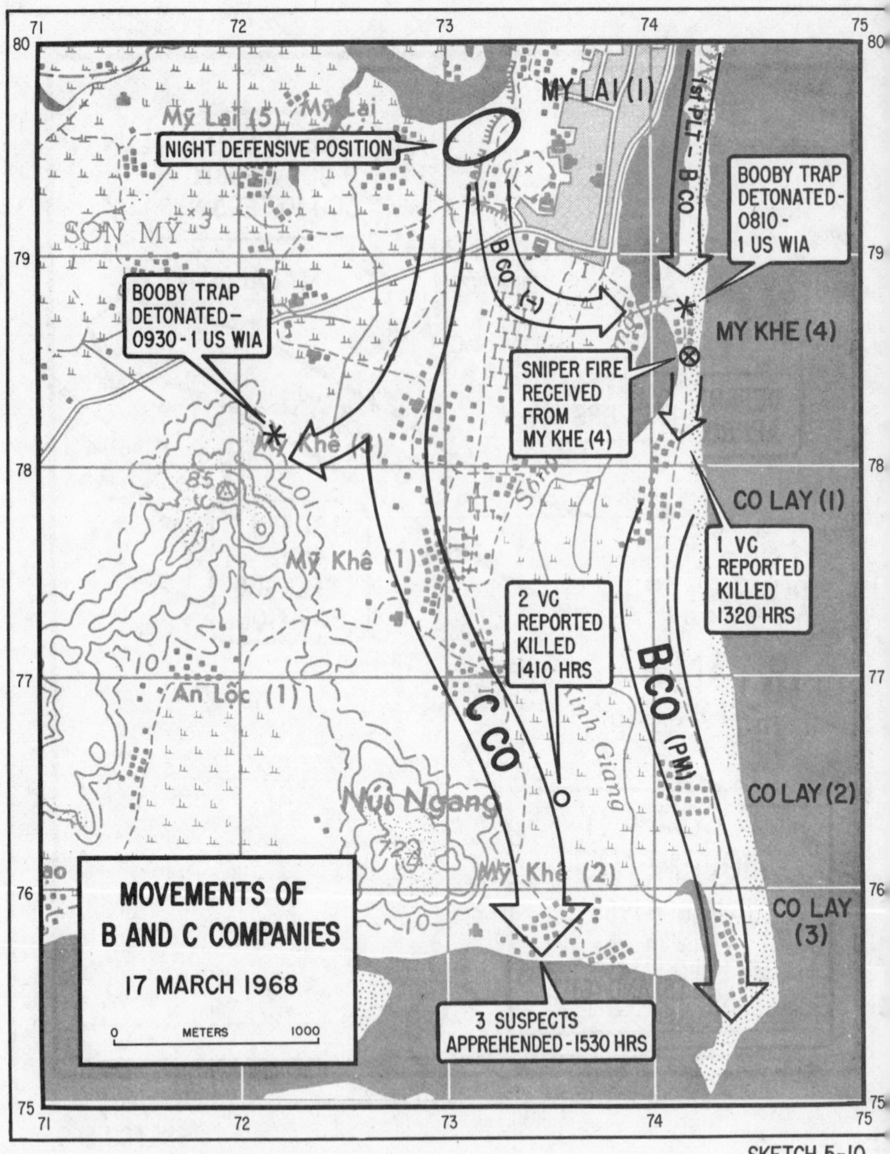

MY LAI (1)
1st PLT - B CO
NIGHT DEFENSIVE POSITION
BOOBY TRAP DETONATED-0810-1 US WIA
SON MY
BOOBY TRAP DETONATED-0930-1 US WIA
B CO (-)
MY KHE (4)
SNIPER FIRE RECEIVED FROM MY KHE (4)
CO LAY (1)
1 VC REPORTED KILLED 1320 HRS
2 VC REPORTED KILLED 1410 HRS
B CO (PM)
C CO
CO LAY (2)
CO LAY (3)
MOVEMENTS OF B AND C COMPANIES
17 MARCH 1968
0 METERS 1000
3 SUSPECTS APPREHENDED-1530 HRS

SKETCH 5-10

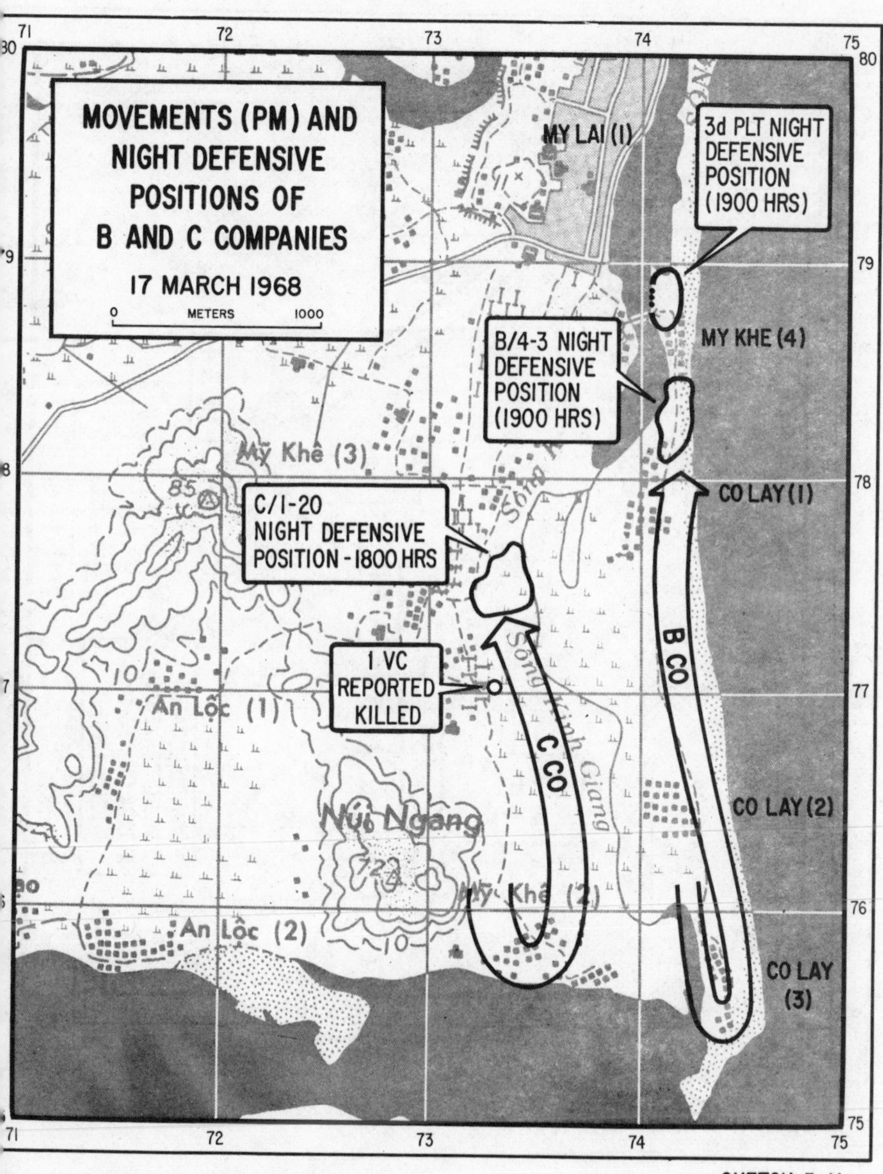

MOVEMENTS (PM) AND
NIGHT DEFENSIVE
POSITIONS OF
B AND C COMPANIES
17 MARCH 1968
0 METERS 1000
MY LAI (1)
3d PLT NIGHT
DEFENSIVE
POSITION
(1900 HRS)
MY KHE (4)
B/4-3 NIGHT
DEFENSIVE
POSITION
(1900 HRS)
Mỹ Khê (3)
C/1-20
NIGHT DEFENSIVE
POSITION - 1800 HRS
CO LAY (1)
1 VC
REPORTED
KILLED
B CO
C CO
An Lộc (1)
Núi Ngang
CO LAY (2)
Mỹ Khê (2)
An Lộc (2)
CO LAY
(3)

SKETCH 5-11

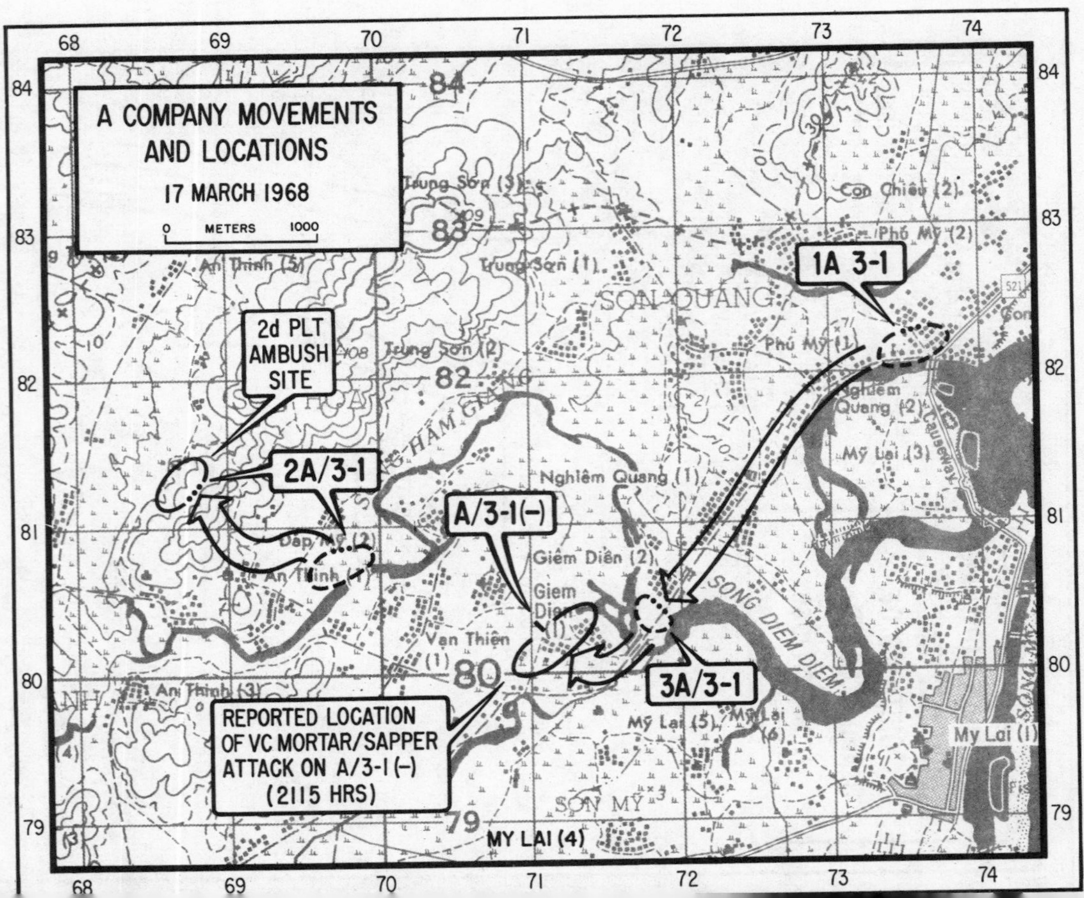

A COMPANY MOVEMENTS
AND LOCATIONS
17 MARCH 1968
0 METERS 1000
2d PLT
AMBUSH
SITE
2A/3-1
A/3-1(–)
1A 3-1
3A/3-1
REPORTED LOCATION
OF VC MORTAR/SAPPER
ATTACK ON A/3-1 (–)
(2115 HRS)
MY LAI (4)
SONG DIEM DIEM
SON QUANG
SON MY
Causeway
My Lai (1)
Mỹ Lai (3)
Mỹ Lai (5)
Nghiêm Quang (1)
Nghiem Quang (2)
Giem Diên (2)
Van Thiện (1)
Phú Mỹ (1)
Phó Mỹ (2)
Con Chiêu (2)
Trung Sơn (1)
Trung Sơn (2)
Trung Sơn (3)
An Thinh (3)
An Thinh (5)
Dap Mỹ (2)

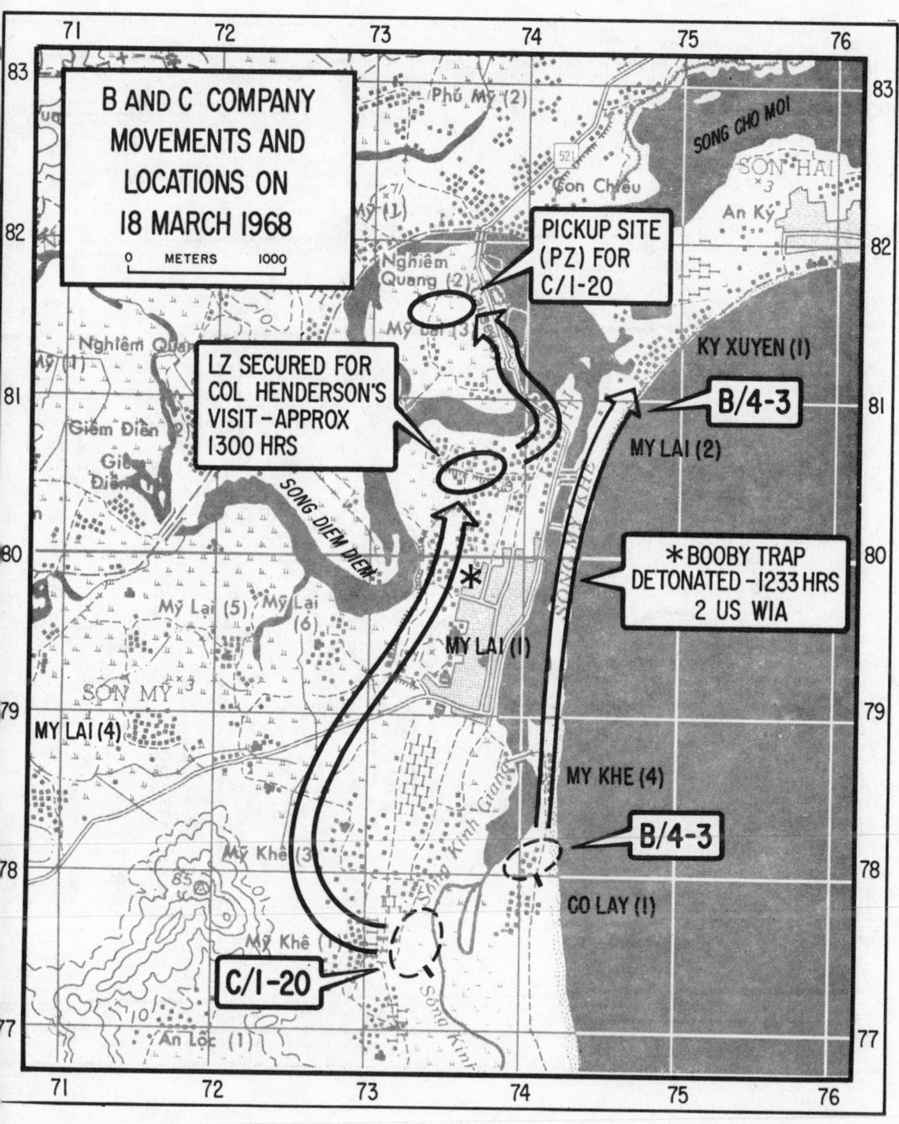
B AND C COMPANY MOVEMENTS AND LOCATIONS ON 18 MARCH 1968
0 METERS 1000
PICKUP SITE (PZ) FOR C/1-20
LZ SECURED FOR COL HENDERSON'S VISIT - APPROX 1300 HRS
B/4-3
* BOOBY TRAP DETONATED - 1233 HRS 2 US WIA
B/4-3
C/1-20
SONG CHO MOI
KY XUYEN (1)
MY LAI (2)
MY LAI (1)
MY LAI (4)
MY KHE (4)
CO LAY (1)
SONG DIEM DIEM
SONG MY KHE

SKETCH 5-13

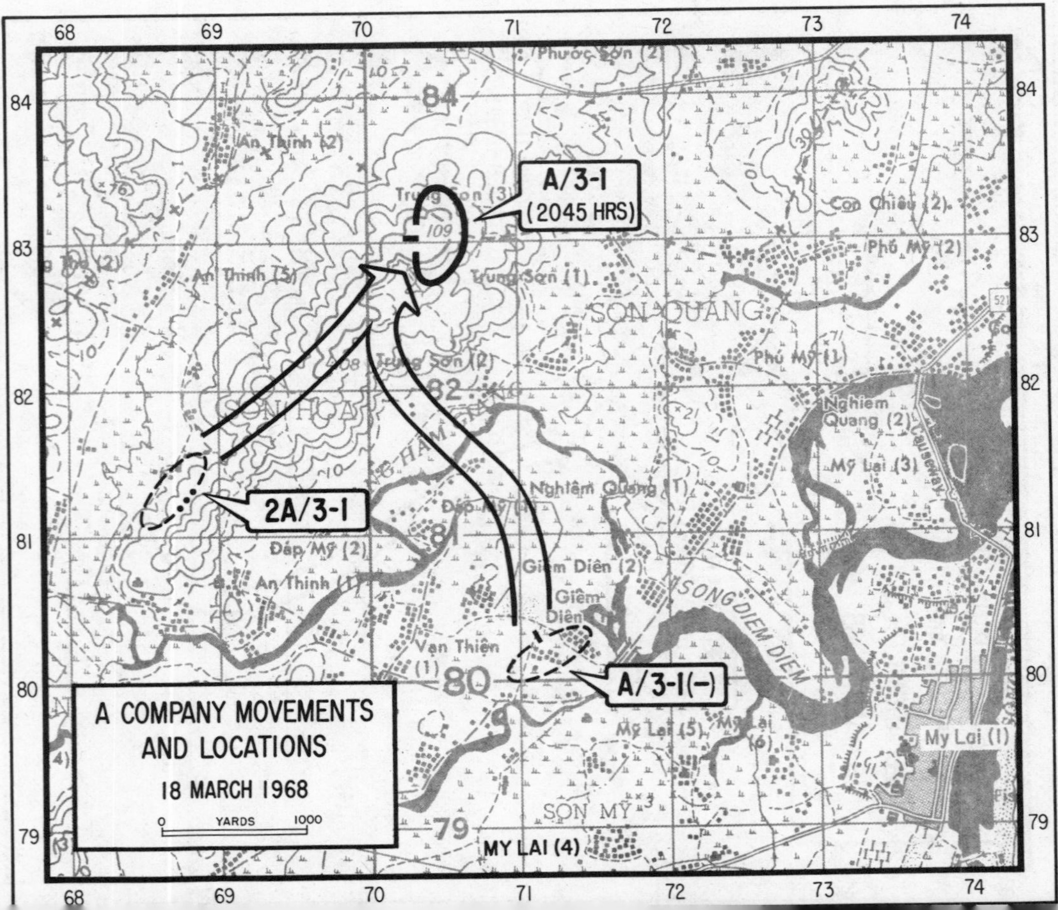
A COMPANY MOVEMENTS AND LOCATIONS
18 MARCH 1968
0 YARDS 1000
A/3-1
(2045 HRS)
2A/3-1
A/3-1(–)
MY LAI (4)
SONG DIEM DIEM
SON QUANG
SON MY
Causeway
My Lai (1)
My Lai (3)
Nghiem Quang (2)
Trung Son (3)
Trung Son (1)
Trung Son (2)
An Thinh (2)
An Thinh (5)
An Thinh (1)
Dap My (2)
Giem Dien (2)
Van Thien (1)
Phu My (1)
Phu My (2)
Con Chieu (2)
Phuoc Son (2)

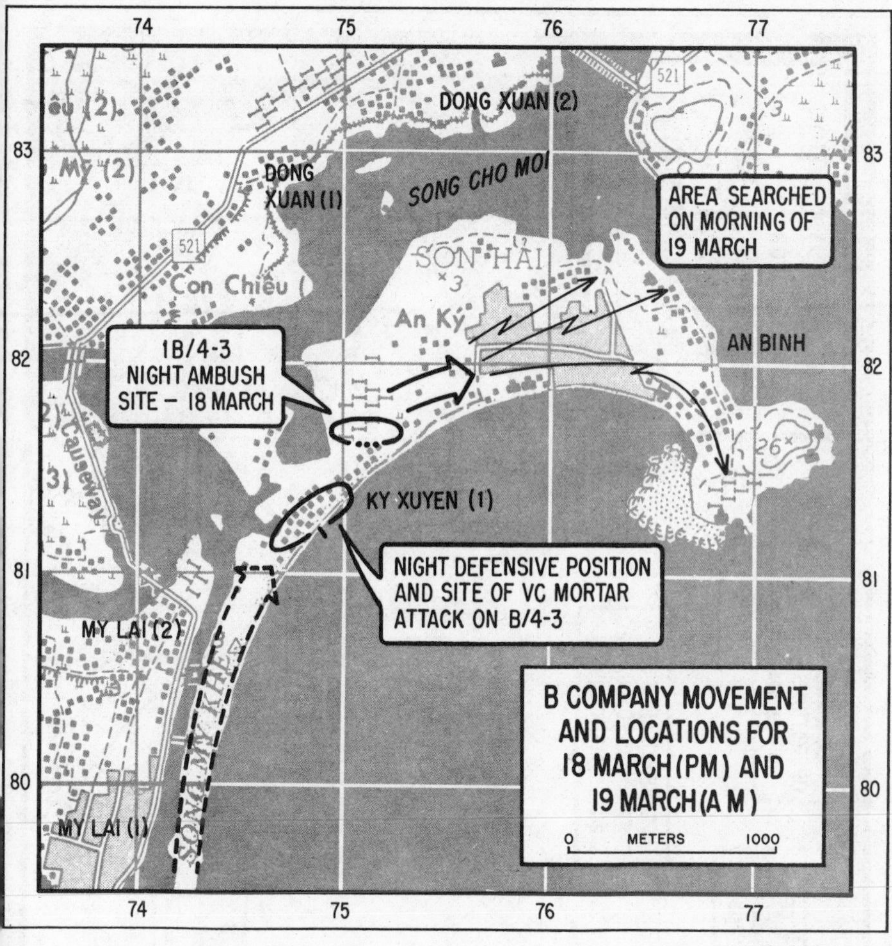

74
75
76
77
83
82
81
80
DONG XUAN (2)
DONG XUAN (1)
SONG CHO MOI
521
Con Chieu (
SON HAI
An Ky
AREA SEARCHED ON MORNING OF 19 MARCH
AN BINH
1B/4-3 NIGHT AMBUSH SITE – 18 MARCH
Causeway
KY XUYEN (1)
NIGHT DEFENSIVE POSITION AND SITE OF VC MORTAR ATTACK ON B/4-3
MY LAI (2)
SONG MY KHE
MY LAI (1)
B COMPANY MOVEMENT AND LOCATIONS FOR 18 MARCH (PM) AND 19 MARCH (A M)
0 METERS 1000

SKETCH 5-15

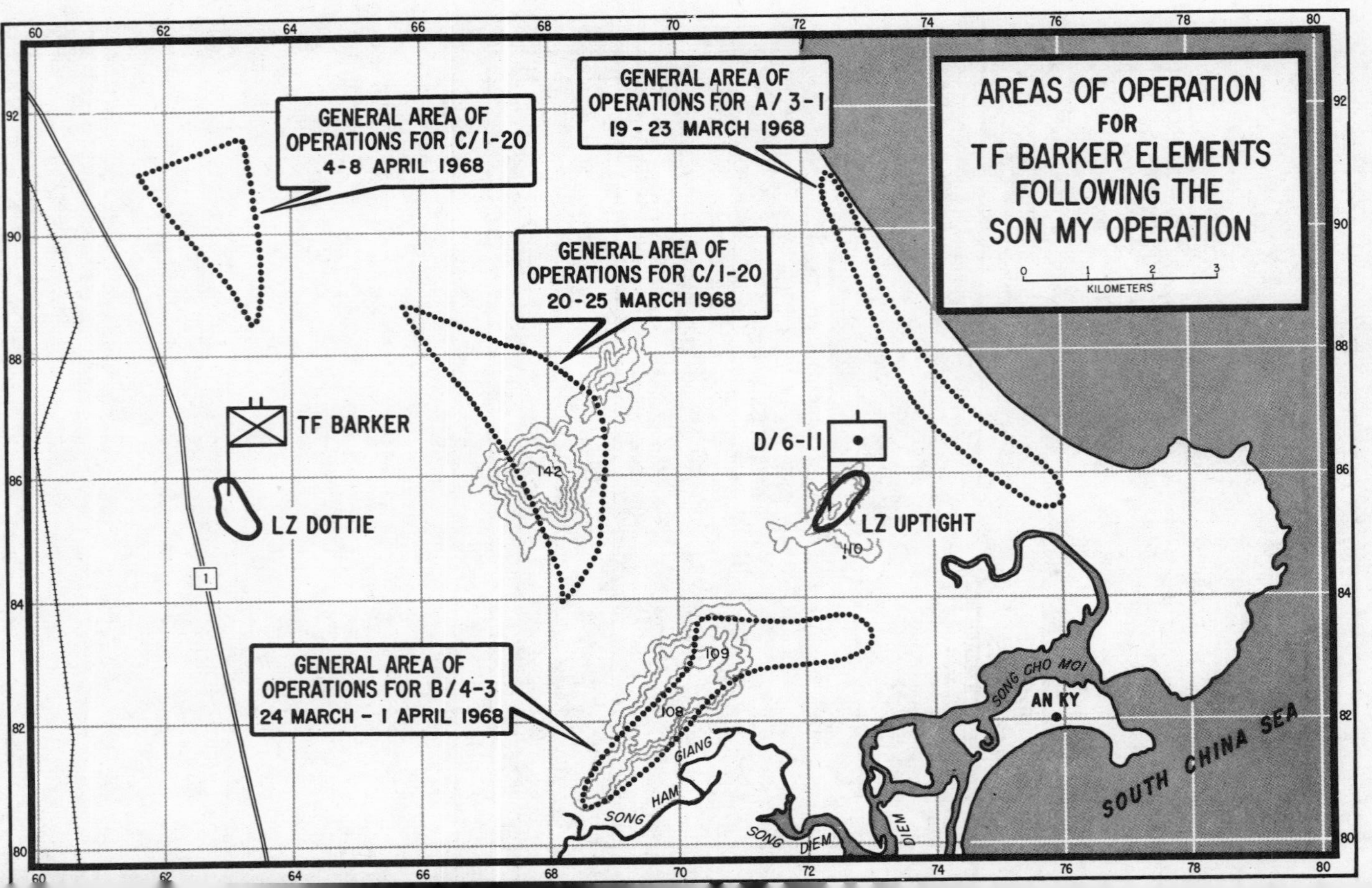
AREAS OF OPERATION
FOR
TF BARKER ELEMENTS
FOLLOWING THE
SON MY OPERATION
0 1 2 3
KILOMETERS
GENERAL AREA OF
OPERATIONS FOR C/1-20
4-8 APRIL 1968
GENERAL AREA OF
OPERATIONS FOR A/3-1
19-23 MARCH 1968
GENERAL AREA OF
OPERATIONS FOR C/1-20
20-25 MARCH 1968
TF BARKER
LZ DOTTIE
D/6-11
LZ UPTIGHT
142
110
GENERAL AREA OF
OPERATIONS FOR B/4-3
24 MARCH - 1 APRIL 1968
109
108
SONG HAM GIANG
SONG DIEM
DIEM
SONG CHO MOI
AN KY
SOUTH CHINA SEA

Chapter 6. Company C, 1st Battalion, 20th Infantry: Actions on 16 and 17 March 1968

The purpose of this chapter is to describe in detail those events involving actions of Company C, 1st Battalion, 20th Infantry (C/1–20 Inf) and its supporting elements in and around My Lai (4) on 16 March, and in My Khe Hamlet on 17 March.

A. Operations on 16 March

1. 0700–0750 HOURS: THE COMBAT ASSAULT PHASE

Shortly before 0700 hours, the men of C Company completed the issuance of ammunition and made final checks of their weapons and equipment. They then moved to the loading area at Landing Zone (LZ) Dottie where the lift helicopters and gunships were arriving (see exhibit P–26).

LTC Baker had departed earlier in his command and control helicopter and began to make final coordination for the artillery preparation and subsequent combat assault.

At approximately 0720 hours, "War Lord" gunships from the aero-scout team, which had flown from their base at Chu Lai, approached the Son My area from the north. The lead gunship contacted Task Force (TF) Barker by radio and advised the net control station that the team would remain over the operational area pending commencement of the combat assault.

At 0722 hours, the first elements of C Company were lifted off from LZ Dottie and headed to the southwest. The selected flight path was intended to serve as a diversionary move away from the target area, and to permit the lift ships to make their final approach into the LZ (from south to north) without having to cross the gun-target line for the artillery preparation (see sketch 6–1).

The artillery preparation began at 0724 hours and continued for about 5 minutes. The rounds impacted on the LZ and portions of My Lai (4). As the preparation began, those inhabitants of My Lai (4) who had been working in the rice paddies surrounding the hamlet sought cover along dikes and in the numerous buffalo wallows which dotted the rice fields. Inside the hamlet, other inhabitants took cover in homemade shelters or bunkers adjacent to their houses and in the several wells located throughout My Lai (4).

The artillery preparation ceased just prior to 0730 hours, as the troop lift helicopters were inbound on their final approach to the LZ. Smoke and fires, caused inside the hamlet by the artillery preparation, were clearly visible from the inbound helicopters (see exhibit P–195). Accompanying "Shark" gunships preceded the C Company insertion by placing rocket and machinegun fires on both flanks of the LZ and probably into the western portion of My Lai (4). The first lift of C Company touched down at 0730 hours.

CPT Medina testified that upon landing he reported the LZ as "cold" (free of enemy fire). Shortly thereafter, according to Medina, a helicopter pilot cut in on the radio and reported "Negative, negative—the LZ is hot. You are receiving fire. We are taking fire. There are VC with weapons running from the village, and we are engaging them now" or words to that effect. Medina has further testified that based on this information, he immediately informed his platoon leaders that the LZ was "hot." Medina's recollection of this event is substantiated neither by the TF Barker Journal, which officially recorded the LZ as "cold," nor by the record of LTC Barker's radio conversation with the leader of the lift ships who confirmed that the LZ was free of enemy fire. It is possible that CPT Medina gained the impression that the LZ was "hot" by monitoring transmissions between LTC Barker and the "Shark" and/or "War Lord" gunships which were, in fact, then in the process of engaging a few armed enemy fleeing from the hamlet. Whether CPT Medina's orders to his platoon leaders were based on facts or on an assumption it seems likely that such orders, if issued, may have served as a final release for the events which followed.

As the first elements of C Company began to deploy on the LZ, an OH-23 helicopter from the aero-scout team arrived in the area south of My Lai (4). The pilot of the scout ship immediately spotted an armed Viet Cong (VC) south of Route 521 running toward the south-southwest (see sketch 6–2). The door gunner in the scout ship fired at the VC but missed. Accompanying "War Lord" gunships then set up and made a northeast to southwest rocket run on his last observed location. Subsequently they were unable to confirm that the VC had been killed.

While the lift helicopters returned to LZ Dottie for the second lift of C Company, their accompanying "Shark" gunships began to orbit counterclockwise over the area to the north of Route 521. As they passed along the southern edge of My Lai (4), an airborne forward air controller (FAC) spotted an armed VC running to the east on a trail along the southern edge of the hamlet. The FAC immediately notified the "Sharks" who took the VC under fire, missed him, turned out to the northeast, and set up for a south to north rocket run. After coordinating air space with the "War Lords," the "Sharks" engaged and apparently killed the man in the extreme southeastern edge of the hamlet. After shifting their orbit back to the north of Route 521, the "Sharks" were notified by the FAC that he had spotted two more armed VC fleeing to the northeast of the LZ. The VC were quickly engaged and killed by "Shark" door gunners. In a subsequent orbit to the south, the "Sharks" spotted a fourth individual (equipped with web gear) who was running to the south of the hamlet. He was also engaged and reported as killed. The "Sharks" then began to drop smoke markers near the bodies to mark their locations for subsequent retrieval of weapons and equipment by elements of C Company.

Because of the congestion of air space around My Lai (4), the "War Lord" aero-scout team decided to shift its orbit farther to the southeast and shortly thereafter began to reconnoiter along the coastal peninsula.

From the LZ, the 1st Platoon of C Company had moved east-southeast for about 150 meters and set up its portion of the security perimeter with the 1st Squad on the right (south) and the 2d Squad to the left (north) (see sketch 6–3).

Elements of the 2d Platoon moved approximately 200 meters to the east-northeast and established a partial perimeter extending from the western edge of My Lai (4) back to the northwest.

While the platoons moved to establish the security perimeter, CPT Medina and the command group remained near the center of the LZ (see exhibit P–202).

As the platoons moved away from the LZ, Vietnamese began to appear from various shelters and hiding areas in and around the rice paddies. They were taken under fire by elements of both the 1st and 2d Platoons and a number of them (approximately 4–9) were killed.

The 1st Platoon was halted when it reached the western edge of the hamlet and set up security positions along the dikes in that area, with SGT Mitchell's 1st Squad on the right (south). SSG Bacon's 2d Squad set up to the left (north) flank of the platoon and quickly opened fire on what was reported to be an armed individual or group of armed individuals observed inside the southwestern edge of the hamlet. Most of the remainder of the platoon then began firing toward the hamlet into "suspected enemy positions" such as bushes, bunkers, and wells, and at Vietnamese fleeing to the southwest of the hamlet.

After halting and attempting to tie in its right flank with the 1st Platoon, the 2d Platoon also began to fire upon Vietnamese in the rice paddies to its north, and placed a heavy volume of fire into the northwestern portion of My Lai (4). Several Vietnamese were hit and apparently killed as a result of this fire.

The second and final lift of C Company departed LZ Dottie at 0738 hours (see exhibit P–27). As the lift ships were making their final approach into the secured LZ, CPT Medina marked the designated touchdown point with smoke and assisted in guiding the ships in. The second lift touched down at 0747 hours (see exhibits P–65 and P–29). As the lift ships were departing the LZ, the lead pilot reported to LTC Barker, who was overhead in his helicopter, that the lift had received fire from one of the surrounding hamlets as they were making their descent into the LZ. Based on this information, the LZ was recorded in the TF Journal as "hot." Neither the helicopters nor their passengers sustained any hits from the fire.

To the south of the LZ, the "Sharks" threw smoke markers near the body of the VC killed previously to the north of Route 521. They requested that Barker dispatch ground elements to the south to retrieve the man's equipment. The "War Lords" who were by that time conducting aerial reconnaissance along the coast, reported to Barker that they had also killed two additional armed enemy south of the LZ. Based on this information, Barker directed Medina to dispatch an element to the south.

Almost immediately after landing, the 3d Platoon Leader (LT [now Mr.] LaCross) received orders from CPT Medina to send an element from his platoon to retrieve the enemy equipment and weapons to the south (see sketch 6–4).

LT LaCross directed his 3d Squad Leader, SP4 (now Mr.) Grimes, to move his men out to the south toward the smoke markers dropped by the "Sharks" gunships. As they moved out (see exhibit P–64), they were accompanied by LaCross, his radio operator, and two 11th Brigade Public Information Office (PIO) men. The remainder of the 3d Platoon and a mortar squad from the company weapons platoon had meanwhile moved a short distance off the LZ to the northwest. They oriented their defensive perimeter generally toward the west.

The remaining elements of the 2d Platoon, who had landed in the second lift, moved rapidly to the northeast and assembled with the rest of the platoon. After link-up, the platoon was deployed with SGT Hodges' 1st Squad on the left (north), CPL (now SGT) Schiel's 2d Squad in the center, and SGT LaCroix's 3d Squad on the right (south).

The 1st and 2d Platoons were deployed generally along the western edge of the hamlet, and at approximately 0750 hours began moving to the east. As they entered My Lai (4), CPT Medina and the command group moved a short distance to the northeast and set up a temporary command post location outside the hamlet.

2. 0750–0845 HOURS: ACTIONS OF 3D PLATOON, AVIATION, AND COMMAND ELEMENTS OUTSIDE OF MY LAI (4)

At about 0755 hours, LTC Barker contacted his tactical operations center (TOC) at LZ Dottie to notify them that all of C Company's elements were on the ground and that the 3d Platoon element was moving out to secure weapons and equipment from VC killed by the gunships. He also reported that C Company had had no contact as of that time but was informed by the TOC that C Company had already been credited with 15 VC killed. These apparently had been reported previously by CPT Medina.

As LT LaCross and his 3d Squad approached the area where the VC body had been marked by the "Sharks," the smoke markers burned out (see sketch 6–5). They searched the area for a short time but were unable to find the weapon, and consequently began to move back toward the LZ. LT LaCross contacted CPT Medina and advised him that they were returning to My Lai (4). Medina, however, ordered them to remain in that area and continue their search for weapons and equipment. To their south, the "Sharks" had spotted another armed VC running southwest along the southern edge of Route 521. The "Sharks" took him under fire as he evaded toward a small tree line running south from the road.

By 0800 hours, several groups of Vietnamese from My Lai (4) and surrounding subhamlets had begun moving out of the area to the southwest along Route 521. As the "Sharks" fired on the VC south of the highway, many of the Vietnamese squatted along the road. These groups were composed primarily of old men, women, and children.

After apparently killing the armed VC, the "Sharks" began dropping smoke markers on his location and the location of several ammo boxes which the VC had discarded in his attempts to evade. The "Sharks" notified LTC Barker of the details, and LT LaCross' 3d Squad, which was already moving farther south, was told to orient its movement on the "Sharks" smoke markers.

At approximately 0800 hours, LTC Barker was contacted by MAJ McKnight, who was airborne over the area with COL Henderson, and was informed about the large number of people moving out along Route 521 to the southwest. MAJ McKnight also indicated that COL Henderson's command and control helicopter was orbiting over the departing group of people.

As LT LaCross and SP4 Grimes' 3d Squad approached Route 521, they observed the group of Vietnamese moving to the southwest. The squad took the group under fire (see exhibit P–30). Members of the squad and "Shark" crew members who were overhead testified that from three to 15 Vietnamese were killed by the squad's initial volley (see exhibits P–31, P–38).

Following the killing of the Vietnamese, a part of the 3d Squad remained along the road to search for documents and equipment (see exhibit P–26). The remainder of the squad proceeded across the road to the south. As they crossed the road, a woman (possibly accompanied by a small girl) was observed hiding in a ditch which paralleled the road. "Shark" crew members who were still orbiting over the area observed an individual, followed by a radio operator, shoot and kill the woman (see P–32). (The two PIO men who had accompanied the 3d Squad to the south also observed the woman when she was alive and subsequently saw her after she had been killed.) The squad element then moved farther south and retrieved a weapon and two ammunition boxes, probably from the body of the VC killed by the "Sharks." After recovering the weapon, the soldiers who had gone south of the road, returned to rejoin the rest of the squad.

At approximately 0810 hours, the aero-scout team contacted COL Henderson's helicopter and notified MAJ McKnight that two VC suspects had been separated from the large group of Vietnamese moving to the southwest, and that the two suspects were stripped down (i.e., had taken their shirts off) and were available for pickup. Shortly thereafter, COL Henderson's helicopter landed 400–500 meters southwest of the 3d Squad's location and picked up the two suspects. WO1 (now 1LT) Thompson was pilot of the scout ship that had separated and cornered the suspects.

After assisting COL Henderson with the apprehension of the two VC suspects, WO1 Thompson began aerial reconnaissance of the area around the crest of Hill 85 and discovered a cache of enemy 60mm mortar ammunition. An infantry platoon from the aero-scout company was subsequently inserted on the hill to capture and destroy the ammunition. Because of its involvement with the capture of the ammunition, and because of its return to LZ Dottie for refueling, the aero-scout team was somewhat separated from the actions in and around My Lai (4) from about 0815 hours until after 0900 hours. The "Shark" gunships also returned to LZ Dottie for refueling and rearming between 0845 and 0900 hours.

The 3d Squad left Route 521 and began retracing its route back to the north toward the LZ (see sketch 6–6). En route, members of the squad detected two Vietnamese running southwest from the vicinity of My Lai (4) across the squad's path. They were fired on by the squad and were either killed or wounded. There is evidence to indicate that at least one of the individuals was a child. The evidence also indicates that these two people, or a subsequent group of Vietnamese encountered by the 3d Squad (before reaching the LZ), were killed or "finished off" at close range by a machinegunner working with the squad (see exhibit P–39). As the squad continued north, at least one of its members observed a large group of Vietnamese, under the guard of US soldiers, off to his east near the southern edge of My Lai.

The squad returned to the southwest corner of the hamlet at approximately 0845 hours. The entire 3d Platoon then began moving into the western edge of My Lai (4), for the mop-up operation. The PIO men who had accompanied SGT Grimes's squad to the south, observed the squad as it began to burn the houses in the southwestern portion of the hamlet (see exhibits P–60, 59, 69, and 68) and then moved off to the northwest where CPT Medina and the command group were still located just inside the western edge of the hamlet.

3. 0750–0845 HOURS: INITIAL ACTIONS OF 1ST PLATOON INSIDE MY LAI (4)

In the 1st Platoon sector, LT Calley and his radio operator followed behind the right (1st) squad led by SGT Mitchell. The platoon sergeant, SFC Cowan, moved behind SSG Bacon's 2d Squad. (The general directions of squad movements shown in sketch 6–7 result from a detailed reconstruction based on witness statements as to location/distance/time where they observed or participated in certain actions. The routes portrayed are at best the central axes of the paths followed by most members of the squads.)

As the 1st Platoon moved into the hamlet, its soldiers began placing heavy fire on fleeing Vietnamese, throwing grenades into houses and bunkers, slaughtering livestock, and destroying foodstuffs. Several witnesses testified to having observed an old Vietnamese man being bayoneted to death by a member of the platoon and to having seen another man thrown alive into a well and subsequently killed with a hand grenade. Several members of the platoon also testified to having participated in "mercy" killings of badly wounded Vietnamese as the platoon advanced. The 1st Platoon's actions in the southwestern portion of My Lai (4) were characterized by one notable, albeit transient, difference from the actions of the 2d Platoon—live detainees were rounded up, in the midst of the scattered killing and destruction. As the villagers were collected, they were moved generally eastward to the main north-south trail running through the center of the village (see sketch 6–7). After reaching the trail, they were moved south in two main groups toward LT Calley's location. The first group consisted of 60–70 people, comprised primarily of women and children. A few elderly males were also among the group. After reaching the southern edge of the hamlet, the first group was escorted by a few soldiers from the 1st Squad to a ditch located approximately 100–150 meters to the east of the southeastern edge of the village. After reaching the ditch they were herded into it and kept under guard.

A second group of villagers, numbering between 20 and 50, also was moved south along the main north-south trail and then moved out into the rice paddies where they were placed under the guard of several men (probably a fire team) from the 1st Squad. This second group of villagers reached the southern edge of the hamlet at approximately 0830 hours.

4. 0750–0845 HOURS: INITIAL ACTIONS OF 2D PLATOON AND COMMAND ELEMENTS IN AND NORTH OF MY LAI (4)

As the 2d Platoon entered My Lai (4), LT Brooks (2d Platoon Leader) followed behind the right flank (3d) squad led by SGT LaCroix. Platoon Sergeant Buchanon testified that he generally followed behind SGT Hodges' left flank (1st) squad. CPL Schiel led the 2d Squad located in the center (see sketch 6–8). As the platoon advanced through the northwestern and north-central part of the hamlet, members of the various squads became intermingled with each other and, in some cases, with elements of the 1st Platoon located to their right flank.

Members of the 2d Platoon began killing Vietnamese inhabitants of My Lai (4) as soon as they entered its western edge. The evidence available indicates they neither sought to take nor did they retain any prisoners, suspects, or detainees while in My Lai (4). As they advanced and discovered homemade bunkers or bomb shelters, many of the soldiers yelled "Lai Day" (the Vietnamese words for "come here"). Failing any response from the Vietnamese inside the bunkers, the soldiers tossed fragmentation grenades into the bunkers, and followed up by spraying the inside with small arms fire. Many witnesses also testified that when Vietnamese did respond most of them were shot down as they exited the bunkers. In at least three instances inside the village, Vietnamese of all ages were rounded up in groups of 5–10 and were shot down. Other inhabitants were shot down in the paddies bordering the northern edge of the hamlet while attempting to escape. Women and children, many of whom were small babies, were killed sitting or hiding inside their homes. At least two rapes were participated in and observed by members of the platoon. Most of the livestock and fowl inside the hamlet were also slaughtered. A precise determination of the number of Vietnamese killed by the 2d Platoon is virtually impossible. However, the preponderence of the evidence indicates that at least 50 and perhaps as many as 100 inhabitants, comprised almost exclusively of old men, women, children, and babies, were killed by members of the 2d Platoon while they were in My Lai.

As the platoon approached the northeastern portion of the village, LT Brooks received a call from CPT Medina directing him to move the entire platoon to the north to secure two weapons from VC killed earlier by "Shark" gunships which were, by this time, re-marking the location of the VC bodies with smoke. The 2d Platoon exited the northern edge of My Lai (4) at approximately 0830 hours. Up to that time it had taken no casualties, and the preponderence of the testimony strongly indicates it had received no enemy fire.

COL Henderson had continued to orbit the operational area after his pickup of the two VC suspects, and after observing the B Company combat assault, returned to the area where "Shark" gunships were marking the location of the two VC they had killed to the north of My Lai (4). The smoke was used to assist in orienting the movements of the 2d Platoon which was moving north from the hamlet toward the smoke markers. After observing the ground troops move to within 100–150 meters of the two bodies and weapons, COL Henderson apparently departed for LZ Dottie to refuel and drop off the two suspects.

LTC Barker also had been orbiting over the operational area for most of the morning. After coordinating the B Company combat assault on My Lai (1), he made a final check with CPT Medina and then headed back to LZ Dottie for refueling. During the conversation with CPT Medina, he was apparently informed that C Company had accounted for a total of 84 enemy killed. Fifteen enemy killed had been reported earlier by CPT Medina to the TF TOC. En route, LTC Barker contacted the TOC and advised them that he was returning to refuel and would bring them up to date on the results of the operation. LTC Barker arrived at LZ Dottie at approximately 0835 hours. An entry, crediting C Company with the additional 69 enemy killed, was made on the TF Barker Journal as of 0840 hours.

Using the smoke markers of the "Sharks" to guide on, the 2d Platoon found the two VC bodies north of My Lai (4) and retrieved a carbine and an M–1 rifle from nearby. The two VC had been killed while running from the vicinity of the small subhamlet of Binh Tay (see sketch 6–9) located to the northwest of the 2d Platoon's position. The platoon was consequently ordered to proceed to Binh Tay to check it out and reached its southern edge at approximately 0845 hours.

5. 0845–0945 HOURS: LOCATION AND ACTIONS OF COMMAND ELEMENTS, AND C COMPANY AT MY LAI (4) AND BINH TAY

By 0855 hours, LTC Barker completed his refueling stop at LZ Dottie and was airborne over the operational area.

COL Henderson, who arrived at LZ Dottie at approximately 0845 hours, apparently remained there until after 0950 hours.

Between 0845–0900 hours, the group of villagers (20–50) who had been moved by the 1st Platoon to the south of the hamlet and held under guard in the rice paddies were shot down by members of the platoon (see sketch 6–10). Following the killing, the fire team that had guarded the villagers was sent through the southeastern portion of the hamlet to round up additional villagers and move them farther east to the ditch. LT Calley and the command group moved from south of the hamlet to the east and arrived at the ditch at approximately 0900 hours. SGT Mitchell's 1st Squad (minus a fire team) had set up a defensive perimeter just to the east of the ditch. SSG Bacon's 2d Squad, which was moving through the northeastern portion of the hamlet, subsequently set up defensive positions as the left flank element of the platoon.

The fire team of the 1st Squad, which had searched through the southeastern portion of the hamlet, arrived at the ditch at about 0900 hours and brought with it approximately 10 additional villagers. The villagers were herded into the ditch with the larger group of 60–70. (There has been testimony from Vietnamese witnesses that an additional number of villagers, possibly 50 or more, were either brought to the ditch from surrounding subhamlets or sought refuge in the ditch from the C Company action. Testimony from US personnel to substantiate the Vietnamese statements has not been developed by this Inquiry.) At approximately 0900–0915 hours, Vietnamese personnel who had been herded into the ditch were shot down by members of the 1st Platoon.

Inside the subhamlet of Binh Tay, the 2d Platoon continued the pattern of burning, killings, and rapes which it had followed in My Lai (4). Besides scattered killing which took place inside the subhamlet, a group of Vietnamese women and children (approximately 10–20) were rounded up, brought to the southern end of Binh Tay, and made to squat in a circle. Several 40 mm rounds from an M–79 grenade launcher were fired into their midst, killing several and wounding many. The wounded were subsequently killed by small arms fire from members of the platoon. Witnesses from the platoon have testified to observing at least one gang-rape of a young Vietnamese girl, an act of sodomy, and several other rape/killings while inside Binh Tay.

On the LZ, the 3d Squad of the 3d Platoon had returned at approximately 0845 hours from its movement to the south. LT LaCross left the squad and moved to the northwest corner of the hamlet where he conferred with CPT Medina for a short while. CPT Medina told him to have his platoon begin moving through the village for the mop-up operation. LT LaCross followed behind SGT (now Mr.) Smail's 1st Squad on the left (north) flank (see sketch 6–11). SGT Grimes' 3d Squad moved on the southern flank. The platoon, accompanied by SFC Maroney's mortar squad, entered the western edge of the hamlet between 0845–0900 hours. CPT Medina and his command group followed behind the platoon.

After CPT Medina and the command group had moved into the hamlet for a short distance (see sketch 6–12), an old Vietnamese man with two children was apprehended and brought to their location. He was interrogated by SGT Phu, CPT Medina's Vietnamese interpreter (see exhibits P–66 and 67). The old man informed Medina that 30–40 VC had been in My Lai (4) the previous evening but had departed the hamlet that morning prior to the combat assault. (This information was reported and recorded on the 11th Brigade Journal.) The command group then moved farther into the village toward the east and southeast.

Forward of the command group, the 3d Platoon went about the destruction of crops and the burning of houses in a thorough and systematic manner (see exhibits P–15, 35, 16, 33, 56, and 14). Throughout the hamlet, members of the platoon and the two PIO men who accompanied them observed the bodies of Vietnamese killed earlier during the 1st and 2d Platoons' advance (see exhibits P–34, 37, and 32). Members of the 3d Platoon slaughtered most of the remaining livestock, and in at least one instance participated in the killing of about five or six seriously wounded Vietnamese to "put them out of their misery" since "they did not give them medical aid."

After completion of his first refueling stop at LZ Dottie, at approximately 0845–0900 hours, WO1 Thompson returned to the My Lai (4) area. MAJ Watke testified that since the "Shark" gunships had departed at this time, he had received permission for the aero-scout team to commence reconnaissance in the area north of Route 521. After arriving in the area, Thompson noticed numerous wounded Vietnamese south of the hamlet and observed the women killed earlier by the 3d Platoon south of Route 521. Thompson testified that he marked the location of the wounded with smoke and contacted his lower gunship to request that the ground elements provide medical aid to the wounded. (The lower gunship had the only radio with which Thompson could communicate. His transmissions were then relayed by the low gunship to the high gunship which in turn passed the information on to TF Barker elements over the TF command net.) While reconnoitering for additional wounded to the east of the hamlet, his crew chief spotted the ditch containing the bodies of Vietnamese killed earlier by the 1st Platoon. Seeing that some of the Vietnamese were still alive, Thompson landed between the ditch and the 1st Platoon's defensive perimeter at approximately 0915–0930 hours. While on the ground, he spoke to a fire team leader in the 1st Squad and then with LT Calley. Thompson testified that the sergeant's response to his question about helping the wounded was to the effect that the only way he could help them was to kill them. Thompson states that he thought the sergeant was joking. (The substance of Thompson's conversation with LT Calley is unknown, inasmuch as Thompson did not recall LT Calley at the ditch and LT Calley elected to remain silent before this Inquiry. Several members of the 1st Platoon, including the sergeant with whom WO1 Thompson spoke, testified or made sworn statements that LT Calley and WO1 Thompson did talk with each other during the incident at the ditch.) Thompson subsequently took off, and his crew chief observed a sergeant shooting into the ditch. Thompson did not personally observe the shooting.

Following WO1 Thompson's departure, several members of the 1st Squad of the 1st Platoon were ordered to return to My Lai (4) to assist the 3d Platoon in searching the eastern portion of the hamlet.

In the subhamlet of Binh Tay, the killing and rapes of Vietnamese by the 2d Platoon were stopped when LT Brooks received an order from CPT Medina at approximately 0915–0930 hours telling him to "cease fire" or "stop the killing," to round up the remaining inhabitants and move them out of the area, and to burn the houses. (Whether this same order was also received by the 1st and 3d Platoons is not entirely clear inasmuch as additional killing, involving members of both the 1st and 3d Platoons, apparently did occur after this time. The basis for CPT Medina's order is even less clear. Since Medina and the command group were apparently moving inside My Lai (4) at this time, what Medina observed inside the hamlet may have caused him to issue the 0915–0930 order. If that were the case, however, it would appear that the same order would also have been issued to the 1st and 3d Platoons. The evidence indicates that killing by members of the company, except for those in the 2d Platoon, continued until at least 1015 hours.) Testimony conclusively indicates that following receipt of the order from CPT Medina, the remaining inhabitants of Binh Tay (consisting of about 50–60 people) were rounded up by the 2d Platoon and instructed to move out of the area. They departed to the southwest without further harm being done to them.

6. 0945–1045 HOURS: CONTINUING ACTIONS INVOLVING C COMPANY AND AVIATION ELEMENTS AROUND MY LAI (4)—RETURN OF 2D PLATOON FROM BINH TAY

Following WO1 Thompson's departure from the ditch east of My Lai (4), several members of the 1st Platoon returned to the hamlet to assist the 3d Platoon in clearing the eastern portion. They became intermingled with members of the 3d Platoon in the vicinity of the main north-south trail running through the center of the hamlet (see sketch

6–13). Various members of both platoons observed numerous dead Vietnamese along the north-south trail inside the hamlet and several drifted far enough to the south that they observed the group killed earlier in the rice paddies (see exhibit P–41). During the time that the two elements were together, additional killings also took place. In one incident, a group of 7–12 women and children were herded together, and members of the 3d Platoon attempted to rip the blouse off a Vietnamese girl. They halted their attempts after observing that the PIO photographer was near their location and had taken a picture of the scene (see exhibit P–40). The women and children were then killed.

At approximately 0930–0945, the 2d Platoon departed Binh Tay and headed southeast toward the northeastern corner of My Lai (4) (see sketch 6–14). As they approached My Lai (4) some of the members of the platoon re-entered the northern edge of the hamlet. Other elements of the platoon apparently moved farther to the east toward a point where they were eventually to establish a part of the company's defensive perimeter. The platoon arrived in the area at approximately 0945–1000 hours.

Following the ditch incident with the 1st Platoon, WO1 Thompson had returned to the area south of My Lai (4) where he had earlier marked the positions of wounded Vietnamese. He testified that he contacted his low gunship to request that ground elements be sent to assist the wounded. His intent was evidently misunderstood by the gunships, for at approximately 0945 hours the high gunship contacted LTC Barker and identified the wounded/killed to the south of My Lai (4) as "8–9 'dinks' . . . with web gear and everything." The gunship also suggested that ground elements pick up the web gear and equipment from the bodies. (The probability that Thompson's message was either garbled or misunderstood by the gunships is further substantiated by the fact that during the events which followed there is no evidence to indicate that either wounded or killed VC [or any enemy equipment] were discovered by the C Company command element.)

After directing CPT Medina to recover the equipment from the bodies being marked by Thompson, LTC Barker proceeded to the B Company area where he landed to pick up three soldiers wounded by a boobytrap. He had his command and control helicopter then drop him off at LZ Dottie at approximately 0950 hours, while the B Company wounded were flown to a medical facility at Chu Lai.

The C Company command group had exited the southern edge of My Lai (4) at approximately 0930–0945 hours (see sketch 6–15). They moved farther south after CPT Medina received LTC Barker's call indicating that VC bodies and weapons were being marked by smoke in that area. CPT Medina testified that he decided to check the area out himself since the platoons were engaged elsewhere. He stated that en route to the smoke markers he observed three dead Vietnamese, consisting of a man, a woman, and a child (see sketch 6–15). Both he and LT (now Mr.) Alaux, his artillery forward observer (FO), testified that the appearance of the bodies indicated they had been killed by artillery or gunships. LT Alaux also testified that as they were approaching the smoke, he believes someone in the command group fired at and hit a fleeing Vietnamese who was subsequently determined to be a woman. (The details surrounding CPT Medina's subsequent killing of the woman are, of course, a matter of current criminal investigation. CPT Medina admitted shooting the woman. The truth concerning the circumstances which caused him to shoot her is outside the scope of this Inquiry.) Following the shooting of the woman, CPT Medina and the command group searched the surrounding area for a short while, and then headed back toward My Lai (4).

LT LaCross, 3d Platoon Leader, reached the northern edge of the hamlet and tried unsuccessfully to contact CPT Medina by radio. He testified that he wanted Medina to pass on to LT Brooks that he (LaCross) had spotted 15–20 Vietnamese males running in the vicinity of Binh Tay. LT LaCross' platoon medic testified that LaCross had tried, unsuccessfully, to contact Medina in an effort to find out the reason for all the killing. In any event, LaCross decided to move south to personally contact Medina who was then approaching the southern edge of the hamlet from the southwest. LaCross went south on the main north-south trail as he traveled to meet Medina.

After the command group returned to My Lai (4) (see sketch 6–16), CPT Medina spoke to LT LaCross for a few minutes and then directed him to return to the northern part of the hamlet to complete the sweep through the eastern edge of the hamlet. Evidence indicates that during the time frame in which Medina spoke to LaCross, various members of the command group strayed from Medina's location and were involved in random killing of wounded Vietnamese located in the vicinity of the intersection formed by the north-south trail and the east-west trail at the southern edge of the hamlet. After LaCross left, Medina proceeded farther east, along the east-west trail, and observed the bodies of the villagers located to the south in the rice paddies. He testified that he observed 20–24 bodies. He did not examine the bodies to actually determine the cause of death, but testified that he considered them "innocent civilians." There is evidence that during the time he observed the bodies, a member of his command group also shot and killed a small child who was standing, crying, in the midst of the group of bodies.

Following the incident involving CPT Medina's shooting of the woman, WO1 Thompson continued to reconnoiter the area east of My Lai (4). While so engaged, Thompson's crew chief spotted a bunker occupied by Vietnamese children (see sketch 6–17). Thompson observed US troops approaching the area and landed near the bunker. SP4 (now Mr.) Colburn, Thompson's door gunner, testified that Thompson told his crew that if the American troops fired on the Vietnamese, while he (Thompson) was trying to get them out of the bunker, the crew was to fire back at them. Thompson then got out of the aircraft. Thompson testified that he spoke with a lieutenant and told him there were women and children in the bunker, and asked if the lieutenant would help get them out. According to Thompson, "he [the lieutenant] said the only way to get them out was with a hand grenade." Thompson testified he then told the lieutenant to "just hold your men right where they are, and I'll get the kids out." (In June 1969, Thompson identified the lieutenant, from a personnel lineup, as having been LT Calley. While the evidence is clear that Thompson had spoken to LT Calley earlier at the ditch, there is evidence to indicate that it was probably the 2d Platoon leader, LT Brooks, who talked with Thompson at the bunker.) Thompson then walked over to the bunker, motioned for the Vietnamese to come out, and discovered that there were approximately 12–16 people consisting of one or two old men, several women, and children. Thompson then went back to his aircraft and called the low gunship pilot, WO1 (now CW2) Millians. He asked Millians to set down and assist in the evacuation. WO1 Millians landed just north of the bunker. He subsequently made two or three trips to evacuate the Vietnamese from the bunker to a safe area southwest of My Lai (4) along Route 521.

WO1 Thompson, WO1 Millians, and other "War Lords" crew members who were airborne over the area during this time testified that several large groups of bodies were clearly visible from the air—one group was located along Route 521, another in the ditch, a further one south of the hamlet, and another north of the hamlet.

COL Henderson testified that after departing LZ Dottie (at approximately 1000 hours) he returned to and overflew the operational area for a period of time. He departed the area at approximately 1030 hours.

After observing the bodies of the villagers located in the rice paddies to his south, CPT Medina and the command group probably moved east from the intersection of the north-south trail and east-west trail (see sketch 6–18). As they were moving, CPT Medina received a report that a member of the 1st Squad, 1st Platoon, had been wounded inside the village. The soldier, PFC (now Mr.) Carter, shot himself through the foot while trying to clear his .45 caliber pistol. This pistol jammed while being used by a member of CPT Medina's command group. Several members of the squad testified that the pistol was used to finish off wounded Vietnamese, including one 4–5 year old child.

Carter's wound was initially treated inside the village where he had discharged the weapon (see exhibits P–6 and 7). He was then carried south on the north-south trail (see exhibit P–9) and was held near the north-south and east-west trail intersection until a medical evacuation helicopter could be provided (see exhibits P–8, 10, and 36).

LTC Barker's command and control helicopter, which had just returned from taking the B Company wounded to Chu Lai, was dispatched to My Lai (4) to pick up Carter and return him to LZ Dottie. LTC Barker remained at Dottie during the medical evacuation.

LTC Barker's helicopter arrived in an area just southwest of the intersection of the two trails and Carter was brought out into the rice paddy for pickup (see exhibits P–11 and 12). The copilot of the helicopter testified that he observed the group of bodies on the north-south trail, while waiting for Carter to be put aboard. Carter was evacuated to LZ Dottie at 1025 hours.

Following Carter's medical evacuation, the command group remained in the general area of the intersection for approximately 15–20 minutes (see sketch 6–19). Several witnesses testified that during this period, a few remaining Vietnamese were rounded up and interrogated by CPT Medina and the attached military intelligence (MI) team, while most of the command group rested (see exhibits P–4, 3, 2, and 13). There is some evidence to indicate that one of the Vietnamese, an elderly male, may have been shot and killed by a Vietnamese interpreter, subsequent to interrogation.

During this same period, the attached PIO and MI teams requested and received a helicopter to take them from My Lai (4) to the B Company area (see exhibit P–17).

At approximately 1030–1045, CPT Medina received an order from MAJ Calhoun, TF S3, to "stop the killing" or "stop the shooting." CPT Medina testified that he assumed the order was generated by the helicopter pilot (WO1 Thompson) having observed his shooting of the woman. MAJ Calhoun admits that he issued such an order, but was not clear as to the timing involved. His testimony is also inconclusive as to whether the order was based on an accumulation of indicators of unnecessary killing of civilians by TF elements or merely the report of the Medina/woman incident. Following the issuance of the order to all of his platoon leaders, CPT Medina and the command group began to move to the northeast through the hamlet (see sketch 6–19). 1LT Alaux, who was with CPT Medina throughout the operation, testified that during this time he observed 17–18 bodies along the north-south trail inside the hamlet and had observed a total of 60–70 throughout the area, excluding those probably killed in bunkers.

7. 1045–1330 HOURS: ACTIONS INVOLVING C COMPANY AND AVIATION ELEMENTS EAST OF MY LAI (4)

WO1 Thompson testified that following the evacuation of the Vietnamese from the bunker, he again flew over the ditch to the east of the hamlet. Observing that some of the Vietnamese in the ditch were still alive, he stated that he landed his helicopter in approximately the same area as on his first trip. According to Thompson and his door gunner, the door gunner and crew chief went down into the ditch and found a small boy who was slightly wounded. The door gunner and crew chief told Thompson that others were still alive in the ditch at the time, but since the OH–23 had room for only one person (the boy was held on the crew chief's lap) the boy was evacuated to the Vietnamese hospital at Quang Ngai. Following this, Thompson and his crew returned to LZ Dottie, where Thompson contacted his company commander, MAJ Watke, and rendered what is now referred to as the "Thompson Report" (see chap. 10).

After reaching the eastern edge of My Lai (4), CPT Medina stopped, ordered a lunch break, and called a meeting with his platoon leaders. MAJ Calhoun arrived over the area in LTC Barker's helicopter at approximately 1145. During the time that he was over the area, he received from LTC Barker and relayed to CPT Medina an order to make sure there was no unnecessary killing/burning or words to that effect. Barker's order was apparently issued in response to information which he had received from MAJ Watke concerning the "Thompson Report."

At approximately 1245 hours, WO1 Thompson returned to the My Lai (4) area, and while in the process of conducting low-level reconnaissance of the area, his helicopter struck some tree limbs, suffered minor damage to its main rotor blade, and he had to land near C Company positions. An element from the company secured the helicopter for a short while until the rotor blade was checked and Thompson departed for LZ Dottie.

COL Henderson returned to the operational area at approximately 1330 hours. He testified that he overflew the area at least twice during the afternoon. LTC (now COL) Luper, who had flown with COL Henderson during the morning hours, testified that during the morning he had observed approximately 15–20 bodies south of My Lai (4). SGT (now Mr.) Adcock, COL Henderson's radio operator, testified that during their overflights of My Lai (4) during the morning hours, he had also observed 35–40 bodies from the air.

8. 1330 HOURS: SUMMARY OF RESULTS OF C COMPANY ACTIONS IN AND AROUND MY LAI (4)

Based exclusively on the testimony of US personnel who participated in or observed the actions in and around My Lai (4) on 16 March, it is evident that by the time C Company was prepared to depart the area, its members had killed no less than 175–200 Vietnamese men, women, and children. The company suffered only the one casualty previously discussed. From among the group of Vietnamese killed, the evidence indicates only three or four were confirmed VC. There were quite possibly several unarmed VC (men and women) among the group and many more who were active and passive supporters of and sympathizers with the VC forces. Three enemy weapons, and allegedly several sets of web gear and grenades were also captured. There is no substantive evidence to indicate that the company received any enemy fire or any other form of resistance during its movement through the area.

The Vietnamese casualty figures cited above are based on those incidents in and around My Lai (4) (including the subhamlet of Binh Tay) wherein clearly identifiable killings of Vietnamese (individuals and groups) were testified to and corroborated by US witnesses who were on the scene. It is considered that the figures are conservative as many of the Vietnamese killed inside bunkers and houses were not observed by the witnesses. The figures do not include additional killings which may have taken place as C Company passed through the several subhamlets east of My Lai (4) en route to their night defensive position, nor do they include additional killings which did take place late on the afternoon of 16 March, after C Company had reached the night defensive position.

In a separate study (see exhibit M–124) the Criminal Investigation Division (CID) agency estimates that 347 Vietnamese residents of My Lai (4) were killed on 16 March. This figure, which is based on a population census of My Lai (4) (i.e., before and after the 16 March operation) does not include Vietnamese who lived in the several subhamlets around My Lai (4) (such as Binh Tay) nor does it include those who may have come to My Lai (4) from surrounding subhamlets on the morning of the operation.

Additional killings which apparently occurred in the B Company area are not included in the 175–200 figure cited above nor in the CID agency's estimate.

9. 1330–1530 HOURS: MOVEMENT OF C COMPANY FROM MY LAI (4) TO NIGHT DEFENSIVE POSITION

At approximately 1330 hours, C Company departed My Lai (4) and moved northeast toward the link-up position with B Company. C Company apparently brought no detainees from the My Lai (4) area. En route, however, the 2d Platoon which was moving on the northern flank of the company passed through the subhamlet of My Lai (5) (Binh Dong) and rounded up approximately 50–75 villagers. Eight to 10 military aged males were separated from the group and were taken with the company to the night defensive position. The remainder of the villagers were told by CPT Medina's interpreter to move out of the area and head southwest toward Quang Ngai City.

There was some testimony to the effect that additional killing and burning of houses occurred as C Company elements passed through subhamlets east of My Lai (4). The preponderance of the testimony, however, does not support this contention.

10. 1530–1700 HOURS: THE NIGHT DEFENSIVE POSITION

After reaching the night defensive position and linking up with B Company, the VC suspects who had been brought into the area by both C Company and B Company were interrogated by the Vietnamese National Police. The police had been brought into the area via helicopter by the S2. The S2 also participated in the interrogation. During the course of the interrogation, one of the suspects was tortured and maimed. He was subsequently shot and killed along with several (1–7) additional suspects. Both the torture and the killings were witnessed by a significant number of C Company soldiers and officers. (This matter is also currently under investigation by the CID.)

At 1555 hours, CPT Medina notified the TF headquarters that approximately 10–11 women and children had been killed (earlier) by gunships or artillery, but were not included in his previous report of enemy killed.

B. Operations on 17 March

C Company departed the night defensive position early on the morning of 17 March and moved toward the south (see sketch 6–20). As the lead elements of the company passed to the east of Hill 85, the 1st Platoon, which was on the right (western) flank of the company, was ordered to establish an observation post on the high ground. CPT Medina testified the observation post was set up to detect any efforts by the VC to flank or strike the rear of the company. In the process of establishing the outpost, the 1st Platoon's point man detonated and was severely wounded by an enemy mine or boobytrap. He was evacuated by helicopter at 1000 hours. The platoon then rejoined the company.

As C Company moved south through the subhamlets of My Khe (3), (1), and (2) it burned the houses in those areas. CPT Medina testified that the subhamlets were deserted and that he had received permission to destroy the houses. As My Khe (2) was being burned, members of the 1st Platoon detected and apprehended four suspects consisting of three males and one female who was brought to CPT Medina's location with her blouse off.

During interrogation of the suspects, CPT Medina testified that two of the males were identified as VC and the female as a VC nurse. He admitted hitting one of the male suspects sufficiently hard to cause profuse bleeding from a skin laceration. He also testified to the effect that after discussing this individual with SGT Phu (his Vietnamese interpreter) he decided to make the suspect "talk." CPT Medina placed the individual against a tree and testified to the effect that he personally induced the suspect to "talk" by firing an M–16 round into the tree approximately 8 inches over the man's head (from a distance of 10–15 meters). Failing a response from the individual, CPT Medina fired a second round from the same distance to a point 4–5 inches over the man's head. After indicating to the individual that the third round would hit "right between the eyes," CPT Medina then moved away to fire a third round. Medina testified the man talked before the third round was fired and that he admitted being a "card carrying member in the Communist Party for 13 years." CPT Medina's recollection of firing over the man's head is essentially substantiated by the testimony of many other C Company witnesses. The testimony of several witnesses also indicates that the female suspect may have been mistreated during this same period. The suspects were subsequently evacuated from the area by helicopter. A readout of official interrogation reports concerning the four suspects indicates that two of the males and the female were subsequently classified as civil defendants. The remaining male was classified as a VC.

Following interrogation of the VC suspects, C Company turned back to the north toward their night defensive position arriving at that location by late evening.

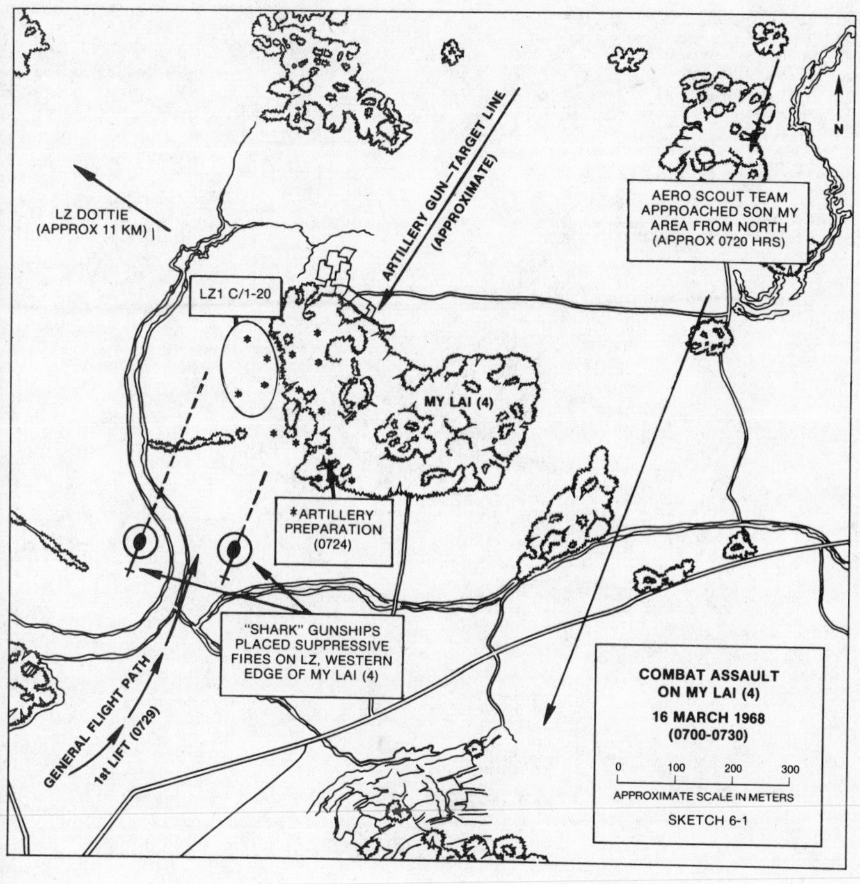
LZ DOTTIE
(APPROX 11 KM)
ARTILLERY GUN—TARGET LINE
(APPROXIMATE)
AERO SCOUT TEAM
APPROACHED SON MY
AREA FROM NORTH
(APPROX 0720 HRS)
N
LZ1 C/1-20
MY LAI (4)
*ARTILLERY
PREPARATION
(0724)
"SHARK" GUNSHIPS
PLACED SUPPRESSIVE
FIRES ON LZ, WESTERN
EDGE OF MY LAI (4)
GENERAL FLIGHT PATH
1st LIFT (0729)
COMBAT ASSAULT
ON MY LAI (4)
16 MARCH 1968
(0700-0730)
0
100
200
300
APPROXIMATE SCALE IN METERS
SKETCH 6-1

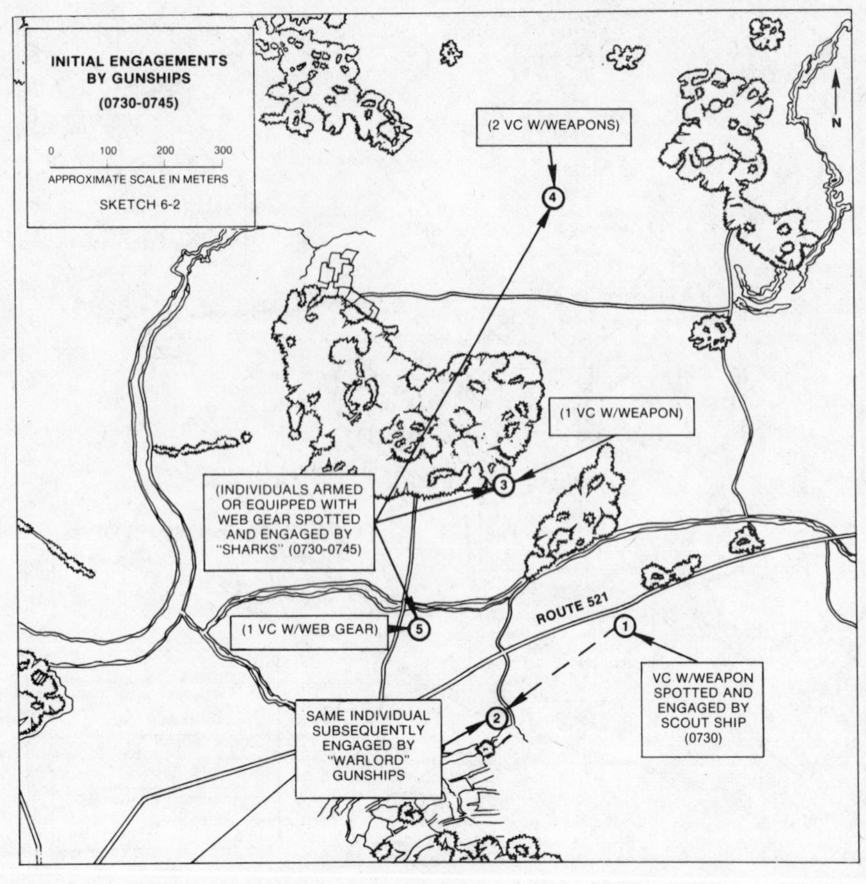
INITIAL ENGAGEMENTS
BY GUNSHIPS
(0730-0745)
0
100
200
300
APPROXIMATE SCALE IN METERS
SKETCH 6-2
N
(2 VC W/WEAPONS)
4
(1 VC W/WEAPON)
3
(INDIVIDUALS ARMED
OR EQUIPPED WITH
WEB GEAR SPOTTED
AND ENGAGED BY
"SHARKS" (0730-0745)
ROUTE 521
(1 VC W/WEB GEAR)
5
1
VC W/WEAPON
SPOTTED AND
ENGAGED BY
SCOUT SHIP
(0730)
2
SAME INDIVIDUAL
SUBSEQUENTLY
ENGAGED BY
"WARLORD"
GUNSHIPS

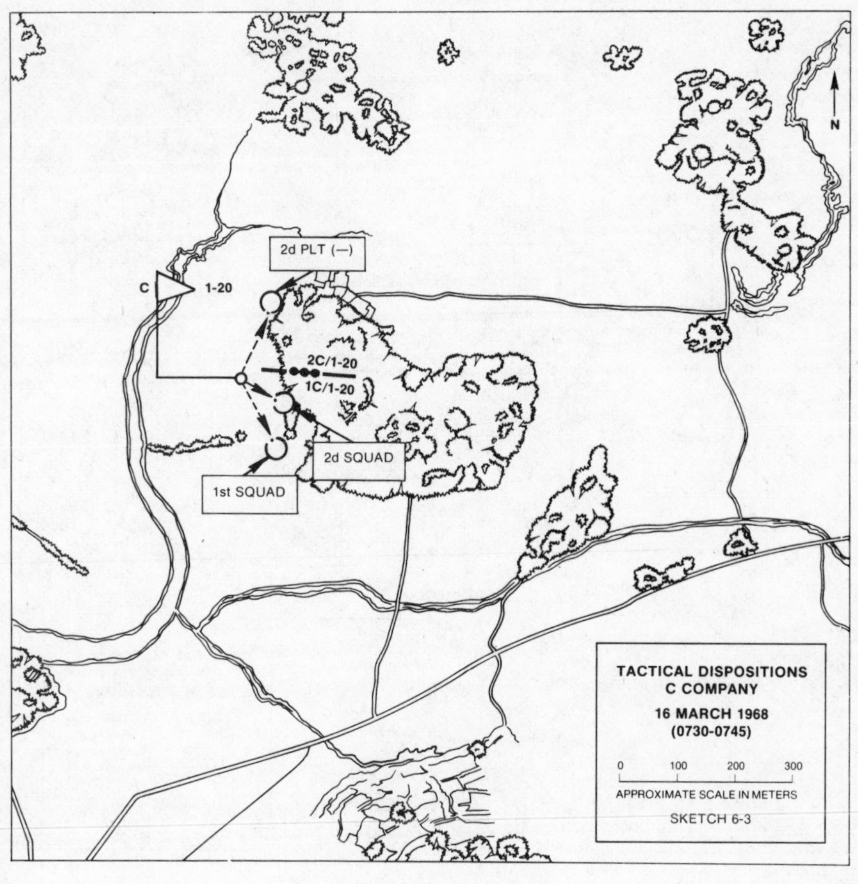
2d PLT (—)
C
1-20
2C/1-20
1C/1-20
2d SQUAD
1st SQUAD
N
TACTICAL DISPOSITIONS
C COMPANY
16 MARCH 1968
(0730-0745)
0
100
200
300
APPROXIMATE SCALE IN METERS
SKETCH 6-3

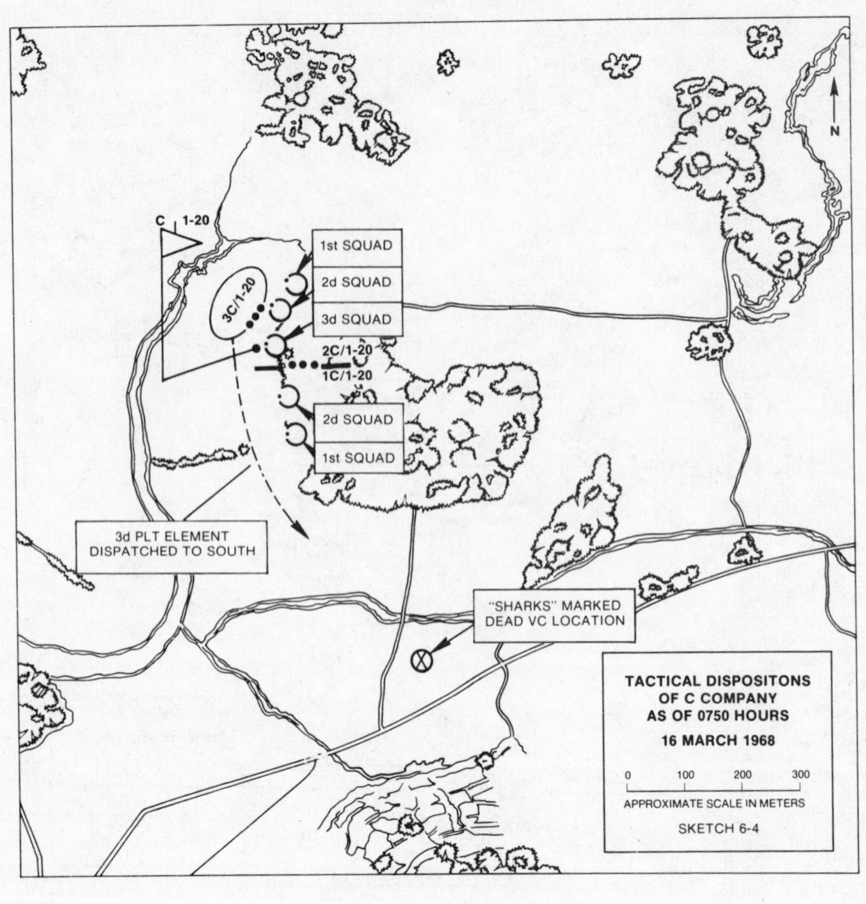

N
C 1-20
3C/1-20
1st SQUAD
2d SQUAD
3d SQUAD
2C/1-20
1C/1-20
2d SQUAD
1st SQUAD
3d PLT ELEMENT
DISPATCHED TO SOUTH
"SHARKS" MARKED
DEAD VC LOCATION
TACTICAL DISPOSITONS
OF C COMPANY
AS OF 0750 HOURS
16 MARCH 1968
0 100 200 300
APPROXIMATE SCALE IN METERS
SKETCH 6-4

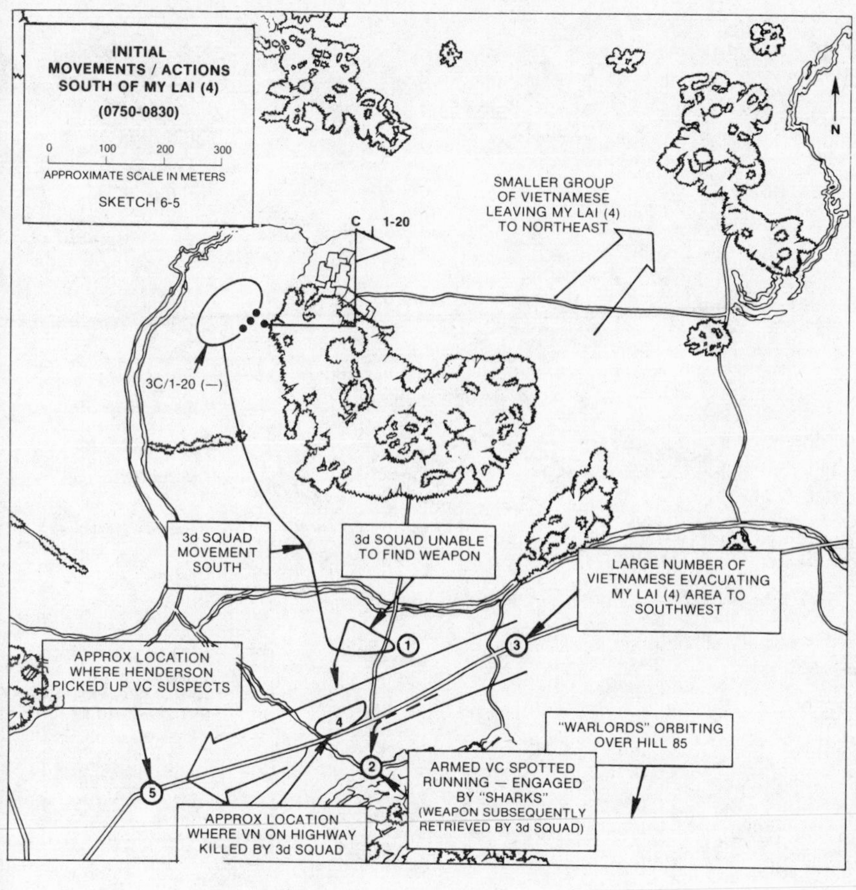

INITIAL
MOVEMENTS / ACTIONS
SOUTH OF MY LAI (4)
(0750-0830)
0 100 200 300
APPROXIMATE SCALE IN METERS
SKETCH 6-5
N
C 1-20
SMALLER GROUP
OF VIETNAMESE
LEAVING MY LAI (4)
TO NORTHEAST
3C/1-20 (—)
3d SQUAD
MOVEMENT
SOUTH
3d SQUAD UNABLE
TO FIND WEAPON
LARGE NUMBER OF
VIETNAMESE EVACUATING
MY LAI (4) AREA TO
SOUTHWEST
1
2
3
4
5
APPROX LOCATION
WHERE HENDERSON
PICKED UP VC SUSPECTS
"WARLORDS" ORBITING
OVER HILL 85
ARMED VC SPOTTED
RUNNING — ENGAGED
BY "SHARKS"
(WEAPON SUBSEQUENTLY
RETRIEVED BY 3d SQUAD)
APPROX LOCATION
WHERE VN ON HIGHWAY
KILLED BY 3d SQUAD

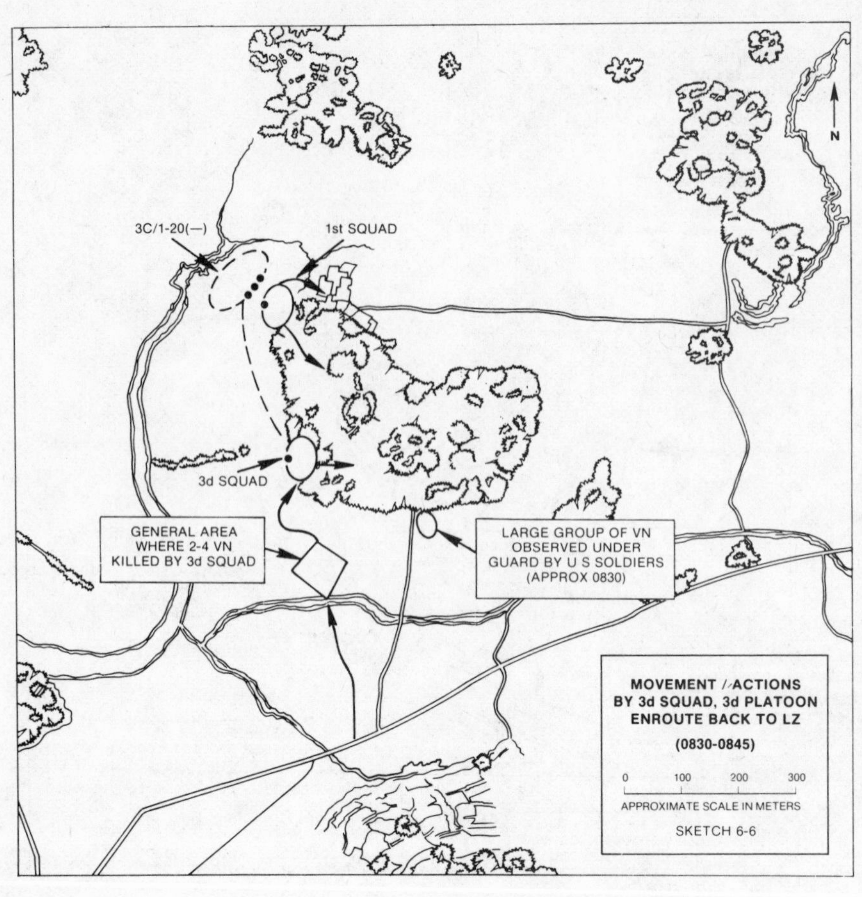
3C/1-20(—)
1st SQUAD
3d SQUAD
GENERAL AREA
WHERE 2-4 VN
KILLED BY 3d SQUAD
LARGE GROUP OF VN
OBSERVED UNDER
GUARD BY U S SOLDIERS
(APPROX 0830)
N
MOVEMENT /-ACTIONS
BY 3d SQUAD, 3d PLATOON
ENROUTE BACK TO LZ
(0830-0845)
0
100
200
300
APPROXIMATE SCALE IN METERS
SKETCH 6-6

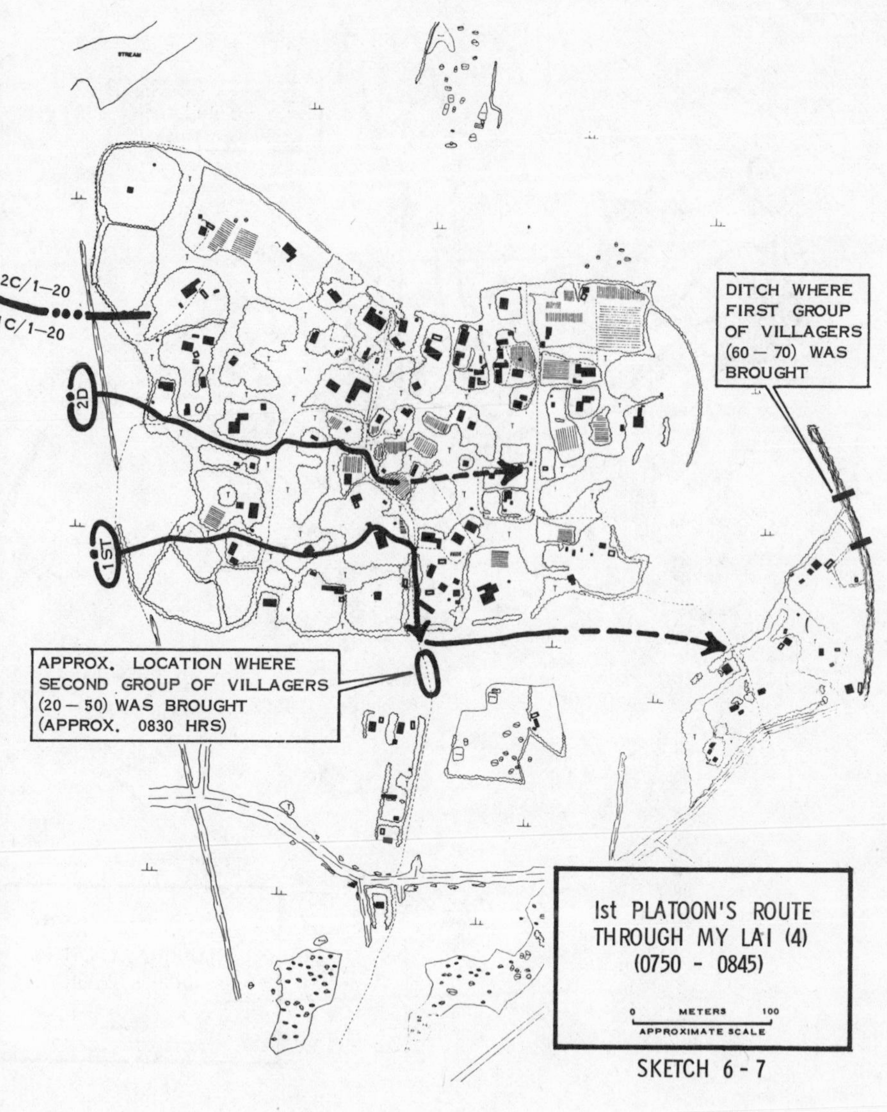

Ist PLATOON'S ROUTE THROUGH MY LAI (4) (0750 - 0845)

SKETCH 6 - 7

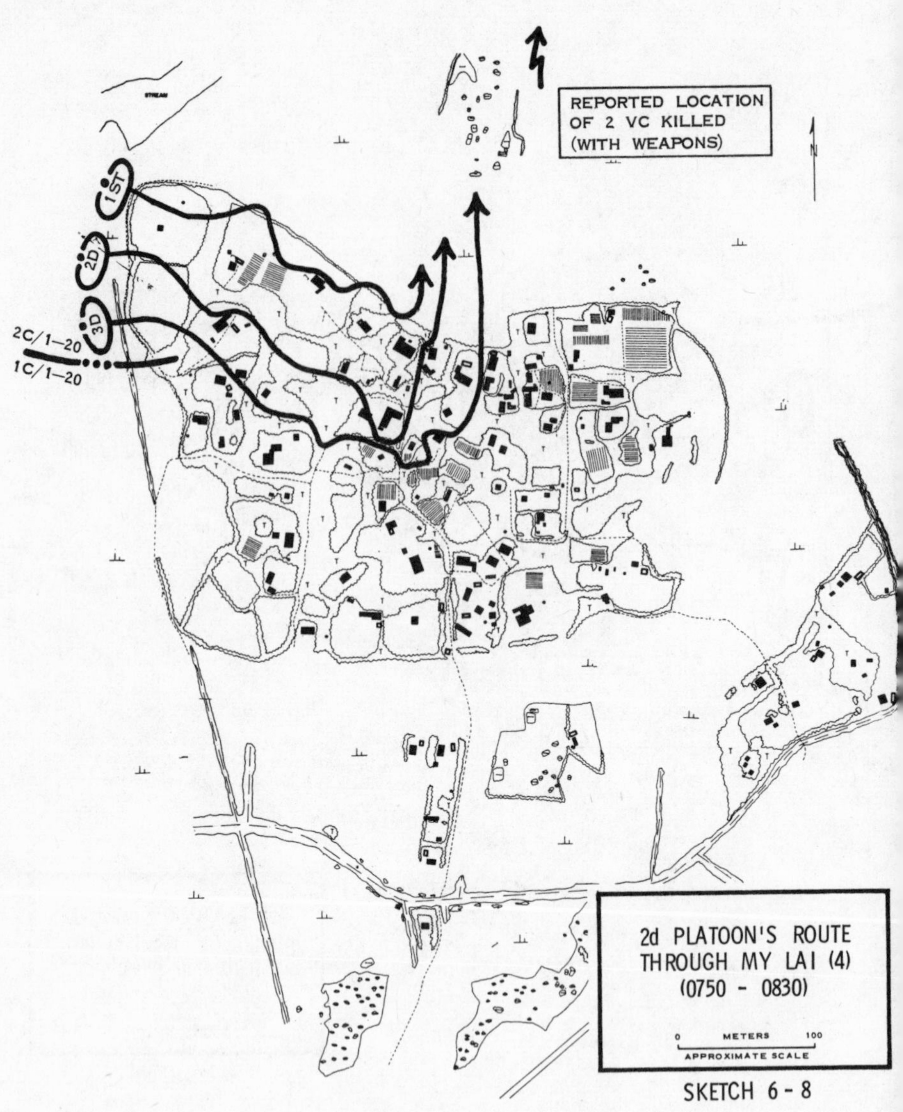
REPORTED LOCATION
OF 2 VC KILLED
(WITH WEAPONS)
N
STREAM
1ST
2D
3D
2C/1—20
1C/1—20
2d PLATOON'S ROUTE
THROUGH MY LAI (4)
(0750 - 0830)
0 METERS 100
APPROXIMATE SCALE

SKETCH 6 - 8

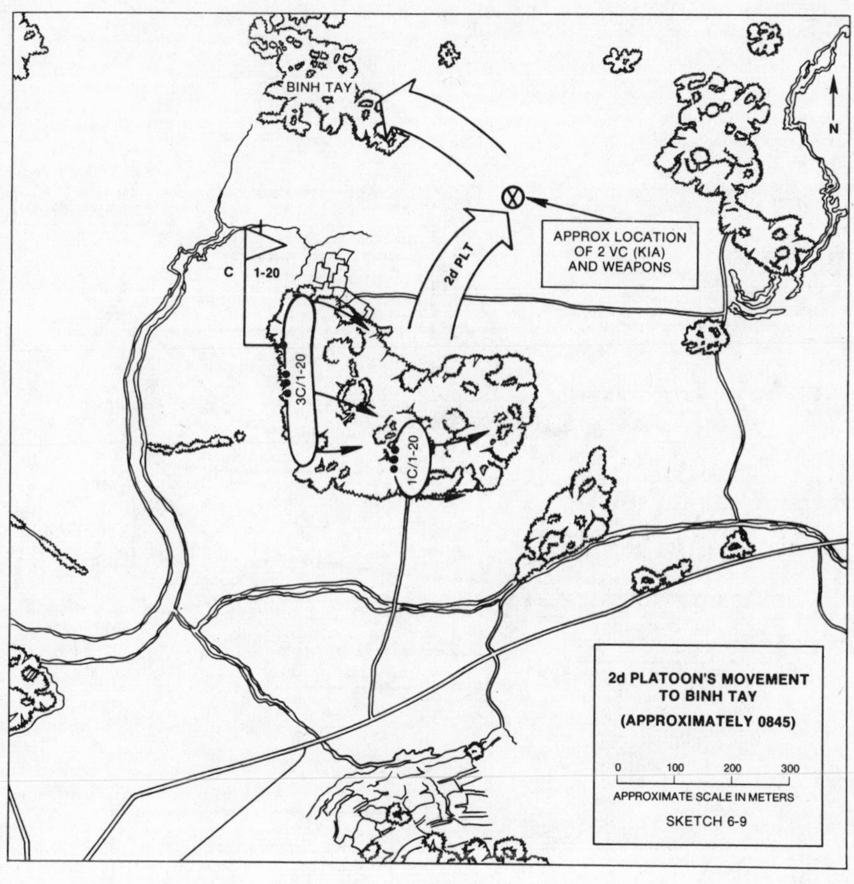
BINH TAY
N
APPROX LOCATION
OF 2 VC (KIA)
AND WEAPONS
2d PLT
C 1-20
3C/1-20
1C/1-20
2d PLATOON'S MOVEMENT
TO BINH TAY
(APPROXIMATELY 0845)
0 100 200 300
APPROXIMATE SCALE IN METERS
SKETCH 6-9

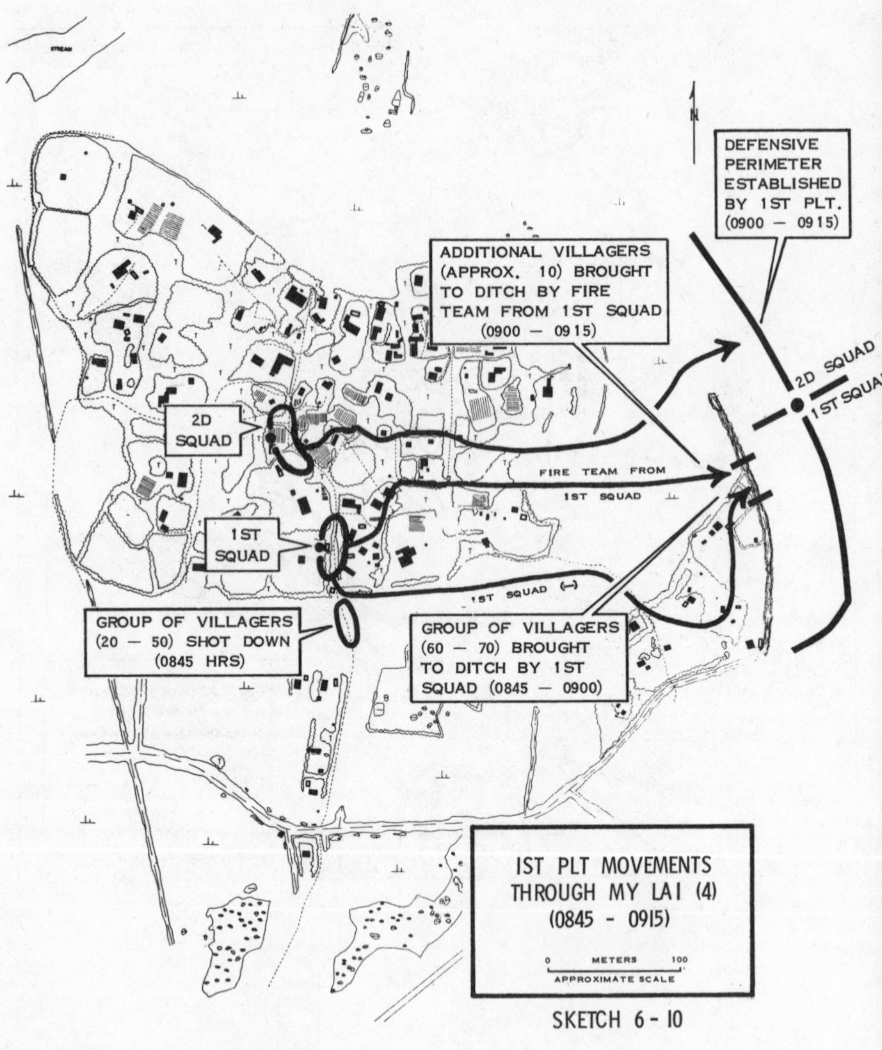
STREAM
N
DEFENSIVE PERIMETER ESTABLISHED BY 1ST PLT. (0900 — 0915)
ADDITIONAL VILLAGERS (APPROX. 10) BROUGHT TO DITCH BY FIRE TEAM FROM 1ST SQUAD (0900 — 0915)
2D SQUAD
1ST SQUAD
2D SQUAD
FIRE TEAM FROM 1ST SQUAD
1ST SQUAD
1ST SQUAD (—)
GROUP OF VILLAGERS (20 — 50) SHOT DOWN (0845 HRS)
GROUP OF VILLAGERS (60 — 70) BROUGHT TO DITCH BY 1ST SQUAD (0845 — 0900)
IST PLT MOVEMENTS THROUGH MY LAI (4) (0845 - 0915)
0 METERS 100
APPROXIMATE SCALE

SKETCH 6 - 10

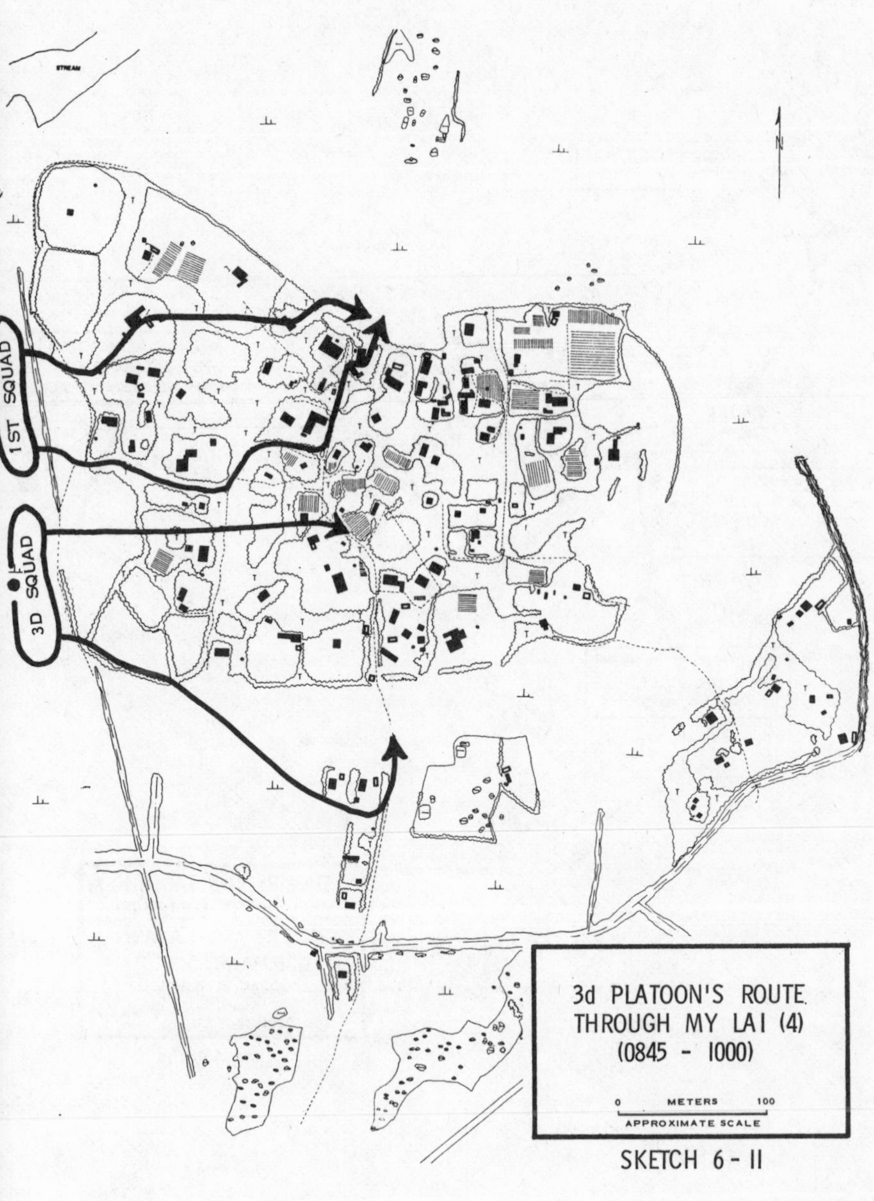
STREAM
N
1ST SQUAD
3D SQUAD
3d PLATOON'S ROUTE THROUGH MY LAI (4)
(0845 - 1000)
0 METERS 100
APPROXIMATE SCALE

SKETCH 6 - II

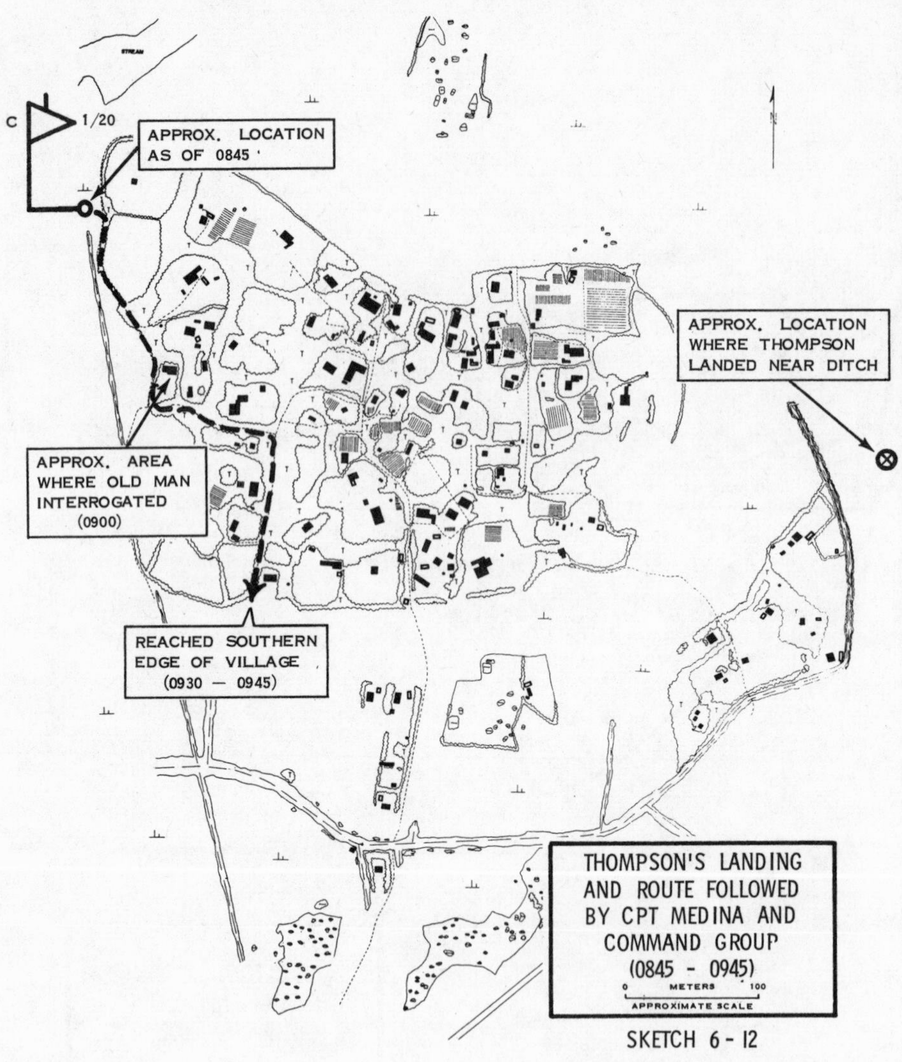

THOMPSON'S LANDING AND ROUTE FOLLOWED BY CPT MEDINA AND COMMAND GROUP (0845 - 0945)

SKETCH 6 - 12

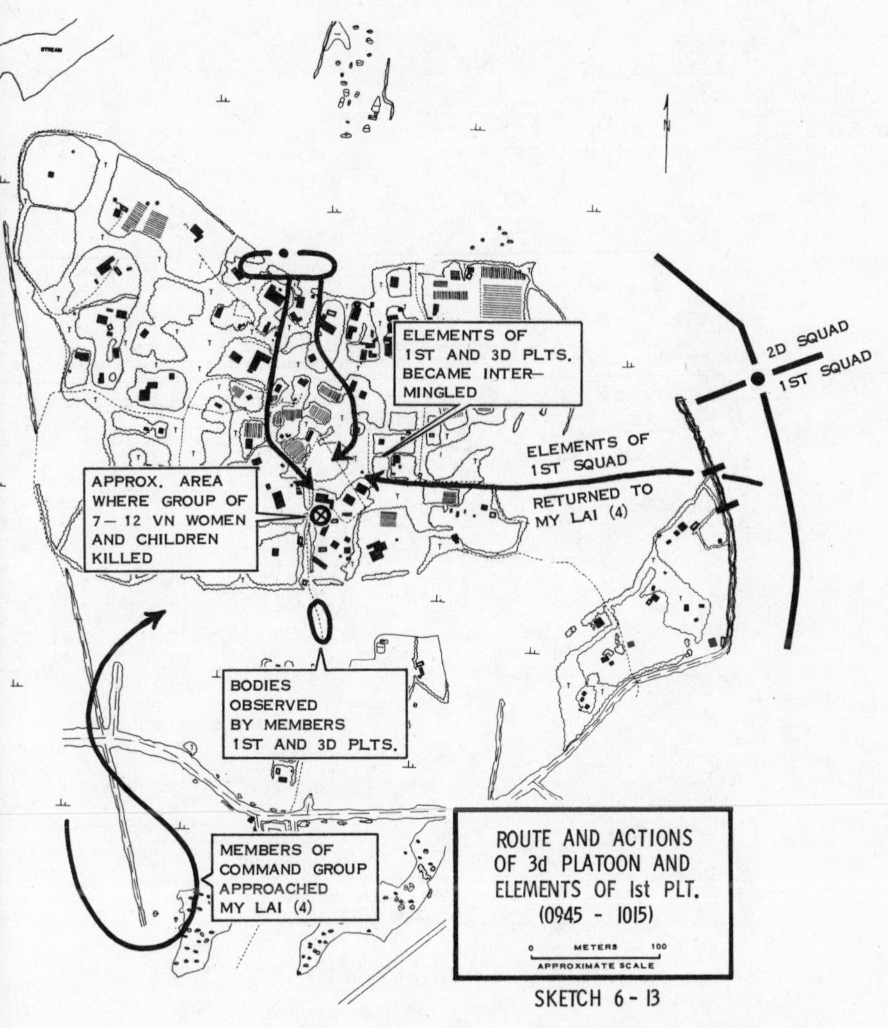
STREAM
N
ELEMENTS OF 1ST AND 3D PLTS. BECAME INTER-MINGLED
2D SQUAD
1ST SQUAD
ELEMENTS OF 1ST SQUAD RETURNED TO MY LAI (4)
APPROX. AREA WHERE GROUP OF 7— 12 VN WOMEN AND CHILDREN KILLED
BODIES OBSERVED BY MEMBERS 1ST AND 3D PLTS.
MEMBERS OF COMMAND GROUP APPROACHED MY LAI (4)
ROUTE AND ACTIONS OF 3d PLATOON AND ELEMENTS OF 1st PLT. (0945 - 1015)
0 METERS 100
APPROXIMATE SCALE

SKETCH 6 - 13

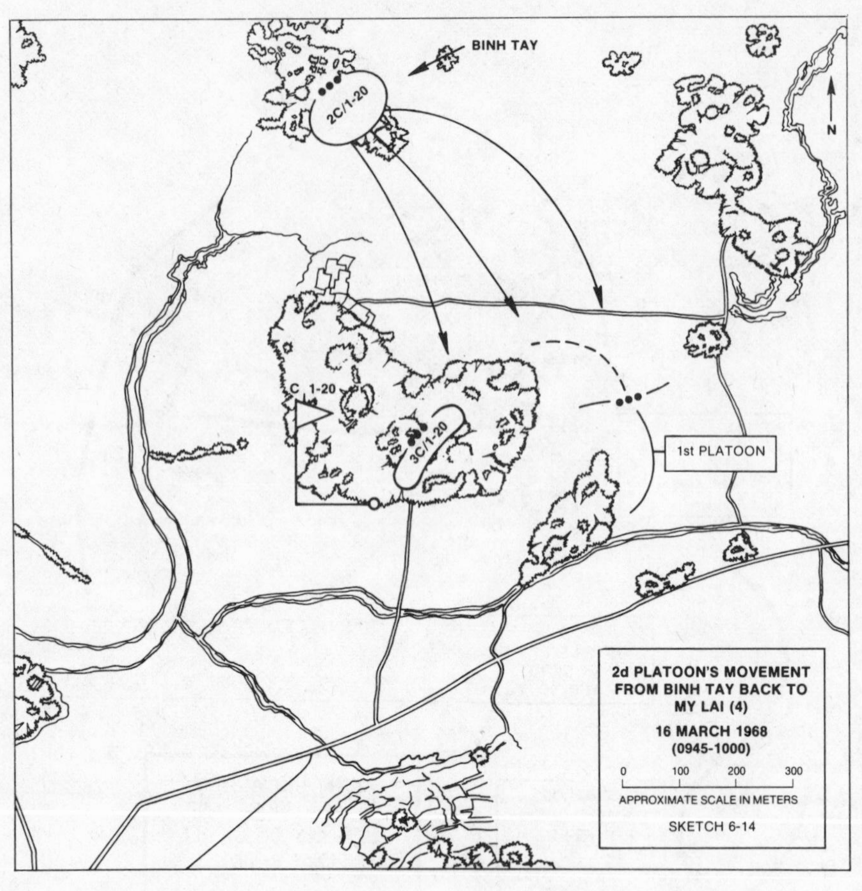
BINH TAY
N
2C/1-20
C 1-20
3C/1-20
1st PLATOON
2d PLATOON'S MOVEMENT
FROM BINH TAY BACK TO
MY LAI (4)
16 MARCH 1968
(0945-1000)
0
100
200
300
APPROXIMATE SCALE IN METERS
SKETCH 6-14

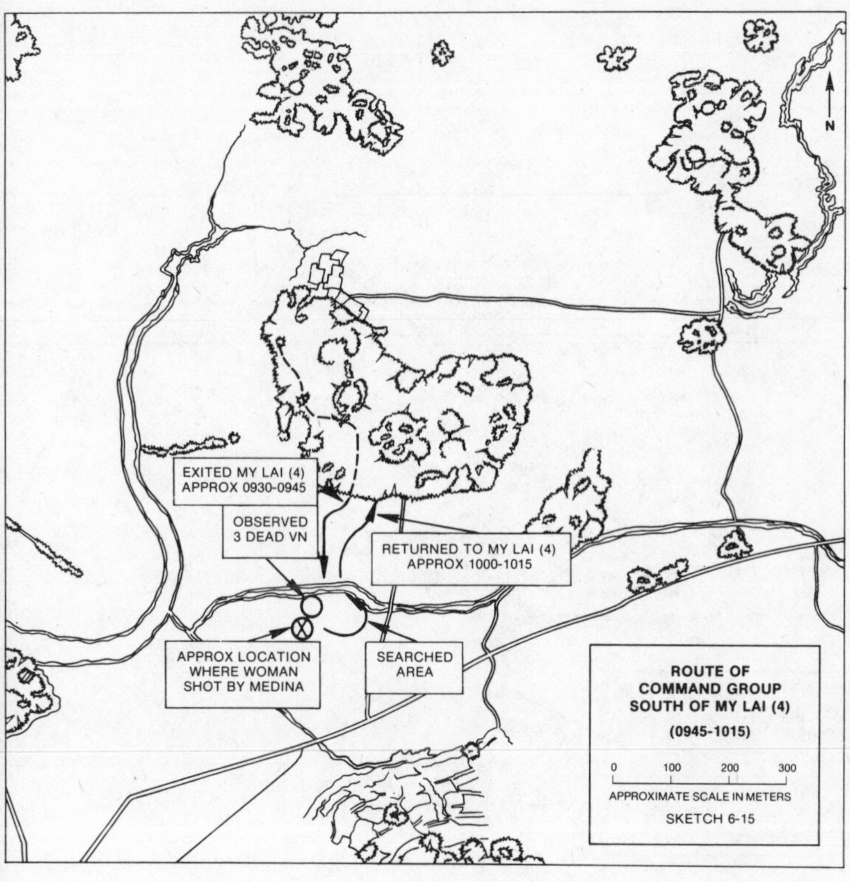
N
EXITED MY LAI (4)
APPROX 0930-0945
OBSERVED
3 DEAD VN
RETURNED TO MY LAI (4)
APPROX 1000-1015
APPROX LOCATION
WHERE WOMAN
SHOT BY MEDINA
SEARCHED
AREA
ROUTE OF
COMMAND GROUP
SOUTH OF MY LAI (4)
(0945-1015)
0 100 200 300
APPROXIMATE SCALE IN METERS
SKETCH 6-15

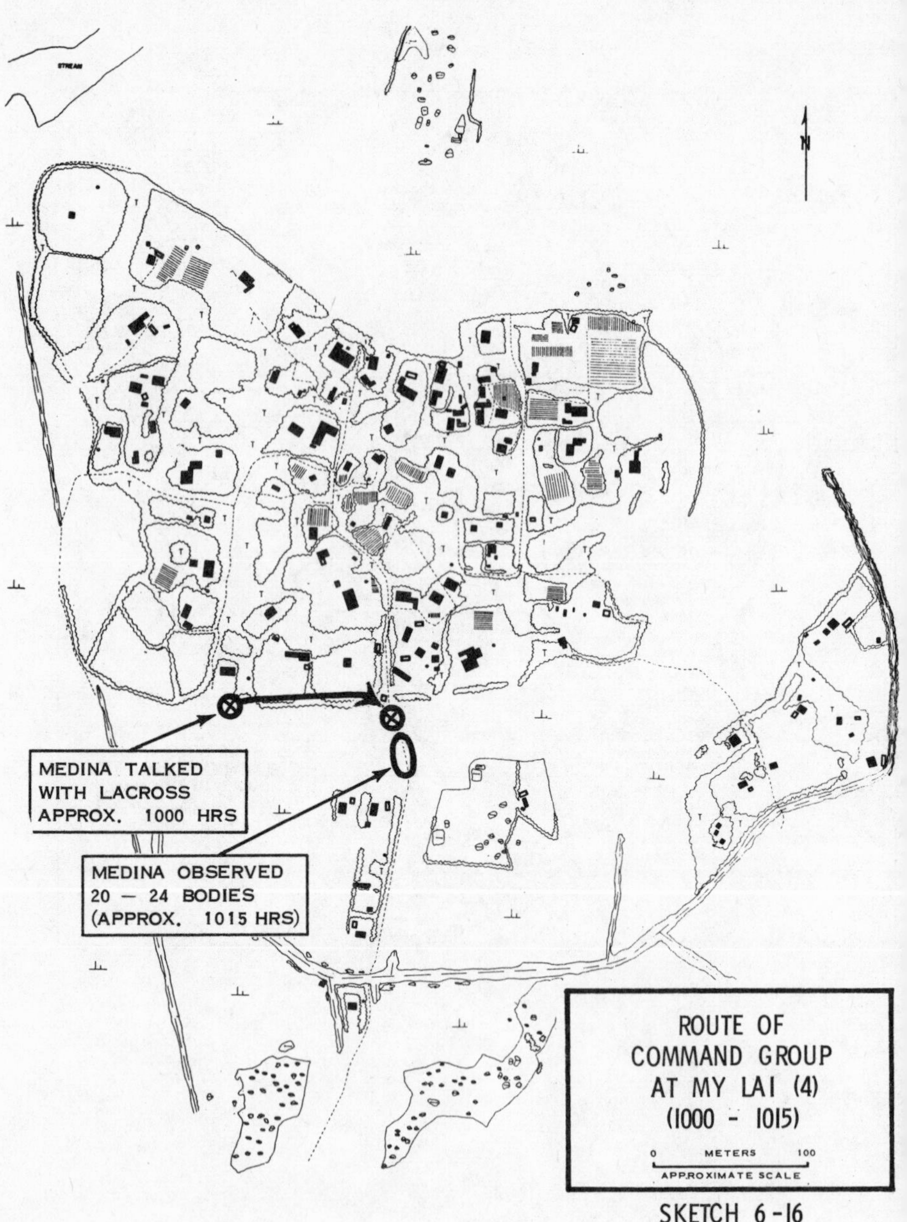
STREAM
N
MEDINA TALKED
WITH LACROSS
APPROX. 1000 HRS
MEDINA OBSERVED
20 — 24 BODIES
(APPROX. 1015 HRS)
ROUTE OF
COMMAND GROUP
AT MY LAI (4)
(1000 - 1015)
0 METERS 100
APPROXIMATE SCALE

SKETCH 6-16

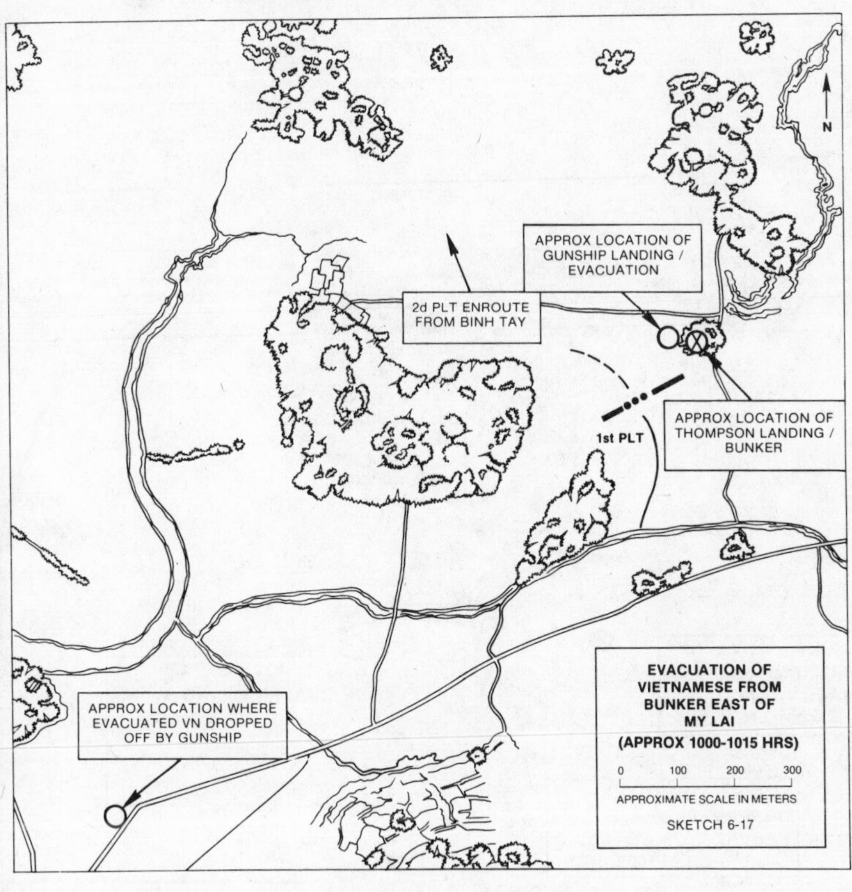
N
APPROX LOCATION OF
GUNSHIP LANDING /
EVACUATION
2d PLT ENROUTE
FROM BINH TAY
1st PLT
APPROX LOCATION OF
THOMPSON LANDING /
BUNKER
APPROX LOCATION WHERE
EVACUATED VN DROPPED
OFF BY GUNSHIP
EVACUATION OF
VIETNAMESE FROM
BUNKER EAST OF
MY LAI
(APPROX 1000-1015 HRS)
0 100 200 300
APPROXIMATE SCALE IN METERS
SKETCH 6-17

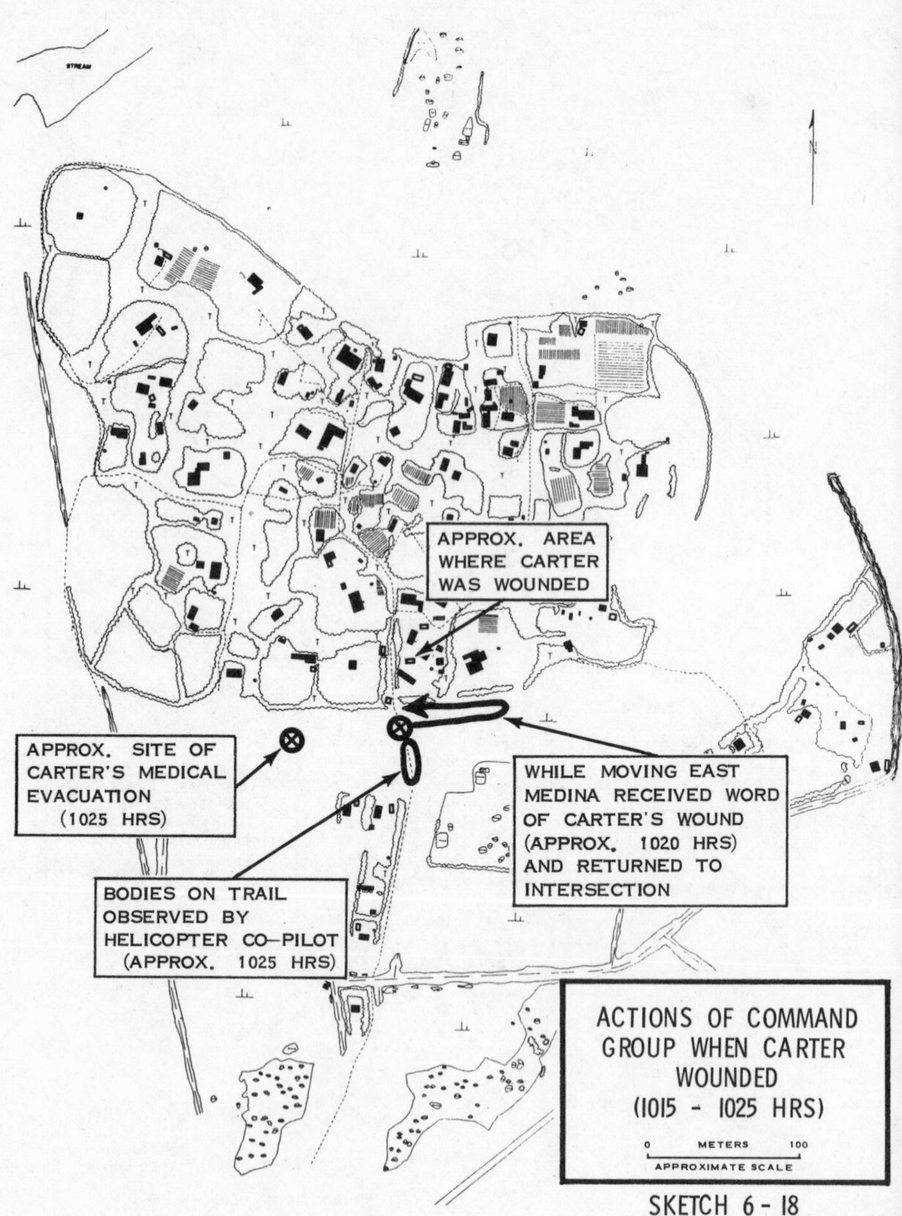
STREAM
N
APPROX. AREA WHERE CARTER WAS WOUNDED
APPROX. SITE OF CARTER'S MEDICAL EVACUATION (1025 HRS)
WHILE MOVING EAST MEDINA RECEIVED WORD OF CARTER'S WOUND (APPROX. 1020 HRS) AND RETURNED TO INTERSECTION
BODIES ON TRAIL OBSERVED BY HELICOPTER CO-PILOT (APPROX. 1025 HRS)
ACTIONS OF COMMAND GROUP WHEN CARTER WOUNDED (1015 - 1025 HRS)
0 METERS 100
APPROXIMATE SCALE

SKETCH 6 - 18

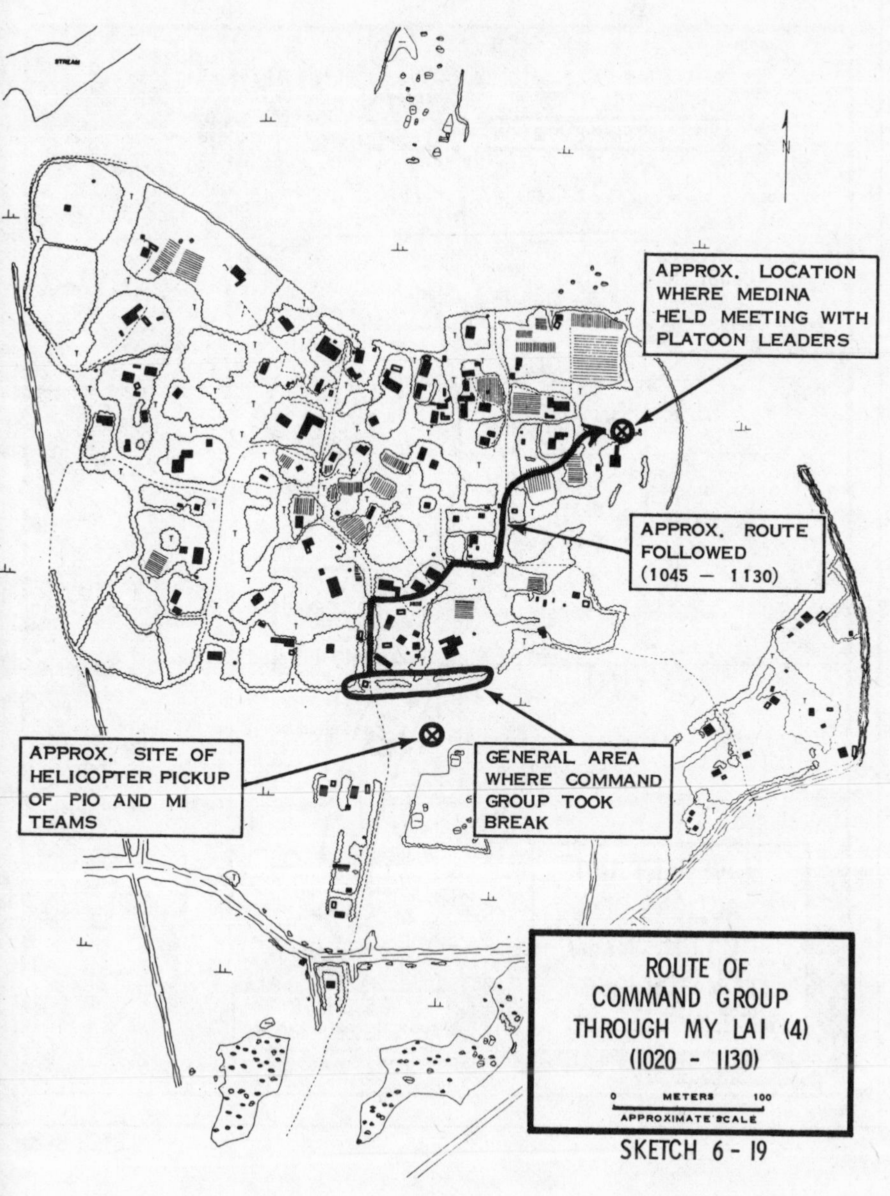
STREAM
N
APPROX. LOCATION WHERE MEDINA HELD MEETING WITH PLATOON LEADERS
APPROX. ROUTE FOLLOWED (1045 — 1130)
APPROX. SITE OF HELICOPTER PICKUP OF PIO AND MI TEAMS
GENERAL AREA WHERE COMMAND GROUP TOOK BREAK
ROUTE OF COMMAND GROUP THROUGH MY LAI (4) (1020 - 1130)
0 METERS 100
APPROXIMATE SCALE

SKETCH 6 - 19

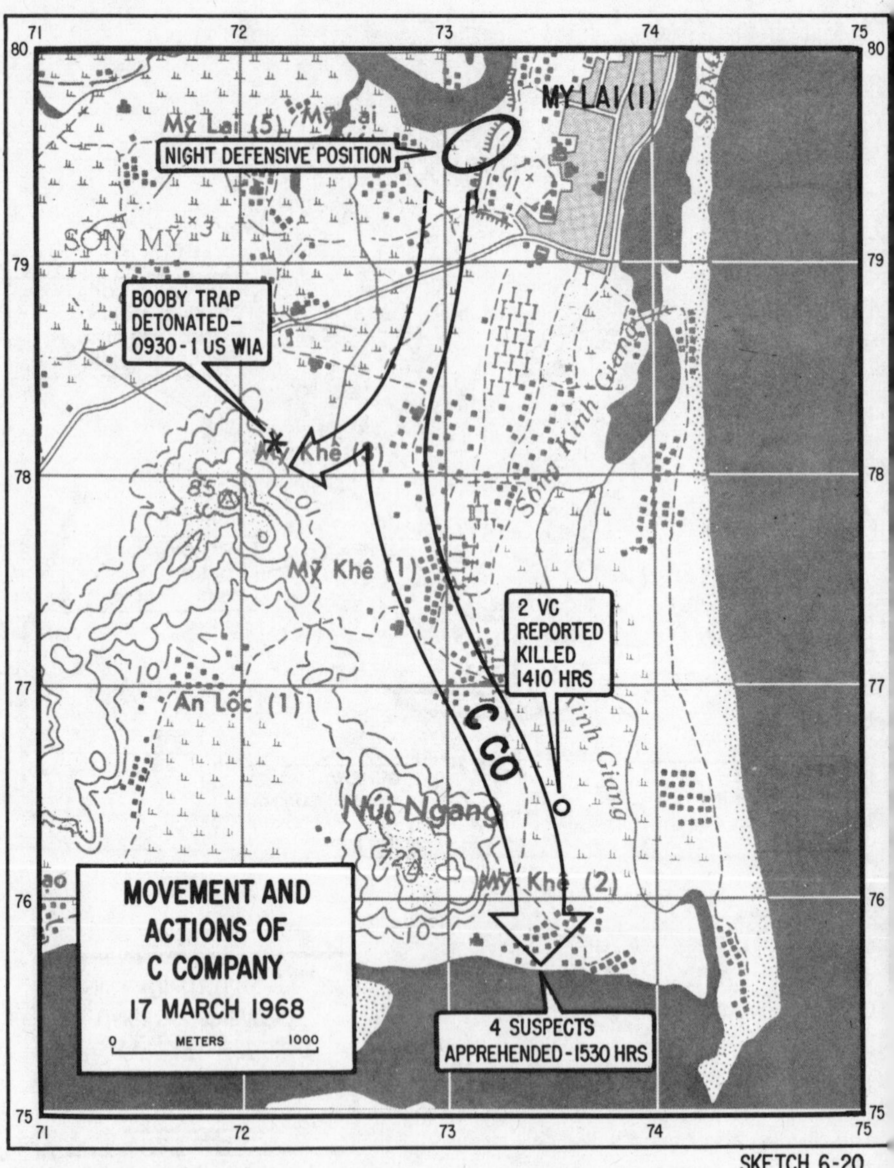

MY LAI (1)
Mỹ Lai (5)
NIGHT DEFENSIVE POSITION
SON MY
BOOBY TRAP
DETONATED–
0930-1 US WIA
Mỹ Khê (3)
Mỹ Khê (1)
Sông Kinh Giang
2 VC
REPORTED
KILLED
1410 HRS
An Lộc (1)
C CO
Núi Ngang
Mỹ Khê (2)
MOVEMENT AND
ACTIONS OF
C COMPANY
17 MARCH 1968
0 METERS 1000
4 SUSPECTS
APPREHENDED-1530 HRS

SKETCH 6-20

Chapter 7. Company B, 4th Battalion, 3D Infantry: Actions on 16-19 March 1968

A. Introduction

In the course of the investigation of Task Force (TF) Barker's operations in Son My Village on 16–19 March 1968, evidence was received of the possible commission of war crimes and violations of regulations by members of B Company, 4th Battalion, 3d Infantry (B/4–3 Inf) and the US and Vietnamese personnel working with the company. Although there are no indications that any of these activities were either reported to or investigated by higher headquarters, an attempt has been made by this Inquiry to establish the facts relating to these incidents in order to present the most complete picture of the Son My operation possible under the circumstances.

In the gravest of the incidents, a number of Vietnamese sources alleged that on 16 March 1968 approximately 80–90 noncombatants, including women and children, were killed by US soldiers in My Hoi subhamlet of Co Luy Hamlet, a coastal area of Son My Village shown on US maps as "My Khe (4)."

This allegation was included in a number of contemporary reports submitted through Government of Vietnam (GVN) channels in March and April 1968, copies of which were obtained by the Inquiry from GVN sources. A Census Grievance cadreman submitted a report, dated 18 March 1968, which included the statement that "at Co Luy Hamlet 80 people, young and old, were killed" by US forces. On 22 March 1968, the Village Chief of Son My wrote a report to the Son Tinh District Chief concerning the operations in his village on 16 March which stated that 90 civilians had been killed in Co Luy Hamlet on that day. The District Chief passed this allegation on to the Quang Ngai Province Chief in a letter dated April 11, 1968.

More recent statements by a Vietnamese woman, who claims to have been present at My Khe (4) on 16 March 1968, and by the Chief of Co Luy Hamlet (who has not been in the area since before the incident), also alleged that approximately 90 people were killed there on 16 March 1968. Finally, a National Liberation Front Committee notice, dated 28 March 1968, charged that 92 civilians were killed in Co Luy Hamlet on 16 March 1968.

Considerable evidence has been developed tending to show that elements of B Company's 1st Platoon did in fact kill a number of Vietnamese women and children at My Khe (4) early on 16 March, but it has not been possible to establish either the full circumstances or the number of victims of this incident.

Only 22 men of B Company's 1st Platoon appear to have witnessed or participated in the My Khe (4) incident. Of these men, two were later killed in action, eight have refused to answer questions about the incident, and several others who testified claimed to have little or no recollection of their actions and observations on 16 March 1968. In addition, the entire coastal area in which My Khe (4) is located has been virtually leveled in the period since the incident took place. The dwellings, trails, and much of the foliage existing in the area in 1968 have been obliterated, and the surviving populace has moved out of the area. These and other factors have precluded a reconstruction of what occurred at My Khe (4) on the morning of 16 March in the same detail given in the preceding chapter to the events in My Lai.

In addition to events of My Khe (4) on 16 March, there is evidence that detainees held by the company on 19 March were beaten and tortured by both US and Army of the Republic of Vietnam (ARVN) personnel. On 17 March, the company destroyed three subhamlets by burning. Thereafter, the company's modus operandi changed, and on 18 March it assembled hundreds of Vietnamese for a TF-supported Medical Civic Action Program (MEDCAP).

The purpose of this chapter is to present such facts and evidence as have been developed bearing upon B/4–3 Inf participation in the Son My Village operation. While this is an expansion of information relating to B Company presented in Chapter 5, the full story must await the completion of ongoing criminal investigations and any resulting prosecutions.

B. Operations 16 March

1. 0800–0830 HOURS: THE COMBAT ASSAULT

The men of B Company were assembled at the loading area at Landing Zone (LZ) Uptight prior to 0800 hours for a planned combat assault at about 0900 hours. Issuance of ammunition and final checks of weapons and equipment were completed, and CPT Michles reminded his men to be alert for the mines and boobytraps they could expect to encounter in the Son My area.

After completing the combat assault of C Company into My Lai (4) at 0751 hours, the lift helicopters proceeded immediately to LZ Uptight (see exhibit P–203) to pick up the first lift of B Company troops. LTC Barker had changed the operation plan by advancing by one hour the scheduled pickup time for B Company.

The artillery preparation of B Company's LZ south of My Lai (1) commenced at 0808 hours, about the time the first lift was departing LZ Uptight. Avoiding the gun/target line from LZ Uptight to the objective LZ the helicopters flew southeast over the South China Sea to a point near the mouth of the Song Tra Khuc (see exhibit P–205) before turning inland and then north toward the LZ located just south of Route 521 near the southwest corner of My Lai (1) (see sketch 7–1). As the helicopters approached the LZ, the artillery preparation did not terminate as planned, with the result that the helicopters were forced to make a 360 degree go-around in order to delay their arrival at the LZ. When the artillery ceased firing, LTC Barker marked the LZ with violet smoke and the first lift touched down at 0815 hours (see exhibit P–207). No resistance was encountered as the troops secured the LZ and it remained "cold" as the second lift touched down at 0827 hours.

2. 0830–0845 HOURS: DEPLOYMENT FROM THE LANDING ZONE

Some members of B Company believed that sniper fire was received from the west as the company moved out from the LZ, but it is possible that these individuals mistook for hostile fire some occasional rounds landing in the area which had been fired by C Company as it advanced in their direction some 2,000 meters to the west. No serious resistance was encountered as the company deployed from the LZ.

The 2d Platoon, led by 1LT Roy B. Cochran, had the mission of searching the subhamlet proper of My Lai (1), and it moved directly north across Route 521 toward its objective (see sketch 7–2). To the west, the 3d Platoon toegther with the Weapons Platoon and company command group also moved north to Route 521 where they halted temporarily to secure the area along and just to the north of that trail (see sketch 7–2).

The 1st Platoon, under 1LT (now CPT) Thomas K. Willingham, had preceded the 2d Platoon north to Route 521 and then moved east along that road toward the cement bridge over the Song My Khe (also called Song Kinh Giang) which had to be crossed to reach its objective, My Khe (4) (see sketch 7–2). The 1st Platoon's mission was to search the area around My Khe (4) and to block any enemy attempt to escape to the east from the My Lai (1) area. For the remainder of 16 March and until the following morning, the 1st Platoon was to be separated physically from CPT Michles and the rest of B Company, although they were in continuous contact by radio.

3. 0845–0945 HOURS: THE ATTEMPT TO ENTER MY LAI (1)

Within 15 minutes of touchdown of the second lift, B Company experienced its first casualties. After leading the 2d Platoon across Route 521, LT Cochran was killed by a land mine while attempting to cross a hedgerow at the perimeter of My Lai (1) (see sketch 7–3). Four members of his platoon were wounded by the same explosion. A dust off was requested, and all of the company except the 1st Platoon held in place until the medical evacuation of dead and wounded was completed about 0915 hours.

At that time a second attempt to enter My Lai (1) began with the platoon sergeant commanding the 2d Platoon. When the platoon had moved approximately 150 meters north along the perimeter of My Lai (1), a second mine was detonated at 0930 hours wounding three more men of the 2d Platoon.

The TF commander, LTC Barker, was airborne over the area when B Company reported encountering the second mine, and he notified CPT Michles and the TF tactical operations center (TOC) that he would pick up the additional casualties in his command and control helicopter. Landing in a field just west of My Lai (1) about 0940 hours, LTC Barker took the three wounded men aboard and immediately departed for LZ Dottie where he was dropped off before the command and control helicopter took the wounded to medical facilities at Chu Lai.

Although he did not meet with CPT Michles while his helicopter was on the ground, LTC Barker at this time apparently rescinded the order for the planned search of My Lai (1) as a result of the heavy casualties already suffered by the 2d Platoon in its efforts to enter the hamlet. The remaining men of the 2d Platoon were ordered by CPT Michles to withdraw from the approaches to My Lai (1) by retracing their steps. B Company made no further attempts to enter My Lai (1) during the operation.

4. 0845–0930 HOURS: 1ST PLATOON MOVEMENT TO MY KHE (4)

The 1st Platoon, commanded by LT Willingham, was provisionally organized into two rifle squads and a point team with a machinegun team attached to each rifle squad. The point team was composed of four soldiers who had volunteered to act as the platoon's permanent point element and who were widely respected in the platoon for their courage and their ability to locate mines and boobytraps. They also handled demolitions for the platoon and had a PRC–25 radio for communication with the platoon leader. The point team led the order of march from the LZ to Route 521 followed in order by the 1st Squad, the platoon leader with his radio/telephone operator (RTO) and mortar forward observer (FO), 2d Squad, and the medic and platoon sergeant.

The movement from the LZ to the cement bridge leading to My Khe (4) was completed without significant resistance or casualties. While on the trail south of My Lai (1), a member of the point team reported seeing a dud grenade hurled in the vicinity of the point team (see sketch 7–3). The platoon took evasive action by falling to the ground and firing in the direction from which the grenade was believed to have been thrown. After an unsuccessful search for the grenade, movement toward the bridge continued at a slow pace.

At or shortly after 0900 hours, the point team reached the western approach to the bridge and LT Willingham transmitted a request to CPT Michles for gunships to support his platoon's crossing. The gunships were rearming and not immediately available, so LTC Barker advised the company to use its mortar in place of gunship fire to support the bridge crossing.

The FO attached from the Weapons Platoon came forward to adjust 81mm mortar fire into the area across the Song My Khe near the eastern approaches to the bridge. Four or five rounds were fired and the mission terminated because a majority of the rounds were duds. Personnel on a Navy "Swift Boat" off the coast observed two of these rounds impacting "on the beach," which was east of the target area. CPT Michles then instructed LT Willingham to clear the area across the bridge with a machinegun.

The platoon deployed along the river in order that the majority of its members could cover the far bank of the river. One machinegun was set up near the trail leading onto the bridge, and the area around the far end of the bridge was taken under fire. The point team began crossing the bridge at approximately 0915 hours.

Members of the 1st Platoon heard the explosions of the mines encountered by the 2d Platoon and word of the casualty reports was also passed along. LT Cochran had formerly led the 1st Platoon and the news of his death strongly affected some of the men.

There is some conflicting testimony as to whether the platoon received sniper fire either before or in the process of crossing the bridge. The platoon leader stated that his platoon received heavy sniper fire and was driven back in its initial attempt to cross the bridge. The platoon sergeant and several others testified that a few rounds of sniper fire were received either before or during the crossing. The rifle squad leaders and others present at the scene recalled no sniper fire, and there is no record of any report being made of this alleged enemy contact. The procedures used in crossing the bridge, including the preparatory fires, appear tactically sound whether the platoon received fire or not. Members of the platoon were wary of the area; they would be exposed to enemy fire without available cover while on the bridge; and the news of the casualties suffered by the 2d Platoon added emphasis to their caution.

5. 0945–1500 HOURS: B COMPANY (–) MOVEMENT TO NIGHT DEFENSIVE POSITION WITH C COMPANY

It appears that the heavy casualties suffered by the 2d Platoon before it had even reached its objective area had a demoralizing effect not only upon the remainder of the 2d Platoon but also upon the members of the 3d Platoon, Weapons Platoon, and command group, who were close to the scene and observed both the explosions and the resulting casualties. Whether for morale reasons or because the elimination of the mission to search My Lai (1) left them with no tactical objectives, these elements of B Company had no further activity of any significance before linking up with C Company in the afternoon.

B Company (–) did move several hundred meters to the northeast late in the morning where the 3d Platoon searched the small hamlet shown on US maps as My Lai (6) (see sketch 7–3). The inhabitants were collected and screened, and several were detained, but in contrast to the actions of other units earlier that day, including those of its own 1st Platoon 1,000 meters to the east, B Company (–) neither harmed the inhabitants nor burned the dwellings in My Lai (6). Later in this chapter it will be noted that CPT Michles had issued an order to the 1st Platoon to insure that women and children were not killed. It is possible that events prompting this order also influenced the conduct of the search of My Lai (6).

Between 1100 and 1200 hours, the reporter and photographer covering the operation for the Brigade Public Information Detachment arrived by helicopter from the C Company area. They stayed with B Company (–) until midafternoon, taking a number of photographs which tend to confirm the complete contrast between the activities of B Company at this time and the actions recorded earlier in the day by the same photographer in My Lai (4) (see exhibits P–18 and 19).

Arriving with the reporter and photographer were 1LT (now CPT) Dennis H. Johnson, from the Brigade's attached Military Intelligence Detachment, and his ARVN interpreter. They interrogated some of the retained inhabitants before returning to LZ Dottie at approximately 1700 hours. They were joined at 1500 hours by the TF S2 who arrived with five ARVN soldiers and three National Policemen. The ARVN soldiers and National Policemen had been brought to the field to identify the VC from among the detained inhabitants.

After remaining for several hours in the area of My Lai (6), B Company (less the 1st Platoon) linked up at about 1500 hours with C Company which moved in from the southwest after completing its sweep through My Lai (4) and My Lai (5). The two units established a joint night defensive position. The events which took place in the night defensive position after the link-up of the two companies have been treated in Chapter 6.

6. 0930–1500 HOURS: THE 1ST PLATOON IN MY KHE (4)

The 1st Platoon crossed the bridge over the Song My Khe in single file and widely spaced to limit the number of men exposed on the bridge at one time. All of the men were across the bridge and the platoon was moving out to search the My Khe (4) area by about 0930 hours. Two men (later joined by a third) were ordered to remain at the bridge to secure the platoon's rear and to prevent enemy movement across the Song My Khe.

There is some doubt as to the exact location of the trails leading from the bridge and as to the number and location of the dwellings and other structures in My Khe (4). As previously noted, little trace remains of the terrain features existing in March 1968. On the basis of available evidence, including contemporary maps, it appears that a trail led east-northeast from the bridge for about 200 meters before turning due south parallel to and about 100 meters inland from the coast line (see sketch 7–4). Between the north-south portion of this trail and the South China Sea is a noticeable ridge or rise which prevents observation of the beach and the sea from the trail and vice versa. The 15 to 20 dwellings in My Khe (4) at that time were located on both sides of the trail and extended along it for about 200 meters, beginning about 100 meters south of the point where the trail curves to the south.

The point team with its RTO led the platoon movement along the trail leading from the bridge, followed in order by the 1st Squad (with attached machinegun team), the platoon command group, and the 2d Squad. The platoon moved in single file, staying on the trail to avoid boobytraps. At about 0935 hours, the point team and 1st Squad had approached to within about 75 meters of My Khe (4) at which time they opened fire on the hamlet (see sketch 7–4).

It has not been established whether the lead elements of the platoon opened fire in accordance with a previous plan, upon orders from the platoon leader, in response to sniper fire, or spontaneously. There is evidence to support each of these possibilities. In any case, an intense volume of fire from M–16 rifles and the M–60 machinegun attached to the 1st Squad was directed into and around the hamlet for 4 or 5 minutes. During this period, a radio operator aboard a Navy "Swift Boat" just offshore reported that "there is a lot of small arms fire coming from that direction on the beach." Inhabitants of the hamlet, mostly women and children, were cut down as they ran for shelter or attempted to flee over the ridge of higher ground toward the beach. At about 0940 hours, LT Willingham gave the order to cease fire, and the point team, together with a machinegun team, then moved south along the trail into the hamlet.

At 0955 hours, CPT Michles reported to TF Barker that the 1st Platoon had killed 12 VC with web equipment in My Khe (4). There is no reliable evidence to support the claim that the persons killed were in fact VC.

LT Willingham's order to cease fire prior to moving into the village may have resulted from instructions received from CPT Michles. At about this time, CPT Michles directed LT Willingham to insure that women and children were not killed. This order may have originated with TF Barker, which was issuing similar instructions to C Company about this time. On the other hand, several RTO's with B Company believe that these instructions were given by CPT Michles either upon hearing the heavy volume of fire in the direction of the 1st Platoon, or in response to LT Willingham's report of killing 12 VC. A number of witnesses testified that CPT Michles continually stressed to his company the importance of safeguarding noncombatants and avoiding indiscriminate firing, and the RTO with the 1st Platoon testified that this order was received before the platoon had even crossed the bridge into the My Khe (4) area.

The 1st Platoon stayed in the general area of My Khe (4) until about 1500 hours. After the initial firing into the hamlet, the point team and the 1st Squad moved down the trail searching and then burning the houses and destroying the bunkers or shelters which each family had constructed in or near their home. The 2d Squad remained to the north of the hamlet. The elements of the platoon searching the hamlet killed an undetermined number of noncombatants in the process.

The destruction of bunkers was accomplished by the point team using one or two pound TNT charges, which would at least collapse the entrances to most shelters if they did not destroy them entirely. Some witnesses alleged that the members of the point team made no attempt to determine if shelters were occupied before throwing explosives into the entrances, and that in some cases unarmed Vietnamese were shot down as they exited from their shelters.

It is believed that only 10 men directly participated in the search and destruction of My Khe (4), and of these two are dead and all the others have either refused to testify about the event or disclaimed any recollection of their observations. For this reason, it has not been possible to establish the facts with any degree of certainty. However, both testimony and circumstantial evidence strongly suggest that a large number of noncombatants were killed during the search of the hamlet.

In response to a request by LT Willingham, a resupply helicopter delivered a case of TNT and additional ammunition to the platoon some time before 1200 hours. At 1025 hours, LT Willingham reported to CPT Michles that the platoon had killed 18 more VC, and at 1420 hours he reported killing an additional 8 VC, making a total of 38 for the day.

No casualties were suffered by the platoon; it made no requests for fire support after crossing the bridge; and it captured no weapons. LT Willingham's RTO testified that he accompanied LT Willingham in a walk down the trail leading through the hamlet later in the morning, and he (the RTO) observed the bodies of about 20 dead Vietnamese—all women and children.

A Vietnamese woman, Nguyen Thi Bay, claims to have been present in the area of My Khe (4) on 16 March 1968. Although she is classified as a civil defendant by RVN authorities, Mrs. Bay's account of her experiences on 16–17 March was corroborated in some respects by members of the 1st Platoon. According to Mrs. Bay, about 20 US soldiers came into My Khe (4) between 0900–1000 hours on 16 March. There were no VC troops in the hamlet and the US soldiers were not fired upon, but 90 people present in the hamlet were killed, many being shot as they emerged from their shelters. She was hiding in a bunker or shelter with two other women and three children. They were not shot when they came out, but Mrs. Bay claims that she was raped by two soldiers, one of whom also struck her and the other woman with the butt of his rifle. About noontime, she was taken into a hootch where she was shown two spent cartridges tied with a rubber band (perhaps an expended boobytrap) and was accused of being a VC, which she denied. Later, she was taken away from the hamlet and made to spend the night in a field with the soldiers. The next morning she was told by the soldiers to take them back to My Khe (4). After doing so, she encountered ARVN soldiers who had come across the bridge.

Testimony from numerous members of the 1st Platoon closely parallels certain aspects of Mrs. Bay's story. A boobytrap consisting of a cartridge rigged with a firing mechanism was discovered during the search of My Khe (4). A woman captured by the point team was used to lead the platoon to its night ambush position a mile north of My Khe (4). The woman stayed in the open with the platoon overnight and the following morning led them back down the trail to the bridge, at which time the other elements of B Company, accompanied by the ARVN soldiers, joined the 1st Platoon. The woman was then turned over to the attached ARVN soldiers.

The above facts concerning the woman used as a point by the 1st Platoon (recalled by many witnesses) tend to corroborate Mrs. Bay's story and lend credence to her account of the killing of 90 noncombatants at My Khe (4) early on 16 March.

The Chief of Co Luy Hamlet (of which My Hoi or "My Khe (4)," is a subhamlet) has stated that 87 people were killed in the area of My Khe (4) on 16 March 1968. Although he was not present at the time and has not returned to the area since the event, he provided the following breakdown of victims: 15 VC soldiers; 20 VC cadre; 25 VC guerrilla and supply personnel; 13 VC female cadre; and 14 civilians. It should be noted that the hamlet chief's analysis of the casualties is based primarily on Communist affiliation rather than sex or age. For example, the category of "VC female cadre" included mothers of VC soldiers.

7. 1500–1800 HOURS: DISPLACEMENT TO NIGHT DEFENSIVE POSITION

Sometime after 1500 hours the platoon moved north approximately 2,000 meters from My Khe (4) and established its night defensive position. A Vietnamese female, tied with a rope, probably Mrs. Bay, walked in front of the platoon as point (see sketch 7–5). It was assumed she would know if the trails were mined and, if so, lead the platoon safely around them.

After the platoon arrived at its night defensive position on 16 March, Navy "Swift Boats" caused six sampans to beach near the 1st Platoon's position. These boats were manned by men and young boys. There were approximately 20 persons on board and they were detained until an interrogation team arrived. After interrogation, approximately five of the detainees were evacuated to Duc Pho for further screening. The others were released. There were no significant activities reported during the hours of darkness.

C. Operations 17 March

1. 0730–0930 HOURS: COMPANY LINKS UP

By 0730 hours, B Company had begun moving for link-up with the 1st Platoon just north of My Khe (4) (see sketch 7–6). The order of march from the company night defensive position west of My Lai (1) was the 3d Platoon, company command group, Weapons Platoon, and 2d Platoon.

An ARVN interpreter and several ARVN soldiers, who had been brought to the field by the TF S2, were attached to and moving with B Company. They moved south to Route 521 and followed it to the east. Concurrently, the 1st Platoon was moving south along the coast. The female apprehended in My Khe (4) was still in their custody and continued to walk in front of the 1st Platoon as point.

During the course of crossing the Song My Khe, one man from the 1st Platoon was wounded at 0810 hours from a boobytrap detonated near the eastern end of the bridge. After his evacuation and a thorough check of the bridge for mines, the 3d Platoon began crossing at approximately 0835 hours. At this time the company received sniper fire from the vicinity of My Khe (4). This fire was suppressed by company elements supported by two helicopter gunships that made strafing passes from north to south over the village. The sniper fire caused no US casualties and no enemy casualties were reported from the ground and gunship fires.

2. 0900–1800 HOURS: COMPANY SEARCHES CO LUY HAMLET

After crossing the Song My Khe, CPT Michles assigned missions to each platoon (see sketch 7–7). The 2d Platoon moved south near the seacoast while the 1st Platoon followed the inland trail through Co Lay (1), Co Lay (2), and Co Lay (3).

The 3d Platoon secured the bridge across the Song My Khe and sent one squad north approximately 1,000 meters to establish a blocking position across the peninsula (see sketch 7–7). The Weapons Platoon positioned the 81mm mortar at the bridge in the 3d Platoon area in order to cover the movements of the company.

While the company was between My Khe (4) and Co Lay (1), 1LT (now Mr.) John E. Mundy, the company executive officer, arrived by helicopter. He was accompanied by 2LT Michael L. Lewis, a newly assigned officer. LT Lewis was assigned to the 2d Platoon and joined his platoon on the beach north of Co Lay (1) where they halted for lunch. When the company commenced moving after lunch, hootches in Co Lay (1) were destroyed by burning.

Shortly after lunch, members of the 2d Platoon sighted two Vietnamese males. The Vietnamese began running and were engaged by small arms fire. One was apparently hit and seen dropping to the ground. The area was searched, but a body was not located. Nevertheless, this action was recorded in the TF Barker Journal at 1320 hours as "Co B-20 element engaged 2 VC Vic 742781, 1 VC KIA."

The subhamlets of Co Lay (1), Co Lay (2), and Co Lay (3) appeared to have been recently vacated, and the company did not encounter a sizable number of inhabitants. These subhamlets were searched and most of the hootches destroyed by burning. Demolition of most bunkers and tunnels was accomplished by the 1st Platoon's point team. The two attached engineer demolition specialists were instructed to destroy only two bunkers.

The two platoons and command group returned north along the trail to an area near Co Lay (1) and went into position for the night (see sketch 7–8). The Weapons Platoon displaced from the 3d Platoon area and closed into the company position.

All that day, the 3d Platoon had secured the area near the bridge and maintained a blocking position to the north. There was no activity in these areas. Members of the platoon did not visit My Khe (4). Toward evening, as the perimeter was being pulled in, a female body with a neck wound was discovered along the ridge near the sea. She was buried in a shallow grave the next morning.

D. Operations 18 March

1. 0730–1000 HOURS: COMPANY DEPLOYS TO KY XUYEN (1)

The primary company activity on 18 March was searching the upper peninsula. Operations on this date exhibited a stark contrast to the previous days' activities. Destruction was discontinued; burning and demolition did not occur; and the entire attitude seemed to be benevolent. The inhabitants of the upper peninsula were collected in the vicinity of Ky Xuyen (1) and a MEDCAP team was dispatched to this area in the afternoon.

Movement north from the company night defensive position had begun by 0730 hours. When the company reached the 3d Platoon's position north of My Khe (4), CPT Michles had the Weapons Platoon emplace its mortar to cover elements of the company moving toward Ky Xuyen (1). The 2d Platoon remained there to provide security for the Weapons Platoon. These platoons are believed to have begun moving north prior to 0930 hours.

The company reported its location at 0955 hours as Ky Xuyen (1). There were no engagements or other significant events recorded during its movement to this location (see sketch 7–9).

2. 1000–1700 HOURS: COMPANY SEARCHES UPPER PENINSULA

Two rifle platoons continued along the shore beyond An Ky. From this position, one of the platoons moved inland and together they began searching the area and directing inhabitants west toward Ky Xuyen (1). The company's other rifle platoon searched and collected the inhabitants of Ky Xuyen (2) while the Weapons Platoon joined and remained with the company command group.

At 1135 hours, TF Barker notified the 11th Infantry Brigade that it was sending a MEDCAP team to B Company's location. The Task Force reported that there were approximately 1,000 people in B Company's area and that the people did not appear to be VC.

Medical treatment and screening of the inhabitants for VC suspects were performed in the vicinity of Ky Xuyen (1) that afternoon. The three rifle platoons spent the day searching the upper peninsula and sending the inhabitants to the Ky Xuyen (1) area. There were no reports of finding enemy equipment and no casualties. Approximately seven Vietnamese were detained overnight.

3. 1700–2000 HOURS: NIGHT DEFENSIVE POSITION SECURED

The night defensive position was established several hundred meters up the shore line from Ky Xuyen (1) (see sketch 7–10). Before dusk, the artillery observer with the company fired in marking rounds. Later that evening, the Vietnamese brought to the company position a female who apparently had been wounded by the artillery adjustment. A dust off was requested at 1900 hours and completed at 1925 hours.

E. Operations 19 March

1. 0130–0600 HOURS: COMPANY POSITION ATTACKED

At 1030 hours, 60 mm mortar rounds began impacting within the company perimeter. Enemy personnel manning the mortar were positioned from 300 to 400 meters northeast of the company position and succeeded in "walking" six to ten rounds through the position. A machinegunner from the 1st Platoon was killed when a mortar round impacted in his foxhole. Five other men were wounded, one of whom died later. All but one of the casualties were from the 1st Platoon.

Personnel on guard observed the muzzle flashes at the enemy mortar position. The company opened fire with small arms all around the perimeter. Countermortar concentrations were fired by the company's 81mm mortar and the artillery located at LZ Uptight. There were some men who believed the company position received small arms fire from the north in conjunction with the mortar attack.

A dust off and an accompanying light fire team were requested by the company at 0143 hours, followed by a casualty report at 0146 hours. Later, LT Willingham had one of his men illuminate an open area along the beach with trip flares, which may have been for the purpose of identifying the company position to the dust-off pilot. Evacuation of the wounded was completed at 0244 hours and the helicopter light fire team remained on station over the company until 0300 hours. Instructions to "really dig in" were issued in preparation for an expected major attack.

Prior to the departure of the light fire team, an AC-47 ("Spooky") had been requested through the 11th Infantry Brigade. This aircraft arrived in the area at 0325 hours and remained there until 0600 hours. Radio communication was established with the "Spooky" and the company location was identified to the crew by using a flashlight. The area to the northeast of the company was intermittently "hosed down" by the miniguns of the "Spooky."

Two additional mortar rounds were received at 0440 hours. There were no casualties or reports of observing the muzzle flash.

2. 0630–1030 HOURS: SEARCH OPERATIONS

At daylight, a squad patrol from the 1st Platoon began searching for the mortar position. They were successful in locating the firing site but nothing more. During this search, two Vietnamese who had been held overnight in the company position walked point for the patrol. The patrol leader, a close friend of the man killed during the mortar attack, began beating one of the Vietnamese with his weapon. He was physically restrained by another member of the squad. Failing to find the mortar and concluding that further search would be useless, the patrol returned to the company command post.

During the morning, an American assisted by the ARVN interpreter interrogated detainees held in the company position. A field telephone with leads attached to various parts of the body to produce electric shocks was one technique being employed to obtain information. Knife wounds were inflicted across the back of the hand of one detainee who was then taken to the beach where salt was rubbed in the flesh wounds. These wounds were probably inflicted by the same American using the field telephone. The detainees were also being kicked and severely beaten by the ARVN interpreter.

One of the detainees promised to show the interrogation team a tunnel entrance leading to a weapons cache. CPT Michles, the ARVN interpreter and three ARVN soldiers, and the 1st Platoon followed the detainees. En route to the supposed tunnel location, one of the detainees broke and ran. He was not immediately fired upon and escaped (see exhibit P–215).

Thereafter, the other detainees either declared they had no knowledge of a tunnel entrance or refused to lead their captors to its location. The platoon returned to the company position and then prepared for extraction.

3. 1050–1340 HOURS: COMPANY RETURNS TO BASE CAMP

Extraction of the company began at 1050 hours and was completed at 1342 hours. The 1st Platoon was extracted first and taken to LZ Uptight, and the remainder of the company was taken to LZ Dottie. B Company's return to LZ Dottie on 19 March concluded TF Barker's operation in the Son My Village area.

During the operation, B Company reported killing a total of 39 VC, of which all but one were reported killed in My Khe (4) on 16 March. Although the number killed may be substantially higher than reported, and the total certainly included women and children, there is no indication that the Task Force and other higher headquarters ever became aware of the actual results of the attack on My Khe (4). In the afternoon of 16 March, CPT Michles reported to TF Barker that there were no women and children among the 38 VC reported as killed. Additionally, the fact that some of the victims were apparently killed in bunkers or shelters may have further assisted in concealing the actual number of persons killed from both the men on the ground and anyone flying over My Khe (4). It should nevertheless be noted that although 39 VC KIA were reported, no weapons were reported captured, no casualties were suffered, and there were no other indications that the 1st Platoon was engaging in armed force. These circumstances should have prompted inquiries from higher headquarters, but apparently none was made.

Although there was some subsequent talk among the men in B Company concerning the people killed by the 1st Platoon in My Khe (4), they recalled no inquiries or investigations about B Company's participation in the operation.

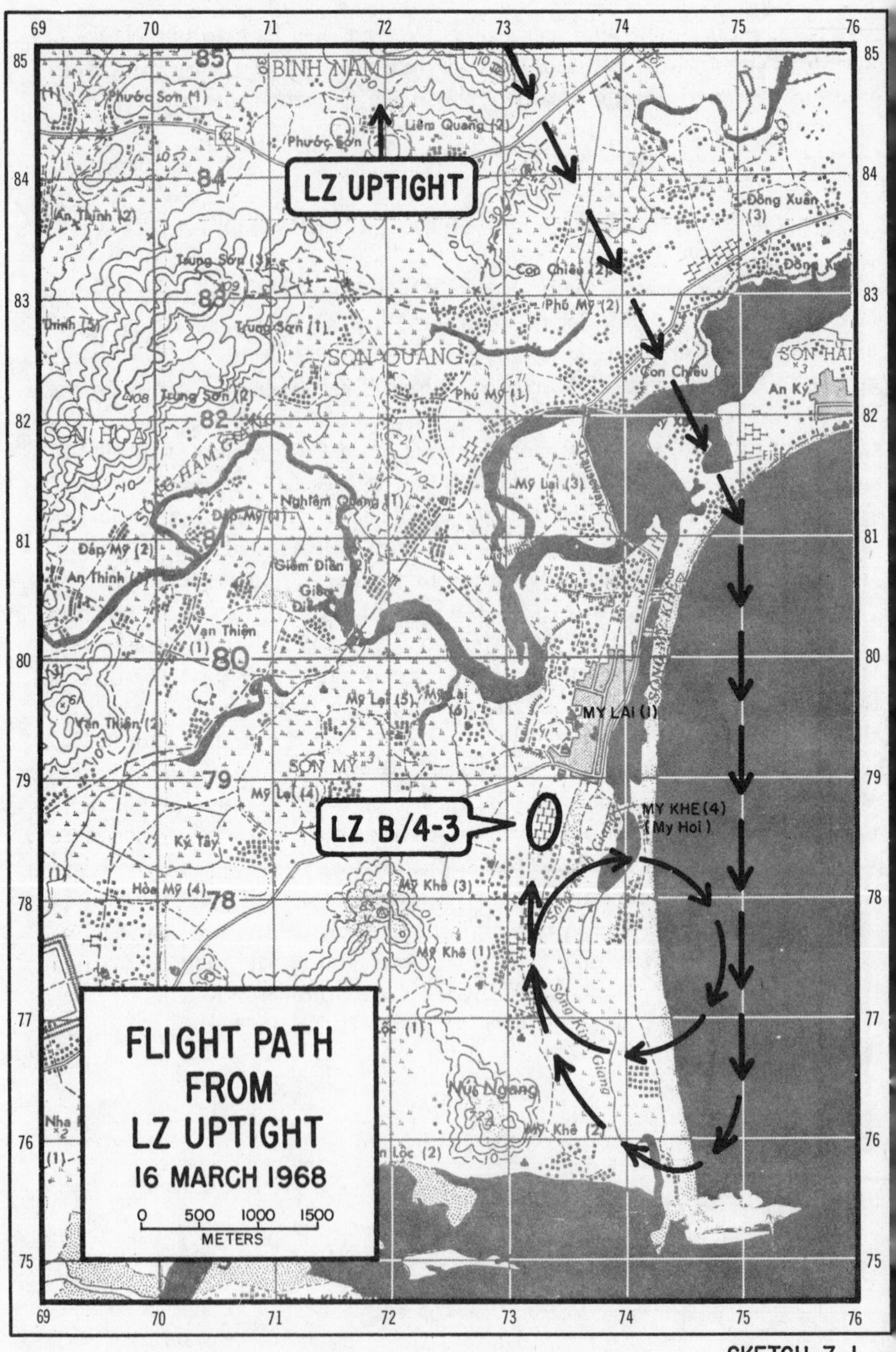

LZ UPTIGHT
LZ B/4-3
MY LAI (1)
MY KHE (4)
(My Hoi)
BINH NAM
SON QUANG
SON MY
SON HOA
SON HAI
FLIGHT PATH
FROM
LZ UPTIGHT
16 MARCH 1968
0 500 1000 1500
METERS

SKETCH 7-1

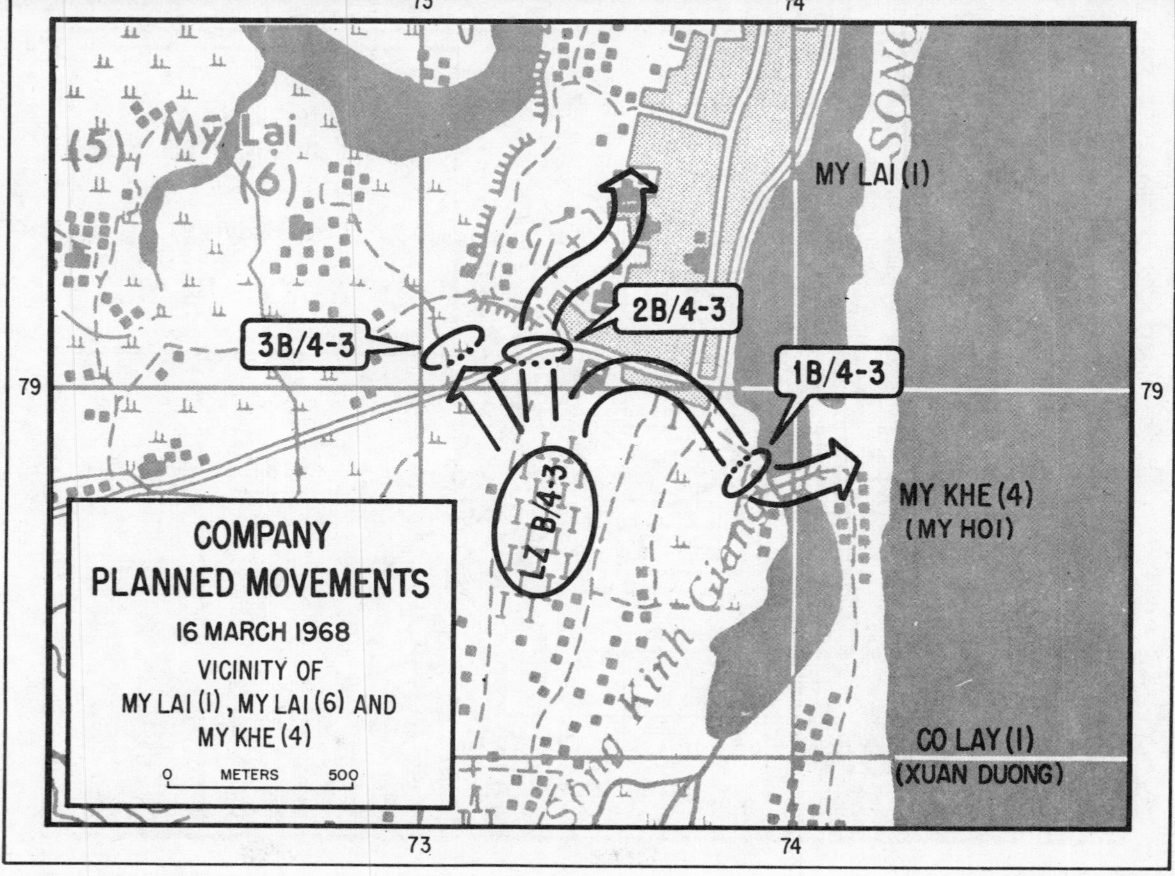
COMPANY
PLANNED MOVEMENTS
16 MARCH 1968
VICINITY OF
MY LAI (1), MY LAI (6) AND
MY KHE (4)
0 METERS 500
3B/4-3
2B/4-3
1B/4-3
LZ B/4-3
MY LAI (1)
MY KHE (4)
(MY HOI)
CO LAY (1)
(XUAN DUONG)
(5)
My Lai
(6)
Song Kinh Giang
79
73
74
79

SKETCH 7-2

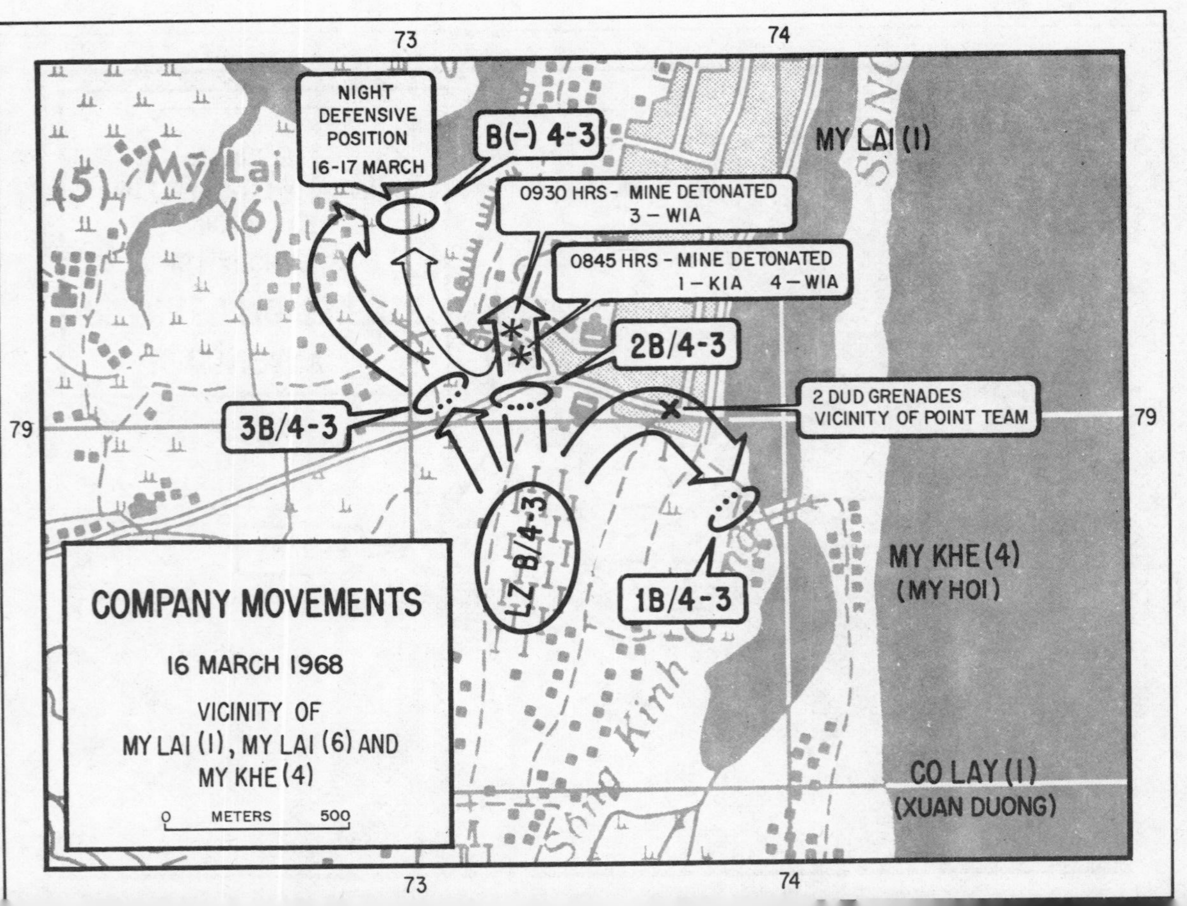

COMPANY MOVEMENTS
16 MARCH 1968
VICINITY OF
MY LAI (1), MY LAI (6) AND
MY KHE (4)
0 METERS 500
NIGHT
DEFENSIVE
POSITION
16-17 MARCH
B(-) 4-3
0930 HRS - MINE DETONATED
3 - WIA
0845 HRS - MINE DETONATED
1 - KIA 4 - WIA
2B/4-3
3B/4-3
1B/4-3
LZ B/4-3
2 DUD GRENADES
VICINITY OF POINT TEAM
MY LAI (1)
My Lai (6)
(5)
MY KHE (4)
(MY HOI)
CO LAY (1)
(XUAN DUONG)
73
74
79

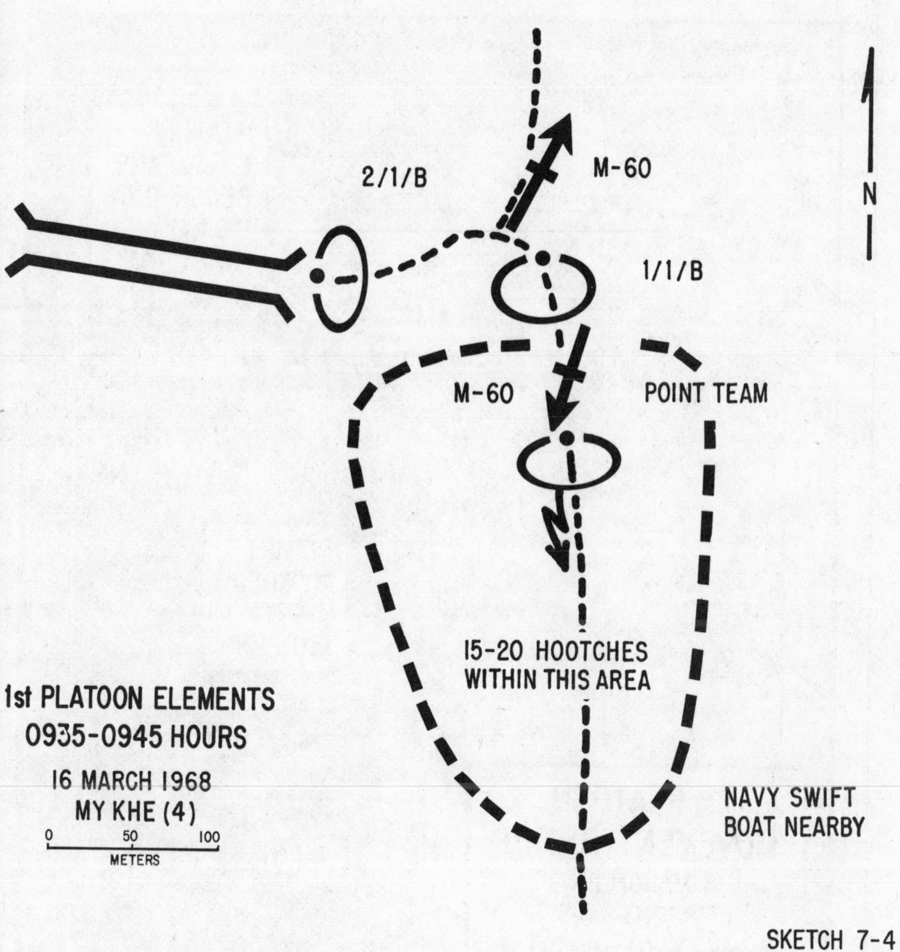
2/1/B
M-60
N
1/1/B
M-60
POINT TEAM
15-20 HOOTCHES
WITHIN THIS AREA
1st PLATOON ELEMENTS
0935-0945 HOURS
16 MARCH 1968
MY KHE (4)
0
50
100
METERS
NAVY SWIFT
BOAT NEARBY

SKETCH 7-4

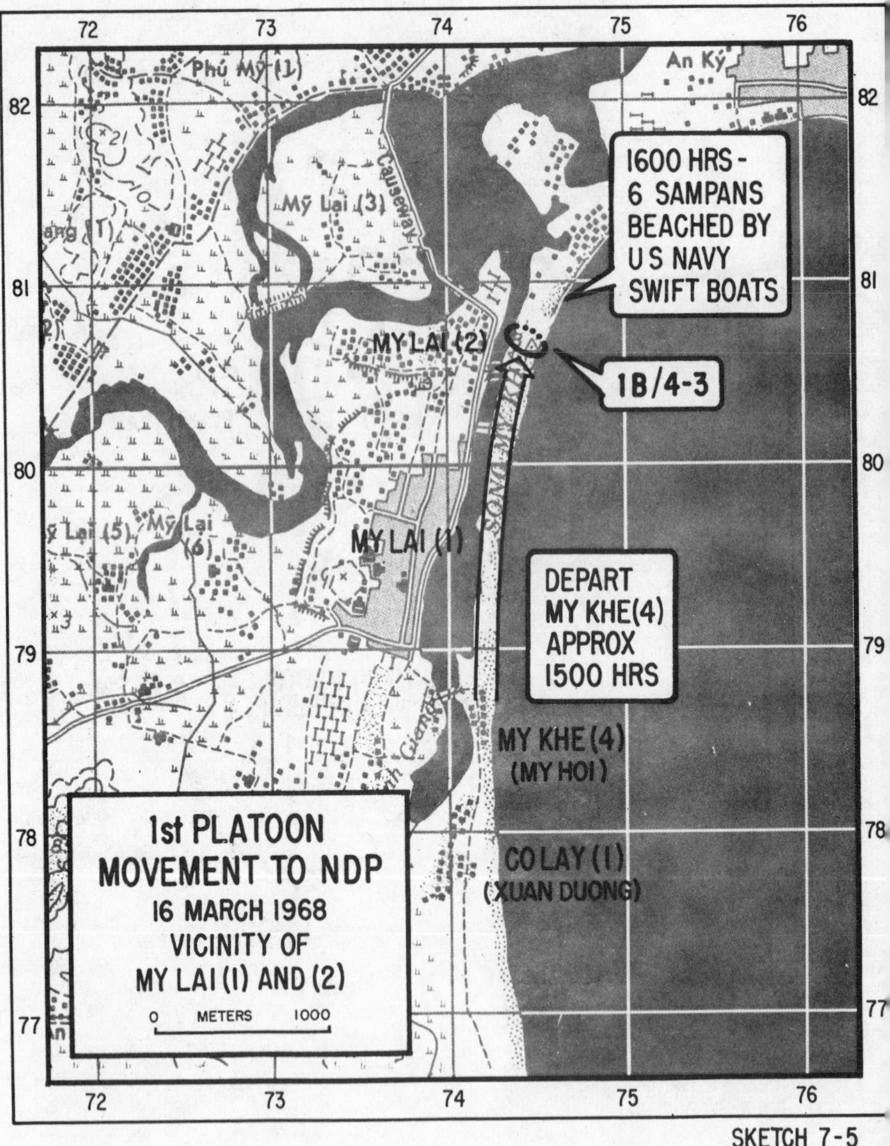

1600 HRS -
6 SAMPANS
BEACHED BY
U S NAVY
SWIFT BOATS
1B/4-3
MY LAI (2)
MY LAI (1)
SONG MY KHE
DEPART
MY KHE(4)
APPROX
1500 HRS
MY KHE (4)
(MY HOI)
CO LAY (1)
(XUAN DUONG)
Causeway
An Kỳ
Phú Mỹ (1)
Mỹ Lai (3)
Mỹ Lai (5)
Mỹ Lai (6)
1st PLATOON
MOVEMENT TO NDP
16 MARCH 1968
VICINITY OF
MY LAI (1) AND (2)
0 METERS 1000
72
73
74
75
76
82
81
80
79
78
77

SKETCH 7-5

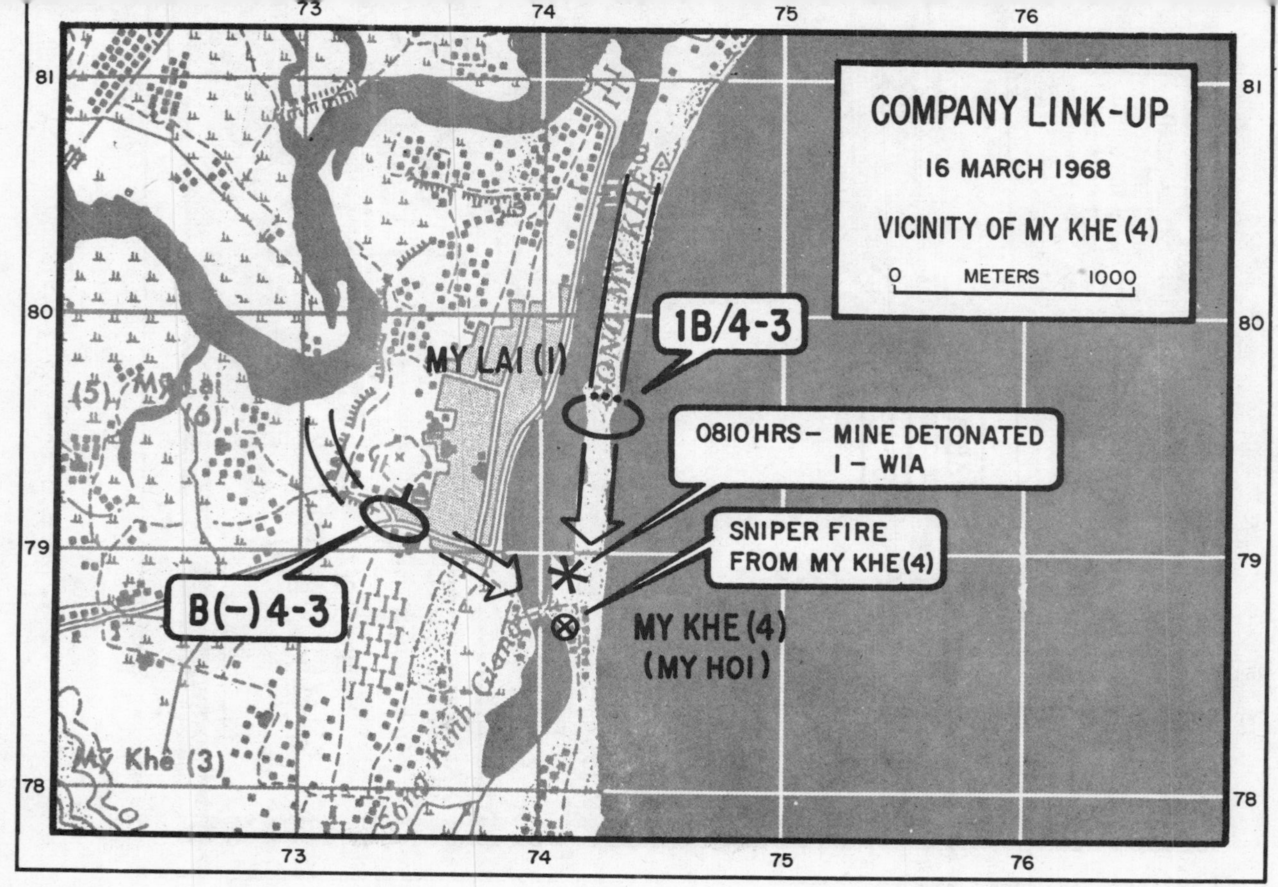
COMPANY LINK-UP
16 MARCH 1968
VICINITY OF MY KHE (4)
0 METERS 1000
1B/4-3
0810 HRS – MINE DETONATED
1 – WIA
SNIPER FIRE
FROM MY KHE (4)
MY KHE (4)
(MY HOI)
MY LAI (1)
B(–)4-3
My Khe (3)

SKETCH 7-6

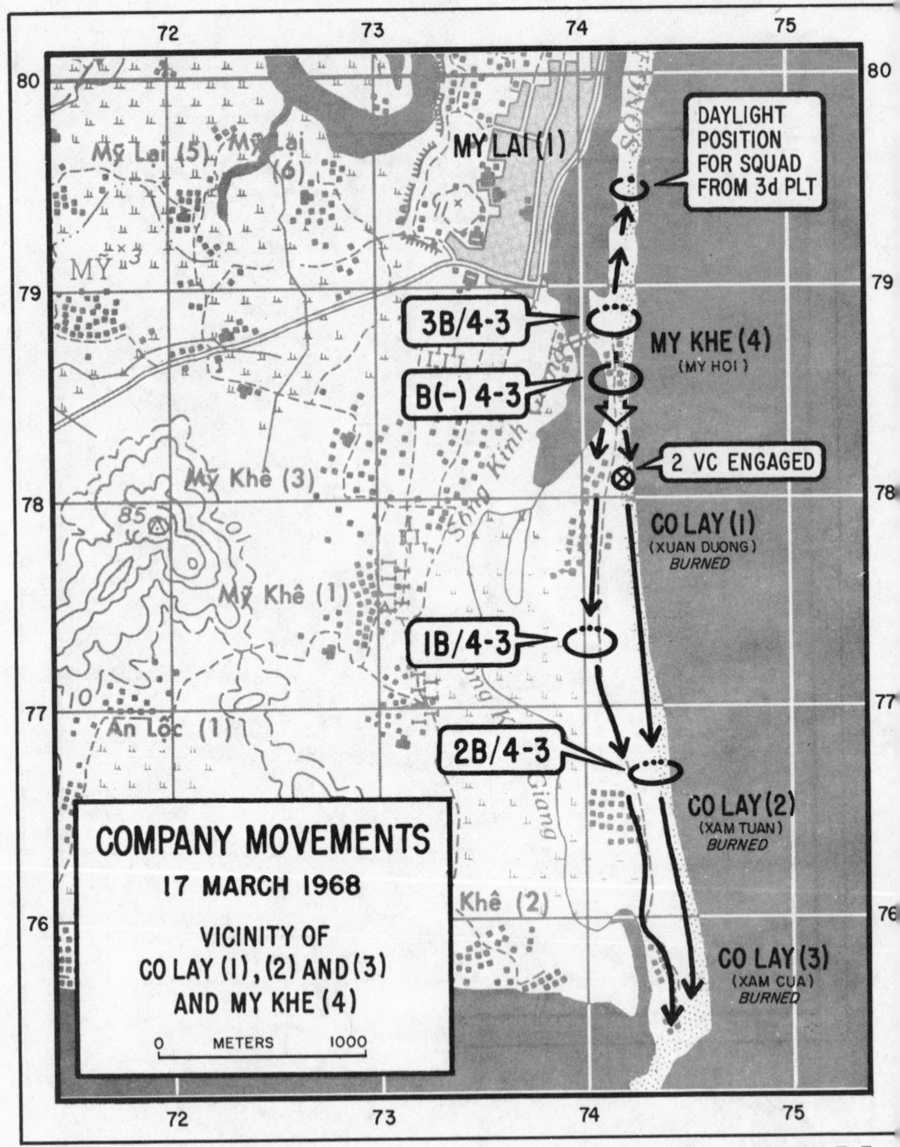
72
73
74
75
80
79
78
77
76
Mỹ Lai (5)
Mỹ Lai (6)
MY LAI (1)
DAYLIGHT POSITION FOR SQUAD FROM 3d PLT
3B/4-3
MY KHE (4)
(MY HOI)
B(-) 4-3
2 VC ENGAGED
Mỹ Khê (3)
85
CO LAY (1)
(XUAN DUONG)
BURNED
Mỹ Khê (1)
1B/4-3
An Lộc (1)
2B/4-3
CO LAY (2)
(XAM TUAN)
BURNED
COMPANY MOVEMENTS
17 MARCH 1968
VICINITY OF
CO LAY (1), (2) AND (3)
AND MY KHE (4)
0 METERS 1000
Khê (2)
CO LAY (3)
(XAM CUA)
BURNED

SKETCH 7-7

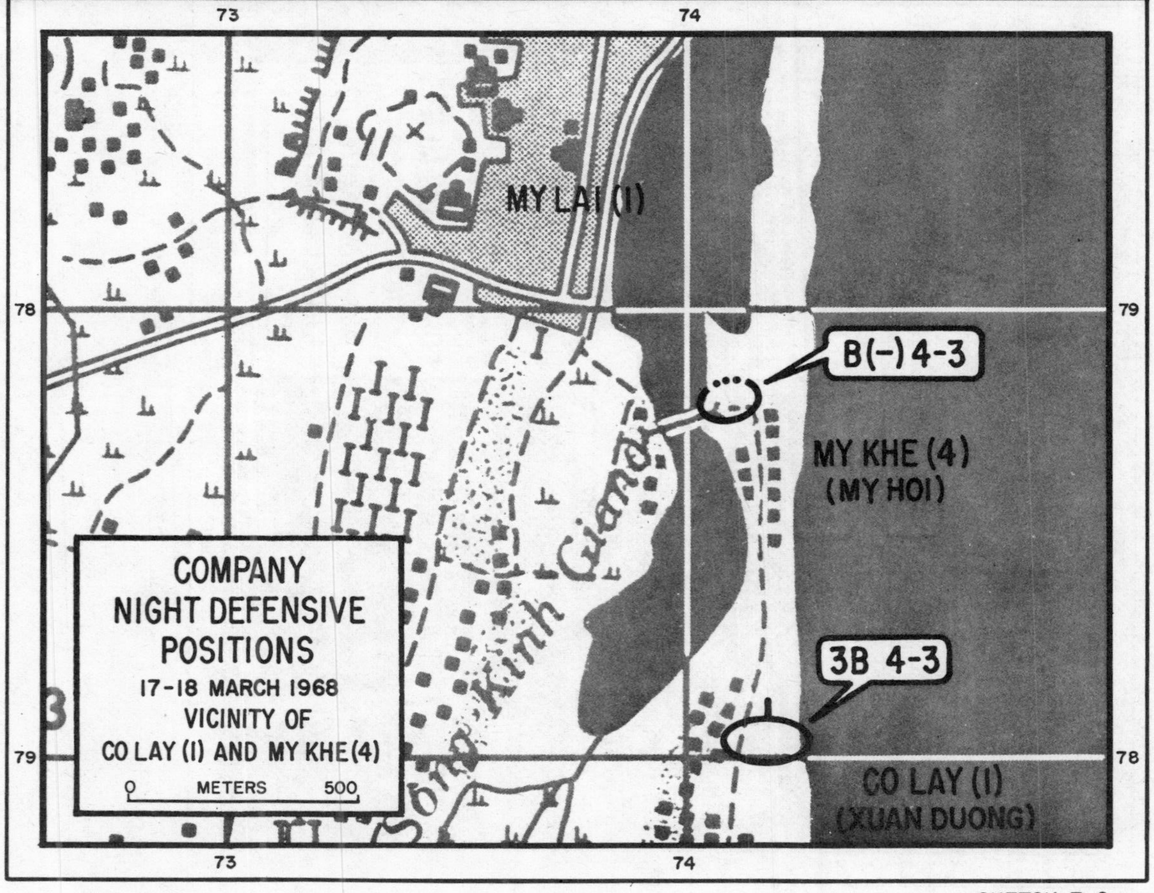

73
74
78
79
MY LAI (I)
B(-) 4-3
MY KHE (4)
(MY HOI)
3B 4-3
CO LAY (I)
(XUAN DUONG)
Song Kinh Giang
COMPANY
NIGHT DEFENSIVE
POSITIONS
17-18 MARCH 1968
VICINITY OF
CO LAY (I) AND MY KHE (4)
0 METERS 500

SKETCH 7-8

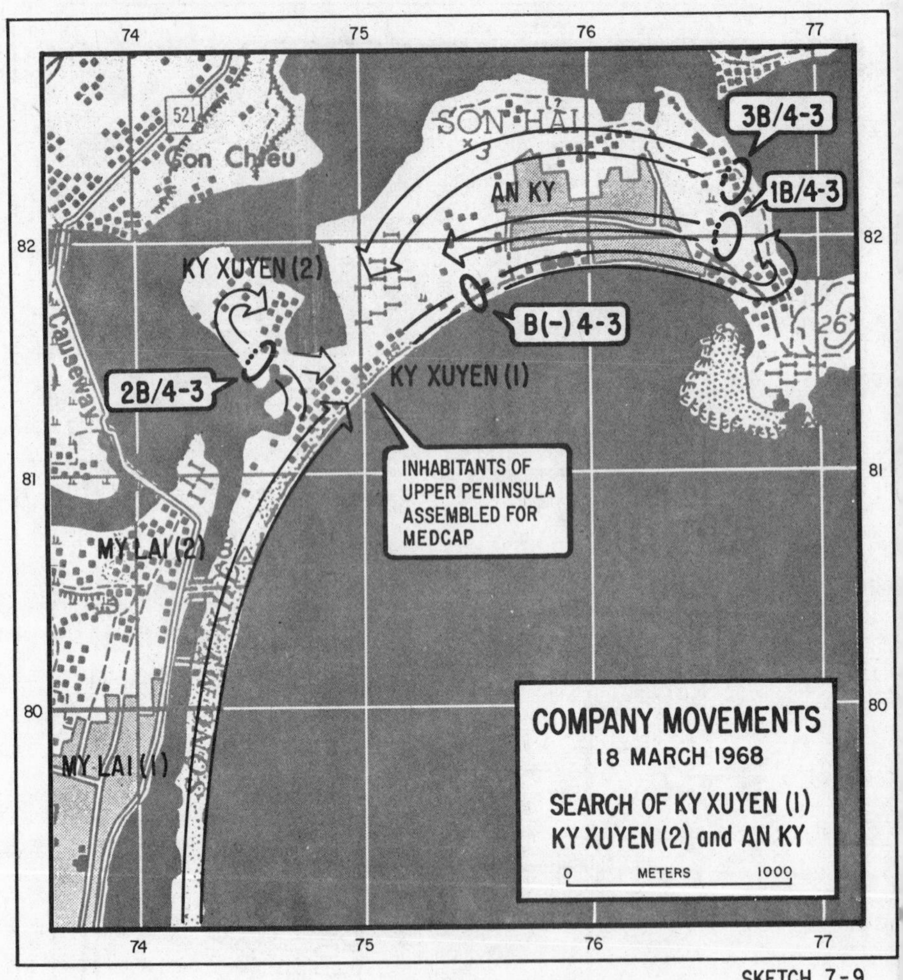

74
75
76
77
82
81
80
521
Son Chieu
SON HAI
AN KY
3B/4-3
1B/4-3
KY XUYEN (2)
B(-) 4-3
2B/4-3
KY XUYEN (1)
Causeway
INHABITANTS OF UPPER PENINSULA ASSEMBLED FOR MEDCAP
MY LAI (2)
MY LAI (1)
COMPANY MOVEMENTS
18 MARCH 1968
SEARCH OF KY XUYEN (1) KY XUYEN (2) and AN KY
0 METERS 1000

SKETCH 7-9

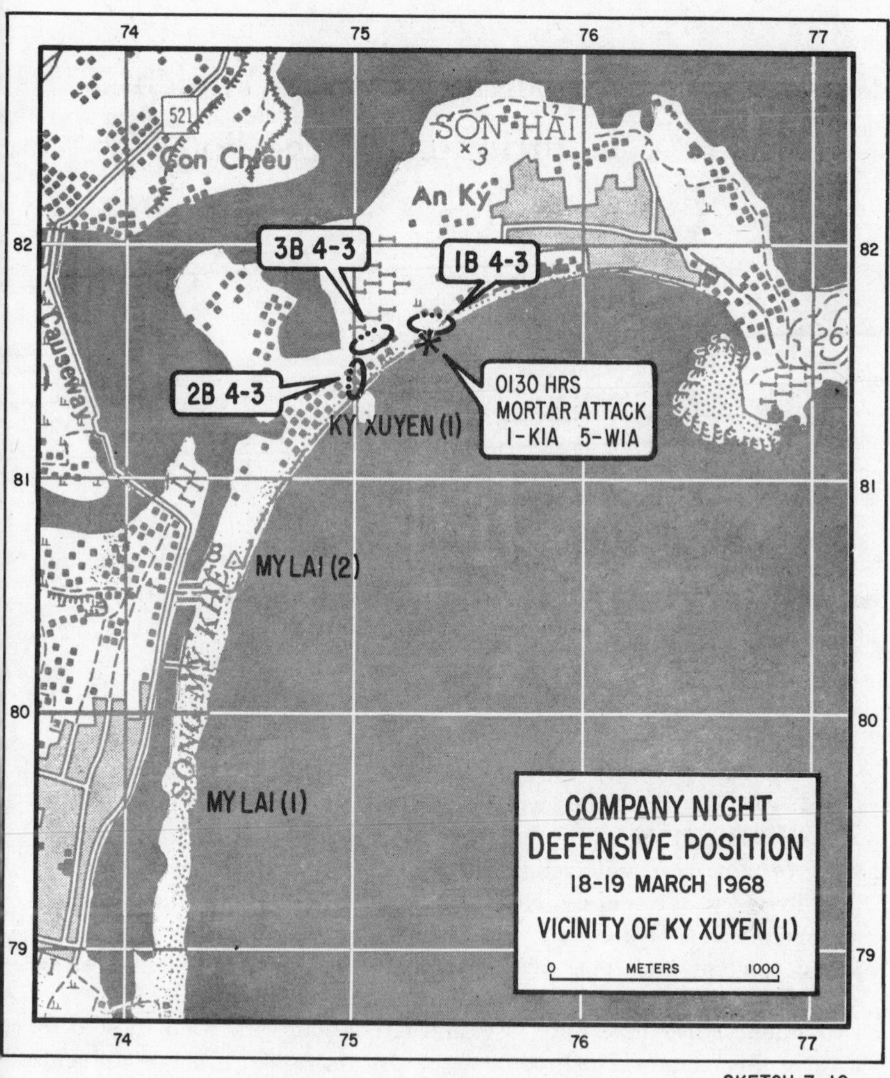
74
75
76
77
82
81
80
79
521
SON HAI
An Ky
Con Chieu
Causeway
3B 4-3
1B 4-3
2B 4-3
0130 HRS
MORTAR ATTACK
1-KIA 5-WIA
KY XUYEN (1)
MY LAI (2)
SONG MY KHE
MY LAI (1)
COMPANY NIGHT
DEFENSIVE POSITION
18-19 MARCH 1968
VICINITY OF KY XUYEN (1)
0 METERS 1000

SKETCH 7-10

Chapter 8. Significant Factors Which Contributed to the Son My Tragedy

The purpose of this chapter is to provide a brief discussion of some of the major factors which appear to the Inquiry to have contributed to the tragedy of Son My.

A. General

In reviewing the events which led up to the Son My operation of 16 March 1968 and the military situation that existed in the area at that time, certain facts and factors have been identified as having possibly contributed to the tragedy. No single factor was, by itself, the sole cause of the incident. Collectively, the factors discussed in this chapter were interdependent and somewhat related, and each influenced the action which took place in a different way.

Undoubtedly, there were facts and circumstances beyond those dealt with in this chapter which could be said to have had a major influence upon the event. The discussion which follows is not intended to be exhaustive, nor a definitive explanation of why Son My happened. Such an effort would be clearly beyond the competence of this Inquiry. Consideration of the following factors does, however, tend to highlight the differences between the Son My operation and numerous other operations conducted throughout South Vietnam over a period of years. It also points up the potential dangers inherent in these operations, which require constant vigilance and scrupulous attention to the essentials of discipline and the unique responsibilities of command. Consideration of these factors also may assist in understanding how the incident could have occurred.

B. Plans and Orders

There is substantial evidence that the events at Son My resulted primarily from the nature of the orders issued on 15 March to the soldiers of Task Force (TF) Barker. Previous chapters of this report have described the content of the different orders issued by LTC Barker, CPT Medina, CPT Michles, and the various platoon leaders and have indicated the crucial errors and omissions in those orders. The evidence is clear that as those orders were issued down through the chain of command to the men of C Company, and perhaps to B Company, they were embellished and, either intentionally or unintentionally, were misdirected toward end results presumably not foreseen during the formative stage of the orders.

The orders derived from a plan conceived by LTC Barker and approved by several of his immediate superiors. There is no evidence that the plan included explicit or implicit provisions for the deliberate killing of noncombatants. It is evident that the plan was based on faulty assumptions concerning the strength and disposition of the enemy and the absence of noncombatants from the operational area. There is also evidence to indicate widespread confusion among the officers and men of TF Barker as to the purpose and limitations of the "search and destroy" nature of the operation, although the purpose and orientation of such operations were clearly spelled out by MACV directives in effect at that time. The faulty assumptions and poorly defined objectives of the operation were not explored nor questioned during such reviews of the plan as were made by MG Koster, BG Lipscomb, and COL Henderson. LTC Barker's decision and order to fire the artillery preparation on portions of My Lai (4) without prior warning to the inhabitants is questionable, but was technically permissible by the directives in effect at that time. The implementing features of that decision were inadequate in terms of reasonable steps that could have been taken to minimize or avoid consequent Vietnamese casualties from the artillery preparation. The orders issued by LTC Barker to burn houses, kill livestock, destroy foodstuffs (and possibly to close the wells) in the Son My area were clearly illegal. They were repeated in subsequent briefings by CPT Medina and possibly CPT Michles and in that context were also illegal.

While the evidence indicates that neither LTC Barker nor his subordinates specifically ordered the killing of noncombatants, they did fail, either intentionally or unintentionally, to make any clear distinctions between combatants and noncombatants in their orders and instructions. Coupled with other factors described in this report, the orders that were issued through the TF Barker chain of command conveyed an understanding to a significant number of soldiers in C Company that only the enemy remained in the operational area and that the enemy was to be destroyed.

C. Attitudes toward the Vietnamese

TF Barker had some men who had been law violators and hoodlums in civilian life and who continued to exercise those traits, where possible, after entering the Army. It appears from the evidence, however, that the men were generally representative of the typical cross-section of American youth assigned to most combat units throughout the Army. Like the men in those other units, the men of TF Barker brought with them the diverse traits, prejudices, and attitudes typical of the various regions of the country and segments of society from whence they came.

There has been testimony to the effect that a "dink" or "slope" complex may have existed among many of the men of C Company. These terms were in fact used frequently by C Company witnesses in referring to Vietnamese in general. For some, the terms were apparently used in the same context in which "kraut," "Jap," and "gook" were used in referring to the enemy in past wars. For others, its use evidently suggested subordination (in their view) of the Vietnamese to an inferior status. For still others, the use of these terms appears to have been simply a case of going along with the majority, using the terms used by most of the other men, to describe Vietnamese (whether friendly or enemy). The available evidence does not indicate that the use of the term "dink," "slope," or "gook" by the men of C Company signified any widespread subliminal classification of Vietnamese as subhuman, however distasteful such terms might be. In fact, some of the men were fond of the Vietnamese nationals. Many indicated a dislike for and, on a recurring basis, mistreated Vietnamese civilians. Many of the men accepted Vietnamese noncombatants on a neutral basis prior to the Son My operation. Additionally, there is evidence that a substantial number of the men in C Company did not trust the Vietnamese. Part of the reason for this lay in previous experiences during which Vietnamese villagers had failed to warn them of the presence of mines and boobytraps which, when subsequently detonated, wounded and killed many of their fellow soldiers. Several of the men apparently felt, with some justification, that if the Vietnamese involved had been truly "friendly" they would have warned the soldiers about the mines and boobytraps. Whether the various commanders in TF Barker had detected this general feeling of mistrust and had attempted to prevent it from developing into a dangerous tendency to categorize all Vietnamese, not specifically identified otherwise, as being the "enemy" is not clear from the testimony available.

While it is impossible to judge the matter with precision, it is considered likely that the unfavorable attitude of some of the men of TF Barker toward the Vietnamese was a contributing factor in the events of Son My.

D. Casualties from Mines and Boobytraps

A significant number of witnesses testified concerning the effect of mine and boobytrap casualties on the morale and attitudes of the soldiers of TF Barker. Besides the generally demoralizing effect which these incidents had upon the men, it is apparent from the evidence that they also served to aggravate a feeling of frustration among the men which derived primarily from their previous failures to come to grips with the enemy.

The men of C Company had specifically been subjected to such frustrations during the previous operations conducted by TF Barker in Son My. While employed outside the principal area where solid enemy contacts were developed by other TF elements (on 13 February and again on 23 February), C Company sustained, during the same time frames, a total of 15 casualties from enemy mines and boobytraps. It had suffered another five casualties from enemy boobytraps 2 days before the Son My operation. The company had not encountered identifiable enemy forces during either period of time.

It is evident that the enemy's extensive use of mines and boobytraps had a considerable effect upon the men and contributed significantly to the events of Son My.

E. Prior Failure to Close with the Enemy

One of LTC Barker's major frustrations was the past failure of the TF to come to grips with, in his words "to do battle" with, the VC 48th Local Force (LF) Battalion. These failures had been highlighted by BG Lipscomb in previous after-action critiques, and were underscored again by COL Henderson in his remarks to TF personnel on the afternoon of 15 March. Given the competitive nature of command assignments and the general tendency to evaluate command performance on the basis of tangible results, it appears that LTC Barker and his subordinate commanders probably viewed the Son My operation as a real opportunity to overcome their past failures (or lack of opportunity) to close effectively with and defeat a major identifiable enemy force. Whether this factor had an effect on the lack of discrimination shown in their planning and orders is not clear from the evidence.

As indicated previously, past failure or lack of opportunity to fight an enemy force had also had a significantly frustrating effect on the morale and attitudes of the soldiers of C Company. Rather than the continuation of essentially nonproductive reconnaissance-in-force operations with attendant high casualties from mines and boobytraps, the Son My operation offered them the opportunity to fight what was (described to them as) almost certainly the 48th VC Local Force Battalion, under conditions and at a time favorable to them. Given their past failure or lack of opportunity to do battle with the enemy and the information which they were provided by CPT Medina, the evidence is clear that many of them also considered the Son My operation as a tangible chance to alleviate some of their past frustrations.

F. Organizational Problems

In previous chapters, this report has provided an examination of the organizational difficulties which confronted the Americal Division and its subordinate elements at the time of the Son My operation. To attach undue importance to this fact would involve ignoring similar organizational difficulties faced and successfully resolved by other US Army divisions in Vietnam and in other wars. Nevertheless, it is apparent from the evidence and testimony made available to the Inquiry that the Americal Division's organizational process, coupled with other factors, detracted from the ability of key personnel to properly supervise to insure that combat operations were being conducted in the appropriate manner. This was most evident in the apparent demands placed on the time available to the various commanders who had direct or indirect responsibilities for supervising the preparation and execution of the Son My operation, and in the evidence which indicates that during the post-*Tet* 1968 time frame there was a lack of any positive enforcement (by means of disciplinary action) of the provisions of division and brigade directives dealing with the treatment of noncombatants.

A commander at the battalion (task force), brigade, or higher level normally depends heavily upon his staff to assist him in planning, coordinating, influencing, and supervising his subordinate units and the men in those units. At the 11th Brigade level, creation of TF Barker apparently resulted in a weakening of the brigade staff because of the loss of the former S3/XO, LTC Barker, the former S1, MAJ Calhoun, and several other officers and noncommissioned officers. Coupled with the brigade change of command which occurred on 15 March, these factors probably contributed to a decline in the proficiency and supervisory capability of the 11th Brigade headquarters.

TF Barker was organized with an austere staff and had no individual who performed exclusively as the TF executive officer. The evidence indicates that the austere staffing of the TF may have had some influence on the Son My operation, particularly in terms of the adequacy of the planning phase, and that a disproportionate amount of LTC Barker's time and effort may have been spent on matters which, under ordinary circumstances, would have been handled by the staff.

It is evident that the organizational problems involving the Americal Division and subordinate elements contributed to inadequate supervision of the planning phase for the Son My operation and, in that sense, played a part in the events which followed.

G. Lack of Command Rapport within TF Barker

There is substantial evidence that LTC Barker did not have a close personal relationship with his company commanders. This may have been Barker's chosen method of operating as TF commander. A more tangible factor was the apparent necessity for Barker to devote a disproportionate amount of his time and effort to matters which an adequate staff might otherwise have been capable of handling.

From LTC Barker's vantage point, his was solely a tactical mission. The majority of the routine administrative and logistical support for the rifle companies still came from their parent battalions. The evidence indicates that such an arrangement probably had a detrimental effect on the morale of the soldiers and their commanders, and may well have caused the company commanders and their men to feel that they were a transient element in a temporary organization.

Whatever the cause, the evidence suggests that the lack of command rapport within TF Barker may have given rise to a void in communications between Barker and his subordinates. This void was apparently filled in part by the TF S3, MAJ Calhoun. Given the interim nature of the TF, the demands on Barker's time in order to overcome difficulties arising from the austere staffing of the TF, and the understandable loyalties of the three company commanders toward their parent battalions and battalion commanders, Barker's detachment from his subordinates may have been more apparent than real. Of more significance is the probability that the absence of a close personal relationship between Barker and his subordinates may have given rise to a lack of understanding on his part as to the professional capabilities of each of his company commanders, and an uncertainty on their part as to what he specifically expected of them and their companies. Ultimately the lack of personal rapport and contact between LTC Barker and his company commanders may have influenced the general breakdown in discipline, restraint, and control which were evident on the first day of the Son My operation.

H. Attitude of Government of Vietnam (GVN) Officials

The general policy and attitude of Vietnamese officials toward the Son My area has been described elsewhere in this report. The Army, Republic of Vietnam forces were, during the post-*Tet* period, reluctant to conduct sustained operations in the area. This fact, coupled with GVN treatment of the area as a free fire zone and the automatic, perfunctory clearances by GVN officials to fire ordnance into the area, were generally known by key members of the TF. It is evident that GVN officials considered Son My as long-standing VC-controlled territory and that its inhabitants were considered as low priority and of little immediate consequence to GVN interests at that time. These general attitudes were well known by key members of the 11th Brigade and TF Barker and undoubtedly affected their feelings toward the area and its people.

I. Nature of the Enemy

While the Communist forces had achieved a substantial psychological impact on the American public during the *Tet* offensive of 1968, they had also taken substantial losses in men and equipment. Time to refit, recruit, and retrain their forces was of critical importance to their future staying power. To provide the requisite time, their forces were, during the post-*Tet* period, seeking to attain sanctuary and protection by melting back into the populace and by retreating into their base areas. In the initial phase of the stepped-up level of actions by US forces, taken to deny the Communists needed time and concealment, there was a consequent and unfortunately high level of civilian casualties throughout most of the Republic of Vietnam.

The Communist forces in South Vietnam had long recognized our general reluctance to do battle with them among the civilian populace and had used that knowledge to our tactical and strategic disadvantage throughout the history of the war in Vietnam. Exploitation of that reluctance by Viet Cong (VC) and North Vietnamese Army (NVA) ground forces caused a distortion of the classic distinction between combatants and noncombatants. (It is important to bear in mind that the old distinctions have been distorted by Communist, not US, forces.) In a war replete with instances of VC women bearing arms and killing US soldiers and children of VC serving as boobytrap specialists and would-be assassins, it became a life and death matter for US soldiers and their commanders to make and adhere to distinctions between combatant and noncombatant, primarily on the basis of whether the individuals in question were armed, were committing hostile acts, or were otherwise endangering the lives of allied troops, rather than on the basis of sex or age. (Such distinctions must, of course, exclude helpless persons such as babies from the list of combatants.)

The Son My area was populated principally by VC, their sympathizers and supporters, and their respective families. It had been controlled by the VC for years and most of the men in TF Barker were aware of this fact. They were also aware that the 48th VC LF Battalion was a tough, well-disciplined guerrilla unit which had not only played a major part in the *Tet* offensive but reportedly had also fought well against TF Barker elements in two previous contacts in the Son My area. It is apparent from the testimony of these soldiers that the entire area and its population were considered as belonging to the enemy, and that they had little apparent understanding of the probability that a significant part of Son My's unarmed population were dominated by the VC because the VC represented the only continuing presence in the area.

The tactical difficulties involved in ferreting enemy forces out of populated areas, the practical difficulties involved in clearly identifying friend from foe, and a generally widespread knowledge of VC control of the Son My area unquestionably played a major role in the events of Son My.

J. Leadership

During the latter stages of this Inquiry, it became apparent that if on the day before the Son My operation only one of the leaders at platoon, company, task force, or brigade level had foreseen and voiced an objection to the prospect of killing noncombatants, or had mentioned the problem of noncombatants in their preoperational orders and instructions, or if adequate restraining orders had been issued early on the following day, the Son My tragedy might have been averted altogether, or have been substantially limited and the operation brought under control. Failures in leadership appear, therefore, to have had a direct bearing on the events of Son My.

COL Henderson had served with the 11th Brigade as the Deputy CO or Acting CO from the time of the brigade's activation in Hawaii until his assumption of formal command on 15 March 1968. Perhaps more than any other single individual, he should have recognized the strengths and weaknesses of the key personnel and operating procedures within the brigade. He testified that his job as Deputy CO under BG Lipscomb was basically administrative in nature and did not allow him as much time as he would have liked to learn the various operational areas assigned to the brigade and the subordinate commanders who were subsequently to serve under him. This is not an uncommon predicament for a second-in-command. It also should have emphasized to him the necessity and importance of going over LTC Barker's plan in detail. There is always a balance to be struck in the amount of latitude and authority to be vested in a subordinate commander when weighed against the commander's overall responsibility for what happens or fails to happen in his unit. In COL Henderson's case, the evidence is clear that he elected during the initial phase of his command to vest maximum latitude in Barker, and in so doing, he treated superficially an operational plan which deserved detailed examination.

The testimony available indicates that LTC Barker was considered by BG Lipscomb and by COL Henderson to be an outstanding officer. His selection to command the TF was reportedly based on their evaluation of his excellence in having performed as the brigade S3 and executive officer. His performance as TF commander up until the time of the Son My operation appears to have been creditable in terms of reported results achieved.

It is apparent that LTC Barker was highly motivated and enthused by the prospect of coming to grips with what was believed to be the same enemy force which had previously fought against and inflicted casualties upon TF elements. His frustrations from previous failures by the TF, his decision to fire the artillery preparation on a part of My Lai (4), and the nature of his orders have been noted elsewhere in this report. In assessing other aspects of his leadership which had an influence on the events of Son My, the evidence indicates that his assumptions, plans, decisions, and orders reflected a degree of incompetence, including an inability to make the kind of distinctions required of successful commanders in the Vietnam war.

CPT Medina was older than most company commanders in Vietnam (his early 30's), and, as a former noncommissioned officer, had gained broad experience in dealing with soldiers. From the evidence developed, it is clear that he was almost unanimously respected by his men and by his superiors and was, in their opinion, an outstanding company commander who held the welfare of his men as one of his primary concerns. His no-nonsense approach to his mission and single-mindedness of purpose in achieving that mission caused him to be the object of respect, but in some cases fear, by some of his men and by his platoon leaders. The evidence indicates that Medina was a strict authoritarian concerning most matters involving his men and exerted an extraordinary degree of influence over them. There was also testimony to indicate that he adopted a condescending and sometimes disparaging manner in dealing with his platoon leaders. The evidence indicates that his principal leadership weakness prior to Son My was in not exercising firm control over the actions of his men toward Vietnamese. The evidence indicates that callousness was not a part of his attitude toward his own men, whose welfare was apparently of primary concern to him.

While most of the men of C Company respected CPT Medina, the evidence indicates that similar feelings of respect apparently did not exist toward the platoon leaders. Any assessment of the C Company platoon leaders, however, must take into account their relative inexperience and the influence exerted over them by CPT Medina. Perhaps the most revealing aspect of testimony concerning the platoon leaders is that each, with the exception of LT Calley, was considered a "nice guy" by many of his men. The implications of this classification are substantiated by evidence which indicates that each lacked any real internal system for control and discipline of his platoon. What control and discipline did exist emanated from the company commander. It is also apparent that each platoon leader was, to an extent, fearful of his men and hesitant in trying to lead. Instead, they attempted to become "buddies" with their noncommissioned officers and men and, in more than one instance, allegedly joined with their men in immoral and illegal acts against Vietnamese prior to the Son My operation. It should also be pointed out that most of the noncommissioned officers in C Company were young and, in general, had no more combat experience than the men themselves. The general lack of experienced leadership for the men of the platoons was not uncommon in other Army units at that time.

CPT Michles was regarded by his men as a good officer and a scrupulous person. From the evidence developed, it is apparent that he was genuinely concerned with the welfare of his men. While it is clear that he was also mission-oriented, he was not regarded by his men as a harsh disciplinarian and was not held in the same light of awe and fear as CPT Medina. The indications are that he was a conscientious career officer who enjoyed the respect and esteem of most of his men.

The available testimony suggests that CPT Michles' relationship with his company officers was unstrained and, while they did not regard him as unapproachable, they clearly respected his position. There is no evidence to suggest that any of the B Company platoon leaders were particularly weak or strong as combat leaders. At the time of the Son My operation, the B company platoon leaders apparently commanded a reasonable degree of respect from their men and had the fortitude to discipline them when required.

The evidence indicates that there was a high degree of competitiveness between CPT Michles and CPT Medina, and a portion of this feeling was undoubtedly communicated to their respective platoon leaders and men and probably played a part in the attitudes of their men toward the forthcoming operation.

Americal Division leaders, down to and including the TF level, failed to supervise properly the planning of the Son My operation. This gave rise to a loosely conceived plan with a poorly defined purpose. These failures resulted in the issuance of ambiguous, illegal, and potentially explosive orders by LTC Barker and CPT Medina, and possibly CPT Michles, who failed, either deliberately or unintentionally, to provide in their plans and orders for the possibility that noncombatants might be found in the objective areas. Implementation of these orders ultimately became the task of generally weak and ineffective leaders at the platoon level and below. Collectively, these factors had a pronounced impact on the results of the Son My operation.

K. Permissive Attitude

The evidence developed during this Inquiry strongly indicates that a dangerously permissive attitude toward the handling and safeguarding of Vietnamese and their property existed within elements of the 11th Brigade chain of command prior to the Son My operation. Evidence also indicates varying degrees of concern by MG Koster, BG Lipscomb, COL Henderson, and LTC Barker concerning the subject, but in the light of the mistreatment, raping, and some indiscriminate killing of Vietnamese known to have occurred prior to Son My, and in view of the events at Son My itself, it is evident that if such concern did exist, it had not been communicated effectively to the soldiers of TF Barker. There had been little in the way of positive enforcement by responsible commanders (in the form of disciplinary action) of the provisions of division and brigade directives dealing with the treatment and safeguarding of noncombatants and their property prior to Son My.

While COL Henderson was officially the brigade commander at the time of the Son My operation, the evidence indicates that BG Lipscomb, the previous brigade commander, may have contributed to the attitude of permissiveness which existed within the brigade. This assumption is warranted in that the attitudes of the 11th Brigade soldiers who characteristically mistreated Vietnamese nationals did not develop overnight nor did they come into being concurrently with the change in brigade commanders. Evidence of scattered incidents involving the mistreatment, rape, and possibly the murder of Vietnamese by 11th Brigade soldiers prior to the Son My operation indicates that a permissive attitude existed and was not uncovered and corrected under BG Lipscomb's command.

The fact that both COL Henderson and LTC Barker were both relatively new in their command assignments may have contributed to some uncertainty among their subordinates as to exactly what was expected of them and their soldiers in the handling of Vietnamese noncombatants, but did not relieve either from the command responsibility for the actions of their units.

The evidence indicates that a number of C Company soldiers were involved in the illegal acts against Vietnamese prior to the Son My operation. These acts may have mirrored a permissive and calloused attitude by CPT Medina, or they may have resulted from the fact that the company was essentially a one-man show run by CPT Medina who was, regardless of his intentions, incapable of exercising single-handed control of 100-plus soldiers. The evidence is inconclusive in this regard, but suggests the latter situation. As indicated previously, the reticence and lack of leadership among the platoon leaders of C Company also contributed to the general permissiveness which existed in the company at the time of the operation.

There was no evidence developed to indicate the existence of a permissive attitude among key members of B Company. To the contrary, the evidence indicates that CPT Michles neither condoned nor tolerated mistreatment of Vietnamese by B Company soldiers prior to the Son My operation.

It is evident that the generally permissive attitude which existed in some of the units of the 11th Brigade prior to Son My was brought into sharp focus for the men of TF Barker by the orders issued on 15 March by LTC Barker, CPT Medina, and possibly CPT Michles, and significantly influenced the events of the following day.

L. Lack of Affirmative Command and Control

A variety of factors, which became evident during the Inquiry, collectively indicate that there was a general lack of affirmative command and control throughout the 11th Brigade, and particularly in TF Barker at the time of the Son My operation.

The evidence of previous mistreatment of Vietnamese by soldiers of the 11th Brigade and TF Barker, testimony concerning previous scattered destruction and burning of Vietnamese homes, the method in which earlier TF operations were conducted, the austere staffing of the TF, and the superficial treatment of plans for the Son My operation all point to the lack of an effective system of controlling combat operations.

The evidence indicates that LTC Barker visited his companies infrequently while they were operating in the field. It is also evident that the facilities and equipment provided or made available to his interim organization were marginal at best. This was particularly true with respect to the communications facilities used in his command and control helicopter, and in his tactical operations center (TOC). This equipment had been drawn from other organizations of the brigade at the time that the TF was established.

A general pattern which emerged during this Inquiry was that some Americal commanders failed to get on the ground with operating units. This was most pronounced on the day of the Son My operation when not a single commander above company level landed in the Son My area to personally communicate with the ground forces despite clear indications that unusual events, of a nature requiring command attention, were taking place on the ground. This is brought into even sharper focus by the fact that this was, on the face of it, the most successful operation ever conducted by an element of the 11th Brigade.

M. Lack of Emphasis in Training

Early in the Inquiry, there was a suspicion that the manner in which the 11th Brigade was activated, trained, prepared for overseas movement, and deployed to Vietnam might have had some impact upon the events of Son My. Investigation revealed that this was the case to a limited extent.

11th Brigade elements underwent an accelerated training program, received a substantial input of replacement personnel shortly before deploying, and eventually deployed earlier than originally had been scheduled. Shortly after arriving in Vietnam, planned makeup training was affected by another infusion of replacements (to overcome a projected rotation "hump") and by early commitment of brigade elements to active combat operations.

As a net result of these actions, the evidence indicates that, at best, the soldiers of TF Barker had received only marginal training in several key areas prior to the Son My operation. These areas were (1) provisions of the Geneva Conventions, (2) handling and safeguarding of noncombatants, and (3) rules of engagement.

The problem of training and instruction having to do with identification of and response to "illegal" orders is addressed elsewhere in this report. The evidence indicates that training deficiencies in this area, together with deficiencies in those training areas described above, played a significant part in the Son My operation.

N. Psychological Buildup

In the case of B Company, no firm conclusions can be drawn as to either the nature or effect of any preoperational psychological buildup that may have been given to the men. CPT Michles did not personally brief his company, and there is some evidence that the content of the briefings given by the platoon leaders was not uniform throughout the company. All the men apparently were told that the area was populated entirely by "VC and VC sympathizers" and that the mission was to "clean the place out," but there was no suggestion made of getting revenge for previous friendly casualties. Any attempt to evaluate the psychological preparation given to B Company is complicated by the fact that (a) the main elements of B Company suffered heavy casualties and had their principal mission aborted almost immediately after the combat assault, and (b) the separated 1st Platoon knew about those casualties (including the death of their former platoon leader) before entering My Khe (4). Undoubtedly, the casualties suffered early on 16 March had a psychological effect upon B Company. Those effects may have influenced, possibly in different ways and to a greater extent than preoperational factors, the subsequent actions of various elements of the company.

The men of C Company who participated in the Son My operation testified, without exception, that their actions in and around My Lai (4) were "different" from anything they had ever been involved in before and from anything that they were ever involved in afterward. From their testimony it is clear that a large part of the difference derived from their understanding of the nature and purpose of the operation. Their understanding and the attitudes that prevailed before the operation appear to have been primarily a product of the factors previously described in this chapter. These factors were apparently brought to a sharp focus by the briefing which they received on the day before the Son My operation.

In retrospect, it is clear that in his preoperational briefing to the men of C Company, CPT Medina "painted the picture" too vividly, and exercised no discrimination and little restraint in his implementing orders. He may also have drawn some erroneous conclusions from LTC Barker's briefing, or simply twisted certain elements of Barker's briefing to suit his own undiscriminating purposes. CPT Medina, like his commander, issued illegal orders to burn and destroy property in the target area, failed to provide in his briefing for the possibility that noncombatants might be found in the area, and further influenced the events to follow by failing to make any distinctions in his orders concerning the treatment to be accorded armed combatants, suspected (but unarmed) sympathizers, and outright noncombatants. CPT Medina's effectiveness in getting his men psychologically "up" for the expected fight is quite clear from the evidence presented to this Inquiry.

Up until the time of the Son My operation, the men of C Company had participated in largely unproductive operations and had suffered significant casualties from enemy mines and boobytraps. During the course of those previous operations, several of them had participated in the mistreatment, rape, and possible murder of Vietnamese, with no apparent retribution. They were told by their company commander that they were going to face an enemy battalion the following day in the Son My area. They were told that an artillery preparation would be placed on the target area before they arrived and that the landing zone (LZ) would probably be "hot." They were given the impression that the only people left in the area would be the enemy and that their mission was to destroy the enemy and all his supplies. They were told that the best way to prevent the enemy from recovering weapons from the battlefield was to close with the enemy aggressively. They were reminded that some of them would probably become casualties in the operation and were enjoined to look out for each other. They were reminded of their past losses to enemy boobytraps and their failure to get revenge for those losses. They were told that the forthcoming operation would provide the opportunity to obtain that revenge. They were not told of any restrictions of any kind that would be imposed on them in accomplishing the assigned mission.

O. Summary

The factors described in this chapter are considered relevant to the purpose of this Inquiry to the extent that they assist in understanding what happened at Son My, and, to a lesser extent, why it happened.

In the time available to this Inquiry, there was no attempt to analyze the factors in depth, nor to evaluate psychological aspects of what happened. This is considered a task that can be best performed by a team of highly qualified research analysts with the technical talents and experience necessary to do justice to the subject.

Chapter 9. Policy and Directives as to Rules of Engagement and Treatment of Noncombatants

A. US Obligations under the Law of War

The conduct of war among civilized nations is regulated by certain well-established rules known as the rules or law of war. This law regulates warfare on both the land and the sea. That which pertains particularly to war on land is called the law of land warfare.

Much of the law of war has been set out in treaties or conventions to which the United States is a party. It is commonly called the written law of war.

Some of the law of war never has been incorporated in any treaty or convention to which the United States is a signatory. This law is commonly called the unwritten or customary law of war. For the most part it is well defined by recognized authorities on international law and is firmly established by the custom and usage of civilized nations.

The primary source of the written law of war as it applies to the United States is international conventions (lawmaking treaties to which the United States is a party). Some of the more important of these are:

1. Hague Convention No. IV Respecting the Laws and Customs of War on Land and the Annex thereto which embodies the Regulations Respecting the Laws and Customs of War on Land.
2. The four 1949 Geneva Conventions for the protection of the wounded and sick of armed forces in the field; wounded, sick, and shipwrecked members of armed forces at sea; prisoners of war; and civilian persons in times of war.
3. The 1929 Geneva Conventions relative to the treatment of prison-

ers of war and amelioration of the conditions of the wounded and sick of armies in the field.

The law of war, both written and customary, had the principal purpose of diminishing the evils of war by:

a. Protecting both noncombatants and combatants from unnecessary suffering;
b. Safeguarding certain fundamental human rights of persons who fall into the hands of the enemy, particularly prisoners of war, the wounded and sick, and civilians; and
c. Facilitating the restoration of the peace.

The United States recognizes the conflict in Vietnam as an international conflict to which both customary and written or conventional laws of war apply, and the United States has declared its intent to observe this law.

The United States has an obligation to instruct its military personnel concerning the conventional law of war which the United States has recognized. This obligation is in part fulfilled by formal military instructions and directives. Further, the United States has affirmative responsibilities to investigate alleged violations of the pertinent conventions. Its obligations under the "grave breaches" article of each of the 1949 Geneva Conventions are quite specific:

> The High Contracting Parties undertake to enact any legislation necessary to provide effective penal sanctions for persons committing, or ordering to be committed, any of the grave breaches of the present Convention defined in the following Article.
>
> Each High Contracting Party shall be under the obligation to search for persons alleged to have committed, or to have ordered to be committed, such grave breaches, and shall bring such persons, regardless of their nationality, before its own courts. It may also, if it prefers, and in accordance with the provisions of its own legislation, hand such persons over for trial to another High Contracting Party concerned, provided such High Contracting Party had made out a *prima facie* case.
>
> Each High Contracting Party shall take measures necessary for the suppression of all acts contrary to the provisions of the present Convention other than the grave breaches defined in the following Article.
>
> In all circumstances, the accused persons shall benefit by safeguards of proper trial and defense, which shall not be less favorable than those provided by Article 105 and those following of the Geneva Convention Relative to the Treatment of Prisoners of War of August 12, 1949.
>
> Grave breaches to which the preceding Article relates shall be those involving the following acts, if committed against persons or property protected by present Convention: wilful killing, torture or inhuman treatment, including biological experiments, wilfully causing great suffering or serious

> injury to body or health, unlawful deportation or transfer or unlawful confinement of a protected person, . . . taking of hostages and extensive destruction and appropriation of property, not justified by military necessity and carried out unlawfully and wantonly.

Most of the "grave breaches" listed above had been considered as violations of customary law or were denounced in other conventions prior to the 1949 Geneva Conventions.

Both US military law and international law place certain responsibilities upon military commanders to control their troops, to investigate alleged violations of the law of war, and to take appropriate action. Furthermore, many offenses against the law of war are violations of the Uniform Code of Military Justice.

The United States, as a civilized nation and as a signatory of Hague Convention No. IV (1907) and its Annex and the four Geneva Conventions of 1949, is obligated to observe the law of war, to investigate alleged war crimes, and, in appropriate cases, to bring alleged offenders to trial.

The term "war crime" is the technical expression for a violation of the law of war by any person or persons, military or civilian. Every violation of the law of war is a war crime.

B. United States Directives

1. POLICY GUIDANCE

A. GENERAL

The military departments within the Department of Defense (DOD) have promulgated regulations providing guidance to military personnel on customary and treaty law applicable to the conduct of warfare. As noted previously, the law of land warfare regulates the conduct of armed hostiles and is inspired by the desire to diminish the evils of war.

Within the guidance established by DOD, each of the military services has published regulations pertaining to both sources of the law of war, as well as detailed instructions regarding the engagement, apprehension, and classification of individuals present in a hostile environment. Specifically, the Department of the Army (DA) has directed actions through the chain of command to insure that the US soldier knows his responsibilities in the conduct of war that are based on the rules of land warfare. This is accomplished through the publication system which spells out the individual's responsibilities.

To accomplish the requisite training, DA has defined two broad objectives:

1. Definition of the US national policy in the conduct of land warfare to include the rules and law of war.
2. Training required to insure that the individual soldier understands his specific duties and obligations in the pursuit of the US national policy.

B. GENEVA CONVENTIONS TRAINING

By Army Regulation (AR) 350–216, commanders are required to provide instruction that is adequate to insure that all members of their commands understand the principles and the provisions of the Geneva and Hague Conventions, which are binding on the United States. [6] This training is designed to be conducted in a manner that will provide each individual with an understanding of his responsibility under the provisions of these conventions to afford humane treatment both to prisoners of war and the enemy civilian population. As a first step, the soldier receives in Basic Combat Training (BCT) an hour of instruction based on Army Subject Schedule 21–18. [8] This subject schedule is published to provide uniformity in the familiarization of military personnel with the Geneva Conventions of 1949. The lesson outline, text and publication references, and training films are designed to provide the requisite background and supplemental instruction material. The scope of this instruction includes the specific provisions of the Geneva Conventions of 1949 and a discussion of individual duties, rights, and obligations thereunder.

AR 350–216 also directs that commanders will take action to insure that each member of their command receives training in the conventions each 12-month period. Suitable entries will be made annually in the individual's personnel record indicating the date that such instruction was last completed. Qualified legal officers are required to conduct this annual instruction.

Therefore, the individual soldier receives the foundational instruction in basic training, and this training is continually updated on an annual basis using Field Manual (FM) 27–10, several DA pamphlets, and current training films.

As early as 1964, Military Assistance Command, Vietnam (MACV) directives and regulations had been published that pertained to the individual soldier's duties and obligations under the rules of warfare. Subsequently, these directives were expanded, updated, and clarified as subordinate headquarters were activated. By 1967–68, directives and regulations were in effect that pertained to all phases of military operations and training.

Army personnel normally arrived in the Republic of Vietnam (RVN) at a replacement unit where it was required by United States Army Vietnam (USARV) Regulation 612–1 that all military personnel would receive, among others, the following information cards:

1. "The Enemy in Your Hands";
2. "Nine Rules";
3. "Code of Conduct"; and
4. "Geneva Convention."

In addition, all commissioned officers would receive a card entitled "Guidance for Commanders in Vietnam." These cards were to be kept in the individual's possession at all times because of the usefulness of the information they contained.

These cards stressed humanitarian treatment and respect for the Vietnamese people and stipulated that each individual would comply with the Geneva Conventions of 1949. Individual methods of capture, care, and treatment were specifically included in the cards.

c. Rules of Engagement

The rules of engagement (ROE) for military operations in Vietnam are based on specific authority granted by the Joint Chiefs of Staff (JCS). In 1966, Commander, United States Military Assistance Command Vietnam (COMUSMACV) established a policy of republishing the ROE every 6 months to insure maximum visibility to all US personnel during their tour. These ROE provided the guidance for the conduct of combat operations within RVN and directed that all practicable means be employed to limit the risk to the lives and property of friendly forces and civilians.

The control of combat operations and application of the ROE pertaining to the individual soldier were vested in the commander at each subordinate level who, among other responsibilities, was directed to "use your firepower with care and discrimination, particularly in populated areas." The chain of command was to be utilized to the fullest extent to insure success in battle with the minimum expenditure of resources. The soldier was regarded as a member of a team responsive to his leader, yet responsible for his individual actions.

Early in the conflict, the magnitude of the firepower available for employment was recognized. The individual soldier's rifle fire was supplemented by huge quantities of direct and indirect firepower from a large variety of sources. All means of firepower had to be carefully controlled and coordinated to insure successful, yet proper, employment. Fire control and coordinating elements were organized at each level of command down to and including rifle companies. These elements had the capability to coordinate and control all available means and sources of supporting firepower. However, because the varied sources of firepower had different delivery means and accuracy, the rules of employment for each varied. It was clear at an early date that the means of control and the rules that governed the employment of the different types and sizes of ordnance were extremely important.

MACV Directives 95–4 and 525–18 were in effect in early 1968. These regulations dealt with combat operations and, more particularly, with the control of firepower delivered by artillery, mortar, air, and naval means.

MACV Directive 95–4 stipulated that airpower should be employed with the objective of eliminating "incidents involving friendly forces, noncombatants, and damage to civilian property." In operational planning of battalion-level operations, it was required that representatives of aviation units participate in the tactical ground planning to provide for the necessary coordination and control of the firepower available within the aviation units.

The specific restrictions and ROE for US aircraft in RVN were amplified in Annex D to MACV Directive 95–4 which directed that "all pilots will endeavor to minimize noncombatant casualties and civilian property damage." This annex also stated that "if the target involves noncombatants, such as in a hamlet or village, whenever possible a Republic of Vietnam Air Force (RVNAF) observer will be aboard the helicopter and US–GVN–RVNAF approval of fire must be obtained unless the situation clearly presents an immediate threat to lives of the crew."

Certain areas in RVN were uninhabited or had been identified as such by Government of Vietnam (GVN) authorities. In 1966, certain of these areas were designated as cleared areas to all Free World Military Assistance Forces (FWMAF) by the GVN and became known as "free fire zones." Simply stated, a free fire zone was a specifically delineated geographic area, usually free of any known populace, that had been previously approved for use of all means of fire and maneuver. Such an area was cleared for employment of firepower unless notification to the contrary was given. In 1967 MACV replaced its use with the term "specified strike zone (SSZ)." An SSZ was defined as "those areas approved by a province chief where strikes may be conducted without additional political clearance."

The control of artillery/mortar and naval gunfire support was directed by MACV Directive 525–18. Restrictive controls were to be held to the minimum necessary to insure that civilians and their property were not destroyed or damaged. This directive stated, however, that fire missions directed against known or suspected VC/NVA targets in villages and hamlets occupied by noncombatants "will be" controlled by an observer and "executed only after Province Chief or District Chief approves as appropriate." Under certain specified conditions, however, this regulation did authorize striking areas known to be inhabited by noncombatants. It states: "Villages and hamlets may be attacked without prior warning if the attack is in conjunction with a ground operation involving maneuver of ground forces through the area, and if in the judgment of the ground commander, his mission would be jeopardized by such warning."

During the 1968 *Tet* offensive, Headquarters, MACV (Forward), issued temporary modifications to MACV Directive 525–18 for specific purposes in designated areas of I Corps Tactical Zone (ICTZ). Some commanders were authorized to attack inhabited areas with weapons and forces most appropriate to insure prompt restriction of the enemy. Even with these temporary modifications, however, commanders were enjoined to exercise prudent judgment to protect noncombatants and private property.

D. Treatment of Noncombatants and Private Property

MACV directives in effect at the time of the Son My operation dealt specifically with the subject of minimizing noncombatant casualties and the control of Vietnamese property, captured materiel, and food supplies. These directives were policy directives pertaining to combat operations in general.

MACV Directive 525–3 dealt with minimizing noncombatant casualties. Noncombatants were generally described as the "hapless rice farmer and the small town inhabitant, whether at any one time [he] lives in a VC or a GVN controlled hamlet" noting that where he lives depends "to a large extent upon factors and forces beyond his control." Commanders were directed to control force and not use "unnecessary force leading to noncombatant battle casualties in area temporarily controlled by the VC."

The exercise of restraint by soldiers to reduce to a minimum the casualties inflicted on the noncombatant populace was stressed. Commanders were directed to "maintain and conduct a thorough and continuing program to emphasize both the short- and long-range importance of minimizing noncombatant casualties." Troop indoctrination briefings were to be held before each operation. Each briefing was to include the location of noncombatants and other friendly forces, measures to prevent mutual interference, safety precautions for fire control support, rules of engagement, identification and recognition signals, emergency procedures, and other appropriate matters.

Several other significant points were covered in the directive:

1. The VC fully exploit incidents of noncombatant casualties and destruction of property by US forces.
2. Commanders will consider the psychological as well as the military objectives. Reconnaissance by fire and poorly selected harassing fires are counterproductive in the long run.
3. Specified strike zones should be configured to exclude populated areas.

4. Established rules of good military conduct and discipline must be enforced.
5. Implementing instructions and SOP's concerning this directive, fire control support and safety precautions will be issued by major commanders. Commanders will insure distribution to the lowest echelons.

MACV Directive 525–9 established policies and procedures for control, disposition, and safeguarding of private property and food supplies as well as captured materiel and supplies during combat operations. Long-term US and GVN objectives were stressed and continuing command emphasis was directed to the preclusion of destruction. Specifically, this document directed that the disposition of private property and supplies is the responsibility of GVN officials and that civilian dwellings or private property, including livestock, will not be destroyed by US forces except as an unavoided consequence of combat actions. If destruction is to be accomplished as a denial measure, such action will be left to GVN authorities or RVNAF units.

E. DETAINING INDIVIDUALS

In addition to the cards previously mentioned, policy and guidance for the apprehension, detention, and treatment of individuals suspected of hostile acts were covered in several MACV directives.

The Combined Campaign Plan for 1968 directed prompt, thorough and effective screening, segregation, and disposition of suspected enemy civilian personnel captured or detained by friendly forces. The screening process was to be accomplished in screening centers established jointly with US and Vietnamese military and civilian representation. Screening and segregation were to identify the detainees as either apparent prisoners of war (PW's), known VC identified by blacklists, suspected civil defendants, or innocents. Once an individual's status was determined, the Combined Tactical Screening Centers (CTSC) were to release those not under suspicion. Suspected civil defendants were to be released to Vietnamese civil authorities after interrogation by military intelligence (MI) and ARVN investigators. The specifics of the screening process were covered in MACV Directive 381–46. The value of human source intelligence was described in MACV Directive 381–11.

When an individual was classified as a PW in accordance with MACV Directive 381–46, certain specific handling procedures became effective. The MACV policy and guidance for these procedures were contained in MACV Directive 190–3. This document stated that "all personnel detained by US forces will be extended the full protection of the Geneva Convention of 12 August 1949."

MACV Directive 20–5 directed "policies and procedures for determining whether personnel in the custody of the United States who have committed belligerent acts are entitled to prisoners of war status." During this determination, however, and while detained, the suspected PW is protected by the Geneva Conventions. Article 5 of the Geneva Conventions "requires that the protections of the Conventions be extended to a person who has committed a belligerent act and whose entitlement to Prisoner of War (PW) status is in doubt until such time as his status has been determined by a competent tribunal." Until such time as an individual's status has been determined, the Geneva Conventions and MACV Directives previously indicated protect the individual's rights.

F. War Crimes

Combat operations during the 1968 *Tet* offensive were reported in a sensational manner. At times, some reports and photographs purported to depict a flagrant disregard for human life, inhumane treatment, and brutality in the handling of detainees and PW's. Because of this situation, on 21 February 1968, GEN Westmoreland wrote a personal letter to GEN Cao Van Vien, Chief of Joint General Staff, RVNAF, reiterating the necessity for observing the Geneva Conventions and taking "appropriate action against those who offend against the law of war." As an inclosure to this letter, GEN Westmoreland included a copy of a confidential message he had dispatched to all US forces concerning the mistreatment of detainees and PW's. This message, signed by MG Walter T. Kerwin, Jr., Chief of Staff MACV, directed vigorous and immediate command action "to insure that all personnel are familiar with and observe strictly FM 27–10, UCMJ [Uniform Code of Military Justice] Article 93, Geneva Conventions relative to treatment of PW (Articles 12 through 121), Geneva Conventions for amelioration of wounded and sick armed forces in the field, Articles 12, 17, and 50, and MACV Directives 20–4, 27–5, and 190–3." The message also reaffirmed that: "All known, suspected or alleged war crimes or atrocities committed by or against US personnel will be investigated IAW [in accordance with] MACV Directive 20–4."

MACV Directive 20–4 has as a stated purpose: "To provide uniform procedures for the collection and perpetuation of evidence relative to war crimes incidents and to designate the agencies responsible for the conduct of investigations for alleged or apparent violations of the Geneva Conventions of 12 August 1949 For the Protection of War Victims."

War crimes were defined in this directive by reference to FM 27–10. Paragraph 499 of FM 27–10 states "the term war crime is the technical expression for a violation of the law of war by any person or persons, military or civilian. Every violation of the law of war is a war crime." (See also MACV Directive 27–5.)

Directive 20–4 further elaborated on the definition of war crimes by stating in part that a "grave breach" of the Geneva Conventions constitutes a war crime. Some examples of "grave breaches" were explained (when committed against persons taking no active part in the hostilities, including members of armed forces who laid down their arms and those placed *hors de combat* by sickness, wounds, detention, or any cause) as wilful killing, torture, or inhuman treatment, or wilfully causing great suffering or serious injury to body or health.

The directive also provided detailed guidance to all personnel for investigating alleged or apparent war crimes against an individual who, in the context of the definition, was mistreated in any way subsequent to apprehension and/or detention. The directive further stated in part:

a. It is the responsibility of all military personnel having knowledge or receiving a report of an incident or an act thought to be a war crime to make such incident known to his commanding officer as soon as practicable. Personnel performing investigative, intelligence, police, photographic, grave registration, or medical functions, as well as those in contact with the enemy, will, in the normal course of their duty, make every effort to detect the commission of war crimes and will report the essential facts to their commanding officer. Persons discovering war crimes will take all reasonable action under the circumstances to preserve physical evidence, to note identity of witnesses present, and to record (by photograph, sketch, or descriptive notes) the circumstances and surroundings.

b. Commanders and MACV Staff sections receiving reports of probable war crimes will, in addition to any other required reports, report the fact as soon as practicable to the Staff Judge Advocate, USMACV, and will make pertinent collateral information available to the appointing authority and investigating officers.

c. Investigations of alleged or apparent war crimes will be coordinated with the Staff Judge Advocate, USMACV.

The appointing authority under the directive:

a. Will appoint an investigating officer and, if appropriate, designate a qualified criminal investigator or CID agent as technical assistant. Upon receipt of notification of an alleged or apparent war crime concerning a member of his command, one of the following appointing authorities will, with all dispatch, appoint an investigating officer to prepare and transmit to him a report of investigation.

b. Officers who exercise General Court-martial jurisdiction (or their designees) are appointing authorities for cases involving personnel under their General Court-martial jurisdiction. The Commanding General, Headquarters Detachment, US Army Element, USMACV (or his designee) is the appointing authority for cases involving US Army personnel assigned to USMACV and any other person believed to be a US serviceman but not sufficiently

> identified or otherwise provided for by another appointing authority. Commanders of brigades (or their designees), who have Judge Advocate assigned to their staff, are appointing authorities for cases involving personnel of their brigades.

MACV Directive 27–5 reaffirmed the "prohibition against commission of war crimes and related acts" and defined, as well as illustrated, what constitutes a war crime. In part some of the examples indicated in this regulation included: Maltreatment of prisoners of war or detainees; killing without trial spies or other persons who have committed hostile acts; torture or inhuman treatment of a prisoner of war or detainee; and depriving PW's or detainees of the right to a fair trial. This directive was "applicable to all US military personnel and to US civilian personnel serving with or accompanying the armed forces in the field." Continuing, it stated "Commission of any act enumerated . . . or constituting a war crime is prohibited. Violation of this directive will be punishable in accordance with the provisions of the Uniform Code of Military Justice."

The commission of a war crime or the knowledge of and failure to report an alleged war crime was thus a punishable offense. Reporting any incident that could be construed as a war crime was mandatory.

MACV Directive 335–1 directs the procedures for reporting "all serious crimes or incidents occurring within RVN involving US Forces personnel." A serious incident is defined as "any incident which may result in damaging public confidence in the US Armed Forces." A specific example of a reportable serious incident is one "involving detainees and prisoners of war for which the US has responsibility under the Geneva Conventions, including death, maltreatment, serious injury, riots, and successful escapes."

G. Reporting of Incidents

The very nature of the conflict in RVN necessitated an increased awareness of the possibility of accidental injury to friendly military or civilian noncombatants. The frequent employment of massed firepower from a variety of sources increased the likelihood of misdirected ordnance incidents. The intermingling of the nonuniformed foe and the populace not only made positive identification of hostile forces difficult but also contributed to the possibility of accidental injury or death to the inhabitants of some areas. Early in the conflict, these factors and many others associated with this unique war caused great concern at the highest levels for the protection of the noncombatants and the minimization of casualties to those persons not directly involved. Further, when incidents involving either friendly military personnel or civilian nationals occurred, investigating and reporting procedures were mandatory so that proper corrective action could be initiated immediately.

In November 1966, MACV Directive 335–12 was first published and was subsequently modified in November 1967. This directive prescribed the format for reporting significant events without delay. Significant events include, but are not limited to:

1. All incidents, accidental or deliberate, including disasters resulting in major property destruction or loss to friendly personnel, or the killing, wounding, or mistreating of friendly personnel by US, RVN, or Free World Forces.
2. Incidents which could be detrimental to US/GVN relationship. Such incidents include, but are not limited to, the following when caused by Americans:
   a. Injury, death, or mistreating of noncombatants or significant damage to Vietnamese property in the course of tactical operations.
   b. Riots or disorders and involvement in criminal incidents of a serious nature.
   c. Incidents which, because of their nature or the personnel involved, reasonably may be expected to arouse public interest, or which are of sufficient importance to receive widespread publicity.

Initial reports were to be followed by detailed and complete reports in the directed format.

MACV Directive 335–1, as previously indicated, established reporting procedures for all serious incidents or crimes. Any incident which could arouse public interest or cause unfavorable publicity required reporting under this directive and generally covered those incidents not specifically mentioned by MACV Directive 335–12.

H. MILITARY ASSISTANCE COMMAND, VIETNAM (MACV) EMPHASIS

MACV published several other documents pertaining to US policy with regard to ROE, treatment of Vietnamese nationals, and the reporting of war crimes. Letters, memoranda, and messages emphasizing COMUSMACV's concern for these subjects, and reaffirmations of MACV policy were published on many occasions. In addition, the COMUSMACV command policy file emphasized these subjects. At his Commander's Conferences, COMUSMACV repeatedly discussed the necessity for proper treatment of Vietnamese nationals and proper control of firepower. For instance, on 28 August 1966, GEN Westmoreland emphasized the following:

> I have five points to cover before we conclude. At your desks are rules of engagement and procedures on control of fires of all types. It is extremely important that we do all we can to use our fires with discrimination, and avoid noncombatant battle casualties. This is a very sensitive subject, both locally, and among our own press corps. Unfortunately, we've had a rash of incidents caused by everything from mechanical failure to human error. I would appreciate your reviewing now, and your continued review, of your safety precautions and procedures on control of fires. Make sure your commanders are thoroughly familiar with the appropriate documents. Henceforth my staff will republish these quarterly, to counter loss of familiarity through turnover of personnel. The percentage of incidents has been minuscule; nonetheless, every civilian killed is a calamity, and we must cut the percentage to the minimum possible.

On 3 December 1967, GEN Westmoreland closed his Commander's Conference by directing each commander to reduce firing accidents, report all accidents/incidents direct to MACV, and insure that all troops understand the "Nine Rules" that govern their conduct in RVN. Documentation of COMUSMACV policy and interest in these areas was and is plentiful.

The necessity for subordinate commanders to implement the MACV directives as well as the stated and implied policies was also emphasized. The chain of command within the MACV unified command afforded the means for the necessary delegation of authority to implement MACV policies. Within the chain of command, subordinate units usually published directives elaborating upon the regulations of the higher headquarters and insuring that at their lower level of command the specifically directed responsibilities assigned to them were further implemented. Another factor used by subordinate headquarters in determining applicability or the requirement to implement the directives of a higher headquarters was the mission assigned to the subordinate unit. In the case of USARV, for instance, the absence of an operational combat mission negated the need for combat operations orders, whereas III Marine Amphibious Force (MAF) had a requirement for operational combat missions as well as logistical and administrative support activities. For directives or regulations that were applicable to all personnel regardless of position or mission, the subordinate headquarters might elect not to publish a duplicate directive or regulation.

In such instances, as a general rule, the commander was then held responsible for insuring that individuals within his command were made aware of the provisions of the regulation or directive from higher headquarters which pertained to an individual's actions or inactions. The source of the regulation or directive was therefore not legally important, and the necessity for a subordinate unit to republish each directive of a higher headquarters was not absolute.

2. IMPLEMENTING DIRECTIVES

A. UNITED STATES ARMY, VIETNAM (USARV)

USARV, as the US Army component command headquarters, published directives not only implementing MACV policy, but also initiating internal policy.

Policy and guidance for all echelons of command in planning, conducting, and supervising the military training of individuals and units assigned to or attached to USARV are published in USARV Regulation 350–1, dated 10 November 1967. This regulation prescribed the policy and guidance for all echelons of command in planning, conducting, and supervising the military training of individuals and units assigned or attached to USARV. All units were directed, as a minimum, to schedule orientation and refresher training for all replacements and to strive to achieve the completion of DA mandatory training requirements. In this regard, the requirement for annual refresher training in the Geneva Conventions as prescribed by AR 350–216 was listed as mandatory training. Training in the rules of land war and the handling of PW's and detainees was required to be integrated in other training as the need for such training was ascertained. The status of individual or unit proficiency dictated the frequency and amount of training to be given.

Procedures for the issuance of the guidance cards to individuals were found in USARV Regulation 612–1. This regulation also established policy with regard to the possession of information cards by all US Army personnel assigned to Vietnam. It specified that upon arrival at either of the replacement battalions, all incoming officer and enlisted personnel would receive the information cards entitled "The Enemy in Your Hands," "Tips on VC Mines and Booby Traps," "Nine Rules," "Standing Orders, Rogers' Rangers," "Tips on the M–16 Rifle," "Code of Conduct," and "Geneva Convention." These cards contain information useful in the performance of the duties assigned to the personnel assigned to USARV. Each individual was to keep these cards in his possession at all times.

USARV implemented the MACV Directive (335–12) pertaining to artillery incidents by publishing USARV Regulation 527–7. This regulation provided the same type information as the MACV 335–12 except that reports were to be immediately electronically transmitted direct to USARV, and followup investigations (either formal or informal) were to be submitted within 15 days to Headquarters, USARV. CG, Americal Division, was specifically cited as a recipient of this directive.

MACV policy with regard to serious incident reports (SIR) was implemented at USARV by Regulation 335–6. Major commands subordinate to USARV were directed to report serious incidents (defined) direct to CG, USARV. Definitions of serious incidents contained in the MACV directive were provided, and initial reports, as well as interim and final reports, were required in a specific format.

USARV also published regulations that provided implementing policy for the evacuation, processing, and accounting for detained personnel (USARV Regulation 190–2). This regulation also directed that detained personnel would be provided humane treatment under the provisions of the Geneva Conventions.

USARV apparently did not publish an implementing directive to MACV Directive 20–4; however, this MACV regulation was applicable throughout the chain of command and did in fact establish the basis and requirement to inform each individual soldier within RVN of his specific responsibilities.

b. III Marine Amphibious Force (III MAF)

III MAF was an operational headquarters subordinate to MACV. The Americal Division was assigned to USARV for administrative and logistical support, and, in April 1967, was directed to receive operational direction from III MAF. Formally, the Americal Division was under the operational control (OPCON) of III MAF. III MAF published an extensive set of force orders and I Corps coordinating instructions that provided guidance and policy to the US Marine forces, and other US forces in ICTZ including the Americal Division.

Directives published by III MAF covered training in the Geneva Conventions (Force Order 1570.1A) as well as operational/reporting matters. Instructions were published by III MAF that were designed both to prevent and to prescribe certain conduct which was inimical to the accomplishment of the mission of US forces in Vietnam. This directive referred to the "Nine Rules" for personnel in RVN stating that, in concise terms, this card was the standard of conduct required of all US personnel.

The control of firepower in ICTZ was directed by III MAF Force Order 3330.1 implementing and referencing MACV Directive 525–18. Definitions of a SSZ were included as well as the restrictions previously quoted (MACV 525–18) for the conduct of fire by artillery, mortar, or naval weapons. Inhabited areas could be fired upon "if, in the judgment of the ground commander, his mission would be jeopardized" by warning. This III MAF Force Order was to serve as the standing operating procedure (SOP) as well as have "the force of a USMACV Directive."

The ROE were specified in Force Order 3121.5 which recognized that the requirements for control of firepower were greater than ever before. It stated that, "on the other hand, maximum effectiveness must be achieved in operations against the VC; on the other hand, a conscientious effort must be made to minimize battle casualties among noncombatants and destruction of their property." III MAF stressed the need for individual responsibility and awareness at the lowest levels. The decisions made were recognized as requiring "keen, swift, decisive analysis of the factors involved and must be based on a thorough understanding of the legal and moral principles concerned" especially when dealing with both noncombatants and PW's. III MAF Force Order 3460.3 specifically directs that "No violence will be done to their life or person, no outrages of any kind committed upon them, and, pending delivery to higher headquarters, the wounded and sick will be cared for."

Processing, screening, classifying, accounting, and evacuating PW's are thoroughly discussed in Force Order 3451.2A which includes definitions of the classifications to be accorded individuals prior to determining that they are PW's.

War crimes investigations and the reporting requirements implementing MACV Directive 20–4 are published in Force Order 5820.1.

Serious incident reporting was directed by III MAF I Corps Coordinating Instruction 5830.1A. This document referred to MACV Directives 335–1 and 335–12, and reiterated the requirement for "immediate reports to higher headquarters of any incident that results in death or serious injury to friendly forces or noncombatants."

c. AMERICAL DIVISION

The Americal Division, initially TF Oregon, was responsive to III MAF regulations after being placed under the operational control of III MAF on 22 April 1967. Additionally, the Americal Division was administratively subordinate to USARV. Both III MAF and USARV were well organized, and, as previously indicated, had published many directives dealing with ROE, required reports, minimizing noncombatant casualties, artillery incident requirements, and war crimes investigative procedures. These directives were directly applicable to the Americal Division.

TF Oregon published Regulation 335–6 on 21 March 1967. This directive required immediate reports in a prescribed format for serious incidents, which were defined and illustrated in the same manner as in MACV Directive 335–1 and USARV Regulation 335–6. The TF Oregon directive served as division-level policy guidance for Americal Division troops at the time of the Son My incident.

Division policy with reference to the control of firepower was published as Americal Regulation 525–4 on 16 March 1968. This regulation referenced MACV Directives 95–4, 525–3, 525–9, and 525–18. Although the regulation was not published until 16 March 1968, testimony indicates that Americal Regulation 525–4 was written, staffed, and coordinated prior to the Son My incident; and the policies stipulated therein were well known within the division. This regulation contains no indication, however, that it was intended to supersede earlier regulations of either TF Oregon or the Americal Division. The specifics of Americal Regulation 525–4 include definitions of areas, e.g., SSZ, guidance concerning the conduct and control of firepower, the necessity for minimizing friendly and noncombatant casualties, and the requirement for subordinate units to develop SOP's and implementing instructions.

The TF Oregon SOP was the primary directive in effect through 1967 and early 1968 providing guidance and policy to subordinate units. The Americal Division apparently did not publish many regulatory directives during its early stages of formation and organization. The SOP is dated 21 March 1967 and did provide, in one volume, specific procedures concerning operations, intelligence, personnel and administration, logistics, and other matters. Direct reference was made in this document to minimizing casualties (friendly and noncombatant) and handling of detainees. In addition, the requirement for spot reporting was covered in some detail and directed that spot reports be made expeditiously in a prescribed format.

As TF Oregon became the Americal Division, the SOP was augmented by directives that specifically covered the areas of interest involved in the III MAF, USARV, and MACV directives. On 1 December 1967, Americal Division Artillery published a SOP which provided routine and recurring field operational procedures within the artillery units assigned or attached to the Americal Division. Clearance for artillery fires in or near inhabited areas was in accordance with the ROE stipulated by III MAF and MACV directives, and specifically required spot reports to be rendered without delay in the event of heavy friendly or civilian casualties occurring in short period of time. Supplementing this SOP, the division artillery commander issued several directives further reiterating the requirement for reports of artillery incidents or misdirected ordnance.

Until 15 April 1968, the Americal Division operated under the TF Oregon SOP of March 1967. On 15 April 1968, the Americal Division published a SOP of their own. Thereafter, other directives, regulations, messages, and letters were issued supplementing those in effect and providing implementing instructions for those of higher headquarters. It was only by mid-1968 that the Americal Division achieved, to a reasonable degree, an adequate series of policy guidance directives.

D. 11TH BRIGADE

The 11th Brigade developed a SOP during their organization phase in Hawaii. In September 1967, prior to their deployment to RVN, the brigade received a copy of the Americal SOP (presumably the TF Oregon SOP) and other pertinent regulations that provided the directives and documentation policies of the division. As previously indicated, the subordinate units of the 11th Brigade were subjected to an accelerated training program from late April until deployment on or about 4 December 1967, and, therefore, did not develop detailed regulations concerning operational activities in RVN.

Soon after deployment, however, the 11th Brigade was committed to combat operations. At this time, 11th Brigade operational directives were practically nonexistent except for the SOP developed during training. According to the testimony, this SOP was in effect during the Son My incident although the publication date was not indicated. The SOP was applicable to field combat operations in a counterinsurgency environment.

The ROE indicated in the 11th Brigade SOP were generally in accordance with MACV guidance. The SOP stated:

> b. Missions against known or suspected NVA/VC targets in hamlets and villages occupied by noncombatants will be conducted as follows:
>
> 1. All fire missions on hamlets or villages will be controlled by an airborne or ground observer (FO) and will be executed only after the target has been declared hostile by GVN, Bde FSCC [Brigade Fire Support Coordination Center] and/or Bn Arty LNO [Liaison Officer].
> 2. Hamlets or villages not associated with ground operations will not be attacked by gunfire without prior warning (by leaflets and/or speaker systems or other appropriate means) even though light fire is received from them.
> 3. Hamlets and villages may be attacked without prior warning if the attack is in conjunction with a ground operation involving the movement of ground forces throughout the area, and if, in the judgment of the ground commander (Bn or higher), his mission would be jeopardized by such warnings.
>
> c. All missions fired on targets or target areas that are in the coastal waters of RVN must be cleared by the Bde FSCC (clearance from GVN Sector US Advisor required).
>
> d. Free-fire areas are coordinated with the sector/subsector US advisor and his VN counterpart, the province/district chief. The province/district chief will establish the restrictions on firing into these areas.
>
> e. Temporary free-fire areas may be negotiated for a specific operation effective for the period of the operation, and are normally more restrictive.

Considerable emphasis was placed on minimizing noncombatant casualties. The SOP directed that "maximum effort will be made to minimize noncombatant casualties during tactical operations" and "troops will be informed of the importance of minimizing casualties and the destruction of property, including livestock."

The SOP further indicated that detainees were to be properly processed by stating that "all personnel captured by US forces as enemy or suspected enemy shall be referred to as a detainee until his status is determined by a brigade interrogator" as a PW, civil defendant, returnee, or doubtful case. The policy for handling of detainees was to be in accordance with MACV Directives 20–5 and 190–3.

Although no reference is made to reporting alleged or apparent war crimes, the requirement for spot reporting of incidents is directed by the SOP. Reporting of serious incidents was directed by the 11th Brigade Regulation 1–3, dated 31 March 1967. The incidents directed to be reported by this regulation included "deaths from other than natural cause to include deaths of foreign national personnel when US Army personnel or equipment are involved." These reports were to be submitted to the Brigade S1.

On 30 January 1968, the first operational directive was published establishing the "criteria for engaging targets by direct and indirect fire in combat operations." This 11th Brigade Regulation, 525–1, directed the ROE for the organic firepower available within the 11th Brigade. The ROE for artillery, mortar, naval gunfire, and aircraft, as directed by MACV and the 11th Brigade SOP, were reiterated. In addition, the individual soldier was provided definitive ROE by this regulation. It stated that, in the employment of small arms and automatic weapons, the utmost care must be exercised to minimize noncombatant casualties and property damage. Specifically, the soldier was directed by this regulation to identify the enemy before engaging:

> Personnel who attempt to evade and are identified as members of NVA or VC Forces by the wearing of a uniform, web gear or pack and/or have possession of a weapon may be engaged. Every attempt will be made to halt these personnel by giving the command halt (*Dung Lai*) and firing warning shots overhead. If attempts to halt evading personnel fail they will then be engaged by fire with intent to wound by firing at lower extremities. The wounded captive will then be treated and evacuated as rapidly as possible for exploitation of intelligence he may possess.

The requirement to minimize casualties and property damage in the employment of all forms of firepower was adequately presented by this regulation. Following higher headquarters guidance, commanders were directed that:

> Immediately following the attack of areas inhabited by noncombatants, the force commander will insure that an explanation is given to the populace of the need for firing, stressing the point that the enemy forced the action.

> If noncombatant casualties occur regardless of safeguards, medical treatment and evacuation should be provided by the responsible commander, subject to tactical considerations and resources available.
>
> Every possible safeguard short of endangering friendly lives will be used to avoid noncombatant casualties and indifference and indiscriminate destruction of private property when such action is being conducted in populated areas.
>
> Individuals that appear to be attempting to escape or evade may be frightened, innocent civilians. The commander on the site must exercise judgment as to whether to engage these individuals or not. The commander must base his decisions on his overall knowledge of the area, situation, mission, and safety of his command.

This regulation, which had been published in late January 1968, provided the initial framework which guided the actions of subordinate elements of the 11th Brigade. During the early months of 1968, however, the brigade depended primarily upon the SOP for operational guidance, policy, and direction.

It is evident that on 16 March 1968, the personnel within the 11th Brigade were subject to and responsible for not only the provisions of the various directives and regulations published by MACV, USARV, III MAF, and the Americal Division but also those contained in their own SOP. Implementation of the broad SOP guidance which was later spelled out in 11th Brigade regulations was, at the time of the Son My operation, resting on the shoulders of the leaders within the brigade. The need for professional leadership, mature judgment, sound analytical decisions, and effective control of combat actions was clearly evident.

3. ANALYSIS

A. EMPLOYMENT OF FIREPOWER AND SAFEGUARDING OF NONCOMBATANTS

From the outset of US involvement, Headquarters MACV recognized that the application of military force in Vietnam must be carefully controlled at all times. The very nature of counterinsurgent warfare generally precluded the massing of firepower unless the target was well away from inhabited areas or positive target identification could be achieved. The US soon attained a vast superiority in firepower that could be properly exploited only when the elusive foe allowed himself to be caught in the open and away from the populace. However, the tactic generally used by the VC/NVA in their attempt to negate the US firepower advantage was to intermingle themselves with the Vietnamese civilian population.

Recognizing that a lack of positive control of firepower in such circumstances would not be in the best interests of the US efforts in Vietnam, MACV developed and promulgated extensive ROE and command directives governing the employment of firepower by ground, naval, and air forces in Vietnam. By such directives, MACV established that the safeguarding of the lives and property of noncombatants was a matter of prime importance to all elements of the command. MACV directives governing the use of firepower were constantly updated, explained, and clarified; and from 1965 to the present the policy they set forth has been consistent in adhering to the humane standard of protecting the civilians within the combat zone. Other MACV directives in effect during the Son My incident provided guidance and policy with respect to serious incident reporting and spot reports that also were clearly adequate in quantity and scope. At the same time, MACV consistently recognized that correct application of these policies in the Vietnam environment required a high calibre of leadership and a special degree of judgment and discrimination.

MACV Directives 95–4 and 525–18, which were in force in March 1968, provided the ROE and reiterated in detail the objectives previously described. The necessity was clearly stated for all commanders to exercise prudent judgment and restraint in the application of firepower to insure the overall policies and missions of FWMAF. Subordinate headquarters, in some instances, implemented the MACV policies with definitive and specific rules more appropriate to their specific situations. In a few cases, the subordinate headquarters modified the MACV directives. Many of the MACV directives should not have been modified nor implementing regulations published by subordinate headquarters. MACV policy directives that establish the ROE, the procedures for handling of detainees and PW's, and the definitive need to minimize casualties were applicable without modification or amplifying instructions. The Inquiry, during its visit to South Vietnam, noted that several of the more recent MACV directives include instructions precluding any modification or implementing directives by subordinate commands.

It should be noted, however, that the exercise of judgment demanded by COMUSMACV during the time of the incident was retained in the directives of subordinate commands. All such directives emphasized that positive control and prudent judgment had to be exercised in the application of firepower. By regulation, local commanders were required to insure that their subordinates were trained in and controlled by the ROE as well as the MACV policy to minimize senseless destruction and needless casualties during all combat operations. The policies were clearly defined charging all commanders with the tasks of training, directing, and controlling their subordinates, and the responsibility for the orders and actions of their commands.

B. REPORTING OF WAR CRIMES

The term war crime is a technical expression of a violation of the law of war by any individual—every violation of the law of war is defined as a war crime. The soldier receives training in war crime definitions and illustrations initially in basic training and annually thereafter at unit level. He is taught that war crimes are not condoned and are a punishable offense. MACV Directive 20–4 directed that all war crimes—or an incident or act thought to be a war crime—were to be reported and investigated. This directive provided definitions and examples of war crimes in addition to specifically directing that any individual having knowledge of any act thought to be a war crime had the responsibility to report the act to his commanding officer. Investigative procedures were also indicated.

This MACV directive was implemented by III MAF, but not by USARV or the Americal Division. In the III MAF regulation, the commanding officer receiving the report of a suspected war crime was required to transmit this report to III MAF utilizing the spot report format. No other channel for reporting suspected crimes other than to his commanding officer was afforded the individual rifleman. If his commander participated in a war crime, the individual soldier's recourse was not specified, although it is apparent that an alternative is required. Channels for reporting over the chain of command are provided, and are available to the soldier, but their use needs to be strengthened. Regulations directing individuals to report incidents such as suspected war crimes should reiterate the use of not only the primary reporting channels but the alternate channels as well.

C. ILLEGAL ORDERS

The term illegal order is not defined in the dictionary of Army terms. A soldier is taught that an order is lawful unless for some reason it is beyond the authority of the official issuing it. He is also taught as a part of the Geneva Conventions training that persons taking no active part in hostilities or who have laid down their arms shall be treated humanely.

It is apparent that directives and training are inadequate concerning an individual's responsibilities and actions concerning illegal orders. There is a dearth of written information concerning this subject. There is but little discussion of illegal orders in Army regulations or training manuals and even less at subordinate levels. What little discussion is included in any publication is cumbersome and indecisive, and presented in such a manner that it takes a legal officer to interpret it. Indeed, the average officer or enlisted man would have difficulty comprehending it.

Further, the directives and regulations are deficient in explaining that a soldier is a reasoning human being who is expected to exercise judgment in obeying the orders of a superior. Also lacking is sufficient instruction providing guidance to the soldier that when an order is beyond the scope of the issuing authority and is so obviously illegal, he is expected to recognize that fact as a man of ordinary sense and average understanding. An individual is not expected to blindly obey all orders.

The actions an individual should take when he receives an unlawful order are not clearly defined in any publication. He is most often (and properly) told that disobedience of orders is at his own peril, and acts involved in the disobedience of an illegal order will normally result in a charge of insubordination with its attendant disciplinary action.

The Department of the Army needs to promulgate guidance that will more clearly define illegal orders and individual responsibilities and actions related thereto, yet continue to insure the proper balance between this guidance and the normal requirements of command and control and the traditions regarding discipline within the Army.

D. Directives Not a Substitute for Leadership

The early part of 1968 and especially the *Tet* offensive presented great difficulties for the units and commanders charged with implementing these policies. The enemy forces had infiltrated into the cities and villages and had become intermingled with the populace. Terrorism and acts of sabotage were rampant, and the individual soldier had become increasingly wary of the local population. The VC disregarded civilian lives in their wanton attacks and suicidal defenses, while FWMAF were determined to rout the infiltrators from among the populace. Firepower was employed inside many inhabited areas by both friendly and enemy forces. The purposes may have been different but at times achieved the same results.

Adequate directives and publications that regulated the control of firepower, stipulated the ROE and directed the handling of detainees were in effect during this period, and many were re-emphasized. However, it is a fact that, although the published policies were clear, their application in the circumstances that existed in Vietnam at the time of the Son My incident required above all professional leadership, mature judgment, and sound decisions.

C. Government of Vietnam Policy/Directives as to Son My

Son My Village was located within that section of Quang Ngai Province which had been designated as a priority area for military offensive operations and for pacification in 1968. The I ARVN Corps/III MAF Combined Campaign Plan 1–68 specified that GVN pacification activities would be increased by 50 percent over the 1967 level within Quang Ngai Province. However, since Son My Villages and the surrounding area were under VC control, and had been since 1964, the primary effort was devoted to conducting military offensive operations within that area to force the VC out so as to create conditions favorable to pacification. In early 1968, US and ARVN forces had separately assigned areas of operation in which they normally conducted independent operations. Coordination was required only if operations outside the normally assigned AO were planned and on matters of special interest. ARVN forces had the primary responsibility for the Son My area. However, since they lacked the capability to operate in the area, or at least were reluctant to, US forces frequently obtained an extension of their AO from the 2d ARVN Division in order to engage the 48th Local Force Battalion and other VC forces.

Son My, being VC controlled, had no GVN administrative authorities living there. The government had repeatedly encouraged all the residents to move into established secure areas, as many had done. The remaining residents of Son My were considered to be VC, or VC sympathizers at a minimum, by GVN authorities. For all practical purposes, the local GVN authorities considered the area a free fire zone (unrestricted) for artillery fires; they placed no restriction on the targets which could be engaged. However, the District Chief did retain the final authority for approving fires in the area to insure that Vietnamese forces (ARVN, RF/PF) were at a safe distance from proposed targets. An area's being considered a free fire zone did not negate the established ROE which should have been considered before engaging any target. The GVN officials recognized their responsibility for civilians remaining in the area but accepted the fact that these people would, by their own choice, be subjected to artillery fire and the results of any offensive action necessary to free the area of VC. According to the deputy Province Senior Advisor, Quang Ngai Province officials placed no restrictions on Vietnamese forces operating in this area. The District Senior Advisor stated that it was normal practice for the Vietnamese forces, if they were successful in penetrating the area, to burn the hootches and to destroy the bunkers and tunnels.

Even though an area might be VC controlled, specific rules, applicable to both US and RVN forces, were established for the safeguarding of Vietnamese property. The I ARVN Corps/III MAF Combined Campaign Plan 1–68 specified that:

> In VC controlled areas, RVNAF, US and other FWMAF must take all practicable measures to minimize the destruction of both public and private property and take appropriate measures as feasible to protect such property. It must be remembered that civilians who live in VC controlled areas may

be under VC control against their will and may not be sympathetic to the enemy. Treating such persons like enemies, destroying their property or depriving them of their goods is incompatible with long range objectives of expanding the influence of the GVN throughout RVN.

Policy stated in the Combined Campaign Plan regarding private property and goods is as follows:

1. Disposition of private property and supplies is the responsibility of GVN officials.
2. Destruction of private property, homes, livestock, and goods is forbidden except in cases of overriding operational necessity.
3. The destruction of dwellings and livestock as a denial measure, is the responsibility of GVN authorities for employment of US forces in the deliberate destruction of noncombatants' property as a denial measure will be referred to Headquarters MACV for the personal decision of COMUSMACV. [69]

No specific GVN policy statements or directives pertaining solely to Son My were obtained by the Peers Inquiry. However, the policy regarding the protection of Vietnamese citizens and their property was clearly stated in the 1968 Combined Campaign Plan. It is equally clear that the GVN/ARVN authorities within Quang Ngai did not apply this policy to VC-controlled areas, especially Son My. Because Son My was a VC stronghold, and had been for many years, GVN officials had little interest in the area. They were primarily concerned with the reestablishment of GVN control in areas lost during *Tet* and the prevention of a second attack on Quang Ngai City which was believed to be imminent. As a practical matter, GVN authorities imposed no restrictions on operations conducted in the Son My area.

Chapter 10. Reports, Investigations, and Reviews

A. The Immediate Reports, Investigations, and Reviews, March–Early April 1968

1. OPERATIONAL AND INTELLIGENCE REPORTS

Significant reports concerning Task Force (TF) Barker's operations on 16 March commenced shortly after the unopposed landing of the lead elements of C Company at 0730 hours. For this period there is no record of the operational reports submitted by the rifle companies of TF Barker to their control headquarters; such reports were normally submitted via radio to the TF Barker Tactical Operations Center (TOC), recorded in the Operations Journal there, and if deemed of significant importance, relayed to the 11th Light Infantry Brigade for recording and possible further transmittal to headquarters of the Americal Division.

a. Reports of Enemy Casualties

The first report from TF Barker to the 11th Brigade concerning enemy casualties came at 0735 hours and noted that one Viet Cong (VC) had been killed in the vicinity of the landing zone (LZ) by C Company. Within 25 minutes of the initial report, gunships supporting the helicopter lift had reported killing an additional six VC; four of these in an area 500 meters west of C Company's LZ and the remaining two at a location approximately 2 kilometers south-southwest of the same LZ. At 0758 hours, 11 minutes after the last elements of C Company had landed on the LZ, the TF reported to 11th Brigade that C Company reported killing an additional 14 VC approximately 200–300 meters east of the LZ. The next report of casualties is recorded in an 0840 entry in the TF Barker Journal which states that C Company had counted 69 VC killed in action (KIA) at the same location where the previous 14 VC casualties were reported being killed. The journal entry also indicates that the 11th Brigade was notified.

Entries in both the 11th Brigade and Americal Division Journals identify 69 VC KIA in the C Company area; however, they cite the location as 600 meters northwest of that reported in the TF Barker Journal and attribute the casualties to artillery fire. No explanation can be found for the discrepancy in these reports; however, since TF Barker in a subsequent report identifies 68 casualties as being killed by artillery fire, it is reasonable to conclude that this cause of death was specified by TF Barker during some communication with 11th Brigade. This discrepancy is examined in detail in a later section of this chapter.

No further enemy casualties were reported by C Company on 16 March although an entry in the TF Barker Journal at 1555 hours states that C Company had reported "10–11 women and children killed by artillery or gunships" and that this figure was not included in previous reports of VC casualties. This information is not reflected in journal entries for the 11th Brigade or the Americal Division although the TF Barker entry indicates the 11th Brigade was notified. This same TF Barker Journal entry also reports that none of the previously reported body count of B Company were women and children. A total of three enemy weapons was reported captured by C Company; these were the only weapons reported captured by TF Barker on this date.

In summary, TF Barker reported a total of 90 VC killed in C Company area of operations (AO) within a period of 70 minutes following the initial touchdown of its forces in the LZ; after 0840 hours, no additional VC casualties were recorded in the C Company area. Throughout the day C Company experienced only one US casualty, an apparent accident in which a soldier shot himself in the foot.

In the area to the east of C Company, B Company was reported by TF Barker to have killed 12 VC at 0955, 18 more killed at 1025, and an additional 8 killed at 1420 hours; all at a location approximately 700 meters east of the B Company LZ. This total of 38 VC KIA by B Company, when added to those reported by C Company, represented a VC body count of 128 and a total of three weapons captured which was reported to the 11th Brigade and Americal Division by the evening of 16 March. The Americal Division Journal initially reflected a total of six weapons captured; this was later changed to three. This discrepancy is not explained.

B. Reports of US Casualties

Total US casualties for TF Barker on 16 March were two killed, ten wounded, and one self-inflicted wound. Eleven of the casualties caused by enemy action were a result of mines and boobytraps. Only one casualty, a man from A Company, was wounded by small arms fire. No casualties were caused by direct contact with the enemy in the C Company or B Company areas.

c. REPORTS OF CIVILIAN CASUALTIES

First reports of possible casualties among noncombatants occurred as a result of COL Henderson's flight over the Son My area after C Company had landed in its LZ. COL Henderson stated that he descended to an altitude of 100–200 feet to examine the bodies of two armed and uniformed VC who had been killed earlier by gunships of the 174th Avn Co. During this maneuver he observed two separate groups of bodies which appeared to be noncombatants. One group consisting of an old man, a woman, and a child, was located about 150 meters south of My Lai (4), on a trail leading to Route 521. Approximately 150 meters farther south, lying in a small ravine near a trail, was another group consisting of two men and a woman. Neither the location nor the number of these casualties coincides with any casualty report submitted by elements of TF Barker.

COL Henderson further stated that at about 0930 hours, while at LZ Dottie, he met with MG Koster who had landed there to refuel, and advised the latter that he observed what he believed to be six to eight noncombatant casualties in the area of C Company's operation. COL Henderson recalls MG Koster's reaction to this as a directive to COL Henderson to determine how these casualties had been incurred. In his appearance before the Inquiry, MG Koster could not recall this specific incident but did say that on two separate occasions on 16 March, COL Henderson advised him of noncombatant casualties.

COL Henderson, in a prepared statement dated 27 November 1969 (exhibit S–3), stated that after speaking to MG Koster, he returned over the area of My Lai (4) and discovered that TF Barker was not submitting the "required reports" to the 11th Brigade TOC. Henderson stated that he then directed LTC Barker to bring the TF headquarters "up-to-date" and to insure that required reports were submitted to the brigade TOC. He stated that at that time he also told Barker to "determine how many civilians had been killed and whether they had been killed by artillery, air, or small arms fire." In this same statement, which is in conflict with testimony Henderson presented to this Inquiry, he also stated that he talked to Barker twice on the afternoon of the 16th, periodically overflying the AO of the TF until 1900 hours that date. During these discussions, according to Henderson, Barker advised him that a total of 128 enemy and 24 civilians had been killed in the operation.

In contrast to his prepared statement (exhibit S–3), COL Henderson in his testimony before this Inquiry stated that he received a report from

LTC Barker during the afternoon of 16 March that from 12 to 14 noncombatants had been killed thus far in the operation. He further stated that LTC Barker was unable to provide detailed information concerning these casualties, and that he directed Barker to obtain an exact count of noncombatant casualties and information concerning the age, sex, and apparent cause of death of each.

As a result of COL Henderson's interest in the matter, at about 1530 hours TF Barker operations section received a requirement from 11th Brigade to determine the number of civilian casualties and the manner in which they were killed or wounded. It is this request which probably resulted in the TF Barker Journal entries at 1555 hours on 16 March which state that B Company reports that none of the VC body count previously reported by that unit includes women or children and that C Company reports "approximately 10 to 11" women and children were killed by artillery or gunships.

The next incident concerning casualties is the subject of considerable conflict in the testimony of the principals involved. This matter concerns the issuance of an order by COL Henderson to TF Barker to have C Company reverse direction and sweep back through My Lai (4) to determine the exact count of civilian and/or VC casualties. Testimony confirms that such an order was issued, received by TF Barker, and relayed by MAJ Calhoun to CPT Medina between 1500 and 1530 hours on 16 March. The evidence further confirms that its issuance to CPT Medina via radio was monitored by MG Koster who countermanded the order shortly thereafter and directed that COL Henderson be so advised. Both COL Henderson and MG Koster contended in their testimony, however, that this action occurred at a later date; Henderson recalled it as an action resulting from his interview with a helicopter pilot and an 18 March order to investigate certain aspects of the Son My operation. MG Koster was less certain of his recollection but recalled it as occurring late in the afternoon on 17 or 18 March while he was returning to his command post at Chu Lai, and related it to the critical nature of helicopter airlift and the extraction of C Company from the Son My area. In his testimony, MG Koster did not dismiss the possibility of the event's having occurred on 16 March. All other personnel related to this incident i.e., 11th Brigade S3, TF Barker S2 and S3, and the CO, C Company were certain the event transpired on 16 March. A review of all available evidence and analysis of events as they occurred during the period 16–18 March, leads to the conclusion that this action occurred on the afternoon of 16 March, about the time C Company had closed into its night defensive position.

During the course of the radio conversation between MG Koster and CPT Medina, in which the former countermanded COL Henderson's order, CPT Medina stated he advised his commanding general that C Company had observed 20–28 civilian casualties during the day. Later that same day, at about 1900 hours, COL Henderson stated he called MG Koster by telephone and advised him that his most recent report from LTC Barker revealed an increase in the civilian casualty toll from "12 to 14" to 20. He also stated he informed MG Koster that he had directed LTC Barker to obtain information concerning the age, sex, and cause of death of these casualties. According to COL Henderson, MG Koster replied that he was also interested in obtaining this information. MG Koster testified that he did not recall the details of this conversation. According to COL Henderson, LTC Barker subsequently provided a more detailed report of the 20 civilian casualties which identified the cause of death as artillery and gunship fire.

On 18 March, sometime prior to 1400 hours, COL Henderson visited C Company's location in the field to question CPT Medina about the allegations made by WO1 (now 1LT) Thompson, which are discussed in detail in a later portion of this chapter. CPT Medina stated that at that time he reported to COL Henderson that he believed approximately 20 to 28 noncombatants had been killed during the operation—which compares with the 20–28 reported by CPT Medina on 16 March to MAJ Calhoun and MG Koster, and the 20 which had been reported to COL Henderson by LTC Barker on the 16th and 17th and relayed by him to MG Koster.

To this date there is no satisfactory explanation for the conflict in civilian casualty figures of "12 to 14" reported by Barker on 16 March and the "10 to 11" reported in TF Barker's Journal at that same time; of the figure 20 submitted by Barker on the evening of 16 March and the "20 to 28" reported by CPT Medina shortly before that period. It can only be concluded that neither commanders nor staff officers checked reports of noncombatant casualties or gave substantial attention in this instance to such matters.

Regardless of the discrepancies in figures, it is clear that LTC Barker, COL Henderson, and MG Koster all had knowledge, as early as the morning of 16 March, that a number of noncombatants had been killed in My Lai (4). It is equally clear that no action was taken to report such casualties to any headquarters outside of the Americal Division despite the fact that Military Assistance Command, Vietnam (MACV) and III Marine Amphibious Force (III MAF) directives required this action.

2. INFORMATION AND ORDERS TRANSMITTED ON 16 MARCH

During the operation of 16 March, information concerning irregularities in My Lai (4) was transmitted over the various command and control radio nets being used by units involved in the operation. Similarly, orders were issued over these same networks which reflected a knowledge by various command elements of these irregularities and an attempt to regain control over combat units. Fixing the exact times and sequence of such radio transmissions was made difficult because of the inability of some witnesses specifically to recall times and events and of the efforts of others to withhold information from the Inquiry. However, the principal significance of the following reconstruction of message traffic of 16 March does not lie in the time or the sequence of individual messages. Rather, the significance is the information these messages contain and the awareness of events in My Lai (4) which had been gained by persons who heard such traffic.

The first of these transmissions probably occurred around 0900 hours and was attributed by three witnesses to COL Henderson. In this transmission to elements of TF Barker, COL Henderson is quoted as saying, "I don't want any unnecessary killing down there." Such a report could have been a logical result of COL Henderson's earlier sightings of noncombatant casualties. This transmission may explain a subsequent action by CPT Medina at about 0915 hours when he issued an order to at least the 2d Platoon, to stop the shooting.

The next message which referred to casualties among noncombatants probably occurred around 1000 hours and was broadcast over the air-ground radio net and monitored by the operations sergeant of B Company, 123d Aviation Battalion, SP5 (now SSG) Kubert. The message came from an unidentified pilot who stated that "Shark" gunships (174th Avn Co) were making a gun run on civilians. SP5 Kubert stated that this message prompted a telephone call from either CPT Moe, the operations officer, or MAJ Watke, the company commander, to TF Barker, advising the TF of the message. The preponderance of the evidence available to the Inquiry indicates that such a gun run probably was not made and that the casualties observed in the vicinity of Route 521 were caused by ground troops.

Approximately 30 minutes later, at about 1030 hours, as the helicopter which was evacuating an accidentally wounded soldier from C Company was departing the area, the pilot broadcast a message to the effect that he had seen a large number of bodies at My Lai (4). CPT Medina stated that it was shortly after this that he received a call from MAJ Calhoun stating that a helicopter pilot had said he thought some noncombatants had been shot and killed. CPT Medina stated that MAJ Calhoun advised that he wanted to make sure this was not being done. MAJ Calhoun denied knowledge of this event.

There is testimony from CPT Kotouc, that sometime during the morning of the 16th he heard a radio transmission from the aero-scout team of Company B, 123d Aviation Battalion, in which the sender reported that an unarmed person was being shot at by a machinegun.

CPT Kotouc goes on to say that MAJ Calhoun then called both CPT Michles and CPT Medina and told them to be sure that they were not killing any civilians. In his testimony before the Inquiry, MAJ Calhoun confirmed the events as related by CPT Kotouc.

Also about midmorning another call came in to the TF Barker TOC from Company B, 123d Aviation Battalion advising MAJ Calhoun that noncombatants were being killed in My Lai (4). SFC Stephens, the intelligence sergeant for TF Barker, overheard this message and a subsequent message by MAJ Calhoun to LTC Barker, advising him of the report. MAJ Calhoun denied knowledge of this event in his testimony.

A series of messages which were said to have been transmitted over the C Company command net are also of significance. The first of these probably occurred at about 1030 and was purportedly made by MAJ Calhoun to CPT Medina. The message was an instruction "not to kill women and children." MAJ Calhoun in his testimony denied knowledge of this transmission. The second message was purportedly from an unidentified helicopter pilot who, according to the witness, stated that "from up here it looks like a blood-bath. What the hell are you doing down there?" The witness could not recall the time of the message or to whom it was directed. The third in this series of messages was overheard by another soldier from C Company who testified that shortly after noon, LTC Barker called CPT Medina. Barker purportedly advised Medina that he had a report "from higher headquarters that there were some civilians being killed," to which Medina replied that he "was positive it wasn't his people." It is appropriate to note that one of the reasons why Barker and Calhoun may have used the C Company radio net rather than the TF net, was to preclude the transmissions being monitored by commanders and staff officers at higher headquarters.

A further message of significance was said to have been transmitted over the air-ground radio net and was monitored by SGM Kirkpatrick, the 11th Brigade operations sergeant at Duc Pho. The message was not a report but apparently a conversation between two individuals, one of whom said, "If you shoot that man, I'm going to shoot you," or words to that effect. The nature of the transmission prompted CPT Henderson, Assistant S3, 11th Brigade, to call the TF Barker TOC by telephone and inquire as to the reason for that kind of radio traffic. In their testimony, TF Barker personnel who were in the TOC at the time, denied recollection of the incident.

Each of these radio transmissions reflected the existence of unusual circumstances concerning the event at Son My. To the commanders and staff officers monitoring the command nets, these messages should have acted to alert them that the operation of TF Barker was not a normal combat assault. No conclusions can be reached solely on the basis of these transmissions; however, when viewed in light of other actions and reports which occurred during this same time period, it would appear that commanders in the Son My area should have been alerted to the unusual nature of TF Barker operations during the morning hours of 16 March.

3. REPORT OF WO1 THOMPSON AND OTHER AVIATION PERSONNEL

As part of the combat support being provided TF Barker on 16 March, an aero-scout team consisting of one light observation helicopter, OH–23, and two UH–1B gunships from Company B, 123d Aviation Battalion, was providing aerial surveillance to locate and take under fire enemy forces in and around the area of Son My. As part of this team, the OH–23 performed the scouting or reconnaissance function, flying close to the ground to detect enemy locations and movements, while the two gunships flew at higher altitudes, protecting the OH–23 and providing firepower to engage the enemy. The pilot of the OH–23 was WO1 (now 1LT) Hugh C. Thompson. He was accompanied on this operation by his crew chief SP4 Glenn W. Andreotta and gunner, SP4 (now Mr.) Lawrence M. Colburn.

Because of the configuration of the aircraft, communications between the aero-scout team and the ground unit they were supporting was limited to intermittent frequency modulated (FM) voice between the high gunship and the TF Barker command net. Neither the OH–23 scout nor the low gunship was in direct contact with the ground unit they were supporting. For WO1 Thompson to communicate with ground elements, it was necessary for him to transmit to the high gunship, which in turn would contact the ground unit. This information is useful in understanding the actions of the aero-scout team, which follow.

This aero-scout team arrived in the vicinity of My Lai (4) in time to observe the artillery preparation terminating at C Company's LZ and commenced its reconnaissance at around 0730 hours in the area generally south of Route 521. It continued to operate south of Route 521 until such time as the helicopter gunships supporting the combat assault of C Company had cleared the area, at which time it began reconnoitering north of the road in the vicinity of My Lai (4). From 0745 hours until approximately 0830 hours, the aero-scout team performed its mission without unusual incident. One enemy was taken under fire south of the hamlet, approximately 40 rounds of 60mm mortar ammunition were discovered southeast of My Lai (4) on Hill 85, and a number of dead and wounded civilians were noted along the road and in the rice paddy south of My Lai (4). Noting the absence of enemy fire, Thompson told the gunship that he would mark the location of the wounded with smoke grenades and that the infantry unit should send assistance to these personnel. Thompson proceeded to mark the location of the wounded during his reconnaissance south and west of My Lai (4) until approximately 0830 hours when he departed for LZ Dottie to refuel.

WO1 Thompson and his aero-scout team returned to the My Lai (4) area at approximately 0900 hours and resumed their reconnaissance. From this point forward there is some contradiction in testimony concerning the exact time and sequence of events observed by WO1 Thompson. These differences do not extend to any significant variance in the substance of testimony and are not considered critical to the investigation. The events related below follow the version reported by WO1 Thompson and include only the major incidents experienced by him. The facts and their sequence are generally corroborated by other members of the aero-scout crew who were present in the area.

Upon resumption of the reconnaissance mission over My Lai (4), WO1 Thompson and his crew noted that many of the wounded civilians previously identified to the ground elements were now dead. At about 0915 hours, WO1 Thompson noted the approach of US military personnel to a location Thompson had previously marked with a colored smoke grenade. Both Thompson and his gunner, SP4 Colburn, stated that they observed an individual wearing a captain's insignia of grade on his helmet approach a wounded girl who was lying on the ground. The captain walked up to the woman, according to Colburn, prodded her with his foot, and then stepped back several paces and fired into her body with his M–16 rifle. There is considerable testimony from other witnesses who reported this as an act of self-defense.

The OH–23 helicopter then moved eastward to an irrigation ditch which ran along a tree line approximately 100 meters east of My Lai (4) and 300 meters east of the location where TF Barker TOC had recorded 84 VC having been killed some 90 minutes earlier. As they approached this ditch, both WO1 Thompson and his gunner noted that it contained a number of bodies which they later reported as between 50 and 100 persons. Upon closer investigation, Thompson noted that some of the persons in the ditch were still alive. He stated he landed his helicopter in close proximity to the ditch and spoke to a "colored sergeant" who was standing nearby, advising him that there were wounded women and children in the ditch and asking if there were not some way in which the sergeant could help the wounded. The sergeant replied in words to the effect that "the only way he could help them was to kill them." Thompson considered the reply to have been made in jest and did not take the response seriously. Instead, he stated to the sergeant, "Why don't you see if you can help them," and returned to the helicopter to resume his reconnaissance. As the helicopter was leaving the ground, the crew chief, SP4 Andreotta, who was sitting in an outside seat, reported over the intercom that a sergeant (not the one to whom Thompson had previously spoken) was shooting into the ditch. WO1 Thompson turned and saw the soldier holding a weapon which was pointed toward the ditch. Testimony of other witnesses before the Inquiry generally substantiated the facts as related by Thompson except that the sergeant to whom he originally spoke was identified by members of the platoon as an individual of Philippine ancestry who could not understand Thompson. Witnesses stated that the sergeant called to a lieutenant standing nearby and the conversation actually ensued between Thompson and this lieutenant—later identified as 2LT (now 1LT) William Calley.

The series of events so far—the shooting of the wounded girl; the discovery that during the period of refueling, the wounded civilians had died; the large number of bodies in the ditch; the shooting into that ditch by the sergeant; and the number of bodies along Route 521 and in the village—all combined to cause great concern on the part of WO1 Thompson. In this frame of mind, Thompson flew east of My Lai (4) and observed in front of the advancing US forces a small bunker into which a group of Vietnamese—old men, women, and children—were moving. Having seen his previous efforts to save noncombatants frustrated, Thompson elected to land his helicopter between the advancing troops and the bunker containing the noncombatants. WO1 Thompson then directed his crew chief and gunner to take the M–60 machineguns which were mounted on their aircraft, and to cover his movements "real close." WO1 Thompson then walked from his helicopter toward the US lines and spoke to an individual whom he later identified as LT Calley. It is possible that this identification has been confused by Thompson with the officer he previously spoke to at the ditch; there is some evidence that this officer probably was the platoon leader of C Company's 2d Platoon.

WO1 Thompson stated that he advised the individual of the Vietnamese in the bunker and sought his assistance in getting them out of the bunker alive. According to Thompson, when this individual replied with words to the effect that "the only way to get them out is with a hand grenade" Thompson responded with the remark that the ground commander should "just stop his men and I'd get them out without killing them." Witnesses agreed that Thompson then left the individual, walked forward of the friendly lines toward the bunker, and signalled for the bunker occupants to come forward. The occupants left the bunker; Thompson gathered them together and radioed for one of his gunships which landed and, in two trips, evacuated the civilians to the southwest near Route 521, without further incident.

Becoming airborne once again, WO1 Thompson queried his crew to determine if they wished to return to the location of the ditch where they had seen the sergeant firing in order to determine if there were survivors. The crew responded affirmatively and so, once again, Thompson landed the OH–23. Thompson dismounted with the M–60 machinegun to provide security. His two crew members went into the ditch and removed a small child who had been shielded by the body of a young woman. Thompson was told by his crew that there were other survivors; however, the capacity of the helicopter precluded evacuating more than the one child. One of the crewmen then held the child on his lap while Thompson flew the helicopter to a Vietnamese hospital at Quang Ngai. After this they once again returned to LZ Dottie to refuel the aircraft.

WO1 Thompson arrived at LZ Dottie between 1100 and 1130 hours. He was greatly concerned over the "unnecessary killing" he had seen and determined that this matter would be reported through proper channels. On the flight-line at LZ Dottie he encountered other pilots and crew members from his company who were also concerned over similar incidents they had seen. In testimony before the Inquiry, witnesses stated that several of the air-crew members were voicing complaints and at least initially, joined with WO1 Thompson in stating their protests.

Upon landing, WO1 Thompson encountered his section leader, CPT (now Mr.) Barry C. Lloyd, and related to him his deep concern over the events he had observed that morning. Both Thompson and Lloyd, possibly in the company of other aviation company personnel, went to the B Company operations van where Thompson reported to his commanding officer, MAJ Frederic Watke. Part of the ensuing conversation was heard by SP5 Lawrence Kubert who was on duty in the van at the time.

There is some discrepancy between what WO1 Thompson believed he told his commanding officer and that which MAJ Watke in his testimony claimed he received and subsequently reported through his chain of command. WO1 Thompson stated he believed he gave MAJ Watke the complete contents of what has been referred to as the Thompson Report. Watke on the other hand acknowledged that Thompson told him of lots of "unnecessary" and "needless" killing—"principally women, children, and older men"; of the confrontation between Thompson and the ground commander; the evacuation of civilians by gunship; and the evacuation of a child to the hospital. Watke claimed no recollection of a captain (or any individual) shooting a woman; of a ditch containing bodies; any grouping of more than 2 or 3 bodies; or of any person shooting into bodies. MAJ Watke stated he thought his subordinates were "over-dramatizing" what they saw, but nevertheless gained the impression that about 30 noncombatants had been killed.

Those personnel who were present for at least part of the time that Thompson reported to Watke—CPT Lloyd and SP5 Kubert—in their testimony generally agreed with what Watke stated was told him by Thompson. Both agree that Thompson was angered, but neither could recall Thompson's mentioning anyone shooting a wounded woman, anything about a ditch containing bodies, or anyone shooting into such a ditch. They also agreed that the allegation of needless killing was clearly stated (Kubert stated the term "murder" was used) and that after Thompson had completed his report, there was a clear understanding that a serious charge had been alleged against TF Barker. It is appropriate to note that much of what MAJ Watke received from WO1 Thompson was reinforced by the complaints of other members at the time Thompson made his report and later on during the day when, according to MAJ Watke, other people who were witnesses to the events at My Lai (4) "came to me (and said) . . . that there were people killed out there."

In succeeding parts of this report, references will be made to the Thompson Report—as such, the Thompson Report is considered an outline of the experiences of WO1 Thompson from the time he arrived over My Lai (4) at 0730 hours, 16 March, until he returned to LZ Dottie to refuel at approximately 1130 hours.

4. COMMAND RESPONSE TO THE THOMPSON REPORT

At this point, there was a requirement for immediate and positive reaction to the Thompson Report. Instead, MAJ Watke stated he "thought the matter over" for 15 minutes and then went to the TF Barker TOC to report the allegation to LTC Barker. Barker was reported by Watke to have evinced no surprise at the charge—probably because he had already gained a knowledge of some of the incidents through radio transmissions and telephone calls already discussed—and advised Watke that he would look into the matter. According to Watke, LTC Barker then made arrangements to depart the area and visit the unit involved in the allegation. Watke stated he was satisfied that the matter was now in the hands of someone who could take the necessary corrective action.

Watke's subsequent actions during the afternoon of 16 March are not clear since of the three principals involved—Barker, Calhoun, and Watke—LTC Barker is deceased and MAJ Calhoun refused to testify further on the grounds that such action might be self-incriminating. Watke stated that sometime during the afternoon of the 16th, he again saw LTC Barker who advised Watke that after visiting C Company's location and speaking to people on the ground, he could not locate the individual with whom Thompson had had the confrontation. MAJ Watke testified that Barker further advised him that while a small number of noncombatants had been killed in My Lai (4), it was "a result of justifiable situations" and that Barker had found nothing to indicate that a large number of people had been killed. In considering the adequacy of MAJ Watke's subsequent actions, it should be noted that he (Watke) "didn't believe Colonel Barker."

Watke's next known action relevant to this matter came at about

2200 hours 16 March, 10 hours after Thompson had made his report. At this time, MAJ Watke at last went to his immediate superior, LTC Holladay, commander of the 123d Aviation Battalion.

It is difficult to understand why MAJ Watke, after receiving a report which he recognized as "very severe," would initially content himself with advising only the commander of the TF. While he had received considerable corroboration of Thompson's story from other personnel, it would have been a simple and logical step to have confirmed some of the allegations through low-level reconnaissance, using one of Watke's available aero-scout teams. The need for such action should have become even more apparent later in the afternoon of 16 March when LTC Barker told Watke that he had found no substance to the Thompson Report. It should have been clear to MAJ Watke, after receipt of LTC Barker's denial, that no further action would be taken unless Watke initiated it. Yet despite his belief that Barker was lying, Watke took no further action until late that night when he reported to LTC Holladay at the latter's quarters in Chu Lai.

Testimony concerning the details of the information which Watke passed to Holladay in their meeting contains some discrepancies. LTC Holladay's version of Watke's report to him on 16 March cited specific items of the Thompson Report which Watke did not recall providing him. Holladay stated that Watke informed him at that time of such things as the bodies in the ditch and the sergeant shooting into the ditch—items which Watke did not remember, but did not dispute hearing from Thompson or reporting to Holladay.

While puzzling, such discrepancies do not affect the conclusion that allegations of a major war crime were transmitted by Watke to Holladay. Both LTC Holladay and Watke agreed that Watke reported Thompson's charge that there had been lots of "unnecessary" and "needless" killing—"primarily women, children, and older men." LTC Holladay stated that he was greatly concerned over the seriousness of the matter, but after "agonizing" over the report for a long time, decided against awakening his superior, BG George Young, Assistant Division Commander.

It is difficult to understand why LTC Holladay took no steps to verify the allegations made or to obtain information first-hand from Thompson or any of the other pilots or crew members who were living at Chu Lai. This omission was to be repeated at the Assistant Division Commander and Division Commander levels and was a major reason why the full contents of the Thompson Report, and an appreciation of the enormity of the atrocity, apparently did not reach those levels of command. Until the Department of the Army investigation was initiated a year later, only MAJ Watke and COL Henderson (which will be explained in more detail later) had interviewed WO1 Thompson concerning his observations and actions on 16 March.

At 0800 the following morning, 17 March, LTC Holladay and MAJ Watke reported to the Assistant Division Commander, BG Young. MAJ Watke recounted for BG Young the allegations he had received from Thompson and other personnel of his unit. In his account of this meeting, BG Young stated that he was not apprised of any charges of indiscriminate or unnecessary killing of noncombatants; he gained the impression from MAJ Watke that the matter of major concern was the fact that there had been a confrontation between the ground forces and an aviation unit resulting from the fact that noncombatants had been caught in a cross-fire between US and VC forces. By BG Young's account, Watke made no mention of a large number of bodies in a ditch; of an individual firing into a ditch containing bodies; of a captain shooting a woman; of any reference to noncombatant casualties; or of other aviation personnel confirming Thompson's Report. LTC Holladay was equally clear that at this meeting MAJ Watke told BG Young of the allegations concerning the bodies in the ditch, the sergeant firing into the ditch, the confrontation between Thompson and a ground commander, and the excessive killing of noncombatants by TF Barker. MAJ Watke testified that he repeated to BG Young the same account he had heard from his men and related to LTC Holladay the night before, including the fact that Thompson was not the only source of the allegations.

At about noon on the same day (Sunday, 17 March), BG Young advised MG Samuel Koster, the Commanding General of the Americal Division, of the allegations he had received from the Aviation Battalion. The testimony of both MG Koster and BG Young is in general agreement that only a very small part of the Thompson Report was given to the Division Commander. In his testimony before this Inquiry, MG Koster specifically denied receiving any report of a captain shooting a woman, of bodies in a ditch, of an individual shooting into a ditch, of unnecessary killing of noncombatants, or of the fact that other aviation personnel had confirmed Thompson's allegations. MG Koster testified that as a result of the meeting, his two primary concerns were that ground troops had endangered civilians by firing more than the circumstances required, and that there had been a confrontation between ground and aviation units. However, in a previous statement given to the Criminal Investigation Division (CID), MG Koster acknowledged that during this meeting with BG Young he was advised that there had been some "indiscriminate shooting of Vietnamese civilians." In any event, the meeting terminated with MG Koster's directing BG Young to instruct COL Henderson to investigate at least two matters, i.e., the confrontation and the allegations that troops had fired more than was required.

The discrepancies in the testimony of BG Young and that of LTC Holladay and MAJ Watke as to what MAJ Watke reported to BG Young is of crucial significance in the evaluation of all that followed. In his testimony MG Koster confirmed parts of BG Young's account of their conversation on 17 March, which would tend to support BG Young's version of what MAJ Watke had reported to him that morning. On the other hand, it seems most unlikely that Holladay and Watke would have relayed a version of the Thompson Report which emphasized the confrontation between members of their unit and the ground forces and omitted mention of the indiscriminate killing of noncombatants that had caused the confrontation. Having every reason to expect that their report would initiate an immediate investigation, Holladay and Watke had no discernible reason for eliminating from the Thompson Report the allegations of indiscriminate killing of noncombatants by TF Barker when they relayed it to BG Young. The testimony of LTC Holladay and MAJ Watke, supported by all considerations of logic and self-interest of the parties, compel the conclusions: (1) that BG Young was told about Thompson's charges of indiscriminate killing of noncombatants, and (2) that BG Young passed such information on to MG Koster.

It would appear that both general officers sought in their testimony to understate the complaint of WO1 Thompson as relayed to them and to rationalize in this way their subsequent lack of affirmative action. Such a conclusion suggests that these two individuals sought to suppress the true facts concerning the events surrounding the Son My operation. The evidence indicating such suppression of information is presented in Chapter 11.

5. INDICATORS OF UNUSUAL EVENTS

During the Son My operation of 16–18 March, there were many indicators of unusual events. These should have aided in making the chain of command aware of the unusual events which transpired on 16 March. Certain of these acts were identified previously as incidents which were cited in oral and written reports submitted through the normal chain of command. There were, however, additional incidents which, when observed by or brought to the attention of experienced personnel, should have been sufficient cause to alert commanders and/or staff officers of the existence of an unusual situation. The primary purpose of this section is to identify and discuss specific incidents relevant to the Son My operation which are not treated as special subjects in other sections of the report, and which are considered to be indications of the occurrence of an unusual event. The list of indicators is not all inclusive; only those incidents are discussed which, when considered in the context of the tactical situation which existed at the time, should have caused a reaction on the part of the commander and/or staff officer.

The reaction to each specific indicator should be considered in light of an awareness or knowledge of other events or indicators by the individual concerned. As an aid in making this judgment, the following is a list of incidents which have already been discussed in this chapter of the report and are considered to have been an indication that an unusual event had occurred during the Son My operation:

1. Reports and/or Observations of Noncombatant Casualties
2. Reports of Confrontation Between WO1 Thompson and a Ground Unit Commander
3. Reports of a Captain Shooting a Wounded Woman
4. Reports of Bodies Observed in a Ditch
5. Reports of Indiscriminate/Unnecessary Firing
6. Reports of a Soldier Firing into a Ditch Containing Bodies
7. Reports of Helicopter Gunships and Scout Ship Landing in My Lai (4)
8. Reports of Complaints by WO1 Thompson and other Aviation Personnel

In addition there were incidents not previously identified which indicate the occurrence of an unusual event in Son My. Such incidents or indicators are listed in chronological sequence and are followed by a discussion of each indicator to include information concerning the reaction of commanders and staff officers at each level of command:

1. Artillery Planned and Fired on My Lai (4)
2. Gunships and Liftships Fire on My Lai (4)
3. The Exodus of Civilians
4. Observation of Burning Buildings
5. Initial Report of High VC Body Count
6. Report of High VC Body Count Attributed to Artillery Fire
7. Low Ratio of Weapons Captured to VC KIA
8. Absence of Reports of Enemy Contact and Requests for Fire Support
9. Report of Departure of VC from My Lai (4)
10. Low Ratio of US Casualties to VC Casualties
11. Commander's Order to Return to My Lai (4)

a. Artillery Planned and Fired on My Lai (4)

One of the first indications that the Son My operation was to be conducted without regard to the welfare of noncombatants is in the planning of artillery support for the combat assault of C/1–20 Inf. From the outset, it was planned for artillery fire to fall on or alongside the inhabited hamlet of My Lai (4). LTC Luper, the artillery battalion commander; MAJ Calhoun, TF Barker S3, CPT Vazquez, the artillery liaison officer with TF Barker; and CPT Medina, the C Company commander, all agreed that it was part of LTC Barker's plan for the artillery preparation for the combat assault to land on the edge of the hamlet. While such action was within the legal limits of the rules of engagement (ROE) in effect at that time, it was clearly in violation of the spirit of the policy and without regard for the lives of the inhabitants of My Lai (4).

The hamlet of My Lai (4) was located in an area identified as under VC domination and control. Clearance to fire was obtained from Vietnamese authorities after a check on their part revealed no Vietnamese military units operating in the area. No check was made or assurance given that noncombatants were not present in the area. For all practical purposes, Province and District authorities regarded Son My Village as a free-fire zone and would approve any request for fire if Army Republic of Vietnam (ARVN) units or personnel were not endangered. This was known by LTC Barker and his staff.

The inhabitants of VC-dominated areas, such as My Lai (4) were frequently encouraged through Government of Vietnam (GVN) and US efforts to evacuate these areas since they were subject to unannounced fires by artillery and air. It was known, however, that many persons elected or were forced to accept the risks attendant in remaining and thus there were villages and hamlets such as My Lai (4) where relatively large numbers of persons, both willingly and unwillingly, lived in VC-controlled areas. This principle was recognized in MACV Directive 525–3 (exhibit D–6) which states that personnel living in VC-controlled areas will not be considered VC solely on the basis of their presence in these areas.

While MG Koster and COL Henderson both stated it was not their policy to employ artillery on inhabited villages, the facts of 16 March reveal little in the way of controls to prevent such incidents. Even if one were to assume ignorance on the part of 11th Brigade personnel concerning knowledge that My Lai (4) was populated—an assumption not borne out in fact—such an assumption was clearly destroyed when, after the artillery preparation was completed, large groups of people were seen departing the village by all of the commanders directly concerned with the operation: CPT Medina, MAJ Watke, LTC Barker, LTC Luper, and COL Henderson. Concurrently, with the observation of civilian casualties on the ground by each of these same individuals, less MAJ Watke, when denied seeing civilian casualties, it should have been apparent that US firepower had inflicted casualties among the noncombatants in My Lai (4). Despite these observations, no action was taken to provide relief or assistance to the noncombatant casualties nor was any significant effort initiated to determine the extent of such casualties until much later in the day when COL Henderson directed TF Barker to send C Company back through My Lai (4) to determine the exact nature of noncombatant casualties. This belated effort was stopped by MG Koster who countermanded the order of COL Henderson, at a time when he already had knowledge that at least "20 to 28" noncombatants had been killed.

B. Gunships and Liftships Fire on My Lai (4)

Another early indicator that commanders in the Son My operation disregarded the safety and welfare of noncombatants is the fact that the firepower of available helicopters was used freely and in some cases indiscriminately in and around the inhabited hamlet of My Lai (4).

CPT Medina stated that as the liftships made their approach to the LZ, the gunships were firing suppressive fire, utilizing 40mm grenades, 2.75 inch rockets, and 5.56mm "miniguns," on both sides of the LZ. As the liftships came in, the door gunners on the outside of the "V" fired M–60 machineguns in suppressive fire directly into the hamlet until the helicopters touched down. Many of the troops on the first lift corroborated CPT Medina's testimony.

LT (now Mr.) Alaux (the artillery forward observer attached to the company) stated that gunships fired "into the trees and the hootches" along the outskirts of the hamlet using rockets and miniguns. Alaux testified that at least one of the bodies he observed had been killed by miniguns.

CPT Vazquez indicated that the gunships fired along the sides of the LZ and on the outskirts of the hamlet, but he did not believe they fired directly into the hamlet itself.

WO1 Hugh Thompson stated that he observed gunships accompanying the liftships "shooting it up pretty good." He also observed these same gunships "working over" the area where he later observed numerous Vietnamese casualties.

A tape recording made by CPT Lewellen in the TF Barker TOC reveals that LTC Barker ordered "no restrictions on door gunners" which had the effect of permitting them to fire suppressive fires into the hamlet of My Lai (4) on the final approach to the LZ.

As was the case in the indiscriminate use of artillery, a knowledge of the planned or actual use of helicopter firepower in support of the Son My operation, despite its tactical desirability, carried with it the awareness that the operation was being conducted with an unusual disregard for the safety of noncombatants. Even again assuming an ignorance of the inhabited status of My Lai (4) prior to the operation—and such an assumption cannot be substantiated—such ignorance was dispelled when people commenced departing My Lai (4) in large numbers, immediately following the landing of US troops.

Again, as was the case in the use of artillery fire, commanders did not react when faced with the knowledge that noncombatant casualties had been unnecessarily caused by US firepower.

c. THE EXODUS OF CIVILIANS

Another early indication that the Son My operation was not a normal, routine, combat assault occurred shortly after the artillery preparation at C Company's LZ terminated. At this point, the area in the vicinity of My Lai (4) which was to be clear of all "friendly inhabitants" by 0730, suddenly became the scene of a mass exodus of personnel. COL Henderson, aboard his command and control helicopter with LTC (now COL) Luper and the 11th Brigade S3, MAJ McKnight, observed approximately 300 Vietnamese exiting the hamlet of My Lai (4) along Route 521.

According to the tape recording of a portion of the radio transmissions made during the operation on the morning of 16 March, LTC Barker was informed by the 174th Aviation Company gunships commander that most of the Vietnamese in the group moving along the route "look like women and children and farmers." There is no indication that LTC Barker admonished CPT Medina to exercise caution at this time because there were noncombatants in the operational area, contrary to the intelligence given him earlier in the operations order.

CPT Vazquez, who was accompanying LTC Barker on his command and control helicopter, noted that many villagers evacuated the hamlet after the gunships had expended their suppressive ordnance around the LZ. He also noted the bodies of Vietnamese in an area where the gunships had made a firing run.

MAJ Watke observed the exodus while flying as copilot on one of the gunships, and participated in the screening of the Vietnamese from the air.

It is clear that at this point in the Son My operation it should have been apparent to commanders from the platoon to the brigade level that something had gone wrong in the operation. The fire support plan for the assault at My Lai (4) was based on an assumption that the hamlet would either be occupied by the 48th Local Force (LF) Battalion or uninhabited; the events described in the preceding paragraphs establish that this assumption relating to the absence of inhabitants was false and that noncombatants had been killed. Except for the reported admonition by COL Henderson at about 0900 hours that he did not "want any unnecessary killing going on down there"—an order COL Henderson specifically denied issuing—all commanders concerned apparently elected to ignore the situation.

D. Observation of Burning Buildings

During the Son My operation on 16 March, many individuals noticed burning buildings in the My Lai (4) hamlet complex. According to COL Henderson's testimony, he observed several buildings burning while he was orbiting over the operational area in his command and control helicopter. He contacted LTC Barker to ascertain the reason for the burnings and Barker, in turn, contacted CPT Medina on the ground and posed the question to him. LTC Barker, after his call to CPT Medina, then informed COL Henderson that the structures were being destroyed by the Vietnamese National Police who were accompanying Company C on the operation. (In fact, there were no National Police with Company C at this time.) The National Police had reportedly found "weapons, or hand grenades, or ammunition, or items of military equipment" in the houses and were burning them for this reason. COL Henderson stated he then informed LTC Barker that any National Police accompanying TF Barker forces fell under his (Barker's) operational control and ordered LTC Barker to have the burning of structures stopped immediately because "we had no authority to burn houses." Although COL Henderson claimed to have taken action to halt the burning of structures, there is considerable evidence in the testimony by members of Company C that the burning of hamlets continued throughout the remainder of the operation.

It is clear that, once again, commanders from the platoon to the brigade level witnessed the occurrence of incidents which were in themselves illegal, but even more important in the instant case, were yet another indication that elements of TF Barker were engaged in an unusual operation. While MG Koster and COL Henderson in their appearance before this Inquiry both maintained the existence of a firm policy against the burning of Vietnamese structures, this policy was patently ineffective in TF Barker on 16 March.

E. Initial Report of High Viet Cong Body Count

Another indication of the unusual nature of events at My Lai (4) is the report concerning casualties inflicted against the enemy force. Within 70 minutes of its touchdown, C Company had reported 90 VC killed in its area of operation. Such reports could be expected to reflect a high degree of satisfaction in the success of TF Barker and could logically expect to cause inquiries concerning tactics used, enemy units encountered, and similar requests for information. It is essential to note that this apparently resounding success passed with no substantive inquiry by commanders at task force, brigade, or division level—this despite the fact that all three were in the area for varying lengths of time on the morning of 16 March. There is little to explain why none of these three commanders ever landed in the immediate vicinity of My Lai (4) or observed what should have been readily apparent to anyone overflying the area at less than 1,000 feet.

The minimum command reaction to the initial report of high VC casualties should have included inquiry concerning location and size of enemy force, unit identification, and the possibility of exploitation. There is no evidence that any such inquiry was made.

F. REPORT OF HIGH VIET CONG BODY COUNT ATTRIBUTED TO ARTILLERY FIRE

At 0840 hours, 16 March, TF Barker personnel recorded in their operations journal that C Company had "counted 69 VC KIA" at a location which is almost the center of the hamlet of My Lai (4). This same entry states that the 11th Brigade was advised of this information. However, the Brigade Journal reflects no information concerning this subject until 55 minutes later when the location is shifted to a point over 600 meters northwest of the original site and the cause of death is stated as "artillery fire." This same information is recorded in the Americal Division Journal at 0940 hours and notes that the G2, G3, CofS, and III MAF have been notified. The delay in reporting this information, the significant change in location, and the identification of artillery fire as the cause of death have not been satisfactorily explained. While the truth of the report is certainly in question, the fact remains that shortly after 0940 hours, 16 March, every headquarters in the chain of command from TF Barker to III MAF was aware of the report that artillery fire had killed 69 VC in the Son My operation.

Testimony of all personnel concerned with the Son My operation reveals that this report of outstanding artillery success caused little reaction among either artillery or infantry commanders. The artillery battalion commander, LTC Luper, stated that he received notice of these casualties about 0930 hours, 16 March, while flying aboard COL Henderson's helicopter and after he had seen 15–20 bodies, a number of which were women and children, located on the road south of My Lai (4). When questioned concerning his reaction to this matter, LTC Luper stated that he did not check into it further since he considered it a "normal operation" and that the killing of 69 VC in an artillery preparation of 100 rounds is not unusual "if you are fortunate enough to catch the enemy in the open." There is nothing to indicate that LTC Luper or any other person either saw or received a report of VC in the open. To the contrary, LTC Luper's suspicions should have been aroused when the first large group of people he observed was approximately 50 civilians departing the area of My Lai (4) immediately following the artillery preparation on a village which he had believed was "not populated." Despite the fact that

LTC Luper knew that women and children had been killed in this operation, and by his own admission, he was aware of the fact that 20 civilians were reported killed by "artillery and/or gunships," Luper made no effort to determine if artillery from his unit had killed noncombatants nor did he question his artillery liaison officer (LNO) at TF Barker, the artillery forward observer with the rifle company in My Lai (4), or the artillery battery commander concerning this matter.

It would appear that the single positive action in response to the high casualty count attributed to artillery was taken by COL Henderson. While COL Henderson indicated his order to turn C Company around and return to My Lai (4) occurred 2 days later, there is little doubt that this occurred on the afternoon of 16 March. In COL Henderson's words, he was "suspicious of the body count" and "didn't believe it was correct, particularly the artillery fire." While there is some question concerning MG Koster's knowledge of the report of 69 VC KIA by artillery at the time he countermanded this order, there is no question that he was, at that time, aware of the fact that from "20 to 28" noncombatants had been killed in My Lai (4), and that the VC body count had reached 128.

G. Low Ratio of Weapons Captured to Viet Cong Killed in Action (VC KIA)

Another fact concerning the Son My operation of TF Barker which indicated an operation of an unusual nature was the paucity of captured weapons experienced by TF Barker. While the TF had a generally low ratio of weapons captured to VC KIA—it averaged approximately 1 to 10—the ratio of less than 1 to 40 experienced on 16 March should have caused some inquiry. The combined effect of many small incidents related to this low ratio and the general nature of the operation reported by TF Barker on 16 March was sufficient cause for considerable concern and suspicion.

On 15 March the brigade commander visited TF Barker and, in discussing the Son My operation with the assembled commanders and staff officers of TF Barker, made the subject of capturing enemy weapons a matter of primary concern. COL Henderson stated he advised all concerned that they should make a much greater effort to improve their performance in regard to capturing and recovering enemy weapons. Yet on the following day, when the enemy was purportedly caught by surprise in large numbers, the number of weapons captured dropped to a token figure. Again COL Henderson's "suspicions" concerning body count appear to have been well founded. What is difficult to understand is that no such "suspicions" existed at division level. The most cursory analysis of TF Barker's operation of 16 March would have revealed inconsistencies which, as a minimum, dictated a need for guidance from senior commanders. First, there were 90 enemy reported killed in a period of 70 minutes—69 of which had been killed by an artillery preparation lasting only 5 minutes and which was followed immediately by a combat assault of one rifle company. No further enemy contact was reported by this company for the remainder of the day and yet no command attention was placed on the fact that the unit had not only failed to exploit its initial success, but also had failed to police the battlefield. Either that conclusion must be drawn or the alternate and more logical conclusion must be examined, viz., unarmed casualties were being identified as VC. The logic of this latter thesis should have been apparent to those who flew in the vicinity of My Lai (4) and observed the large number of people evacuating the area along Route 521. As previously noted, commanders who did overfly the area that morning included: MAJ Watke, LTC Barker, COL Henderson, and MG Koster.

H. ABSENCE OF REPORTS OF ENEMY CONTACT AND REQUESTS FOR FIRE SUPPORT

One of the most significant facts to emerge from an examination of events of 16 March 1968 concerning TF Barker is the almost total absence of reports of enemy contact. Except for a single radio report by an unidentified liftship or gunship pilot during the initial landing of C Company, not one member of TF Barker reported any exchange of fire on 16 March.

Commencing at 0735 hours elements of TF Barker reported killing VC; reports of enemy casualties continued to be received until 1420 hours. Not a single journal entry at the TF Barker or 11th Brigade reflects any enemy contact or activity except reports of enemy killed.* During the course of this Inquiry, no individual was encountered who could recall enemy contact on 16 March, other than a few isolated reports

* A search of Americal Division files by an investigation team from the Office of the Provost Marshal General (OPMG) in Oct 1969 discovered what purported to be a carbon copy of the Division Journal for 16 March 1968 (exhibit M–138). The copy was found in the Division Historian's files, the original reportedly having been forwarded to the USARV records holding area.

A search of the USARV Adjutant General's files in November 1969 uncovered a purported record copy of the 16 March 1968 Americal Division Journal which contains one substantive difference when compared with the carbon copy. In the carbon copy there is an item #94, a 2400 hours summary item concerning TF Barker which reads: "Heavy combat resulted in the area and continued until approximately 1500 hours." This sentence does not appear in the record copy uncovered at USARV, although the journal in general, and item #94 in particular, are essentially the same in all other respects.

This difference raises suspicions which have not been satisfactorily explained. An investigation of the matter is being conducted by OPMG.

of sniper fire, nor could any recall requests for supporting fires which would normally have been required when enemy contact was made.*

After the artillery preparation was fired, no supporting fires were requested—no tactical air, no gunships, no artillery—a most unusual occurrence in the Vietnam conflict where contact with the enemy is typified by a heavy reliance on supporting fire.

Equally difficult to comprehend is the absence of inquiry from commanders at the brigade and division level for information concerning current operations. As the situation was reported on 16 March, a battalion-size task force was engaged in a highly successful operation, yet there were no reports being forwarded outside the TF concerning anything except final results. Even the most cursory inquiry by a senior commander concerning type of opposition, location of enemy, unit identification of VC KIA, nature or size of enemy force, would have revealed the existence of a highly unusual situation requiring a more detailed study. As a minimum, an inquiry should have been made as to the reasons for success and its tactical and intelligence significance.

It is also appropriate to note at this point that the unique nature of combat operations in Vietnam creates an immediate high level of communications activity when contact is made with an enemy force. Radio networks suddenly come alive with a continuing series of messages; supporting arms are employed via radio; helicopter assists are controlled by radio; and higher headquarters are either kept advised of developments through radio messages or inquiries begin to flow to subordinate units. In the case of TF Barker on 16 March, the sense of urgency and closeness of combat which follows from this communications activity could not have existed in the absence of request for supporting fires. To the experienced combat commander, this absence of activity and lack of enemy contact could not be equated with the success being reported by TF Barker.

I. Reports of Departure of VC from My Lai (4)

As has been previously stated, the Son My operation was planned by the 11th Brigade and TF Barker to destroy 48th LF Battalion. Witnesses testified that at the brigade and task force level, intelligence indicated

* It has not escaped the Inquiry's attention that statements supporting recommendations for a posthumous award to SP4 Glenn W. Andreotta (exhibit M–42) and awards to WO1 Thompson (exhibit M–44) and SP4 Lawrence M. Colburn (exhibit M–43) for their performances on 16 March 1968 referred to hostile fire or crossfire in the area of My Lai (4); nor that certain of these recommendations were signed or indorsed by MAJ Watke and LTC Holladay. Such references to enemy action on 16 March are entirely inconsistent with the evidence before this Inquiry including the testimony given by these individuals. It is recognized that the desire to give recognition to personnel in a combat environment sometimes leads to certain liberties being taken in the description of the attendant conditions.

this enemy battalion was located in and near the hamlet of My Lai (4). Assuming such intelligence was valid—and there is a preponderance of the evidence to indicate it was not—the high VC body count reported by TF Barker on 16 March 1968 should not have caused any great surprise among commanders and staff officers in the 11th Brigade.

In view of the intelligence basis for the Son My operation, there should have been suspicions aroused when, early in the operation, it was discovered that the VC had, in fact, left the area before the operation commenced! At 0900 hours the 11th Brigade recorded in its journal a report received from Barker TOC to the effect that information obtained from inhabitants of My Lai (4) revealed that "30–40 VC had departed the area at 0700 hours. . . ." The journal entry also states that both the brigade S2 and S3 were notified of this fact—the brigade S3 at this time was the brigade commander at LZ Dottie.

LT (now CPT) Johnson, the Military Intelligence (MI) officer who accompanied C Company in the field on 16 March, testified that after landing in My Lai (4) and interrogating village inhabitants, he learned that "the VC had departed the village prior to the combat assault."

LT Alaux, the C Company forward observer (FO) stated in his testimony he recalled receiving information that interrogation of a Vietnamese in My Lai (4) had revealed information that an enemy platoon had been in the village but had departed just prior to the operation.

From the foregoing, it is evident that by 0915 hours, at least the commander of C Company (who is the most probable source of the report which originated with LT Johnson and was transmitted through TF Barker TOC to the 11th Brigade TOC); the commander, S2 and S3 of TF Barker; and the commander, S2 and S3 of the 11th Brigade were all aware of this significant report. Journal entries at the Americal Division do not reflect this information and MG Koster testified that he does not recall receiving such a report.

At the same time these officers possessed information concerning this intelligence report, they were also cognizant of the report of high VC body count, the low ratio of weapons captured to VC killed, the absence of reports of enemy contact, and many of the other "indicators" which have been discussed in this chapter. What is difficult to understand is why none of the officers—especially those in the intelligence field—acted on this information. If the VC had left the hamlet, who were the people C Company had reported killing? To what unit did the "30–40" VC belong? Where did they go—and a host of other questions all required answers. Yet apparently none of the commanders or staff officers asked these questions, sought additional information, or connected this report with other information they had concerning the unique nature of the Son My operation.

As stated previously, the Americal Division Operations Journal for

16 March 1968 does not reflect this report of 30–40 VC departing My Lai (4). It does, however, contain entries concerning the Vietnamese personnel who were detained by C/1–20 Inf at that time. One significant entry concerning the only status that this individual reports "lots of VC" at the map coordinates which coincide with those recorded in the 11th Brigade Journal as the location at which C Company interrogated the Vietnamese detainees. The significance of this erroneous and/or altered report is discussed in Chapter 11.

J. Low Ratio of United States Casualties to Viet Cong Casualties

One fact which should have become increasingly evident to commanders as the events at Son My unfolded on 16 March 1968, especially in the C Company area. By 1030 hours, TF Barker had reported a total of 120 VC killed and 13 US casualties—2 KIA, 10 WIA, and 1 self-inflicted wound. Of the 12 casualties caused by enemy contact, that one individual was shot by enemy small arms fire in the area of A/3–1 Inf. On the surface, this ratio of 10 to 1 might be considered the result of a highly successful operation. However, when consideration is given to the fact that C Company, which accounted for 84 VC casualties in 70 minutes, experienced only one casualty, a self-inflicted wound, there is cause for inquiry.

An awareness at the company and TF level of the details concerning US casualties is presumed because of the involvement of commanders in medical evacuation procedures and similar actions requiring radio transmissions. As a minimum, the commanders at these levels, if they were not aware of the true conditions at My Lai (4), should have been making efforts to determine what tactics and/or procedures were causing such remarkable success. It is clear that any such probing would probably have revealed the true events which had transpired in My Lai (4).

At the 11th Brigade level, COL Henderson acknowledged that he was suspicious of the C Company body count and ordered C Company back through My Lai (4) to resolve the matter. Yet when the order was countermanded by MG Koster, COL Henderson took no further action to allay his suspicions until directed to investigate WO1 Thompson's allegations 2 days later.

At the Americal Division headquarters, knowledge of a better than 10 to 1 ratio of VC casualties was known not later than the evening briefing of 16 March. Taken at face value and viewed in isolation from other information, these statistics reflected an outstanding tactical success on the part of TF Barker and 11th Brigade. This conclusion is reflected in the congratulatory message which was sent to the Americal Division by Commander, United States Military Assistance Command, Vietnam (COMUSMACV) as a result of receiving a statistical summary of the Son

My operation. That such a conclusion could be reached at the Americal Division headquarters is not as readily understood. By the time the 16 March evening briefing was conducted and an announcement made concerning friendly casualties, the following additional information had also been provided to the division commander:

1. Approximately 20–28 noncombatant casualties had occurred in the C/1–20 Inf area of operations.
2. The 11th Brigade Commander had indicated his concern over irregularities in My Lai (4) to the extent of directing a rifle company to retrace its steps.

Information concerning these items was not transmitted outside the Americal Division.

K. COMMANDER'S ORDER TO RETURN TO MY LAI (4)

Of all the events which transpired on 16 March, the one which most clearly indicated that something had gone wrong in the Son My operation was the order issued by COL Henderson to have C Company return through My Lai (4) to count civilian casualties and to determine the age, sex, and cause of death of each. Issued to TF Barker at about 1530 hours, it was transmitted to CPT Medina and almost immediately countermanded by MG Koster. Although both MG Koster and COL Henderson believed that this order was given on 18 March, the preponderance of the testimony and the surrounding circumstances established that the order was given on 16 March.

COL Henderson testified that at the time he gave the order he was aware of from "12 to 14" civilian casualties, which had been reported to him by LTC Barker, and that he was "suspicious" of the 128 body count because the number of weapons captured (3) was too low. He stated that he directed LTC Barker to have a company return to My Lai (4) to examine the bodies to determine the exact number of noncombatant casualties, by sex, age group, and apparent cause of death. He also stated that LTC Barker then suggested that C Company should return to make the count since they were more familiar with the area and because they knew where the bodies were.

Both CPT Medina, the company commander, and MAJ Calhoun, the TF S3, agreed in their testimony that this command to return to My Lai (4) was relayed to CPT Medina by MAJ Calhoun over the radio; and that CPT Medina contested the order because of the late hour and the possibility of mines and boobytraps; that CPT Medina reported 20 to 28 civilian casualties had occurred during the operation; and that MG Koster broke into the series of transmissions and countermanded the order.

MG Koster did not recall talking to either MAJ Calhoun or CPT Medina but stated that he believed his conversation over the radio was with LTC Barker. He further stated that he knew at the time he countermanded the order that at least 20 noncombatant casualties had been reported, and that the purpose of the order to return to My Lai (4) was to recount the noncombatant casualties and determine the cause of death. According to MG Koster, he based his decision to countermand the order on the mines and boobytraps reportedly infesting the area, the late hour, his feeling that the cause of death probably could not be determined accurately by the soldiers, and the shortage of helicopters. MG Koster decided to countermand the order despite the fact that he knew there had been at least 20 noncombatants reported killed during the operation, and that the brigade commander was apparently concerned enough about these casualties to order a return to My Lai (4) for the purpose of determining the number of and the reason for these casualties. MG Koster contended that his action did not preclude COL Henderson's sending the unit back the following day. In countermanding the order he specifically directed LTC Barker to insure that COL Henderson was advised of the action.

The point in issue is not whether the order should have been countermanded, but rather, that the issuance of the order itself should have been a signal to MG Koster that one of his senior subordinate commanders suspected something had gone awry. The fact that CPT Medina advised MG Koster of 20–28 civilian casualties should have acted to reinforce that suspicion or to cause MG Koster to consider a substitute course of action; available testimony indicates it did neither.

6. INITIAL INVESTIGATION AND REVIEW

As a result of instructions received from MG Koster to have COL Henderson initiate an investigation of WO1 Thompson's allegations, BG Young after departing MG Koster's office on 17 March, made arrangements for a meeting of the five principals in the chain of command who were involved: himself, COL Henderson, LTC Barker, LTC Holladay, and MAJ Watke. The meeting was inexplicably not scheduled until 0900 hours the following day, 18 March. However, BG Young did make a visit to LZ Dottie on the afternoon of 17 March and, according to MAJ Calhoun, was briefed by him.

MG Koster testified that on the afternoon of 17 March he too went to LZ Dottie and spoke to LTC Barker concerning the allegations of WO1 Thompson. MG Koster stated that Barker advised him that either he or MAJ Calhoun had been over the area of My Lai (4) throughout the morning of 16 March and that they had not witnessed or heard of any irregularities. MG Koster stated that Barker gave him every assurance that the incident alleged by Thompson had not taken place.

During the initial phase of this Inquiry, considerable disagreement was experienced among witnesses concerning the time and date of this meeting arranged by BG Young. It was finally fixed after MAJ Watke produced a series of letters written to his wife and dated 16, 17, and 18 March 1968. The last of these letters made specific reference to this meeting and established the date as 18 March.

On the morning of the meeting, the five officers concerned met at TF Barker's Command Post at LZ Dottie at about 0900 hours. BG Young stated that he met with the group only briefly, addressing himself primarily to COL Henderson and repeating the allegation as understood by BG Young, i.e., that there had been a confrontation between personnel of TF Barker and Company B, 123d Aviation Battalion and that forces of TF Barker had fired into noncombatant civilians while engaging an enemy force. Young advised Henderson of the Division Commander's directive to conduct an immediate investigation and to report the results to MG Koster as soon as possible. BG Young stated that without waiting to hear any explanation of the allegations by Watke or Holladay, he departed LZ Dottie. While such action is possible, it seems quite unusual if not unlikely that an Assistant Division Commander, having been charged by his Commanding General with the task of directing a brigade commander to initiate an investigation, would depart before he was reasonably sure that the brigade commander understood the mission. The contention that BG Young remained at Dottie for more than a few minutes is supported by entries in the TF Barker Journal which indicate that BG Young spent a total of 20 minutes at LZ Dottie at this time.

LTC Holladay recalled the incident as a brief introduction by BG Young and a complete recitation of the Thompson Report by MAJ Watke. MAJ Watke agreed in his testimony that he presented an explanation in the presence of BG Young which was the same in content as his two previous recitations of the event.

COL Henderson related the events of 18 March as commencing with an encounter at LZ Dottie with the Executive Officer of Company B, 123d Aviation Battalion, MAJ (now Mr.) Wilson, who introduced WO1 Thompson as an individual with a serious matter to report. According to Henderson, Thompson then described the events of "extremely wild shooting" by troops and helicopters; troops shooting at everything that moved; of having seen "a lot of civilian bodies on the ground" and an incident where a captain shot a unarmed and wounded female civilian. COL Henderson further stated that within an hour of this meeting with Thompson and Wilson, the meeting with BG Young took place during which the confrontation between the helicopter pilot and ground troops and other incidents which occurred on 16 March was discussed. MAJ Wilson stated that he had no knowledge of taking WO1 Thompson to LZ Dottie to see COL Henderson on any occasion and denies any knowledge of the event related by COL Henderson.

Once again, after considering all available evidence, it appears that the events as related by LTC Holladay and MAJ Watke represent the most probable occurrences of that time. BG Young's contention that he merely summarized the allegations of WO1 Thompson and then departed, is refuted by the testimony of Watke and Holladay and is incompatible with the conduct that would be normal for a general officer under the circumstances.

There is general agreement that the exchange of information between WO1 Thompson and COL Henderson did not occur before the meeting with BG Young but took place after that event. The previous paragraph provides a summary of COL Henderson's version of the meeting between these two individuals which is in substantive conflict with WO1 Thompson's recollection that he told COL Henderson all the details of the incident at My Lai (4) in an interview which took from 20 to 30 minutes. COL Henderson also stated that he spoke to no other pilot or crewmen concerning this matter. However, MAJ Watke stated he sent three individuals to see him. There is testimony by WO1 Thompson, SP4 Colburn, and CWO Culverhouse that each of these individuals was interviewed by COL Henderson and that each provided him detailed information concerning the incidents which occurred at My Lai (4) on the morning of 16 March.

It is significant to note that during these interviews, none of the individuals was placed under oath nor were any statements reduced to writing; records of the event were limited to notes COL Henderson made in a small green notebook which was subsequently destroyed.

While there is some evidence to indicate that two of these individuals may have spoken to "another colonel at LZ Dottie" other than COL Henderson, there is little doubt concerning the extent of COL Henderson's knowledge at this point in time. There is no other evidence to show that there was another officer in the grade of Colonel at LZ Dottie on that day. All available evidence confirms the fact that not later than the morning of 18 March, COL Henderson was in receipt of all allegations contained in the Thompson Report; that these allegations had been presented to him by at least one and probably three eyewitnesses; and that he was aware of the existence of many more possible eyewitnesses.

There are other inconsistencies in COL Henderson's testimony at this point, but for the purpose of continuing with a presentation of facts concerning the chain of events following My Lai (4), it is sufficient to state that following the meeting at LZ Dottie, BG Young departed with the understanding that COL Henderson was to undertake a prompt and thorough investigation into the allegation made by WO1 Thompson concerning the operations of TF Barker on 16 March 1968.

A brief summary reveals the following significant facts which emerge at this point: first, COL Henderson had been charged with investigating events which actually represent only a part of what happened at My Lai (4); second, COL Henderson was aware of a disparity between the allegation he was charged with investigating and the dimensions of the events which had been observed and described by eyewitnesses; and finally and most significantly, COL Henderson may well have concluded that MG Koster and BG Young were not aware that extensive killing of noncombatants had occurred on 16 March 1968. It is in the context of this knowledge that COL Henderson's subsequent actions will be considered.

As previously mentioned, there is disagreement concerning both the sequence of events as they occurred on the morning of 18 March and the substance of the information discussed by personnel interviewed by COL Henderson. For the purpose of relating later events, it is sufficient at this point to state that on the morning of the meeting with BG Young at LZ Dottie, COL Henderson also met with WO1 Thompson and, as a result of this meeting, flew directly to the field location of C Company to speak to CPT Medina about the Thompson allegation. CPT Medina explained the shooting incident to COL Henderson's satisfaction—a matter of self-defense—but could not satisfy COL Henderson's requirements for detailed information concerning noncombatant casualties. CPT Medina explained at this point that he had seen "between 20 and 28" civilian casualties. COL Henderson contended in his testimony that it was at this point that he alerted C Company to a possible requirement to move back through My Lai (4) to conduct a count of all noncombatant casualties. COL Henderson stated that he issued the order for such a move shortly after the meeting, and after discussing the matter with LTC Barker. The evidence to refute this contention is overwhelming and it is clear that such an order was issued on the afternoon of 16 March.

There is agreement in the testimony of Henderson and Medina that the substance of this meeting concerned the incident of Medina's shooting the wounded woman and a discussion concerning noncombatant casualties and the body count of 128 VC KIA. No mention was made of such incidents as the confrontation, the bodies in the ditch, or the firing into the ditch.

In his testimony, LTC (now ret.) Blackledge stated that he especially recalled this meeting because of the subject matter discussed and the extent to which COL Henderson questioned Medina. Blackledge stated he had not been advised of the purpose of the meeting and observed that Henderson pursued the matter of civilian casualties to a point that Blackledge considered a "little unusual" and in a matter which seemed to be investigative. It is significant to note that this constituted the only meeting of COL Henderson with CPT Medina at which the subject of Thompson's allegations was discussed. Again, as was the case in the interviews with aviation unit personnel, no oaths were administered nor were statements reduced to writing.

The next step of COL Henderson's "inquiry" involved a visit with troops of C Company as they deplaned on the afternoon of 18 March at LZ Dottie. COL Henderson assembled a group of 30 to 40 soldiers primarily from the 1st and 2d Platoons of C Company who had just debarked from helicopters. After complimenting them on their performance during the previous few days, he told them that there had been some "unsubstantiated reports that we had killed some noncombatants" and then asked the group if any of them had any knowledge of "anybody killing civilians during this operation." COL Henderson testified that the response to this was silence and he then directed his comments to specific individuals, saying: "How about you?" and pointing to an individual or small group. The response in each case, COL Henderson stated, was a "loud and clear, 'No sir!' " This totally meaningless action constituted the entire effort by COL Henderson to interrogate members of Company C. Testimony by individuals who were present during COL Henderson's interrogation of this group revealed that, in at least one case, when addressed individually by COL Henderson, a sergeant responded to his question concerning possible irregularities during the My Lai (4) operation with "no comment" but, inexplicably, he was not questioned further.

COL Henderson stated that he then departed LZ Dottie and returned to his headquarters at Duc Pho and either at that time, or after the evening briefing on 18 March, spoke to MAJ Gibson, CO, 174th Aviation Company. COL Henderson related that he advised MAJ Gibson of the allegations made by WO1 Thompson concerning wild shooting and killing of civilian noncombatants and asked MAJ Gibson to survey all of his pilots who had participated in this operation to determine if any of them could provide further information. COL Henderson further stated that after the evening briefing on either the 18th or 19th of March at brigade headquarters, he called MAJ Gibson aside and asked for his report. According to Henderson, Gibson replied that he had spoken to each of the pilots who had been involved in the My Lai operation and that "not a single one of them observed any noncombatants being killed nor were any (174th) gunships out of control. . . ." MAJ Gibson denied that he was ever requested to provide the information and that he made such a report to Henderson.

Except for COL Henderson's claim of an 18 March visual reconnaissance over the village of My Lai (4) in which field glasses were used to aid in observation, the aforementioned actions constitute the total effort expended in the initial inquiry by COL Henderson. It should be noted that at no time during COL Henderson's "inquiry" was there ever an effort made to put people on the ground at My Lai (4) or even to make a meaningful reconnaissance of the area. In summary, COL Henderson's investigative efforts, by his own account, were completed not later than the evening hours of 18 March except for the report he had purportedly requested from MAJ Gibson.

COL Henderson testified that on 19 March he advised BG Young of the people to whom he had spoken and the negative findings he had reached and was advised by BG Young to make his report to MG Koster on 20 March.

COL Henderson stated that on the morning of 20 March he reported to the Chief of Staff of the Americal Division, COL Parson, advising him of the purpose of the meeting and then, before completing the substance of the report, was ushered in to see MG Koster. COL Parson was unable to shed additional light on this matter since he stated he could not recall the incident. COL Henderson stated that his oral report was submitted with no witnesses present. He recounted that he commenced his discussion by first advising the Commanding General that the total number of civilian casualties reported by TF Barker for 16 March was 20. He then proceeded to advise MG Koster that reports of indiscriminate killing were not substantiated; that CPT Medina had been able to provide a satisfactory explanation for the shooting of the wounded female; that the matter of the confrontation had been "put to bed" with the re-establishment of a rapport between MAJ Watke and LTC Barker; and that after completing the inquiry, WO1 Thompson was the only individual COL Henderson could find who could allege that "something" happened in My Lai (4).

COL Henderson stated that MG Koster then replied that Henderson's report had already been discussed with him by BG Young, that he wanted to discuss it once more with BG Young and he gave Henderson no further instructions. COL Henderson stated that he also mentioned to MG Koster the incident of the latter's countermanding his order to move C Company back through My Lai (4) but that MG Koster's response to this matter indicated "disinterest" and a tendency to minimize the importance of any information which might have been obtained as a result of the operation. COL Henderson then departed to await further developments.

MG Koster testified that he received this initial report in a series of conversations; some with BG Young who relayed interim reports from COL Henderson, and the remainder as direct discussions with Henderson. MG Koster did not recall a meeting in which the entire report was presented as a "single wrap-up." However, his recollection of the substance of all the conversations is in general agreement with what Henderson testified that he presented in his 20 March report, MG Koster's testimony is in general agreement with that of BG Young who also recalled that Henderson's report was a series of conversations with BG Young, conversations which Young then relayed to MG Koster. BG Young also recalled that Henderson told him he had delivered an oral report to MG Koster who had instructed him to reduce the report to writing. BG Young testified that he confirmed this with MG Koster, but he could not recall any of the details of the discussion for this Inquiry.

There was a further report reaching the Americal Division command group which deserves mention. LTC Holladay stated that after the meeting with himself, Watke, and BG Young, he went to the Division Chief of Staff and related to him the allegations which had been made by WO1 Thompson. It is significant to note that Holladay's version of the allegations included all of MAJ Watke's version plus information concerning a ditch containing bodies, an individual shooting into that ditch, and the use of the term "murder." COL Parson testified that he did not pass this information on to BG Young or MG Koster because "In my mind, the generals were doing what needed to be done. The generals took this part over." Such a detached attitude on the part of a division chief of staff of the rank and experience of COL Parson seems unlikely.

COL Henderson stated that the matter was next brought to his attention approximately 2 weeks after the 20 March meeting, when BG Young advised him that MG Koster desired the oral report of 20 March be submitted in writing, as a matter of record.

COL Henderson testified that he then prepared a three-to-five-page typewritten report and personally delivered it to COL Parson at division headquarters on either 4, 5, or 6 April and that several days after, BG Young advised him that MG Koster had seen the report, passed it on to BG Young, and that BG Young believed MG Koster to be satisfied with the report. MG Koster denied ordering such a report prepared; BG Young denied advising COL Henderson to prepare it; and COL Parson denied any knowledge of it.

There is some corroboration of COL Henderson's statement regarding this written report. MAJ McKnight testified that he read a written report which was shown to him by COL Henderson "in late March or early April"; however, when shown exhibit R–1 (a report submitted on 24 April by COL Henderson and which is discussed in detail in section B), McKnight identified the exhibit as the report he had read in 1968. CPT Henderson, who was MAJ McKnight's assistant, testified that he recalled seeing a one-page written report "about a week after 16 March." CPT Henderson stated that McKnight was in possession of the report which concerned the matter of civilian casualties and allegations by helicopter pilots. When asked if he could identify the previously mentioned 24 April 1968 report of COL Henderson (exhibit R–1), CPT Henderson stated he could not and that he was certain exhibit R–1 was not the report he had seen in MAJ McKnight's hands.

A thorough search of currently available records and files failed to reveal a trace of any report which could possibly fit the description which COL Henderson provided. To date, the only written report recovered has been the report of 24 April 1968.

There is considerable conflict in the testimony of MG Koster, BG Young, and COL Henderson concerning the actual submission of the initial report by the latter and the subsequent events and directives as they concern additional investigative efforts. MG Koster was clear that he considered BG Young to be his principal agent in overseeing the investigative efforts of COL Henderson; BG Young, on the other hand, took the position that after the initial directive was issued to COL Henderson, and the oral report was made to MG Koster, the matter became one of direct contact between the Division Commander and the CO of the 11th Brigade, and largely excluded the Assistant Division Commander. According to BG Young's testimony, after 20 March, when MG Koster received a preliminary report from COL Henderson, BG Young took no further action in pursuing the allegations made by WO1 Thompson or in supervising the investigative efforts of COL Henderson. However, MG Koster and others stressed the continuing contact of BG Young with the matter and the fact that this, as other division business, was routinely shared with the maneuver ADC.

As concerns actions between MG Koster and COL Henderson, conflicts in testimony can be resolved to the extent that an oral report was received by MG Koster from COL Henderson sometime between 20 March and early April. As a result of this report, MG Koster concluded that COL Henderson had interrogated responsible personnel in the chain of command, as well as a cross-section of both aviation and ground troops, and that there was no basis for a formal investigation. MG Koster considered the matter closed and placed no further requirement on COL Henderson concerning this matter until sometime in mid-April when receipt of VC propaganda and further information from GVN channels reopened the question of civilian casualties in the Son My operation.

7. REPORT THROUGH CHAPLAIN CHANNELS

There is one further report which was made during the Son My operation and which concerned the actions of C Company as observed by WO1 Thompson. On either 16 or 17 March, WO1 Thompson went to see the Division Artillery Chaplain, CPT (now Rev.) Carl Creswell, regarding the events he had witnessed at My Lai (4). Thompson was at the time taking instructions regarding confirmation in his faith by Chaplain Creswell and in the course of such instructions, he saw the chaplain regularly.

According to Chaplain Creswell, when Thompson came to see him, he was "terribly upset" and asked for advice concerning what actions he should take. WO1 Thompson related to the chaplain the substance of his observations, and Chaplain Creswell advised him that he should make his official protest through command channels while he, CPT Creswell, would do the same thing through "Chaplain Channels."

Chaplain Creswell then went to see LTC Lewis, the Division Chaplain, related the story told to him by WO1 Thompson, and recommended that an investigation be conducted. Chaplain Creswell stated that Chaplain Lewis assured him that he would take the matter up with the appropriate authorities. Approximately 3 weeks later, after continual prodding of Chaplain Lewis by Chaplain Creswell and repeated assurances by Chaplain Lewis that an official investigation was underway, Chaplain Creswell acknowledged with remorse that he did nothing further.

Chaplain Lewis recalled that Chaplain Creswell came to see him on 17 March with information concerning WO1 Thompson's complaints. Chaplain Lewis could not recollect the details of the conversation but did recall that it included the specific allegation that a sergeant had fired into women and children and that the general content of the allegation dealt with the unnecessary killing of women and children. When questioned concerning the order of magnitude of the killings, Chaplain Lewis stated that while he was not sure of the source of the figure, the figure 124 is what he seemed to recall as the number of noncombatants killed.

In reconstructing Chaplain Lewis' actions relevant to this event, it can be established that he spoke to the Americal Division CofS, COL Parson, and the G5, LTC Anistranski. LTC Lewis stated he also spoke to the G1, LTC Qualls; the G2, LTC Trexler; and the G3, LTC Balmer. These latter three, in their testimony, denied any recollection of an occasion wherein LTC Lewis made inquiry concerning serious allegations against TF Barker, the 11th Brigade, or any operations which involved WO1 Thompson. In the two instances where key staff officers recollected a discussion with Chaplain Lewis, it is clear that the discussion was not one of an official nature concerning a serious allegation but rather, a request from Chaplain Lewis concerning the status of any investigation concerning "some pretty bad things" that Lewis had heard. From the testimony of individuals familiar with Chaplain Lewis, it was common practice for him to visit with key members of the staff on an informal basis and during such visits the Chaplain would frequently make reference to rumors or reports he had heard concerning the unnecessary use of force or firepower by combat troops. It appears probable that any "reports" Chaplain Lewis may have made concerning WO1 Thompson's allegations were most likely delivered and received in that context. It is clear that Chaplain Lewis did not make any timely effort to transmit the information he received from Chaplain Creswell to the command group of the Americal Division. By his own recollection, it was approximately 10 days after receiving the report from Creswell that he made his "informal" call on the CofS.

Chaplain Lewis stated he continued his personal inquiry into the matter, speaking to LTC Barker and MAJ (now LTC) Hoffman, 11th Brigade Chaplain. Chaplain Lewis stated that LTC Barker assured him that while there had been some casualties among the noncombatants, these were inadvertent and were a natural consequence of the type of combat units faced in inhabited areas.

MAJ Hoffman in testifying before the Inquiry stated that Chaplain Creswell said that he had heard reports that "our people had fired into women and children." Chaplain Hoffman further stated that Creswell continually "ragged" him and "pulled his leg" and Hoffman did not take him seriously. Chaplain Hoffman stated that after this matter was brought up on several occasions, he replied to Creswell that the 11th Brigade had not killed the civilians, "it was Div Arty firing the (artillery) prep." Chaplain Hoffman stated that this caused Creswell to "stop his ragging a little bit." Hoffman went on to state that Creswell never gave him specific information nor did he make any specific allegations. He also stated that he was quite certain that Chaplain Lewis did not speak to him about this matter at any time.

It is clear from the actions—and the acts of omission—of Chaplains Lewis and Creswell, that while both were aware of the serious nature of the charges alleged by WO1 Thompson, neither took adequate or timely steps to bring these charges to the attention of his commander. It should have been evident to both these chaplains that the idea of conducting an investigation of a war crime through chaplain channels was preposterous.

8. SUMMARY OF THE INITIAL REPORTS, INVESTIGATIONS, AND REVIEWS

In concluding this portion of the report, it should be noted that the Inquiry has been faced with a difficult task of attempting to determine precisely what actions transpired among the members of the Americal Division command groups upon receipt of the Thompson Report. No written record of anything pertaining to Thompson's complaint has been found——if one ever did exist. All references to the Thompson Report and its allegations were omitted from such written reports as have been found. Thus it was solely through testimony that the facts have been reconstructed. The task has been complicated by the apparent reluctance of some of the principals to testify frankly on the matter and by the significant contradictions in their testimony.

While there is evidence that the seriousness of the Thompson Report may have been muffled in the process of being passed to BG Young and MG Koster, it is clear that there was available at the time the report was received, sufficient information of an operational and intelligence nature available from other sources, which should have placed the recipients on notice that the events at Son My were of an exceptional nature.* Evaluation of subsequent actions by key personnel of the Americal Division indicates that such notice was not acknowledged. Instead, it seems likely that when the Thompson Report was received at Division Headquarters it was related to the report concerning 20–28 noncombatants deaths which MG Koster had previously received.

There was at least a tacit decision to withhold from higher headquarters any information concerning the incident. Adopting a "close-hold" attitude concerning all information relating to this matter, MG Koster directed the incident be investigated by COL Henderson, but neither MG Koster nor others in the Division command element took any steps to insure that an adequate investigation would be conducted. From the start, COL Henderson must have recognized the lack of any real appreciation at Division for the enormity of the incident and it appears that he deliberately set about to conceal information which would indicate its true nature.

The Inquiry does not exclude the possibility that from an early time there was a greater appreciation at Division as to the seriousness of the situation. MG Koster acknowledged that he and BG Young at some time discussed and dwelt upon the implications of the allegations. However, in the absence of more specific proof, the Inquiry cannot conclude that in March and early April the Division command element was aware of the nature and extent of the events which had transpired at Son My.

In the section which follows, the actions of the principals will be examined in light of the additional information received from Vietnamese sources.

B. The Subsequent Reports (the Absence of Further Investigation or Review) April–May 1968

1. INTRODUCTORY

Almost immediately following the events of 16 March 1968, rumors, reports, and VC propaganda relating to the operation began to move

* See Inclosure 1 for graphic portrayal of knowledge possessed by key individuals.

from the VC-controlled Son My Village area in Vietnamese channels. While it appears that these did not come immediately to the attention of responsible US personnel, such information did begin to reach some US military and possibly civilian personnel at least by the early days of April 1968.

The surfacing of this information from Vietnamese sources in the first half of April resulted in further reports but virtually no additional investigation or review within the US chain of command, and a lost opportunity for the Americal command again to review what had transpired. In this section of the report these events are examined.

2. REPORTS WITHIN VIETNAMESE CHANNELS

In March 1968, since Son My Village and the surrounding area were VC-controlled, no Government of Vietnam (GVN) officials resided in the village or its hamlets. The Son My Village Chief, Do Dinh Luyen, and the Tu Cung Hamlet Chief, Do Tan Nhon, lived in exile at Son Tinh approximately 10 kilometers from Son My Village. Accordingly, information available to GVN officials regarding activities in the village was based primarily on information obtained from residents of the village who, from time to time, visited the market in Son Tinh. Through this means, and through VC propaganda, some information regarding the US operation in Son My Village on 16 March 1968 reached the appropriate officials and was reported through GVN channels.

A. CENSUS GRIEVANCE REPORT

Based on information obtained from unspecified sources, a Census Grievance Cadreman of Son My Village submitted a written report to the Census Grievance Chief, Quang Ngai, on 18 March 1968, summarizing the results of the allied operation in Tu Cung Hamlet on 15 March 1968. This report indicated that:

1. After a fierce battle with district VC and local guerrillas, the allies killed 320 people at subhamlets Thuan Yen and Binh Dong.
2. Twenty-seven people were killed at My Lai.
3. Eighty people, young and old, were killed at Co Luy hamlet.
4. During the 3-day operation, a total of 427 civilians and guerrillas were killed.

While this report refers to an operation on "15 March," it apparently referred to the events of 16 March since no operations were conducted in that area on the preceding day. This is the earliest report submitted through GVN channels regarding the incident which the Inquiry found. The report contained no explanatory details. A copy of the report was provided to the Inquiry in early 1970 from the files of the Quang Ngai Census Grievance Committee, but there were no indications that it had been forwarded to Province Headquarters; hence it appears that no action was taken on it. The Census Grievance report, referred to later in this section, which is said to have contained different information, was not located by the Inquiry.

B. Report of the Son My Village Chief

Mr. Do Dinh Luyen, Son My Village Chief, submitted a written report, dated 22 March 1968, to the Son Tinh District Chief providing the results of the 16 March 1968 allied operation at Tu Cung and Co Luy hamlets [My Lai (4) is a subhamlet of Tu Cung and My Khe (4) of Co Luy]. The report specified that:

1. One US soldier was killed in action (KIA) and two wounded in action (WIA) at Thuan Yen subhamlet.
2. Forty-eight VC were KIA and 52 WIA.
3. 570 civilians were killed; 480 in Tu Cung and 90 in Co Luy.
4. Animals, property, and houses were 90 percent destroyed.

The Son Tinh District Chief stated to this Inquiry that this report had been submitted pursuant to his direction following the receipt of an earlier oral report from the Hamlet Chief and Village Chief. Mr. Luyen stated that his report to the District Chief had been based on hearsay information obtained from people who had talked with residents of Thuan Yen subhamlet [My Lai (4)]. Prior to the Inquiry's locating a copy of his report in the District Chief's files, Mr. Luyen recalled that he had submitted only an oral report to the District Chief and he did not recall writing a letter. He tended to play down the substance of his report, stating that the people had reported that not more than 30 civilians were killed in Thuan Yen, and that hundreds of VC were killed. He further volunteered to the Inquiry that, according to the rumors which he had heard, the deaths were the result of artillery, gunships, and small arms fire during the battle to enter the hamlet and the Americans had not assembled the people and shot them. Luyen stated his belief that most of the information he had received was VC propaganda and thus he had not gotten particularly concerned about it.

The written report of Mr. Luyen dated 22 March 1968 which was in fact passed in GVN channels contained substantially different allegations from those suggested by his statement to this Inquiry.

C. THE INITIAL REPORT OF THE SON TINH DISTRICT CHIEF, 28 MARCH 1968

LT (now CPT) Tran Ngoc Tan, the Son Tinh District Chief, as a result of the report from the Son My Village Chief, submitted an initial report to the Quang Ngai Province Chief on 28 March 1968 indicating that US forces had conducted an operation at Tu Cung Hamlet on "19 March 1968" (an apparent error) which resulted in injuries to a number of hamlet residents. It was reported that when the US force entered the hamlet, one soldier was killed and others wounded by a VC boobytrap following which the VC opened fire from their positions within the hamlet. The US forces responded with intense firepower, including artillery and air, causing injury to hamlet residents with whom the VC force was intermingled. The report stated, additionally, that Tu Cung Hamlet, and other hamlets of Son My Village, had been under VC control since 1964 and that the VC would possibly take advantage of the incident to undermine, through propaganda, the prestige of the Republic of Vietnam Armed Forces and the Government's pacification program.

In addition to submitting the report to the Province Chief, a copy was also forwarded to the S2 and S3 of Quang Ngai Sector. The Province Chief, LTC Ton That Khien, acknowledged receipt of this report in addition to having previously heard about the incident from the District Chief and through some rumors from the people. From the information which is available, indications are that the Province Chief took no specific action in response to this report, but he may have informed the Commanding Officer of the 2d ARVN Division.

D. THE SECOND REPORT OF THE SON TINH DISTRICT CHIEF, 11 APRIL 1968

Following up his initial report, the District Chief submitted a subsequent report to the Province Chief dated 11 April 1968 providing more definite information regarding the incident of 16 March and including the allegation that a US Army unit had assembled and killed civilian residents of Son My Village. LT Tan stated that this report was based on additional information provided by the Village Chief, including a list of residents killed. Although LT Tan stated that the list of civilians that had been killed would be found in the files of Son Tinh District, when the files were searched the list could not be located. The 11 April report specified that, after detonating a VC mine and receiving fire from Tu Cung, the US Army unit attacked the hamlet, assembled the people, and shot and killed more than 400 inhabitants. An additional 90 people were said to have been killed at Co Luy Hamlet.

The District Chief added that he believed the US unit acted in anger and killed too many civilians in this case even though Son My had long been under VC control and allied forces frequently operated in the area without restriction. He stated that, if true, he considered this an act of insane violence and requested the Province Chief to intervene on behalf of the people.

This report of the District Chief was not based on any investigation of the incident, but as already noted, on reports received by the Village Chief from residents of Son My who came out from the area to visit the market in Son Tinh and for other reasons. Since Son My was under VC control, no effort was made to corroborate the report at that particular time by an on-site investigation, although the Hamlet Chief and Village Chief were purportedly able to develop a list of residents who had been killed.

According to the distribution stated on LT Tan's 11 April report, copies of this report were forwarded to Headquarters, 2d ARVN Division, and MACV, Quang Ngai Sector [US Advisors] with a courtesy copy to the Major, US Advisor, Son Tinh District. While in Vietnam, the Inquiry was provided copies of this report from the files of both the Province Chief and the District Chief. However, neither a copy of the report nor any reference to it could be found in the files of the US Advisory Teams at Quang Ngai Province and Son Tinh District although exhaustive searches were made.

E. Memorandum to the Commanding Officer of the 2d ARVN Division

Based on the District Chief's 11 April report and VC propaganda which he had received, the G2, 2d ARVN Division, submitted a memorandum, dated 12 April 1968, to the CG, 2d ARVN Division, summarizing the allegations regarding the incident. A copy of the VC propaganda message (which is discussed in the following section of this chapter) describing the incident and a copy of the District Chief's report were attached to the memorandum. Upon receiving this information, COL Toan directed that Quang Ngai Sector investigate the incident. In a marginal note on the G2's memorandum, COL Toan stated: "Quang Ngai Sector review this investigation. If there is nothing to it, have the District rectify the report—If it is true, link-up with the Americal Division to have it stopped." Thereafter, on 15 April 1968, a message, signed by the Chief of Staff, directing the investigation in accordance with COL Toan's guidance, was dispatched to Quang Ngai Sector. COL Toan stated to this Inquiry that he recognized that the area was under VC control and that in fact it had not been possible to conduct an on-site investigation.

COL Toan subsequently discussed the incident with LTG Hoang Xuan Lam, CG, I CTZ. This discussion appears to have been the only report during 1968 by either Quang Ngai Province or the 2d ARVN Division to a higher authority in the GVN chain of command.

3. VC PROPAGANDA

During 1967 and 1968, it was a common technique of the VC to attempt to exploit actions in which they had suffered heavy losses by disseminating propaganda claiming that allied forces had killed many civilians, burned houses, destroyed property, and committed other such acts. This was done through a variety of means including public gatherings, broadcasts, and published leaflets or letters. Such propaganda was regularly monitored by US and Vietnamese intelligence teams, but its grossly exaggerated and drumbeat quality resulted in any purported specific information it might contain being treated with considerable skepticism and more frequently than not, dismissed as pure fabrication.

It would appear that much of the VC propaganda issued concerning the Son My incident was dismissed in this fashion although some of it did contain an unusual number of specific charges. While the propaganda was in some respects an obvious distortion, it recited some of the events of that day with reasonable accuracy. In fact, this particular propaganda, especially when combined with other information available to US and Vietnamese command elements should have prompted follow-up action.

The following is a summary of the propaganda which this Inquiry found, which in varying degrees came to the attention of US and/or ARVN personnel in the Spring of 1968. This summary of propaganda is in addition to the rumors heard by village, district, and province officials which, for the most part, appear to have been dismissed by these officials as VC-initiated and to which their reaction was tempered by past experience with VC propaganda, a small concern for VC-controlled areas, and an obvious reluctance on the part of GVN officials to embarrass their US allies.

The Inquiry obtained in Vietnam a copy of a Quang Ngai National Liberation Front Committee notice which was dated 28 March 1968. This notice was entitled "Concerning the Crimes Committed by US Imperialists and Their Lackeys Who Killed More Than 500 Civilians of Tinh Khe Village (Son My), Son Tinh District." It specified that:

> Xam Lang (Thuan Yen) Subhamlet of Tu Cung Hamlet and Xom Go Subhamlet of Co Luy were pounded by artillery for hours. After shelling, nine helicopters landed troops who besieged the two small hamlets. The US soldiers were like wild animals, charging violently into the hamlets, killing and destroying. They formed themselves into three groups: one group was

> in charge of killing civilians, one group burned huts, and the third group destroyed vegetation and trees and killed animals. Wherever they went, civilians were killed, houses and vegetation were destroyed and cows, buffalo, chickens, and ducks were also killed. They even killed old people and children; pregnant women were raped and killed. This was by far the most barbaric killing in human history.

The notice stated that 502 people were massacred at Tu Cung and Co Luy Hamlets, including 67 old people, 170 children, and 130 women. Although dated 28 March 1968, the copy of this notice which appears in the record was captured by the Americal Division on 11 December 1969 approximately 20 kilometers northwest of Son My Village. While there is no reliable evidence one way or the other it is possible that a pre-dated notice was published in late 1969 in order to capitalize on the widespread publicity at that time concerning the Son My incident. The Inquiry found no indication that it in fact reached GVN or US hands at any time prior to December 1969.

One item found by early April 1968 was a script for a proposed VC broadcast entitled "American Evil Appears." It is not clear how it was obtained. The script indicated that the proposed broadcast was to be used in coordination with VC leaflets with the title "Let American Enemy Pay This Bloody Debt." In addition to the general charges of murder, mistreatment of Vietnamese people, and the destruction of property by US forces, the script specifically highlighted the Son My incident. This was the item of VC propaganda that the G2 of the 2d ARVN Division brought to the attention of COL Toan. The script as provided to COL Toan stated, in part, in translation:

> In the operation of 15 March 1968, in Son Tinh District the American enemies went crazy. They used machineguns and every other kind of weapon to kill 500 people who had empty hands, in Tinh Khe (Son My) Village (Son Tinh District, Quang Ngai Province). There were many pregnant women some of which were only a few days from childbirth. The Americans would shoot everybody they saw. They killed people and cows, burned houses. There were some families in which all members were killed.

The propaganda went on to encourage ARVN soldiers to use their guns against American personnel. Several later enemy propaganda broadcasts were made from Hanoi during the period April–June 1968 along the theme that allied forces were committing atrocious war crimes in South Vietnam by murdering innocent civilians, burning houses, abusing women, and destroying property. The Son My incident was cited as one specific example of such an atrocity in each of these broadcasts. Broadcasts are known to have been made on 16 April (2), 17 April, 23 April, and 2 June which provided generally the same description of the incident as the propaganda messages previously discussed.

An intelligence report which was received in April 1968 indicated that soldiers of the Viet Cong were wearing red arm bands on which was a slogan expressing determination to avenge the massacre or murder at Son My. A VC who subsequently returned to government control also indicated that arm bands with a slogan concerning the incident were worn at Binh Duc, an area in eastern Binh Son District. This same individual also reported that he had attended two propaganda lectures in Tu Cung concerning the incident.

On 16 July 1969, a propaganda message published in May 1968 and entitled "The American Aggressors Must Pay For Their Debts in Blood Against the People of Son My" was captured approximately 50 kilometers northwest of Son My. This message, as others, provided a summary of the events of 16 March plus a vivid description of the alleged atrocities against the residents of Son My. The message encouraged the people to hate the Americans and to seek revenge for the murder of their relatives.

From the foregoing, it is apparent that by mid-April 1968, reports and propaganda relating to Son My were circulating in Vietnamese channels which continued for at least several months thereafter. In the next section, the information received by US officials from these sources and the resulting actions are examined.

4. INFORMATION RECEIVED FROM VIETNAMESE SOURCES AND FURTHER US ACTION

A. The Problem of Contradictory Testimony

The Inquiry met with a welter of contradiction, denials of knowledge, and vague recollections when examining what, when, and how information relating to the alleged incident passed from Vietnamese sources to US personnel. But with the aid of documents and information obtained from GVN authorities and the testimony of a few individuals who were in positions to observe portions of the events it has been possible to reconstruct in at least broad outline the information received and to determine those who had the knowledge and were principally responsible for the lack of any effective response in the chain of command.

B. Information Received and Actions Taken By the US Advisory Teams

LTC William D. Guinn was the Deputy Province Senior Advisor of Quang Ngai Province in March, April, and May 1968. He testified that in March 1968 he received a handwritten translation of a report that he was told had come through Census Grievance channels in Quang Ngai. He could not recall who specifically had given it to him. As LTC Guinn variously recalled the report in his testimony in 1969, it had stated that American forces had killed 1,000 or 1,500 or 2,000 in an operation in eastern Son Tinh District. When initially questioned about the report in May 1969, LTC Guinn, testified that "because of the seriousness of the allegation" he carried the report immediately to COL Henderson at his headquarters in Duc Pho so that COL Henderson "could start conducting an investigation on his own." He later testified that he had taken the report to COL Henderson just as soon as he could get a helicopter, but was unable to recall the exact date. When Guinn retold the story in his testimony in December 1969 before this Inquiry, he added that the report, in addition to stating the large number of casualties resulting from the action of the US forces, had said that they had been killed "by bombing and artillery" and that there was "no indication in there that they had been killed by small arms or ground action." LTC Guinn explained that in his opinion he had no duty to report the matter since no war crime was alleged, it being expressly stated that the casualties had resulted from bombing and artillery.

LTC Guinn further explained that he had not believed the report and had not considered that any atrocity had been committed. He also stated that he had told COL Henderson of the unreliability of its source, but that he, Guinn, had made no effort to check out the report. According to Guinn, COL Henderson stated that he would check out the report. Henderson flatly denied that he received any such report from Guinn, either orally or in writing, and stated that he believed that he had not even met Guinn up to that time.

In addition to these conflicts in testimony, Guinn's refusal upon being recalled as a witness to answer further questions left unresolved just what report he did receive in March 1968 and specifically how and from whom he received it. Guinn previously had told the Inquiry that he had maintained no file of such things as the Census Grievance report and that accordingly the only place a copy could possibly be found would be at the Census Grievance office. Thereafter, when this Inquiry obtained from the Census Grievance office in Quang Ngai a copy of the Census Grievance report of 18 March 1968 (exhibit M–31), Guinn, exercising his privilege, refused further to testify and accordingly, it was not possible to ascertain whether the 18 March Census Grievance report was in fact the one which he recalled having received. His previous description of the document and its contents is not consistent with Exhibit M–31, hence there may have been another Census Grievance report.

LTC Guinn testified, on his first appearance before this Inquiry, that the report from Census Grievance was the only one of which he had heard covering the killing of Vietnamese civilians by Americans. However, in prior testimony given to the IG in May 1969, he had stated that LTC Khien, the Province Chief, had received the same information regarding the alleged killing of civilians by US forces and had forwarded it to the 2d ARVN division. He further stated his understanding that COL Toan, LTC Khien, and MG Koster all had conducted investigations to find out what had happened. As previously noted, when this Inquiry went to Vietnam it obtained copies of both the 22 March 1968 report from Mr. Luyen, the Son My Village Chief, to the Son Tinh District Chief (exhibit M–49) and the 11 April 1968 report from LT (now CPT) Tan, the Son Tinh District Chief, to LTC Khien containing allegations of a mass killing in Son My Village (exhibits M–29, M–34, M–36).

The evidence does not establish that either LTC Guinn or MAJ (now LTC) Gavin, the Son Tinh District Advisor, or any member of their advisory teams had any immediate knowledge of the village Chief's report at the time it was made. Nor does it appear that members of either advisory team saw LT Tan's first report of 28 March 1968 to LTC Khien (exhibit M–5). Although Tan states that he discussed it with Gavin, Gavin denies this. However, despite the denials by Guinn and Gavin of knowledge of this Vietnamese complaint, it is clear that LT Tan's 11 April 1968 letter, referring to the Village Chief's complaint, was provided to both their headquarters and was the subject of considerable discussion.

MAJ Hancock, the G3 advisor to the 2d ARVN Division, has traced to the District Advisory Team and presumably MAJ Gavin, the initial Vietnamese report concerning the Son My incident. He stated that LTC Guinn told him in late March or early April that Gavin had received from the Son Tinh District Chief a report of several hundred civilians having been killed by US forces. MAJ Hancock apparently fixed the time of this oral report as preceding the District Chief's 11 April letter.

Shortly after hearing through Guinn of this information received from the District Advisory team, MAJ Hancock recalled having seen the script for the propaganda broadcast (exhibit M–33) and talking about it with Guinn. He further stated that he later saw in an Advisory Team reading file at the 2d ARVN Division the memorandum from the G2 of the division to COL Toan on which COL Toan had noted his direction for sector to investigate.

MAJ Earle, the G2 Advisor of the 2d ARVN Division, further corroborates LTC Guinn's knowledge and participation in the actions which ensued. He testified that LTC Guinn, in April 1968, spoke both of the District Chief's report and of the VC propaganda relating to the incident.

Guinn also mentioned CPT Rodriguez, the Assistant Son Tinh District Advisor. Guinn further mentioned that he was having someone look into the matter and was seeking additional information. Guinn also stated that he was passing the information up through his channels.

CPT Rodriguez confirms that he received a request from the Province Advisory Team, during MAJ Gavin's temporary absence from Son Tinh between 10 and 16 April, to obtain information regarding the allegations contained in LT Tan's 11 April letter. Since Son My Village was in VC-controlled area, an on-site investigation by CPT Rodriguez was not possible. He stated that, in response to this request, he limited his actions to discussing the matter with LT Tan and preparing a statement, dated 14 April 1968, in which he expressed the conclusion that LT Tan did not give the Village Chief's complaint much importance (exhibit M–30).

The attitude of LT Tan as thus reflected in the Rodriguez statement appears to contrast with the serious allegations in Tan's 11 April letter. During interrogation by the Inquiry in Vietnam, LT Tan stated that he had seen and agreed with Rodriguez's statement. He added that the substance and intent of his discussion with Rodriguez had not been that the information provided by the Village Chief was invalid or incorrect; rather that in view of the situation throughout Son Tinh District, which was under extreme pressure from the VC with outposts being attacked nightly, he considered a report alleging that some civilians had been killed in a VC-controlled area to be of less importance under the circumstances.

CPT Rodriguez testified that two copies of his 14 April statement were sent to the Province Advisor's office in Quang Ngai and one copy was placed in the files of the Son Tinh Advisory Team. When the Inquiry team was in Vietnam, the only copy of the 14 April statement which could be found was in the personal files of LTC Khien who made available files to the Inquiry and provided the copy entered in the record. The office files of the District, Province, and 2d ARVN Division Advisory teams were similarly bereft of any paper relating to the 1968 reports.

CPT Rodriguez stated that following the forwarding of his 14 April statement to the Province Advisory office he could recall discussing the matter with no one other than MAJ Gavin, whom he briefed on the matter and showed a copy of his 14 April statement upon MAJ Gavin's return to Son Tinh on 16 April. LT Tan and LT Dawkins, the intelligence advisor at the District Headquarters, recalled talking to both CPT Rodriguez and MAJ Gavin about the incident, but MAJ Gavin, despite the fact that he was the addressee of a courtesy copy of Tan's 11 April letter and the contrary testimony noted above, claimed he was kept entirely in the dark regarding the reports on Son My and knew nothing of what CPT

Rodriguez had done or of his discussion with LT Tan during Gavin's absence.

Although LTC Khien stated that he had talked with both Mr. James May, the Province Senior Advisor, and LTC Guinn, who was May's deputy, about the 11 April letter, Mr. May was apparently absent from Quang Ngai at the time the letter was received and he denied ever having heard of the letter or of the Rodriguez 14 April statement. No other evidence links Mr. May directly to the letter or the statement.

As to LTC Guinn, his refusal to answer any questions regarding the materials found by the Inquiry in RVN through the cooperation of the GVN authorities—including the Tan 11 April letter and the Rodriguez 14 April statement—has prevented the development of evidence as to the specific manner in which Rodriguez's 14 April statement was subsequently transmitted to COL Henderson at Duc Pho. Moreover, when Guinn first testified before the Inquiry, he was shown the version of the 14 April statement found in the files of the S2 at the 11th Brigade (from which CPT Rodriguez's signature block had been eliminated) and he professed not having seen the statement before. Disassociating himself from the matter, Guinn before this Inquiry denied discussing the allegations regarding the incident with LTC Khien, COL Toan, MG Koster, BG Young or Mr. May, and he did not mention either MAJ Earle or MAJ Hancock. He insisted that his only discussion had been the one with COL Henderson when he brought the Census Grievance report to Duc Pho.

The surrounding circumstances and the testimony of various witnesses place LTC Guinn squarely in the central position at Quang Ngai both in handling Tan's 11 April letter—of which he was an addressee—and in arranging for the preparation and subsequent distribution of Rodriguez's 14 April statement concerning Tan's letter.

BG Young (like MAJ Earle) stated that Guinn expressly told him about the District Chief's report and COL Henderson confirmed that Guinn was present when he talked to LTC Khein regarding "this allegation against US troops." Similarly, MG Koster confirmed that he also talked with Guinn about the District Chief's report to the Province Chief when he had gone to Quang Ngai to speak with LTC Khien regarding these matters. Another apparently knowledgeable member of the advisory teams who has sought to disassociate himself from the events is COL Hutter, the US Senior Advisor to COL Toan. Both MG Koster and MAJ Hancock as well as COL Toan and MAJ Pho, place him at critical meetings in this time frame.

Whatever may have been the extent and detail of Guinn's report to the 11th Brigade and the Americal Division regarding these matters, or the knowledge of COL Hutter, there is no evidence that they ever brought these matters to the attention of their superiors within their respective chains of command (DCORDS and DSA I CTZ), or took any steps to see that such matters were included in the monthly Advisory Team report or any other reports submitted by the 2d ARVN Division or Province Advisory Teams. (Ironically, the monthly province reports contained laudatory accounts concerning TF Barker.)

c. Information Recieved and Actions Taken by the 11th Brigade

As previously noted, MAJ McKnight, the S3 of the 11th Brigade, testified that by late March or early April 1968 COL Henderson's investigation concerning the Son My operation was completed and closed with the preparation of a letter to the CG Americal Division giving an explanation of this operation and of what had occurred. He further testified, however, that the matter was reopened in the first half of April because of the receipt of a VC propaganda leaflet alleging that US forces had massacred 300–400 people in the 16 March operation. MAJ McKnight knew nothing of a report from Census Grievance channels, and the testimony of LTC Guinn and COL Henderson is in conflict as to whether the first report reaching the 11th Brigade from Vietnamese sources was delivered by Guinn. Nevertheless, it is clear that it was information from Vietnamese channels which prompted further action by COL Henderson.

LTC Blackledge confirms the receipt at the 11th Brigade of a report on such VC propaganda. He testified that he "seized" on the fact that this piece was of a different kind than the usual run of VC propaganda and brought it to COL Henderson's attention around the middle of April. He recalled receiving one or two later pieces of VC propaganda of similar import which he also showed to COL Henderson. COL Henderson acknowledged having been shown some such report around mid-April (which he thought had been obtained by the intelligence liaison officer to Quang Ngai Province) and stated that it had alleged that US forces had killed some 470 civilians on 16 March and on an earlier operation.

LTC Blackledge also recalled a further intelligence report which he received about the same time indicating that soldiers of the Viet Cong were wearing arm bands on which was a slogan expressing determination to avenge the massacre or murder at Son My.

The evidence indicates that COL Henderson moved quickly to allay any suspicions raised by the VC propaganda and the reports emanating from Son Tinh District. He testified that he went "immediately" to see COL Toan and LTC Khien within 24 to 36 hours. However, his description of the discussions which ensued is confused, contradictory, and belied by other testimony and the documentary record. MAJ Hancock, the S3 advisor to the 2d ARVN Division, was present when Henderson spoke to Toan, as apparently were MAJ McKnight, COL Hutter, and possibly MAJ Earle. He seemed to recall that the meeting took place after 12 April when the G2, 2d ARVN Division, sent his memorandum to COL Toan. MAJ Hancock stated further that COL Henderson, when asked by COL Toan about the allegations of the killing of civilians at Son My, assured COL Toan that the matter had been fully investigated by Henderson himself, that he had landed in the objective area and questioned the troops in the field about the alleged killing of civilians, and that he had been assured in talking with the men that there was nothing to the charges. Apparently no reference was made by Henderson to the earlier allegations in the Thompson Report which had led to Henderson's initial investigation. Hancock recalled that Toan seemed to accept the explanation and that he, Hancock, regarded the matter as closed and concluded that nothing wrong had happened. MAJ McKnight in his description of the meeting stated that while COL Toan regarded the charges as a VC propaganda stunt, there was an ARVN investigation of the matter which was apparently in progress at the time of the meeting.

COL Henderson, in his account of the meeting with COL Toan, stated that he had told COL Toan that he was very disturbed by the allegations and asked whether he had any knowledge or information that Henderson did not have. COL Toan apparently told Henderson that he had received the District Chief's letter and the VC propaganda message a day or two earlier and that he had directed an investigation which was in progress. In his testimony Henderson said nothing about telling Toan of having made his own investigation in March, rather that he simply told Toan that he was very much interested in the matter and that he too "was trying to ferret out the truth." Henderson attributed the ARVN investigation to a directive from LTG Lam, CG I CTZ, and claimed that he offered to make available to COL Toan any number of troops to go into the area and help him secure it while the matter was looked into. COL Henderson further testified that COL Toan replied: "No. This is VC propaganda. There is no truth to this," and that when Henderson pressed him to accept the assistance, Toan replied that he had told LTC Khien, the Province Chief, to handle the investigation.

From MAJ Hancock's testimony it would appear that the meeting with Toan terminated on a note suggesting that the allegations were groundless and the matter was closed (or at least Hancock so regarded it), but apparently COL Henderson, still very much concerned, went directly to see LTC Khien.

COL Henderson's account of his visit to LTC Khien in his testimony before this Inquiry follows generally his description of his meeting with COL Toan but was at substantial variance with his testimony in May

1969 before the IG. In his May testimony he stated that the province advisors arranged the meeting and that he believed that this was the first time that he had met LTC Guinn. Since Guinn denied ever having such a meeting with Henderson and Henderson's testimony on the point is completely vague, it is left to conjecture what Guinn and Henderson actually said to each other regarding the allegations from the District Chief and the VC propaganda. It was just about this time that the Province Advisory Team was obtaining the statement prepared by CPT Rodriguez on 14 April which COL Henderson used in his later report to MG Koster. LTC Khien was also given a copy of the Rodriguez statement, presumably by LTC Guinn. It seems reasonable to assume that LTC Guinn provided Henderson a copy of the Rodriguez statement at this time or arrangements were made to provide a copy.

As to the meeting with LTC Khien, Henderson testified before this Inquiry that he expressed to him "my regret and how disturbed I was over this thing, and that I wanted to get to the bottom of it, and if there was any truth to it I would make troops available to go with his RF/PF forces, or any other forces, into the area if he was going to conduct such an investigation." (At this point it should be noted that COL Henderson had available to him sufficient assets in terms of ground forces, airlift, and fire support to go into the area at any time, had he really desired to ascertain the facts.) COL Henderson made no mention in his testimony of what he might have told LTC Khien regarding his own investigation in March which he had already completed. Instead, he testified only about what Khien had said to him regarding the Village Chief's allegations. According to COL Henderson, LTC Khien described them as VC propaganda and explained his plan to conduct a counterpropaganda campaign. Henderson also stated that Khien showed him either the Village Chief's or the District Chief's letter which stated that the US forces had gathered up groups of civilians and killed a total of 470 in two operations. Henderson at one time acknowledged that he obtained a copy of some such letter from Khein, but he was not clear as to which one it was. LTC Khien purportedly stated to Henderson that he did not consider an investigation to be appropriate. LTC Khien has no recollection of such a discussion with COL Henderson.

In contrast to his testimony to this Inquiry, COL Henderson told the IG in May 1969 that the Province Chief, LTC Khien, requested Henderson to assist in his investigation: "He asked if I would send US forces into that area with his ARVN and Local Forces to get some truth out of this. I assured him that I would and told him that I would conduct the operation anytime that he was ready." Henderson went on to state that they conducted such an operation in July 1968 but that it was abortive. Nevertheless, LTC Khien told him afterwards "that from his investigation that he could find no truth to the allegations that US forces had killed some 400 civilians in this area."

Although Henderson acknowledged in his testimony before this Inquiry in December 1969 that he had obtained from Khien a copy of a letter containing the Village Chief's allegations on recall in February 1970, after the Inquiry had succeeded in obtaining copies of both the Village Chief's 22 March 1968 letter (exhibit M–49) and the District Chief's 11 April 1968 letter (exhibit M–34), COL Henderson denied that he had ever seen either of them.

COL Henderson testified to this Inquiry that it was immediately after his visit to COL Toan and LTC Khien in mid-April that he furnished to the Americal Division copies of the Vietnamese documents, with English translations, in which the allegations were contained. According to Henderson this "tripped" MG Koster's memory and led to a request, delivered to him by BG Young, that Henderson should reduce his earlier oral report to writing so there would be "some back-up in the files here if anything further should develop on the matter." However, according to Henderson, BG Young made it clear that MG Koster did not want to re-open the matter or to conduct a formal investigation.

The testimony given by MG Koster tends to confirm COL Henderson's testimony in this respect. He indicated that the receipt in mid-April 1968 of VC propaganda, "plus something from the District Chief" reopened the subject of civilian casualties in the 16 March operation, but that it did not stimulate any fresh inquiry since COL Henderson had already completed his investigation and had reported upon it at least orally. Rather, the receipt of the VC propaganda led MG Koster to direct COL Henderson to commit his original report to writing. He stated he did not remember that his instructions to Henderson were in writing, but if they were he would say that either BG Young or COL Parson would have prepared the letter. Neither of them recalls having given nor having prepared any such instructions to COL Henderson nor having seen any written instructions in this regard. However, SGM Gerberding, from the S2 office of the 11th Brigade, seemed to recall at one time having seen such a directive from MG Koster in the file at Duc Pho. Although it is possible that such a letter was sent by MG Koster to COL Henderson, and might be anticipated had the matter in other respects been handled with greater formality, since SGM Gerberding is the only person who stated that he had seen such a document, this Inquiry cannot place much credence upon its existence.

In any event, it was at this time in the second half of April that COL Henderson prepared and submitted to MG Koster his so-called Report of Investigation dated 24 April 1968. COL Henderson confirmed that in accordance with the instructions he had received he conducted no additional interrogation and merely put down in letter form the information from his notebook which he had recorded at the time of his earlier investigation. "And with this I prepared what I termed a report of investigation which I acknowledge loud and clear is not a report of investigation." This so-called Report of Investigation was written in longhand by COL Henderson and when typed consisted of a two-page letter with two inclosures. Because of the importance of this so-called Report of Investigation to an evaluation of what took place, the letter is set forth in full. The letter read as follows:

DEPARTMENT OF THE ARMY
Headquarters, 11th Infantry Brigade, Americal Division
APO San Francisco 96217

XICO 24 April 1968

SUBJECT: Report of Investigation

Commanding General
Americal Division
APO SF 96374

1. (U) An investigation has been conducted of the allegations cited in Inclosure 1. The following are the results of this investigation.

2. (C) On the day in question, 16 March 1968, Co C 1st Bn 20th Inf and Co B 4th Bn 3d Inf as part of Task Force Barker, 11th Inf Bde, conducted a combat air assault in the vicinity of My Lai Hamlet (Son My Village) in eastern Son Tinh District. This area has long been an enemy strong hold, and Task Force Barker had met heavy enemy opposition in this area on 12 and 23 February 1968. All persons living in this area are considered to be VC or VC sympathizers by the District Chief. Artillery and gunship preparatory fires were placed on the landing zones used by the two companies. Upon landing and during their advance on the enemy positions, the attacking forces were supported by gunships from the 174th Avn Co and Co B, 23d Avn Bn. By 1500 hours all enemy resistance had ceased and the remaining enemy forces had withdrawn. The results of this operation were 128 VC soldiers KIA. During preparatory fires and the ground action by the attacking companies 20 noncombatants caught in the battle area were killed. US Forces suffered 2 KIA and 10 WIA by booby traps and 1 man slightly wounded in the foot by small arms fire. No US soldier was killed by sniper fire as was the alleged reason for killing the civilians. Interviews with LTC Frank A. Barker, TF Commander; MAJ Charles C. Calhoun, TF S3; CPT Ernest L. Medina, CO Co C, 1-20; and CPT Earl Michles, CO Co B, 4-3 revealed that at no time were any civilians gathered together and killed by US soldiers. The civilian habitants in the area began withdrawing to the southwest as soon as the operation began and within the first hour and a half

all visible civilians had cleared the area of operations.*

3. (C) The Son Tinh District Chief does not give the allegations any importance and he pointed out that the two hamlets where the incident is alleged to have happened are in an area controlled by the VC since 1964. COL Toan, Cmdr 2d Arvn Div reported that the making of such allegations against US Forces is a common technique of the VC propaganda machine. Inclosure 2 is a translation of an actual VC propaganda message targeted at the ARVN soldier and urging him to shoot Americans. This message was given to this headquarters by the CO, 2d ARVN Division o/a 17 April 1968 as a matter of information. It makes the same allegations as made by the Son My Village Chief in addition to other claims of atrocities by American soldiers.

4. (C) It is concluded that 20 non-combatants were inadvertently killed when caught in the area of preparatory fires and in the cross fires of the US and VC forces on 16 March 1968. It is further concluded that no civilians were gathered together and shot by US soldiers. The allegation that US forces shot and killed 450-500 civilians is obviously a Viet Cong propaganda move to discredit the United States in the eyes of the Vietnamese people in general and the ARVN soldier in particular.

5. (C) It is recommended that a counter-propaganda campaign be waged against the VC in eastern Son Tinh District.

2 Incl
a/s

ORAN K. HENDERSON
COL, Infantry
Commanding

Although SGM Gerberding stated that four copies of this report were typed (COL Henderson put the number at three), the only copy of this report which was found was a carbon copy retained in a separate personal folder in the S2 office of the 11th Brigade by SGM Gerberding who was given it by LTC Blackledge, the Brigade S2, in April 1968. SGM Gerberding testified that he had been instructed by LTC Blackledge "to keep it confidential," to insure that it received no publicity and not too many people should hear or know about it. Found with the carbon copy of the letter were carbon copies of the two documents which apparently were the inclosures to the letter. The first inclosure was a typed copy of the Rodriguez 14 April 1969 statement, but with the signature block entirely omitted. It read as follows:

* It will be noted that there is no reference in this paragraph to any member of the 123d Aviation Bn or to WO1 Thompson's complaint.

Statement 14 April 1968

This statement is in reference to letter from the Son Tinh District Chief to the Quang Ngai Province Chief Subject: Allied Forces Gathered People of Son My Village for Killing, dated 11 April 1968.

The Son Tinh District Chief received a letter from the Village Chief of Son My Village containing the complaint of the killing of 450 civilians including children and women by American troops. The Village Chief alleged that an American unit operating in the area on 16 March 1968 gathered and killed these civilians with their own personal weapons. The incident took place in the hamlets of Tu-Cong and Co-Luy located in the eastern portion of Son Tinh District. According to the Village Chief the American unit gathered 400 civilians in Tu-Cong hamlet and killed them. Then moved to Co-Luy hamlet. At this location the unit gathered 90 more civilians and killed them.

The Son-My Village Chief feels that this action was taken in revenge for an American soldier killed by sniper fire in the village.

The letter was not given much importance by the District Chief but it was sent to the Quang Ngai Province Chief. Later the Son Tinh District Chief was called and directed by the 2d Division Commander, Col Toan, to investigate the incident and prepare a report. The District Chief proceeded to interview the Son-My Village Chief and got the same information that I have discussed above. The District Chief is not certain of the information received and he has to depend on the word of the Village Chief and other people living in the area.

The two hamlets where the incident is alleged to happen are in a VC controlled area since 1964.

There was nothing on this document itself which disclosed its authorship; and none of the witnesses interrogated by the Inquiry, before a copy of the Rodriguez Statement was obtained from Vietnamese sources, disclosed from where it came. Those questioned included Henderson, McKnight, Blackledge, Guinn, and Gavin. Most of them denied any knowledge as to the origin of the statement. At one point in his testimony, COL Henderson seems to suggest that he obtained the information for the statement (or perhaps a copy of CPT Rodriguez' Statement) from MAJ Gavin at Son Tinh District. It also appears possible that he, COL Henderson, could have obtained it from LTC Guinn. Irrespective of how COL Henderson may have obtained the statement, the impression conveyed in his so-called Report of Investigation was that the statement was of Vietnamese origin and was actually a translation of a statement prepared by a Vietnamese official.

As previously noted, it was only when the Inquiry obtained from LTC

Khien in Quang Ngai a signed copy of the Rodriguez 14 April statement that it was possible to establish the origin of this document which COL Henderson used in his so-called Report of Investigation as the basis for summarily dismissing the allegations in the Son Tinh District Chief's letter of 11 April 1968 regarding the gathering and killing by US forces of people in Son My Village. It appears that COL Henderson and those who participated with him in making this report of his investigative efforts tried to make it appear that the evaluation of the Village Chief's allegations came from Vietnamese and not American sources. Taken with the total absence in any US unit's files of a copy of either the Rodriguez statement or the 11 April letter, it strongly suggests a conscious effort to deceive.

The second inclosure found with the copy of COL Henderson's 24 April letter was an English translation of the script for a VC propaganda broadcast which COL Henderson identified as having been furnished to him on or about 17 April 1968 by COL Toan. This is the same script for a VC broadcast which was attached to the memorandum dated 12 April 1968 from the G2 of the 2d ARVN Division to COL Toan as described above. (See exhibit M-36.) The full text of this piece of VC propaganda is set forth as Inclosure 2 to this chapter.

It will be noted that COL Henderson in his 24 April report, on the basis of his earlier "investigation" of the incident summarily dismissed all of the new allegations as "obviously a Viet Cong propaganda move to discredit the United States in the eyes of the Vietnamese people in general and the ARVN soldier in particular." He, accordingly, recommended that a counterpropaganda campaign be waged against the VC in eastern Son Tinh District.

The evidence establishes that despite some testimony from MG Koster and COL Henderson to the contrary, to which reference is made in the following section, neither COL Henderson nor anyone in the 11th Brigade took any further action with respect to the investigating or reporting of the Son My operation of 16 March 1968, after the delivery of this so-called Report of Investigation to the Americal Division.

D. INFORMATION RECEIVED BY THE AMERICAL DIVISION AND THE TERMINATION OF ALL INVESTIGATION

No question was more difficult for this Inquiry to answer than precisely when and what information reached Americal Division headquarters from Vietnamese channels regarding the killing of civilians in the Son My operation. The testimony is confusing as to the time at which particular information reached various individuals and the extent of that information. There is some evidence that the seriousness of the allegations may have been muted by the time they came to the attention of the division command element. Nevertheless, the evidence is convincing that division headquarters was put firmly on notice by several indications that something most unusual had taken place in Son My Village on 16 March and therefore is responsible for the further suppression of crucial information regarding the incident.

Knowledge of the allegations of the Son My Village Chief as set forth in the District Chief's 11 April report and of the VC propaganda relating to the events in Son My came to division headquarters in at least three ways, although there remains a question as to when it reached division in each way. First, from LTC Guinn: as previously noted, BG Young stated that he received a report regarding the District Chief's letter which he passed to MG Koster; moreover, MG Koster himself met with LTC Guinn during this time frame. Second, from the 2d ARVN Division Commander and the Sector Commander: MG Koster briefly discussed the allegations with both COL Toan and LTC Khien. Finally, from COL Henderson and the 11th Brigade: the 24 April Report of Investigation is specific evidence of what was provided from this source. MG Koster was asked who had provided him the information regarding the VC propaganda, and that from the District Chief, before he ordered COL Henderson's 24 April report. He replied: "I'm kind of foggy. It could have come directly from the province, 2d ARVN Division, 11th Brigade, I'd say those were the most likely sources." In his testimony to the IG in May 1969 LTC Guinn, omitting reference to his own contacts with MG Koster, stated that he thought COL Toan had passed the information to MG Koster.

BG Young recalled having been told by Guinn of the village chief's allegations during one of Young's visits to the Quang Ngai Province headquarters. According to BG Young, Guinn told him that the Province Chief had received a letter from the Village Chief indicating that a number of civilians had been killed north and east of Quang Ngai City. He believed that Guinn mentioned the District Chief's 11 April report although he stated that he was not shown a copy of the letter. Guinn apparently indicated to Young that LTC Khien was going to investigate the matter. Although BG Young placed LTC Guinn's report in late May 1968, from all the surrounding circumstances it appears most unlikely that it was later than mid-April. In view of BG Young's frequent visits to Province headquarters and contact with the Province Advisory team, it is quite possible that Guinn's report to Young was among the earliest of the reports to division on these allegations. Guinn's general denial of discussing the District Chief's report and his subsequent refusal to testify further prevented the Inquiry from determining more precisely the content and fixing the time and circumstances of this report to BG Young. Despite the tandem in which the District Chief's report and the VC propaganda repeatedly appear, BG Young insisted that he was not aware of the VC propaganda; yet various individuals specifically recalled seeing some of the VC propaganda relating to Son My in Division headquarters.

With respect to information obtained from LTC Guinn by division headquarters, it should also be noted that MG Koster in his testimony in February 1970 recalled discussing with Guinn the allegations of the local officials. To fix the time, he stated that the only time he recalled being in a conversation with Guinn was when Guinn accompanied him on a visit to LTC Khien at which the allegations were discussed. He had the impression that Guinn and Khien had done some checking on the matter prior to the time he talked to them. Subsequently, before this Inquiry when shown the 11 April letter from the District Chief to the Province Chief, MG Koster said that he did not recall seeing the letter and did not specifically remember any references to it by LTC Guinn, LTC Khien, or COL Toan. But when pressed on interrogation, his reply was equivocal, "I can't say that I've seen it. I don't know."

Regarding information furnished to MG Koster by the CO of the 2d ARVN Division and LTC Khien, the evidence indicates that some information regarding both the VC propaganda and the allegations in the District Chief's 11 April report was given to MG Koster by COL Toan. MG Koster acknowledged that he had a meeting with COL Toan in mid-April 1968 at the latter's headquarters in Quang Ngai. COL Toan remembered such a meeting with a general from the Americal Division sometime in the first half of April, and MAJ Pho, the ARVN G2 and the author of the 12 April memorandum to COL Toan, fixed the date as several days following his memorandum and indicated that MG Koster was accompanied by COL Hutter, the Senior Advisor of the 2d ARVN Division. Pho recalled being asked to bring his memorandum with its attachments into the meeting and MG Koster confirmed that the overall subject of discussion related, although he could not be specific, to the District Chief's letter and the VC propaganda. MG Koster recalled that COL Toan either had investigated or was investigating the allegations and Koster asked him to let them know if anything thereafter turned up.

MG Koster further stated that he told COL Toan that he had made a check of the Son My operation due to the helicopter pilot's report and had not been able to determine that there was any such thing taking place as had been alleged. Toan recalled speaking about the "rumor" with Koster so he could check out if anything had happened, but indicated that he did not give Koster a copy of either the VC propaganda or the District Chief's letter. This accorded with Koster's recollection that he learned of the allegations either from "seeing the propaganda leaflet or possibly the letter" before he visited Toan. MG Koster was unable to state who had earlier shown him this material. At another point in his testimony, he said that he met with Toan immediately following his visit with Guinn to Khien. But he seemed to recall that his visits to both Khien and Toan were stimulated by what he already had heard and seen.

While at times suggesting that his meetings with Toan and with Khien were in May rather than in April, at other times MG Koster indicated that they could have preceded COL Henderson's 24 April written report. This is consistent with his statement to the CID early in December 1969: "I had been informed of the allegations made by villagers. As I recall, although these appeared to be VC propaganda, they prompted my direction for a written report." Later, to this Inquiry, he stated that he directed COL Henderson to put his oral report in writing to rebut VC allegations of an atrocity.

Further indications that some of these documents reached Division headquarters is found in COL Parson's testimony. He stated that following the Thompson Report: "I recall I dropped the incident in my mind because I don't recall hearing any more about it. Sometime later there was a document which I believe was on the same subject written by either the Province Chief or the 2d ARVN Division Commander. I recall the subject had to do with the killing or the unnecessary killing of civilians, possibly [by] artillery. . . ." COL Parson stated that he believed he saw the document in MG Koster's office. Also in his statement to the CID on 14 January 1970 COL Parson stated "I saw a letter that had been written by a Vietnamese official about this incident. Here again, I am not sure what it said, and I am sure that I gave it to the Division Commanding General."

When recalled to testify, COL Parson was shown the District Chief's 11 April letter and asked if that was the document he had seen. Having before him both the District Chief's letter of 28 March and of 11 April, he stated, "I'm unable to say which of these two—I don't recall two, I recall one." From all the circumstances, it seems clear that if COL Parson saw either one of the District Chief's letters to the Province Chief it necessarily would have been the 11 April report of which both LTC Guinn and MAJ Gavin were indicated as receiving copies; whereas, the 28 March letter did not indicate any US recipients.

SGM Gerberding lent some support for the fact that a copy of the District Chief's 11 April letter reached Division headquarters and MG Koster. As previously noted, he recalled that he had seen a personal letter from MG Koster to COL Henderson stating that the District Chief of Son Tinh had made a complaint to the Province Chief in Quang Ngai that during the operation in March by TF Barker some 450 civilians were killed by TF Barker. He stated that a letter in Vietnamese was attached, together with an English translation. In the letter, as Gerberding recalled it, MG Koster asked COL Henderson to answer the allegations made by the District Chief. As previously stated, the Inquiry was unable either to accept or to reject SGM Gerberding's recollection on this point. He was the custodian of the file copy of Henderson's 24 April Report of Investigation and undoubtedly was in a unique position to see what papers were at the brigade headquarters at that time. However, no other witness recalls any written directive with respect to the investigation and no copy of any such communication has been found.

As already noted, the third channel through which the information from the Vietnamese sources reached Americal Division headquarters was by way of COL Henderson and the 11th Brigade. COL Henderson clearly furnished some information, both as to the District Chief's 11 April report and the VC propaganda, with his 24 April so-called Report of Investigation; but the evidence already outlined, including the wording of the 24 April letter itself, strongly suggests that MG Koster was aware of these matters and, in fact, had requested that Henderson reduce to writing his earlier oral report because of the information that already had been received at division. However, by the 24 April letter it is conclusively established that the command element at division headquarters no later than the time of reading that report, with its inclosures, was expressly informed of the information coming from Vietnamese channels and on notice of what was being said: namely, that in each of the two hamlets where C/1–20 and B/4–3 operated on 16 March large numbers of civilians had been killed.

SGM Gerberding who prepared the letter from COL Henderson's handwritten draft recalled that the 24 April Report of Investigation was delivered to division by the daily courier in a double sealed envelope marked "Eyes of the CG only." On the other hand, COL Henderson testified at one time that he personally carried the "report" to Chu Lai and handed it to COL Parson, which Parson said was a possibility; but Henderson later stated that he believed he gave one report to the liaison officer for delivery to division. MG Koster recalled that he did not see the report until he returned from R & R on about 8 May. Although BG Young was the acting Division Commander during MG Koster's absence and the one to whom matters would normally be referred in the CG's absence, he testified that he did not see the 24 April report until he was shown a copy by this Inquiry on 13 December 1969. However, he did say that he was certain that Henderson had submitted a written report (but not as late as 24 April) and that he did not believe that Henderson submitted two written reports.

LTC Holladay testified that he was unofficially shown the 24 April Report by COL Parson and upon reading the paper made clear in an epithet his personal view that there had been a cover-up. COL Parson stated that he did not recall this incident, but added "I'm sure it happened, if he said so." As to the 24 April report itself, he said that he could not specifically recall having seen it but that he "might very well have seen it." Later, however, in response to a question he expressly based his answer upon the 24 April report, that he recalled "principally this paper [the 24 April report] here as refuting this as a war crime."

The view was universally expressed by the witnesses that the 24 April letter was a totally inadequate report for any investigation. It was entirely unresponsive to the allegations of WO1 Thompson (which MG Koster stated he had intended it to cover). The omission of any reference to either the Thompson Report or any personnel of the aviation unit indicates a design to delete from the record any reference to the fact that such a complaint had been made.

MG Koster and COL Henderson were so clear as to this inadequacy of the 24 April report when they reviewed it in 1969 that in conversations before they gave testimony they apparently concluded that there must have been a further investigation and later report. MG Koster stated that because the 24 April report was unsatisfactory, he directed BG Young or COL Parson, or possibly both, to have a formal investigation conducted as BG Young had recommended. BG Young, however, denied this. He stated: ". . . I cannot recall him directing me to pass these instructions to COL Henderson. . . . I'm not aware that a formal investigation was conducted. I cannot recall a formal investigation being conducted." COL Parson also stated that he had no recollection of ever being informed that MG Koster desired that a formal investigation be conducted.

According to COL Henderson, BG Young told him in early May that MG Koster had directed that a formal investigation be conducted. Henderson went on to say that he also discussed with BG Young the fact that he intended to appoint LTC Barker as the investigating officer and that BG Young concurred. Regarding his instructions to LTC Barker, Henderson stated: "The requirement was that he conduct a formal investigation of the 16 March incident. I believe I also told him that as far as I knew nothing new had developed. This was to have first priority and either at that time or a few days later I told him it was to be completed before he went on R & R on the 20th of May. . . ."

Both Koster and Henderson testified that in May 1968 a formal report was prepared and submitted. Both contended that the report was approximately three pages in length and had attached to it the signed statements of 15 to 20 witnesses. The Inquiry expressly interrogated each individual who might have given such a signed statement and not one could recall ever having made such a statement. No trace of such a document has been found, and not only BG Young and COL Parson, but also other personnel of the Americal headquarters all testified that they had never seen or heard of such a report of investigation. The inescapable conclusion is that no such formal report of investigation ever existed.

From what we were able to ascertain MG Koster apparently accepted the 24 April report without any critical review of its content. The document had been requested in order to make a record of COL Henderson's investigative efforts in March—in MG Koster's words. "To show what we had done in this case"—and it was assumed that this had been done. The reference in the inclosed 14 April statement to an 11 April letter of the Son Tinh District Chief brought forth no request to provide a copy of that letter, nor did the absence of any indication on that statement as to its origins evoke any questions. As MG Koster stated in his testimony before the Inquiry in February 1970 when shown the original Rodriguez statement: "I wondered whose statement that was. I have never really known."

It also is appropriate to note that when MG Koster returned from R & R in early May 1968 and the 24 April report probably came to his attention for the first time, he was almost immediately involved in a major operational problem relating to the relief and evacuation of Kham Duc which conceivably pushed to one side other matters requiring the CG's attention.

In all events, conditioned by what Henderson had reported to the command element regarding the results of his immediate investigative efforts in March and their acceptance of his oral report, when the allegations of the Son My villagers and the VC propaganda reached division headquarters those who learned of them were quick to dismiss them as bogus propaganda. In his testimony before this Inquiry MG Koster described his own reaction: "I just didn't feel that an incident like this was apt to have happened." Thus MG Koster assured both COL Toan and LTC Khien that the matter had already been investigated and found to be without substance. COL Henderson delivered a similar message to the GVN officials.

Against this background, MG Koster further stated in his testimony that he had not believed that a war crime had been alleged because the information came from a VC area; it did not correlate with the information from Henderson's investigation; the allegations concerned many more civilian casualties than the number of civilians reported to live in the area; and "the document I read" indicated that the District Chief did not give importance to the matter.

The combination of a natural predisposition to discount all charges from VC-controlled areas as baseless propaganda, a natural reticence on the part of GVN and ARVN officials to express forthrightly any criticism of US forces, the failure of US personnel to recognize the seriousness of the allegations as subtly passed to them, and an apparent deception on the part of the Brigade Commander all contributed to a completely negative command response to the additional allegations that came to division from the Vietnamese sources.

C. GVN/ARVN Investigations

Information regarding Quang Ngai Sector's efforts to investigate the Son My Village incident, as directed by COL Toan, is confusing. The Province Chief did initiate an operation on 11 June 1968, which continued until 13 June, which he stated had the purpose of going to Thuan Yen subhamlet for an on-site investigation of the incident. However, Thuan Yen was never reached supposedly because of the VC strength and fire from the subhamlet and because the operation was diverted to secure a helicopter (in which LTC Barker and CPT Michles were passengers) and an 0–2 aircraft which had collided and crashed in the immediate vicinity.

Any suggestion that the operation was for the purpose of investigating the incident is negated almost totally by the testimony of MAJ William Ford who accompanied the operation. MAJ Ford stated that the RF Group, which he served as a Mobile Advisory Team (MAT) advisor, secured the right flank of the aircraft crash site and in doing so passed through, stopped in, and returned through Thuan Yen subhamlet. MAJ Ford talked with some of the remaining inhabitants, but stated that he had never received a request to check the earlier incident, nor did he believe that his RF counterpart had been so directed. That the purpose of the operation was not to investigate the Son My incident is further substantiated by the interrogation reports of the three prisoners captured during the operation. All questions posed to these prisoners were biographic in nature; no questions were asked concerning the incident.

In his efforts to reach Thuan Yen, either in June or during a later operation in August or September, the Province Chief stated that he did meet and interrogate approximately 20 residents of Thuan Yen about 2 kilometers west of the subhamlet. Mr. Burke, the then Province Senior Advisor, and LTC Green of the advisory team, both confirm seeing the Province Chief talking to residents in this area in an operation in the late summer or fall of 1968. These people had no specific information regarding the events of 16 March but apparently reported that some residents had been killed. They indicated that when the Americans and the VC began to shoot, the people moved to their shelters or ran to other hamlets and thus they were unable to see how many people were killed. The following day they went to the hamlet and buried an unknown number of bodies, which they estimated to be about 100.

The Province Chief stated that he did not submit a formal after action report covering this operation or a report of investigation, since he had been unable to reach Thuan Yen.

Apparently there were no further efforts by the GVN to investigate the events of 16 March 1968 until 1969 when the incident was brought to public attention.

KNOWLEDGE OF INCIDENTS RELATED TO THE SON MY OPERATION

	MG KOSTER CG AMERICAL DIV	BG YOUNG ADC AMERICAL DIV	COL PARSON CofS AMERICAL DIV	COL HENDERSON CO 11TH BDE	LTC BARKER CO TF BARKER	LTC HOLLADAY CO 123D AVN BN	LTC (CHAP) LEWIS CHAPLIN AMERICAL DIV	LTC LUPER CO 6—11TH ARTY	MAJ CALHOUN XO,S3,TF BARKER	MAJ MC KNIGHT S3 11TH BDE	MAJ WATKE CO Co B, 123D AVN BN	CPT (CHAP) CRESSWELL CHAPLIN AMERICAL DIV	CPT JOHNSON DIV INTERROGATOR,52D MI	CPT KOTOUC S2 TF BARKER
ARTILLERY PLANNED AND FIRED ON MY LAI (4)				15M	15 M			15M	15 M	15 M	15 M			15 M
GUNSHIPS AND LIFTSHIPS FIRE ON MY LAI (4)					16 M				16 M		16 M			
REPORTS OF DEPARTURE OF VC FROM MY LAI (4)				16M	16 M			16 M	16 M	16 M			16 M	16 M
EXODUS OF CIVILIANS FROM MY LAI (4)	16 M			16 M	16 M			16 M	16 M	16 M	16 M		16M	16M
REPORTS AND OBSERVATIONS OF NONCOMBATANT CASUALTIES	16 M	17 M	17 M	16M	16 M	16M	17M	16 M	16 M	16 M	16 M	16M	16M	16 M
REPORTS AND OBSERVATIONS OF BURNING BUILDINGS	16 M	18 M		16 M	16 M			16 M	16M	16 M	16 M		16M	16 M
INITIAL REPORT OF HIGH VC BODY COUNT	16 M	16 M	16 M	16 M	16 M			16 M	16 M	16 M	16 M		16M	16 M
REPORT OF 69 VC KIA BY ARTILLERY	16 M	16 M	16 M	16 M	16 M	16M	16 M	16 M	16 M	16 M	16M	16 M	16 M	16 M
ABSENCE OF REPORTS OF ENEMY CONTACTS & REQUESTS FOR FIRE SUPPORT	16 M	16 M	16 M	16 M	16 M	16M		16 M	16 M	16 M	16 M		16 M	16M
LOW RATIO OF US CASUALTIES TO VC CASUALTIES	16 M	16 M	16 M	16 M	16 M	16 M	16 M	16 M	16 M	16 M	16 M	18 M	16 M	16 M
LOW RATIO OF WEAPONS CAPTURED TO VC KIA	16 M	16 M	16 M	16 M	16M	16 M	16 M	16 M	16 M	16 M	16 M	18 M	16 M	16 M
WO1 THOMPSON'S COMPLAINT	17 M	17 M	17 M	18 M	16 M	16 M	17 M		16 M	18 M	16 M	16 M		16 M
COMMANDER'S ORDER TO RETURN TO MY LAI (4)	16 M	16 M		16 M	16 M			16 M	16 M	16 M				16M

LEGEND

M=MARCH
A=APRIL

INCLOSURE 1

Broadcast American Evil Appears
(Coordinate this broadcast with leaflets:"Let American Enemy Pay This Bloody Debt.)

American imperialists make Vietnam aggressive war, but he said that he came here to "help" our people and he calls himself as our friends.

When he arrives in South Vietnam he tries to hide his bad aggressive ambition. He told his troopers to respect Vietnamese people and make good relationship with them. His psyops also give troops "commandments" whose contents are "Have to respect women and Vietnamese traditions and customs."

When American troops had just arrived in Vietnam, they tried to show themselves as "Honorable gentlemen" selling or buying fair and square, even, paying higher than market prices. When they destroyed something, they paid for it with money. Then some posts allowed people to come, and doctors were sent to some where to give people medical aid. American press shows some pictures of Americans and Vietnamese shaking hands - Americans kiss Vietnamese people and give them candies - or Americans with Red Cross signs at their arms give medical aid to Vietnamese people ... and they boast that this is one of familiar pictures around American troops locations.

This demagogy makes some ARVN troops believe Americans are good friends. How happy it is if we have such good and rich friends!

But any play has to end, although the actors are skillful, but they play only one act, they will become soon unskillful - and the play will become a bad one. So the damagogy will become "true", "unmask", easier than any plays.

The role can be played more beautifully if U.S. troops collect more victories every year, but they are beaten more heavily by our people year by year. So the demagogy is unmasked more easy. Now, U.S. troops can not hide anything, they have shown all bad ambition which belongs to any aggressive troops. In sweep operations, they loot people's properties, destroy everything, rape women, they have shown their animal ambition, their civilization. In Saigon one American had put his penis outside his pants, and one dollar was put on it, which he paid to a girl. U.S. troops play girls every public areas: beach, roadside ... they do not care about people passing by. In U.S. troop locations, they search people to get piaster, gold rings, watches, ear rings, they are so cunning that they do not pick up false gold.

Due to their great defeats in the recent Spring, they are like wild wounded animal, the more they wriggle, the more bad actions are done - definitely inhuman doings. They had dropped bombs at random onto populous areas and cities such HUE, SAIGON, BEN TRE. They confirmed that 90% of houses were destroyed in HUE City. Thousands of our people were killed or homeless. Western newspapers and radio stations also confirmed that all the damages of houses in South Vietnam cities came from American bombs and ammo because U.S. has more fire power than NLF troops. British newspapers said Americans bombed cities, especially Saigon City, it would be condemned by opinion it was too much when Americans did that. Japanese public opinion said: America would be isolated and lose appreciation when they bomb South Vietnamese cities. It would make an anti-American wave in the South Vietnam, unless the world public opinion protested, and also there was not a unanimity of Allies. Americans still close their eyes, shut their ears to perform their cruel acts.

A sweep operation was conducted on 15 Mar 68 recently in SON TINH. Crazy American enemy used light machineguns and all kinds of weapons to kill our innocent civilian people in TINH KHE Village (SON MY (V)). Most of them were women, kids, there were some just born babies and pregnant women. They shot everything they saw, they killed all domestic animals, they burned all people's houses. There were 26 families killed completely - no survivors.

The fierce devil Americans dropped down their priest covers to become barbarous, and cruel.

American wolf forgot their good sheeps' appearance. They opened mouth to eat, drink our people blood with all their animal barbarity.

Our people have only one way, it is to kill them so they can not bite around anymore.

Vietnam officers, soldier brothers, it is about time to know the true face of Americans. There were so many times they forgot you when you were bitten by NLF's troops but they have never fired any mortar round to support you. Even they are right beside you and they also dropped bombs on puppet dead bodies to suppress and sometimes they mortared right on your formation.

The position of puppet troops as their targets are so clear. Any one still doubt, just look at the 39th Ranger Battalion stationed in KHE SANH area. They used the unit as an obstacle in the front for American Marines, you already know they offered this battalion as "ready to die" but it doesn't mean the same as the meaning of "die for fatherlands" as NLF soldiers, they said that because they wanted to protect 6000 American troops there.

So it is the American civilization it is the good of friend as you see them - a murderer, killed your blood people - made a vietnamese blood stream running as blood in our own bodies - as an allied or not?

What are you waiting for! Use right American guns to shoot right their heads in order to avenge our people, to wash out insult to our nation and save your proud and your own life.

This time: more than ever before
American guns are in your hands
Point to American heads and shoot!

A TRUE TRANSLATION TO THE BEST OF MY KNOWLEDGE, CHU LAI, REPUBLIC OF VIETNAM

1 JANUARY 1970

BILLY M. STANBERRY
Lieutenant Colonel, US Army

Chapter 11. Suppression and Withholding of Information

A. Introduction

One aspect of the Son My operation most difficult to comprehend is that the facts remained hidden for so long. Within the Americal Division, at every command level from company to division, actions were taken or omitted which together effectively concealed from higher headquarters the events which transpired in TF Barker's operation of 16–19 March 1968. Some of these acts and omissions were by design, others perhaps by negligence, and still others were the result of policies and procedures. Outside the Division, personnel in the Province and District and possibly the 2d ARVN Division Advisory Teams also contributed to the end result.

The purpose of this chapter of the report is to identify, insofar as it is possible at this time, those acts and omissions which aided in the concealment from appropriate authorities of the true facts of the Son My operation. In this connection, it should be noted that efforts to withhold information continue to this date. Six officers who occupied key positions during the Son My operation exercised their right to remain silent before this Inquiry. There is evidence that an even larger number of witnesses either withheld information or gave false testimony, and no trace has been found in US files of several contemporaneous documents bearing upon the incident. Despite such obstacles to the complete development of the facts, it seems clear that the following acts and omissions constituted or contributed to the suppression or withholding of information concerning the events which took place in Son My Village of 16 March 1968.

B. C Company, 1st Battalion, 20th Infantry

1. FAILURE TO REPORT ACTS OF MURDER AND OTHER WAR CRIMES

It has been established elsewhere in this report that members of C/1–20 Inf did not report the crimes perpetrated by that unit in Son My Village on 16 March 1968. While no explanation is needed in the case of those members who actively participated in criminal acts, C Company's collective failure to make any reports of crimes committed on the operation probably resulted from the large proportion of its members implicated in such acts and from the apparent sanction given to the entire operation by company officers. The sheer enormity of the acts committed by some and observed by all on 16 March caused many of the men to put the Son My operation out of their minds and to avoid talking about it even among themselves. This collective reluctance to expose what had occurred was facilitated by the nature of the operation, which isolated C/1–20 Inf from other elements of TF Barker, by the fact that the company was detached from its parent battalion at the time of the operation and remained so for some weeks thereafter, and by the fact that Son My Village was located in a VC-controlled area.

2. FALSE REPORT OF 20–28 NONCOMBATANT CASUALTIES

It is clear from the testimony of persons who were with the C/1–20 Inf command group on 16 March that a far greater number of noncombatant casualties was observed by CPT Medina than the 20–28 he reported. That CPT Medina reported any noncombatant casualties at all is probably due to the fact that COL Henderson had observed some bodies of women and children on the ground and questioned LTC Barker about them, or to the circumstance that a large group of bodies (largely women and children) were lying in the open on the trail leading south from My Lai (4), in plain view of anyone flying overhead. In any event, the result of CPT Medina's admission that some noncombatants had been killed, coupled with the false attribution of such casualties to artillery and gunships, provided the basis subsequently used by COL Henderson to explain and dismiss the Thompson Report.

3. INSTRUCTIONS NOT TO DISCUSS OR REPORT THE OPERATION OF 16 MARCH

Upon their return to LZ Dottie on 18 March, the members of C/1–20 Inf were advised by CPT Medina that the incidents of 16 March were to be investigated and that they were not to discuss them except in the course of the investigation. This action, combined with the natural reluctance of many of the men to discuss the acts they had participated in, proved an effective means of containing the story of Son My within C Company. In the same sense, CPT Medina advised a member of C/1–20 Inf, who had indicated an intention to write his Congressman concerning the operation, not to do so "until the investigation was complete."

C. B Company, 4th Battalion, 3d Infantry

1. REPORTS OF VC KILLED

On 16 March, B/4–3 Inf reported a total of 38 VC killed in action (KIA) at My Khe. Testimony reveals that, at a minimum, such reports included women and children killed by B Company's 1st Platoon. While there is no testimony to indicate that CPT Michles had knowledge of this, there is evidence that 1LT (now CPT) Willingham was aware that the majority (if not all) the persons reported as VC KIA were women and children. On the afternoon of 16 March, in response to a request for information concerning the number of women and children who may have been killed, CPT Michles submitted a negative report to TF Barker. It is not known whether CPT Michles made this report knowing it was false or innocently transmitted a false report made to him by 1LT Willingham.

2. FAILURE TO REPORT ACTS OF MURDER AND OTHER WAR CRIMES

Testimony presented to this Inquiry indicates that acts of murder and aggravated assault were committed by members of B/4–3 Inf during the Son My operation. None of these criminal acts was reported outside the company, probably as a result of factors similar to some of those mentioned above in connection with C/1–20 Inf.

D. Task Force Barker and 11th Brigade

Some of the most significant acts of suppression and withholding of information concerning the Son My incident involved the commanders and certain key staff officers and other personnel of TF Barker and the 11th Brigade. Due to the fact that several of these individuals (other than LTC Barker, who is dead) either gave false testimony before this Inquiry or refused to give further testimony, or both, it has not been possible to sort out acts of concealment that may have been initiated by and known only to TF Barker from those done or approved by the 11th Brigade as well. False and misleading testimony by COL Henderson; the death of LTC Barker; the refusal to testify further by MAJ McKnight, MAJ Calhoun, and CPT Kotouc; and the professed inability of LTC Blackledge, MSG Johnson, and other key personnel to recall any significant information have together precluded a reconstruction of exactly what transpired between the two headquarters. For this reason, the roles played by TF Barker and the 11th Brigade in the suppression and withholding of information are considered jointly.

1. FAILURE TO REPORT CASUALTIES INFLICTED BY C/1–20 INF AFTER 0840 HOURS

Until 0840 hours on 16 March, C/1–20 Inf had apparently been reporting to TF Barker as VC KIA all persons they had killed in My Lai (4), although few if any of the victims had actually been identified as VC. After 0840 hours, no further reports of VC KIA by C Company were recorded by TF Barker and the 11th Brigade, or reported to Division headquarters. The discontinuance of these reports conceivably was initiated by C Company even though there is some evidence that CPT Medina did make further reports of VC KIA. More probably, recording and reporting of VC dead reported by C Company was halted by TF Barker either in response to the order from COL Henderson to stop the "unnecessary killing," or to avoid attracting undue attention to C Company's operations in My Lai (4). It is entirely possible that such action was either ordered or condoned by COL Henderson, who was present in the TF Barker TOC between 0840 and 1000 hours on 16 March.

2. FAILURE TO REPORT NONCOMBATANT CASUALTIES

It is clear from the testimony of many witnesses that any overflight of My Lai (4) on the morning of 16 March, at an altitude of less than 1,000 feet, would have permitted observation of a large number of bodies of noncombatants. According to COL Henderson's testimony, he observed 6–8 such bodies early on the 16th and discussed this matter with MG Koster about 0935 hours at LZ Dottie. Others in COL Henderson's aircraft admit to seeing 15–20 bodies. By noon, LTC Barker had been advised of the Thompson Report by MAJ Watke, and during the afternoon hours LTC Barker and MAJ Calhoun were both aware of a report from CPT Medina that 20–28 noncombatants had been killed. A 1555 hours entry in the TF Barker Journal recorded that "10–11 women and children were killed" in the C Company area of operations. By early evening, COL Henderson was admittedly aware that at least 20 noncombatants had been killed.

While some of this information may have been given by COL Henderson to MG Koster in oral reports, such reports could not have been considered a substitute for the normal spot report required when any friendly forces, any enemy forces, or any civilians are known to have been killed.

In addition to the requirement for an immediate spot report, concerning casualties of any type, directives from MACV, USARV, and III MAF in effect at the time clearly required civilian casualties to be reported as a special matter. Had such a report been made as required, it might well have generated a thorough investigation of the Son My operation.

3. CHANGES IN REPORT OF 69 VC KILLED BY C COMPANY

One of the most obvious efforts to suppress information uncovered by this Inquiry concerns the matter of 69 VC purportedly killed by artillery. The source of this false report has not been established, but it is known that by 0758 hours on 16 March C Company had reported 14 VC KIA in the hamlet of My Lai (4) and one VC KIA at the LZ just west of My Lai (4). It is also known that LTC Barker, who was flying over My Lai (4), received a radio message at about 0830 hours advising him that C Company's VC body count had reached 84. Shortly after receiving this message, Barker advised the TOC that he was coming in and would bring them "up to date." Returning to the TOC at LZ Dottie, Barker met with COL Henderson, LTC Luper, MAJ McKnight, and MAJ Calhoun. An entry was made in the TF Barker Journal as of 0840 hours of 69 VC KIA at a location (by map coordinates) in the hamlet of My Lai (4). Inexplicably, this report of 69 VC KIA was not reported to the 11th Brigade TOC for about an hour. The delay alone is suspicious for several reasons. First, there is the operational requirement to report immediately information of this type—a requirement which TF Barker fulfilled in transmitting all other VC body count reports on 16 March. Secondly, the natural reaction of a combat unit in reporting such obvious proof of success is haste, not an hour's delay.

During this period of almost one hour during which the report of 69 VC KIA was held at the TF Barker TOC, a decision was apparently made to attribute the cause of death to the artillery preparation and to shift the location at which the VC were reported killed from inside the hamlet to a point 600 meters outside the hamlet and generally on the gun-target line from LZ Uptight to the C Company LZ. This decision was reflected in an entry at 0930 hours in the 11th Brigade Journal and in a report made by the 11th Brigade at the same time to Division. There was no factual basis for attributing the killing to artillery, and the change of map coordinates cannot reasonably be explained as resulting from a transposition of numbers or some other inadvertent error.

A reasonable inference is that the changes effected in the original report of the 69 VC killed by C Company were made to lessen the attention which might have been attracted had the original report reached Division headquarters. Such a report would have reflected a total of 83 VC killed by small arms fire at a single location inside the hamlet of My Lai (4). Coupled with the absence of any casualties to C Company personnel and the few weapons captured, it might have prompted inquiries that could not readily have been answered.

4. FAILURE TO REPORT ALLEGATIONS OF WAR CRIMES

A most significant act of withholding information is the apparent failure of TF Barker to report to 11th Brigade (or, alternatively, the failure of the Brigade to report to the Americal Division) the allegations of WO1 Thompson, which were reported by MAJ Watke to LTC Barker shortly after noon on 16 March. There is some testimony that after MAJ Watke apprised LTC Barker of the complaints of WO1 Thompson, Barker left LZ Dottie ostensibly to visit C Company. There is little evidence to show that he made any real effort to investigate the charges; in fact, the Inquiry has failed to uncover a single member of C Company who recalls Barker landing at Son My at any time during the operation. There is a similar absence of any evidence that Barker reported Thompson's allegations to 11th Brigade. If he did, his report was neither recorded nor relayed to Division by the 11th Brigade.

5. FAILURE TO REPORT ACTS OF DESTRUCTION OF PRIVATE PROPERTY

During the course of the Son My operation, both B and C Companies engaged in extensive destruction of private dwellings and structures through demolition and burning. There is ample testimony to establish that such destruction had been ordered by LTC Barker and must have been observed by COL Henderson and MAJ McKnight. Although such acts violated MACV directives and the strong policy within the Americal Division against the burning and destruction of houses, no report of these violations was made.

6. CHANGE IN REPORT OF 30–40 VC DEPARTING MY LAI (4)

At about 0900 hours on 16 March, during the interrogation of a Vietnamese inhabitant of My Lai (4), C/1–20 Inf received information that 30–40 VC had departed the hamlet prior to the combat assault. This information was apparently transmitted to the TF Barker TOC where, for reasons unknown, it was not recorded in the unit journal. The records at 11th Brigade, however, do reflect this information in a journal entry made at 0915 hours. At the Americal Division TOC, however, it was recorded that the prisoner "so far has said their (sic) lots of VC in vic BS716788." The reason for this erroneous entry has not been explained. It may have resulted from a simple error in the transmission of information, or from a deliberately false report made to withhold from Division the fact that the VC had departed the area prior to the combat assault and to create the impression that C/1–20 Inf was involved in a contested combat action. This matter is discussed in more detail in Chapter 10.

7. TF BARKER'S COMBAT ACTION REPORT

Periodically, the Americal Division would direct subordinate elements to prepare special after-action reports on operations which appeared to have been particularly successful. The Son My operation was selected as the subject of such a report, and on 28 March 1968, LTC Barker submitted a Combat Action Report (CAR) to the 11th Brigade, covering the period of 0730–1800 hours, 16 March 1968.

In this report, LTC Barker made no mention of the many noncombatants killed by C Company on 16 March, although US and claimed VC casualties were reported. He disingenuously explained the problem of "population control and medical care of those civilians caught in fires of the opposing forces," but there was no mention of the magnitude of the problems of that type which TF Barker actually encountered on 16 March. In an apparent reference to WO1 Thompson's aero-scout unit, he reported that helicopters assisted civilians in leaving the area, but again there was no indication of the true circumstances of this aspect of the operation.

The report contained a narrative description of the operations of B and C Companies on 16 March that was pure fabrication. It described an artillery preparation on the enemy "combat post positions" which killed 68 VC. It reported contact with "two local force companies and two or three guerrilla platoons" until 1630 hours when "surviving enemy elements had broken all contact."

An appreciation of the misleading and deceptive nature of LTC Barker's report can be gained from the following extract:

> *Commander's Analysis:* This operation was well planned, well executed, and successful. Friendly casualties were light and the enemy suffered heavily. On this operation the civilian population supporting the VC in the area numbered approximately 200. This created a problem in population control and medical care of those civilians caught in fires of the opposing forces. However, the infantry unit on the ground and helicopters were able to assist civilians in leaving the area and in caring for and/or evacuating the wounded.

The Combat Action Report can only be considered an effort by LTC Barker deliberately to suppress the true facts and to mislead higher headquarters into believing that there had been a combat operation in Son My Village on 16 March involving a hotly contested action with a sizable enemy force.

8. WITHHOLDING AND SUPPRESSION OF KNOWLEDGE AND EVIDENCE OF WAR CRIMES BY INFORMATION OFFICE PERSONNEL

On 16 March, a two-man team from the 31st Public Information Detachment, a part of the 11th Brigade, accompanied C/1–20 Inf on the combat assault. These men, SGT (now Mr.) Ronald Haeberle, photographer, and SP5 (now Mr.) Jay Roberts, journalist, witnessed numerous war crimes committed by members of C/1–20 Inf in My Lai (4). SGT Haeberle took a series of photographs using both personal and government owned cameras. He used the color film to record scenes of atrocities and the black and white for other pictures. Both men remained with C/1–20 Inf until approximately 1100 hours, when they departed for B/4–3 Inf. They observed nothing unusual in the B Company area.

After leaving the operations area, they discussed what they had seen and during the discussion, according to SP5 Roberts, SGT Haeberle mentioned that he was curious concerning "what the press would do with photos like that," referring to the pictures taken at My Lai (4).

Later that evening SP5 Roberts wrote a story concerning the incident, making no mention of the atrocities he had seen and lauding the efforts of TF Barker. His account was relayed to the Americal Division Information Office and was the basis for a misleading article in the 11th Brigade news sheet. Indicative of the misleading nature of the article was the statement that a suspect had "told an interpreter that 35 VC had moved into the village [My Lai (4)] two hours earlier," when in fact an inhabitant of the hamlet interrogated by C/1–20 Inf that morning had said that a comparable size force had departed My Lai (4) prior to the combat assault.

Neither SGT Haeberle nor SP5 Roberts took any action to report what they had seen, nor did SGT Haeberle make available to proper authority the photographic evidence of war crimes he had obtained. SGT Haeberle retained the color film he had exposed during the operation as personal property and shortly thereafter rotated to the United States for eventual discharge. Late in 1969, and after his separation from the service, SGT Haeberle sold the photographs to a publisher.

It is apparent that both these individuals had firsthand knowledge of the incident, and that neither took any action to report it. To the contrary, both actively contributed to the suppression of information concerning the incident. It should be noted also that neither of these men was under command of TF Barker and, in contrast to the other enlisted personnel in My Lai (4) that day, they were in a position to report what they had seen without the same fear of retaliation.

E. COL Henderson's Reports

After being charged to investigate the allegations made by WO1 Thompson, and after hearing directly from Thompson and other aviation personnel accounts of what they had observed on the ground on 16 March, COL Henderson failed to make any real investigation of the matter. His subsequent oral reports to BG Young and MG Koster with respect to the scope and findings of his so-called investigation were knowingly false and deceptive.

COL Henderson's deception of his commanders as to what he had done to investigate the matter and as to the facts he had learned probably played a larger role in the suppression of the facts of Son My than any other factor. Whatever may be said of the failure of BG Young and MG Koster to subject COL Henderson's reports to adequate review, they had to rely upon the veracity of what Henderson told them. In misrepresenting to his commanders that he had made a real effort to determine the facts and that WO1 Thompson was the only individual he could find who had seen anything unusual on 16 March, COL Henderson effectively closed off the full exposure of the facts of the Son My incident that would have resulted from a real investigation and a factual report.

COL Henderson's written "Report of Investigation," according to MG Koster, was supposed to have put in writing the details of his previous oral report in response to WO1 Thompson's allegations. In fact, however, it made no mention of Thompson's complaints and is addressed solely to the allegations from Vietnamese sources (VC propaganda and the Son Tinh District Chief's letter of 11 April 1968). It dismissed these allegations as baseless propaganda and restated the fiction that 20 noncombatant casualties had been inadvertently killed on 16 March. There had been no further investigation, and the manner in which the statement by CPT Rodreguez was appended to the "Report of Investigation" suggests that the intent was to imply a Vietnamese origin and concurrence from that source in Henderson's findings.

F. Company B, 123d Aviation Battalion

There is no evidence to establish that members of Company B, 123d Avn Bn deliberately set about to withhold or suppress information concerning the Son My incident. There were, however, several acts of omission and commission by this unit which contributed to those ends.

1. FAILURE TO MAKE A SPOT-REPORT OF ALLEGED WAR CRIMES

Upon receipt of the complaints of WO1 Thompson and other members of his unit, MAJ Watke acted only to report the matter to the commander of the Task Force charged with the offense. Later in the day, after being advised by Barker that he could find nothing to substantiate the charges and despite the fact that he "didn't believe Colonel Barker" Watke did nothing further until approximately 2200 hours. The fact that WO1 Thompson's complaint did not reach the Division Commander until almost 24 hours after it was received by MAJ Watke, and the fact that it never reached the Division Staff, is due in large part to Watke's failure to make the complaint the subject of a spot-report.

2. FAILURE TO REPORT THE COMPLETE FACTS CONCERNING ALLEGATIONS OF WAR CRIMES

The disparity between what WO1 Thompson saw at My Lai (4) and what MAJ Watke stated he reported to BG Young was discussed in detail in Chapter 10. The fact that the complete story did not reach BG Young and subsequently the Division Commander is largely attributable to MAJ Watke's failure to confirm or document the complaints of WO1 Thompson and others. If MAJ Watke did not gain a full appreciation of Thompson's complaint on the basis of what Thompson told him, a full awareness of the nature of the incident would have been obtained through any efforts to confirm the allegations. MAJ Watke had available to him other pilots and crew members who had been over the area as well as the complete "aero-scout" team which could have been used for aerial reconnaissance.

3. INSTRUCTIONS TO MEMBERS OF THE UNIT TO CURB DISCUSSION OF THE SON MY OPERATION

Testimony by former members of the unit reveals that following the Son My operation there was considerable discussion among members of Company B concerning what had occurred in My Lai (4). MAJ Watke has testified that he was aware of this general unrest and approximately two days after the operation, he spoke to the assembled company and "asked them not to discuss the matter any further (that) nothing good could come of their discussion of it and . . . it would be taken care of." At this time MAJ Watke was aware that COL Henderson was conducting an investigation and, according to his testimony, he had no reason to suspect the investigation would not be thorough. While MAJ Watke's intent may have been the elimination of rumors and stories while the incident was being investigated, the effect was largely to silence further discussion of the matter within the company.

4. FAILURE TO TAKE APPROPRIATE ACTION WHEN CONVINCED A "COVER-UP" WAS TAKING PLACE

MAJ Watke testified that he was convinced a "cover-up" was taking place after he observed that no serious effort . . . was being made to interrogate the members of his unit. This conviction reinforced his earlier impression that LTC Barker was lying when Barker said he could not substantiate WO1 Thompson's allegations. Having once come to this conclusion, Watke was faced with a difficult decision and elected not to pursue the matter further. MAJ Watke has testified that he was reluctant to go outside the division with the charge, and could not offer an explanation for his failure to document Thompson's allegations with statements from his pilots and crewmen or to take any other steps to make the allegations a matter of record.

5. FAILURE TO ACT ON REPORTS OF EXTENSIVE CIVILIAN CASUALTIES

Several former members of Company B have testified that they submitted written reports concerning the events of 16 March. These reports were submitted through the Company Operations Section and made reference to as many as 150 civilian casualties. There has been no satisfactory explanation concerning the disposition of these reports and no indication that any action was initiated as a result of their submission. It would appear that MAJ Watke considered his obligations to report the incident satisfied once he delivered his report to BG Young.

G. Headquarters, 123d Aviation Battalion

The actions at this level in the chain of command in suppressing information are similar to those taken by B Company of the same unit. Both LTC Holladay and MAJ Watke have testified that they were in agreement concerning two facts: First, that the allegations made by WO1 Thompson and others were true; and second, that there had been a "cover-up." In considering the reaction of these two officers to the situation, it should be noted they possessed the capability to do much that was not done: to obtain sworn statements from the many eyewitnesses within the unit; to conduct a low-level aerial reconnaissance of My Lai (4); and to seek approval for employment of a small infantry unit into the area to confirm or deny suspicions.

H. Headquarters, Americal Division

On 16 March 1968, the Americal Division was the principal headquarters to which information and reports concerning the Son My operation was directed. Subsequent to that date, other reports and allegations concerning that operation, from both US units and GVN sources, were channeled to that headquarters. Except for routine operational data forwarded on 16 March, none of these reports and allegations were transmitted by the Americal Division to higher headquarters, even though information had been received by 17 March concerning the events at My Lai (4) that warranted a thorough investigation.

While it is clear that information which should have been reported was withheld by the Americal Division from III MAF and MACV, the matter of motivation and intent is difficult to determine. There is little evidence to warrant a conclusion that the Americal Division headquarters actually had an awareness of the full dimension of what had taken place at Son My. While such a possibility cannot be entirely excluded, there is no direct evidence to that effect, and it appears much more likely that (at least prior to mid-April) the CG, ADC, and the Chief of Staff believed they were dealing with the killing of 20–28 noncombatants by TF Barker.

Although the reports they received to that effect were false and they were negligent to have believed them, they probably thought they were withholding information concerning a much less serious incident than the one which had actually occurred.

It is also clear that some information reaching the command element of the division in April indicated that a much more serious event had taken place on 16 March. The command reaction to these subsequent reports was so inadequate to the situation and so inconsistent with what ordinarily would be expected of officers of the ability and experience of MG Koster and BG Young, that it can only be explained by a refusal or an inability to accept or give any credence to evidence or reports which were not consistent with their original, and erroneous, conclusion.

The following is a summary of specific acts of omission or commission taken at the Americal Division headquarters which contributed to the concealment of the true facts of the incident:

1. FAILURE TO REPORT INFORMATION CONCERNING NONCOMBATANT CASUALTIES

MG Koster has testified that by 1600 hours on 16 March, he was aware that at least 20 noncombatants had been killed by elements of TF Barker. As commander of a major combat unit, he was aware of the concern expressed by COMUSMACV concerning noncombatant casualties and of the requirement that such matters be reported as a serious incident. No such report was made by the Americal Division.

2. FAILURE TO REPORT ALLEGATIONS OF SUSPECTED WAR CRIMES

While there is some conflict in testimony concerning the extent to which MG Koster, BG Young, and COL Parson were apprised of the full contents of the Thompson Report, there is sufficient testimony to establish that these three individuals had been advised of the allegation that noncombatants had been indiscriminately killed in My Lai (4). MACV directives in effect at that time clearly required that such allegations be reported. No such report was made by the Americal Division.

3. FAILURE TO INSURE A THOROUGH AND IMPARTIAL INVESTIGATION OF ALLEGATIONS OF WAR CRIMES

Upon receipt of the Thompson Report, MG Koster directed an investigation by the commander of the unit accused in the allegation. Such an investigation, subject to a thorough and impartial review, might have been an acceptable response to the allegations. However, it is clear from the testimony of the principals concerned that the investigation was a pretense and the review inadequate.

4. EFFORTS BY THE DIVISION COMMAND GROUP TO LIMIT INFORMATION CONCERNING NONCOMBATANT CASUALTIES AND ALLEGED WAR CRIMES

From the testimony of MG Koster, BG Young, and COL Parson, it appears that each individual acted to restrict knowledge of matters being investigated by COL Henderson. Specific actions included the failure to include pertinent information in daily staff briefings; the failure properly to employ the investigative resources of the division staff; the failure to advise key staff members concerning the allegations and investigations; and the failure to advise the staff of matters which should have been reported to higher headquarters. Testimony indicates that members of the General and Special Staffs had but little information concerning the incident or of the subsequent investigation or review.

5. FAILURE OF THE DIVISION CHAPLAIN TO REPORT ALLEGATIONS OF WAR CRIMES

As discussed in Chapter 10, shortly after 16 March 1968, WO1 Thompson went to the Division Artillery Chaplain, CPT Carl Creswell, with a report of what he had seen at My Lai (4). Chaplain Creswell in turn, without reporting the matter to his commander, went to the Division Chaplain, LTC Francis Lewis, with the story. As previously discussed, LTC Lewis' efforts at investigation were futile and he allowed the matter to pass without substantive effort to bring it to the attention of his superiors.

I. Actions by Personnel Outside the Americal Division

Among the Vietnamese officials who came in contact with information concerning possible war crimes in Son My during the period 16–19 March, there was a natural reluctance to confront their American counterparts with such a serious allegation and to insist on inquiry into the matter. Such information as did reach US advisory channels was not forwarded through advisory channels but referred only to the Americal Division and its 11th Brigade. There is evidence that at least at the Quang Ngai Province and Son Tinh District levels, and possibly at the 2d ARVN Division, the senior US military advisors aided in suppressing information concerning the incident.

J. Summary

It is evident that efforts to suppress and withhold information concerning the Son My incident were made at every level in the Americal Division. These efforts, coupled with the false and misleading reports by COL Henderson, were successful in containing the story of Son My within the division. It is evident to this Inquiry, after interviewing most of those who witnessed the events at Son My, that any serious attempt to interrogate such individuals immediately following the incident would have resulted in full disclosure of the event. Many testified in a manner which showed an eagerness to express what had apparently caused them great concern. If there had been real concern in the chain of command, if anyone had taken action to ask questions, they would have had full and complete answers.

One matter which casts further suspicion on the Americal Division is the almost total absence of files and records of documents relating to the Son My incident and its subsequent investigation. With few exceptions the files have been purged of these documents and records of their removal or destruction have not been maintained. The single notable exception to this has been the copy of COL Henderson's 24 April report, and this document was found in the files of the 11th Bde S2 where it would not normally have been filed. The files of US advisory teams which had knowledge of the Son My incident were similarly barren.

Another factor which may have contributed to suppression was the manner in which information concerning the Son My incident was handled in Vietnamese circles. Such information was apparently not discussed to any extent in GVN channels as witnessed by the number of US personnel who worked closely with Province, District, and ARVN authorities and yet had no knowledge that the incident had occurred. Even on the Vietnamese civilian side, a measure of silence fell over the community. Without exception, Americans who worked and lived closely with Vietnamese in both official and social circles in Quang Ngai Province, stated that they had not obtained an inkling of the incident.

Chapter 12. Findings and Recommendations

I. On the Basis of the Foregoing, the Findings of the Inquiry Are as Follows:

A. CONCERNING EVENTS SURROUNDING THE SON MY OPERATION OF 16–19 MARCH 1968

1. During the period 16–19 March 1968, US Army troops of TF Barker, 11th Brigade, Americal Division, massacred a large number of noncombatants in two hamlets of Son My Village, Quang Ngai Province, Republic of Vietnam. The precise number of Vietnamese killed cannot be determined but was at least 175 and may exceed 400.
2. The massacre occurred in conjunction with a combat operation which was intended to neutralize Son My Village as a logistical support base and staging area, and to destroy elements of an enemy battalion thought to be located in the Son My area.
3. The massacre resulted primarily from the nature of the orders issued by persons in the chain of command within TF Barker.
4. The task force commander's order and the associated intelligence estimate issued prior to the operation were embellished as they were disseminated through each lower level of command, and ultimately presented to the individual soldier a false and misleading picture of the Son My area as an armed enemy camp, largely devoid of civilian inhabitants.
5. Prior to the incident, there had developed within certain elements of the 11th Brigade a permissive attitude toward the treatment and safeguarding of noncombatants which contributed to the mistreatment of such persons during the Son My operation.
6. The permissive attitude in the treatment of Vietnamese was, on

16–19 March 1968, exemplified by an almost total disregard for the lives and property of the civilian population of Son My Village on the part of commanders and key staff officers of TF Barker.

7. On 16 March, soldiers at the squad and platoon level, within some elements of TF Barker, murdered noncombatants while under the supervision and control of their immediate superiors.
8. A part of the crimes visited on the inhabitants of Son My Village included individual and group acts of murder, rape, sodomy, maiming, and assault on noncombatants and the mistreatment and killing of detainees. They further included the killing of livestock, destruction of crops, closing of wells, and the burning of dwellings within several subhamlets.
9. Some attempts were made to stop the criminal acts in Son My Village on 16 March; but with few exceptions, such efforts were too feeble or too late.
10. Intensive interrogation has developed no evidence that any members of the units engaged in the Son My operation was under the influence of marijuana or other narcotics.

B. CONCERNING THE ADEQUACY OF REPORTS, INVESTIGATIONS AND REVIEWS

11. The commanders of TF Barker and the 11th Brigade had substantial knowledge as to the extent of the killing of noncombatants but only a portion of their information was ever reported to the Commanding General of the Americal Division.
12. Based on his observations, WO1 Thompson made a specific complaint through his command channels that serious war crimes had been committed but through a series of inadequate responses at each level of command, action on his complaint was delayed and the severity of his charges considerably diluted by the time it reached the Division Commander.
13. Sufficient information concerning the highly irregular nature of the operations of TF Barker on 16 March 1968 reached the Commanding General of the Americal Division to require that a thorough investigation be conducted.
14. An investigation by the Commander of the 11th Brigade conducted at the direction of the Commanding General of the Americal Division, was little more than a pretense and was subsequently misrepresented as a thorough investigation to the CG, Americal Division in order to conceal from him the true enormity of the atrocities.

15. Patently inadequate reports of investigation submitted by the Commander of the 11th Brigade were accepted at face value and without an effective review by the CG, Americal Division.
16. Reports of alleged war crimes, noncombatant casualties, and serious incidents concerning the Son My operation of 16 March were received at the headquarters of the Americal Division but were not reported to higher headquarters despite the existence of directives requiring such action.
17. Reports of alleged war crimes relating to the Son My operation of 16 March reached Vietnamese government officials, but those officials did not take effective action to ascertain the true facts.
18. Efforts of the ARVN/GVN officials discreetly to inform the US commanders of the magnitude of the war crimes committed on 16 March 1968 met with no affirmative response.

C. CONCERNING ATTEMPTS TO SUPPRESS INFORMATION

19. At every command level within the Americal Division, actions were taken, both wittingly and unwittingly, which effectively suppressed information concerning the war crimes committed at Son My Village.
20. At the company level there was a failure to report the war crimes which had been committed. This, combined with instructions to members of one unit not to discuss the events of 16 March, contributed significantly to the suppression of information.
21. The task force commander and at least one, and probably more, staff officers of TF Barker may have conspired to suppress information and to mislead higher headquarters concerning the events of 16–19 March 1968.
22. At the 11th Brigade level, the commander and at least one principal staff officer may have conspired to suppress information to deceive the division commander concerning the true facts of the Son My operation of 16–19 March.
23. A reporter and a photographer from the 11th Brigade observed many war crimes committed by C/1–20 Inf on 16 March. Both failed to report what they had seen; the reporter submitted a misleading account of the operation; and the photographer withheld and suppressed (and wrongfully misappropriated upon his discharge from the service) photographic evidence of such war crimes.
24. Efforts within the 11th Brigade to suppress information concerning the Son My operation were aided in varying degrees by members of US Advisory teams working with ARVN and GVN officials.

25. Within the Americal Division headquarters, actions taken to suppress information concerning what was purportedly believed to be the inadvertent killing of 20 to 28 noncombatants effectively served to conceal the true nature and scope of the events which had taken place in Son My Village on 16–19 March 1968.
26. Failure of the Americal Division headquarters to act on reports and information received from GVN/ARVN officials in mid-April served effectively to suppress the true nature and scope of the events which had taken place in Son My Village on 16–19 March 1968.
27. Despite an exhaustive search of the files of the 11th Brigade, Americal Division, GVN/ARVN advisory team files, and records holding centers, with few exceptions, none of the documents relating to the so-called investigation of the events of 16–19 March were located.

D. WITH RESPECT TO INDIVIDUALS

1. During the period March–June 1968 a number of persons assigned to the Americal Division and to US Advisory elements located in Quang Ngai Province had information as to the killing of noncombatants and other serious offenses committed by members of TF Barker during the Son My operation in March 1968 and did one or more of the following:

   a. Failed to make such official report thereof as their duty required them to make;
   b. Suppressed information concerning the occurrence of such offenses acting singly or in concert with others;
   c. Failed to order a thorough investigation and to insure that such was made, or failed to conduct an adequate investigation, or failed to submit an adequate report of investigation, or failed to make an adequate review of a report of investigation, as applicable;

   or committed other derelictions related to the events of the Son My operation, some constituting criminal offenses.
2. Attached to this chapter at Inclosure 1 is a list of such persons and the omissions and commissions of which they are suspected and upon which the above findings are based.

   a. The officers named in Inclosure 1, their position in 1968, and their current grade and status, are listed below:

NAME	GRADE	POSITION	CURRENT STATUS
Koster, Samuel W.	MG	CG, Americal Div	Active Duty
Young, George H.	BG	ADC (OPS), Americal Div	Active Duty
Henderson, Oran K.	COL	CO, 11th Inf Bde	Active Duty
Hutter, Dean E.	COL	Senior Advisor 2d ARVN Div	Active Duty
Luper, Robert B.	COL	CO, 6–11th Arty	Active Duty
Parson, Nels A.	COL	Chief of Staff Americal Div	Active Duty
Barker, Frank A.	LTC	CO, TF Barker	Deceased
Gavin, David C.	LTC (then MAJ)	Senior District Advisor, Son Tinh District	Active Duty
Guinn, William D.	LTC	Deputy Senior Advisor, Quang Ngai Province	Active Duty
Holladay, John L.	LTC	CO, 123d Avn Bn	Active Duty
Lewis, Francis R.	LTC (Ch)	Div Chaplain, Americal Div	Active Duty
Calhoun, Charles C.	MAJ	XO/S3, TF Barker	Active Duty
McKnight, Robert W.	MAJ	S3, 11th Inf Bde	Active Duty
Watke, Frederic W.	MAJ	CO, Co B, 123d Avn Bn	Active Duty
Boatman, Kenneth W.	CPT (then 1LT)	Forward Observer, Command Group, B/4–3	Active Duty
Creswell, Carl E.	CPT (Ch)	Div Arty Chaplain Americal Div	Civilian
Johnson, Dennis H.	CPT (then 1LT)	Military Intelligence officer in support of TF Barker	Active Duty
Kotouc, Eugene M.	CPT	S2, TF Barker	Active Duty
Medina, Ernest L.	CPT	CO, C/1–20 Inf	Active Duty
Michles, Earl A.	CPT	CO, B/4–3 Inf	Deceased
Vazquez, Dennis R.	CPT	Artillery Liaison officer in support of TF Barker	Civilian
Willingham, Thomas K.	CPT (then 1LT)	Plt Ldr, 1st Plt, B/4–3 Inf	Active Duty
Calley, William L., Jr.	1LT (then 2LT)	Plt Ldr, 1st Plt, C/1–20 Inf	Active Duty
Alaux, Roger L., Jr.	2LT	Arty Forward Observer attached to C/1–20 Inf	Civilian
Brooks, Steven K.	2LT	Plt Ldr, 2d Plt, C/1–20	Deceased
LaCross, Jeffrey U.	2LT	Plt Ldr, 3d Plt, C/1–20	Civilian
Lewis, Michael L.	2LT	Plt Ldr, 2d Plt, B/4–3	Deceased
Mundy, John E.	2LT	Executive Officer, B/4–3	Civilian

b. The following enlisted members of the Army operating in support of TF Barker, on 16 March 1968 and now civilians, by reason of their military training and assignment, and having a particular duty to report any knowledge of suspected or apparent war crimes which came to their attention, failed to perform this duty:

Name	Grade	Position
Haeberle, Ronald L.	SGT	Photographer, Info Office, 11th Inf Bde (31st PID)
Roberts, Jay A.	SP5	Senior Correspondent, Info Office, 11th Inf Bde (31st PID)

3. Evidence adduced in this Inquiry also indicates that numerous serious offenses in violation of the Uniform code of Military Justice and the law of war may have been committed by military personnel who participated in the TF Barker operation in Son My during the period 16–19 March 1968. Evidence of these suspected offenses has been furnished to representatives of the Provost Marshal General of the Army for further investigation.
4. Some of the officers and enlisted men concerned fulfilled their minimum obligation to report their knowledge of crimes committed during the Son My operation to their commanding officers. However, had they exhibited deeper concern for their units, the United States Army and the Nation by taking action beyond that which was technically required, it is probable that the details of the Son My incident would have come to light promptly. Those who failed to do so have contributed to a serious obstruction of justice.

E. CONCERNING THE ADEQUACY OF CERTAIN POLICIES, DIRECTIVES, AND TRAINING

1. In 1968 the then existing policies and directives at every level of command expressed a clear intent regarding the proper treatment and safeguarding of noncombatants, the humane handling of prisoners of war, and minimizing the destruction of private property.
2. Directives prescribing the procedures for the reporting of war crimes were not clear as to the action which should be taken by subordinates when their unit commander participated in or sanc-

tioned a war crime. Directives prescribed only that war crimes would be reported to the commanding officer.

3. Many soldiers in the 11th Brigade were not adequately trained as to:
   a. Their responsibilities regarding obedience to orders received from their superiors which they considered palpably illegal.
   b. Their responsibilities concerning the procedures for the reporting of war crimes.
   c. The provisions of the Geneva Conventions, the handling and treatment of prisoners of war, and the treatment and safeguarding of noncombatants.

F. PERIPHERAL ISSUES

Findings regarding peripheral issues are discussed in Annex B.

II. It Is Recommended That:

A. You take cognizance of the findings set forth above.

B. The names of the members of the Army listed in paragraph D (2) a, above, together with information concerning their omissions and commissions, be referred to their respective general court-martial convening authorities for possible disciplinary or administrative action.

C. Consideration be given to the modification of applicable policies, directives, and training standards in order to correct the apparent deficiencies noted in paragraph IE above.

Omissions and Commissions by Individuals

Following is a listing of individuals and the omissions and commissions of which they are suspected pertaining to the planning, conduct, reporting, and investigation of the operation by TF Barker in the Son My area and the related incidents. The terms omissions and commissions are used here to denote, respectively, instances in which an individual may have failed to perform his duty or may have performed his duty improperly, measured in terms of those responsibilities which were reasonably his under the attendant circumstances. It is recognized that some of the omissions and commissions may involve criminal offenses.

1. MG Samuel W. Koster

a. He did not insure that the plan for the Son My operation included provisions for the handling, screening, and treatment of the noncombatant inhabitants of the area.

b. About midmorning of 16 March 1968 when informed by COL Henderson that he had observed 6 to 8 dead civilians, he (MG Koster) did not take positive action to insure that such casualties were reported through the proper chain of command nor is there any indication that he took any strong positive action to prevent any further killing or to otherwise minimize noncombatant casualties.

c. On the afternoon of 16 March 1968, he countermanded an order which had been issued by a subordinate commander, COL Henderson, directing that C/1–20 Inf return to My Lai (4) to determine the number of civilian casualties, old men, women, and children; and apparently at no time did he obtain COL Henderson's reasons for directing C Company to return to make the count of civilian casualties nor is there any evidence that he discussed this matter with COL Henderson at any later time.

d. By the evening of 16 March 1968, he knew that at least 20 civilians had been killed in or around My Lai (4), purportedly as a result of artillery, gunship, and small arms fire. However, he did not:

   1. Provide such information to other command and staff elements of the Division headquarters with the result that such information was not entered into the operations log of the division nor reported to higher headquarters in the Division SITREP and/or INTSUM.
   2. Initiate a Serious Incident Report (SIR) to be submitted to higher headquarters in accordance with regulations.
   3. Direct the initiation of an artillery incident report as required by regulations even though some of the civilian casualties were reported as having resulted from artillery fire.

e. At or about noontime on 17 March 1968, BG Young, an ADC, informed him of the details of WO1 Thompson's report which had been relayed through LTC Holladay and MAJ Watke. According to MG Koster, the essence of the report was that there had been indiscriminate firing, that extensive firepower had been directed at civilians thereby causing casualties and that a confrontation had taken place between elements of the 123d Aviation Battalion and elements of TF Barker. Although he directed that an investigation be made in response to this information, he failed to:

1. Issue proper instructions to insure that a thorough investigation would be conducted.
2. Insure that the information was forwarded to CG III MAF and possibly COMUSMACV.
3. Inform appropriate elements of the command and staff of the Thompson Report, or advise them that he had directed an investigation.
4. Properly utilize the investigative elements of the Division staff to insure that an appropriate investigation would be conducted.

f. On or about 20 March 1968, he accepted an oral report of investigation presented by COL Henderson and did not:

1. Ascertain that an appropriate in-depth investigation had been conducted.
2. Require that a report of investigation be submitted in writing along with necessary documentation.
3. Notify appropriate elements of the Division command and staff that he had received and accepted the oral report of COL Henderson which indicated that the complaints registered by WO1 Thompson were invalid.
4. Inform the commander of the 123d Aviation Battalion of the submission of COL Henderson's oral report nor in any other way inform WO1 Thompson that his complaints were not supported.

g. About mid-April 1968, he received information that the Chief, Son Tinh District, had submitted a report to the Chief, Quang Ngai Province, alleging that American forces had killed approximately 500 civilians in Tu Cung and Co Luy hamlets of Son My Village on 16 March 1968. He also received information that VC propaganda broadcasts were stressing that American forces had killed a large number of noncombatants (some broadcasts indicated 500) in Son My Village on or about 16 March. Having received this information, he failed to:

1. Initiate a staff analysis of these items of information in combination with COL Henderson's report and the operational data resulting from TF Barker operations on 16 March 1968.
2. Inform higher headquarters of the allegations contained in the District Chief's report to the Province Chief or those made in in the VC propaganda.
3. Have orders prepared appointing an investigating officer along

with appropriate CID support, as required by MACV Directive 20–4 to insure that the allegations were properly investigated by an independent, disinterested party.
4. Direct his G2 to initiate an aggressive intelligence collection effort to obtain additional information concerning what might have taken place in Son My on 16 March 1968.

h. He indicates that he considered COL Henderson's so-called report of investigation of 24 April to be an inadequate report. However, he failed to:

1. Insure that COL Henderson had conducted an adequate investigation.
2. Require information as to who had prepared the statement at Inclosure 1 and the reasons therefor.
3. Give proper consideration to the reports cited in Inclosure 1, specifically the Son Tinh District Chief's report and the Son My Village Chief's report.
4. Inform authorities in I Corps, i.e., CG III MAF and LTG Lam, CG ICTZ, concerning the actions he had taken with respect to the allegations and the investigation.

i. As noted in paragraph h above, when he found COL Henderson's report of 24 April to be inadequate, he stated in testimony that he directed that a formal investigation be conducted. However, there is no record of an investigating officer having been appointed nor is there any record in the division of a report of the investigation having been prepared or submitted.

j. Besides the commissions and omissions cited above, there is no testimony to indicate that at any time he took any additional positive or aggressive command action to determine the true facts surrounding the operation of TF Barker on 16 March 1968.

k. By retaining unto himself information that at least 20 civilians had been killed and by not reporting such facts, he effectively suppressed information concerning the Son My incident both within and outside the Division.

l. In restricting knowledge of the incident, the investigations, reports, and reviews to a group consisting of BG Young, COL Parson, and himself, he may have initiated a conspiracy to withhold the facts concerning the actions of elements of TF Barker on 16 March 1968.

m. He may have falsely testified on several matters before this Inquiry. For example, he stated that he always kept BG Young and

COL Parson completely informed, whereas both of them indicated that they had only a minimum of knowledge concerning his actions. He also indicated that he directed a formal investigation and that he had received a report of said investigation from COL Henderson. This Inquiry did not locate such a formal report of investigation nor is there any indication other than from MG Koster and COL Henderson that such a report was ever prepared or submitted.

2. BG George H. Young

a. Having received a report from LTC Holladay and MAJ Watke to the effect that WO1 Thompson and other members of the 123d Aviation Battalion had observed a large number of civilian noncombatants who had been killed unnecessarily during TF Barker's operation of 16 March 1968, and that there had been a confrontation between air elements of the 123d Aviation Battalion and the ground elements of TF Barker, he failed:

1. To convey this same information or the severity of the incident to the Commanding General, according to his own and MG Koster's testimony.
2. Either to direct or to recommend to the CG that the Commanding Officer of the 123d Aviation Battalion obtain specific details and written statements from the pilots and other crew members who participated in supporting the operation of TF Barker on 16 March.
3. To recommend to the CG that III MAF, MACV, and USARV be notified immediately and that a SIR should be rendered or an investigation of an artillery incident be initiated.

b. Having received instructions from the CG at about 1200 hours on 17 March to initiate an immediate investigation, he:

1. Visited TF Barker at LZ Dottie early on the afternoon of 17 March and was briefed by the TF S3 but took no action to employ a ground element, either by land movement or by combat air assault, or an aerial reconnaissance element to ascertain the facts relative to noncombatant casualties in My Lai (4) on the previous day.
2. Delayed almost 24 hours before issuing such instructions although he had ample opportunity to do so early on the afternoon of 17 March.

c. On the morning of 18 March, he met with COL Henderson and three others in LTC Barker's van at LZ Dottie to discuss the incident. But if his testimony is accurate, he did not issue appropriate instructions to COL Henderson to insure that a proper investigation would be conducted.

d. He had knowledge of the burning of dwellings and shelters in the area of Son My Village and knew this to be contrary to regulations and policy, but took no action to have it officially reported or investigated.

e. Without assuring himself that a proper investigation had been conducted by COL Henderson, he reported its progress and status to the CG. In doing so, he may have contributed to the impression that a proper investigation had been conducted and thereby influenced the acceptance by the CG of COL Henderson's report of investigation.

f. Having knowledge of the acceptance of COL Henderson's oral report by MG Koster, he did not inform LTC Holladay or MAJ Watke of the results of COL Henderson's investigation or its acceptance by the CG.

g. Having been advised by LTC Guinn, Deputy PSA Quang Ngai Province, concerning the Son My District Chief's report to the Province Chief of the killing of large numbers of civilians by Americans in Son My Village, he failed:

  1. To take positive action to obtain a copy of the report.
  2. To discuss the report in depth with the Province Chief and/or other GVN officials.
  3. To seek out additional information concerning the data included in the report.

h. Having knowledge of (1) the information contained in the District Chief's report, (2) the previously reported activities of TF Barker, (3) the information provided through WO1 Thompson's report, and (4) COL Henderson's oral report of investigation, he failed to correlate the aforesaid information and to advise MG Koster that the information indicated an allegation of major war crimes.

i. Together with the CG, he failed to inform the Division staff of the complaints and allegations which had been made and the actions which had been taken, thereby contributing to the suppression of information concerning the activities of TF Barker on 16 March.

j. Although he virtually disassociated himself from events following COL Henderson's oral report of investigation on about 20 March, the evidence suggests that he was well informed with respect to the issues involved and may have contributed to a conspiracy to suppress information of the incident.

k. There were several instances in his testimony before this Inquiry where he may have testified falsely concerning that which was told to him by LTC Holladay and MAJ Watke and what he reported to the CG. He repeatedly insisted that the civilian casualties were the result of having been caught in a "cross-fire" yet there was no evidence of the ground troops involved having received any opposition.

3. COL Oran K. Henderson

a. When briefed on the concept of the operation of TF Barker into the Son My area, he did not insure that the plan included provisions for handling, screening, and treatment of noncombatants and refugees.

b. After observing the bodies of noncombatants in and around My Lai (4) during the morning of 16 March, and despite his knowledge that C Company had not encountered resistance, he failed to take effective action to prevent further killing of noncombatants by C Company.

c. He failed to take any action to insure that medical treatment was provided to noncombatants in the Son My area on 16 March.

d. After C Company had reported killing 84 VC in My Lai (4) by 0840 hours on 16 March, he either participated in or condoned the making of fictitious reports to higher headquarters and false entries in official records to the effect that 69 VC had been killed by artillery at a location north of My Lai (4).

e. Having observed on 16 March that many of the dwellings and other structures in My Lai (4) were being burned in violation of division policy and the provisions of pertinent directives, he failed to take any effective action to:

1. Stop such destruction.
2. Report the facts to higher headquarters.

f. Having observed the bodies of women and children in and around My Lai (4) on 16 March, and after receiving subsequent reports and information on the same day indicating that many additional noncombatants may have been killed by artillery or gunship, he failed to initiate:

1. An immediate investigation to determine the extent and the causes of the casualties.
2. An investigation of an artillery incident, or to recommend that such an investigation be initiated, as required by USARV and Americal Division directives.
3. A SIR as required by regulations.

g. Having been directed to investigate and report to his commanding officer concerning the Thompson Report and after personally hearing from WO1 Thompson, CWO Culverhouse, and SP Colburn accounts of their observations of the events in Son My Village, he failed to make an appropriate investigation to determine the truth of such reports.

h. Having been directed to investigate and report to his commanding officer concerning the report of WO1 Thompson; having personally interrogated Thompson, Culverhouse, and Colburn; and having failed to make a genuine investigation of their reports, he:

1. Made a series of false and misleading reports to his commanding officer to the effect that:

   a. He had made a thorough investigation of the Thompson Report.
   b. He had interrogated all of the commanders and many of the soldiers and aviation personnel involved.
   c. WO1 Thompson was the only person he had found who had seen anything unusual on 16 March.
   d. There was no substance to Thompson's allegations.

2. Concealed the existence of war crimes.

i. About mid-April 1968, having received information that (1) the Son Tinh District Chief had submitted a report to the Quang Ngai Province Chief alleging that US forces had killed approximately 500 noncombatants in Tu Cung and Co Luy hamlets of Son My Village on 16 March 1968, and (2) VC propaganda broadcasts were stressing that US forces had killed a large number of noncombatants in the Son My Village on 16 March 1968, he:

1. Failed to conduct any investigation of the allegations of the District Chief.
2. Falsely informed the CG, 2d ARVN Division, and the Province Chief that he had previously investigated similar allegations

respecting the 16 March operation and had found them to be entirely without substance.

j. Having been subsequently directed to investigate the allegations of the District Chief and the VC propaganda, and to submit a written report incorporating the evidence he claimed to have collected in response to the Thompson Report, and having made no investigation of such allegations, he submitted to his commanding officer a written Report of Investigation, dated 24 April 1968, which was false and misleading in the following particulars:

1. While the document purported to be a "Report of Investigation" and implied that he had made an investigation in response to the allegations of the District Chief, no proper investigation was ever conducted.
2. It avoided any reference to the Thompson Report.
3. It falsely stated that his interviews with the TF Barker S3 and the commanders involved revealed that at no time were civilians gathered together and killed by US soldiers.
4. It falsely stated that 20 noncombatants were inadvertently killed by preparatory fires and in the cross fires of US and VC forces on 16 March 1968.

k. It appears that in conjunction with one or more members of his command, and possibly of the Province Advisory Team, he conspired to withhold and suppress facts concerning the actions of elements of TF Barker on 16 March and information regarding the origin of and basis for a statement dated 14 April 1968 prepared by CPT Rodriguez.

l. He gave false testimony before the Inquiry in a manner calculated to mislead this Inquiry in many particulars. For example, he testified that:

1. On 16 March 1968 he observed the bodies of only 6–8 women and children in and around My Lai (4).
2. He directed LTC Luper to investigate whether any artillery rounds landed on My Lai (4) and that LTC Luper thereafter reported to him that an investigation had been made and had disclosed that no artillery had struck the village.
3. WO1 Thompson was the only individual he spoke with who had observed anything unusual on 16 March.
4. He had not been directed to submit his written Report of Investigation, dated 24 April 1968, and that the Report was prepared and submitted in order to bring to MG Koster's attention reports and propaganda received from Vietnamese sources.

5. In May 1968, MG Koster directed a formal investigation be conducted and that he (COL Henderson) directed LTC Barker to conduct such an investigation.
6. In May 1968, LTC Barker conducted an investigation and prepared a formal report of investigation, including 15–20 written statements of witnesses, which he (COL Henderson) then transmitted to Division.

4. COL Dean E. Hutter

a. He may have testified falsely before this Inquiry in a manner calculated to be misleading when he stated he had no knowledge of any reports of civilians being killed by Americans in Son My Village on 16 March 1968, and that he had not attended any meeting wherein such a subject was discussed.

b. Having information available to him of possible war crimes and not ascertaining all of the facts pertaining to the incident and reporting them through his chain of command, DSA ICTZ, he may have contributed to the suppression of information relating to the incident in Son My Village on 16 March 1968.

5. COL (then LTC) Robert B. Luper

a. After observing the bodies of noncombatants in and around My Lai (4) during the morning of 16 March 1968, and despite his knowledge that C Company had not encountered resistance, he failed to take any action.

b. Having observed on 16 March that many of the dwellings and other structures in My Lai (4) were being burned in violation of division policy and the provisions of pertinent directives, he failed to take any action or to insure that the facts were reported to higher headquarters.

c. He failed to report the killings in and around My Lai (4) as a possible war crime in accordance with MACV Directive 20–4.

d. Having received a report that noncombatants had been killed by artillery, he failed to advise the Division Artillery Commander, and he failed either to initiate an investigation of an artillery incident or to recommend that such an investigation be initiated.

6. COL Nels A. Parson

a. Having received information relating to the Son My incident, he failed to:

1. Insure that such information was made available to proper elements of the Division staff, especially the Staff Judge Advocate and the Inspector General.
2. Take steps to insure that a proper investigation was conducted.
3. Require that a report of suspected war crimes and/or SIR be be submitted to III MAF, MACV, and USARV.
4. Initiate action through the Division Artillery Commander for the investigation of an artillery incident.

b. He failed officially to inform LTC Holladay of COL Henderson's oral report of investigation or its acceptance by the CG.

c. In response to an informal inquiry from CH Lewis concerning the incident, COL Parson:

1. Contributed to the suppression of information concerning the activities of TF Barker on 16 March 1968 by telling CH Lewis that an investigation was being conducted and that he should not discuss it.
2. Took no action to insure that such a proper investigation was being conducted.
3. Took no action to insure that the information he had given CH Lewis was correct.

d. Having knowledge that (1) some civilians had been killed in TF Barker's operation on 16 March 1968, (2) GEN Young had related WO1 Thompson's complaint to the CG, (3) COL Henderson had conducted a so-called investigation, and (4) MG Koster had received and accepted the results of the so-called investigation, COL Parson may have participated in or contributed to a conspiracy to suppress information of the Son My incident.

e. Knowing that the 24 April 1968 Report of Investigation was inadequate, he did not insure that a proper investigation was conducted by issuing orders designating a disinterested investigating officer in accordance with appropriate regulations.

f. He failed to assure the proper control and retention of documents (with the exception of those classified SECRET or higher) such as those relating to the investigation of the Son My incident.

g. Having knowledge of (1) the "close hold" manner in which information concerning the incident was being handled, (2) the fact that the CG had not informed the division staff of his actions in this matter, and (3) LTC Holladay's suspicions of a cover-up expressed upon being shown the 24 April report, COL Parson should have been aware that efforts were being made to suppress information concerning the incident. If he in fact had such a suspicion, his failure to initiate action to conduct an adequate investigation contributed to the suppression of information regarding the incident.

7. LTC Frank A. Barker (Deceased)

a. He planned, ordered, and actively directed the execution of an unlawful operation against inhabited hamlets which included destruction of houses by burning, killing of livestock, and destruction of crops and other foodstuffs, and possibly the closing of wells. Moreover, he knew there were noncombatants living in Son My Village and, while he did not directly order the killings of such persons, he may have created a belief in the minds of some of the unit commanders that they were authorized to kill any persons found there.
b. He planned an artillery preparation on an inhabited village with disregard for the lives of the inhabitants, in violation of the intent of MACV and III MAF regulations.
c. He failed, in preparing the plans for the Son My operation, to provide for the evacuation and safekeeping of the noncombatants residing in the objective areas.
d. He intentionally or negligently provided to the TF Barker company commanders false intelligence that civilians would be out of the hamlets in the Son My Village area by 0700 hours, 16 March 1968, and indicated that only VC and VC sympathizers would be in the village, thereby contributing to the killing of numerous noncombatants on that date.
e. Having become aware early on the morning of 16 March that many noncombatant residents of Son My were being killed by C/1–20 Inf, he probably conspired with MAJ Calhoun and others to:
    1. Conceal the number of civilian casualties inflicted by C/1–20 Inf in My Lai (4).
    2. Make a false report that 69 VC were killed by artillery fire during the assault on My Lai (4).
f. He probably conspired with MAJ Calhoun and others to suppress information concerning the war crimes committed during the Son My operation.

g. He failed to report the suspected war crimes committed in My Lai (4) as required by MACV Directive 20–4.

h. He failed to report that dwellings were burned in My Lai (4) and other hamlets by C/1–20 Inf and B/4–3 Inf in violation of division policy and the provisions of pertinent directives.

i. He failed to include in operational reports to higher headquarters the 20–30 noncombatant casualties of which he had knowledge.

j. He prepared and submitted a deliberately false and misleading combat after action report covering the 16 March 1968 operation in Son My Village.

k. As the responsible commander, he failed to investigate indications of war crimes as reported to him by MAJ Watke.

8. LTC (then MAJ) David C. Gavin

a. Having knowledge that his District Advisory Team had received (1) information from the Son Tinh District Chief regarding allegations that American forces had killed approximately 500 civilians at Tu Cung and Co Luy Hamlets of Son My Village on 16 March 1968; (2) information that the District Chief had reported this to the Quang Ngai Province Chief; and (3) a request from the Province Advisory Team for further information regarding these allegations, he:

   1. Did not take the necessary steps to familiarize himself with the available information or to see that a proper investigation was made through resources available to him.
   2. May not have fully informed himself as to the conduct of his command in his absence but, in all events, failed to assure himself that those matters dealt with in his absence were adequately handled.
   3. Failed to report to higher headquarters the allegations of a serious war crime as required by MACV Directive 20–4.

b. By retaining unto himself information possibly received from the Son Tinh District Chief, he may have effectively suppressed information concerning the Son My incident.

c. By action within his District Advisory Team and in conjunction with the Province Advisory Team and TF Barker, he may have participated in a conspiracy to withhold facts concerning the actions of elements of TF Barker on 16 March 1968.

d. He may have falsely testified before this Inquiry in a manner calculated to be misleading when he asserted that he had no knowledge of the allegations that American forces had killed a substantial number of civilians in Son My Village on 16 March 1968.

9. LTC William D. Guinn, Jr.

a. Having received (1) information through Census Grievance Channels regarding the killing of a large number of civilians in Tu Cung Hamlet by an American unit; (2) a copy of the Son Tinh District Chief's report to the Quang Ngai Province Chief alleging that US forces had killed approximately 500 noncombatants in Tu Cung and Co Luy Hamlets of Son My Village on 16 March 1968; (3) information from the Quang Ngai Province Chief concerning the incident; and (4) information that VC propaganda broadcasts were stressing that US forces had killed a large number of noncombatants in Son My Village on 16 March 1968, he:

1. Failed to report to his superiors and higher headquarters the allegations of a serious war crime as required by MACV Directive 20–4.
2. Failed to have such information included in the regular monthly report of the Quang Ngai Province Advisory Team.

b. By his handling of information which he received regarding the allegations of a massacre by elements of TF Barker on or about 16 March 1968, he effectively suppressed that information.

c. Having provided certain documents to the CO, 11th Brigade, and in conjunction with members of the 11th Brigade, he possibly participated in a conspiracy to:

1. Withhold the true facts concerning the actions of elements of TF Barker on 16 March 1968.
2. Suppress information regarding the origin of and basis for the statement dated 14 April 1968 prepared by CPT Rodriguez.

d. He probably gave false testimony before this Inquiry in a manner calculated to be misleading when he:

1. Asserted he had only a limited knowledge regarding the reports and investigations in April 1968 relating to the actions of elements of TF Barker in Son My Village on or about 16 March 1968.
2. Gave contradictory testimony with that previously given by him to a representative of the Office of the Inspector General.

10. LTC John L. Holladay

a. Having received information that possible war crimes had been committed, he failed to interview or obtain statements from any individual witnesses prior to or immediately following his oral report to BG Young.
b. He failed to follow up on his report to BG Young to determine if a report of investigation had been submitted and reviewed and, as a consequence, failed to provide information concerning the results of the investigation to the officers and men of his battalion who had witnessed the events at Son My.
c. Believing that information pertaining to a possible war crime was being suppressed, he failed to bring this to the attention of higher headquarters.

11. Chaplain (LTC) Francis R. Lewis

a. Having received from CH Creswell an account of WO1 Thompson's serious allegations of improper conduct by elements of TF Barker, he failed to make a timely and proper report of the matter and to assure that there was an adequate investigation conducted. He limited his action at the division headquarters to informal discussions with various staff officers.
b. Having accepted the assertion that an investigation was being conducted, and while disregarding any admonition not to talk about the matter, he still avoided ascertaining the results of such investigation and made no report back to CH Creswell concerning the results of the investigation.

12. MAJ Charles C. Calhoun

a. Participated in the planning of and assisted in the direction of an unlawful operation by TF Barker against inhabited hamlets which included destruction of houses by burning, killing livestock, destruction of crops and foodstuffs and possibly the closing of wells. Moreover, knowing that there were noncombatants living in the hamlets, and by indicating that only VC and VC sympathizers were living there, he may have contributed to the killing of noncombatants.

b. He participated in planning an artillery preparation on an inhabited village with disregard for the lives of the inhabitants in violation of the intent of MACV and III MAF regulations.

c. As TF Barker S3, he failed in preparing the plans for the Son My operation to provide for the evacuation and safekeeping of the noncombatants residing in the objective areas.

d. Having become aware early on the morning of 16 March 1968 that many noncombatant residents of Son My were being killed by C/1–20 Inf, he may have conspired with LTC Barker and probably others to:

   1. Conceal the number of civilian casualties inflicted by C/1–20 Inf in My Lai (4).
   2. Make a false report that 69 VC were killed by artillery fire during the assault on My Lai (4).

e. He may have conspired with LTC Barker and probably others to suppress information concerning the war crimes committed during the Son My operation.

f. He failed to report that dwellings were burned in My Lai (4) and other hamlets by C/1–20 Inf and B/4–3 Inf in violation of directives.

g. He failed to include in operational reports to higher headquarters the 20–30 noncombatant casualties of which he had knowledge.

h. He failed to report the suspected war crimes committed in My Lai (4) as required by MACV Directive 20–4.

i. He probably gave false testimony before this Inquiry in a manner calculated to be misleading when he stated that:

   1. The company commanders were not told to burn the villages and destroy livestock.
   2. COL Henderson's investigation concerned only the killing of one civilian.
   3. He recalled nothing unusual about the radio transmissions monitored in the TF Barker TOC on the morning of 16 March 1968.
   4. To his knowledge, the only rumor of suspicious activity at My Lai (4) was that a pilot had seen an American shoot one Vietnamese.
   5. There was an actual count of 128 VC KIA during the first day of the Son My operation, verified by someone in TF Barker actually seeing or touching each body.
   6. He never heard of a confrontation between a helicopter crew and members of C/1–20 Inf.

13. MAJ Robert W. McKnight

a. He did not take action to insure that the plan for the Son My operation included provisions for the handling, screening, and treatment of noncombatants and refugees.

b. After observing the bodies of noncombatants in and around My Lai (4) during the morning of 16 March 1968, and despite his knowledge that C Company had not encountered resistance, he failed to take any action.

c. Having observed on 16 March that many of the dwellings and other structures in My Lai (4) were being burned in violation of division policy and the provisions of pertinent directives, he failed to take any effective action to:

   1. Stop the destruction.
   2. Recommend to his commander that the burning should be stopped.
   3. Report the facts to higher headquarters.

d. He failed to take any action to insure that medical treatment was provided to noncombatants in the Son My area on 16 March.

e. After C Company had reported killing 84 VC in My Lai (4) by 0840 hours on 16 March, he either participated in or condoned the making of fictitious reports to higher headquarters and false entries in official records to the effect that 69 VC had been killed by artillery at a location north of My Lai (4).

f. Having received a report that noncombatants had been killed by artillery, he failed to recommend to his commander that an investigation of an artillery incident be initiated as required by USARV and Americal Division directives.

g. He failed to report the killings of noncombatants in and around My Lai (4) as a possible war crime as required by MACV Directive 20–4.

h. In conjunction with COL Henderson and possibly members of the Province Advisory Team, he may have conspired to withhold and suppress facts concerning the actions of elements of TF Barker on 16 March 1968 and information regarding the origin of and basis for a statement dated 14 April 1968 prepared by CPT Rodriguez.

i. He may have given false testimony before the Inquiry in a manner calculated to be misleading when he testified that:

   1. On 16 March 1968 he observed only 5 bodies in and around My Lai (4).
   2. He had no knowledge concerning war crimes and violations of regulations committed by TF Barker on 16 March 1968.

3. He had never heard any report of 69 VC being killed by artillery.
4. He did not know who had prepared Inclosure 1 to Exhibit R–1.

14. MAJ Frederic W. Watke

a. He gave misleading testimony before the Inquiry in that he withheld details and provided information that was not completely accurate or factual.
b. Having received reliable information of the possible commission of war crimes on 16 March 1968 and, by his own testimony, being of the belief that the ground commander concerned (LTC Barker) had not taken adequate action, he failed to pursue the matter by either aerial reconnaissance of the area or by obtaining additional evidence from those members of his unit who had observed the possible war crimes.
c. Having been apprised of possible war crimes by members of his command and having reported this through the chain of command, he failed to follow through to keep himself and the members of his unit informed as to the progress and results of the subsequent investigation.
d. Believing that information pertaining to a possible war crime was being suppressed he failed to bring this matter to the attention of higher headquarters.

15. CPT (then 1LT) Kenneth W. Boatman

a. Having witnessed, according to his own testimony, the killings of 8 VC suspects by RVN National Police on 16 March 1968 and recognizing that it was a violation of the law of war, he did not attempt to stop the killings and did not report them to his commanding officer as required by MACV Directive 20–4.
b. He observed the burning of subhamlets Co Lay (1), Co Lay (2), and Co Lay (3) by B/4–3 Inf on 17 March 1968 but failed to report this destruction of private property to his commanding officer.

16. Rev. (then CPT, CH) Carl E. Creswell

a. Having received from WO1 Thompson serious allegations of improper conduct by elements of TF Barker, he failed to report the matter to his commanding officer (Division Artillery Commander) or to the SJA, or the IG.

b. After he reported the matter to CH Lewis and received no satisfactory response, he took no effective action to insure that a proper investigation would be conducted.

17. CPT (then 1LT) Dennis H. Johnson

a. During the morning of 16 March 1968, he observed numerous killings in and around My Lai (4) and, even though as an intelligence officer he was specifically charged by MACV Directive 20–4 to report such crimes, he failed to report them to anyone in authority.

b. He was asked by his interpreter, SSG Minh (ARVN), to intercede with CPT Medina concerning the killing of women and children and, subsequently, to report the war crimes which they had observed to his commanding officer, CPT Labriola, but failed to do so.

c. Despite his position as an intelligence officer, he failed to take positive action to stop the killing of women, children, and other noncombatants.

d. Having knowledge that 4 or 5 VC suspects had been killed by the RVN National Police in the night defensive position of Companies B and C, he did not report such information to any of his superiors.

e. On the afternoon or early evening of 16 March 1968, he may have left the field without authority by departing from the night defensive position of B and C Companies and returning to LZ Dottie with his interpreter.

f. He may have given false testimony to the Inquiry in a manner calculated to be misleading when he stated that:

1. He provided information of the activities of 16 March 1968 to his commanding officer, CPT Labriola.
2. SSG Minh and he returned to Duc Pho the evening of 16 March 1968.

18. CPT Eugene M. Kotouc

a. Participated in the planning of and the issuance of orders for an unlawful operation by TF Barker against inhabited villages which included destruction of houses by burning, killing of livestock, destruction of crops and foodstuffs, and possibly the closing of wells. Moreover knowing that there were noncombatants living in the hamlets, and indicating that only VC and VC sympathizers were living there, he may have contributed to the killing of noncombatants.

b. He intentionally or negligently provided to the TF Barker company commanders false intelligence that civilians would be out of the hamlets in the Son My Village area by 0700 hours, 16 March 1968, thereby contributing to the killing of numerous noncombatants on that date.

c. He became aware early on the morning of 16 March that many noncombatant Vietnamese residents of My Lai (4) were being killed by C/1–20 Inf. He may have conspired with LTC Barker and probably others to:

   1. Conceal the number of noncombatants killed by C/1–20 Inf in My Lai (4).
   2. Make a false report that 69 VC were killed by artillery fire during the assault on My Lai (4).

d. He may have conspired with LTC Barker and probably others to suppress information concerning the killing of noncombatants during the Son My operation.

e. He failed to report the killings of noncombatants in and around My Lai (4) as a possible war crime as required by MACV Directive 20–4.

f. He authorized the killing of at least one VC suspect by members of the RVN National Police in violation of MACV Directive 20–4.

g. He committed an aggravated assault by repeatedly striking a VC suspect on the back of the hand with the dull edge of a knife.

h. He committed the offense of maiming by cutting off the finger of a VC suspect with a knife during the suspect's interrogations.

i. He may have given false testimony before this Inquiry in a manner calculated to be misleading when he stated that:

   1. The inhabitants of the objective area had been told to leave the area and go to Quang Ngai.
   2. The plan of the Son My operation called for moving the civilians found in the area to Quang Ngai.
   3. The RVN National Police while in support of TF Barker on 17 March 1968 were not under US control.

19. CPT Ernest L. Medina

a. He informed the men of C/1–20 Inf that nearly all the civilian residents of the hamlets in Son My Village would be gone to market by 0700, 16 March 1968, and that any who remained would be VC or VC sympathizers. This caused many of the men in C/1–20 Inf to believe that they would find only armed enemy in the hamlets and directly contributed to the killing of noncombatants which followed.

b. He planned, ordered, and supervised the execution by his company of an unlawful operation against inhabited hamlets in Son My Village which included the destruction of houses by burning, killing of livestock, and the destruction of crops and other foodstuffs, and the closing of wells; and impliedly directed the killing of any persons found there.

c. There is evidence that he possibly killed as many as three noncombatants in My Lai (4).

d. He probably conspired with LTC Barker and others to suppress information concerning the killing of noncombatants during the Son My operation.

e. He actively suppressed information concerning the killing of noncombatants in Son My Village on 16 March 1968 by:

   1. Telling the men of C/1–20 Inf not to talk about what happened in Son My Village on 16 March.
   2. Advising at least one member of his company not to write to his Congressman.
   3. Giving false reports as to the number of noncombatants killed by the men of C/1–20 Inf and the cause of death.

f. He failed to report the killings in and around My Lai (4) as a possible war crime as required by MACV Directive 20–4.

g. If he in fact believed that 20–28 civilians had been killed in My Lai (4) by artillery or gunship fire, he failed to request an artillery incident investigation.

h. He obstructed an inquiry into the killing of civilians in My Lai (4) by objecting to orders to return C/1–20 Inf to the hamlet for that purpose.

i. He failed to prevent the killing of VC suspects by the RVN National Police on 16 March 1968 and subsequently failed to report these killings as required in MACV Directive 20–4.

j. He personally mistreated a VC suspect during an interrogation on 17 March 1968 by striking him on the head and repeatedly firing an M–16 close to the prisoner's head to induce him to talk.

k. He failed to determine the cause of death of the 20–24 people whose bodies he admitted seeing on the trail leading south from My Lai (4).

l. He gave false testimony before this Inquiry in a manner calculated to be misleading when he stated that:

1. He did not see any bodies or wounded as he moved within My Lai (4).
2. Only 20 to 28 civilians were killed by C/1–20 Inf in and around My Lai (4) on 16 March 1968.
3. He questioned his platoon leaders about killing of civilians in My Lai (4).

20. CPT Earl R. Michles (Deceased)

a. During the afternoon of 16 March 1968, he made a false report that there were no women and children included in the previous reports of 38 VC KIA.
b. Possibly having knowledge of war crimes committed in My Khe (4) on 16 March 1968, he failed to report them as required by MACV Directive 20–4.
c. He failed to prevent the killing of VC suspects by the RVN National Police on 16 March 1968 and failed to report these killings as required by MACV Directive 20–4.
d. On 17 March 1968, he ordered the destruction of the subhamlets Co Lay (1), Co Lay (2), and Co Lay (3) in violation of regulations.
e. During the morning of 19 March 1968, he permitted VC suspects to be severely beaten and subjected to electrical shocks administered to their bodies.

21. Mr. (then CPT) Dennis R. Vazquez

a. While serving as artillery liaison officer with TF Barker on 16 March 1968, he indiscriminately adjusted an artillery concentration onto the populated hamlet of My Lai (4).
b. Although he felt the report of 69 VC KIA by artillery might have been the result of the rounds falling in My Lai (4), he:

    1. Made no attempt to determine whether or not civilians had been killed.
    2. Failed to initiate an artillery incident investigation in accordance with USARV and Americal Division Artillery Regulations.

c. He may have given false testimony before this Inquiry in a manner calculated to be misleading when he stated that he received the report from LT Roger Alaux of 69 casualties by artillery fire which the latter denied.

22. CPT (then 1LT) Thomas K. Willingham

a. During the morning of 16 March 1968, he directed the placing of indiscriminate fire into the inhabited subhamlet of My Khe (4).
b. He permitted his men to fire indiscriminately into and detonate explosives in dwellings and shelters at My Khe (4) resulting in the death of at least 15 to 20 women and children.
c. Having knowledge during the morning of 16 March 1968 that the majority of those killed were noncombatants (women and children), apparently he submitted three subsequent reports to his company commander indicating that 12, 18 and 8 VC respectively had been killed.
d. He failed to report the killings of noncombatants in and around My Khe (4) as possible war crimes as required by MACV Directive 20–4.
e. He gave false testimony before a representative of the Inspector General's office in a manner calculated to be misleading pertaining to the number of Vietnamese casualties counted in My Khe (4) on 16 March 1968, and the extent of the enemy resistance encountered during the operation.

23. 1LT (then 2LT) William L. Calley

a. He ordered the execution by his platoon of an unlawful operation against inhabited hamlets in Son My Village, which included the destruction of houses by burning, killing of livestock, the destruction of crops and other foodstuffs, and the closing of wells; and expressly ordered the killing of persons found there.
b. He directed and supervised the men of his platoon in the systematic killing of many noncombatants in and around My Lai (4).
c. He personally participated in the killing of some noncombatants in and around My Lai (4).
d. He failed to report the killings of noncombatants in and around My Lai (4) as a possible war crime as required by MACV Directive 20–4.

24. Mr. (then 1LT) Roger L. Alaux, Jr.

a. Having knowledge of war crimes committed in and around My Lai (4), he failed to report them as required by MACV Directive 20–4.

b. Having witnessed the killings of 4 or 5 VC suspects by RVN National Police on 16 March 1968 and recognizing that it was a violation of the law of war, he did not attempt to stop the killings and did not report them to his commanding officer as required by MACV Directive 20–4.

25. 2LT Steven K. Brooks (Deceased)

a. He ordered the execution by his platoon of an unlawful operation against inhabited hamlets in Son My Village, which included the destruction of houses by burning, killing of livestock, and the destruction of crops and other foodstuff, and the closing of the wells; and expressly or impliedly ordered the killing of persons found there.
b. He directed and supervised the men of his platoon in the systematic killing of at least 60–70 noncombatants in the subhamlets of My Lai (4) and Binh Tay.
c. Although he knew that a number of his men habitually raped Vietnamese women in villages during operations, on 16 March 1968, he observed, did not prevent, and failed to report several rapes by members of his platoon while in My Lai (4) and Binh Tay on 16 March.
d. He failed to report the killings of noncombatants in and around My Lai (4) as a possible war crime as required by MACV Directive 20–4.

26. Mr. (then 2LT) Jeffrey U. LaCross

a. He ordered the execution by his platoon of an unlawful operation against inhabited hamlets in Son My Village, which included the destruction of houses by burning, killing of livestock, and the destruction of crops and other foodstuffs, and the closing of the wells; and expressly or impliedly ordered the killing of persons found there.
b. He directed and supervised the men of his platoon in the systematic killing of many noncombatants in and around My Lai (4).
c. It is possible that he killed at least one noncombatant female near My Lai (4) during the Son My operation.
d. He failed to report that a VC suspect had been beaten and maimed during his interrogation in violation of MACV Directive 20–4.
e. He failed to report the killings of noncombatants in and around

My Lai (4) as a possible war crime as required by MACV Directive 20–4.

27. 2LT Michael L. Lewis (Deceased)

Having witnessed the destruction of the subhamlets Co Lay (1), Co Lay (2), and Co Lay (3) during the afternoon of 17 March 1968, he failed to report the destruction of private property in violation of division policy and the provisions of pertinent directives.

28. Mr. (then 1LT) John E. Mundy

Having witnessed the destruction of the subhamlets Co Lay (1), Co Lay (2), and Co Lay (3) during the afternoon of 17 March 1968, he failed to report the destruction of private property in violation of division policy and the provisions of pertinent directives.

29. Mr. (then SGT) Ronald L. Haeberle

a. He made no attempt to stop any of the acts he witnessed on 16 March 1968 despite the fact that such acts violated the law of war.
b. He failed to report the killings of noncombatants in and around My Lai (4) as required by MACV Directive 20–4.
c. He withheld and suppressed photographic evidence of war crimes in violation of MACV Directive 20–4.
d. He failed to report the crimes he had witnessed to CPT Medina; the TF Commander, LTC Frank A. Barker; or to his superiors, LT John W. Moody, LT Arthur J. Dunn, Jr., or SGT John Stonich.
e. He may have wrongfully appropriated and disposed of photographs taken as an Army photographer on an assigned operational mission in support of a combat unit.

30. Mr. (then SP5) Jay Roberts

a. As stated before this Inquiry, during the morning of 16 March 1968 while in support of C/1–20 Inf, he:

1. Made no attempt to stop any of the acts he witnessed despite the fact that he realized that such acts violated the law of war.
2. Failed to report the killings of noncombatants in and around My Lai (4) as required by MACV Directive 20–4.
3. Failed to report the crimes he had witnessed to CPT Medina; the TF Commander, LTC Frank A. Barker; or to his superiors, LT John W. Moody, LT Arthur J. Dunn, or SGT John Stonich.

b. He subsequently prepared an article for the brigade newspapers which omitted all mention of the war crimes he had observed and gave a false and misleading account of the Task Force Barker operation.

Annex A. Peers Inquiry Organization and Procedures

1. Executive Direction

As indicated in Chapter 1, the Secretary of the Army and the Chief of Staff of the Army on 26 November 1969 directed Lieutenant General William R. Peers, Chief, Office of Reserve Components, Headquarters, Department of the Army, to conduct the Inquiry which is the subject of this report (Inclosure 1, chap. 1). Mr. Bland West, Assistant General Counsel, Department of the Army, was designated as General Peers' deputy by the same directive.

LTC James H. Breen, Office, Deputy Chief of Staff for Military Operations was selected to serve as the executive officer and to be responsible for the required administrative and logistical support, and COL Joseph R. Franklin was selected to supervise the operational functions of the Inquiry.

By a message dated 9 December 1969, the Chief of Staff requested all agencies of the Department of the Army to provide assistance to General Peers and members of his team as required (Inclosure 5). In this same message, it will be noted, the Inquiry was given the formal title, "The Department of the Army Review of the Preliminary Investigations Into the My Lai Incident" and the short title of "Peers Inquiry."

2. Special Civilian Counsel

On 30 November 1969, General Peers addressed a memorandum to the Secretary of the Army and the Chief of Staff of the Army requesting that a "distinguished jurist of impeccable integrity" be designated to serve as his legal counsel (Inclosure 4, chap. 1). In response, the Secretary of the Army obtained the services of two distinguished attorneys engaged in private practice in the City of New York, Mr. Robert MacCrate and Mr. Jerome K. Walsh, Jr., to serve as General Peers' Special Counsel and Associate Special Counsel respectively. Both served in that capacity throughout the Inquiry, participating fully in all major activities, including the trip to Vietnam.

3. Organization and Rules of Procedure

Office space for the Inquiry was made available in the Army Operations Center (AOC), Pentagon, and the initial meeting of the investigating team was held on 28 November 1969. The following key decisions were made:

a. AR 15–6 would be used as a general guide for the proceedings of the Inquiry, with the understanding that the nature of the mission would require liberal exceptions to its provisions.
b. Witnesses would be called to Washington for interrogation to the extent possible.
c. Interrogation of witnesses in Washington would begin on 2 December 1969.
d. A trip to Vietnam would be an essential part of the Inquiry.
e. The report submitted by General Peers would be classified "confidential." Witnesses would be told that their testimony would be so classified, but that it was possible that it would be released to the public at a later date.
f. The Inquiry would be conducted as speedily as possible consistent with thoroughness.

Tasks were assigned and performed on an *ad hoc* basis initially. When the full scope of the Inquiry became apparent, a formal organization was established (Inclosure 1) and the staff substantially augmented.

Additional details as to the organization of the Inquiry are provided in subsequent paragraphs describing various functions.

4. Personnel

The original members of the team were:

LTG William R. Peers
Mr. Bland West, OGC, Deputy
LTC James H. Breen, ODCSOPS, Executive Officer
COL W. V. Wilson, OTIG
COL R. W. Miller, OTJAG

MAJ E. F. Zychowski, OTPMG
Mr. R. E. Montgomery, Jr., OGC

Mr. James S. Stokes, III, OGC, replaced Mr. Montgomery on 29 November 1969 and served briefly during the early stages of the Inquiry.

Mr. MacCrate and Mr. Walsh joined the team on 5 December 1969.

As the operations and functions of the team progressed, additional personnel requirements rapidly developed until the team reached its maximum strength of 32 officers, 44 enlisted men, and 10 civilians (Inclosure 2, roster; Inclosures 3 and 4, photographs).

The officers serving with the Peers Inquiry were, for the most part, selected from agencies and commands in the Washington area. Due to the unusual personnel requirements of the Inquiry [e.g., many court reporters and Magnetic Tape/Selectric Typewriter (MTST) operators], it was necessary to levy upon agencies outside the Washington area for a considerable number of enlisted specialists.

5. Administration and Logistics

All administrative functions (personnel, security, filing, correspondence, etc.) and logistic functions (office space and supplies, transportation, and housing of witnesses, etc.) were supervised and coordinated by the Executive Officer and a staff of four assistants. With respect to security, MAJ Edward F. Zychowski conducted necessary inspections and interrogations. The Executive Officer also supervised the activities of the reporters and tape operators.

Early in the Inquiry the Son My Army Staff Monitor Group was established in the Office of the Secretary of the General Staff and a major portion of the Inquiry's routine administration and staffing was thereafter handled by that office.

The Inquiry was physically located in a suite of offices in the AOC, in a restricted area of the Pentagon. This simplified the administration of security measures and provided ready access to optimum communications, graphics, and reproduction facilities. However, limited space within that facility required that many functions of the Inquiry be performed in ten offices outside of the AOC.

The administrative and logistics functions of the Inquiry were performed by the following persons:

LTC James H. Breen, Executive Officer
SP6 John R. Stremikis, Stenographer/Administrative NCO
PFC Thomas R. Broderick, Clerk Typist
PV2 William H. Wanlund, Clerk Typist

Mrs. Rita Collins, Stenographer
Mrs. Maureen Marshall, Stenographer
Mrs. Dorothy Staron, Stenographer
Miss June Roth, Stenographer

6. Production of Testimonial Evidence

A. INTERROGATION TEAMS

Initially the Inquiry functioned with one interrogation team chaired by General Peers. The interrogations were continued while General Peers and other members of the Inquiry were in Vietnam (26 Dec 1969–8 Jan 1970) by a panel headed by Mr. West which heard only testimony concerning the activities of Company C, 1st Battalion, 20th Infantry (C/1–20 Inf) during the Son My operation. Two interrogation teams functioned in Vietnam, one headed by General Peers and the other by Mr. Walsh (see para. 9 below).

Upon the return of the party from Vietnam, three interrogation teams were formed. Team A, headed by General Peers and with Mr. MacCrate as a principal, had general coverage, but primarily took testimony bearing upon the adequacy of the preliminary investigations into the Son My incident and whether there had been a "cover-up." Team B, headed by Mr. West and with COL Franklin and LTC Patterson as principals took additional testimony on the activities of C/1–20 Inf during the Son My operation and also interrogated pilots and crews of supporting helicopters. Team C, headed by COL Wilson and with Mr. Walsh as a principal, focused on the activities of Company B, 4th Battalion, 3d Infantry (B/4–3 Inf) during the operation. During the latter part of February and early March 1970, a fourth team was formed to examine witnesses from Company A, 3d Battalion, 1st Infantry (A/3–1 Inf). Team D, headed by COL John W. Armstrong, heard 16 witnesses and terminated its interrogations after finding no basis for concluding that A/3–1 Inf had killed any noncombatants during the Son My operation.

The officers listed below served as required on any of the interrogation teams:

Colonels John W. Armstrong, Joseph R. Franklin, Robert E. Miller, and William V. Wilson.

Lieutenant Colonels Charles J. Bauer, Leo M. Brandt, Fred K. Mahaffey, Wallace W. Noll, James H. Patterson, and John E. Rogers, Majors Edward F. Zychowski and Joseph I. Apici.

Many supplemental interrogations, in which witnesses marked on vertical aerial photographs the locations of things they had seen and the routes which they and their units had taken through the Son My operational area, were conducted by COL William V. Wilson, LTC James H. Patterson, and MAJ Edward F. Zychowski.

The following officers served as Recorders for the interrogation teams:

Majors Clyde D. Lynn (Team A), Harold L. Coop (Teams B and D) and Joe C. Thomas (Team C).

B. CONDUCT OF THE INVESTIGATIONS

Each witness was given an explanation of the nature and purpose of the Inquiry (see exhibit M–57 for a sample explanation). If the witness was suspected of an offense relevant to the Inquiry, he would be advised of his testimonial rights and right to counsel by COL Robert E. Miller, JAGC, who also arranged for counsel for the witness if desired.

All witnesses were sworn prior to giving testimony. Their testimony was elicited by interrogation and questions and answers recorded by a reporter and by tape recorder. Exhibits consisting of documents, photographs, maps and other physical evidence were introduced during testimony and made a part of the record.

C. WITNESSES

At the outset, COL Wilson was responsible for identifying and scheduling witnesses and the Executive Officer, aided by MAJ Coop and SP5 Machusick, for locating and making arrangements to bring them to the Pentagon to appear before an interrogation team. Witnesses interrogated in Vietnam (see para. 9 below) were arranged for on an *ad hoc* basis. As the rate of interrogation increased, it became necessary to establish a witness section, headed by MAJ Joseph I. Apici, to locate witnesses and make all necessary arrangements for their travel to the Pentagon and return. In addition, MAJ Stanley Kraus spent about 3 weeks with the Inquiry identifying and locating helicopter pilots and crews who had participated in the Son My operation.

Military witnesses could be ordered to appear before the Inquiry. As General Peers lacked subpoena power, civilian witnesses could not be required to appear. Nevertheless, MAJ Apici and his principal assistants, SP5 Richard F. Machusick and SP5 Gregory A. Bentley, were almost uniformly successful in persuading civilian witnesses to make the trip to Washington, many coming from thousands of miles away.

MAJ Apici's section also included several assistants who manned a waiting room for witnesses and served as their escorts to and from the interrogation rooms located in restricted areas. These assistants were:

SP5 Peter D. Hallock, SP5 Robert M. Hamilton, SP4 Paul D. Searle, and PV2 Paul L. Hull.

D. REPORTERS

The Inquiry utilized members of the Army trained in reporting court-martial trials as reporters. The majority used the stenomachine system; the balance were stenotype operators. Initially, four reporters were assigned, but the number was augmented substantially as the hours spent in taking testimony increased, primarily through simultaneous operation of more than one interrogation team. The names of the reporters follow:

SP7 Lee B. Edmonds (Chief Reporter)
SP7 Milton J. Brown
SP7 Kenneth Betteridge
SP6 Arthur B. Reid, Jr.
SP5 Richard Tjosvold
SP5 James V. Link
SP5 Viola L. Parrish (also assisted in preparation of report)
SP4 Allan A. Brockman
SP4 Gary E. France
SP4 James L. Thill
PFC Dennis G. Bull
PFC James Christian
PFC James L. Holland
PFC Joseph Lavieri

E. PROCESSING OF TRANSCRIPTS

COL Robert E. Miller, JAGC, in addition to serving as the legal member of the interrogation teams, was responsible for the processing of all transcripts of testimony, an operation which required more personnel than any other function of the Inquiry.

Uncorrected reporter transcripts were converted to final copy through a series of edits, reviews, and retypings designed to insure factual, format, spelling, and punctuation accuracy insofar as practicable.

A team of four officer editors read each transcript in its entirety and made format, spelling, and punctuation corrections. They also spent many hundreds of hours comparing reporter drafts with tape recordings and making corrections to assure substantive accuracy.

Each edited draft transcript was then reviewed by a senior officer or civilian member of the Inquiry, usually one who had participated in the questioning of the witness whose testimony was being reviewed. This was primarily a substantive review for the purpose of further assuring the accuracy of the transcript.

The next step was production of a MTST typed draft. In this process the testimony was recorded on MTST tapes, which facilitated materially the further correction of drafts and production of final copy. At peak strength 19 MTST operators were operating 5 machines 24 hours a day and 2 machines 16 hours a day. Several of these operators had never operated an MTST before and on-the-job training was required.

Four additional officer editors reviewed each MTST draft for substantive, format, spelling and punctuation errors, and the corrected draft was returned to the MTST operators for a clean draft. This process was repeated as many times as necessary to produce acceptable final copy.

Four Judge Advocate General's Corps (JAGC) captains spent approximately one month as editors and in becoming familiar with the evidence. They developed a format for summarizing testimony and beginning in early January devoted their full time to preparation of summaries of testimony, with cross-references to transcript pages. They were assisted by one WAC stenographer who did virtually all of their draft and final summaries.

General Peers and his principal assistants had a continuing and immediate need for testimony as background for interrogations. Several copies of the first reporter draft were prepared and distributed for this purpose. Extensive and detailed controls were required to insure that all transcripts in all stages of processing were accounted for, were being worked on, and were available. Two enlisted assistants maintained all work status and flow charts, prepared copies of and distributed transcripts, and maintained accountability records.

The following persons accomplished the tasks described above:

Chief	COL Robert E. Miller
Chief Clerk	PFC Alan L. Butler
Asst Chief Clerk	SP4 Edward P. Nalevanko
Editorial Supervisor	CPT Michael H. Clark

Editors

MAJ Jon A. Kosty
PT Gary Eifried
CPT Lloyd L. Chester

MTST Draft Editors

MAJ John G. Connor
MAJ Howard C. Jacobson
CPT William R. Porter
1LT Robert L. Bruer

MTST Operators

SGT Kenneth B. Crenshaw
SGT Charles E. Olson
SP5 Rodney H. Pearce
SP5 Stephen A. Wright
SP4 Loren B. Havekost
SP4 Dennis P. McCoy
SP5 Thomas W. Petersik
SP4 John R. Somers
SP4 David F. Stone
PFC Ronald L. Blakely

Summarizers

CPT James F. Clark
CPT Thomas M. Jackson
CPT Alex B. Shipley, Jr.
CPT Frank B. Stahl, Jr.

Stenographer

SP5 Viola L. Parrish

PFC Donald P. Boudreaux
PFC Joseph S. W. Brasher
PFC Leslie W. Dyson
PFC Dennis A. Gibbs
PFC Craig Hill
PFC Joseph N. Hollerich
PFC Roger F. Presnell
PFC Thomas J. Zakovitch
PV2 Alan J. Towson

7. Production of Physical Evidence

A. ORGANIZATION

COL Thomas F. Whalen initially was made responsible for the production of physical evidence for the Inquiry. When he was dispatched to Vietnam in mid-December to establish the Saigon office (see para. 10, below), LTC James H. Patterson assumed overall responsibility for production of physical evidence. Colonel Whalen's duties in Vietnam included responsibility for the collection of testamentary as well as physical evidence. As noted elsewhere, he was assisted in Vietnam by LTC Leo M. Brandt.

SP6 James R. Thomas assisted LTC Patterson in the Pentagon office of the Inquiry.

B. IDENTIFICATION

Prior to the beginning of the collection process, a list of documents of an evidentiary nature was prepared, representing those that were required by regulation to be initiated and maintained by all units associated with the Son My incident. Added to this list were other documents and records that could have been initiated and maintained, although not required. This listing was continually revised during the Inquiry to insure that all possible documentary evidence was identified. Other types of physical evidence were also considered and listed, including pictorial and topographic material.

C. COLLECTION PROCEDURES

After the identification procedure, the collection process began. It included the tracing of documents from source to storage.

1. Method

The collection process was decentralized. Individuals and agencies were tasked to provide a physical on-site search and collection effort. Team members of the Inquiry supervised the collection at the various headquarters and agencies. Overseas members of the Inquiry were involved in this effort as well as Continental United States (CNOUS) personnel, but the direction of the entire effort was retained in Washington, DC.

2. Searches

The collection of all types of evidence was initiated at Department of the Army level. A search was conducted within the headquarters to include all staff sections for the availability of any listed evidentiary material. Subsequent searches at subordinate headquarters were conducted. The object of the searches was to procure the planning, policy, and guidance directives applicable to Task Force (TF) Barker, the 11th Brigade and the Americal Division during March 1968.

The storage records centers, to include intermediate record holding areas, were physically searched by members of the Inquiry, and pertinent records, documents and/or receipts procured. The facilities searched included the National Records Center, Suitland, Maryland; US Army Records Holding Area, Okinawa; and the Vietnam Records Holding Area at Long Binh, Vietnam. Searches were also conducted in Japan and Hawaii, as well as in Vietnam.

3. Witnesses

The collection of documents and physical evidence was a continuing process. Witnesses appearing before the Inquiry were queried in an effort to procure any physical evidence in their possession. Several had evidentiary matter such as letters and photographs which they furnished willingly to the Inquiry.

D. CERTIFICATES OF SEARCH

Upon completion of the search at each of the various units and agencies, a certificate was obtained to indicate the extent of the search. A record of the documents obtained and the specific location of each was prepared to accompany the search certificate. In some cases Inquiry personnel executed the search certificates, while in the larger headquarters the certificates were prepared by responsible commanders. These certificates were made a permanent part of the record of the Inquiry.

E. PROCESSING

Processing the documents and physical evidence was accomplished as they were received. Locator cards and files were established to provide ready accessibility and reference, and each item was carefully analyzed for pertinency. Each document was read by General Peers or his deputy, Mr. West. In like manner, other forms of evidence were studied. Based on General Peers' guidance, all documents were highlighted or extracted, distributed for information to all interrogators, and a determination made as to whether they would be given exhibit status. Reproduction was necessary in most cases, with original copies retained in file for the final report. Control of all documentary evidence was administered centrally to insure the necessary security and correlation with other requirements.

F. TYPES OF PHYSICAL EVIDENCE

The types of physical evidence collected were as varied as the sources. Regulations, directives, orders, plans, reports, messages, letters, and photographs are representative of the basic evidence collected. In addition, the search and collection efforts uncovered diaries, tape recordings, diagrams, news articles, propaganda leaflets, and maps, to a few of the nonstandard types of data obtained and used. The volume of documentary and physical evidence identified, collected, processed, analyzed, correlated, and disseminated amounted to approximately 30 linear feet.

8. Support by Other Offices and Agencies

A. SPECIAL SUPPORT

1. Office of the General Counsel (OGC)

The General Counsel of the Department of the Army, Mr. Robert E. Jordan, III; the Deputy General Counsel, Mr. R. Kenly Webster; and Mr. Robert E. Montgomery, Jr., Assistant to the General Counsel, provided special support to the Inquiry on a variety of legal and other matters, including policy guidance as to the release of information to Congressional committees, the news media, and others.

2. Office of the Chief of Information (OCINFO)

Because of the extraordinary interest in the activities of the Inquiry displayed by the news media, BG Winant Sidle, CINFO, assigned LTC

Daniel R. Zenk, an experienced senior information officer, to serve as the Inquiry's public relations officer. MAJ Jeffrey Scribner served briefly in this capacity during the early days of the Inquiry. MAJ William F. Gabella was the information officer on the Vietnam trip.

3. Office of the Chief of Staff of the Army (OCSA)

Responsibility for providing whatever support was needed for effective functioning of the Inquiry was assumed by OCSA. MAJ L. Dilworth, OCSA, provided major administrative and logistical support to the Inquiry. As indicated, the Son My Army Staff Monitor Group, established in the Office of the Secretary of the General Staff (SGS) and headed by COL G. W. Everett, was most helpful in coordinating the Inquiry's requirements within the Army Staff and in obtaining assistance from external agencies.

4. Office of the Provost Marshal General of the Army (OPMG)

Since OPMG was charged in August 1969 with investigating the criminal aspects of the Son My incident, there was a substantial community of interest between OPMG and the Inquiry. MAJ Edward F. Zychowski, an experienced member of OPMG's Criminal Investigation Division (CID), was made available by OPMG to serve as a full member of the Inquiry staff. One of his principal duties was to maintain close liaison with the headquarters of the Army CID Agency in Washington to arrange for the mutual exchange of information on the Son My incident.

B. GENERAL SUPPORT

1. Other Service Support

The United States Navy, the United States Marine Corps, and the United States Air Force were very cooperative in arranging the appearance before the Inquiry of witnesses assigned to those services.

2. Office of the Deputy Chief of Staff for Military Operations (ODCSOPS)

ODCSOPS provided excellent support in the preparation of background papers and fact sheets necessary to the reconstruction of relevant military operations in Vietnam in 1968 for background purposes. In addition, the AOC provided extremely effective support in the areas of communications, graphics and reproduction facilities, in addition to housing the bulk of the Inquiry organization.

3. Office of the Deputy Chief of Staff for Personnel (DCSPER); Office of Personnel Operations (OPO)

Under the policy guidance of ODCSPER, personnel requirements of the Inquiry were filled on an immediate priority by the Office of Personnel Operations with personnel of extremely high calibre. This fine response was a major factor in the successful functioning of the Inquiry.

4. Office of the Adjutant General (TAG)

TAG support in the areas of personnel location, records consolidation and statistical information was of critical importance to the Inquiry. All requirements were met in a most timely and effective manner.

5. Corps of Engineers

Over 500 photographs of high professional quality were reproduced expeditiously for the Inquiry by the Corps of Engineers.

6. Other Offices of the Department of the Army Which Provided Immediate and Helpful Support

a. Office, Chief of Military History (OCMH)
b. Office of the Provost Marshal General
c. Office of the Judge Advocate General (JAG)
d. Office of the Assistant Chief of Staff for Intelligence
e. Office of the Inspector General
f. Army Photographic Agency
g. Defense Printing Office

9. Saigon Office

A. ORGANIZATION

COL Thomas F. Whalen and LTC Leo M. Brandt proceeded to Vietnam on 13 December 1969. Their primary mission was to coordinate the collection of pertinent documents and other evidence from Military Assistance Command, Vietnam (MACV) staff agencies and subordinate commands and to conduct a detailed physical search of records and files of various units and agencies in Vietnam.

B. OFFICE ESTABLISHED

Upon arrival, the team established a liaison office in MACV headquarters, near Saigon. The MACV Inspector General (IG) served as the sponsoring staff agency and provided administrative support. The team from Washington was supplemented with the services of several commissioned JAG, IG and Combined Intelligence Center, Vietnam (CICV) personnel.

C. LIAISON ARRANGEMENTS

Each MACV staff agency designated a point of contact. Liaison visits were conducted with representatives from the MACV staff, Hq USARV, III MAF, Hq Americal Division, the 11th LIB, the Senior Province Advisor, the 2d ARVN Div Advisor, and the District Advisory Team. The criminal investigation (CID) team chief from the Office of the Provost Marshal General of the Army was contacted and arrangements made for exchange of information as well as coordination of future collection efforts.

D. REVIEW OF REQUIREMENTS

Upon completion of the initial coordination, a review of the material previously collected by the MACV IG was conducted. Responsible organization and staff points of contact were notified of additional requirements that were developed. This became a continuing process.

E. HOME OFFICE GUIDANCE

Daily telecons with Inquiry personnel in Washington facilitated the proper channeling of, and fixing of priorities for, the collection effort in Vietnam, as well as providing timely information to support the ongoing interrogation of witnesses. Requirements based on testimony were identified and efforts directed toward location and recovery of key documentation.

F. RE-INSPECTIONS AND FOLLOWUP SEARCHES

1. Upon completion of initial searches conducted by assigned unit personnel, the in-country personnel of the Inquiry conducted a

followup search of records. Augmented by additional members of the Inquiry, who arrived in Vietnam on 28 December 1969, the effort was intensified. This search encompassed the available files of all units engaged in, or in support of, the operations of TF Barker in mid-March 1968, as well as the files of all staff sections of immediate and intermediate headquarters.

2. Based on information received during testimony in Washington, a number of facilities and staff records were reinspected to assure that no pertinent document had been overlooked. Personnel conducting the search were interchanged to increase the thoroughness and possibility for recovery. Effort was concentrated in those areas identified as the most logical depositories, in the judgment of persons with administrative experience in the unit.

G. ASSISTANCE BY VIETNAMESE AUTHORITIES

Vietnamese officials who assisted the in-country collection effort include the I Corps and 2d ARVN Division Commanders, and the Quang Ngai Province and Son Tinh District Chiefs. In addition, many Vietnamese civilian witnesses were located and made available by the GVN to facilitate the investigation. The cooperation by GVN/ARVN officials was outstanding.

H. SEARCHES IN OKINAWA AND HAWAII

To insure complete coverage, a search was made through files of the Records Holding Area in Okinawa, as well as those of the Overseas Record Center at Kapalama, Hawaii. In addition, the records of USARHAW and USARPAC were screened.

10. Vietnam Trip

A. ORGANIZATION

1. Planning for a visit to Vietnam began in mid-December when General Peers designated the team members to accompany him. Necessary coordination for in-country clearance, special air mission aircraft and preparation for overseas movement of the members of the team was accomplished. An advance party arrived in Vietnam on 15 December 1969, and in conjunction with the appointed

project officer from the MACV Inspector General's office, the necessary arrangements were made for the visit of General Peers and team to arrive in-country on 28 December 1969.

2. General Peers was accompanied by:

Mr. Robert MacCrate, Civilian Counsel
Mr. Jerome K. Walsh, Jr., Civilian Counsel
LTC John E. Rogers, Interrogation Team
MAJ David D. Dantzscher, Interpreter
MAJ William F. Gabella, Information Officer
MAJ Clyde D. Lynn, Recorder
SP7 Milton J. Brown, Reporter
SP6 James R. Thomas, Stenographer
SP5 Robert F. Fromme, Photographer
PVT James C. Holland, Reporter

In addition, personnel were requested and provided from MACV as follows:

LTC Billy J. Stanberry, Interpreter
CMDR William J. Davis, JAG Representative
CPT Werner Unzelmann, Intelligence
CW4 Andre C. Feher, CID Representative

3. Upon arrival in Vietnam, the official party organized into two interrogation teams, a document collection team and an administration team. The first interrogation team consisted of General Peers, Mr. MacCrate, LTC Stanberry and PVT Holland. The second interrogation team consisted of Mr. Walsh, MAJ Dantzscher, and SP7 Brown. The document collection team consisted of MAJ Lynn and SP6 Thomas.

B. VISITS

General Peers, Mr. MacCrate, Mr. Walsh and selected team members visited the following offices while in Vietnam:

1. Military and Advisory Units

a. USMACV HQ
b. USARV HQ
c. III MAF HQ
d. Americal Division HQ
e. 11th Infantry Brigade
f. Quang Ngai Province Advisory Staff

g. 123d Aviation Battalion HQ
h. Son Tinh District Advisory Staff

2. ARVN and GVN Authorities/Units

a. MG Hoang Xuan Lam, CG I Corps
b. BG Nguyen Van Toan, CG 2d ARVN Division
c. COL Nguyen Van Binh, Quang Ngai Province Chief
d. COL Ton That Khien, former Quang Ngai Province Chief to 31 December 1969
e. LTC Ha Thuc Ung, Deputy Sector Commander Quang Ngai
f. CPT Tran Ngoc Tan, former Son Tinh District Chief
g. Mr. Nguyen Duc Te, Census Grievance Chief

3. US Embassy

General Peers and Mr. MacCrate visited Ambassador Ellsworth Bunker, Deputy Ambassador Samuel D. Berger and other officials in the US Embassy.

C. RECONNAISSANCE OF AREA

1. On-Site Inspection

On 3 January 1970, General Peers, Mr. MacCrate and Mr. Walsh conducted a ground survey of the subhamlet of Thuan Yen [My Lai (4)]. This inspection served to familiarize the members of the Inquiry with Thuan Yen, to identify and locate key structures and terrain features, and to assist in resolving conflicts in testimony given by witnesses (see exhibit M–111).

2. Aerial Inspection

On 1 January 1970 General Peers and WO1 Thompson made a low-level reconnaissance of the Thuan Yen subhamlet in a light observation helicopter piloted by CPT Gary E. Hickman. The reconnaissance was conducted at altitudes of 30–100 feet and on occasion as low as 5 to 10 feet. All sites were located on an aerial photo and subsequently replotted and identified on an aerial photo (see exhibit M–110). WO1 Thompson made another low-level reconnaissance on 3 January 1970 for the purpose of rechecking the location of the ditch.

D. INTERROGATION

Formal interrogation transcripts were prepared on 31 Vietnamese and 9 American witnesses. Mr. Walsh's team conducted interrogations of Vietnamese civilians at Quang Ngai during the period 31 December 1969 to 5 January 1970. The interrogation teams interviewed several Vietnamese people for which a formal transcript was not prepared. These interviews provided background and familiarization type information.

E. COLLECTION OF DOCUMENTS

The document collection team selectively reviewed the files of headquarters, USMACV, USARV, and III MAF. These offices had previously searched their files for all pertinent information. While the team had specific instructions to look for key documents, an exhaustive search also was made for all pertinent material. The team was able to inspect thoroughly the files of the Americal Division, 11th Infantry Brigade, and advisory staffs. Documents collected during the inspection were turned over to the Inspector General's representative accompanying the team. This representative prepared logs and supervised the reproduction and receipting for each document. General Peers and Mr. MacCrate were successful in having many of the ARVN files made available to them during their visits, resulting in the collection of many key documents. Approximately 6 linear feet of documents were brought back with the team and an equal quantity identified for reference.

F. ADMINISTRATION

Office space was allocated for the advance party and for General Peers' visit by COMUSMACV in the Headquarters building. The Americal Division provided an office and court room building for the use of the interrogation and administrative teams. The administrative team accompanied the members of the Inquiry while in RVN and provided the necessary office support.

11. Preparation of Report

A. ORGANIZATION

Preliminary planning for the report of the investigating officer began during the first week of the Inquiry with a decision to prepare suitable background chapters as early as possible and to follow on with the substantive chapters as rapidly as progress of the Inquiry permitted. Augmentation of the staff began on 8 December 1969. COL Joseph Franklin was assigned overall responsibility for preparation of a draft report for the investigating officer. Dr. Walter G. Hermes, Office of the Chief of Military History, was made available as a full-time member of the Inquiry to serve as an advisor and writer. A number of officers with combat experience in Vietnam and recognized writing ability were then assigned to the staff as writers, namely, Lieutenant Colonels Charles J. Bauer, Fred K. Mahaffey, John E. Rogers, James H. Patterson and Wallace W. Noll. Also assigned to the staff as operational analysts were MAJ George K. Garner and CPT Thomas Kennan.

SGM John W. Griney provided required administrative support for the report effort, assisted by SP5 Don A. Evans and PV2 William H. Wanlund. Mrs. Mary R. Boothe and Mrs. Mary H. Conroy served as copy editors.

Members of the writing group also were designated on an *ad hoc* basis to assist in the interrogation of witnesses, and were asked to make recommendations for the gathering of evidence and to review physical evidence collected by the Inquiry.

B. WRITING PHASE

After an initial period of orientation by the writers and analysts, a tentative outline of the report was approved by General Peers and specific subject areas were assigned to members of the writing group. The writers progressively screened and analyzed the statements, directives, reports and other evidence that was being gathered by the interrogation and document teams for substantive facts and drafted the background and early portions of the report. Aerial photographs annotated by the witnesses, sketches, and information received from the aerial and ground reconnaissance made in RVN contributed to the reconstruction of events that took place in the subhamlets of Thuan Yen and My Hoi on 16 March 1968.

By the time the Inquiry neared the end of its interrogations, the writers had prepared drafts of several of the planned chapters of the report. These formed the basis of a preliminary report prepared by General Peers and forwarded to the Secretary of the Army and the Chief of Staff of the Army. Subsequently, the remaining chapter drafts were completed and all were reviewed by the principal members of the Inquiry and General Peers and rewritten until each chapter was ready for final editing, typing, and printing.

C. PRINTING PHASE

Concurrent with the writing phase, consideration was being given to the editing and printing of the report, to include the testimony and documentary evidence. Mr. Ralph A. Rollins, Office of the Adjutant General of the Army, joined the staff as an adviser on publication matters early in the Inquiry. Mr. James Breedlove, graphic illustrator from OTAG, provided Cartographic assistance and prepared final artwork for the sketches in the report. MAJ Clyde D. Lynn joined the report staff as the interrogations neared completion to expedite preparation of the final report manuscript for printing.

The editing was performed simultaneously with the writing phase to the extent possible, so that each phase would merge into the finalization and printing of the report. Necessary arrangements were made with the Army Photographic Agency for the reproduction of photographs, the Army Topographic Command for the reproduction of maps and aerial photographs, and the Defense Printing Office for printing and binding of the final report. Due to the mass of material collected during the Inquiry and the great volume of testimony, it was decided to print the final report in volumes as follows:

a. Volume I—The narrative report with findings and recommendations, attendant sketches, tables of contents and other material.
b. Volume II—Testimony and summaries of testimony, subdivided into books of 300 pages.
c. Volume III—Evidentiary material entered as exhibits, also subdivided into books. Oversize exhibits were photographed and reduced or folded so that the longest book would not exceed 16 inches by 20 inches.
d. Volume IV—Statements made by individuals to the CID Agency, bound in one book.

D. PUBLICATION IN BOOK FORM

Publication of the report in book form was explored. It was decided, however, that this was a matter for subsequent consideration and decision by the Secretary and the Chief of Staff of the Army.

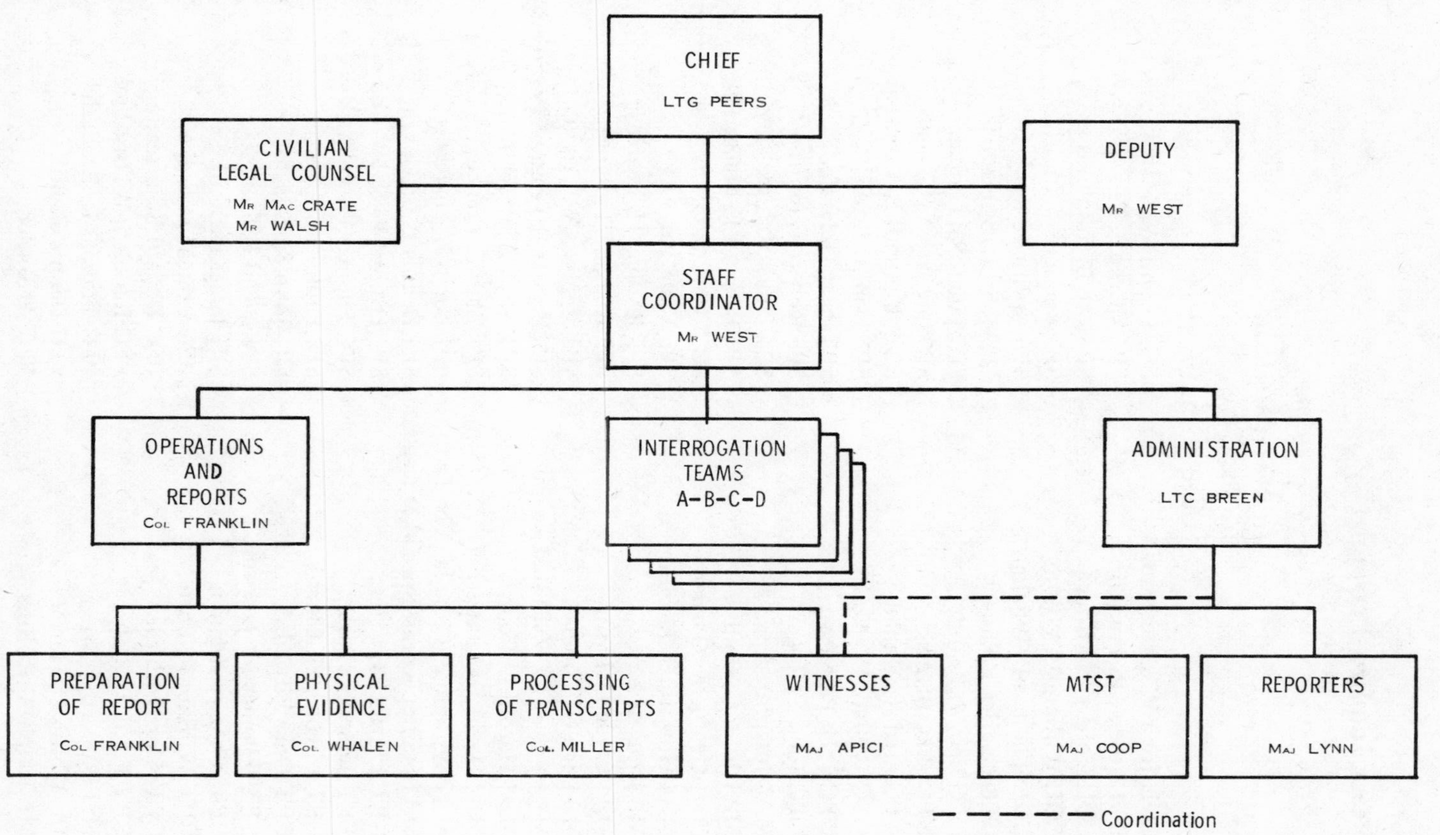
CHIEF
LTG PEERS
CIVILIAN LEGAL COUNSEL
Mr MacCRATE
Mr WALSH
DEPUTY
Mr WEST
STAFF COORDINATOR
Mr WEST
OPERATIONS AND REPORTS
Col FRANKLIN
INTERROGATION TEAMS A-B-C-D
ADMINISTRATION
LTC BREEN
PREPARATION OF REPORT
Col FRANKLIN
PHYSICAL EVIDENCE
Col WHALEN
PROCESSING OF TRANSCRIPTS
Col MILLER
WITNESSES
Maj APICI
MTST
Maj COOP
REPORTERS
Maj LYNN
Coordination

Peers Inquiry Personnel

LTG W. R. Peers
Mr. Robert MacCrate
Mr. Bland West
Mr. Jerome K. Walsh, Jr.

COL John W. Armstrong
COL Joseph R. Franklin
COL Robert E. Miller
COL William V. Wilson
COL Thomas F. Whalen
LTC Charles J. Bauer
LTC Leo M. Brandt
LTC J. H. Breen
LTC Fred K. Mahaffey
LTC Wallace W. Noll
LTC J. H. Patterson
LTC John E. Rogers
MAJ Joseph I. Apici
MAJ John G. Connor
MAJ George K. Garner
MAJ Howard C. Jacobson
MAJ Jon A. Kosty
MAJ Clyde D. Lynn
MAJ Joe C. Thomas
MAJ Edward F. Zychowski
MAJ Harold L. Coop
MAJ David D. Dantzscher (VN Trip)
MAJ William F. Gabella (VN Trip)
MAJ Stanley Kraus (Special Duty)
CPT Lloyd L. Chester
CPT James F. Clark
CPT Michael H. Clark
CPT Gary Eifried
CPT Thomas M. Jackson
CPT Thomas Kennan
CPT William R. Porter
CPT Alex B. Shipley, Jr.
CPT Frank B. Stahl, Jr.
1LT Robert L. Bruer
Dr. Walter G. Hermes
Mr. Ralph A. Rollins

SGM John W. Griney
SP7 Milton J. Brown
SP7 Lee B. Edmonds
SP7 Kenneth Betteridge
SP6 Arthur B. Reid, Jr.
SP6 John R. Stremikis
SP6 James R. Thomas
SP5 Gregory A. Bentley
SGT Kenneth B. Crenshaw
SP5 Don A. Evans
SP5 Peter D. Hallock
SP5 Robert Hamilton
SP5 James V. Link
SP5 Richard F. Machusick
SGT Charles Olson
SP5 Viola Parrish
SP5 Rodney H. Pearce
SP5 Richard Tjosvold
SP5 Stephen A. Wright
SP5 Robert F. Fromme (VN Trip)
SP4 Allan A. Brockmann
SP4 Gary E. France
SP4 Loren B. Havekost
SP4 Dennis P. McCoy
SP4 Edward P. Nalevanko
SP4 Thomas W. Petersik
SP4 Paul Searle
SP4 John Somers
SP4 David F. Stone
SP4 James L. Thill
PFC Ronald L. Blakely
PFC Donald Boudreaux
PFC Joseph S. W. Brashier
PFC Thomas R. Broderick
PFC Dennis G. Bull
PFC Al Butler

Mr. James Breedlove
Mrs. Rita F. Collins
Mrs. Maureen Marshall
Miss Dorothy A. Staron
Miss June Roth
Mrs. Mary R. Boothe
Mrs. Mary H. Conroy

PFC James Christian
PFC Leslie W. Dyson
PFC Dennis A. Gibbs
PFC James L. Holland
PFC Craig Hill
PFC Joseph N. Hollerich
PFC Joseph Lavieri
PFC Roger F. Presnell
PFC Thomas J. Zakovitch
PV2 Alan J. Towson
PV2 William H. Wanlund
PV2 Paul L. Hull

Annex B. Peripheral Issues

During the conduct of this investigation, several matters, not within the specified scope of the investigation, were identified. Some of them appear to warrant follow-up action by responsible staff agencies of the Department of the Army. The following is a brief summary of these peripheral issues for action as deemed appropriate.

1. Records Management and Disposition

a. In reconstructing the events of Son My, much reliance had to be placed on official records of activities during that period. Consequently, exhaustive searches were made of all available files at all headquarters and records holding areas. The records of interest dated back over 18 months, but those found in the files or logged in were in most cases minimal, generally unsatisfactory. Examples of deficiencies noted include:

1. *Incomplete permanent records files.* Many of the permanent record files contained documents which were not necessarily of a permanent nature while documents which should have been retained, such as reports of investigations, were missing. Daily staff journals were found to be poorly prepared and incomplete in most cases.
2. *Destruction of records.* There appears to be a tendency among units to destroy records rather than to retire them in accordance with established procedures. In some cases "probably destroyed prior to the last IG [Inspector General] inspection" was cited as the possible reason for documents missing from the files. In one case, the Son Tinh District Advisory Team files, a headquarters critical to this investigation, had been "cleaned out" in preparation for the IG Inspection scheduled for August 1969. If records are arbitrarily destroyed at the unit level, the Army's historical records obviously

will never be complete. Action appears to be required throughout the Army to emphasize the importance of periodic screening of records to insure that documents of historical significance are retired and not destroyed.

3. *Accounting for sensitive correspondence.* There is no system established to account for important correspondence except for documents classified secret or higher. While similar controls may be established for special correspondence on a local level, this practice appears to be the exception. Thus, with the passage of time, recovery of a specific document becomes increasingly difficult unless the correspondence has been afforded a security classification requiring control. Adoption of a uniform system for the control of sensitive or important documents of an unclassified nature would be particularly useful in units and areas where personnel turbulence is experienced.
4. *Retired records.* Files transferred to records holding areas were poorly selected, poorly organized and, in some cases, inaccurately identified, thus making it difficult to locate any specific document without a detailed, document-by-document search of all records applicable to a given period. The selection of documents for retirement at unit level appears weak and requires increased attention. In the records holding areas, files appear to have been consolidated in boxes without consideration as to headquarters, time, or subject matter; there was no index system or cross referencing available to facilitate the rapid identification and location of documents. In the retirement process, general lack of supervision was obvious, especially at the unit level, where apparently each unit wrote its own rules. This appears to be an area appropriate for special emphasis during future Annual General Inspections.

b. Based on the generally poor conditions found by the Inquiry, it appears that the entire records maintenance and retirement process should be reviewed to insure that existing directives are adequate and additional emphasis placed on strict adherence to these details.

2. Aviation Records

a. TM 38–750, Army Equipment Record Procedures, prescribes aviation maintenance records which will be maintained. While this system provides for "complete" records from a maintenance point of view, it does not necessarily meet all requirements for aviation records and does not require the retention of all records on a permanent basis. The Army Aviation Flight Record, for example (DA Form 2408–12), the only record which identifies the crew assigned to the aircraft each day, is maintained for only three months. No other records required by TM 38–750 reflect crew or operational data. However, some units do maintain informal "Mission Sheets" which provide detailed operational data as to the exact tasks accomplished by each aircraft daily. Since these are not required, they are often destroyed with changes in personnel or after a period of three to six months. Such a document appears to provide useful information not available through other records.

b. Consideration should be given to establishing a formal procedure for maintaining daily aircraft and unit operational data in addition to the currently required aviation maintenance records. A record of the operational data should be kept on file in the unit, probably for a period of one year and then retired, not destroyed.

3. Use of Personal Cameras by Army Photographers

a. There appears to be no clear policy regarding the ownership and release (US Army versus individual) of film exposed by Army photographers using personal cameras while on official missions. The pictures related to the Son My incident which were released to *Life* magazine by a former Army photographer were made under such conditions. According to the testimony of personnel from the Americal Division Public Information Office (PIO), there was no established policy in March 1968 regarding the use of personal cameras. Because of the lack of unit cameras, the use of private cameras by photographers was encouraged. Likewise, the 11th Brigade had no established policy, but according to some testimony, there was an unwritten understanding that negatives taken on official missions were not to be removed from the PIO office. While the use of personal cameras by photographers is apparently desirable and continues as a common practice, review of applicable regulations and directives indicates that there is still no established policy either with respect to the use of the cameras or the future ownership of any pictures taken.

b. It therefore appears that a policy should be established clarifying the ownership and release authority of film exposed by Army photographers using their personal cameras while on official missions to preclude the unauthorized release of Army photographs in the future. Such policy must be effective throughout the Army and not subject to local interpretation. It is understood that ACSC–E is taking action to issue appropriate guidance to all commanders.

4. Use of Smoke Grenades

a. While not an issue in the Son My incident, the random use of colored smoke by aviators and ground troops to mark both enemy and friendly locations could easily cause confusion. This is an area where positive understanding by all parties as to the meaning or purpose of a specific color of smoke is essential in order to prevent false identification. For example, if the ground troops used red smoke to mark a no–fire area, and the gunships flying overhead assumed that red smoke marked an enemy location, the result could prove disastrous. Many units in Vietnam have recognized this problem and routinely publish within their Signal Operating Instructions (SOI), or by other means, the purpose for which specific colors of smoke will be used during a given period.

b. In view of the potential for misunderstanding in this regard, a review of the use of smoke grenades from a doctrinal point of view appears warranted. Further, it appears desirable that an Army-wide policy be established requiring that all units, probably at division level, announce in the SOP or SOI procedures for the use of various colors of smoke for identification purposes. Although the impetus for such a policy should come from the top echelon, its implementation must be delegated to the lowest level wherein employment will depend on the weather, terrain, enemy, and several other factors.

5. Selection and Training of Liaison Officers

Some of the officers interviewed by the Inquiry who had filled liaison officer positions did not appear particularly well qualified, nor were there any indications that they had received special guidance or training for the job. In view of the important function performed by liaison officers, especially in Vietnam, it appears that the criteria followed for the selection of liaison officers and the training conducted to prepare officers for liaison duty are areas which require additional emphasis within the Army school system.

6. Personnel Turbulence

One of the most significant problems faced by the Americal Division, and probably by other units in Vietnam, was the personnel turbulence created by the one-year rotational policy, the rest and recuperation (R&R) program, the policy of rotating commanders and staff officers normally after six months on the job, and the infusion program. While these are all excellent programs and each served a most useful and valid purpose, this Inquiry found that the resulting lack of continuity and the problems created within the personnel replacement process were detrimental to unit effectiveness. No change is suggested; however, it does appear that a thorough review should be undertaken to determine if the impact of these, or similar programs, on combat readiness can be reduced in the future.

7. Utilization of First Sergeants

a. While the use made of a first sergeant is the prerogative of the unit commander, the generally accepted policy is that a rifle company first sergeant is most effectively employed in the field with his company. It is perhaps significant that none of the first sergeants of TF Barker were in the field for other than short visits during the Son My operation; they had all remained behind at their unit's base camp. Had they been in the field following the activities of their companies, setting the example and influencing the actions of other NCO's and enlisted men, the results of the operation might have been different.

b. It is suggested that additional emphasis be placed upon the position of the first sergeant and the role he should play in the administration and, particularly, the operations of his unit in the field. This could be accomplished through the Army school system, the Command Sergeants Major program and command emphasis.

Annex C. Glossary

AB–143	Designation for MACV Combined Campaign Plan, 1968
AC	Aircraft commander. Aviator in charge of piloting the helicopter.
ADC	Assistant Division Commander.
Aero-Scouts	See aircraft names.
After Action Report	See Combat Action Report.
AG	Adjutant General. The adjutant of a unit authorized a General Staff. See Staff.
Aircraft Names	
Aero-Scouts	Helicopters from Co B, 123 Avn Bn.
"Bubble"	Nickname for OH–6, OH–13, or OH–23 helicopter.
"Dolphins"	Liftship, 174th Assault Helicopter Company.
"Firebirds"	Gunship, 71st Avn Co.
"Gunship"	UH–1 helicopter armed with miniguns, rockets, 40 millimeter grenade launchers, or any combination thereof.
"Helix"	FAC, light fixed wing aircraft.
"Hook"	CH–47 helicopter. Used for heavy cargo and troop transport.
"Huey"	UH–1 helicopter.
"Liftship"	Helicopter used to transport troops during a combat assault.

LOH	Light observation helicopter.
"Minute men"	Liftships for 176th Assault Helicopter Company.
"Medevac"	Medical evacuation helicopter.
"Muskets"	Gunships for 176th Assault Helicopter Company.
"PRIMO"	11th Bde C&C helicopter.
"Puff the Magic Dragon"	AC–47 aircraft armed with multibarreled, 7.62 millimeter, extremely high rate of fire weapon. Also called "Spooky."
"Rattlers"	Liftships 71st Assault Helicopter Company.
"Scorpions"	Old name for 123d Avn Bn gunships.
"Sharks"	Gunship 174th Assault Helicopter Company.
"Skeeter"	LOH, Co B, 123d Avn Bn.
"Slick"	UH–1 helicopter used for cargo and troop transport. May or may not have door gunners armed with M–60 machineguns.
"Spooky"	AC–47 aircraft armed with multibarreled, 7.62 millimeter, extremely rapid fire weapon. Also called "Puff the Magic Dragon."
"War Lords"	Gunship Co B, 123d Avn Bn.
AIT	Advanced Individual Training.
ALO	Air Liaison Officer. A tactical Air Force Officer attached to a ground force as air advisor.
Ammo	Ammunition.
"Animals"	Nickname for infantrymen of Co B, 123d Avn Bn.
Antipersonnel mine	A mine designed to cause casualties to personnel.
AO	Area of Operations. An area where US/FWMAF conduct operations during a specific period of time. An AO is assigned normally for a specific operation which may be within or outside of a TAOR.

APC — Armored personnel carrier.

Arty — Artillery.

ARVN — Army of the Republic of Vietnam; Vietnamese soldier.

ATP — Army Training Program.

ATT — Army Training Test.

Avn — Aviation.

Bde — Brigade.

BG — Brigadier General.

"Blow away" — To kill. (GI slang)

Blown in place — Destruction by demolition without removing the object to another location.

Bn — Battalion.

Body Count — Procedure whereby enemy bodies are counted to provide a statistic for measuring degree of success of an operation and to be used in developing data concerning enemy order of battle.

Boobytrap — Usually an explosive charge which is exploded when an unsuspecting person disturbs an apparently harmless object or performs a presumably safe act. Can also be a spear trap or similar mechanical device which does not employ an explosive charge.

"Bought it" — Killed. (GI slang)

Bounding mine — Type of antipersonnel mine, usually buried just below the surface of the ground. It has a small charge which throws the case up into the air; this explodes at a height of 3 or 4 feet, throwing shrapnel or fragments in all directions.

Break — Radio procedure signifying a break between one conversation or idea and another.

"Bubble" — See aircraft names.

Bunker — A fortified structure for the protection of personnel, defended gun position or a defensive position.

CA	Combat assault. Usually used in reference to an assault utilizing helicopters to transport the troops.
Cal	Caliber.
"C&C" "C&C ship (or helicopter)"	Command and control. Used in reference to the helicopter utilized by the tactical commander during a tactical operation.
CD	Civil defendant. Persons who are suspected of being spies, saboteurs, terrorists, or criminals and who do not qualify as prisoners of war.
Census Grievance Committee	GVN agency which accepts and processes complaints from citizens.
CG	Commanding General.
CH	Chaplain.
"Charlie Bird"	Command and control helicopter. See C&C.
"Charlie Charlie"	Command and control helicopter. See C&C.
CHICOM	Chinese Communist.
Chieu Hoi	Vietnamese program whereby Viet Cong or North Vietnamese who surrender voluntarily are given amnesty. Means "open arms."
CID	Criminal Investigation Division (Provost Marshal's Office).
CIDG	Civilian Irregular Defense Group (RVN). Vietnamese irregulars, often advised by U.S. Special Forces.
"Claymore"	M–18 mine series. A type of antipersonnel mine developed by the Army, which propels pellets in the direction employed. The VC and CHICOM have devised similar mines, which are also referred to as "claymores."
"Click"	Kilometer.
CO	Commanding Officer.
Co	Company.
COL	Colonel.
"Cold"	Not receiving fire, i.e., a "cold LZ."

Combat Action Report (CAR)	Report detailing plan and conduct of tactical operation and its results.
Command and Control	An arrangement of personnel and facilities, employed by a commander in planning, directing, and controlling operations. Also used in reference to the commander's helicopter.
Command detonated mine	A mine which is detonated electrically utilizing wires and a detonating generator (blasting machine) or a battery.
Command net	A communications network which connects an echelon of command with some or all of its subordinate echelons for the purpose of command control.
Command Post	In combat, the echelon in which the commander is located. Frequently the field commander is located in a C&C helicopter; thus the helicopter becomes the command post.
COMUSMACV	Commander, United States Military Assistance Command Vietnam.
Console	A grouping of radios in a helicopter which enables the user to have a multiple frequency radio capability.
CORDS	Civil Operations Revolutionary Development Support. US Agency which channels funds and materials for civil works.
"Coyote"	See radio call signs.
CP	Command Post.
CPT	Captain.
C Rations	Special type ration designed for troops under combat conditions.
CSCC	Combat Support Coordination Center. The CSCC is a facility within which are grouped representatives of artillery, air, naval gunfire, and other agencies deemed necessary by the commander(s).
CSM	Command Sergeant Major.
CSWC	Crew served weapons captured.

CTZ — Corps Tactical Zone. Military subdivision in Vietnam, providing areas of responsibility to ARVN corps and US Field Force headquarters. Divided into 4 zones, i.e., I CTZ, II CTZ, III CTZ, IV CTZ.

CWO — Chief Warrant Officer.

CYA — GI slang expression, usually used among staff personnel when referring to a paper or action prepared as a defense against some future charge. Means "Cover Your Action."

DAO — Division aviation officer.

DEROS — Date eligible for return from overseas.

Detainees — Vietnamese who have been detained but whose final status, i.e., innocent civilian, returnee, civil defendant or prisoner of war, has not yet been determined.

"Di Di" — Vietnamese words meaning "to run."

"Di Di-ing" — Running.

"Dink" — Vietnamese person (GI slang).

DIOCC — District Intelligence and Operations Coordinating Center.

Direct Support (DS) — Mission in which a field artillery unit is primarily responsive to fire missions in support of a particular ground force.

District — Political subdivision in RVN, roughly equivalent to a county.

District Chief — GVN official governing a district containing several villages, usually a military officer.

Division Support Command — An organic divisional unit responsible for providing division level supply, transportation, maintenance, medical, and miscellaneous services for all elements of the division.

"Dolphin" — See radio call signs; aircraft names.

DSA — District Senior Advisor. Senior US advisor to the District Chief.

Dud	Explosive munition which has failed to explode after being armed; an individual who does not perform properly.
"Dung Lai"	Vietnamese words meaning "halt."
Dust Off	Term used for medical evacuation helicopters. Also used referring to being evacuated from the battlefield because of wounds.
EOD	Explosive Ordnance Disposal unit. Personnel with special training and equipment who render explosive ordnance safe (such as bombs, mines, projectiles and boobytraps), make intelligence reports on such ordnance and supervise the safe removal thereof.
Extracted	To be removed by helicopter.
FAC	Forward Air Controller. An officer (Air Force Pilot) member of the tactical air control party who controls aircraft engaged in close air support of ground troops. In Vietnam the FAC controls airstrikes from a light fixed-wing aircraft such as the 0–1 (Piper Cub).
FDC	Fire Direction Center. That element of a command post by means of which the commander exercises fire direction and/or fire control.
FDO	Fire Direction Officer.
Fire for effect	Fire which is delivered after the burst is within the desired distance of the target; term in a fire message to indicate the adjustment is satisfactory and fire for effect is desired.
Firepower	The amount of fire which may be delivered by a position, unit, or weapons system; ability to deliver fire on an overall basis.
"Flap"	A situation of confusion or chaos.
FO	Forward Observer. A front line observer trained to adjust ground or naval gunfire and pass back battlefield information.
Fortified Village or Hamlet	A hamlet which has been fortified with bunkers, fighting positions, communications trenches, interconnecting tunnel networks, hiding places, etc.

"Fox Mike" Frequency modulated (FM) radio.

Freq Radio frequency.

FSB Fire Support Base. Base of operations from which fire support may be delivered.

FWMAF Free World Military Assistance Forces.

Garble An error in transmission or reception which renders a message or portion thereof incorrect or unintelligible.

"Gook" Vietnamese person. (GI slang)

"Grunts" Nickname for infantrymen.

GT Line Gun-target line. An imaginary straight line from the gun to the target.

"Gunnie" Aviator who flies a gunship.

GVN Government of South Vietnam.

G1, G2, G3, etc. See Staff.

Hamlet The political subdivision in the RVN governmental structure immediately below village level.

Hamlet Chief GVN official governing a hamlet, usually a civilian.

"H&I" Harassing and interdiction fire. Fire designed to disturb the rest of the enemy troops, to curtail movement, and, by threat of losses, to lower morale. Fire placed on an area or point to prevent the enemy from using the area or point.

"Hard core" "Hard core Viet Cong" are those who are completely indoctrinated toward and dedicated to the Viet Cong.

HE High explosive (projectile).

HES Hamlet Evaluation System. US program which evaluates GVN control over hamlets.

"Higher" Higher headquarters or higher authority.

"High gun" UH-1 armed helicopter in Co B, 123d Avn Bn, which was the controlling commander's air-

	craft. It was so named because it flew higher than the rest of the aero-scout team.
"Hit the LZ"	Land in the landing zone.
"Hook"	See aircraft names.
"Hootch"	Term used for hut or structure made of rice straw and bamboo or similar material. (GI slang)
"Hot"	Receiving hostile fire (i.e., a "hot LZ").
"Huey"	See aircraft names.
Hustle	To move rapidly.
IG	Inspector General. A Special Staff officer who examines and reports on every phase of activity that affects a command, installation, or activity. See staff.
IG Inspection	Inspector General Inspection. An examination by an inspector general into the performance of a mission and the state of discipline, efficiency, and economy of a command, installation, or activity of the Department of the Army.
III MAF	Third Marine Amphibious Force.
"Incoming"	Receiving hostile fire.
In-country	Physically located within the country.
Inf	Infantry.
Info	Information.
Infrastructure	The basic economical, social, or military facilities and installations of a community, state, etc. See Viet Cong Infrastructure.
Innocent Civilians	Members of the civilian population of Son My Village, who were unarmed and committing no hostile acts. (Also called noncombatants.)
INTSUM	Intelligence summary. A specific report providing a summary of items of intelligence information, usually at 6 hour intervals.
IWC	Individual weapons captured.

JAG	Judge Advocate General. See Staff.
Journal	A record of significant events, see log.
J1, J2, J3, etc.	See Staff.
"KHA"	Killed due to hostile action.
KIA	Killed in action.
Laager	South African term used during the Boer War. Used to mean a defensive position.
"Lai day"	Vietnamese words meaning "come here."
LAW	See weapons.
"Lead"	The leader of a flight. See call signs.
LF	Local Force. VC military units which are directly subordinate to a provincial or district party committee and normally operate only within a specific VC province or district.
Lift	A flight of troop-carrying helicopters.
"Lift Ship"	See aircraft names.
"Lima Zulu"	Landing zone.
LNO	Liaison officer.
LO	Liaison officer.
Log	A record of significant events. See Journal.
Logged	Entered into a Log or Journal.
Logging Time	Keeping a record of hours of flight.
LOH	Light observation helicopter.
"Low Gun"	UH–1 armed helicopter flying at a low altitude with mission of protecting the light observation helicopter.
LRRP	Long Range Reconnaissance Patrol.
LT	Lieutenant.
LTC	Lieutenant Colonel.
LTL	Lien tinh-lo. Vietnamese designation for an interprovincial highway or route.
LZ	Landing zone.

MACV	Military Assistance Command, Vietnam.
MAJ	Major.
"Mama San"	An old woman. (GI slang)
MEDCAP	Medical Civic Action Program. A military operation during which a hamlet is secured by a military force, and medical care, medicine, food, and clothing are dispensed to the villagers.
MEDEVAC	Medical evacuation. Removed from the battle field because of wounds. Also term used to identify a helicopter used in the medical evacuation.
Medic	A member of the Army Medical Corps, especially one who gives first aid in combat.
MG	Major General.
MI	Military Intelligence branch.
"Mike Mike"	Millimeter, i.e. 60 Mike Mike mortar.
Mine	An explosive designed to destroy or damage vehicles, boats, or aircraft or designed to kill or incapacitate personnel. It may be detonated by the action of its victim, by the passage of time, or by controlled means.
Mine sweeper	A device which detects metallic objects; used to detect mines.
"Minigun"	An extremely rapid firing machinegun using multiple barrels, 5.56 millimeters.
"Misprison of a felony"	The offense of concealing knowledge of a felony by one who has not participated or assisted in it.
mm	Millimeter, i.e. 60 mm mortar.
Monitoring	The act of listening to, reviewing and/or recording enemy or friendly communication for the purpose of maintaining standards, improving communications, or for reference.
M–1, M–16, M–60, etc.	See weapons.
NCO	Noncommissioned officer. Ranks Corporal through Sergeant Major.

NCS	Net Control Station. A station designated to control traffic and enforce circuit discipline within a given net.
Net	An organization of (radio) stations capable of direct communications on a common channel or frequency.
NLF	National Liberation Front. Political arm of the Viet Cong.
Noncombatant	Members of the civilian population of Son My Village, who were unarmed and committing no hostile acts. (Also called "innocent civilians.")
"Nuoc mam"	Vietnamese fish sauce.
NVA	North Vietnamese Army.
OB	Order of Battle. The identification, strength, command structure, and disposition of the personnel, units, and equipment of any military force.
OBJ	Objective. A definite tactical feature, the seizure and/or holding of which is essential.
OJT	On the Job Training. A training process whereby students or trainees acquire knowledge and skill through actual performance of duties.
OPCON	Operational Control. The authority granted to a commander to direct forces assigned so that the commander may accomplish specific missions, or tasks which are usually limited by function, time, or location.
OPREP	Operations Report.
Orbiting	Flying in circles over an area.
"Out"	Radio procedure signifying end of transmission.
"Over"	Radio procedure signifying a reply to the preceding transmission is anticipated.
Paddy	Rice field.
"Papa San"	An old man. (GI slang)

Pax	Passenger(s).
PD	Point detonating fuze for an artillery projectile. Located in the nose of a projectile, which is initiated upon impact.
"Peter Pilot"	Pilot of a helicopter, as differentiated from the aircraft commander.
PFC	Private First Class.
PHOENIX Program	Coordinated effort to attack the Viet Cong infrastructure on a nationwide basis.
Phonetic Alphabet	A list of standard words used to identify letters in a message transmitted by radio or telephone:
A—Alpha	N—November
B—Bravo	O—Oscar
C—Charlie	P—Papa
D—Delta	Q—Quebec
E—Echo	R—Romeo
F—Foxtrot	S—Sierra
G—Golf	T—Tango
H—Hotel	U—Uniform
I—India	V—Victor
J—Juliet	W—Whiskey
K—Kilo	X—Xray
L—Lima	Y—Yankee
M—Mike	Z—Zulu
PIC	Province Interrogation Center.
"Pinkville"	Nickname for My Lai (1).
PIOCC	Province Intelligence and Operations Coordinating Center.
Plt	Platoon.
POL	Petroleum, Oils, and Lubricants.
"Pop Smoke"	To employ a smoke grenade in order to identify a location.
POR	Preparation of Replacement for oversea movement.
"Pot"	Marijuana. A hallucinatory drug.

POW	Prisoner of war. Correct term is "PW".
Prep	Shortened term for preparation or preparatory fire. A heavy volume of prearranged ground or aircraft fire delivered to destroy, disrupt, disorganize, and neutralize the enemy and to demoralize and destroy the defending forces prior to the initiation of the attack. Fire delivered on a target preparatory to an assault.
"Prick 9"	AN/PRC 9 portable, man-carried radio.
"Prick 25"	AN/PRC 25 portable, man-carried radio.
Province	Political division in RVN, roughly equivalent to a state.
Province Chief	GVN official governing a Province, usually a military officer, roughly equivalent to a governor.
Provost Marshal	Staff officer who supervises all activities of military police of a command and who advises the commander on military police matters, prisoners of war, military prisoners, and other matters of concern to the commander.
PSA	Province Senior Advisor. Senior US advisor to the Province Chief.
PSYOPS	Psychological Operations. These operations include psychological warfare, and in addition, encompass those political, military, economic, and ideological actions planned and conducted to create in neutral or friendly foreign groups the emotions, attitudes, or behavior to support the achievement of national objectives.
"Puff the Magic Dragon"	See aircraft names.
"Push"	Term used to mean a radio frequency.
PVT	Private.
PW	Prisoner of war. (Incorrectly called "POW")
PZ	Pickup zone.

QL	Quoc-lo. Vietnamese designation for a national highway or route.
Radio Call Sign	A group of letters, numerals, or a combination of both which identifies a radio station.
"Coyote"	TF Barker.
"Coyote 3"	MAJ Calhoun.
"Coyote 6"	LTC Barker.
"Coyote 23"	Pickup zone control, LZ Dottie.
"Coyote 65"	Net Control Station, MSG Johnson.
"Coyote Alpha 6"	A Company Commander, CPT Riggs.
"Coyote Bravo 6"	B Company Commander, CPT Michles.
"Coyote Charlie 6"	C Company Commander, CPT Medina.
"Coyote Charlie 81"	81mm Mortar FDC, located at LZ Uptight.
"Dolphin"	Liftships, 174th Avn Co.
"Dolphin Lead"	Leader of liftships, 174th Avn Co.
"Dolphin 2, 3, 4, 5"	Individual liftships, 174th Avn Co.
"Dust Off"	Medevac helicopter.
"Helix 32"	FAC.
"Helix 22"	FAC.
"Lobo 65"	Net Control Station, 4th Bn, 3d Inf.
"Newsboy India Two Zero"	US Navy "Swift Boat."
"Rawhide"	11th Bde.
"Rawhide 6"	COL Henderson, Bde Co.
"Rawhide 3"	MAJ McKnight, 11th Bde S3.
"Saber"	Americal Division.
"Saber 6"	MG Koster, CG Americal Division.
"Sane Drank Delta Mike (Same Drink)"	US Navy "Swift Boat."
"Shark"	Gunships, 174th Avn Co.

"Shark 6"	Gunship platoon commander, 174th Avn Co.
"Skeeter"	OH–23 helicopter, Aero-Scout team, Co B, 123d Avn Bn (flown by WO1 Thompson on 16 Mar 68).
"War Lord"	Gunships, Co B, 123d Avn Bn.
"War Lord Alpha Lead"	Aero-Scout team leader, Co B, 123d Avn Bn.
R&R	Rest and Recuperation. The withdrawal of individuals from combat or arduous duty for short periods of rest and recuperation.
"Rawhide"	See radio call signs.
RD	Revolutionary Development. The formalized GVN program in specified hamlets located generally with RD campaign areas. It includes the local security for those hamlets and the political, economic, and social activities at that level.
RD Cadre	Revolutionary Development Cadre. Vietnamese team which implements the Revolutionary Development program within the community.
Recon	Reconnaissance.
Reconnaissance	A mission undertaken to obtain, by visual observation or other detection methods, information about the activities and resources of an enemy or potential enemy; or to secure data concerning the meteorological, hydrographic, or geographic characteristics of a particular area.
Reconnaissance by fire	Employment of artillery, mortar, aircraft, or small arms fire to cause the enemy to disclose his position.
Reconnaissance in Force	A limited objective operation by a considerable force to discover and test the enemy's dispositions and strengths, or to develop other intelligence.
Report of Investigation	An official written record of all pertinent information obtained in an inquiry concerning a crime, offense, accident, or allegation.

RF/PF	Regional Forces/Popular Forces; GVN Paramilitary units.
"Roger"	Radio procedure meaning "I understand".
ROK	Republic of Korea.
Round	All the parts that make up the ammunition necessary in firing one shot; One shot fired by a weapon.
RTO	Radio-telephone operator. The man who carried the radio or whose job is to operate the radio.
"Ruff Puff"	Regional Forces/Popular Forces.
RVN	Repubic of Vietnam.
RVNAF	Republic of Vietnam Armed Forces.
"Saber"	See radio call signs.
Safe-haven hamlet	A hamlet under Viet Cong domination, which provides the VC with aid and comfort, and in which the VC feel safe from Allied attack.
"S&C"	See Search and Clear.
"S&D"	See Search and Destroy.
Sapper	VC/NVA soldiers who infiltrate friendly positions in order to employ explosives.
Satchel charge	A number of blocks of explosive taped to a board fitted with a rope or wire loop for carrying and attaching.
"Scarf up"	To seize or capture.
Search and clear	Clearing operations. Military operation to clear an area permanently of organized VC/NVA main forces, including the provincial battalions, in order to eliminate the immediate enemy threat.
Search and destroy	Military operation conducted for the purpose of seeking out and destroying enemy forces, installations, resources, and base areas. This term is no longer used.
Sector	Province military structure.

SFC	Sergeant First Class.
SGM	Sergeant Major.
SGT	Sergeant.
"Shark"	See aircraft names; call signs.
SHELREP	Shelling report. A report of enemy shelling containing information on caliber, direction, time, density, and area shelled.
SIR	Serious Incident Report. Report of any incident which may result in damaging public confidence in the US Armed Forces and cause continued or widespread adverse publicity.
SITREP	Situation report. A report giving the situation in the area of a reporting unit or formation.
SIW	Self-inflicted wound.
"Six"	Radio call sign normally assigned to a unit commander.
SJA	Staff Judge Advocate. See Staff.
"Skeeter"	See Radio call signs; aircraft names.
"Slick"	See aircraft names.
"Slope"	Vietnamese person. (GI slang)
Small arms	All arms, including automatic weapons, up to and including .60 caliber and shotguns.
Solatium	Payment as compensation for loss or injury.
"Song"	Vietnamese word for river.
SOP	Standing operating procedure.
Sortie	An operational flight by one aircraft.
SP	Specialist.
"Spooky"	See aircraft names.
Spot Report	A concise narrative report of essential information covering events or conditions that may have an immediate and significant effect on current planning and operations.
Sqd	Squad.

SSG	Staff Sergeant.
Staff	Officers who are specifically ordered or detailed to assist the commander in his exercise of command.
General Staff (GS)	A group of officers in the headquarters of Army divisions or similar or larger units which assist their commanders in planning, coordinating, and supervising operations. Consists of four or more principal functional systems: personnel (G–1), military intelligence (G–2), operations and training (G–3), logistics (G–4), civil affairs (G–5). G–2 Air and G–3 Air are Army officers assigned to G–2 or G–3 who assist in planning and coordinating joint operations or ground and air units.
Joint Staff	The staff of a commander of a unified command (such as MACV) which includes members for the services comprising the force. A joint staff may be designated J–1, J–2, J–3, etc. J–5 is Plans and Policy.
Personal Staff	Such staff officers as the commander elects to coordinate and administer directly, instead of through the chief of staff. The commander's aides are members of his personal staff.
Special Staff	All staff members having duties at a headquarters and not included in the general staff group or in the personal staff group. Special staff includes aviation officer, staff judge advocate (SJA or JAG), chaplain, Inspector General (IG), provost marshal, adjutant general (AG), etc.
Unit Staff	In brigades and smaller units, staff sections are designated S1, S2, S3, etc., with duties corresponding to those of the general staff.
"Stand Down"	Assume a lower level of readiness, as to "stand down" from an alert.
"STRAC"	An expression meaning "sharp" or on top of the situation. Formerly "Strategic Army Corps".
Subhamlet	Subdivision of a hamlet.

Subsector	District military structure.
Support Command	See Division Support Command.
Suppressive fire	Firepower delivered upon a target to discourage or preclude the enemy from returning the fire.
"Swift Boat"	Vessel employed by the Navy to screen river banks and coast lines.
S1, S2, S3, etc.	See Staff.
TAOI	Tactical area of interest. An area including, but not necessarily limited to, the TAOR in which the designated US/FWMAF commander is knowledgeable of the location, activities, and operations of all GVN forces and installations, CIDG camps, and RD areas. The TAOI differs from the TAOR in that US/FWMAF commanders are not charged with primary tactical responsibility in the TAOI.
TAOR	Tactical area of responsibility. An area assigned to a commander who is responsible for installations, the control of movement, and the conduct of tactical operations with troops under his control. All fire and maneuver conducted within the TAOR must be coordinated with the commander.
Task Force	A temporary grouping of units under one commander, formed for the purpose of carrying out a specific operation or mission.
TF	Task Force.
"That's affirm"	Affirmative.
The 5 S's	Procedures for handling prisoners of war, i.e., "Search, Silence, Segregate, Speed, Safeguard".
TL	Tinh-lo. Vietnamese designation for a provincial highway or route.
TOC	Tactical operations center. A physical groupment of those elements of an Army general and special staff concerned with current operations and the tactical support thereof.

Track	Tracked vehicles, i.e. tanks, 'APC's'.
UHF	Ultra high frequency radio.
USARPAC	United States Army, Pacific.
USARV	United States Army, Vietnam.
VC	Viet Cong.
VCI	Viet Cong Infrastructure.
VCS	Viet Cong suspect or Viet Cong sympathizer.
VHF	Very high frequency radio.
Viet Cong	Vietnamese words meaning Vietnamese Communist.
Viet Cong Infrastructure	The political and administrative organization through which the Viet Cong control or seek to control the South Vietnamese people.
Village	Political subdivision below district level, consists of several hamlets, roughly equivalent to a metropolitan area.
Village Chief	GVN official governing a number of hamlets, usually a civilian.
VIP	Voluntary Informant Program. Program whereby Vietnamese are paid for information leading to the capture of weapons, ammunition, equipment, or Viet Cong personnel.
VR	Visual reconnaissance.
VR Aircraft	Aircraft utilized to conduct a visual reconnaissance.
VT	Variable time fuse. A fuse designed to detonate a projectile when activated by external influence other than contact in the close vicinity of a target.
"War Lord"	See radio call signs; aircraft names.
"Waste"	Term meaning to shoot or to kill. (GI slang)
Web gear	Military equipment consisting of a belt and harness made of webbing, designed to carry pack, canteen, ammunition pouches, etc.

Weapons

AK 47	Communist-made automatic rifle.
C–4	Plastic explosive. More powerful than an equivalent weight of TNT.
LAW	Light antitank weapon. Lightweight weapon carried by an individual soldier which delivers a high explosive projectile against a target.
Minigun	5.56 millimeter, multi-barreled, extremely high rate of fire weapon.
M–1	US rifle, caliber .30, M–1, semiautomatic. World War II vintage weapon, no longer issued to US units.
M–16	US rifle, 5.56 millimeter, M–16, automatic or semiautomatic. Also known as AR–15.
M–18	US mine, M–18 series. Also known as "claymore".
M–60	US Machinegun, 7.62 millimeter, M–60. Also known as "60".
M–79	US grenade launcher, M–79, propels a 40 millimeter grenade.
SKS	Communist-made carbine.
"8 inch"	8 inch howitzer.
"16"	See M–16.
"45"	US pistol (automatic), caliber .45.
"50"	US heavy machinegun, caliber .50.
"60"	See M–60.
"60mm"	60 millimeter mortar.
"79"	See M–79.
"81mm"	81 millimeter mortar.
"105"	105 millimeter howitzer.
"155"	155 millimeter howitzer.
"175"	175 millimeter gun.

"Willy Peter"	White phosphorus artillery projectile.
WO1	First Warrant Officer rank.
"8 inch"	See weapons.
"16"	See weapons.
"45"	See weapons.
"50"	See weapons.
"60"	See weapons.
"60mm"	See weapons.
"79"	See weapons.
"81mm"	See weapons.
"105"	See weapons.
"155"	See weapons.
"175"	See weapons.

SUPPLEMENT

From World War II and Nuremberg

1. Allied Powers, Moscow Declaration, 30 October 1943

. . .

The United Kingdom, the United States and the Soviet Union have received from many quarters evidence of atrocities, massacres and cold-blooded mass executions which are being perpetrated by Hitlerite forces in many of the countries they have overrun and from which they are now being steadily expelled. The brutalities of Hitlerite domination are no new thing and all peoples or territories in their grip have suffered from the worst form of Government by terror. What is new is that many of these territories are now being redeemed by the advancing armies of the liberating powers and that in their desperation, the recoiling Hitlerite Huns are redoubling their ruthless cruelties. This is now evidenced with particular clearness by monstrous crimes of the Hitlerites on the territory of the Soviet Union which is being liberated from Hitlerites, and on French and Italian territory.

Accordingly, the aforesaid three Allied Powers, speaking in the interests of the thirty-three United Nations, hereby solemnly declare and give full warning of their declaration as follows: At the time of granting of any armistice to any government which may be set up in Germany, these German officers and men and members of the Nazi Party who have been responsible for or have taken a consenting part in the above atrocities, massacres and executions will be sent back to the countries in which their abominable deeds were done in order that they may be judged and punished according to the laws of these liberated countries and of the free governments which will be erected therein. Lists will be compiled in all possible detail from all these countries, having regard especially to invaded parts of the Soviet Union, to Poland and Czechoslovakia, to Yugoslavia and Greece including Crete and other islands, to Norway, Denmark, Netherlands, Belgium, Luxembourg, France and Italy.

Thus, Germans who take part in wholesale shooting of Polish officers or in the execution of French, Dutch, Belgian or Norwegian hostages or of Cretan peasants, or who have shared in slaughters inflicted on the people of Poland or in territories of the Soviet Union which are now being swept clear of the enemy, will know they will be brought back to the scene of their crimes and judged on the spot by the peoples whom they have outraged. Let those who have hitherto not imbrued their hands with innocent blood beware lest they join the ranks of the guilty, for most assuredly the three Allied Powers will pursue them to the uttermost ends of the earth and will deliver them to their accusers in order that justice may be done.

The above declaration is without prejudice to the case of German criminals, whose offenses have no particular geographical localization and who will be punished by joint decision of the Governments of the Allies.

2a. London Agreement of 8 August 1945

Agreement [in accord with the Moscow Declaration of 30 October 1943] *by the Government of the United States of America, the Provisional Government of the French Republic, the Government of the United Kingdom of Great Britain and Northern Ireland, and the Government of the Union of Soviet Socialist Republics for the Prosecution and Punishment of the Major War Criminals of the European Axis.*

. . .

Article 1. There shall be established after consultation with the Control Council for Germany an International Military Tribunal for the trial of war criminals whose offenses have no particular geographical location whether they be accused individually or in their capacity as members of organizations or groups or in both capacities.

Article 2. The constitution, jurisdiction, and functions of the International Military Tribunal shall be those set out in the Charter annexed to this Agreement, which Charter shall form an integral part of this Agreement.

Article 3. Each of the Signatories shall take the necessary steps to make available for the investigation of the charges and trial the major war criminals detained by them who are to be tried by the International Military Tribunal. The Signatories shall also use their best endeavors to make available for investigation of the charges against and the trial before the International Military Tribunal such of the major war criminals as are not in the territories of any of the Signatories.

Article 4. Nothing in this Agreement shall prejudice the provisions established by the Moscow Declaration concerning the return of war criminals to the countries where they committed their crimes.

Article 5. Any Government of the United Nations may adhere to this Agreement by notice given through the diplomatic channel to the Government of the United Kingdom, who shall inform the other signatory and adhering Governments of each such adherence.*

Article 6. Nothing in this Agreement shall prejudice the jurisdiction or the powers of any national or occupation court established or to be established in any Allied territory or in Germany for the trial of war criminals.

Article 7. This Agreement shall come into force on the day of signature and shall remain in force for the period of one year and shall continue thereafter, subject to the right of any Signatory to give, through the diplomatic channel, one month's notice of intention to terminate it. Such termination shall not prejudice any proceedings already taken or any findings already made in pursuance of this Agreement.

In witness whereof the Undersigned have signed the present Agreement.

Done in quadruplicate in London this 8th day of August 1945 each in English, French, and Russian, and each text to have equal authenticity.

For the Government of the United States of America
/s/ ROBERT H. JACKSON

For the Provisional Government of the French Republic
/s/ ROBERT FALCO

For the Government of the United Kingdom of Great Britain and Northern Ireland
/s/ JOWITT

For the Government of the Union of Soviet Socialist Republics
/s/ I. NIKITCHENKO
/s/ A. TRAININ

* In accordance with Article 5, the following Governments of the United Nations have expressed their adherence to the Agreement: Greece, Denmark, Yugoslavia, the Netherlands, Czechoslovakia, Poland, Belgium, Ethiopia, Australia, Honduras, Norway, Panama, Luxembourg, Haiti, New Zealand, India, Venezuela, Uruguay, and Paraguay.

2b. Charter of the International Military Tribunal

I. Constitution of the International Military Tribunal

Article 1. In pursuance of the Agreement signed on the 8th day of August 1945 . . . there shall be established an International Military Tribunal (hereinafter called "the Tribunal") for the just and prompt trial and punishment of the major war criminals of the European Axis.

Article 2. The Tribunal shall consist of four members, each with an alternate. One member and one alternate shall be appointed by each of the Signatories. The alternates shall, so far as they are able, be present at all sessions of the Tribunal. . . .

Article 3. Neither the Tribunal, its members nor their alternates can be challenged by the Prosecution, or by the defendants or their counsel. . . .

Article 4.

a. The presence of all four members of the Tribunal or the alternate for any absent member shall be necessary to constitute the quorum.
b. The members of the Tribunal shall, before any trial begins, agree among themselves upon the selection from their number of a President, and the President shall hold office during that trial, or as may otherwise be agreed by a vote of not less than three members. The principle of rotation of presidency for successive trials is agreed. If, however, a session of the Tribunal takes place on the territory of one of the four Signatories, the representative of that Signatory on the Tribunal shall preside.

c. Save as aforesaid the Tribunal shall take decisions by a majority vote and in case the votes are evenly divided, the vote of the President shall be decisive: provided always that convictions and sentences shall only be imposed by affirmative votes of at least three members of the Tribunal. . . .

II. Jurisdiction and General Principles

Article 6. The Tribunal established by the Agreement referred to in Article 1 hereof for the trial and punishment of the major war criminals of the European Axis countries shall have the power to try and punish persons who, acting in the interests of the European Axis countries, whether as individuals or as members of organizations, committed any of the following crimes.

The following acts, or any of them, are crimes coming within the jurisdiction of the Tribunal for which there shall be individual responsibility:

a. *Crimes against Peace:* namely, planning, preparation, initiation or waging of a war of aggression, or a war in violation of international treaties, agreements or assurances, or participation in a Common Plan or Conspiracy for the accomplishment of any of the foregoing;
b. *War Crimes:* namely, violations of the laws or customs of war. Such violations shall include, but not be limited to, murder, ill-treatment or deportation to slave labor or for any other purpose of civilian population of or in occupied territory, murder or ill-treatment of prisoners of war or persons on the seas, killing of hostages, plunder of public or private property, wanton destruction of cities, towns, or villages, or devastation not justified by military necessity;
c. *Crimes against Humanity:* namely, murder, extermination, enslavement, deportation, and other inhumane acts committed against any civilian population, before or during the war,* or persecutions on political, racial, or religious grounds in execution of or in connection with any crime within the jurisdiction of the Tribunal, whether or not in violation of domestic law of the country where perpetrated.

Leaders, organizers, instigators, and accomplices participating in the formulation or execution of a Common Plan or Conspiracy to commit any of the foregoing crimes are responsible for all acts performed by any persons in execution of such plan.

* Comma substituted in place of semicolon by Protocol of 6 October 1945.

Article 7. The official position of defendants, whether as Heads of State or responsible officials in Government departments, shall not be considered as freeing them from responsibility or mitigating punishment.

Article 8. The fact that the defendant acted pursuant to order of his Government or of a superior shall not free him from responsibility, but may be considered in mitigation of punishment if the Tribunal determine that justice so requires.

Article 9. At the trial of any individual member of any group or organization the Tribunal may declare (in connection with any act of which the individual may be convicted) that the group or organization of which the individual was a member was a criminal organization.

After receipt of the Indictment the Tribunal shall give such notice as it thinks fit that the Prosecution intends to ask the Tribunal to make such declaration and any member of the organization will be entitled to apply to the Tribunal for leave to be heard by the Tribunal upon the question of the criminal character of the organization. The Tribunal shall have power to allow or reject the application. If the application is allowed, the Tribunal may direct in what manner the applicants shall be represented and heard.

Article 10. In cases where a group or organization is declared criminal by the Tribunal, the competent national authority of any Signatory shall have the right to bring individuals to trial for membership therein before national, military, or occupation courts. In any such case the criminal nature of the group or organization is considered proved and shall not be questioned.

Article 11. Any person convicted by the Tribunal may be charged before a national, military, or occupation court, referred to in Article 10 of this Charter, with a crime other than of membership in a criminal group or organization and such court may, after convicting him, impose upon him punishment independent of and additional to the punishment imposed by the Tribunal for participation in the criminal activities of such group or organization.

Article 12. The Tribunal shall have the right to take proceedings against a person charged with crimes set out in Article 6 of this Charter in his absence, if he has not been found or if the Tribunal, for any reason, finds it necessary, in the interests of justice, to conduct the hearing in his absence.

Article 13. The Tribunal shall draw up rules for its procedure. These rules shall not be inconsistent with the provisions of this Charter.

III. Committee for the Investigation and Prosecution of Major War Criminals

Article 14. Each Signatory shall appoint a Chief Prosecutor for the investigation of the charges against and the prosecution of major war criminals.

The Chief Prosecutors shall act as a committee for the following purposes:

a. to agree upon a plan of the individual work of each of the Chief Prosecutors and his staff,
b. to settle the final designation of major war criminals to be tried by the Tribunal,
c. to approve the Indictment and the documents to be submitted therewith,
d. to lodge the Indictment and the accompanying documents with the Tribunal,
e. to draw up and recommend to the Tribunal for its approval draft rules of procedure, contemplated by Article 13 of this Charter. The Tribunal shall have power to accept, with or without amendments, or to reject, the rules so recommended.

The Committee shall act in all the above matters by a majority vote and shall appoint a Chairman as may be convenient and in accordance with the principle of rotation: provided that if there is an equal division of vote concerning the designation of a defendant to be tried by the Tribunal, or the crimes with which he shall be charged, that proposal will be adopted which was made by the party which proposed that the particular defendant be tried, or the particular charges be preferred against him.

Article 15. The Chief Prosecutors shall individually, and acting in collaboration with one another, also undertake the following duties:

a. investigation, collection, and production before or at the Trial of all necessary evidence,
b. the preparation of the Indictment for approval by the Committee in accordance with paragraph (c) of Article 14 hereof,
c. the preliminary examination of all necessary witnesses and of the defendants,
d. to act as prosecutor at the Trial,
e. to appoint representatives to carry out such duties as may be assigned to them,

f. to undertake such other matters as may appear necessary to them for the purposes of the preparation for and conduct of the Trial.

It is understood that no witness or defendant detained by any Signatory shall be taken out of the possession of that Signatory without its assent.

IV. Fair Trial for Defendants

Article 16. In order to ensure fair trial for the defendants, the following procedure shall be followed:

a. The Indictment shall include full particulars specifying in detail the charges against the defendants. A copy of the Indictment and of all the documents lodged with the Indictment, translated into a language which he understands, shall be furnished to the defendant at a reasonable time before the Trial.
b. During any preliminary examination or trial of a defendant he shall have the right to give any explanation relevant to the charges made against him.
c. A preliminary examination of a defendant and his trial shall be conducted in, or translated into, a language which the defendant understands.
d. A defendant shall have the right to conduct his own defense before the Tribunal or to have the assistance of counsel.
e. A defendant shall have the right through himself or through his counsel to present evidence at the Trial in support of his defense, and to cross-examine any witness called by the Prosecution.

V. Powers of the Tribunal and Conduct of the Trial

Article 17. The Tribunal shall have the power:

a. to summon witnesses to the Trial and to require their attendance and testimony and to put questions to them,
b. to interrogate any defendant,
c. to require the production of documents and other evidentiary material,
d. to administer oaths to witnesses,
e. to appoint officers for the carrying out of any task designated by

the Tribunal including the power to have evidence taken on commission.

Article 18. The Tribunal shall:

a. confine the Trial strictly to an expeditious hearing of the issues raised by the charges,
b. take strict measures to prevent any action which will cause unreasonable delay, and rule out irrelevant issues and statements of any kind whatsoever,
c. deal summarily with any contumacy, imposing appropriate punishment, including exclusion of any defendant or his counsel from some or all further proceedings, but without prejudice to the determination of the charges.

Article 19. The Tribunal shall not be bound by technical rules of evidence. It shall adopt and apply to the greatest possible extent expeditious and non-technical procedure, and shall admit any evidence which it deems to have probative value.

Article 20. The Tribunal may require to be informed of the nature of any evidence before it is offered so that it may rule upon the relevance thereof.

Article 21. The Tribunal shall not require proof of facts of common knowledge but shall take judicial notice thereof. It shall also take judicial notice of official governmental documents and reports of the United Nations, including the acts and documents of the committees set up in the various Allied countries for the investigation of war crimes, and the records and findings of military or other Tribunals of any of the United Nations.

Article 22. The permanent seat of the Tribunal shall be in Berlin. The first meetings of the members of the Tribunal and of the Chief Prosecutors shall be held at Berlin in a place to be designated by the Control Council for Germany. The first trial shall be held at Nuremberg, and any subsequent trials shall be held at such places as the Tribunal may decide.

Article 23. One or more of the Chief Prosecutors may take part in the prosecution at each trial. The function of any Chief Prosecutor may be discharged by him personally, or by any person or persons authorized by him.

The function of counsel for a defendant may be discharged at the defendant's request by any counsel professionally qualified to conduct cases before the Courts of his own country, or by any other person who may be specially authorized thereto by the Tribunal.

Article 24. The proceedings at the Trial shall take the following course:

a. The Indictment shall be read in court.
b. The Tribunal shall ask each defendant whether he pleads "guilty" or "not guilty."
c. The Prosecution shall make an opening statement.
d. The Tribunal shall ask the Prosecution and the Defense what evidence (if any) they wish to submit to the Tribunal, and the Tribunal shall rule upon the admissibility of any such evidence.
e. The witnesses for the Prosecution shall be examined and after that the witnesses for the Defense. Thereafter such rebutting evidence as may be held by the Tribunal to be admissible shall be called by either the Prosecution or the Defense.
f. The Tribunal may put any question to any witness and to any defendant, at any time.
g. The Prosecution and the Defense shall interrogate and may cross-examine any witnesses and any defendant who gives testimony.
h. The Defense shall address the Court.
i. The Prosecution shall address the Court.
j. Each Defendant may make a statement to the Tribunal.
k. The Tribunal shall deliver judgment and pronounce sentence.

Article 25. All official documents shall be produced, and all court proceedings conducted, in English, French, and Russian, and in the language of the defendant. So much of the record and of the proceedings may also be translated into the language of any country in which the Tribunal is sitting, as the Tribunal considers desirable in the interests of justice and public opinion.

VI. Judgment and Sentence

Article 26. The judgment of the Tribunal as to the guilt or the innocence of any defendant shall give the reasons on which it is based, and shall be final and not subject to review.

Article 27. The Tribunal shall have the right to impose upon a defendant on conviction, death or such other punishment as shall be determined by it to be just.

Article 28. In addition to any punishment imposed by it, the Tribunal shall have the right to deprive the convicted person of any stolen property and order its delivery to the Control Council for Germany.

Article 29. In case of guilt, sentences shall be carried out in accordance with the orders of the Control Council for Germany, which may at any time reduce or otherwise alter the sentences, but may not increase the severity thereof. If the Control Council for Germany, after any defendant has been convicted and sentenced, discovers fresh evidence which, in its opinion, would found a fresh charge against him, the Council shall report accordingly to the Committee established under Article 14 hereof, for such action as they may consider proper, having regard to the interests of justice. . . .

3. Jackson, Robert H., Chief Prosecutor's Opening Speech at the Nuremberg Trials, 11 November 1945 *

. . .

The Law of Individual Responsibility

The Charter . . . recognizes individual responsibility on the part of those who commit acts defined as crimes, or who incite others to do so, or who join a common plan with other persons, groups or organizations to bring about their commission. The principle of individual responsibility for piracy and brigandage, which have long been recognized as crimes punishable under international law, is old and well established. That is what illegal warfare is. This principle of personal liability is a necessary as well as logical one if international law is to render real help to the maintenance of peace. An international law which operates only on states can be enforced only by war because the most practicable method of coercing a state is warfare. Those familiar with American history know that one of the compelling reasons for adoption of our constitution was that the laws of the Confederation, which operated only on constituent states, were found ineffective to maintain order among them. The only answer to recalcitrance was impotence or war. Only sanctions which reach individuals can peacefully and effectively be enforced. Hence, the principle of the criminality of aggressive war is implemented by the Charter with the principle of personal responsibility.

Of course, the idea that a state, any more than a corporation, com-

* 2 Trial of Major War Criminals (Blue Series, 1948), pp. 149–151.

mits crimes, is a fiction. Crimes always are committed only by persons. While it is quite proper to employ the fiction of responsibility of a state or corporation for the purpose of imposing a collective liability, it is quite intolerable to let such a legalism become the basis of personal immunity.

The Charter recognizes that one who has committed criminal acts may not take refuge in superior orders nor in the doctrine that his crimes were acts of states. These twin principles working together have heretofore resulted in immunity for practically everyone concerned in the really great crimes against peace and mankind. Those in lower ranks were protected against liability by the orders of their superiors. The superiors were protected because their orders were called acts of state. Under the Charter, no defense based on either of these doctrines can be entertained. Modern civilization puts unlimited weapons of destruction in the hands of men. It cannot tolerate so vast an area of legal irresponsibility. [Emphasis added.]

Even the German Military Code provides that:

> If the execution of a military order in the course of duty violates the criminal law, then the superior officer giving the order will bear the sole responsibility therefor. However, the obeying subordinate will share the punishment of the participant: (1) if he has exceeded the order given to him, or (2) if it was within his knowledge that the order of his superior officer concerned an act by which it was intended to commit a civil or military crime or transgression. (*Reichsgesetzblatt,* 1926 No. 37, P. 278, Art. 47.)

Of course, we do not argue that the circumstances under which one commits an act should be disregarded in judging its legal effect. A conscripted private on a firing squad cannot expect to hold an inquest on the validity of the execution. The Charter implies common sense limits to liability just as it places common sense limits upon immunity. But none of these men before you acted in minor parts. Each of them was entrusted with broad discretion and exercised great power. Their responsibility is correspondingly great and may not be shifted to that fictional being, "the State," which cannot be produced for trial, cannot testify, and cannot be sentenced.

The Charter also recognizes a vicarious liability, which responsibility is recognized by most modern systems of law, for acts committed by others in carrying out a common plan or conspiracy to which a defendant has become a party. I need not discuss the familiar principles of such liability. Every day in the courts of countries associated in this prosecution, men are convicted for acts that they did not personally commit, but for which they were held responsible because of membership in illegal combinations or plans or conspiracies.

. . .

4. Nuremberg Trial Proceedings, 31 August 1946*

. . .

THE PRESIDENT: I call upon the Defendant Alfred Jodl.

ALFRED JODL (Defendant): Mr. President, may it please the Tribunal, it is my unshakable belief that later historians will arrive at a just and objective verdict concerning the higher military leaders and their assistants, for they, and the entire German Wehrmacht with them, were confronted with an insoluble task, namely, to conduct a war which they had not wanted under a commander-in-chief whose confidence they did not possess and whom they themselves only trusted within limits; with methods which frequently were in contradiction to their principles of leadership and their traditional, proved opinions; with troops and police forces which did not come under their full command; and with an intelligence service which in part was working for the enemy. And all this in the complete and clear realization that this war would decide the life or death of our beloved fatherland. They did not serve the powers of hell and they did not serve a criminal but rather their people and their fatherland.

As far as I am concerned, I believe that no man can do more than try to reach the highest of the goals which appear attainable to him. That and nothing else has always been the guiding principle for my actions, and for that reason, gentlemen of the Tribunal, no matter what verdict you may pass upon me, I shall leave this courtroom with my head as high as when I entered it many months ago.

But whoever calls me a traitor to the honourable tradition of the German Army, or whoever asserts that I remained at my post for personal and egotistical reasons, him I shall call a traitor to the truth. In a war

* 22 Trial of Major War Criminals (Blue Series, 1948), pp. 400, 570–571.

such as this, in which hundreds of thousands of women and children were annihilated by layers of bombs or killed by bullets fired from low-flying aircraft, and in which partisans used every, yes, every means of violence which seemed expedient, harsh measures, even though they may appear questionable from the standpoint of International Law, are not a moral crime.

For I believe and avow that one's duty toward one's people and fatherland stands above every other. To carry out this duty was for me an honour and the highest law.

May this duty be supplanted in some happier future by an even higher one, by the duty toward humanity.

. . .

[Judgment of the Tribunal]:

War Crimes and Crimes Against Humanity

On 18th October, 1942, Hitler issued the Commando Order, and a day later a supplementary explanation to commanding officers only. The covering memorandum was signed by Jodl. Early drafts of the order were made by Jodl's staff with his knowledge. Jodl testified that he was strongly opposed on moral and legal grounds, but could not refuse to pass it on. He insists that he tried to mitigate its harshness in practice by not informing Hitler when it was not carried out. He initialed the OKW memorandum of 25th June, 1944, reaffirming the order after the Normandy landings.

A plan to eliminate Soviet commissars was in the directive for "Case Barbarossa." The decision whether they should be killed without trial was to be made by an officer. A draft contains Jodl's handwriting suggesting this should be handled as retaliation, and he testified that this was his attempt to get around it.

When in 1945 Hitler considered denouncing the Geneva Convention, Jodl argued that the disadvantages outweighed the advantages. On 21st February he told Hitler that adherence to the Convention would not interfere with the conduct of the war, giving as an example the sinking of a British hospital ship as a reprisal and calling it a mistake. He said he did so because it was the only attitude that would be considered by Hitler, on whom moral or legal arguments had no effect, and he argues that by this means he prevented Hitler from denouncing the Convention.

There is little evidence that Jodl was actively connected with the slave labour programme, and he must have concentrated on his task of strategic planning. But in his speech of 7th November, 1943, to the Gauleiter he said it was necessary to act "with remorseless vigor and resolution" in Denmark, France and the Low Countries in order to compel work on the Atlantic Wall.

By teletype of 28th October, 1944, Jodl ordered the evacuation of all persons in Northern Norway and the burning of their houses so that they could not help the Russians. Jodl says he was against this, but Hitler ordered it and it was not fully carried out. A document of the Norwegian Government says such an evacuation did take place in Northern Norway and 30,000 houses were damaged. On 7th October, 1941, Jodl signed an order that Hitler would not accept an offer of surrender of Leningrad or Moscow, but on the contrary he insisted that they be completely destroyed. He says this was done because the Germans were afraid those cities would be mined by the Russians as was Kiev. No surrender was ever offered.

His defence, in brief, is the doctrine of "superior orders," prohibited by Article 8 of the Charter as a defence. There is nothing in mitigation. Participation in such crimes as these has never been required of any soldier and he cannot now shield himself behind a mythical requirement of soldierly obedience at all costs as his excuse for commission of these crimes.

Conclusion

The Tribunal finds that Jodl is guilty on all four counts. . . .

5a. Application of Yamashita, 327 U.S. 1 (1946)

. . .

Mr. Chief Justice Stone delivered the opinion of the Court.

No. 61 Miscellaneous is an application for leave to file a petition for writs of habeas corpus and prohibition in this Court. No. 672 is a petition for certiorari to review an order of the Supreme Court of the Commonwealth of the Philippines (28 U.S.C. § 349, 28 U.S.C.A. § 349), denying petitioner's application to that court for writs of habeas corpus and prohibition. As both applications raise substantially like questions, and because of the importance and novelty of some of those presented, we set the two applications down for oral argument as one case.

From the petitions and supporting papers it appears that prior to September 3, 1945, petitioner was the Commanding General of the Fourteenth Army Group of the Imperial Japanese Army in the Philippine Islands. On that date he surrendered to and became a prisoner of war of the United States Army Forces in Baguio, Philippine Islands. On September 25th, by order of respondent, Lieutenant General Wilhelm D. Styer, Commanding General of the United States Army Forces, Western Pacific, which command embraces the Philippine Islands, petitioner was served with a charge prepared by the Judge Advocate General's Department of the Army, purporting to charge petitioner with a violation of the law of war. On October 8, 1945, petitioner, after pleading not guilty to the charge, was held for trial before a military commission of five Army officers appointed by order of General Styer. The order appointed six Army officers, all lawyers, as defense counsel. Throughout the proceedings which followed, including those before this Court, defense counsel have demonstrated their professional skill and resourcefulness and their proper zeal for the defense with which they were charged.

On the same date a bill of particulars was filed by the prosecution, and the commission heard a motion made in petitioner's behalf to dismiss the charge on the ground that it failed to state a violation of the law of war. On October 29th the commission was reconvened, a supplemental bill of particulars was filed, and the motion to dismiss was denied. The trial then proceeded until its conclusion on December 7, 1945, the commission hearing two hundred and eighty-six witnesses, who gave over three thousand pages of testimony. On that date petitioner was found guilty of the offense as charged and sentenced to death by hanging.

The petitions for habeas corpus set up that the detention of petitioner for the purpose of the trial was unlawful for reasons which are now urged as showing that the military commission was without lawful authority or jurisdiction to place petitioner on trial, as follows:

a. That the military commission which tried and convicted petitioner was not lawfully created, and that no military commission to try petitioner for violations of the law of war could lawfully be convened after the cessation of hostilities between the armed forces of the United States and Japan;
b. that the charge preferred against petitioner fails to charge him with a violation of the law of war;
c. that the commission was without authority and jurisdiction to try and convict petitioner because the order governing the procedure of the commission permitted the admission in evidence of depositions, affidavits and hearsay and opinion evidence, and because the commission's rulings admitting such evidence were in violation of the 25th and 38th Articles of War (10 U.S.C. §§ 1496, 1509, 10 U.S.C.A. §§ 1496, 1509) and the Geneva Convention (47 Stat. 2021), and deprived petitioner of a fair trial in violation of the due process clause of the Fifth Amendment;
d. that the commission was without authority and jurisdiction in the premises because of the failure to give advance notice of petitioner's trial to the neutral power representing the interests of Japan as a belligerent as required by Article 60 of the Geneva Convention, 47 Stat. 2021, 2051.

On the same grounds the petitions for writs of prohibition set up that the commission is without authority to proceed with the trial.

The Supreme Court of the Philippine Islands, after hearing argument, denied the petition for habeas corpus presented to it, on the ground, among others, that its jurisdiction was limited to an inquiry as to the jurisdiction of the commission to place petitioner on trial for the offense charged, and that the commission, being validly constituted by the order of General Styer, had jurisdiction over the person of petitioner and over the trial for the offense charged.

In Ex parte Quirin, 317 U.S. 1, we had occasion to consider at length the sources and nature of the authority to create military commissions for the trial of enemy combatants for offenses against the law of war. We there pointed out that Congress, in the exercise of the power conferred upon it by Article I, § 8, Cl. 10 of the Constitution to "define and punish . . . Offenses against the Law of Nations . . . ," of which the law of war is a part, had by the Articles of War (10 U.S.C. §§ 1471–1593, 10 U.S.C.A. §§ 1471–1593) recognized the "military commission" appointed by military command, as it had previously existed in United States Army practice, as an appropriate tribunal for the trial and punishment of offenses against the law of war. Article 15 declares that "the provisions of these articles conferring jurisdiction upon courts-martial shall not be construed as depriving military commissions . . . or other military tribunals of concurrent jurisdiction in respect of offenders or offenses that by statute or by the law of war may be triable by such military commissions . . . or other military tribunals." See a similar provision of the Espionage Act of 1917, 50 U.S.C. § 38, 50 U.S.C.A. § 38 Article 2 includes among those persons subject to the Articles of War the personnel of our own military establishment. But this, as Article 12 indicates, does not exclude from the class of persons subject to trial by military commissions "any other person who by the law of war is subject to trial by military tribunals," and who, under Article 12, may be tried by court-martial, or under Article 15 by military commission.

We further pointed out that Congress, by sanctioning trial of enemy combatants for violations of the law of war by military commission, had not attempted to codify the law of war or to mark its precise boundaries. Instead, by Article 15 it had incorporated, by reference, as within the preexisting jurisdiction of military commissions created by appropriate military command, all offenses which are defined as such by the law of war, and which may constitutionally be included within that jurisdiction. It thus adopted the system of military common law applied by military tribunals so far as it should be recognized and deemed applicable by the courts, and as further defined and supplemented by the Hague Convention, to which the United States and the Axis powers were parties.

We also emphasized in Ex parte Quirin, as we do here, that on application for habeas corpus we are not concerned with the guilt or innocence of the petitioners. We consider here only the lawful power of the commission to try the petitioner for the offense charged. In the present cases it must be recognized throughout that the military tribunals which Congress has sanctioned by the Articles of War are not courts whose rulings and judgments are made subject to review by this Court. See Ex parte Vallandigham, 1 Wall. 243, . . . In re Vidal, 179 U.S. 126, cf. Ex parte Quirin, supra, 317 U.S. 39. They are tribunals whose determinations are reviewable by the military authorities either as provided in the military orders constituting such tribunals or as provided by the Articles of War. Congress conferred on the courts no power to review their determinations save only as it has granted judicial power "to grant writs of habeas corpus for the purpose of an inquiry into the cause of the restraint of liberty." 28 U.S.C. §§ 451, 452, 28 U.S.C.A. §§ 451, 452. The courts may inquire whether the detention complained of is within the authority of those detaining the petitioner. If the military tribunals have lawful authority to hear, decide and condemn, their action is not subject to judicial review merely because they have made a wrong decision on disputed facts. Correction of their errors of decision is not for the courts but for the military authorities which are alone authorized to review their decisions. . . .

Finally, we held in Ex parte Quirin, supra, 317 U.S. 24, 25, . . . as we hold now, that Congress by sanctioning trials of enemy aliens by military commission for offenses against the law of war had recognized the right of the accused to make a defense. . . . It has not foreclosed their right to contend that the Constitution or laws of the United States withhold authority to proceed with the trial. It has not withdrawn, and the Executive branch of the government could not, unless there was suspension of the writ, withdraw from the courts the duty and power to make such inquiry into the authority of the commission as may be made by habeas corpus.

With these governing principles in mind we turn to the consideration of the several contentions urged to establish want of authority in the commission. We are not here concerned with the power of military commissions to try civilians. See Ex parte Milligan, 4 Wall. 2, 132, . . . ; Sterling v. Constantin, 287 U.S. 378, . . . ; Ex parte Quirin, supra, . . . The Government's contention is that General Styer's order creating the commission conferred authority on it only to try the purported charge of violation of the law of war committed by petitioner, an enemy belligerent, while in command of a hostile army occupying United States territory during time of war. Our first inquiry must therefore be whether the present commission was created by lawful military command and, if so, whether authority could thus be conferred on the commission to place petitioner on trial after the cessation of hostilities between the armed forces of the United States and Japan.

The authority to create the Commission. General Styer's order for the appointment of the commission was made by him as Commander of the United States Armed Forces, Western Pacific. His command includes, as part of a vastly greater area, the Philippine Islands, where the alleged offenses were committed, where petitioner surrendered as a prisoner of war, and where, at the time of the order convening the commission, he was detained as a prisoner in custody of the United States Army. The

Congressional recognition of military commissions and its sanction of their use in trying offenses against the law of war to which we have referred, sanctioned their creation by military command in conformity to long established American precedents. Such a commission may be appointed by any field commander, or by any commander competent to appoint a general court martial, as was General Styer, who had been vested with that power by order of the President. . . .

Here the commission was not only created by a commander competent to appoint it, but his order conformed to the established policy of the Government and to higher military commands authorizing his action. In a proclamation of July 2, 1942 (56 Stat. 1964, 10 U.S.C.A. § 1554 note), the President proclaimed that enemy belligerents who, during time of war, enter the United States, or any territory possession thereof, and who violate the law of war, should be subject to the law of war and to the jurisdiction of military tribunals. Paragraph 10 of the Declaration of Potsdam of July 6, 1945, declared that ". . . stern justice shall be meted out to all war criminals including those who have visited cruelties upon prisoners." U. S. Dept. of State Bull., Vol. XIII, No. 318, pp. 137, 138. This Declaration was accepted by the Japanese government by its note of August 10, 1945. U. S. Dept. of State Bull., Vol. XIII, No. 320, p. 205.

By direction of the President, the Joint Chiefs of Staff of the American Military Forces, on September 12, 1945, instructed General MacArthur, Commander in Chief, United States Army Forces, Pacific, to proceed with the trial, before appropriate military tribunals, of such Japanese war criminals "as have been or may be apprehended." By order of General MacArthur of September 24, 1945, General Styer was specifically directed to proceed with the trial of petitioner upon the charge here involved. This order was accompanied by detailed rules and regulations which General MacArthur prescribed for the trial of war criminals. These regulations directed, among other things, that review of the sentence imposed by the commission should be by the officer convening it, with "authority to approve, mitigate, remit, commute, suspend, reduce or otherwise alter the sentence imposed," and directed that no sentence of death should be carried into effect until confirmed by the Commander in Chief, United States Army Forces, Pacific.

It thus appears that the order creating the commission for the trial of petitioner was authorized by military command, and was in complete conformity to the Act of Congress sanctioning the creation of such tribunals for the trial of offenses against the law of war committed by enemy combatants. And we turn to the question whether the authority to create the commission and direct the trial by military order continued after the cessation of hostilities.

An important incident to the conduct of war is the adoption of measures by the military commander, not only to repel and defeat the enemy, but to seize and subject to disciplinary measures those enemies who, in their attempt to thwart or impede our military effort, have violated the law of war. Ex parte Quirin, supra, . . . The trial and punishment of enemy combatants who have committed violations of the law of war is thus not only a part of the conduct of war operating as a preventive measure against such violations, but is an exercise of the authority sanctioned by Congress to administer the system of military justice recognized by the law of war. That sanction is without qualification as to the exercise of this authority so long as a state of war exists—from its declaration until peace is proclaimed. . . . The war power, from which the commission derives its existence, is not limited to victories in the field, but carries with it the inherent power to guard against the immediate renewal of the conflict, and to remedy, at least in ways Congress has recognized, the evils which the military operations have produced.

We cannot say that there is no authority to convene a commission after hostilities have ended to try violations of the law of war committed before their cessation, at least until peace has been officially recognized by treaty or proclamation of the political branch of the Government. In fact, in most instances the practical administration of the system of military justice under the law of war would fail if such authority were thought to end with the cessation of hostilities. For only after their cessation could the greater number of offenders and the principal ones be apprehended and subjected to trial.

No writer on international law appears to have regarded the power of military tribunals, otherwise competent to try violations of the law of war, as terminating before the formal state of war has ended. In our own military history there have been numerous instances in which offenders were tried by military commission after the cessation of hostilities and before the proclamation of peace, for offenses against the law of war committed before the cessation of hostilities.

The extent to which the power to prosecute violations of the law of war shall be exercised before peace is declared rests, not with the courts, but with the political branch of the Government, and may itself be governed by the terms of an armistice or the treaty of peace. Here, peace has not been agreed upon or proclaimed. Japan, by her acceptance of the Potsdam Declaration and her surrender, has acquiesced in the trials of those guilty of violations of the law of war. The conduct of the trial by the military commission has been authorized by the political branch of the Government, by military command, by international law and usage, and by the terms of the surrender of the Japanese government.

The Charge

Neither Congressional action nor the military orders constituting the commission authorized it to place petitioner on trial unless the charge preferred against him is of a violation of the law of war. The charge, so far as now relevant, is that petitioner, between October 9, 1944 and September 2, 1945, in the Philippine Islands, "while commander of armed forces of Japan at war with the United States of America and its allies, unlawfully disregarded and failed to discharge his duty as commander to control the operations of the members of his command, permitting them to commit brutal atrocities and other high crimes against people of the United States and of its allies and dependencies, particularly the Philippines; and he . . . thereby violated the laws of war."

Bills of particulars, filed by the prosecution by order of the commission, allege a series of acts, one hundred and twenty-three in number, committed by members of the forces under petitioner's command, during the period mentioned. The first item specifies the execution of "a deliberate plan and purpose to massacre and exterminate a large part of the civilian population of Batangas Province, and to devastate and destroy public, private and religious property therein, as a result of which more than 25,000 men, women and children, all unarmed noncombatant civilians, were brutally mistreated and killed, without cause or trial, and entire settlements were devastated and destroyed wantonly and without military necessity." Other items specify acts of violence, cruelty and homicide inflicted upon the civilian population and prisoners of war, acts of wholesale pillage and the wanton destruction of religious monuments.

It is not denied that such acts directed against the civilian population of an occupied country and against prisoners of war are recognized in international law as violations of the law of war. Articles 4, 28, 46, and 47, Annex to Fourth Hague Convention, 1907, 36 Stat. 2277, 2296, 2303, 2306, 2307. But it is urged that the charge does not allege that petitioner has either committed or directed the commission of such acts, and consequently that no violation is charged as against him. But this overlooks the fact that the gist of the charge is an unlawful breach of duty by petitioner as an army commander to control the operations of the members of his command by "permitting them to commit" the extensive and widespread atrocities specified. The question then is whether the law of war imposes on an army commander a duty to take such appropriate measures as are within his power to control the troops under his command for the prevention of the specified acts which are violations of the law of war and which are likely to attend the occupation of hostile territory by an uncontrolled soldiery, and whether he may be charged with personal responsibility for his failure to take such measures when violations result. That this was the precise issue to be tried was made clear by the statement of the prosecution at the opening of the trial.

It is evident that the conduct of military operations by troops whose excesses are unrestrained by the orders or efforts of their commander would almost certainly result in violations which it is the purpose of the law of war to prevent. Its purpose to protect civilian populations and prisoners of war from brutality would largely be defeated if the commander of an invading army could with impunity neglect to take reasonable measures for their protection. Hence the law of war presupposes that its violation is to be avoided through the control of the operations of war by commanders who are to some extent responsible for their subordinates.

This is recognized by the Annex to Fourth Hague Convention of 1907, respecting the laws and customs of war on land. Article I lays down as a condition which an armed force must fulfill in order to be accorded the rights of lawful belligerents, that it must be "commanded by a person responsible for his subordinates." 36 Stat. 2295. Similarly Article 19 of the Tenth Hague Convention, relating to bombardment by naval vessels, provides that commanders in chief of the belligerent vessels "must see that the above Articles are properly carried out." 36 Stat. 2389. And Article 26 of the Geneva Red Cross Convention of 1929, 47 Stat. 2074, 2092, for the amelioration of the condition of the wounded and sick in armies in the field, makes it "the duty of the commanders-in-chief of the belligerent armies to provide for the details of execution of the foregoing articles [of the convention], as well as for unforeseen cases." And, finally, Article 43 of the Annex of the Fourth Hague Convention, 36 Stat. 2306, requires that the commander of a force occupying enemy territory, as was petitioner, "shall take all the measures in his power to restore, and ensure, as far as possible, public order and safety, while respecting, unless absolutely prevented, the laws in force in the country."

These provisions plainly imposed on petitioner, who at the time specified was military governor of the Philippines, as well as commander of the Japanese forces, an affirmative duty to take such measures as were within his power and appropriate in the circumstances to protect prisoners of war and the civilian population. This duty of a commanding officer has heretofore been recognized, and its breach penalized by our own

[Editor's note: Because of excerpting, footnotes in this and subsequent chapters are out of sequence. The authors have retained original footnote numbers for the convenience of the reader who might want to consult the complete documents.]

military tribunals.[3] A like principle has been applied so as to impose liability on the United States in international arbitrations. Case of Jenaud, 3 Moore, International Arbitrations, 3000; Case of "The Zafiro," 5 Hackworth, Digest of International Law, 707.

We do not make the laws of war but we respect them so far as they do not conflict with the commands of Congress or the Constitution. There is no contention that the present charge, thus read, is without the support of evidence, or that the commission held petitioner responsible for failing to take measures which were beyond his control or inappropriate for a commanding officer to take in the circumstances.[4] We do not here appraise the evidence on which petitioner was convicted. We do not consider what measures, if any, petitioner took to prevent the commission, by the troops under his command, of the plain violations of the law of war detailed in the bill of particulars, or whether such measures as he may have taken were appropriate and sufficient to discharge the duty imposed upon him. These are questions within the peculiar competence of the military officers composing the commission and were for it to decide. . . . It is plain that the charge on which petitioner was tried charged him with a breach of his duty to control the operations of the members of his command, by permitting them to commit the specified atrocities. This was enough to require the commission to hear evidence tending to establish the culpable failure of petitioner to perform the duty imposed on him by the law of war and to pass upon its sufficiency to establish guilt.

Obviously charges of violations of the law of war triable before a military tribunal need not be stated with the precision of a common law indictment. Cf. Collins v. McDonald, supra, 258 U.S. 420, . . . But we conclude that the allegations of the charge, tested by any reasonable standard, adequately allege a violation of the law of war and that the commission had authority to try and decide the issue which it raised. . . .

[3] Failure of an officer to take measures to prevent murder of an inhabitant of an occupied country committed in his presence. Gen.Orders No. 221, Hq.Div. of the Philippines, August 17, 1901. And in Gen.Orders No. 264, Hq.Div. of the Philippines, September 9, 1901, it was held that an officer could not be found guilty for failure to prevent a murder unless it appeared that the accused had "the power to prevent" it.

[4] In its findings the commission took account of the difficulties "faced by the accused, with respect not only to the swift and overpowering advance of American forces, but also to errors of his predecessors, weakness in organization, equipment, supply . . ., training, communication, discipline and morale of his troops," and "the tactical situation, the character, training and capacity of staff officers and subordinate commanders, as well as the traits of character of his troops." It nonetheless found that petitioner had not taken such measures to control his troops as were "required by the circumstances." We do not weigh the evidence. We merely hold that the charge sufficiently states a violation against the law of war, and that the commission, upon the facts found, could properly find petitioner guilty of such a violation.

The Proceedings before the Commission

The regulations prescribed by General MacArthur governing the procedure for the trial of petitioner by the commission directed that the commission should admit such evidence "as in its opinion would be of assistance in proving or disproving the charge, or such as in the commission's opinion would have probative value in the mind of a reasonable man," and that in particular it might admit affidavits, depositions or other statements taken by officers detailed for that purpose by military authority. The petitions in this case charged that in the course of the trial the commission received, over objection by petitioner's counsel, the deposition of a witness taken pursuant to military authority by a United States Army captain. It also, over like objection admitted hearsay and opinion evidence tendered by the prosecution. Petitioner argues as ground for the writ of habeas corpus, that Article 25 of the Articles of War prohibited the reception in evidence by the commission of depositions on behalf of the prosecution in a capital case, and that Article 38 prohibited the reception of hearsay and of opinion evidence.

We think that neither Article 25 nor Article 38 is applicable to the trial of an enemy combatant by a military commission for violations of the law of war. Article 2 of the Articles of War enumerates "the persons . . . subject to these articles," who are denominated, for purposes of the Articles, as "persons subject to military law." In general, the persons so enumerated are members of our own Army and of the personnel accompanying the Army. Enemy combatants are not included among them. Articles 12, 13 and 14, before the adoption of Article 15 in 1916, 39 Stat. 653 made all "persons subject to military law" amenable to trial by courts-martial for any offense made punishable by the Articles of War. Article 12 makes triable by general court martial "any other person who by the law of war is [triable] by military tribunals." Since Article 2, in its 1916 form, 39 Stat. 651, includes some persons who, by the law of war, were, prior to 1916, triable by military commission, it was feared by the proponents of the 1916 legislation that in the absence of a saving provision, the authority given by Articles 12, 13 and 14 to try such persons before courts-martial might be construed to deprive the non-statutory military commission of a portion of what was considered to be its traditional jurisdiction. To avoid this, and to preserve that jurisdiction intact, Article 15 was added to the Articles.[7] It declared that

[7] General Crowder, the Judge Advocate General, who appeared before Congress as sponsor for the adoption of Article 15 and the accompanying amendment of Article 25, in explaining the purpose of Article 15, said:

"Article 15 is new. We have included in article 2 as subject to military law a num-

"The provisions of these articles conferring jurisdiction upon courts-martial shall not be construed as depriving military commissions . . . of concurrent jurisdiction in respect of offenders or offenses that by the law of war may be lawfully triable by such military commissions."

By thus recognizing military commissions in order to preserve their traditional jurisdiction over enemy combatants unimpaired by the Articles, Congress gave sanction, as we held in Ex parte Quirin, to any use of the military commission contemplated by the common law of war. But it did not thereby make subject to the Articles of War persons other than those defined by Article 2 as being subject to the Articles, nor did it confer the benefits of the Articles upon such persons. The Articles recognized but one kind of military commission, not two. But they sanctioned the use of that one for the trial of two classes of persons, to one of which the Articles do, and to the other of which they do not apply in such trials. Being of this latter class, petitioner cannot claim the benefits of the Articles, which are applicable only to the members of the other class. Petitioner, an enemy combatant, is therefore not a person made subject to the Articles of War by Article 2, and the military commission before which he was tried, though sanctioned, and its jurisdiction saved, by Article 15, was not convened by virtue of the Articles of War, but pursuant to the common law of war. It follows that the Articles of War, including Articles 25 and 38, were not applicable to petitioner's trial and imposed no restrictions upon the procedure to be followed. The Articles left the control over the procedure in such a case where it had previously been, with the military command. . . .

It thus appears that the order convening the commission was a lawful order, that the commission was lawfully constituted, that petitioner was charged with violation of the law of war, and that the commission had authority to proceed with the trial, and in doing so did not violate any military, statutory or constitutional command. We have considered, but find it unnecessary to discuss other contentions which we find to be without merit. We therefore conclude that the detention of petitioner for trial and his detention upon his conviction, subject to the prescribed review by the military authorities were lawful, and that the petition for certiorari, and leave to file in this Court petitions for writs of habeas corpus and prohibition should be, and they are

---

ber of persons who are also subject to trial by military commission. A military commission is our commonlaw war court. It has no statutory existence, though it is recognized by statute law. As long as the articles embraced them in the designation 'persons subject to military law,' and provided that they might be tried by court-martial, I was afraid that, having made a special provision for their trial by court-martial, [Arts. 12, 13, and 14] it might be held that the provision operated to exclude trials by military commission and other war courts; so this new article was introduced. * * *" [Sen.R. 130, 64th Cong., 1st Sess., p. 40.]

Denied.

Writs denied.

Mr. Justice Jackson took no part in the consideration or decision of these cases.

Mr. Justice Murphy, dissenting.

The significance of the issue facing the Court today cannot be overemphasized. An American military commission has been established to try a fallen military commander of a conquered nation for an alleged war crime. The authority for such action grows out of the exercise of the power conferred upon Congress by Article I, § 8, Cl. 10 of the Constitution to "define and punish . . . Offenses against the Law of Nations. . . ." The grave issue raised by this case is whether a military commission so established and so authorized may disregard the procedural rights of an accused person as guaranteed by the Constitution, especially by the due process clause of the Fifth Amendment.

The answer is plain. The Fifth Amendment guarantee of due process of law applies to "any person" who is accused of a crime by the Federal Government or any of its agencies. No exception is made as to those who are accused of war crimes or as to those who possess the status of an enemy belligerent. Indeed, such an exception would be contrary to the whole philosophy of human rights which makes the Constitution the great living document that it is. The immutable rights of the individual, including those secured by the due process clause of the Fifth Amendment, belong not alone to the members of those nations that excel on the battlefield or that subscribe to the democratic ideology. They belong to every person in the world, victor or vanquished, whatever may be his race, color or beliefs. They rise above any status of belligerency or outlawry. They survive any popular passion or frenzy of the movement. No court or legislature or executive, not even the mightiest army in the world, can ever destroy them. Such is the universal and indestructible nature of the rights which the due process clause of the Fifth Amendment recognizes and protects when life or liberty is threatened by virtue of the authority of the United States.

The existence of these rights, unfortunately, is not always respected. They are often trampled under by those who are motivated by hatred, aggression or fear. But in this nation individual rights are recognized and protected, at least in regard to governmental action. They cannot be ignored by any branch of the Government, even the military, except under the most extreme and urgent circumstances.

The failure of the military commission to obey the dictates of the due process requirements of the Fifth Amendment is apparent in this case. The petitioner was the commander of an army totally destroyed by the superior power of this nation. While under heavy and destructive attack by our forces, his troops committed many brutal atrocities and other high crimes. Hostilities ceased and he voluntarily surrendered. At that point he was entitled, as an individual protected by the due process clause of the Fifth Amendment, to be treated fairly and justly according to the accepted rules of law and procedure. He was also entitled to a fair trial as to any alleged crimes and to be free from charges of legally unrecognized crimes that would serve only to permit his accusers to satisfy their desires for revenge.

A military commission was appointed to try the petitioner for an alleged war crime. The trial was ordered to be held in territory over which the United States has complete sovereignty. No military necessity or other emergency demanded the suspension of the safeguards of due process. Yet petitioner was rushed to trial under an improper charge, given insufficient time to prepare an adequate defense, deprived of the benefits of some of the most elementary rules of evidence and summarily sentenced to be hanged. In all this needless and unseemly haste there was no serious attempt to charge or to prove that he committed a recognized violation of the laws of war. He was not charged with personally participating in the acts of atrocity or with ordering or condoning their commission. Not even knowledge of these crimes was attributed to him. It was simply alleged that he unlawfully disregarded and failed to discharge his duty as commander to control the operations of the members of his command, permitting them to commit the acts of atrocity. The recorded annals of warfare and the established principles of international law afford not the slightest precedent for such a charge. This indictment in effect permitted the military commission to make the crime whatever it willed, dependent upon its biased view as to petitioner's duties and his disregard thereof, a practice reminiscent of that pursued in certain less respected nations in recent years.

In my opinion, such a procedure is unworthy of the traditions of our people or of the immense sacrifices that they have made to advance the common ideals of mankind. The high feelings of the moment doubtless will be satisfied. But in the sober afterglow will come the realization of the boundless and dangerous implications of the procedure sanctioned today. No one in a position of command in an army, from sergeant to general, can escape those implications. Indeed, the fate of some future President of the United States and his chiefs of staff and military advisers may well have been sealed by this decision. But even more significant will be the hatred and ill-will growing out of the application of this unprecedented procedure. That has been the inevitable effect of every method of punishment disregarding the element of personal culpability. The effect in this instance, unfortunately, will be magnified infinitely for here we are dealing with the rights of man on an international level. To subject an enemy belligerent to an unfair trial, to charge him with an unrecognized crime, or to vent on him our retributive emotions only antagonizes the enemy nation and hinders the reconciliation necessary to a peaceful world.

That there were brutal atrocities inflicted upon the helpless Filipino people, to whom tyranny is no stranger, by Japanese armed forces under the petitioner's command is undeniable. Starvation, execution or massacre without trial, torture, rape, murder and wanton destruction of property were foremost among the outright violations of the laws of war and of the conscience of a civilized world. That just punishment should be meted out to all those responsible for criminal acts of this nature is also beyond dispute. But these factors do not answer the problem in this case. They do not justify the abandonment of our devotion to justice in dealing with a fallen enemy commander. To conclude otherwise is to admit that the enemy has lost the battle but has destroyed our ideals.

War breeds atrocities. From the earliest conflicts of recorded history to the global struggles of modern times inhumanities, lust and pillage have been the inevitable by-products of man's resort to force and arms. Unfortunately, such despicable acts have a dangerous tendency to call forth primitive impulses of vengeance and retaliation among the victimized peoples. The satisfaction of such impulses in turn breeds resentment and fresh tension. Thus does the spiral of cruelty and hatred grow.

If we are ever to develop an orderly international community based upon a recognition of human dignity it is of the utmost importance that the necessary punishment of those guilty of atrocities be as free as possible from the ugly stigma of revenge and vindictiveness. Justice must be tempered by compassion rather than by vengeance. In this, the first case involving this momentous problem ever to reach this Court, our responsibility is both lofty and difficult. We must insist, within the confines of our proper jurisdiction, that the highest standards of justice be applied in this trial of an enemy commander conducted under the authority of the United States. Otherwise stark retribution will be free to masquerade in a cloak of false legalism. And the hatred and cynicism engendered by that retribution will supplant the great ideals to which this nation is dedicated.

This Court fortunately has taken the first and most important step toward insuring the supremacy of law and justice in the treatment of an enemy belligerent accused of violating the laws of war. Jurisdiction properly has been asserted to inquire "into the cause of restraint of liberty" of such a person. 28 U. S. C. § 452, 28 U.S.C.A. § 452. Thus the obnoxious doctrine asserted by the Government in this case, to the effect that restraints of liberty resulting from military trials of war criminals are political matters completely outside the arena of judicial review, has been rejected fully and unquestionably. This does not mean, of course, that the foreign affairs and policies of the nation are proper subjects of judicial inquiry. But when the liberty of any person is restrained by reason of the authority of the United States the writ of habeas corpus is available to test the legality of that restraint, even though direct court review of the restraint is prohibited. The conclusive presumption must be made, in this country at least, that illegal restraints are unauthorized and unjustified by any foreign policy of the Government and that commonly accepted juridical standards are to be recognized and enforced. On that basis judicial inquiry into these matters may proceed within its proper sphere.

The determination of the extent of review of war trials calls for judicial statesmanship of the highest order. The ultimate nature and scope of the writ of habeas corpus are within the discretion of the judiciary unless validly circumscribed by Congress. Here we are confronted with a use of the writ under circumstances novel in the history of the Court. For my own part, I do not feel that we should be confined by the traditional lines of review drawn in connection with the use of the writ by ordinary criminals who have direct access to the judiciary in the first instance. Those held by the military lack any such access; consequently the judicial review available by habeas corpus must be wider than usual in order that proper standards of justice may be enforceable.

But for the purposes of this case I accept the scope of review recognized by the Court at this time. . . .

The Court, in my judgment, demonstrates conclusively that the military commission was lawfully created in this instance and that petitioner could not object to its power to try him for a recognized war crime. Without pausing here to discuss the [other] issues, however, I find it impossible to agree that the charge against the petitioner stated a recognized violation of the laws of war.

It is important, in the first place, to appreciate the background of events preceding this trial. From October 9, 1944, to September 2, 1945, the petitioner was the Commanding General of the 14th Army Group of the Imperial Japanese Army, with headquarters in the Philippines. The reconquest of the Philippines by the armed forces of the United States began approximately at the time when the petitioner assumed this command. Combined with a great and decisive sea battle, an invasion was made on the island of Leyte on October 20, 1944. "In the six days of the great naval action the Japanese position in the Philippines had become extremely critical. Most of the serviceable elements of the Japanese Navy had become committed to the battle with disastrous results. The strike had miscarried, and General MacArthur's land wedge was firmly implanted in the vulnerable flank of the enemy. . . . There were 260,000 Japanese troops scattered over the Philippines but most of them might as well have been on the other side of the world so far as the enemy's ability to shift them to meet the American thrusts was concerned. If General MacArthur succeeded in establishing himself in the Visayas where he could stage, exploit, and spread under cover of overwhelming naval and air superiority, nothing could prevent him from overrunning the Philippines." Biennial Report of the Chief of Staff of the United States Army, July 1, 1943, to June 30, 1945, to the Secretary of War, p. 74.

By the end of 1944 the island of Leyte was largely in American hands. And on January 9, 1945, the island of Luzon was invaded. "Yamashita's inability to cope with General MacArthur's swift moves, his desired reaction to the deception measures, the guerrillas, and General Kenney's aircraft combined to place the Japanese in an impossible situation. The enemy was forced into a piecemeal commitment of his troops." Ibid, p. 78. It was at this time and place that most of the alleged atrocities took place. Organized resistance around Manila ceased on February 23. Repeated land and air assaults pulverized the enemy and within a few months there was little left of petitioner's command except a few remnants which had gathered for a last stand among the precipitous mountains.

As the military commission here noted, "The Defense established the difficulties faced by the Accused with respect not only to the swift and overpowering advance of American forces, but also to the errors of his predecessors, weaknesses in organization, equipment, supply with especial reference to food and gasoline, training, communication, discipline and morale of his troops. It was alleged that the sudden assignment of Naval and Air Forces to his tactical command presented almost insurmountable difficulties. This situation was followed, the Defense contended, by failure to obey his orders to withdraw troops from Manila, and the subsequent massacre of unarmed civilians, particularly by Naval forces. Prior to the Luzon Campaign, Naval forces had reported to a separate ministry in the Japanese Government and Naval Commanders may not have been receptive or experienced in this instance with respect to a joint land operation under a single commander who was designated from the Army Service."

The day of final reckoning for the enemy arrived in August, 1945. On September 3, the petitioner surrendered to the United States Army at Baguio, Luzon. He immediately became a prisoner of war and was interned in prison in conformity with the rules of international law. On September 25, approximately three weeks after surrendering, he was served with the charge in issue in this case. Upon service of the charge he was removed from the status of a prisoner of war and placed in confinement as an accused war criminal. Arraignment followed on October 8 before a military commission specially appointed for the case. Petitioner pleaded not guilty. He was also served on that day with a bill of particulars alleging 64 crimes by troops under his command. A supplemental bill alleging 59 more crimes by his troops was filed on October 29, the same day that the trial began. No continuance was allowed for preparation of a defense as to the supplemental bill. The trial continued uninterrupted until December 5, 1945. On December 7 petitioner was found guilty as charged and was sentenced to be hanged.

The petitioner was accused of having "unlawfully disregarded and failed to discharge his duty as commander to control the operations of the members of his command, permitting them to commit brutal atrocities and other high crimes." The bills of particular further alleged that specific acts of atrocity were committed by "members of the armed forces of Japan under the command of the accused." Nowhere was it alleged that the petitioner personally committed any of the atrocities, or that he ordered their commission, or that he had any knowledge of the commission thereof by members of his command.

The findings of the military commission bear out this absence of any direct personal charge against the petitioner. The commission merely found that atrocities and other high crimes "have been committed by members of the Japanese armed forces under your command . . . that they were not sporadic in nature but in many cases were methodically supervised by Japanese officers and noncommissioned officers . . . that during the period in question you failed to provide effective control of your troops as was required by the circumstances."

In other words, read against the background of military events in the Philippines subsequent to October 9, 1944, these charges amount to this: "We, the victorious American forces, have done everything possible to destroy and disorganize your lines of communication, your effective control of your personnel, your ability to wage war. In those respects we have succeeded. We have defeated and crushed your forces. And now we charge and condemn you for having been inefficient in maintaining control of your troops during the period when we were so effectively beseiging and eliminating your forces and blocking your ability to maintain effective control. Many terrible atrocities were committed by your disorganized troops. Because these atrocities were so widespread we will not bother to charge or prove that you committed, ordered or condoned any of them. We will assume that they must have resulted from your inefficiency and negligence as a commander. In short, we charge you with the crime of inefficiency in controlling your troops. We will judge the discharge of your duties by the disorganization which we ourselves created in large part. Our standards of judgment are whatever we wish to make them."

Nothing in all history or in international law, at least as far as I am aware, justifies such a charge against a fallen commander of a defeated force. To use the very inefficiency and disorganization created by the victorious forces as the primary basis for condemning officers of the defeated armies bears no resemblance to justice or to military reality.

International law makes no attempt to define the duties of a commander of an army under constant and overwhelming assault; nor does it impose liability under such circumstances for failure to meet the ordinary responsibilities of command. The omission is understandable. Duties, as well as ability to control troops, vary according to the nature and intensity of the particular battle. To find an unlawful deviation from duty under battle conditions requires difficult and speculative calculations. Such calculations become highly untrustworthy when they are made by the victor in relation to the actions of a vanquished commander. Objective and realistic norms of conduct are then extremely unlikely to be used in forming a judgment as to deviations from duty. The probability that vengeance will form the major part of the victor's judgment is an unfortunate but inescapable fact. So great is that probability that international law refuses to recognize such a judgment as a basis for a war crime, however fair the judgment may be in a particular instance. It is this consideration that undermines the charge against the petitioner in this case. The indictment permits, indeed compels, the military commission of a victorious nation to sit in judgment upon the military strategy and actions of the defeated enemy and to use its conclusions to determine the criminal liability of an enemy commander. Life and liberty are made to depend upon the biased will of the victor rather than upon objective standards of conduct.

The Court's reliance upon vague and indefinite references in certain of the Hague Conventions and the Geneva Red Cross Convention is misplaced. Thus the statement in Article 1 of the Annex to Hague Convention No. IV of October 18, 1907, 36 Stat. 2277, 2295, to the effect that the laws, rights and duties of war apply to military and volunteer corps only if they are "commanded by a person responsible for his subordinates," has no bearing upon the problem in this case. Even if it has, the clause "responsible for his subordinates" fails to state to whom the responsibility is owed or to indicate the type of responsibility contemplated. The phrase has received differing interpretations by authorities on international law. In Oppenheim, International Law (6th ed., rev. by Lauterpacht, 1940, vol. 2, p. 204, fn. 3) it is stated that "The meaning of the word 'responsible'. . . is not clear. It probably means responsible to some higher authority, whether the person is appointed from above or elected from below; . . ." Another authority has stated that the word "responsible" in this particular context means "presumably to a higher authority," or "possibly it merely means one who controls his subordinates and who therefore can be called to account for their acts." Wheaton, International Law (14th ed., by Keith, 1944, p. 172, fn. 30). Still another authority, Westlake, International Law (1907, Part II, p. 61), states that "probably the responsibility intended is nothing more than a capacity of exercising effective control." Finally, Edwards and Oppenheim, Land Warfare (1912, p. 19, par. 22) state that it is enough "if the commander of the corps is regularly or temporarily commissioned as an officer or is a person of position and authority." It seems apparent beyond dispute that the word "responsible" was not used in this particular Hague Convention to hold the commander of a defeated army to any high standard of efficiency when he is under destructive attack; nor was it used to impute to him any criminal responsibility for war crimes committed by troops under his command under such circumstances.

The provisions of the other conventions referred to by the Court are on their face equally devoid of relevance or significance to the situation here in issue. Neither Article 19 of Hague Convention No. X, 36 Stat. 2371, 2389, nor Article 26 of the Geneva Red Cross Convention of 1929, 47 Stat. 2074, 2092, refers to circumstances where the troops of a commander commit atrocities while under heavily adverse battle conditions. Reference is also made to the requirement of Article 43 of the Annex to Hague Convention No. IV, 36 Stat. 2295, 2306, that the commander of a force occupying enemy territory "shall take all the measures in his power to restore, and ensure, as far as possible, public order and safety, while respecting, unless absolutely prevented, the laws in force in the country." But the petitioner was more than a commander of a force occupying enemy territory. He was the leader of an army under constant and devastating attacks by a superior re-invading force. This provision is silent as to the responsibilities of a commander under such conditions as that.

Even the laws of war heretofore recognized by this nation fail to impute responsibility to a fallen commander for excesses committed by his disorganized troops while under attack. Paragraph 347 of the War Department publication, Basic Field Manual, Rules of Land Warfare, FM 27–10 (1940), states the principal offenses under the laws of war recognized by the United States. This includes all of the atrocities which the Japanese troops were alleged to have committed in this instance. Originally this paragraph concluded with the statement that "The commanders ordering the commission of such acts, or under whose authority they are committed by their troops, may be punished by the belligerent into whose hands they may fall." The meaning of the phrase "under whose authority they are committed" was not clear. On November 15, 1944, however, this sentence was deleted and a new paragraph was added relating to the personal liability of those who violate the laws of war. Change 1, FM 27–10. The new paragraph 345.1 states that "Individuals and organizations who violate the accepted laws and customs of war may be punished therefor. However, the fact that the acts complained of were done pursuant to order of a superior or government sanction may be taken into consideration in determining culpability, either by way of defense or in mitigation of punishment. The person giving such orders may also be punished." From this the conclusion seems inescapable that the United States recognizes individual criminal responsibility for violations of the laws of war only as to those who commit the offenses or who order or direct their commission. Such was not the allegation here. Cf. Article 67 of the Articles of War, 10 U.S.C. § 1539, 10 U.S.C.A. § 1539.

There are numerous instances, especially with reference to the Philippine Insurrection in 1900 and 1901, where commanding officers were found to have violated the laws of war by specifically ordering members of their command to commit atrocities and other war crimes. . . . And . . . officers have been held liable where they knew that a crime was to be committed, had the power to prevent it and failed to exercise that power. . . . In no recorded instance, however, has the mere inability to control troops under fire or attack by superior forces been made the basis of a charge of violating the laws of war.

The Government claims that the principle that commanders in the field are bound to control their troops has been applied so as to impose liability on the United States in international arbitrations. Case of Jeannaud, 1880, 3 Moore, International Arbitrations (1898) 3000; Case of The Zafiro, 1910, 5 Hackworth, Digest of International Law (1943) 707. The difference between arbitrating property rights and charging an individual with a crime against the laws of war is too obvious to require elaboration. But even more significant is the fact that even these arbitration cases fail to establish any principle of liability where troops are under constant assault and demoralizing influences by attacking forces. The same observation applies to the common law and statutory doctrine, referred to by the Government, that one who is under a legal duty to take protective or preventive action is guilty of criminal homicide if he willfully or negligently omits to act and death is proximately caused. . . . No one denies that inaction or negligence may give rise to liability, civil or criminal. But it is quite another thing to say that the inability to control troops under highly competitive and disastrous battle conditions renders one guilty of a war crime in the absence of personal culpability. Had there been some element of knowledge or direct connection with the atrocities the problem would be entirely different. Moreover, it must be remembered that we are not dealing here with an ordinary tort or criminal action; precedents in those fields are of little if any value. Rather we are concerned with a proceeding involving an international crime, the treatment of which may have untold effects upon the future peace of the world. That fact must be kept uppermost in our search for precedent.

The only conclusion I can draw is that the charge made against the petitioner is clearly without precedent in international law or in the annals of recorded military history. This is not to say that enemy commanders may escape punishment for clear and unlawful failures to prevent atrocities. But that punishment should be based upon charges fairly drawn in light of established rules of international law and recognized concepts of justice.

But the charge in this case, as previously noted, was speedily drawn and filed but three weeks after the petitioner surrendered. The trial proceeded with great dispatch without allowing the defense time to prepare an adequate case. Petitioner's rights under the due process clause of the Fifth Amendment were grossly and openly violated without any justification. All of this was done without any thorough investigation and prosecution of those immediately responsible for the atrocities, out of which might have come some proof or indication of personal culpability on petitioner's part. Instead the loose charge was made that great numbers of atrocities had been committed and that petitioner was the commanding officer; hence he must have been guilty of disregard of duty. Under that charge the commission was free to establish whatever standard of duty on petitioner's part that it desired. By this flexible method a victorious nation may convict and execute any or all leaders of a vanquished foe, depending upon the prevailing degree of vengeance and the absence of any objective judicial review.

At a time like this when emotions are understandably high it is difficult to adopt a dispassionate attitude toward a case of this nature. Yet now is precisely the time when that attitude is most essential. While peoples in other lands may not share our beliefs as to due process and the dignity of the individual, we are not free to give effect to our emotions in reckless disregard of the rights of others. We live under the Constitution, which is the embodiment of all the high hopes and aspirations of the new world. And it is applicable in both war and peace. We must act accordingly. Indeed, an uncurbed spirit of revenge and retribution, masked in formal legal procedure for purposes of dealing with a fallen enemy commander, can do more lasting harm than all of the atrocities giving rise to that spirit. The people's faith in the fairness and objectiveness of the law can be seriously undercut by that spirit. The fires of nationalism can be further kindled. And the hearts of all mankind can be embittered and filled with hatred, leaving forlorn and impoverished the noble ideal of malice toward none and charity to all. These are the reasons that lead me to dissent in these terms.

Mr. Justice Rutledge, dissenting.

Not with ease does one find his views at odds with the Court's in a matter of this character and gravity. Only the most deeply felt convictions could force one to differ. That reason alone leads me to do so now, against strong considerations for withholding dissent.

More is at stake than General Yamashita's fate. There could be no possible sympathy for him if he is guilty of the atrocities for which his death is sought. But there can be and should be justice administered according to law. In this stage of war's aftermath it is too early for Lincoln's great spirit, best lighted in the Second Inaugural, to have wide hold for the treatment of foes. It is not too early, it is never too early, for the nation steadfastly to follow its great constitutional traditions, none older or more universally protective against unbridled power than due process of law in the trial and punishment of men, that is, of all men, whether citizens, aliens, alien enemies or enemy belligerents. It can become too late.

This long-held attachment marks the great divide between our enemies and ourselves. Theirs was a philosophy of universal force. Ours is one of universal law, albeit imperfectly made flesh of our system and so dwelling among us. Every departure weakens the tradition, whether it touches the high or the low, the powerful or the weak, the triumphant or the conquered. If we need not or cannot be magnanimous, we can keep our own law on the plane from which it has not descended hitherto and to which the defeated foes' never rose.

With all deference to the opposing views of my brethren, whose attachment to that tradition needless to say is no less than my own, I cannot believe in the face of this record that the petitioner has had the fair trial our Constitution and laws command. Because I cannot reconcile what has occurred with their measure, I am forced to speak. At bottom my concern is that we shall not forsake in any case, whether Yamashita's or another's, the basic standards of trial which, among other guaranties, the nation fought to keep; that our system of military justice shall not alone among all our forms of judging be above or beyond the fundamental law or the control of Congress within its orbit of authority; and that this Court shall not fail in its part under the Constitution to see that these things do not happen.

This trial is unprecedented in our history. Never before have we tried and convicted an enemy general for action taken during hostilities or otherwise in the course of military operations or duty. Much less have we condemned one for failing to take action. The novelty is not lessened by the trial's having taken place after hostilities ended and the enemy, including the accused, had surrendered. Moreover, so far as the time permitted for our consideration has given opportunity, I have not been able to find precedent for the proceeding in the system of any nation founded in the basic principles of our constitutional democracy, in the laws of war or in other internationally binding authority or usage.

The novelty is legal as well as historical. We are on strange ground. Precedent is not all-controlling in law. There must be room for growth, since every precedent has an origin. But it is the essence of our tradition for judges, when they stand at the end of the marked way, to go forward with caution keeping sight, so far as they are able, upon the great landmarks left behind and the direction they point ahead. If, as may be hoped, we are now to enter upon a new era of law in the world, it becomes more important than ever before for the nations creating that system to observe their greatest traditions of administering justice, including this one, both in their own judging and in their new creation. The proceedings in this case veer so far from some of our time-tested road signs that I cannot take the large strides validating them would demand.

It is not in our tradition for anyone to be charged with crime which is defined after his conduct, alleged to be criminal, has taken place; or in language not sufficient to inform him of the nature of the offense or to enable him to make defense. Mass guilt we do not impute to individuals, perhaps in any case but certainly in none where the person is not charged or shown actively to have participated in or knowingly to have failed in taking action to prevent the wrongs done by others, having both the duty and the power to do so.

It is outside our basic scheme to condemn men without giving reasonable opportunity for preparing defense; in capital or other serious crimes to convict on "official documents . . . ; affidavits; . . . documents or translations thereof; diaries . . . , photographs, motion picture films, and . . . newspapers" or on hearsay, once, twice or thrice removed, more particularly when the documentary evidence or some of it is prepared ex parte by the prosecuting authority and includes not only opinion but conclusions of guilt. Nor in such cases do we deny the rights of confrontation of witnesses and cross-examination.

Our tradition does not allow conviction by tribunals both authorized and bound by the instrument of their creation to receive and consider evidence which is expressly excluded by Act of Congress or by treaty obligation; nor is it in accord with our basic concepts to make the tribunal, specially constituted for the particular trial, regardless of those prohibitions, the sole and exclusive judge of the credibility, probative value and admissibility of whatever may be tendered as evidence.

The matter is not one merely of the character and admissibility of evidence. It goes to the very competency of the tribunal to try and punish consistently with the Constitution, the laws of the United States made in pursuance thereof, and treaties made under the nation's authority.

All these deviations from the fundamental law, and others, occurred in the course of constituting the commission, the preparation for trial and defense, the trial itself, and therefore, in effect, in the sentence imposed. Whether taken singly in some instances as departures from specific constitutional mandates or in totality as in violation of the Fifth Amendment's command that *no* person shall be deprived of life, liberty or property without due process of law, a trial so vitiated cannot withstand constitutional scrutiny.

One basic protection of our system and one only, petitioner has had. He has been represented by able counsel, officers of the army he fought. Their difficult assignment has been done with extraordinary fidelity, not only to the accused, but to their high conception of military justice, always to be administered in subordination to the Constitution and consistent Acts of Congress and treaties. But, as will appear, even this conceded shield was taken away in much of its value, by denial of reasonable opportunity for them to perform their function.

On this denial and the commission's invalid constitution specifically, but also more generally upon the totality of departures from constitutional norms inherent in the idea of a fair trial, I rest my judgment that the commission was without jurisdiction from the beginning to try or punish the petitioner and that, if it had acquired jurisdiction then, its power to proceed was lost in the course of what was done before and during trial.

Only on one view, in my opinion, could either of these conclusions be avoided. This would be that an enemy belligerent in petitioner's position is altogether beyond the pale of constitutional protection, regardless of the fact that hostilities had ended and he had surrendered with his country. The Government has so argued, urging that we are still at war with Japan and all the power of the military effective during active hostilities in theatres of combat continues in full force unaffected by the events of August 14, 1945, and after.

In this view the action taken here is one of military necessity, exclusively within the authority of the President as Commander-in-Chief and his military subordinates to take in warding off military danger and subject to no judicial restraint on any account, although somewhat inconsistently it is said this Court may "examine" the proceedings generally.

As I understand the Court, this is in substance the effect of what has been done. For I cannot conceive any instance of departure from our basic concepts of fair trial, if the failures here are not sufficient to produce that effect.

We are technically still at war, because peace has not been negotiated finally or declared. But there is no longer the danger which always exists before surrender and armistice. Military necessity does not demand the same measures. The nation may be more secure now than at any time after peace is officially concluded. In these facts is one great difference from Ex parte Quirin, 317 U.S. 1, 63 S.Ct. 2, 87 L.Ed. 3. Punitive action taken now can be effective only for the next war, for purposes of military security. And enemy aliens, including belligerents, need the attenuated protections our system extends to them more now than before hostilities ceased or than they may after a treaty of peace is signed. Ample power there is to punish them or others for crimes, whether under the laws of war during its course or later during occupation. There can be no question of that. The only question is how it shall be done, consistently with universal constitutional commands or outside their restricting effects. In this sense I think the Constitution follows the flag.

The other thing to be mentioned in order to be put aside is that we have no question here of what the military might have done in a field of combat. There the maxim about the law becoming silent in the noise of arms applies. The purpose of battle is to kill. But it does not follow that this would justify killing by trial after capture or surrender, without compliance with laws or treaties made to apply in such cases, whether trial is before or after hostilities end.

I turn now to discuss some of the details of what has taken place. My basic difference is with the Court's view that provisions of the Articles of War and of treaties are not made applicable to this proceeding and with its ruling that, absent such applicable provisions, none of the things done so vitiated the trial and sentence as to deprive the commission of jurisdiction.

My Brother Murphy has discussed the charge with respect to the substance of the crime. With his conclusions in this respect I agree. My own primary concern will be with the constitution of the commission and other matters taking place in the course of the proceedings, relating chiefly to the denial of reasonable opportunity to prepare petitioner's defense and the sufficiency of the evidence, together with serious questions of admissibility, to prove on offense, all going as I think to the commission's jurisdiction. . . .

. . . The difference between the Court's view of this proceeding and my own comes down in the end to the view, on the one hand, that there is no law restrictive upon these proceedings other than whatever rules and regulations may be prescribed for their government by the executive authority or the military and, on the other hand, that the provisions of the Articles of War, of the Geneva Convention and the Fifth Amendment apply.

I cannot accept the view that anywhere in our system resides or lurks a power so unrestrained to deal with any human being through any process of trial. What military agencies or authorities may do with our enemies in battle or invasion, apart from proceedings in the nature of trial and some semblance of judicial action, is beside the point. Nor has any human being heretofore been held to be wholly beyond elementary procedural protection by the Fifth Amendment. I cannot consent to even implied departure from that great absolute.

It was a great patriot who said:

> He that would make his own liberty secure must guard even his enemy from oppression; for if he violates this duty he establishes a precedent that will reach himself.

Mr. Justice Murphy joins in this opinion.

5b. Office of the Theater Judge Advocate, U.S. Army Forces, Pacific, Review of the Record of Trial by a Military Commission of Tomoyuki Yamashita, General, Imperial Japanese Army, 26 December 1945 *

. . .

There can be . . . little doubt that the charge is sufficient, read in conjunction with the items of the Bill of Particulars, aptly to charge violation of the Laws of War. The gist of the offense is that accused wrongfully failed to discharge his duty as a military commander to control the members of his command, permitting them to commit the atrocities alleged. The doctrine that it is the duty of a commander to control his troops is as old as military organization itself and the failure to discharge such duty has long been regarded as a violation of the Laws of War. In the Annex to the Hague Convention No. IV of October 18, 1917, embodying the regulations respecting the laws and customs of war on land, adopted by that Convention, we find:

> The laws, rights and duties of war apply not only to armies but to militia and volunteer corps fulfilling the following conditions:
>
> 1. To be commanded by a person responsible for his subordinates. (FM 27-10, Rules of Land Warfare, Sec 9)

Thus, a necessary prerequisite of the right of an army to conduct

* Memorandum of December 26, 1945, quoted in Whitney, The Case of General Yamashita, Memorandum for the Record of November 22, 1949, pp. 76–77.

hostilities is the requirement that it be commanded by an officer responsible for its actions. It must, however, be conceded that only rarely, if at all, has punishment for failure to exercise control been meted out to an individual commander. Expiation for such failure has, in the past, customarily been required only of the belligerent power itself under the provisions of Article 3, Hague Convention No. IV, 1917, respecting the laws and customs of war on land, which provides:

> A belligerent party which violates the provisions of said regulations shall, if the case demands, be liable to pay compensation. It shall be responsible for all acts committed by persons forming part of its armed forces.

But since the duty rests on a commander to protect by any means in his power both the civil population and prisoners of war from wrongful acts of his command and since the failure to discharge that duty is a violation of the Laws of War, there is no reason, either in law or morality, why he should not be held criminally responsible for permitting such violations by his subordinates, even though that action has heretofore seldom or never been taken. The responsibility of the commander to control his troops is well understood by all experienced military men, including accused, who admitted in writing in open court that failure to discharge such duty would be culpable (R 3674). The accused should thus not be heard to complain of being held criminally responsible for such violation, particularly in view of the solemn warnings given the Axis powers by the Government of the United States on the outbreak of hostilities that all those responsible for war crimes, either directly or indirectly, would be held accountable (Congressional Record, 9 March 1943, page 1773). It should be borne in mind that International Law is not a static body of definite statutes but a living, growing thing. By solemn pronouncement, the United Nations gave warning that a new era had arrived with respect to the conduct of all persons, even high commanders, in their methods of waging war. In the enlightened and newly awakened conscience of the world, there is nothing either legally or morally wrong in now holding to strict accountability not only those who by their own acts violate the laws of humanity, but also those who knowingly or negligently permit such acts to be done. It is only by so holding commanders that any forward progress toward decency may be expected. . . .

6. Geneva Convention Relative to the Protection of Civilian Persons in Time of War, 12 August 1949

The undersigned, Plenipotentiaries of the Governments represented at the Diplomatic Conference held at Geneva from April 21 to August 12, 1949, for the purpose of establishing a Convention for the Protection of Civilians in Time of War, have agreed as follows:

. . .

Article 1

The High Contracting Parties undertake to respect and to ensure respect for the present Convention in all circumstances.

Article 2

In addition to the provisions which shall be implemented in peace time, the present Convention shall apply to all cases of declared war or of any other armed conflict which may arise between two or more of the High Contracting Parties, even if the state of war is not recognised by one of them.

The Convention shall also apply to all cases of partial or total occupation of the territory of a High Contracting Party, even if the said occupation meets with no armed resistance.

Although one of the Powers in conflict may not be a party to the present Convention, the Powers who are parties thereto shall remain bound by it in their mutual relations. They shall, furthermore, be bound by the Convention in relation to the said Power, if the latter accepts and applies the provisions thereof.

Article 3

In the case of armed conflict not of an international character occurring in the territory of one of the High Contracting Parties, each Party to the conflict shall be bound to apply, as a minimum, the following provisions:

1. Persons taking no active part in the hostilities, including members of armed forces, who have laid down their arms and those placed *hors de combat* by sickness, wounds, detention, or any other cause, shall in all circumstances be treated humanely without any adverse distinction founded on race, colour, religion or faith, sex, birth or wealth, or any other similar criteria.

   To this end the following acts are and shall remain prohibited at any time and in any place whatsoever with respect to the above-mentioned persons:

   a. violence to life and person, in particular murder of all kinds, mutilation, cruel treatment and torture;
   b. taking of hostages;
   c. outrages upon personal dignity, in particular humiliating and degrading treatment;
   d. the passing of sentences and the carrying out of executions without previous judgment pronounced by a regularly constituted court, affording all the judicial guarantees which are recognised as indispensable by civilised peoples.

2. The wounded and sick shall be collected and cared for.

An impartial humanitarian body, such as the International Committee of the Red Cross, may offer its services to the Parties to the conflict.

The Parties to the conflict should further endeavour to bring into force, by means of special agreements, all or part of the other provisions of the present Convention.

The application of the preceding provisions shall not affect the legal status of the Parties to the conflict.

Article 4

Persons protected by the Convention are those who, at a given moment and in any manner whatsoever, find themselves, in case of a conflict or occupation, in the hands of a Party to the conflict or Occupying Power of which they are not nationals.

Nationals of a State which is not bound by the Convention are not protected by it. Nationals of a neutral State who find themselves in the territory of a belligerent State, and nationals of a co-belligerent State, shall not be regarded as protected persons while the State of which they are nationals has normal diplomatic representation in the State in whose hands they are.

The provisions of Part II are, however, wider in application, as defined in Article 13.

Persons protected by the Geneva Convention of August 12, 1949 for the Amelioration of the Condition of the Wounded and Sick in Armed Forces in the Field, or by the Geneva Convention of August 12, 1949 for the Amelioration of the Condition of Wounded, Sick and Shipwrecked Members of Armed Forces at Sea, or by the Geneva Convention of August 12, 1949 relative to the Treatment of Prisoners of War, shall not be considered as protected persons within the meaning of the present Convention.

Article 5

Where in the territory of a Party to the conflict, the latter is satisfied that an individual protected person is definitely suspected of or engaged in activities hostile to the security of the State, such individual person shall not be entitled to claim such rights and privileges under the present Convention as would, if exercised in the favour of such individual person, be prejudicial to the security of such State.

Where in occupied territory an individual protected person is detained as a spy or saboteur, or as a person under definite suspicion of activity hostile to the security of the Occupying Power, such person shall, in those cases where absolute military security so requires, be regarded as having forfeited rights of communication under the present Convention.

In each case such persons shall nevertheless be treated with humanity and in case of trial shall not be deprived of the rights of fair and regular trial prescribed by the present Convention. They shall also be granted the full rights and privileges of a protected person under the present Convention at the earliest date consistent with the security of the State or Occupying Power, as the case may be.

Article 6

The present Convention shall apply from the outset of any conflict or occupation mentioned in Article 2.

In the territory of Parties to the conflict, the application of the present Convention shall cease on the general close of military operations.

In the case of occupied territory, the application of the present Convention shall cease one year after the general close of military operations; however, the Occupying Power shall be bound, for the duration of the occupation, to the extent that such Power exercises the functions of government in such territory, by the provisions of the following Articles of the present Convention: 1 to 12, 27, 29 to 34, 47, 49, 51, 52, 53, 59, 61 to 77, 143.

Protected persons whose release, repatriation or re-establishment may take place after such dates shall meanwhile continue to benefit by the present Convention.

. . .

Article 24

The Parties to the conflict shall take the necessary measures to ensure that children under fifteen, who are orphaned or are separated from their families as a result of the war, are not left to their own resources, and that their maintenance, the exercise of their religion and their education are facilitated in all circumstances. Their education shall, as far as possible, be entrusted to persons of a similar cultural tradition.

The Parties to the conflict shall facilitate the reception of such children in a neutral country for the duration of the conflict with the consent of the Protecting Power, if any, and under due safeguards for the observance of the principles stated in the first paragraph.

They shall, furthermore, endeavour to arrange for all children under twelve to be identified by the wearing of identity discs, or by some other means.

. . .

Article 27

Protected persons are entitled, in all circumstances, to respect for their persons, their honour, their family rights, their religious convictions and practices, and their manners and customs. They shall at all times be humanely treated, and shall be protected especially against all acts of violence or threats thereof and against insults and public curiosity.

Women shall be especially protected against any attack on their honour, in particular against rape, enforced prostitution, or any form of indecent assault.

Without prejudice to the provisions relating to their state of health, age and sex, all protected persons shall be treated with the same consideration by the Party to the conflict in whose power they are, without any adverse distinction, based, in particular, on race, religion or political opinion.

However, the Parties to the conflict may take such measures of control and security in regard to protected persons as may be necessary as a result of the war.

Article 28

The presence of a protected person may not be used to render certain points or areas immune from military operations.

Article 29

The Party to the conflict in whose hands protected persons may be is responsible for the treatment accorded to them by its agents, irrespective of any individual responsibility which may be incurred.

. . .

Article 31

No physical or moral coercion shall be exercised against protected persons, in particular to obtain information from them or from third parties.

Article 32

The High Contracting Parties specifically agree that each of them is prohibited from taking any measure of such a character as to cause the physical suffering or extermination of protected persons in their hands. This prohibition applies not only to murder, torture, corporal punishments, mutilation and medical or scientific experiments not necessitated by the medical treatment of a protected person, but also to any other measures of brutality whether applied by civilian or military agents.

Article 33

No protected person may be punished for an offense he or she has not personally committed. Collective penalties and likewise all measures of intimidation or of terrorism are prohibited.

Pillage is prohibited.

Reprisals against protected persons and their property are prohibited.

Article 34

The taking of hostages is prohibited.

. . .

Article 35

All protected persons who may desire to leave the territory at the outset of, or during a conflict, shall be entitled to do so, unless their departure is contrary to the national interests of the State. The applications of such persons to leave shall be determined in accordance with regularly established procedures and the decision shall be taken as rapidly as possible. These persons permitted to leave may provide themselves with the necessary funds for their journey and take with them a reasonable amount of their effects and articles of personal use.

If any such person is refused permission to leave the territory, he shall be entitled to have such refusal reconsidered as soon as possible by an appropriate court or administrative board designated by the Detaining Power for that purpose.

Upon request, representatives of the Protecting Power shall, unless reasons of security prevent it, or the persons concerned object, be furnished with the reasons for refusal of any request for permission to leave the territory and be given, as expeditiously as possible, the names of all persons who have been denied permission to leave.

Article 36

Departures permitted under the foregoing Article shall be carried out in satisfactory conditions as regards safety, hygiene, sanitation and food. All costs in connection therewith, from the point of exit in the territory of the Detaining Power, shall be borne by the country of destination, or, in the case of accommodation in a neutral country, by the Power whose nationals are benefited. The practical details of such movements may, if necessary, be settled by special agreements between the Powers concerned.

The foregoing shall not prejudice such special agreements as may be concluded between Parties to the conflict concerning the exchange and repatriation of their nationals in enemy hands.

. . .

Article 47

Protected persons who are in occupied territory shall not be deprived, in any case or in any manner whatsoever, of the benefits of the present Convention by any change introduced, as the result of the occupation of a territory, into the institutions or government of the said territory, nor by any agreement concluded between the authorities of the occupied territories and the Occupying Power, nor by any annexation by the latter of the whole or part of the occupied territory.

. . .

Article 144

The High Contracting Parties undertake, in time of peace as in time of war, to disseminate the text of the present Convention as widely as possible in their respective countries, and, in particular, to include the study thereof in their programmes of military and, if possible, civil instruction, so that the principles thereof may become known to the entire population.

Any civilian, military, police or other authorities who, in time of war, assume responsibilities in respect of protected persons must possess the text of the Convention and be especially instructed as to its provisions.

Article 145

The High Contracting Parties shall communicate to one another through the Swiss Federal Council and, during hostilities, through the Protecting Powers, the official translations of the present Convention, as well as the laws and regulations which they may adopt to ensure the application thereof.

Article 146

The High Contracting Parties undertake to enact any legislation necessary to provide effective penal sanctions for persons committing, or ordering to be committed, any of the grave breaches of the present Convention defined in the following Article.

Each High Contracting Party shall be under the obligation to search for persons alleged to have committed, or to have ordered to be committed, such grave breaches, and shall bring such persons, regardless of their nationality, before its own courts. It may also, if it prefers, and in accordance with the provisions of its own legislation, hand such persons over for trial to another High Contracting Party concerned, provided such High Contracting Party has made out a *prima facie* case.

Each High Contracting Party shall take measures necessary for the suppression of all acts contrary to the provisions of the present Convention other than the grave breaches defined in the following Article.

In all circumstances, the accused persons shall benefit by safeguards of proper trial and defense, which shall not be less favourable than those provided by Article 105 and those following of the Geneva Convention of August 12, 1949, relative to the Treatment of Prisoners of War.

Article 147

Grave breaches to which the preceding Article relates shall be those involving any of the following acts, if committed against persons or property protected by the present Convention: wilful killing, torture or inhuman treatment, including biological experiments, wilfully causing of great suffering or serious injury to body or health, unlawful deportation or transfer or unlawful confinement of a protected person, compelling a protected person to serve in the forces of a hostile Power, or wilfully depriving a protected person of the rights of fair and regular trial prescribed in the present Convention, taking of hostages and extensive destruction and appropriation of property, not justified by military necessity and carried out unlawfully and wantonly.

Article 148

No High Contracting Party shall be allowed to absolve itself or any other High Contracting Party of any liability incurred by itself or by another High Contracting Party in respect of breaches referred to in the preceding Article.

Article 149

At the request of a Party to the conflict, an enquiry shall be instituted, in a manner to be decided between the interested Parties, concerning any alleged violation of the Convention.

If agreement has not been reached concerning the procedure for the enquiry, the Parties should agree on the choice of an umpire who will decide upon the procedure to be followed.

Once the violation has been established, the Parties to the conflict shall put an end to it and shall repress it within the briefest possible delay.

. . .

7. Department of the Army. The Law of Land Warfare (1956) *

1. PURPOSE AND SCOPE

The purpose of this Manual is to provide authoritative guidance to military personnel on the customary and treaty law applicable to the conduct of warfare on land and to relationships between belligerents and neutral States. Although certain of the legal principles set forth herein have application to warfare at sea and in the air as well as to hostilities on land, this Manual otherwise concerns itself with the rules peculiar to naval and aerial warfare only to the extent that such rules have some direct bearing on the activities of land forces.

This Manual is an official publication of the United States Army. However, those provisions of the Manual which are neither statutes nor the text of treaties to which the United States is a party should not be considered binding upon courts and tribunals applying the law of war. However, such provisions are of evidentiary value insofar as they bear upon questions of custom and practice.

2. PURPOSES OF THE LAW OF WAR

The conduct of armed hostilities on land is regulated by the law of land warfare which is both written and unwritten. It is inspired by the desire to diminish the evils of war by:

a. Protecting both combatants and noncombatants from unnecessary suffering;
b. Safeguarding certain fundamental human rights of persons who

* Field Manual 27-10 (1956), pp. 3–4, 35, 106–107, 178–179, 181–183.

fall into the hands of the enemy, particularly prisoners of war, the wounded and sick, and civilians; and

c. Facilitating the restoration of peace.

3. BASIC PRINCIPLES

A. Prohibitory Effect

The law of war places limits on the exercise of a belligerent's power in the interests mentioned in paragraph 2 and requires that belligerents refrain from employing any kind of degree of violence which is not actually necessary for military purposes and that they conduct hostilities with regard for the principles of humanity and chivalry.

The prohibitory effect of the law of war is not minimized by "military necessity" which has been defined as that principle which justifies those measures not forbidden by international law which are indispensable for securing the complete submission of the enemy as soon as possible. Military necessity has been generally rejected as a defense for acts forbidden by the customary and conventional laws of war inasmuch as the latter have been developed and framed with consideration for the concept of military necessity.

B. Binding on States and Individuals

The law of war is binding not only upon States as such but also upon individuals and, in particular, the members of their armed forces.

. . .

85. KILLING OF PRISONERS

A commander may not put his prisoners to death because their presence retards his movements or diminishes his power of resistance by necessitating a large guard, or by reason of their consuming supplies, or because it appears certain that they will regain their liberty through the impending success of their forces. It is likewise unlawful for a commander to kill his prisoners on grounds of self-preservation, even in the case of airborne or commando operations, although the circumstances of the operation may make necessary rigorous supervision of and restraint upon the movement of prisoners of war.

. . .

Provisions Common to the Territories of the Parties to the Conflict and to Occupied Territories

266. GENERAL

Protected persons are entitled, in all circumstances, to respect for their persons, their honour, their family rights, their religious convictions and practices, and their manners and customs. They shall at all times be humanely treated, and shall be protected especially against all acts of violence or threats thereof and against insults and public curiosity.

Women shall be especially protected against any attack on their honour, in particular against rape, enforced prostitution, or any form of indecent assault.

Without prejudice to the provisions relating to their state of health, age and sex, all protected persons shall be treated with the same consideration by the Party to the conflict in whose power they are, without any adverse distinction based, in particular, on race, religion or political opinion.

However, the Parties to the conflict may take such measures of control and security in regard to protected persons as may be necessary as a result of the war. (*GC, art. 27.*)

. . .

271. PROHIBITION OF CORPORAL PUNISHMENT, TORTURE, ETC.

The High Contracting Parties specifically agree that each of them is prohibited from taking any measure of such a character as to cause the physical suffering or extermination of protected persons in their hands. This prohibition applies not only to murder, torture, corporal punishment, mutilation and medical or scientific experiments not necessitated by the medical treatment of a protected person, but also to any other measures of brutality whether applied by civilian or military agents. (*GC, art. 32.*)

272. INDIVIDUAL RESPONSIBILITY, COLLECTIVE PENALTIES, REPRISALS, PILLAGE

No protected person may be punished for an offence he or she has not personally committed. Collective penalties and likewise all measures of intimidation or of terrorism are prohibited.

Pillage is prohibited.

Reprisals against protected persons and their property are prohibited. (*GC, art. 33.*) (See also pars. 47 and 397.)

. . .

Crimes under International Law

498. CRIMES UNDER INTERNATIONAL LAW

Any person, whether a member of the armed forces or a civilian, who commits an act which constitutes a crime under international law is responsible therefor and liable to punishment. Such offenses in connection with war comprise:

a. Crimes against peace.
b. Crimes against humanity.
c. War crimes.

Although this manual recognizes the criminal responsibility of individuals for those offenses which may comprise any of the foregoing types of crimes, members of the armed forces will normally be concerned only with those offenses constituting "war crimes."

499. WAR CRIMES

The term "war crime" is the technical expression for a violation of the laws of war by any person or persons, military or civilian. Every violation of the law of war is a war crime.

500. CONSPIRACY, INCITEMENT, ATTEMPTS, AND COMPLICITY

Conspiracy, direct incitement, and attempts to commit, as well as complicity in the commission of, crimes against peace, crimes against humanity, and war crimes are punishable.

501. RESPONSIBILITY FOR ACTS OF SUBORDINATES

In some cases, military commanders may be responsible for war crimes committed by subordinate members of the armed forces, or other persons subject to their control. Thus, for instance, when troops commit massacres and atrocities against the civilian population of occupied territory or against prisoners of war, the responsibility may rest not only with the actual perpetrators but also with the commander. Such a responsibility arises directly when the acts in question have been committed in pursuance of an order of the commander concerned. The commander is also responsible if he has actual knowledge, or should have knowledge, through reports received by him or through other means, that troops or other persons subject to his control are about to commit or have committed a war crime and he fails to take the necessary and reasonable steps to insure compliance with the law of war or to punish violators thereof.

. . .

506. SUPPRESSION OF WAR CRIMES

a. Geneva Conventions of 1949

The Geneva Conventions of 1949 contain the following common undertakings:

The High Contracting Parties undertake to enact any legislation necessary to provide effective penal sanctions for persons committing, or ordering to be committed, any of the grave breaches of the present Convention defined in the following Article.

Each High Contracting Party shall be under the obligation to search for persons alleged to have committed, or to have ordered to be committed, such grave breaches, and shall bring such persons, regardless of their nationality, before its own courts. It may also, if it prefers, and in accordance with the provisions of its own legislation, hand such persons over for trial to another High Contracting Party concerned, provided such High Contracting Party has made out a *prima facie* case.

Each High Contracting Party shall take measures necessary for the suppression of all acts contrary to the provisions of the present Convention other than the grave breaches defined in the following Article.

In all circumstances, the accused persons shall benefit by safeguards of proper trial and defence, which shall not be less favourable than those provided by Article 105 and those following of the Geneva Convention relative to the Treatment of Prisoners of War of August 12, 1949. (*GWS, art. 49; GWS Sea, art. 50; GPW, art. 129; GC, art. 146.*)

b. Declaratory Character of Above Principles

The principles quoted in *a,* above, are declaratory of the obligations of belligerents under customary international law to take measures for the punishment of war crimes committed by all persons, including members of a belligerent's own armed forces.

c. Grave Breaches

"Grave breaches" of the Geneva Conventions of 1949 and other war crimes which are committed by enemy personnel or persons associated with the enemy are tried and punished by United States tribunals as violations of international law.

If committed by persons subject to United States military law, these "grave breaches" constitute acts punishable under the Uniform Code of Military Justice. Moreover, most of the acts designated as "grave breaches" are, if committed within the United States, violations of domestic law over which the civil courts can exercise jurisdiction.

507. UNIVERSALITY OF JURISDICTION

a. Victims of War Crimes

The jurisdiction of United States military tribunals in connection with war crimes is not limited to offenses committed against nationals of the United States but extends also to all offenses of this nature committed against nationals of allies and of cobelligerents and stateless persons.

b. Persons Charged With War Crimes

The United States normally punishes war crimes as such only if they are committed by enemy nationals or by persons serving the interests of the enemy State. Violations of the law of war committed by persons subject to the military law of the United States will usually constitute violations of the Uniform Code of Military Justice and, if so, will be prosecuted under that Code. Violations of the law of war committed within the United States by other persons will usually constitute violations of federal or state criminal law and preferably will be prosecuted under such law (see pars. 505 and 506). Commanding officers of United States troops must insure that war crimes committed by members of their forces against enemy personnel are promptly and adequately punished.

508. PENAL SANCTIONS

The punishment imposed for a violation of the law of war must be proportionate to the gravity of the offense. The death penalty may be imposed for grave breaches of the law. Corporal punishment is excluded. Punishments should be deterrent, and in imposing a sentence of imprisonment it is not necessary to take into consideration the end of the war, which does not of itself limit the imprisonment to be imposed.

Section IV. Defenses not Available

509. DEFENSE OF SUPERIOR ORDERS

a. The fact that the law of war has been violated pursuant to an order of a superior authority, whether military or civil, does not deprive the act in question of its character of a war crime, nor does it constitute a defense in the trial of an accused individual, unless he did not know and could not reasonably have been expected to know that the act ordered was unlawful. In all cases where the order is held not to constitute a defense to an allegation of war crime, the fact that the individual was acting pursuant to orders may be considered in mitigation of punishment.

b. In considering the question whether a superior order constitutes a valid defense, the court shall take into consideration the fact that obedience to lawful military orders is the duty of every member of the armed forces; that the latter cannot be expected, in conditions of war discipline, to weigh scrupulously the legal merits of the orders received; that certain rules of warfare may be controversial; or that an act otherwise amounting to a war crime may be done in obedience to orders conceived as a measure of reprisal. At the same time it must be borne in mind that members of the armed forces are bound to obey only lawful orders (*e.g., UCMJ, Art. 92*).

510. GOVERNMENT OFFICIALS

The fact that a person who committed an act which constitutes a war crime acted as the head of a State or as a responsible government official does not relieve him from responsibility for his act.

511. ACTS NOT PUNISHED IN DOMESTIC LAW

The fact that domestic law does not impose a penalty for an act which constitutes a crime under international law does not relieve the person who committed the act from responsibility under international law.

From Vietnam War

8. *United States* v. *Goldman,* 43 C.M.R. 711 (ACMR 1970)

. . .

Opinion of the Court on Reconsideration en Banc

NEMROW, JUDGE:

After a panel of this Court filed its opinion in this case, on 16 September 1970, a majority of the judges directed, on 28 September 1970, and on their own motion . . . the case be referred for reconsideration and review to the Court sitting en banc. . . .

The appellant was tried, on 6–8 September 1968, by a general court-martial, for the following offenses, all in violation of the Uniform Code of Military Justice (UCMJ):

a. Failure to obey a lawful general regulation (paragraph 3, USARV Regulation 335–6, dated 24 June 1967), on 3 June 1968, in the District of Tam Ky, Republic of Vietnam, by failing to report the non-battle death of a female Oriental human being who died as a result of gunshot wounds inflicted while in the custody of his unit (Specification 1 of Charge I, Article 92, UCMJ, 10 USC § 892).

b. Dereliction in the performance of his duties, during the period 2 through 3 June 1968, in the District of Tam Ky, Republic of Vietnam, by negligently failing to enforce adequate safeguards to protect female Orientals, then in the custody of his unit, from physical mistreatment by the members of his unit (Specification 2 of Charge I, Article 92, UCMJ, 10 USC § 892).

c. Misprision of a felony, on 3 June 1968, in the District of Tam Ky, Republic of Vietnam, by wrongfully and unlawfully concealing the murder of a female Oriental human being (Specification of Charge II, Article 134, UCMJ, 10 USC § 934).

He pleaded not guilty to all charges and specifications. The appellant was acquitted of the misprision offense, but convicted of Charge I and its specifications. He was sentenced to a reprimand and to pay a fine of $2,500. The initial reviewing authority approved the sentence.[1] Pursuant to Article 69 of the Code, supra, 10 USC § 869, The Judge Advocate General of the Army referred this case to the Court of Military Review for review in accordance with Article 66 of the Code, supra, 10 USC § 866.

Appellate defense counsel have assigned the following errors:

1. The appellant's conviction of Specification 1 of Charge I is contrary to law and not supported by the evidence of record.
2. The evidence is insufficient as a matter of law to sustain the finding of guilty of Specification 2 of Charge I.

The facts necessary as background to a disposition of the aforementioned issues are as follows:

The events which led up to the charges in this case occurred in June 1968, when the appellant's unit was engaged in combat operations in Dragon Valley, District of Tam Ky, Republic of Vietnam. The appellant resumed command of Company B on 2 June 1968 immediately upon his return from a rest and recuperation (R & R) absence. On the afternoon of 2 June 1968, his unit captured some prisoners, including two females who were described as being NVA or VC nurses. The appellant's unit was operating with Company A, but because of the dense undergrowth it was difficult to maintain visual contact. Company A had moved ahead and had established a defensive "laager" position. While the appellant's unit was moving to the area where Company A was located, one of his squads was ambushed. The squad leader was killed and another soldier was wounded. It was beginning to get dark and the appellant moved his company to the area already occupied by Company A. Because of the recent attack and lack of knowledge as to the location of enemy units, it was necessary for him to integrate his troops with those of A Company.

[1] The case was referred for trial by the Commanding General, 23 Infantry Division (Americal). The "Action" was taken by the Commanding General, I Field Force, Vietnam. The Commanding General, Americal Division, had granted immunity to a prosecution witness, but the allied papers do not contain the letter of transmittal containing a statement of the reasons for the failure of the normal convening authority to act on the record. See para 84c, MCM, 1951. . . .

This caused him concern because of the obvious problem of command and control.

The appellant had informed his battalion headquarters by radio of the fact that he had some detainees in his custody, but was advised that the helicopters had been released for the day and that the detainees would not be picked up. He then directed one of his sergeants to secure the detainees for the night.

The events which transpired during the night are not in dispute; suffice it to say that the two female detainees were subject to multiple rapes, sodomy, and other mistreatment at the hands of various members of the First Platoon of Company B. On the morning of 3 June 1968, these detainees, including the two females, were escorted to the landing zone where one female nurse was murdered by a member of the appellant's unit. Lieutenant D, who had been Acting Company Commander while the appellant was on R & R, had ordered a VC male detainee to shoot the nurse and provided him with a loaded M–16 rifle to accomplish that purpose. The VC shot the nurse in the neck and Lieutenant D thereafter fired two more shots into the nurse's head. The appellant was not present when the killing occurred, and when he was informed of the incident he was advised that "some gink grabbed a rifle and shot one of the nurses."

Appellate defense counsel state in their brief, "It is the appellant's contention that his conviction under Specification 1 of Charge I must fall because he did not have the requisite 'knowledge' of a 'serious incident' as defined in Regulation Number 335–6 and therefore did not violate the regulation; or, in the alternative, that his conviction under the Regulation . . . is violative of due process because of ambiguities in the Regulation which render it unconstitutionally vague." Finally, appellate defense counsel contend that the regulation "is not fit for punitive purposes."

The latter contention need not detain us long. We are of the opinion that the provisions of the regulation in issue are mandatory in nature and that a violation thereof subjects the offender to punitive sanctions. . . .

Our perusal of USARV Regulation No. 335–6 (see Appendix) leads us to conclude that appellant had a duty to render a report as required by its provisions.

The last sentence of subparagraph 2b of the aforementioned regulation expressly provides the following:

> Crimes, offenses, and incidents to be reported include, but are not limited to:
>
> 1. Nonbattle deaths from other than natural causes, to include the deaths of foreign national personnel when US personnel or equipment are involved.

Clearly, under the requirements of those provisions, if one prisoner of war or enemy detainee kills another prisoner of war or enemy detainee while both are in the hands of United States personnel, whether or not the weapon used was obtained as a result of negligence by United States personnel, such crime (see Article 2(9), UCMJ, 10 USC § 802(9)),[3] offense, or incident is reportable. In the words of the author judge in United States v Brooks, 43 CMR—(AFCMR 1970):

> In this case we find that the words involved are words of common usage and understanding, and have a meaning well enough known to those within the reach of the regulation to apply them correctly.

The fact that both the battalion commander and the battalion operations officer may not have regarded the matter as a "serious incident" within the purview of the regulation does not [faze] us one bit. They are charged with knowledge of the laws of war and the provisions of our Governmental treaties in implementation thereof, specifically the various Geneva Conventions. Hence, their ignorance thereof does not help the appellant.

The evidence of record convinces us beyond a reasonable doubt that the appellant had full knowledge of a serious incident which involved Lieutenant D and which had to be reported in accordance with the USARV regulation. We note that immediately after the shooting and in the immediate presence of the appellant, and after Lieutenant D exchanged glimpses with the appellant, a soldier told Lieutenant D that he had blood on him. If the appellant did not hear the three shots (fired when his troops were not engaged in battle), he must have been intentionally deaf. That he was well aware of what had transpired within his "laager," about 60 feet away from his "CP" is evident from his remark to one of his men concerning the remaining female detainee:

> . . . if she's taken back to the MI interrogation and she tells what happened in the field we'll all swing for it.

Moreover, when the appellant spoke to his battalion commander, on 5 June 1968, he admitted that he already knew what had happened to the victim, the Viet Cong nurse; hence, it is clear that he should have reported the incident when he first learned about it. . . .

The appellant's sentence includes a fine although he has not been unjustly enriched by any offense of which he was convicted. Recognizing that the provision in paragraph 127b, Section B, Manual for Courts-Martial, United States, 1951, that a fine should not ordinarily be ad-

[3] A prisoner of war is subject to the laws, regulations, and orders in force in the armed forces of the Detaining Power. The Detaining Power is justified in taking judicial or disciplinary measures with respect to any offense committed by a prisoner of war against such laws, regulations, or orders. Para 158, FM 27-10, The Law of Land Warfare (1956; GPW, Art 82).

judged unless the accused was unjustly enriched by an offense of which he was convicted is directory and not mandatory, we consider it appropriate to conform the sentence with the guidance of the President by affirming a less severe punishment of forfeiture of pay. . . .

Six officers, including a former battalion commander, and two enlisted men testified that the appellant was an outstanding company commander with whom they would like to serve again despite his conviction. The appellant is now 29 years old. His father is a retired lieutenant colonel. After graduation from Georgia Tech in 1964 with a Bachelor of Science degree, the appellant entered the Army as a reserve second lieutenant on 26 February 1966. Thereafter, he attended the Infantry Officers Basic Course and, on 19 November 1966, assumed command of his company in Vietnam. Subsequently, he requested an extension of his Vietnam tour of duty which was approved on 23 March 1968. Captain Goldman's awards include the Ranger Tab, Parachutist Badge, and Combat Infantry Badge.

The findings of guilty are affirmed. Reassessing the sentence on the basis of the foregoing and the entire record, the Court affirms only so much of the sentence, as approved, and ordered into execution, as provides for a reprimand and forfeiture of $100.00 pay per month for 12 months.

In view of the foregoing, the decision rendered by this Court on 16 September 1970 is hereby withdrawn and this decision substituted therefor.

Chief Judge Rogers, Senior Judge Chalk, and Judges Bailey, Collins, Rouillard and Folawn concur.

. . .

FINKELSTEIN, JUDGE, concurring in part and dissenting in part:

That this was a "serious incident" seems to me to be clear, not only from the extracts of the regulation set out in the majority opinion, but also from those portions of the regulation clearly requiring reports in the case of suicides and accidents (see para 2b, USARV Reg. No. 335–6). In my view a report would be required of the non-battle death of a detained person if he or she succumbed to injuries incurred as the result of an accident and three board certified physicians were vainly in attendance. See paragraph 58, *Handling Prisoners of War,* FM 19–40.

That the evidence is sufficient as a matter of law to sustain the findings of guilty as to the dereliction charge is equally clear. What General MacArthur stated in his action as confirming authority in the case of United States v General Tomoyuki Yamashita is shamefully applicable here:

> Rarely has so cruel and wanton a record been spread to public gaze. Revolting as this may be in itself, it pales before the sinister and far reaching implication thereby attached to the profession of arms. The soldier, be he friend or foe, is charged with the protection of the weak and unarmed. It is the very essence and reason for his being. When he violates that sacred trust he not only profanes his entire cult but threatens the very fabric of international society. The traditions of fighting men are long and honorable. They are based upon the noblest of human traits,—sacrifice. This officer, of proven field merit, entrusted with high command involving authority adequate to responsibility, has failed this irrevocable standard; has failed his duty to his troops, to his country, to his enemy, to mankind; has failed utterly his soldier faith. The transgressions resulting therefrom as revealed by the trial are a blot upon the military profession, a stain upon civilization and constitute a memory of shame and dishonor that can never be forgotten.

For this reason I respectfully dissent from the reduction of sentence herein ordered. I would affirm a forfeiture equal to the fine imposed, not because it is appropriate but because it is less inappropriate than that affirmed today.

TAYLOR, Judge, concurring and dissenting:

. . .

The submission of the suggestion for reconsideration by the entire Court was premised, at least in part, on a view that this was a case of exceptional importance because the initial opinion would cause adverse reactions from antiwar groups and could significantly affect the disposition of the notorious, so-called My Lai cases which are presently pending. In my opinion, such considerations may make a *case* important, but they do not create a *question* of exceptional importance under Rule 18a. Unquestionably, what is intended by a question of exceptional importance is a holding which will establish a rule of law that will have a significant influence on the administration of justice. Concern that the original opinion could have a significant effect on the "My Lai" cases is misplaced because the regulation allegedly violated in the majority of those cases is not the same as the one involved in Specification 1, Charge I, in this case and because of the narrow scope of the holding in the original opinion.

9. Howard, Col. Kenneth, Charge to the Jury in *United States* v. *Medina*, September 1971*

. . .

I now call your attention to the Specification of the additional Charge and the additional Charge, both as modified to allege the offense of involuntary manslaughter in violation of Article 119, Uniform Code of Military Justice. Before stating the elements of that offense, I believe it to be prudent and necessary to state certain preliminary matters. As I understand the issues and theories of the prosecution and defense, the specific issues for your determination are represented by the opposing parties to be as follows:

The following statements are prosecution representations and not my conclusions as to the state of the evidence but the prosecution alleges that Captain Medina was the company commander of Charlie Company, 1st Battalion, 20th Infantry of the 11th Brigade. As company commander Captain Medina had briefed the men of his company, assigned them specific missions and dispatched them on a combat assault described as a search-and-destroy mission, into the village of My Lai (4) at about 0730 hours on 16 March 1968. The prosecution alleges that the accused was on the ground in and about the village of My Lai (4) from shortly after 0730 hours, 16 March 1968, until after Charlie Company moved from the village of My Lai (4) into a night laager position in the afternoon of 16 March 1968, as well as thereafter. The prosecution also alleges that Captain Medina was in radio contact throughout the operation with his platoons. It is contended that the accused was aware almost from the beginning of the operation that the units of his company were

* C.M. 427162 (1971).

receiving no hostile fire and in fact early in the morning ordered his men to conserve ammunition. The prosecution also contends that some time during the morning hours of 16 March 1968, the accused became aware that his men were improperly killing noncombatants. It is contended that this awareness arose because of the accused's observations, both by sight and hearing, and because of the conversation between Sgt. Minh and the accused. The prosecution contends this time of awareness on the part of the accused was at least at some time between 0930–1030 hours, 16 March 1968, if not earlier. The contention is further made that the accused, as Company Commander, had a continuing duty to control the activities of his subordinates where such activities were being carried out as part of an assigned military mission, and this became particularly true when he became aware that the military duties were being carried out by his men in an unlawful manner. The prosecution contends that Captain Medina, after becoming aware of the killing of noncombatants by his troops, declined to exercise his command responsibility by not taking necessary and reasonable steps to cause his troops to cease the killing of noncombatants. It is further contended by the prosecution that after the accused became aware of these acts of his subordinates and before he issued an order to cease fire, that a number of unidentified Vietnamese civilians were killed by his troops. The contention is made that Captain Medina did not issue a cease fire order until late in the morning and that when a cease fire order was in fact given, that the troops did cease their fire. It is the prosecution's contention that the accused was capable of controlling his troops throughout the operation, but that once learning he had lost control of his unit, he declined to regain control for a substantial period of time during which the deaths of unidentified Vietnamese civilians occurred. It is finally the prosecution's contention that since as a commander the accused, after actual awareness, had a duty to interfere, he may be held personally responsible because his unlawful inaction was the proximate cause of unlawful homicides by his men.

Contrary to the theory of the prosecution, the defense alleges that Captain Medina never became aware of the misconduct of his men until too late and immediately upon suspecting that his orders were being misunderstood and improper acts occurring, he ordered his men to cease fire. The accused contends that even though he was on the ground he stayed with his command post west of the village for tactical reasons and never saw any evidence of suspicious or unnecessary deaths until immediately prior to the cease fire order. He contends that he was aware of an artillery prep and double coverage of helicopter gunships, and that it was likely that some noncombatants might be killed by such protective fires. He believed that noncombatants, and particularly the women and children, would not be in the village on that particular morning. He contends that though he saw a few bodies near the vicinity of the village of My Lai (4), he believed these to be the results of the artillery and gunship fire. The accused contends that though he became aware that his troops were out of control, by the time of this awareness, the deaths had all occurred and it was too late to prevent what had occurred; but as soon as he became aware he did issue a cease fire order. He asserts that though there was some degree of volume of fire throughout the morning, he was aware that his men were under orders to kill the livestock in My Lai (4) and in the initial stages of the operation his men were advancing toward and through what he believed to be an area heavily infested with a well-armed enemy and his men were laying down a suppressive fire.

In relation to the question pertaining to the supervisory responsibility of a Company Commander, I advise you that as a general principle of military law and custom a military superior in command is responsible for and required, in the performance of his command duties, to make certain the proper performance by his subordinates of their duties as assigned by him. In other words, after taking action or issuing an order, a commander must remain alert and make timely adjustments as required by a changing situation. Furthermore, a commander is also responsible if he has actual knowledge that troops or other persons subject to his control are in the process of committing or are about to commit a war crime and he wrongfully fails to take the necessary and reasonable steps to insure compliance with the law of war. You will observe that these legal requirements placed upon a commander require actual knowledge plus a wrongful failure to act. Thus mere presence at the scene without knowledge will not suffice. That is, the commander-subordinate relationship alone will not allow an inference of knowledge. While it is not necessary that a commander actually see an atrocity being committed, it is essential that he know that his subordinates are in the process of committing atrocities or are about to commit atrocities.

Furthermore you are advised that the conduct of warfare is not wholly unregulated by law. Nations have agreed to treaties limiting warfare; and customary practices governing warfare have, over a period of time, become recognized by law as binding on the conduct of warfare. Some of these deal with the propriety of killing during the conduct of war activities. The killing of resisting or fleeing enemy forces is generally recognized as a justifiable act of war, and you may consider any such killing justifiable in this case. The law attempts to protect those persons not actually engaging in warfare, however, and limits the circumstances under which their lives may be taken.

Both combatants captured by and noncombatants detained by the opposing force, regardless of their loyalties, political views, or prior acts have the right to be treated as prisoners until released, confined, or executed in accordance with law and established procedures, by competent authority sitting in judgment of such detained or captured individuals. Summary execution of detainees or prisoners is forbidden by law. Further, it is clear under the evidence presented in this case, that hostile acts or support of enemy North Vietnamese or Viet Cong forces by inhabitants of My Lai (4) at sometime prior to 16 March 1968, would not justify the summary execution of all or a part of the occupants of My Lai (4) on 16 March 1968, nor would hostile acts committed that day, if, following the hostility, the belligerents either surrendered or were captured, and thus were under the control of our forces. I, therefore, instruct you, as a matter of law, that if unresisting human beings were killed at My Lai (4) while within the effective custody and control of our military forces, their deaths cannot be considered justified.

Considering the theories of the two parties and the general statements of legal principles pertaining to military law and customs and the law of war, you are now advised that the following is an exposition of the elements of the offense of involuntary manslaughter, an offense alleged to be in violation of Article 119 of the *Uniform Code of Military Justice.*

In order to find the accused guilty of this offense, you must be satisfied by legal and competent evidence beyond reasonable doubt, of the following four elements of that offense:

1. That an unknown number of unidentified Vietnamese persons, not less than 100, are dead;
2. That their deaths resulted from the omission of the accused in failing to exercise control over subordinates subject to his command after having gained knowledge that his subordinates were killing noncombatants, in or at the village of My Lai (4), Quahg Ngai Province, Republic of Vietnam, on or about 16 March 1968;
3. That this omission constituted culpable negligence; and
4. That the killing of the unknown number of unidentified Vietnamese persons, not less than 100, by subordinates of the accused and under his command, was unlawful.

You are again advised that the killing of a human being is unlawful when done without legal justification. [*]

[* See note 5, Essay on Limits of Law, supra.]

10. The Case Against Maj. Gen. Samuel W. Koster, Cong. Rec., 4 February 1971*

. . .

Mr. Stratton. Mr. Speaker, the Army made a very grave error last Friday when it dropped all the charges in connection with the Mylai massacre against Maj. Gen. Samuel W. Koster, the commanding general of the Americal Division in Vietnam at the time its subordinate units participated in the assault on Mylai 4 on March 16, 1968.

Dropping charges against the highest ranking officer involved, without any public trial or even discussion of the case against him, and doing so at a time when very grave charges involving the same incident against a junior officer in his command are still in the process of trial, can only result in serious damage to the reputation of the U.S. Army, to the United States, and to the effectiveness of the processes and procedures of military justice in dealing with matters which involve profound national and international concerns.

Mr. Speaker, I am afraid that this is a case where the ground rules of the mythical WPPA, the West Point Protective Association, have taken precedence over the welfare of the Nation and the fundamental right of the American people to know the facts: Never mind what happens to the Army or to the country, just make sure we keep our paid-up members out of embarrassment and hot water.

The dismissal of these charges is not only bad, but it has been carried out in a manner that purports to absolve the top military and civilian leadership of the Pentagon of all responsibility for this action by resting the decision on a single, obscure lieutenant general just a few hours away from retirement.

* Congressional Record, 4 February 1971, pp. H1725 *ff*.

Mr. Speaker, if this decision to drop the Koster charges is not rescinded—by the Army, by the Department of Defense, or by the President—then I predict it will rise up to haunt the entire Military Establishment in months to come, and may very likely end up doing even more serious damage to America's military posture and prestige than did the Army's original handling of the Mylai affair.

I concern myself with this case because for some 7 months last year I served as a member of a four-man congressional subcommittee which made an in depth survey of the whole Mylai incident. Our subcommittee report was issued unanimously on July 15, 1970, was widely hailed for its decisive tone at the time, and is still the most detailed public account in existence of what happened at Mylai, and how that incident was covered up within the Army and the State Department.

The basic point, which our subcommittee was well aware of—and which the Army's action in suddenly dropping all the charges against General Koster still completely fails to understand—is that the Mylai case is not just a strictly internal Army matter. It is a case that has caught the critical eye not only of the Nation but the whole world. And the handling and disposal of the Mylai case will directly affect not only the U.S. Army and the promotional status of its West Point trained generals, but the prestige of the Nation, and the confidence and respect —or rather the lack thereof—in which the American people hold the Army and their other military services. This is not just a question of who spends how many days in the brig for going AWOL. This is a case where the American people rightly insist on knowing the truth about Mylai—what went on there, why it happened, who was responsible for it, and what is going to be done about it.

This fact seemed to have been understood by the Army hierarchy in November 1969, when Secretary Resor and General Westmoreland, the Chief of Staff, took the most unusual step of appointing the Peers committee "to explore the nature and the scope of the original Army investigation of the so-called Mylai incident." They were charged with finding out how it took the top Army brass more than a year to find out what happened at Mylai, and then only as a result of a letter from a former GI long mustered out of the service. The Peers group worked hard and long and came up with a detailed report which was critical of the Army's conduct in this case.

Even more critical, and far more detailed in its published sections, was the report issued by the Hébert subcommittee of the Congress, sections of which I intend to quote as they relate to the strange case of General Koster.

General Koster was the commanding general of the U.S. Americal division in Vietnam in early 1968. As a result of the Peers investigation he was charged on seven counts of covering up the Mylai incident, or more specifically, of a "failure to obey lawful regulations and dereliction of duty" in failing to follow rules that require commanders to report any possible atrocities all the way up the chain of command. Following the lodging of these charges General Koster was relieved as Superintendent of West Point, and since 1969 has been serving on temporary duty at 1st Army Headquarters at Fort Meade in Maryland awaiting the disposition of his case. He testified before the Peers group on several occasions and twice before our Hébert subcommittee.

The statement regarding the dropping of the charges against General Koster was released on January 29. The statement said the decision to drop the charges had been made by Lt. Gen. Jonathan O. Seaman, 1st Army commander, "in the interest of justice," and because "they were not supported by the available evidence." In the case of two of the seven charges involved, however, General Seaman did find evidence to support the charge that General Koster "did not report civilian casualties at My-lai—4," and "did not insure a proper and thorough initial investigation of the reported civilian casualties." But considering the "long and honorable career of General Koster," the statement said, and because "the evidence did not show any intentional abrogation of responsibilities on the part of General Koster," the charges were dismissed.

Shortly after the public announcement of this decision, I issued the following statement:

> The decision of the Army to drop the charges against Major General Koster in the My Lai case is in my opinion a grave miscarriage of military justice.
>
> To drop the charges against the top officer responsible in this situation raises once again the whole question of a military whitewash.
>
> The decision to drop charges against a number of the enlisted men involved makes some sense in the light of the court martial verdicts in the Mitchell and the Hutto cases, but the crime of covering up the My Lai incident is an entirely different, and in my judgment much graver, charge. Our committee found plenty of evidence of what had taken place in this connection.
>
> If the Army system is either unwilling or unable to produce the facts and to punish the guilty in this case then I am inclined to feel that we do need some independent tribunal which will be higher and separate from the ordinary military-controlled court martial proceeding to make a final determination in this case.

The next day in the New York Times Mr. Robert MacCrate, a Wall Street lawyer who had served as special consultant to the Peers group, was quoted as calling the dropping of the charges "a serious disservice to the Army," because, he said, "charges are still pending against men who were within his command" at the time of the massacre.

Then a curious thing happened. That same day, January 30, an unidentified "Army spokesman" announced—in reply to a question—that at the time General Seaman informed General Koster of the dismissal of charges against him, he had also given him a "letter of censure—for his failure to report civilian casualties and to insure that the circumstances of these casualties were investigated promptly and thoroughly." The spokesman also indicated that further "adverse administrative action" might be taken against General Koster by the Secretary of the Army "if warranted."

One cannot help wondering why this censure action was not made public at the time the original announcement was made that charges were being dropped. Why was the impression given that General Koster was being let off completely free and clear? Was the Army perhaps waiting to test the public reaction to their decision to sweep the Koster case under the rug? It is perhaps possible that if there had been no adverse reaction—from Mr. MacCrate of the Peers group or from some member of the congressional investigating subcommittee—then the letter of censure, if indeed it ever existed, would have been torn up?

Actually, there is some question whether all this talk about dark administrative action lurking ahead has any meaning at all, once the really serious business, the formal court-martial charges, have been dropped. If General Koster is adjudged, through the curious processes of military justice on the opinion of one man, to be innocent of any "intentional abrogation of his responsibilities," then how can this process be meaningfully reversed by some unfavorable "administrative action" taken outside the scope of military justice?

Indeed the whole episide reveals one of the grave failings of the military judicial process. One man, in this case General Seaman, makes the crucial "grandjury" decision as to whether the evidence in a pending case in his comamnd is or is not substantial enough to proceed to trial. Yet the man who has the power to make this decision just happens to be the commanding officer in the area in which the individual charged just happens to be currently stationed—the northeastern United States, the First Army area. He has no special expertise in military justice. And he has no special knowledge of the alleged incident—which took place in Vietnam, not in Maryland. Yet he—and he alone—is empowered to make a decision, as in this case, on which the reputation and future of the whole Defense Establishment and even the country may depend. He, and he alone, is empowered to decide whether the issues involved are to be publicly aired, so that the people can judge the evidence themselves and weigh the fairness of the ultimate verdict; or whether the matter is to be swept under the rug, the record locked, and nothing more than a meaningless slap on the wrist administered to the highest ranking officer involved.

Such powers of decision might be appropriate in the case of a soldier who gets drunk off duty and goes AWOL. They are out of place in a case that has aroused the profound national and international concern that Mylai has aroused. We ought to change this procedure and change it swiftly.

Actually, I think we have to recognize that there is some question whether General Seaman is really the culprit in this Koster dismissal action or in somebody else's fall guy. It hardly makes sense to suppose that the Army hierarchy, the Secretary and the Chief of Staff, would have been so deeply concerned about Mylai and a possible Mylai coverup in November 1969, that they would go to the unusual step of creating a special Peers group to make a thorough investigation of the incident; and then, a year later allow one obscure officer—whose only claim to authority is that he happens to be in the right place at the right time—to blow the whole case on his own say so.

I just cannot honestly believe that General Seaman made the decision to drop the charges against General Koster on his own and without any reference to the Pentagon. The precise reverse is probably true. The Pentagon must have decided to let General Koster off the hook, even while subordinates were still being tried on far more serious charges, probably because they feared that a full, public airing of the charges against Koster and of his incredible mismanagement of his command would make the Army look very, very bad. They probably figured that the furor over Mylai had died down, that people were getting bored with the grisly details, and that nobody would really care very much what happened to General Koster anyway. Things would stand or fall, I suppose they reasoned, on the outcome of the Calley case. He was already building up a lot of sympathy. And as long as they went through the motions of prosecuting the coverup aspects of the case with Colonel Henderson—and rubbing off as much of the blame as possible on Lieutenant Colonel Barker, who is dead—that should take care of the matter and none of the tarnish would have to rub off on any of the general officers.

So General Seaman was instructed to let Koster go, I am inclined to believe, and sweep the Koster case under the rug. After all, General Seaman was on the verge of retiring, so he had nothing to lose himself. In fact his retirement was originally scheduled for February 1, but on January 26 orders were issued extending him to March 1 and possibly later. The action with regard to the dropping of the Koster charges was announced 3 days after the order delaying General Seaman's retirement was issued. Perhaps all this is purely coincidental. The Army claims the delay was solely because General Seaman's relief is ill and is now in Walter Reed hospital. Maybe so; but the whole situation smells, and the usual procedure, when a relief is ill, is to go ahead and designate another relief. Was the Pentagon perhaps forced to twist General Seaman's arm a little bit, before letting him go off to a comfortable retirement, to get him to perform the ultimate coverup action in an already tragic coverup case? The circumstances make such a conclusion almost inescapable.

After all, let us not forget that it is the coverup aspects of the Mylai case that have been the most damaging to the reputation of the American military high command. What happened at Mylai on March 16 could have been an aberration of men already bent under all the pressures and tensions of combat. But the failure of the facts about Mylai to surface to the Army high command for more than a whole year, either in Vietnam or in Washington, raises grave questions about the reliability, honor, and integrity of top command officers.

Otherwise, why create a Peers panel in the first place? Yet having created it, and having allowed it to operate in great depth for over 7 months, the Army now suddenly throws all of its work down the drain by blocking a public trial of the commanding general of the division involved. And all on the personal opinion of one man. No report, no summary, no reasoning.

If General Koster were so blameless in the Mylai case, then why not hold the trial and let him exonerate himself publicly? The letter of censure makes it clear that he is not lily white. But what the letter of censure has accomplished—and that apparently is what was most important to the Army's top leadership—is that the general's case will at least stay out of the papers. The public and the public interest be damned.

. . .

11. *United States* v. *Calley,* 46 C.M.R 1131 (ACMR 1973)

. . .

Opinion and Action on Petition for New Trial

ALLEY, JUDGE:

In much publicized proceedings, appellant was convicted by general court-martial of three specifications of premeditated murder and one of assault with intent to commit murder in violation of Articles 118 and 134, Uniform Code of Military Justice, 10 USC §§ 918 and 934, respectively. He was sentenced to dismissal, forfeiture of all pay and allowances, and confinement at hard labor for life. The convening authority approved dismissal and the forfeitures, but reduced the period of confinement to twenty years. The offenses were committed by First Lieutenant William L. Calley when he was performing as a platoon leader during an airmobile operation in the subhamlet of My Lai (4) in Son My village, Quang Ngai Province, Republic of South Vietnam, on 16 March 1968. Although all charges could have been laid as war crimes, they were prosecuted under the UCMJ. *See* paragraph 507b, Field Manual 27–10, The Law of Land Warfare (1956).

Appellate defense counsel have presented thirty-one assignments of error and a petition for new trial. For clarity our opinion will consolidate those assignments which warrant discussion under the broad headings of jurisdiction, publicity, command influence, composition of the court-martial, sufficiency of the evidence, discovery and subpoenas, and petition for new trial.

. . .

III. Command Influence

Appellant's trial and appellate defense counsel have raised allegations of unlawful command influence infecting the entire proceedings, including an unprecedented challenge to this Court's authority and capability to render an impartial decision. Confident of our ability to carry out the responsibilities given us by Article 66 of the Uniform Code of Military Justice we turn to the more serious allegations. . . .

The isolated issue of unlawful influence may be subdivided into three topics warranting discussion: A, whether the Army Chief of Staff at the time of trial, General William C. Westmoreland, was an accuser under the Code, and, if so, whether the convening authority, who was junior to him, lawfully convened the court-martial; B, whether the investigation, preferral and referral of charges, and conduct of the court-martial were free from unlawful command influence; C, whether the court members were prejudicially influenced by statements made by superiors about the My Lai incident.

Appellate defense counsel have recited several generalizations about command influence with which we readily agree—the appearance of command influence gives rise to a presumption of prejudice; unlawful command influence is to be condemned as a denial of military due process; we may look outside the record of trial for evidence of unlawful influence; and military appellate courts are sensitive to the issue. Granting the validity of these general principles, the facts and circumstances of the instant case will dictate our resolution of the issue.

A. In a novel argument, it is contended that Major General Orwin C. Talbott, who served in the dual position of Commanding General, United States Army Infantry Center and Commandant, United States Army Infantry School, Fort Benning, Georgia, was rendered ineligible as convening authority because General William C. Westmoreland, who at the time charges against Lieutenant Calley were referred to trial was serving as the Chief of Staff, United States Army, and at the time of the alleged offenses commanded United States Military Assistance Command, Vietnam, and its service component United States Army, Vietnam, was an "accuser" superior in rank and command to Major General Talbott. General Westmoreland, appellant claims, was an accuser as one who had an interest other than official. He was personally interested in appellant's conviction, the claim proceeds, because he faced possible criminal liability himself should the doctrine of commander responsibility recognized in *In re* Yamashita, 327 US 1 (1945), be extended to United States troop and commanders' conduct in Vietnam; [18] and because his public utterances

[18] Although the *Yamashita* case has engendered much discussion about a commander's responsibility for the conduct of his troops it should be remembered that the Opinion

demonstrated an interest more fervid than the merely official in the enforcement of measures he instituted as senior commander in Vietnam for the prevention and reporting of war crimes.

Our opinion is that Major General Talbott was not incapacitated from convening the general court-martial which convicted Lieutenant Calley even assuming General Westmoreland was an accuser within the meaning of Article 1(9).

. . .

B. *Pretrial Processing.* Trial defense counsel, in support of requests for subpoenas and motions for discovery, suggested that the decision to prosecute Lieutenant Calley might have been made by the President and that this information might have been passed down the chain of command to those who preferred, investigated, and referred the charges against the appellant. The result, defense counsel contend, is that command control infects the entire pretrial proceedings leading to appellant's court-martial and that, at least, the appearance of evil and cumulative effect of the actions of superiors require reversal of his conviction. We disagree.

Shortly after the court-martial commenced, the defense raised command influence issues, citing news magazine and other second-hand reports as the factual basis. Trial counsel vehemently protested that reports of this type, unverified and speculative, were an insufficient basis for requiring the Government to respond and prove the negative—that no unlawful influence was exerted. Judge Kennedy disagreed with trial counsel, and told him:

> . . . [Y]ou better be prepared when you come in here . . . to show by live witnesses whether or not there has been influence on any commanders here at Fort Benning to prefer any charges against Lieutenant Calley. I think the issue is raised squarely by the statements, if true, that the defense has previously introduced in these proceedings, the quotes from *Time* magazine and *Life* and others as to the interest of the President, the Secretary of Defense and the Secretary of the Army. . . . When there is a specter of command influence, the government must dispel it.

Following the directions of the military judge, the Government presented the testimony of the staff judge advocate at Fort Benning, Colonel Robert M. Lathrop; the executive officer of the Student Brigade (the unit having immediate military justice jurisdiction over Lieutenant Calley), who swore as accuser to the initial charge, Lieutenant Colonel Henry E. Vincent; the legal officer for the Student Brigade, who was the accuser on

---

of the Court expressly stated that the evidence was not being appraised but that the Court was only deciding whether the military commission had jurisdicion and the charge alleged a cognizable offense.

the Additional Charge, Captain William R. Hill; the commander of the Student Brigade, who forwarded the charges with a recommendation of general court-martial, Lieutenant Colonel Frank L. Garrison; the commanding general of Fort Benning for the period 11 August to 9 September 1969; Brigadier General Oscar E. Davis; and the commanding general of Fort Benning from 9 September 1969 through the completion of appellant's court-martial, Major General Orwin C. Talbott. These witnesses rendered the following composite narrative of the processing of the allegations against Lieutenant Calley:

In early August 1969 the staff judge advocate first heard of the case upon being called by the deputy chief of staff at Fort Benning, who asked whether he recognized the name "Pinkville." Soon after, an advance copy of the following letter, dated 6 August 1969, was received by the commanding general, Fort Benning from the Office of the Inspector General in Washington.

To: Commanding General
US Army Infantry Center and Fort Benning
Fort Benning, Georgia 21905

1. The Inspector General has received testimony which indicates that acts in violation of the Uniform Code of Military Justice may have been committed by 1LT William L. Calley, a member of your command.
2. The testimony which involved LT Calley was taken 16 July 1969 in Terre Haute, Indiana, from Mr. Paul D. Meadlo, formerly a member of the Army. A copy of this testimony is furnished at Inclosure 1. The Provost Marshal General, Headquarters, Department of the Army, will provide additional information as acquired.
3. This matter is referred to you for information and action deemed appropriate.

By telecommunication (TWX) from the Adjutant General, Department of Army, Fort Benning was informed on 13 August 1969 that Lieutenant Calley could not be retained on active duty beyond 6 September 1969 unless he continued to be under investigation which would lead to court-martial charges. Colonel Lathrop thereupon requested the Office of the Inspector General to give a more detailed briefing, as he felt that evidence available at Fort Benning was insufficient to warrant such action.

A Colonel Wilson from the Inspector General's Office did conduct a briefing at Fort Benning on 19 August. The chief of staff, the staff judge advocate and two members of his office, the commander and legal officer of the Student Brigade, a local representative of the criminal investigation division, and some members of the Fort Benning public information office attended. These officers were informed of the Ridenhour letter which triggered the IG investigation, the organization of Task Force Barker, and the alleged events of 16 March 1968 as had been so far discovered. Colonel Wilson also told them that further investigation had been assumed by the Criminal Investigation Division. All witnesses who were present at this briefing stated that Colonel Wilson did not give or relay any instructions as to what disposition to make of the allegations.

After consulting with his staff judge advocate and chief of staff, who had attended the briefing, General Davis decided that Lieutenant Calley would be continued on active duty pending final disposition of the investigation. A message was sent to the Department of Army advising of this decision.

Colonel Lathrop, the staff judge advocate, then took several actions: he dispatched his Chief of Military Justice, Captain Hammett, to interview former Private First Class Meadlo; he established liaison with the criminal investigation division at Fort Benning to obtain information; he made a trip to the Office of The Judge Advocate General in Washington where he discussed the drafting of the original specifications and other matters; and he caused to be forwarded on 25 August 1969 the official notification of the alleged incident to the Student Brigade.

Upon receipt of the documents forwarded by the staff judge advocate the Student Brigade assigned its executive officer to make a preliminary inquiry. Lieutenant Colonel Vincent obtained several additional statements and discussed the possible number of victims with Captain Hill, the brigade legal officer, and Captain Hammett from the staff judge advocate's office. On the afternoon of 4 September 1969 or early on 5 September, Lieutenant Colonel Vincent decided that there was sufficient evidence to sign as accuser the draft charge sheet received the day before. After requesting the Fort Benning Chief of staff to make available a qualified officer to conduct an Article 32 investigation, the Student Brigade appointed Lieutenant Colonel Cameron to that duty on 5 September.

Communication between Colonel Lathrop and the Office of The Judge Advocate General for informational and technical purposes had remained open. Sometime in late August or early September Colonel Lathrop received a call from Colonel Chilcoat, Chief of Military Justice in the Office of The Judge Advocate General, who stated without giving reasons, "Do nothing until you hear from us." On 4 September Colonel Lathrop received another call to the effect, "It's all yours." He also remembered hearing from someone in the Office of The Judge Advocate General that the matter had gone at some time to San Clemente, where the President was staying. However, there is no evidence that this information was relayed by Colonel Lathrop to the accuser, Lieutenant Colonel Vincent.

In the normal course of his duties in preparing the initial charges with the assistance of the staff judge advocate's office, Captain Hill, the Student Brigade legal officer, had heard that the investigation had apparently gone to the President. However, it was his speculative conclusion after discussion with some younger judge advocates that Presidential interest, if any, would mean the case would *not* be charged because of political repercussions. These young officers decided that one of them would nevertheless prefer charges against Lieutenant Calley if "coverup" attempts occurred.

Captain Hill was later asked by the commander of the Student Brigade to read some additional statements that had been received and to decide whether to prefer an Additional Charge if he felt it was warranted. On 12 September 1969 Captain Hill did swear to the Additional Charge as accuser. This new allegation was also referred to Lieutenant Colonel Cameron for investigation under Article 32.

After granting several defense requests for delay the Article 32 investigating officer conducted an extensive investigation, recommending on 6 November 1969 trial by general court-martial. The Article 32 report was forwarded by the Student Brigade commander to the commanding general with a strong concurring recommendation of trial by general court-martial.

The charge sheets, Article 32 investigation, and pretrial advice by his staff judge advocate were presented to Major General Talbott on 20 November. He stated that he read the lengthy report more than once from cover to cover, discussed the allegations with his staff judge advocate, and thought about it a great deal. On 24 November 1969 he referred the charges to trial by general court-martial, having based his decision "solely on my judgment, on the principles of the law, and the Article 32 investigation."

All of the officers required to make a decision or recommendation in the processing of the charges against Lieutenant Calley testified that they did not receive, directly or indirectly, any instructions as to an appropriate disposition of the case. . . .

On the question of command influence during the pretrial processing of charges the defense did call Colonel Jim D. Kiersey, the Chief of Staff of the U. S. Army Infantry Center, Fort Benning. Colonel Kiersey served all three generals who were participants in processing the instant case. Colonel Kiersey's earliest contact with Lieutenant Calley's case was 23 July 1969 when he received advice from Colonel Wilson, Inspector General investigator, not to reassign the appellant, a circumstance which Colonel Kiersey indicated would only occur with Department of Army approval in any instance. In early August he was asked at home by General Forsythe, then his commander, whether he knew anything about "Pinkville," as the general had been called by General Coates, the Information Officer in Washington. The first definite information he remembers coming to Fort Benning was the Meadlo statement from the Inspector General's Office. After the TWX concerning the retention of Lieutenant Calley on active duty was received, Colonel Kiersey stated he remarked to the staff judge advocate "if this was all we had, that we had no reason to retain Lieutenant Calley." The briefing from Colonel Wilson was therefore requested and held. A short time later Colonel Kiersey received a call from General Reid, his counterpart at Third Army Headquarters, Fort McPherson, Georgia (who undoubtedly saw the referral of testimony from The Adjutant General relaying the direction from Continental Army Command not to place the lieutenant in pretrial confinement and to hold up decisions because additional information may be forthcoming). Colonel Kiersey testified General Reid again called on 4 or 5 September and said, "It's your action. You are not receiving any instructions." Freely admitting these points of contact with other Army offices and headquarters, Colonel Kiersey also avowed he did not receive instructions at any time from these contacts about how to dispose of the case; he made no recommendations; and he had no knowledge of any instructions ever being given to any of the commanding generals. The Chief of Staff, Third Army, was kept advised only of the dates when Lieutenant Calley was granted leave.

After hearing the testimony just summarized, examining the allied papers and the appellate exhibits relating to the pretrial processing, and giving the defense access to the relevant personal notes of the staff judge advocate on the processing of the charges, the military judge declared: "At this point there is absolutely no evidence that these people [the President, Secretary of Defense, Secretary of Army, General Westmoreland] in any way communicated with any of the commanders down here." Thus, the military judge denied requests for subpoenas of these persons subject to permitting the defense to make a further showing. He strongly suggested that the defense interview officials in the Department of Defense and investigate its naked allegations.

Six months later defense counsel renewed their claim of command influence and requests for subpoenas, and made additional discovery motions. However, the military judge was only presented with one additional germ of evidence. A letter from the Chief of Legislative Liaison, Department of Army, dated 5 September 1969, to the Honorable L. Mendel Rivers, Chairman of the House Armed Services Committee, contained the following paragraph:

> The investigation continues however, it has revealed sufficient information to warrant the preferring of charges against a Lieutenant Calley, former Platoon Leader in the unit, for violation of the Uniform Code of Military Justice, Article 118, Murder. The information is in the hands of Lieutenant Calley's Commanding Officer at Fort Benning, Georgia and it is anticipated that charges may be preferred not later than 6 September.

On 15 July 1970 the House Armed Services Committee released the report of its Investigating Subcommittee on the My Lai incident. The introduction contained the sentence:

> By a letter dated September 5th, the Department of the Army advised that, while its investigation was continuing, charges would be preferred against Lt. William L. Calley not later than September 6th.

The transition from "charges *may* be preferred" to "charges *would* be preferred" provided fuel for the defense speculation of improper command influence.

The military judge was unmoved by this shred of evidence and announced:

> . . . I'll give you the opportunity, as I did before, to talk to anyone of the people in Washington, the offices that handled, who handled this correspondence, and if after talking with them, you still are not satisfied that there is no command control exercised by any of those people whose offices appear there, or they won't discuss it with you to your satisfaction, if you want them subpoenaed, I'll consider the issuance of the subpoena. I think it is incumbent upon the defense to do something about it instead of just merely speculate that there may have been some type of command control, and this letter, to me, doesn't show it at all. . . . But once again, I offer to the defense the offer to talk to General Westmoreland, General Parker, any person in Washington who had any dealings with this case prior to the time the charges were preferred, and if you're not satisfied with the answers that you receive from them, or you believe the answers are evasive, or you want him placed under oath, we'll take steps so that you can obtain sworn testimony, whether it be down here, or whether it be done by deposition, as you decide at that time. I don't believe that I can go beyond that.

Trial defense counsel further argued command influence on 13 October 1970. Once again they had declined to avail themselves of the invitation to talk to those alleged to have influenced appellant's pretrial proceedings and had failed to unearth any evidence of unlawful command control. Primarily because of the lack of defense efforts to litigate the issue, the military judge made no direct ruling on the general claim of command influence. He did declare, in view of unsupported impugnings of the Chief of Staff of the Army:

> I find specifically that General Westmoreland did not attempt to influence anyone in the military chain of command in the trial of Lieutenant Calley, that is, thus far. [13 October 1970]

Considering the entire record, including the evidence recounted above, we find no merit to the claim of improper command influence.

There is simply no showing that anyone's decision to prosecute was affected by factors other than the evidence presented to those persons at Fort Benning whose duties required making decisions in the case. The accuser upon the initial charge was unaware of any actions and desires on the part of superiors in Washington; the accuser upon the Additional Charge anticipated that influence, if any should be exerted, would be *not* to pursue court-martial proceedings. The defense expressly declined to call the commander who had immediate military justice jurisdiction over Lieutenant Calley during much of the pretrial processing. The impartiality of the Article 32 officer was stipulated. The forwarding officer who recommended general court-martial was untainted by instructions or knowledge of superiors' desires. The convening authority who referred the case for trial confined the basis for his decision to the file presented to him. He was neither the recipient nor author of any instructions as to any mandated disposition.

The record reveals only that the staff judge advocate and chief of staff at Fort Benning communicated with superior headquarters and that they, but *not* the persons preferring, investigating, or referring, were once requested to hold up processing until further notice. This notice, when received, was the neutral comment, "It's all yours." The argument that communications by staff officers and higher headquarters and through technical channels taints the decision makers denigrates the role of staff officers and commanders. To be meritorious, such an argument would at least have to rest on misrepresentation by staff officers or a showing of other than official conduct.

The most extraordinary action taken by the staff judge advocate at Fort Benning was the seeking of assistance through technical channels in person and not by written or telephonic communication. Colonel Lathrop explained his trip to Washington by describing the case as unusual, which it was. He had questions about the drafting of specifications because of the unnamed victims, uncertain number of victims, and the propriety of laying the charge under Article 134, UCMJ, 10 USC § 934, as alleged violations of the laws of war, rather than premeditated murder under Article 118, UCMJ, 10 USC § 918. Colonel Lathrop stated he also wanted to discuss the possibility of trials of former servicemen because of the bearing this might have in considering grants of immunity to witnesses. We do not find in the record any evidence rebutting Colonel Lathrop's stated purposes and certainly no evidence that he served as a conduit for instructions from Washington to the decision makers at Fort Benning. Neither was Colonel Kiersey, the chief of staff at Fort Benning, a relayer of orders. His communication with his counterpart at Third Army mainly related to the pretrial status of Lieutenant Calley, which we note was remarkably unrestrained for one accused of multiple premeditated murder.

Undeniably officials in Washington had information about the My Lai incident and military officers in the Department of Army contacted officers at Fort Benning. The very fact that the information that launched the investigation into the My Lai incident was mailed to members of Congress and his ranking Defense Department officials made necessary some action on the part of the leadership in the military establishment. The Army Chief of Staff initiated an investigation by the Office of the Inspector

General, the results of which led to the return of Lieutenant Calley from his extended tour in the Republic of South Vietnam before its scheduled expiration. This and subsequent inquiries by Army agencies were not limited to the actions of appellant, but also included probing into the conduct of many others in the Americal Division. Given the genesis of the My Lai inquiry, it is apparent that the Department of the Army would have communicated in some fashion with the immediate commanders of those involved. *A failure to act would have been an evasion of responsibility under domestic and international law*. [Emphasis added.]

From cataloguing the points of contact between officials at Fort Benning and the Department of the Army and the statements of high government officials about the My Lai incident, appellate defense counsel assert that the cumulative effect and appearance of evil created by all this activity requires reversal. This argument if carried to its logical extension is tantamount to asserting that Lieutenant Calley or any other person subject to the Code whose case attracts national interest or is of national significance may not be brought to trial. This we cannot accept. The facts and circumstances in the instant case are not convincing that communications between Fort Benning and Washington were outside the sphere of official interest. . . . The nature of the allegations and the supporting documents in the possession of those called upon to make decisions in the case were such as inevitably would have led to the preferral of charges against Lieutenant Calley and referral to trial by general court-martial.

C. The final claim of unlawful command influence is that publicized statements of policy and factual conclusions made by the President of the United States, Secretary of State, Secretary of Defense, Secretary of Army, and the Chief of Staff prejudicially influenced the court members toward returning findings of guilty against Lieutenant Calley. This assignment of error is not supported in the record.

The following remarks of Government officials are presented to us by counsel as leading "to an inescapable conclusion that it was the policy, dictated from on high, to *try* and *convict* and *punish* the participants in the alleged My Lai incident in order to cleanse the Army of any guilt."

Transcript of President Nixon's News Conference as Recorded by the New York Times on 9 December 1969

"Q. In your opinion, was what happened at My Lai a massacre, an alleged massacre, or what was it, and what do you think can be done to prevent things like this? And if it was a massacre, do you think it was justifiable on military or other grounds?

"A. Well, trying to answer all of those questions, in sorting it out, I would start first with this statement: What appears was certainly a massacre, and under no circumstances was it justified. One of the goals we are fighting for in Vietnam is to keep the people from South Vietnam from having imposed upon them a Government which has atrocity against civilians as one of its policies, and we cannot ever condone or use atrocities against civilians in order to accomplish that goal.

"Now when you used the word 'alleged,' that is only proper in terms of the individual involved. Under our system a man is not guilty until proved to be so. And there are several individuals involved here who will be tried by military courts, and consequently we should say 'alleged' as far as they are concerned until they are proved guilty.

"As far as this kind of activity is concerned, I believe it is an isolated incident. Certainly within this Administration we are doing everything possible to find out whether it was isolated, and so far our investigation indicates that it was. And as far as the future is concerned, I would only add this one point: Looking at the other side of the coin, we have a million, two hundred thousand Americans who have been in Vietnam. Forty thousand of them have given their lives.

"Virtually all of them have helped the people of Vietnam in one way or another. They built roads and schools, they built churches and pagodas. The Marines alone this year have built over 50,000 churches, pagodas and temples for the people of Vietnam. And our soldiers in Vietnam and sailors and airmen this year alone contributed three-quarters of a million dollars to help the people of South Vietnam.

"Now this record of generosity, of decency, must not be allowed to be smeared and slurred because of this kind of an incident. That's why I'm going to do everything I possibly can to see that all the facts in this incident are brought to light, and that those who are charged, if they are found guilty, are punished, because if it is isolated it is against our policy and we shall see to it that what these men did—if they did it—does not smear the decent men that have gone to Vietnam in a very, in my opinion, important cause.

Interview with the Honorable William P. Rogers, Secretary of State, for National Educational Television Network, Wednesday, November 26, 1969

"Mr. Niven: I think enough has been said in the press in the last two or three days about the alleged massacre of Vietnamese civilians, that probably enough has been done to prejudice the court-martial proceedings more than they should be, but in general these things have come and gone before, there was the Green Beret case which was dropped and others. Isn't one of the worst things about this kind of a dirty, jungle war that it brutalizes large numbers of young Americans?

"SECRETARY ROGERS: Yes, I don't think there is any way to deny that. I think that if the allegations are true, it is a shocking, shocking incident and all we can do is to court-martial any responsible persons and to show the world that we don't condone this. Obviously, if anything of this kind happened, it is in direct contradiction of the others.

"MR. NIVEN: As you know, it is big news in Europe, almost bigger than here. Are you getting much heat diplomatically about it?

"SECRETARY ROGERS: Well, we haven't gotten much heat diplomatically. We don't need much heat. It is a tragic event, if it is true. And certainly there is indication of some truth at least. So we are highly concerned; it is a shocking thing.

"The Washington Star on 26 November 1969 reported:

"The testimony of [Secretary of the Army] Resor and Army General Counsel Robert E. Jordan III also comes a day after the release of a letter on the case from Defense Secretary Melvin R. Laird to Senate Foreign Relations Committee Chairman J. William Fulbright, D-Ark. "Laird said he was 'shocked and sick' when he first heard allegations of the massacre, but he said, it would be improper for him to comment on the specific allegations or on the individuals allegedly involved.

" 'This matter first came to my attention in early April,' Laird said. 'I immediately looked into it and shortly thereafter a full investigation was launched by the Army.

" 'I want to make clear, Mr. Chairman, beyond any doubt, that the Nixon administration is determined to insure absolute compliance with our orders and with the laws of war.

" 'I also want to make clear, Mr. Chairman, that the Nixon administration program of Vietnamization . . . is the primary mission of the United States forces in Vietnam.' "

Secretary of the Army Resor Press Conference, 26 November 1969

"It is difficult to convey the feelings of shock and dismay which I and other civilian and military leaders of the Army have experienced as the apparent tragedy of My Lai has gradually unfolded before us. I know all Americans share these emotions and fully appreciate the gravity of the alleged incident.

"I have reviewed the incident at My Lai with a number of officers who have served in Vietnam. It is their judgment—a judgment which I completely endorse and share—that what allegedly occurred at My Lai is wholly unrepresentative of the manner in which our forces conduct military operations in Vietnam. I am convinced that the overall record of the hundreds of thousands of American soldiers who have participated in combat operations in Vietnam is one of deceny [sic], consideration and restraint toward the civilians who find themselves in a zone of military operations."

General William C. Westmoreland Press Conference, Charlotte, North Carolina, 9 December 1969

"*Q:* General, have any new instructions been issued to the men in Vietnam as a result of the My Lai massacre?

"*A:* I don't believe new instructions have been issued, except the instructions that had been previously issued were re-emphasized. At least a recent report from Vietnam indicates that they have taken extraordinary steps to re-emphasize our previous instructions. But I know of no change because the instructions were rather clear.

"*Q:* General, has the special Army panel that's investigating that alleged massacre developed any evidence of an earlier, lower-level cover up?

"*A:* Of course, General Peers and his group—General Peers is also assisted by a very distinguished New York attorney—are in the process of the investigation. They have made no report to me so I do not know what they've turned up.

"*Q:* Do you believe there's been excessive news coverage of this?

"*A:* Well, I don't know whether I'd call it excessive. Needless to say, it's been rather complete news coverage. Many young men who have been involved have been interviewed over television and radio and by reporters and so a great deal of what took place has been made known to the American public, as reported by these individuals. However, how much of this information is hearsay, how much is factual, is another matter; the individuals, who have committed offenses, after appropriate investigation "has been made, of course, will be charged, and if the charges are supported by further investigation, known as a Form 32 investigation, as provided by the Uniformed [sic] Code of Military Justice, they will be court-martialed and they will be appropriately represented by counsel and of course the court will proceed, as any court proceeds where only admissable [sic] evidence will be allowed and all witnesses will have a chance to be cross-examined. In other words, the law of the land which pertains in this case, namely the Uniformed [sic] Code of Military Justice will be followed and the individuals will be given justice. Whether or not this publicity that has been given which has been quite wide spread and very intensive in the last several weeks, will jeopardize a fair trial, I do not know. I think there are mixed opinions in this regard.

"*Q:* General, aside from the My Lai, Senator Kennedy said last week that evidence before his subcommittee on refugees indicated that there may have been as many as 1 million Vietnamese civilians killed so far—casualties so far. Perhaps 300 thousand have been killed and the majority of those Senator Kennedy said by American and South Vietnamese forces. Do you think those figures are correct?

"*A:* I have absolutely no evidence to support figures of that magnitude. It is my opinion that they are tremendously exaggerated based on my four and one half years in Vietnam where extraordinary steps were taken to avoid civilian casualties. There have been many civilian casualties. Some accidental and no doubt many innocent victims have been victims of a battle. This has happened in all wars and this war is no exception, but never in all history have commanders given such extraordinary attention to controlling their fires. It is standing orders that fire "will be used with descrimination [sic]. The clearance procedures were in some cases so time-consuming that we suffered casualties by virtue of these precautionary measures.

"*Q:* I think we all recognize that this is a very unconventional war compared to what we have had in our past history, but can you tell us if there is ever any military justification for eliminating civilians—women and children, as might have happened here?

"*A:* No, unless they were armed and were combatants. There have been cases where women have been armed and where women have killed our soldiers. There have also been cases where young boys have thrown grenades and implanted booby traps and actually served as combatants. These are not unusual, but at the same time, I wouldn't say they are commonplace. But unless they are armed and jeopardize the safety of our troops where a matter of self-defense comes in to play, I would say there is no justification for it whatsoever, and it's contrary to the rules of land warfare which has always governed the conduct of our troops on the battlefield. And strictly contrary to regulations and contrary to the instructions that were issued to the troops in Vietnam."

General Westmoreland was also quoted by the New York Times on 7 December 1969:

> FORT CAMPBELL, KY., DEC. 6 (AP)—Gen. William C. Westmoreland, Chief of Staff of the Army, has declared that an unlawful order from a superior 'does not excuse or justify one of our soldiers in killing an innocent' civilian.

In our considering the fair and reasonable interpretation and impact of these publicized statements, a review of the relevant *voir dire* of the court members is appropriate.

Colonel Ford, the president of the court-martial, was placed under the military judge's order to refrain from reading about the case prior to the time these statements were released to the public. He and Captain Salem, who was on duty in Alaska when he first heard about My Lai, were not queried during *voir dire* as to whether they heard or read public statements of Government officials. Major Bierbaum, upon examination by defense counsel, did not remember reading any statements attributable to the President, Secretary of Defense, Secretary of Army, or members of Congress regarding the My Lai incident.

Major Kinard did not remember any specific statements by the President, Secretary of Defense, or Secretary of Army. When pressed by assistant individual defense counsel, he did connect the use of the word "massacre" with the President but did not recall its context and stated that this remembrance would have no influence on his performance as a court member. Major McIntosh did not hear any remarks by the President but remembered a statement by the Secretary of Defense. He responded negatively to individual defense counsel's question whether he would be affected by statements of high officials to the effect that the prosecution must ensure protecting the image of the Army. Major Brown heard that the President had made a statement but could not recall its content. When asked by individual defense counsel if it sounded similar to, "Lieutenant Calley had to be charged and prosecuted in this case, that the image of the Army should not be tarnished and that the other members of the Army, their character, should not be colored by the evidence of this case," Major Brown answered yes. However, he answered negatively to a question whether such a statement by the President, Secretary of Defense, or Secretary of Army would influence him, and also to the question, "Have you heard anybody in the chain of command senior to you in any position of influence to your future in the Army say anything about this case?"

Influence in the air, so to speak, is a contradiction in terms. An object and effect upon the object must be identified for influence to exist. The *voir dire* facially suffices to rebut a claim of influence due to statements by higher officials. Appellate defense counsel correctly assert that self-proclaimed impartiality by jurors need not, and in some instances should not, be accepted. United States v Zagar, 5 USCMA 410, 18 CMR 34 (1955). However, there is no reason to gainsay *voir dire* responses that a member was not aware of or cannot recall prior expressions by officials, or responses which evince that a member's recollection of an expression is so general or remote as to be easily disregarded. At trial no showing was made that the court members were or felt they were under pressure from higher authority to return any particular finding. Of the members who sat, only Colonel Ford and Major Brown were challenged for cause by trial defense counsel on grounds relating to pretrial publicity. No challenges were expressly based upon the purported grounds about which the defense now complains.

We find as a matter of fact that the statements made by the President, Secretary of State, Secretary of Defense, Secretary of Army, and Chief of Staff had no influence on the court members. Further, the statements made by these officials are not of the kind previously found by military appellate courts to have been generative of unlawful command influence.

Written directives and lectures to prospective court members containing suggestions of the desires and prerogatives of the convening authority, the relationship between performance as a court member and efficiency reports, and the announcement of specific local or service policies inimical to accused persons in general or individually, have long been condemned. . . . The evil of these practices is their tendency to inhibit members in the full and free exercise of that discretion with which they are vested by the Code. Press releases or prior discussions of individual cases by high officials do not *per se* cause the same evil.

The offenses committed at My Lai (4) are not the first to have generated public statements by high-ranking military officers. In United States v Carter, 9 USCMA 108, 25 CMR 370 (1958), the multiple rape of a fifteen year old German girl by seven American enlisted men prompted comments by the Commander-in-Chief of the U. S. Army in Europe before an Ambassador-Army Commanders conference. His remarks, which contained references to this incident among others and called for the elimination of serious incidents between our soldiers and German citizens, were distributed to lower commands with a forwarding letter by the Commanding General of Seventh Army. The Court of Military Appeals, even presuming that the court members had read the documents, found no prejudice in view of the general character of remarks, the lack of direct relationship between the author and the selection of court members, the absence of a fixed opinion as to the facts of culpability of any specific individual, and the responsibility of the General to take some action to prevent future criminal conduct and to soothe "the strain so apparently put upon relations between the two countries by the crimes of this period." Id., at 113. In United States v Hurt, 9 USCMA 735, 27 CMR 3 (1958), the rape and felony murder of a five year old Okinawan girl, for which an Army sergeant was charged, induced Major General Moore, Commander of the Ryukyus Command and Deputy Governor of the Ryukyu Islands, to call a special meeting of the Ryukyuan-American Community Relations Advisory Council at which he expressed his abhorrence of recent child rape incidents and stated that appropriate legal actions were being taken. These remarks were published by the local press, as were responses of the civilian community leaders and interviews with two staff judge advocates regarding court-martial procedure. In affirming this capital case the Court of Military Appeals noted that the statements did not reflect prejudice against the accused but rather concern for maintaining understanding between the Americans and Okinawans and for the right to a fair trial. It was significant that all court members declared that they would not be influenced by the possible political significance of the case. . . .

The statements in question in appellant's case were general in character and made with no evident design to secure conviction of a particular individual. More likely they were made in response to public demand for information. The statements were neither coercive in nature nor specifically directed to potential court members who might serve on appellant's general court-martial. We find no possibility of prejudice considering the timing and content of the statements, as well as the positions of the persons issuing the statements. Undeniably the offices of those making the statements are prestigious, but their utterance almost a year prior to trial, their overall neutral character, and the vague recollection or absence of any recollection of these statements by the court members demonstrate no fair risk of the exertion of improper command influence upon them.

. . .

V. Sufficiency of the Evidence

A. THE EVIDENCE

On 16 March 1968 Lieutenant Calley was the 1st platoon leader in C Company, 1st Battalion, 20th Infantry, 11th Light Infantry Brigade, as he had been since he arrived in the Republic of Vietnam in December 1967. The 11th Brigade was assigned to the Americal Division, itself only formally activated in October 1967.

The Americal Division was assigned a tactical area of operation along the South China Sea Coast from Quang Ngai Province north into Quang Nam Province. That area, approximately 150 kilometers from north to south, was divided among the three constituent brigades, the 11th Brigade receiving the southern-most portion. With the exception of the area in the vicinity of Quang Ngai City, which had been assigned to 2nd Republic of Vietnam Army (ARVN) Division, the 11th Brigade area of operation ran from Duc Pho District north to Binh Son District, and inland for approximately 30 kilometers.

In January 1968, appellant's company; A Company, 3d Battalion, 1st Infantry; and B Company, 4th Battalion, 3d Infantry, were chosen by the brigade commander to compose Task Force Barker. A supporting field artillery battery was organized from the assets of three existing batteries of the brigade's organic field artillery battalion. The Task Force area of operation, designated Muscatine, was located north of the Song Diem-Diem and east of Highway 1 northward for approximately 12 kilometers to Binh Son. Its operations were conducted from two fire support bases, Uptight and Dottie (Task Force Barker Headquarters). (See Appendix A.)

During operations in the southern sector of its area of operation, the units of Task Force Barker drew fire from enemy forces which would withdraw south of the Song Diem-Diem into the area of operations of the 2d ARVN Division. After the Tet offensive in early February 1968 Task Force Barker requested and received authority temporarily to extend its area of operation south of the river into Son My village. Intelligence reports had indicated that the 48th Viet Cong Battalion maintained its base camp in the My Lai (1), or Pinkville, area of Son My. The village reportedly had been controlled by the Viet Cong for twenty years. Prior efforts by friendly forces to enter the area had been sternly resisted. When Task Force Barker made sweeps into Son My later in February, it met only limited success. At the cost of moderate casualties it destroyed some enemy supplies and fortifications, but was unable decisively to engage the main enemy force.

C Company, appellant's unit, had not experienced much combat prior to 16 March 1968. In its three months of overseas duty, two of which were with Task Force Barker, its operations had consisted of uneventful patrolling, attempted ambushes, providing defense for the fire bases, and providing blocking forces for Task Force missions. The casualties it had sustained were mainly from mines and booby traps. While moving into a blocking position on 25 February 1968 the company became ensnared in a mine field, suffering two killed and thirteen wounded. Appellant was not on this operation, for he had just returned from a three day in-country rest and recuperation leave. On 14 March 1968, a popular sergeant in the second platoon was killed and three others were wounded by a booby trap.

The next day, Captain Medina, commander of C Company, was notified that his company would engage in an upcoming offensive action. He was briefed at Task Force headquarters, then called his officers and men together on the evening of 15 March 1968 for a unit briefing. The content of the briefing (a matter of some dispute as will subsequently be discussed) essentially was that the next morning the unit would engage the 48th VC Battalion, from whom it could expect heavy resistance and by whom it would be outnumbered by more than two to one. C Company was to be inserted by airlift to the west of My Lai (4), sweep through it, and continue toward My Lai (1) or Pinkville (Appendices A and C). There they would be joined in a night defensive position by B Company of the Task Force, which would be conducting a similar operation from south to north into My Lai (1), and by A Company which would be in a blocking position north of the river.

The concept of the operation for C Company was for the 1st and 2nd platoons to sweep rapidly through My Lai (4) and the 3rd platoon to follow. The 3rd platoon would thoroughly search the hamlet and destroy all that could be useful to the enemy. A demolition team of engineers was attached to assist in the destruction of enemy bunkers and facilities.

This was to be the unit's first opportunity to engage decisively the elusive enemy they had been pursuing since their arrival in South Vietnam. The men, as is normal in an untried unit, faced the operation with both anticipation and fear, mindful of the recent casualties taken in less perilous missions.

C Company was transported by helicopter from LZ Dottie about six miles southeast to My Lai (4) in two lifts (Appendix B, Point A). The first lift was completed at approximately 0730 hours; the second lift at 0747 hours. The insertion was preceded by five minutes of preparatory fires of 105 howitzer high explosive rounds and by gunship fire. The insertion, although within 100 meters of the western edge of My Lai (4), was not opposed by hostile fire. In formation with the first and second platoons on line from north to south, the third platoon in reserve and the mortar platoon remaining with the rear to provide support if needed, C Company laid heavy suppressive fires into the subhamlet as the first and second platoons began the assault.

Despite expectations of heavy resistance based upon specific intelligence briefings, C Company moved through My Lai (4) without receiving any fire. The only unit casualty on 16 March 1968 was one self-inflicted wound. No mines or booby traps were detonated. Lead elements of the company had no occasion to call for mortar fires from the weapons platoon; the forward observer with C Company had no occasion to call for any fires from artillery units in direct support. In My Lai (4), the unit encountered only unarmed, unresisting, frightened old men, women, and children, and not the expected elements of the 48th Viet Cong Battalion. The villagers were found in their homes eating breakfast and beginning their morning chores.

The members of C Company reacted to the unexpected absence of opposition in diverse ways. Some continued the mission as if the enemy was in fact being engaged. Most recognized the difference between actual and expected circumstances, so while continuing with the destruction of foodstuffs, livestock, and buildings, reverted to the unit standing operating procedures on collecting and evacuating Vietnamese. Many soldiers took no action at all, but stood passively by while others destroyed My Lai (4). A few, after witnessing inexplicable acts of violence against defenseless villagers, affirmatively refused to harm them.

No single witness at appellant's trial observed all that transpired at My Lai (4). The testimony of the 92 witnesses was shaded by the lapse of time between 16 March 1968 and the commencement of trial in November 1970. Even in the voluminous record, all that happened is not fully revealed. One reason for vagueness and confusion in testimony offered by both sides is that the operation itself was confused, having been planned on the basis of faulty intelligence and conducted with inexperienced troops without adequate command control.

With this *caveat* as to the evidence, we come to the events which led to charges against appellant. Twenty out of the twenty-seven persons who were members of Lieutenant Calley's understrength platoon on 16 March 1968 testified at his court-martial.

The first platoon arrived on the first lift about 0730 hours. Its initial task was to provide perimeter defense for the insertion of the remainder of the company. After the company was on the ground and organized for assault, the first platoon moved toward My Lai (4) in formation as follows:

———
(SP4 Turner (fire team ldr)
(PFC Simone (duty not revealed in record)
(PVT E–2 Stanley (ammo bearer & grenadier)
(PFC Bergthold (ass't machine gunner)

(SP4 Maples (machine gunner)
2d Squad (SSG Bacon (sqad ldr)
(PFC Conti (grenadier and minesweeper)
(PFC Doines (rifleman)
(PFC Lloyd (grenadier)
(SP4 R. Wood (fire team ldr)
(PFC Kye (rifleman)
———

Plt Hdg Gp
———
(2LT Calley (plt ldr)
(SP4 J. Wood (RTO)
(SFC Cowan (plt sgt)
(SP4 Lee (medic)
(SP4 Sledge (RTO)
———

———
(PFC Mauro (duty not revealed in record)
(SP4 Boyce (rifleman)

(SP4 Grzesik (fire team ldr)
(PFC Meadlo (rifleman)
(PFC Carter (rifleman)/ tunnel rat)

1st Squad
(SSG Mitchell (squad ldr)
(PFC Dursi (rifleman)
(SP4 Hall (ass't machine gunner)
(PFC Olsen (machine gunner)
(PFC Haywood (rifleman)
(SGT Lagunoy (fire team ldr)
———

This formation quickly became disorganized in the subhamlet. Thick vegetation made it difficult for the troops to see who was near, and for the squad leaders and Lieutenant Calley to maintain visual contact with their men and with each other. However, the principal reason why the formation broke down and leaders lost control was the discovery of unresisting, unarmed old men, women and children instead of the expected enemy. The platoon had not been specifically instructed what to do in this event. No civilian collection point had been designated; and the first platoon was supposed to move through the village quickly, not to return to the rear with detainees.

Some villagers were shot by some members of the first platoon when it first entered the subhamlet. Some members collected groups of Vietnamese, without knowing what to do with them, and others stopped to kill livestock. The platoon assault formation became a meandering troop. Lieutenant Calley started out behind his platoon on the western edge of the subhamlet, but emerged at a ditch on the eastern edge before several members of his platoon (Appendix B, Point C; Appendix D). Sergeant Mitchell similarly lost contact wtih his squad at one time, leaving most of them to search a small cluster of huts and buildings to the southeast of My Lai (4). Sergeant Bacon testified he never saw his platoon leader or even heard from him as he pushed through the subhamlet. Sergeant Cowan lost contact with Lieutenant Calley soon after they entered the village, did not see him inside the village, and came close to him again only as he exited My Lai (4) on the east.

The Vietnamese who were taken in the first platoon's sweep were herded in two general directions, either toward the southern edge of the hamlet near an intersection of trails or easterly in front of the advancing troops.

In the second squad, Sergeant Bacon detailed men to escort a group of men, women and children villagers down a trail (to his right or south) to where he thought the platoon leader would be. Private First Class Doines, a rifleman in Bacon's squad, took ten to fifteen people along a trail running north-south in the middle of the village and left them with Lieutenant Calley. Specialist Four Wood got some people together and sent them toward the right with a guard. Private First Class Kye found about ten old men, women and children in a hootch. They were whisked away to his right by an American soldier. A key witness, Private First Class Conti, stated he encountered Lieutenant Calley on a trail midway through the village. At Lieutenant Calley's direction he rounded up five or six people and put them with a nearby group of thirty to forty, consisting mostly of women and children. At appellant's order he and Private First Class Meadlo, another critical witness, moved these people down the trail and into rice paddies on the southern side of the subhamlet (Appendix B, Point B). Specialist Four Maples searched hootches, gathered some people, and moved them up front as he continued through My Lai (4).

The first squad's contact with the people of My Lai (4) was more significant. Private First Class Meadlo testified that, upon order from Sergeant Mitchell, he collected thirty to forty people near what he remembered as a clearing in the center of the village. Private First Class Dursi recalled that he moved through the village gathering people in a group. He related coming upon PFC Meadlo, who was guarding a group of Vietnamese near some rice paddies next to a trail on the southern side of the village. PFC Dursi later moved his group of fifteen to a ditch on the eastern side. Private First Class Haywood picked up five or six villagers and was told by someone to take the people to Dursi, whom he saw guarding twenty to thirty others on a trail in the south side of the village. A fire team leader in the first squad, Specialist Four Grzesik, stated that he found seven or eight unresisting Vietnamese in a hootch immediately upon entering the village. He left these people with another group of twenty-five farther east in the village, in a small clearing. Specialist Four Boyce rounded up about fifteen people, mostly women and children, and passed them on to someone else. The people assembled in the southern portion of the subhamlet were not the only ones met by the first squad. Specialist Four Hall recalled that thirty to forty people were gathered in front of him, herded easterly through the village, and left at a ditch with Lieutenant Calley, Sergeant Mitchell, and others.

After the first platoon's movement through My Lai (4), which took from ninety minutes to two hours to cover only a third of a mile, the majority of the platoon formed a perimeter defense about 50 to 100 meters east of the ditch on the east side of the subhamlet. The rest of

C Company more thoroughly searched and destroyed My Lai (4). The first platoon remained in its defensive position for another two hours or so until after the company had taken a lunch break. C Company then continued its mission with less eventful forays into two other subhamlets of Song My village. At one time later in the afternoon C Company was ordered by the brigade commander to return to My Lai (4) to verify reports of civilian casualties; but after an estimate of twenty-eight killed was radioed in by Captain Medina, that order was countermanded by the division commander.

The fate of villagers gathered by appellant's platoon in the southern portion of My Lai (4) and at the ditch on the subhamlet's eastern boundary was alleged in the following charges: [20]

CHARGE: VIOLATION OF THE UNIFORM CODE OF MILITARY JUSTICE, ARTICLE 118

"Specification 1: In that First Lieutenant William L. Calley, Jr., US Army, 40th Company, The Student Brigade, US Army Infantry School, Fort Benning, Georgia (then a member of Company C, 1st Battalion, 20th Infantry) did, at My Lai 4, Quang Ngai Province, Republic of South Vietnam, on or about 16 March 1968, with premeditation, murder an unknown number, not less than 30, Oriental human beings, males and females of various ages, whose names are unknown, occupants of the village of My Lai 4, by means of shooting them with a rifle.

"Specification 2: In that First Lieutenant William L. Calley, Jr., US Army, 40th Company, The Student Brigade, US Army Infantry School, Fort Benning, Georgia (then a member of Company C, 1st Battalion, 20th Infantry) did, at My Lai 4, Quang Ngai Province, Republic of South Vietnam, on or about 16 March 1968, with premeditation, murder an unknown number of Oriental human beings, not less than seventy, males and females of various ages, whose names are unknown, occupants of the village of My Lai 4, by means of shooting them with a rifle.

ADDITIONAL CHARGE: VIOLATION OF THE UNIFORM CODE OF MILITARY JUSTICE, ARTICLE 118

"Specification 1: In that First Lieutenant William L. Calley, Jr., US Army, Headquarters Company, The Student Brigade, US Army In-

20 Appellant was originally charged with two other specifications alleging the premeditated murder of seven more persons. These offenses were, however, dismissed upon motion by the Government.

fantry School, Fort Benning, Georgia (then a member of Company C, 1st Battalion, 20th Infantry) did, at My Lai 4, Quang Ngai Province, Republic of South Vietnam on or about 16 March 1968, with premeditation, murder one Oriental male human being, an occupant of the village of My Lai 4, whose name and age is unknown, by shooting him with a rifle.

"Specification 2: In that First Lieutenant William L. Calley, Jr., US Army, Headquarters Company, The Student Brigade, US Army Infantry School, Fort Benning, Georgia (then a member of Company C, 1st Battalion, 20th Infantry) did, at My Lai 4, Quang Ngai Province, Republic of South Vietnam, on or about 16 March 1968, with premeditation, murder one Oriental human being, an occupant of the village of My Lai 4, approximately two years old, whose name and sex is unknown, by shooting him with a rifle."

Upon motion the military judge ruled that the defense was entitled to a Bill of Particulars. The Government presented the following:

I. All of the alleged offenses occurred on a day on or about 16 March 1968, between 0700 hours and 1500 hours. The offense alleged in Specification 1 of the Charge was committed before the offense alleged in Specification 2 of the Charge. The offense alleged in Specification 2 of the Charge was committed after the offense alleged in Specification 1 of the Charge and before the offenses alleged in Specifications 1 and 2 of the Additional Charge. The offense alleged in Specification 1 of the Additional Charge was committed after the offenses alleged in Specifications 1 and 2 of the Charge and before the offense alleged in Specification 2 of the Additional Charge. The offense alleged in Specification 2 of the Additional Charge was committed after the offense alleged in Specifications 1 and 2 of the Charge and Specification 1 of the Additional Charge.

II. The offense alleged in Specification 1 of the Charge occurred somewhere in the southern portion of the village of My Lai 4 or in the vicinity of the southern edge of the village of My Lai 4, Quang Ngai Province, Republic of South Vietnam. The offenses alleged in Specification 2 of the Charge and Specifications 1 and 2 of the Additional Charge occurred somewhere in the eastern portion of the village or in the vicinity of the eastern edge of the said village.

III. Specifications 1 and 2 of the Charge are each alleged by the Government to be a separate offense.

IV. In each of Specifications 1 and 2 of the Charge, the Government will attempt to prove as a matter of fact that the accused personally killed Oriental human beings and that he caused others to kill Oriental human beings.

1. The Trail (Appendix B, Point B)

To Specification 1 of the Charge, alleging premeditated murder of not less than thirty persons, the court members returned a finding of guilty of premeditated murder of not less than one person. As outlined by the Bill of Particulars, this offense was committed in the southern portion of My Lai (4) before the other offenses of which the appellant stands convicted.

As previously described, some of the villagers rooted out of their homes were placed in a group guarded by PFC Paul Meadlo and PFC Dennis Conti. PFC Dursi, who was about fifteen feet from PFC Meadlo watching his own group of Vietnamese, saw Lieutenant Calley come onto the trail and heard him ask Meadlo "if he could take care of that group." A couple of minutes later the appellant returned and, as Dursi remembered, yelled to Meadlo, "Why haven't you wasted them yet?" PFC Dursi turned and started to move his group down the trail when he heard M–16 fire from his rear.

PFC Conti recounted that Lieutenant Calley told him and Meadlo "To take care of the people," left, and returned:

> Then he came out and said, 'I thought I told you to take care of them.' Meadlo said, 'We are. We are watching them' and he said 'No, I mean kill them.'

Conti testified that he saw Lieutenant Calley and Meadlo fire from a distance of ten feet with M–16 rifles on automatic fire into this group of unarmed, unresisting villagers.

Former PFC Meadlo's first appearance as a witness resulted only in his claiming his privilege against self-incrimination. However, he did return to testify at length under a grant of immunity. By the time of trial, he was a civilian. By the time of his testifying, he was presumably satisfied that he was not facing trial himself before a military commission.

Meadlo testified that he was guarding a group of villagers with Conti when Lieutenant Calley approached him and said, "You know what to do with them, Meadlo." He assumed at the time this meant only to continue guarding them. However, appellant returned in ten or fifteen minutes and said, "How come they're not dead?" Meadlo replied, "I didn't know we were supposed to kill them," after which Lieutenant Calley directed, "I want them dead." Meadlo remembered that appellant backed away and began firing into the group before he did the same.

Specialist Four Sledge, a radio operator, remembered moving with appellant to the south side of the village, where they found a group of thirty or forty Vietnamese with Meadlo. After Lieutenant Calley asked the group whether they were Viet Cong, which they naturally disclaimed, Sledge heard him tell Meadlo "to waste them." Sledge was walking away when he heard shooting and screaming from behind him. He glanced back and saw a few people start to fall. He did not see appellant firing.

Appellant, testifying in his own behalf, stated that after he got to the eastern edge of the village he received radio messages from the second platoon leader, who asked him to check out some bunkers in the northeast corner of My Lai (4), and from Captain Medina, who asked what he was doing. He told Captain Medina that he had some bunkers and a small portion of the hamlet to the southeast to check out and that he had a lot of enemy personnel with him. As appellant moved over to Sergeant Mitchell's position to the southeast, he came out of the village and encountered Meadlo with a large group of Vietnamese. Lieutenant Calley recalled he said something to the effect, "Did he know what he was supposed to be doing with those people" and, "To get moving, get on the other side of the ditch." About this time he claimed to have stopped Conti from molesting a female. Instead of continuing to the first squad leader, he returned inside the village to insure that Sergeant Bacon was searching the bunkers and placing his men on perimeter defense. Then, he claims to have received another call from Captain Medina telling him to "waste the Vietnamese and get my people out in line, out in the position they were supposed to be." He yelled to Sergeant Bacon to get moving, and as he passed by Meadlo a second time he told them that if he couldn't move those people to "get rid of them."

There is no doubt that a group of submissive, defenseless Vietnamese, women, children, and old men, being guarded at the trail south of My Lai (4) by PFC Meadlo, were shot down in summary execution either by Meadlo and the appellant or by Meadlo at the order of the appellant. Nor is there doubt that the location of this offense and its occurrence as the first in time of the several charged satisfied the prosecution's responsibility of proof under the specification and Bill of Particulars.

Many of the bodies are depicted in a photograph taken by former Specialist Four Ronald Haeberle near the north-south trail, south of My Lai (4). A great deal of foundation evidence satisfactorily authenticates the photograph as being of the same group of bodies as was the subject of Specification 1 of the Charge and the testimony of Meadlo, Conti, Dursi and Sledge. Although over twenty inert bodies are shown, almost all displaying dreadful wounds, a pathologist-witness could point to only one wound on one body which, in his opinion from viewing the photograph, was certain to have been instantly fatal. Most probably his testimony was the reason for findings amending the charged number of decedents to "not less than one."

2. The Ditch (Appendix B, Point C; Appendix D)

Specification 2 of the Charge alleged the premeditated murder of not less than seventy persons. The court members returned findings of guilty, except the number of victims was reduced to not less than twenty. As outlined by the Bill of Particulars, this offense occurred after the trail incident but before the offenses laid under the Additional Charge.

It is not disputed that during mid-morning on 16 March 1968 a large number of unresisting Vietnamese were placed in a ditch on the eastern side of My Lai (4) and summarily executed by American soldiers. We can best begin a recital of the tragic facts and circumstances surrounding this offense by examining the appellant's testimony.

Lieutenant Calley testified that after he passed PFC Meadlo for the second time at the trail, he moved toward Sergeant Mitchell's location in the southeastern part of My Lai (4). He found him near a ditch that ran through that sector. He walked up the ditch until he broke into a clearing. There he discovered some of his men firing upon Vietnamese in another ditch. Lieutenant Calley admitted that he also fired with them and told Meadlo to get his people over the ditch or, if he couldn't move them, to "waste them." He then went north to check out the positions of his men.

Charles Sledge confirmed some of those movements of his platoon leader. However, Sledge remembers important events differently. He heard someone shout that Sergeant Mitchell had some people at a ditch; moved there; saw twenty to thirty Vietnamese women, children, and a few old men; saw Lieutenant Calley and Sergeant Mitchell shove these Vietnamese down into the ditch and fire into them from four or five feet. The victims screamed and fell. A helicopter landed nearby. Lieutenant Calley went to it to talk with the aviator and returned to say to Sledge, "He don't like the way I'm running the show, but I'm the boss here."

Other important witnesses to the mass murder at the ditch were Conti, Hall, Olsen, Dursi, Meadlo, Grzesik and Turner.

After the killings at the trail, Conti went back into the village. Later he exited the east side and heard firing to his front. When he got to its source, Conti found Lieutenant Calley and Sergeant Mitchell firing from six or seven feet into a ditch filled with people who were screaming and trying to crawl up. He described the scene in court:

> I seen the recoil of the rifles and the muzzle flashes and I looked down, I see a woman try to get up. As she got up I saw Lieutenant Calley fire and hit the side of her head and blow the side of her head off. I left.

Specialist Four Hall collected thirty or forty people, pushed them forward through My Lai (4) to the ditch, left them there, and proceeded to a position in the paddies beyond. He noticed that Sergeant Mitchell, Lieutenant Calley, the platoon's RTO's, and several others stayed behind. Sometime after he got into position Hall heard fully automatic fire behind him coming from the area of the ditch. He saw a helicopter land and appellant converse with its aviator, after which he heard slow, semi-automatic fire from the ditch. Later, when he crossed the ditch on a wooden foot bridge, he saw thirty or forty people in it:

> They were dead. There was blood coming from them. They were just scattered all over the ground in the ditch, some in piles and some scattered out

> 20, 25 meters perhaps up the ditch. . . . They were very old people, very young children, and mothers. . . . There was blood all over them.

Olsen did not see Lieutenant Calley fire into the villagers, but did see him by the ditch when about two dozen Vietnamese were in it.

> They were—the majority were women and children, some babies. I distinctly remember one middle-aged Vietnamese male dressed in white right at my feet as I crossed. None of the bodies were mangled in any way. There was blood. Some appeared to be dead, others followed me with their eyes as I walked across the ditch.

James Dursi, it will be recalled, moved his group away from the trail when appellant yelled to Meadlo there. He moved his people until he came upon the ditch. He stopped. Lieutenant Calley, and then Meadlo, joined him. Dursi heard Lieutenant Calley tell Meadlo, "We have another job to do" and tell Meadlo and him to put the people into the ditch. He and Meadlo complied. The Vietnamese started to cry and yell. Lieutenant Calley said something like, "Start firing," and fired into the group himself. So did Meadlo, but Dursi refused. Asked why, he testified, "I couldn't go through with it. These little defenseless men, women and kids." After the first of the firing ceased, Lieutenant Calley told Dursi to move across the ditch before he (Dursi) got sick. He did move away from the scenes of blood flowing from chest, arm, and head wounds upon the victims. From the perimeter, to the east, he looked back toward the ditch only once and saw the helicopter land.

Meadlo gave the most graphic and damning evidence. He had wandered back into the village alone after the trail incident. Eventually, he met his fire team leader, Specialist Four Grzesik. They took seven or eight Vietnamese to what he labeled a "ravine," where Lieutenant Calley, Sledge, and Dursi and a few other Americans were located with what he estimated as seventy-five to a hundred Vietnamese. Meadlo remembered also that Lieutenant Calley told him, "We got another job to do, Meadlo," and that the appellant started shoving people into the ravine and shooting them. Meadlo, in contrast to Dursi, followed the directions of his leader and himself fired into the people at the bottom of the "ravine." Meadlo then drifted away from the area but he doesn't remember where.

Specialist Four Grzesik found PFC Meadlo, crying and distraught, sitting on a small dike on the eastern edge of the village. He and Meadlo moved through the village, and came to the ditch, in which Grzesik thought were thirty-five to fifty dead bodies. Lieutenant Calley walked past and ordered Grzesik to take his fire team back into the village and help the following platoon in their search. He also remembered that Calley asked him to "finish them off," but he refused.

Specialist Four Turner saw Lieutenant Calley for the first time that day as Turner walked out of the village near the ditch. Meadlo and a few other soldiers were also present. Turner passed within fifteen feet of the area, looked into the ditch and saw a pile of approximately twenty bodies covered with blood. He also saw Lieutenant Calley and Meadlo firing from a distance of five feet into another group of people who were kneeling and squatting in the ditch. Turner recalled he then went north of the ditch about seventy yards, where he joined with Conti at a perimeter position. He remained there for over an hour, watching the ditch. Several more groups of Vietnamese were brought to it, never to get beyond or out of it. In all he thought he observed about ninety or a hundred people brought to the ditch and slaughtered there by Lieutenant Calley and his subordinates.

Other members of the first platoon saw Vietnamese placed into a ditch and appellant and others fire into it. Some members of the third platoon also saw the bloody bodies. Also, the observations of witnesses who were in the supporting helicopters portray a telling, and ghastly, overview of the slaughter at the ditch. Aviators and crew members saw from the air numbers of bodies they variously estimated from about thirty to about one hundred. One aviator, a Lieutenant (then Warrant Officer) Thompson, actually landed near the scene three times. The second time, he spoke with someone, who from the evidence must have been Lieutenant Calley. Thompson succeeded in evacuating a few living Vietnamese despite appellant's deprecations. The evidence from others is certainly persuasive that Lieutenant Calley boasted, "I'm the boss here," after he spoke with an aviator.

There is no dispute as to the fact of killings by and at the instance of appellant at a ditch on the eastern edge of My Lai (4). From appellant's own testimony, and that of his radio operator, it is clear that this second offense preceded those laid under Additional Charge, as was specified in the Bill of Particulars.

That the findings reduced the originally charged number of victims from "not less than seventy" to "not less than twenty" reflects the members' careful adherence to the instructions of the military judge. His instructions permitted findings of guilty only in conformance with the Bill of Particulars, namely, that any deaths found under Specification 2 of the Charge precede those alleged under the Additional Charge. Using the meeting between Lieutenant Calley and the aviator Thompson as a dividing line between the offenses laid under the Charge and those under the Additional Charge, we find the evidence conclusively supports the findings of premeditated murder of not less than twenty human beings.

3. The Additional Charge

Specification 1 of the Additional Charge alleged the premeditated murder of one male human being and Specification 2, the premeditated murder of one human being approximately two years old. Instructions required that the Government prove these offenses to have occurred in sequence after the mass killing offense at the ditch. The findings were guilty as charged as to Specification 1 and guilty of assault with intent to commit murder as to Specification 2.

Appellant's conviction of the Additional Charge and its specifications rests squarely on the resolution of conflicts between his testimony and the testimony of Charles Sledge. The members resolved these against appellant, with ample support in the record.

According to Specialist Four Sledge, five or ten minutes after Lieutenant Calley returned from speaking with a helicopter aviator, he and Calley encountered a forty to fifty year old man dressed in white robes as they moved north up the ditch. Appellant repeatedly questioned the man, "Viet Cong adou?" (Are you Viet Cong), to which the man continually replied, "No viec." Suddenly Lieutenant Calley shot the man in the face at point blank range, blowing half his head away. Immediately after this incident Sledge remembered that:

> Someone hollered, 'there's a child,' You know, running back toward the village. Lieutenant Calley ran back, the little—I don't know if it was a girl or boy—but it was a little baby, and he grabbed it by the arm and threw it into the ditch and fired.

Sledge observed this from a distance of twenty to thirty feet. He recalled that only one shot was fired at the child from a distance of four or five feet. He did not see whether the round struck.

Lieutenant Calley testified that after talking with the aviator, he moved along the platoon's perimeter checking the position of his troops. He did not recall making any statement to Sledge that, "He [the aviator] don't like the way I'm running the show but I'm the boss here." but did claim that he told Captain Medina over the radio that "a pilot don't like the way things were being done down here." As appellant went northerly along the ditch, a man dressed in white was brought to him for interrogation. He admitted butt-stroking the individual with his M–16, bloodying his face, but denies shooting him. Lieutenant Calley also denied the episode concerning a child that Sledge described.

Appellate defense counsel urge us to discount Sledge's testimony about the Additional Charge because of its apparent inconsistency with testimony from other members of the first platoon. However, after a careful review of the evidence we are convinced that any minor disparities in location and time sequence are capable of resolution. Differences in perception or recollection of physical features in the hamlet, including the ditch, and the passage of time are to be expected. Essentially, the defense contends that Sledge should not be believed and that the appellant's remembrances should be accorded greater weight. Our view of the evidence leads us, as it did the court members, to the opposite conclusion. Appellant's account of the facts and circumstances surrounding the Additional Charge (as well as the other offenses) is riddled with inconsistency and selectivity of recall. He purported to be able to recall all exculpatory material in great detail, but became vague when describing any significant features of the village and its environs and events surrounding the offenses which tended to be incriminating.

The evidence in support of the specifications under the Additional Charge is sufficient in itself to be persuasive beyond reasonable doubt. In addition, this is not a case in which the evidence going to these offenses should be viewed in isolation from the rest of the case. The last two offenses are the conclusion of a course of conduct, consistent with and logically following all the carnage which preceded.

B. LEGAL RESPONSIBILITY

Although appellant disputes the assault on the child and killing of the man found under the Additional Charge, his theories of defense at trial and on appeal accept as fact his participation in the killings at the trail and ditch. His testimony differs from others' about the details of his participation, the time spent upon the slayings at the ditch, and the number of the dead. These differences pose no substantial factual issues on appeal.

In an argument of extraordinary scope, appellant asks us to hold that the deaths of the My Lai villagers were not legally requitable in that the villagers had no right to continued life cognizable in our law. The two premises for this view are first, that the history of operations around Pinkville discloses villager sympathy and support for the Viet Cong, so extensive and enduring as to constitute all the villagers as belligerents themselves; and second, that appellant's superiors had determined the belligerent status of the villagers before the operation of 16 March—i.e., as belligerents, the villagers were not entitled to the protections of peaceful civilian status under the Geneva Convention Relative to the Protection of Civilian Persons in Time of War, 12 August 1949 [1956], 6 UST 3516, TIAS No. 3365; 75 UNTS 287, or of prisoner of war status because they did not organize under a responsible commander, bear a fixed distinctive sign recognizable at a distance, carry arms openly, and conduct their own operations in accordance with the laws of war, the four minima which must be satisfied by irregular belligerents in order to be regarded as prisoners of war under Article 4, Geneva Convention Relative to the treatment of Prisoners of War, 12 Aug 1949 [1956], 6 UST 3316, TIAS No. 3364; 75 UNTS 135.

This argument is tainted by several fallacies. One is that participation in irregular warfare is done by individuals, although they may organize themselves for the purpose. Slaughtering many for the presumed delicts of a few is not a lawful response to the delicts. We do not know whether the findings specifically included the deaths of infants in arms or children of toddler age, but the fallacy is clear when it is recalled that villagers this young were indiscriminately included in the general carnage. A second fallacy is that the argument is in essence a plea to permit summary execution as a reprisal for irregular villager action favoring the Viet Cong. Reprisal by summary execution of the helpless is forbidden in the laws of land warfare. *See generally* paragraph 497, Field Manual 27–10, The Law of Land Warfare (July 1956). It is not the law that the villagers were *either* innocent civilians or eligible for prisoner of war status *or* liable to summary execution. Whether an armed conflict be a local uprising or a global war, summary executions as in My Lai (4) are not justifiable. Articles 3, 32, 33, GC, supra.

Though conceding participation in some killings, the defense abstracts appellant's mental state while he was in My Lai to claim that the evidence was insufficient to support the findings under the original charge.

No claim is made that appellant lacked mental responsibility in the sense of the ordinary sanity tests. . . .

Granting his own sanity, appellant contends that he was nevertheless not guilty of murder because he did not entertain the requisite *mens rea*. His specific claims are:

1. He was prompted to kill by provocation such as negated malice and would reduce any offense to manslaughter.
2. Events preceding and during the My Lai operation affected his psychic make-up in a way which deprived him of the capacity to premeditate or to entertain a state of mind of malice.
3. Because he did not bear any individualized ill will toward the villagers, but simply regarded them as enemy in a strict military sense, and because in the context of the operation he was not conscious of any criminal quality to his acts but rather thought that he was properly performing his duty, he is not guilty of unlawful homicide; or at very most is guilty of manslaughter because he was void of malice.
4. His acts were justified because of the orders given to him; or, if the orders and his response do not constitute a complete defense, he is at most guilty of manslaughter.

These claims are inextricably intertwined. To some extent it is necessary that they be taken up individually; however, their aggregate effect may be significant even though the effect of one would not be.

Each claim implies the absence of malice in appellant's mind on 16 March 1968. The defense considers proof of malice to be as indispensable to conviction for murder in violation of Article 118, UCMJ, as it was at common law or under the predecessor Articles of War. *See* paragraph 179a, Manual for Courts-Martial, United States Army, 1949. The Government, on the other hand, asks us to construe Articles 118 and 119 as being supplanting statutory definitions of murder and manslaughter, so complete in their terms as to express all that is encompassed within the current offenses; and to hold that, by omitting reference to malice, Congress rendered the concept immaterial in military prosecutions.

Articles 118 and 119 (10 USC §§ 918, 191) provide:

> § 918. Art. 118. Murder
>
> Any person subject to this chapter who, without justification or excuse, unlawfully kills a human being, when he—
>
> 1. has a premeditated design to kill;
> 2. intends to kill or inflict great bodily harm;
> 3. is engaged in an act which is inherently dangerous to others and evinces a wanton disregard of human life; or
> 4. is engaged in the perpetration or attempted perpetration of burglary, sodomy, rape, robbery, or aggravated arson;
>
> is guilty of murder, and shall suffer such punishment as a court-martial may direct, except that if found guilty under clause (1) or (4), he shall suffer death or imprisonment for life as a court-martial may direct.
>
> § 919. Art. 119. Manslaughter
>
> a. Any person subject to this chapter who, with an intent to kill or inflict great bodily harm, unlawfully kills a human being in the heat of sudden passion caused by adequate provocation is guilty of voluntary manslaughter and shall be punished as a court-martial may direct.
>
> b. Any person subject to this chapter who, without an intent to kill or inflict great bodily harm, unlawfully kills a human being—
>
> 1. by culpable negligence; or
> 2. while perpetrating or attempting to perpetrate an offense, other than those named in clause (4) of section 918 of this title (article 118), directly affecting the person;
>
> is guilty of involuntary manslaughter and shall be punished as a court-martial may direct.

Despite omission of the term in Article 118, we are persuaded that the concept of malice retains vitality in the military law of homicide. Malice is still the proper term for describing that state of mind which distinguishes murder from manslaughter. The concept of malice was expressed during hearings on the Code by a member of the House Armed Services Committee:

> MR. DEGRAFFENRIED. . . . Murder in the first degree is the killing of a human being with premeditation, deliberation, and malice; murder in the second degree is the killing of a human being with malice but without premeditation and deliberation; manslaughter in the first degree is the intentional, unlawful

killing of a human being but without malice and without premeditation or deliberation.

MR. LARKIN. Well, when you delete the malice from the intention, what have you done?

MR. DEGRAFFENRIED. Well, the intent. You have the intent there.

MR. LARKIN. You are intending to act mala in se and you say it is without malice?

MR. DEGRAFFENREID. Yes. The passion that you exist under at the time does away with the malice. You still have the intent to kill. But the heat of passion does away with the idea of malice and premeditation and deliberation.

Hearing on HR 2498 Before a Subcommittee of the House Committee on Armed Services, 81st Congress, 1st Session, 1247, 1248 (1949).

Mr. deGraffenried was speaking about intended killings. There are other kinds of murders and manslaughters, in each of which an inquiry for the presence or absence of malice may be pertinent. The dividing line between the wanton-misconduct murder denounced by Article 118(3) and culpably negligent manslaughter denounced by Article 119(b)(1) is marked out by malice implied in the degree of heedlessness of life evidenced by the wanton misconduct itself. United States v Judd, 10 USCMA 113, 27 CMR 187 (1959). The malice in felony murder, denounced by Article 118(4), is implied in the intent to commit one of the named felonies. *Compare* Article 119(b)(2); *see* United States v Jones, 10 USCMA 122, 27 CMR 196 (1959). In support of conviction for felony murder, there must be proof by competent evidence of attempted or actual commission of one of the felonies named in Article 118(4). United States v Gaines, 44 CMR 375 (ACMR), *pet denied,* 44 CMR 939 (1971). It follows that in wanton misconduct murder and felony murder, the concept of malice is not entirely subjective. Extrinsic facts, i.e., the degree of danger to life from one's conduct, or actual engagement in certain felonies, are ingredients of malice and not merely indicia of malice.

We believe the malice essential in murder by intended killing is similar. The requisite malice is not solely established by subjective and personal norms as appellant maintains. Surrounding circumstances must be taken into account. The following definition is accurate and complete:

> The term [malice], as used in the law of homicide, has often been defined as the *intentional* killing of a human being by another, without legal justification or excuse and under circumstances which are insufficient to reduce the crime to manslaughter. Nunez v State, 383 P2d 726, 729 (Wyo 1963).

Military cases make it clear, as does the last clause of the quoted definition, that murder is the starting point for evaluating the degree of criminality of an intended killing done without justification or excuse. The degree may be reduced to manslaughter given certain circumstances. One does not start with manslaughter and aggravate the degree to murder upon discovering a state of mind even more ferocious than intent to kill. Fundamentally, unmitigated intent to kill *is* the malice. This is why "imperfect self-defense" has been rejected as a defense in military law, and why reduction of intended killing from murder to voluntary manslaughter must be based on objectively adequate provocation. . . . Absent any mental or emotional dysfunction, for a legally cognizable mitigation of intent to kill into some mental state less than malice, there must be objectively adequate provocative cause in real events. Only after some evidence of adequate provocation is presented is the Government faced with bearing the burden of proof that the more serious offense of murder was committed.

The instant record discloses no adequate provocation. To be legally adequate, the provocation must be of a quality which would "excite uncontrollable passion in the mind of a reasonable man." Paragraph 198, *Manual,* supra; United States v Maxie, supra. The insertion of the airmobile ground force at My Lai (4) was not resisted. The overwhelming weight of evidence is that the force drew no fire entering or in the village; the company tripped no mines or booby traps in My Lai (4); the persons at the trail and ditch passively submitted to their movement to those locations; and at no time was appellant confronted with a threat or hostile reaction. Those passages in appellant's brief and utterances in oral argument referring to the terror and horror of a combat assault at My Lai (4) and the circumstances there engendering fear and rage to an irresistible degree are false. Our recitation of the facts, we hope, will put an end to this sort of mythopoesis. No residents of My Lai did anything during the 16 March operation to provoke appellant's killing them and ordering their killing. If any cause could be found in their conduct, it would only be a history of sympathy or support for the enemy as related in available intelligence information. A status of being a sympathizer, collaborator, or Viet Cong proper is not such provocation as would mitigate a summary execution down the scale of unlawful homicide to manslaughter.

A review of the psychiatric and lay witness testimony persuades us also that appellant was not afflicted with any psychic dysfunction which would preclude his premeditating the killings or harboring malice.

Military law takes account of partial mental responsibility. The rules are succinctly put in paragraph 120c, *Manual,* supra:

> A mental condition, not amounting to a general lack of mental responsibility, which produces a lack of mental ability, at the time of the offense, to possess actual knowledge or to entertain a specific intent or a premeditated design to kill, is a defense to an offense having one of these states of mind as an element. For example, if premeditated murder is charged and the court finds that, as a result of mental impairment, not amounting to a general lack of mental responsibility, the accused at the time of the offense lacked the mental ability to entertain a premeditated design to kill, the court must find the

accused not guilty of premeditated murder, but it may find him guilty of the included offense of unpremeditated murder as a premeditated design to kill is not an element of the latter.

To prove a case of murder, the prosecution must of course prove a murderous *mens rea.* An accused may always encounter by putting in issue that he *did* not entertain the *mens rea.* When the basis is that he *could* not entertain it, his evidence must tend to show a total lack of capacity to do so and not merely some lesser extent of impairment. . . . So long as some capacity exists, the question, upon which the prosecution must bear the burden of proof, is simply whether an accused exercised it by premeditating, intending, or knowing, whichever is pertinent. . . .

None of the lay testimony casts doubt on appellant's capacity for a murderous *mens rea.* Two psychiatrists testified for appellant, one from a hypothetical question and one from personal clinical experience with him. Three testified for the prosecution, all from extensive clinical observation and interviews. The two defense psychiatrists gave some testimony in conclusory terms to the effect that appellant was acting "automatically," that he did not have capacity to premeditate because he was effectively without ability to reflect upon alternative courses of action and choose from them; and that he did not have the capacity to "contrive" the deaths of the villagers. However, both agreed that appellant had capacity to perceive and predict, the two functions essential to the pertinent *mens rea.* Appellant knew he was armed and what his weapon would do. He had the same knowledge about his subordinate and their arms. He knew that if one aimed his weapon at a villager and fired, the villager would die. Knowing this, he ordered his subordinates to "waste" the villagers at the trail and ditch, to use his own terminology; and fired upon the villagers himself. These bare facts evidence intent to kill, consciously formed and carried out.

What appellant did and said at My Lai even more clearly evidences premeditation as a conscious process. He told Meadlo, concerning the group collected at the trail, "Take care of them," and left to reenter the village. When he returned, his reaction at observing the group alive was surprise and dismay. His then ordering the killing at the trail was not impulsive; it was, we are satisfied, an instance of supervision over a plan he had conceived.

Indicia of appellant's premeditation of the killings at the ditch are abundant. His attitude toward the persons collected there was expressed in his statement to Meadlo, "We have another job to do" and his order to Meadlo and Dursi to shove the persons into the ditch and "start firing." He personally pushed villagers down into the ditch before firing point blank at the group and ordering subordinates to do the same. Villagers were brought to the ditch in batches; and appellant supervised killing them over an extended period of time. Estimates of the period vary from witness to witness. Understandably, appellant's estimate is among the shortest. Close comparison of all testimony leads us to conclude that appellant's supervising and participating in killings at the ditch lasted from forty-five minutes to an hour. He no doubt fired more than one clip into the ditch. He fired into the ditch even after he spoke with Thompson at Thompson's helicopter. It was after that conversation that appellant boasted of "being the boss here." He asked Grzesik to "help finish off" the villagers, and ask Maples, a machine gunner, if he could use his weapon, and ordered Dursi to "start firing" in the ditch. All refused even though appellant was their commissioned superior. (Appellant stated a lack of recollection of these conversations with Grzesik and Maples, but evidence that they occurred was clear and credible.)

These acts and conversations bespeak premeditation. We find not only that the act of killing was consciously conceived, but also that appellant expressed his conception in so many words to Meadlo, Dursi and Grzesik. Prior consideration of the fatal acts is demonstrated most clearly by appellant's compressing the group into a situs most convenient for the killing, namely the bed of the ditch.

The psychiatric theory that appellant acted automatically, without power of choice, explains his conduct not within conscious operations of mind but instead by unconscious impulse activated by a special set of circumstances. It is proposed that appellant came to the My Lai operation affected by anger, anxiety, and also guilt in that he was not present with his platoon during a prior operation in which it sustained casualties; that appellant's capacity for discrimination among concepts and grasping abstractions was of a low order; that his reaction to training, including indoctrination in obedience to orders, was to exhibit conditioned response; and that one of his strong psychic needs was to satisfy and please others. Given this psychic set, the defense argument proceeds, a combination of the orders he purportedly received or thought he received and a confrontation with the Vietnamese he despised and feared touched off an impelling urge to kill of an involuntary nature.

The defense psychiatrists apparently viewed the urge to kill and the killing as demonstrations of psychological determinism, the outcropping in overt conduct of the force of a dictatorial unconscious. A psychiatrist who holds this view of man is often said to be of the "psychodynamic" school, and one defense psychiatrist so described himself.

In the leading case of State v Sikora, 44 NJ 453, 210 A2d 193 (1965), psychodynamic theory as a basis for reducing the degree of unlawful homicide committed by a concededly sane defendant was emphatically rejected. We have nothing to add to the opinions in *Sikora,* which must be read in full for a full understanding of the several reasons why these theories of "automaton" behavior in a sane accused are repugnant to the rules of law which circumscribe defenses and inquiries into partial mental responsibility. The primary reason, in strict legal analysis, is that deterministic theories of the unconscious are logically irrelevant because the legal definitions of premeditation, intent, and malice are framed in terms of conscious thought. . . .

The remaining defense arguments negating the requisite *mens rea* may be evaluated by reference to conscious processes of the mind, namely, knowledge and intent; and we need say no more about the automaton concept or theories of the unconscious.

That appellant may have regarded his victims impersonally as military enemy to "waste" rather than as objects of individually founded ill will is not inconsistent with the presence of malice. . . . The following approved instruction illustrates the point:

> Malice, as referred to in the law, gentlemen, does not necessarily mean that there shall be entertained by the slayer any hatred, or ill will, or ill feeling, or anything of that character, towards the person killed. It means in law the intention on the part of the slayer to take human life under such circumstances that the law will neither justify nor in any degree excuse or mitigate that intention, if the killing should take place as intended. A man may kill another against whom he entertained no ill will whatever; he may be a stranger to him, and yet be guilty of murder. No particular length of time is required for malice to be generated in the mind of the slayer; it may be formed in a moment, and instantly a mortal blow may be given or a fatal shot fired; yet if malice is in the mind of the slayer at the time of the doing of the act or killing, and moves him to do it, it is sufficient to constitute the homicide murder. Crawford v State, 149 Ga 485, 100 SE 633 (1919) (Syllabus by the Court).

Similarly, even accepting appellant's protestations that he genuinely thought the villagers had no rights to live because they were enemy, and thus was devoid of malice because he was not conscious of the criminal quality of his acts, we find no legal mitigation. To the extent this state of mind reflects a mistake of fact, the governing principle is: to be exculpatory, the mistaken belief must be of such a nature that the conduct would have been lawful had the facts actually been as they were believed to be. United States v Rowan, 4 USCMA 430, 16 CMR 4 (1954). An enemy in custody may not be executed summarily.

Mere absence of a sense of criminality is likewise not mitigating, for any contrary view would be an excrescent exception to the fundamental rule that ignorance of the very law violated is no defense to violating it. The maxim *ignorantia legis neminem excusat* applies to offenses in which intent is an element. United States v Gris, 247 F2d 860 (2d Cir 1957); . . . .

> It matters not whether appellant realized his conduct was unlawful. He knew exactly what he was doing; and what he did was a violation . . . [of a nature

which had to be shown to be knowing and willful.] He intended to do what he did, and that is sufficient. United States v Gris, supra at 864.

Of the several bases for his argument that he committed no murder at My Lai because he was void of *mens rea,* appellant emphasized most of all that he acted in obedience to orders.

Whether appellant was ever ordered to kill unresisting, unarmed villagers was a contested question of fact. The findings of a court-martial being in the nature of a general verdict, we do not know whether the court found that no such orders were given or, alternatively, concluded that the orders were given but were not exculpatory under the standards given to them in instructions.

Responding to a question during direct examination asking why he gave Meadlo the order, "If he couldn't get rid of them to 'waste them' ", Lieutenant Calley replied, "Because that was my order. That was the order of the day, sir." The appellant stated he received that order from Captain Medina, "The night before in the company briefings, the platoon leaders' briefing, the following morning before we lifted off, and twice there in the village."

Lieutenant Calley related what he remembered of Captain Medina's remarks to the company at the evening briefing prior to My Lai (4) operation:

> He [Medina] started off and he listed the men that we had lost, . . . We were down about 50 percent in strength, and that the only way we would survive in South Vietnam would be to—we'd have to unite, start getting together, start fighting together, and become extremely aggressive and we couldn't afford to take anymore casualties, and that it was the people in the area that we had been operating in that had been taking the casualties on us, and that we would have to start treating them as enemy and you would have to start looking at them as enemy, . . . We were going to start at My Lai (4). And we would have to neutralize My Lai (4) completely and not to let anyone get behind us, and then we would move into My Lai (5) and neutralize it and make sure there was no one left alive in My Lai (5) and so until we got into the Pinkville area, and we would completely neutralize My Lai (5)—I mean My Lai (1) which is Pinkville. He said it was completely essential that at no time that we lose our momentum of attack because the other two companies that had assaulted the time in there before had let the enemy get behind him or he had passed through enemy, allowing him to get behind him and set up behind him, which would disorganize him when he made his final assault on Pinkville. It would disorganize him, they would lose their momentum of attack, start taking casualties, be more worried about their casualties than their mission, and that was their downfall. So it was our job to go through destroying everyone and everything in there, not letting anyone or anything get behind us and move on into Pinkville, sir.

Appellant further recalled Captain Medina's saying that "the area had been completely covered by PSYWAR operations; that all civilians had left the area and that there was no civilians in the area and anyone there would be considered enemy," and that the unit had "political clearance to destroy and burn everything in the area."

Lieutenant Calley stated that at a platoon leaders' briefing later in the evening Captain Medina reemphasized "that under no circumstances would we let anyone get behind us, nor would we leave anything standing in these villages."

The next morning at LZ Dottie, according to appellant, he was told by Captain Medina "to hang on to some of the Vietnamese in case we encountered a mine field," and "that everybody in that area would be the enemy and everyone there would be destroyed, all enemies would be destroyed."

Lieutenant Calley testified that during his movement through My Lai (4) he received and made several radio transmissions to Captain Medina. When he reached the eastern part of the village, Captain Medina called to ask what he was doing. Appellant continued:

> I told him I had some bunkers up here to check out—that I wanted to check, and that I had that small portion of the hamlet to the southeast, and also there was still a lot of enemy personnel I still had with me.— . . . he told me to hurry up and get my people moving and get rid of the people I had there that were detaining me.

Appellant said that after he first encountered PFC Meadlo with a group of people and returned to Sergeant Bacon's location, he received another call from his company commander asking "why I was disobeying his order." His remembrance of Captain Medina's reply to his explanation of what was slowing him down was the specific order, "to waste the Vietnamese and get my people out in line, out in the position they were supposed to be."

On cross examination Lieutenant Calley indicated some confusion as to when he first saw the Vietnamese who were slowing his progress. He also admitted that he didn't describe these people to Captain Medina, except perhaps as Vietnamese or VC, and that he knew these people were slowing him down because "anytime you are moving Vietnamese people, you will be moving slowly." Lieutenant Calley denied knowing if any of the persons detained by his platoon were women and children, and claimed to have discriminated between sexes only when he stopped Dennis Conti from molesting a female.

Captain Medina, who was called as a witness at the request of the court members, gave a different version of his remarks to the company on the eve of the operation:

> The briefing that I conducted for my company was that C Company had been selected to conduct a combat assault operation onto the village of My Lai (4) beginning with LZ time 0730 hours on the morning of the 16th of March, 1968. I gave them the enemy situation, intelligence reports where the

> 48th VC Battalion was located in the village of My Lai (4). I told them that the VC Battalion was approximately, numbered approximately 250 to 280 men and that we would be outnumbered approximately two to one, and that we could expect a hell of a good fight and that we probably would be engaged. I told them that even though we were outnumbered that we had a double coverage of gunships that were being provided and that the artillery was being placed onto the village and that this would help make up for the difference in ratio between the enemy forces and our company. I told the people that this would give them a chance to engage the 48th VC Battalion, that the 48th VC Battalion was the one that we had been chasing around the Task Force Barker area of operation, and that we would finally get a chance to engage them in combat, and that we would be able to destroy the 48th VC Battalion. . . . The information that I gave also in the briefing to the company was that the 48th VC Battalion was located at the village of My Lai (4), and that the intelligence reports also indicated that the innocent civilians or noncombatants would be gone to market at 0700 hours in the morning. That this was one reason why the artillery preparation was being placed onto the village at 0720 hours with the combat assault LZ time 0730 hours. I did not make any reference to the handling of prisoners.

Captain Medina recalled that someone at the company briefing asked, "Do we kill women and children," and that his reply was, "No, you do not kill women and children. You must use common sense. If they have a weapon and are trying to engage you, then you can shoot back, but you must use common sense." He remembered instructing during the briefing:

> . . . that Colonel Barker had told me that he had permission from the ARVN's at Quang Ngai to destroy the village of My Lai (4), and I clarified this by saying to destroy the village, by burning the hootches, to kill the livestock, to close the wells and to destroy the food crops.

Captain Medina conceded mentioning to Lieutenant Calley before lift-off "to utilize prisoners to lead the elements through the mine fields." Any congruence between their testimony in regard to communications between them ends here. Although Captain Medina acknowledged that he called the first platoon leader to inform him of the implementation of a contingency plan and so to spread his men out, he denied that Lieutenant Calley ever told him that he had bunkers to check out or that he was having difficulty in handling civilians or that the first platoon had encountered a large number of civilians. Captain Medina further disclaimed that he ever gave an order to the appellant "to move civilians out of the way or get rid of them." He stated he was never informed that the first platoon had gathered women and children and did not know the circumstances under which the inhabitants of My Lai (4) were killed. He came to the pile of bodies at the trail after the killings.

Both appellant and Captain Medina had high stakes in the acceptance of their testimony. Their testimony is not only mutually conflicting, but each conflicts with other witnesses. Of the many witnesses who attended

Captain Medina's briefing to C Company on 15 March, no two had precisely the same recollection of his remarks about treatment of noncombatants during the operation, if any were recalled. The only recollection in common is that members of the unit did not expect noncombatant residents of the village to be there the next day. They expected instead to encounter elements of the 48th VC Battalion, their mission being to destroy it. Three defense witnesses interpreted Captain Medina's answer to a question whether women and children were to be considered as enemy as an affirmative directive to kill them. About twenty prosecution and defense witnesses had no recollection of any briefing directive to kill women and children. Whoever are correct, it is important to place Captain Medina's briefing remarks in the context of everyone's anticipation that the insertion of the ground force into My Lai (4) would be resisted by fire from elements of an enemy battalion. Appellant's testimony that during the operation Captain Medina ordered him by radio to kill villagers is not corroborated by the evidence given by third persons. The two radio operators for Captain Medina recalled no orders of that tenor being communicated by him. One had no recollection either way; the other testified positively that no order to kill or waste went over the unit net to Lieutenant Calley. Further, appellant said he ordered the squad leader Sergeant Bacon to search the bunkers which were mentioned in the first purported Medina-Calley radio conversation; and saw and spoke with Sergeant Bacon both before and after the second, telling him at that time where to deploy his squad. Sergeant Bacon, who had previously been called as a defense witness, denied having any contact with or communication from appellant at any of these times.

If the members found that appellant fabricated his claim of obedience to orders, their finding has abundant support in the record. If they found his claim of acting in obedience to orders to be credible, he would nevertheless not automatically be entitled to acquittal. Not every order is exonerating.

The trial judge's instructions under which he submitted the issues raised by evidence of obedience to orders were entirely correct. After fairly summarizing the evidence bearing on the question, he correctly informed the members as a matter of law that any order received by appellant directing him to kill unresisting Vietnamese within his control or within the control of his troops would have been illegal; that summary execution of detainees is forbidden by law. A determination of this sort, being a question of law only, is within the trial judge's province. Article 51(b), UCMJ, 10 USC § 851(b); paragraph 57b, *Manual,* supra.

The instructions continued:

> The question does not rest there, however. A determination that an order is illegal does not, of itself, assign criminal responsibility to the person following

the order for acts done in compliance with it. Soldiers are taught to follow orders, and special attention is given to obedience of orders on the battlefield. Military effectiveness depends upon obedience to orders. On the other hand, the obedience of a soldier is not the obedience of an automaton. A soldier is a reasoning agent, obliged to respond, not as a machine, but as a person. The law takes these factors into account in assessing criminal responsibility for acts done in compliance with illegal orders.

The acts of a subordinate done in compliance with an unlawful order given him by his superior are excused and impose no criminal liability upon him unless the superior's order is one which a man of ordinary sense and understanding would, under the circumstances, know to be unlawful, or if the order in question is actually known to the accused to be unlawful.

Judge Kennedy amplified these principles by specifying the burden of proof and the logical sequence for consideration of the questions to be resolved. The members were told that if they found beyond reasonable doubt that appellant actually knew the orders under which he asserted he operated were illegal, the giving of the orders would be no defense; that the final aspect of the obedience question was more objective in nature, namely, that if orders to kill unresisting detainees were given, and if appellant acted in response thereto being unaware that the orders were illegal, he must be acquitted unless the members were satisfied beyond reasonable doubt that a man of ordinary sense and understanding would have known the orders to be unlawful.

The literature on the subject of the defense of obedience to orders is extensive. Recent examples include Paust, My Lai and Vietnam: Norms, Myths and Leader Responsibility, 57 Mil L Rev 99, 170–175 (1972); Norene, Obedience to Orders as a Defense to a Criminal Act (unpublished thesis, The Judge Advocate General's School, 1971); Dinstein, The Defense of Obedience to Superior Orders in International Law (1965), all of which contain extensive citations. Interesting as it is to trace history and ponder theory as do these and similar works, we need not do so for the law to be applied in military courts is clear.

Judge Kennedy's instructions were sound and the members' findings correct. An order of the type appellant says he received is illegal. Its illegality is apparent upon even cursory evaluation by a man of ordinary sense and understanding. A finding that it is not exonerating should not be disturbed. . . . The argument is essentially that obedience to orders is a defense which strikes at *mens rea;* therefore in logic an obedient subordinate should be acquitted so long as he did not personally know of the order's illegality. Precedent aside, we would not agree with the argument. Heed must be given not only to subjective innocence-through-ignorance in the soldier, but to the consequences for his victims. Also, barbarism tends to invite reprisal to the detriment of our own force or disrepute which interferes with the achievement of war aims, even though the barbaric acts were preceded by orders for their commission. Casting the defense of obedience to orders solely in subjective terms of *mens rea* would operate practically to abrogate those objective restraints which are essential to functioning rules of war. The court members, after being given correct standards, properly rejected any defense of obedience to orders.

We find no impediment to the findings that appellant acted with murderous *mens rea,* including premeditation. The aggregate of all his contentions against the existence of murderous *mens rea* is no more absolving than a bare claim that he did not suspect he did any wrong act until after the operation, and indeed is not convinced of it yet. This is no excuse in law.

. . .

VIII. Sentence

In the report of the House Armed Services Investigating Subcommittee many of the extenuating circumstances affecting Lieutenant Calley are identified:

> In a war such as that in Vietnam, our forces in the field must live for extended periods of time in the shadow of violent death and in constant fear of being crippled or maimed by booby traps and mines. And added to this is the fact that this is not war in the conventional sense. The enemy is often not in uniform. A farmer or a housewife or a child by day may well be the enemy by night, fashioning or setting mines and booby traps, or giving aid, comfort and assistance to the uniformed enemy troops. Under such circumstances, one can understand how it might become increasingly difficult for our troops to accept the idea that many of those who kill them by night somehow become "innocent civilians" by day. Understandably such conditions can warp attitudes and mental processes causing temporary deviation from normality of action, reason or sense of values. And the degree of deviation may vary with each individual.

These general circumstances, and mitigating factors personal to Lieutenant Calley, were specifically considered by the convening authority who substantially reduced the confinement portion of the sentence to twenty years.

No doubt Lieutenant Calley would never have directed or participated in a mass killing in time of peace. Nevertheless, he committed an atrocity in time of war and it is in the context of war that we judge him. Destructive as war is, war is not an occasion for the unrestrained satisfaction of an individual soldier's proclivity to kill. An officer especially must exert his mind to keep his emotions in check, so that his judgment is not destroyed by fear, hate, or frustration. Probably Lieutenant Calley's judgment, perception, and stability were lesser in quality than the average lieutenant's and these deficiencies are mitigating to some extent. However, the deficiencies did not even approach the point of depriving him of the power of choice. The approved sentence is not too severe a consequence of his choosing to commit mass murder.

12. *United States* v. *Calley,* 22 U.S.C.M.A. 534, 48 C.M.R. 19 (1973)

. . .

Opinion

Quinn, Judge:

First Lieutenant Calley stands convicted of the premeditated murder of 22 infants, children, women, and old men, and of assault with intent to murder a child of about 2 years of age. All the killings and the assault took place on March 16, 1968 in the area of the village of My Lai in the Republic of South Vietnam. The Army Court of Military Review affirmed the findings of guilty and the sentence, which, as reduced by the convening authority, includes dismissal and confinement at hard labor for 20 years. The accused petitioned this Court for further review, alleging 30 assignments of error. We granted three of these assignments.

We consider first whether the public attention given the charges was so pernicious as to prevent a fair trial for the accused. . . .

We have carefully examined the extensive voir dire of the court members in the light of the pretrial materials submitted to us and we are satisfied that none of the court members had formed unalterable opinions about Lieutenant Calley's guilt from the publicity to which they had been exposed and that the total impact of that publicity does not oppose the individual declaration by each member retained on the court that he could, fairly and impartially, decide whether Lieutenant Calley was guilty of any crime upon the evidence presented in open court. . . .

In his second assignment of error the accused contends that the evidence is insufficient to establish his guilt beyond a reasonable doubt. Summarized, the pertinent evidence is as follows:

Lieutenant Calley was a platoon leader in C Company, a unit that was part of an organization known as Task Force Barker, whose mission was to subdue and drive out the enemy in an area in the Republic of Vietnam known popularly as Pinkville. Before March 16, 1968, this area, which included the village of My Lai 4, was a Viet Cong stronghold. C Company had operated in the area several times. Each time the unit had entered the area it suffered casualties by sniper fire, machine gun fire, mines, and other forms of attack. Lieutenant Calley had accompanied his platoon on some of the incursions.

On March 15, 1968, a memorial service for members of the company killed in the area during the preceding weeks was held. After the service Captain Ernest L. Medina, the commanding officer of C Company, briefed the company on a mission in the Pinkville area set for the next day. C Company was to serve as the main attack formation for Task Force Barker. In that role it would assault and neutralize My Lai 4, 5, and 6 and then mass for an assault on My Lai 1. Intelligence reports indicated that the unit would be opposed by a veteran enemy battalion, and that all civilians would be absent from the area. The objective was to destroy the enemy. Disagreement exists as to the instructions on the specifics of destruction.

Captain Medina testified that he instructed his troops that they were to destroy My Lai 4 by "burning the hootches, to kill the livestock, to close the wells and to destroy the food crops." Asked if women and children were to be killed, Medina said he replied in the negative, adding that, "You must use common sense. If they have a weapon and are trying to engage you, then you can shoot back, but you must use common sense." However, Lieutenant Calley testified that Captain Medina informed the troops they were to kill every living thing—men, women, children, and animals—and under no circumstances were they to leave any Vietnamese behind them as they passed through the villages enroute to their final objective. Other witnesses gave more or less support to both versions of the briefing.

On March 16, 1968, the operation began with interdicting fire. C Company was then brought to the area by helicopters. Lieutenant Calley's platoon was on the first lift. This platoon formed a defense perimeter until the remainder of the force was landed. The unit received no hostile fire from the village.

Calley's platoon passed the approaches to the village with his men firing heavily. Entering the village, the platoon encountered only unarmed, unresisting men, women, and children. The villagers, including infants held in their mothers' arms, were assembled and moved in separate groups to collection points. Calley testified that during this time he was radioed twice by Captain Medina, who demanded to know what was delaying the platoon. On being told that a large number of villagers had been detained, Calley said Medina ordered him to "waste them." Calley further testified that he obeyed the orders because he had been taught the doctrine of obedience throughout his military career. Medina denied that he gave any such order.

One of the collection points for the villagers was in the southern part of the village. There, Private First Class Paul D. Meadlo guarded a group of between 30 to 40 old men, women, and children. Lieutenant Calley approached Meadlo and told him, " 'You know what to do,' " and left. He returned shortly and asked Meadlo why the people were not yet dead. Meadlo replied he did not know that Calley had meant that they should be killed. Calley declared that he wanted them dead. He and Meadlo then opened fire on the group, until all but a few children fell. Calley then personally shot these children. He expended 4 or 5 magazines from his M–16 rifle in the incident.

Lieutenant Calley and Meadlo moved from this point to an irrigation ditch on the east side of My Lai 4. There, they encountered another group of civilians being held by several soldiers. Meadlo estimated that this group contained from 75 to 100 persons. Calley stated, " 'We got another job to do, Meadlo,' " and he ordered the group into the ditch. When all were in the ditch, Calley and Meadlo opened fire on them. Although ordered by Calley to shoot, Private First Class James J. Dursi refused to join in the killings, and Specialist Four Robert E. Maples refused to give his machine gun to Calley for use in the killings. Lieutenant Calley admitted that he fired into the ditch, with the muzzle of his weapon within 5 feet of people in it. He expended between 10 to 15 magazines of ammunition on this occasion.

With his radio operator, Private Charles Sledge, Calley moved to the north end of the ditch. There, he found an elderly Vietnamese monk, whom he interrogated. Calley struck the man with his rifle butt and then shot him in the head. Other testimony indicates that immediately afterwards a young child was observed running toward the village. Calley seized him by the arm, threw him into the ditch, and fired at him. Calley admitted interrogating and striking the monk, but denied shooting him. He also denied the incident involving the child.

Appellate defense counsel contend that the evidence is insufficient to establish the accused's guilt. They do not dispute Calley's participation in the homicides, but they argue that he did not act with the malice or *mens rea* essential to a conviction of murder; that the orders he received to kill everyone in the village were not palpably illegal; that he was acting in ignorance of the laws of war; that since he was told that only "the enemy" would be in the village, his honest belief that there were no innocent civilians in the village exonerates him of criminal responsibility for their deaths; and, finally, that his actions were in the heat of passion caused by reasonable provocation.

In assessing the sufficiency of the evidence to support findings of guilty, we cannot reevaluate the credibility of the witnesses or resolve conflicts in their testimony and thus decide anew whether the accused's guilt was established beyond a reasonable doubt. Our function is more limited; it is to determine whether the record contains enough evidence for the triers of the facts to find beyond a reasonable doubt each element of the offenses involved. . . .

The testimony of Meadlo and others provided the court members with ample evidence from which to find that Lieutenant Calley directed and personally participated in the intentional killing of men, women, and children, who were unarmed and in the custody of armed soldiers of C Company. If the prosecution's witnesses are believed, there is also ample evidence to support a finding that the accused deliberately shot the Vietnamese monk whom he interrogated, and that he seized, threw into a ditch, and fired on a child with the intent to kill.

Enemy prisoners are not subject to summary execution by their captors. Military law has long held that the killing of an unresisting prisoner is murder. Winthrop's Military Law and Precedents, 2d ed., 1920 Reprint, at 788–91.

> While it is lawful to kill an enemy "in the heat and exercise of war," yet "to kill such an enemy after he has laid down his arms . . . is murder."

Digest of Opinions of the Judge Advocates General of the Army, 1912, at 1074–75 n. 3.

Conceding for the purposes of this assignment of error that Calley believed the villagers were part of "the enemy," the uncontradicted evidence is that they were under the control of armed soldiers and were offering no resistance. In his testimony, Calley admitted he was aware of the requirement that prisoners be treated with respect. He also admitted he knew that the normal practice was to interrogate villagers, release those who could satisfactorily account for themselves, and evacuate the suspect among them for further examination. Instead of proceeding in the usual way, Calley executed all, without regard to age, condition, or possibility of suspicion. On the evidence, the court-martial could reasonably find Calley guilty of the offenses before us.

At trial, Calley's principal defense was that he acted in execution of Captain Medina's order to kill everyone in My Lai 4. Appellate defense counsel urge this defense as the most important factor in assessment of the legal sufficiency of the evidence. The argument, however, is inapplicable to whether the evidence is *legally* sufficient. Captain Medina denied that he issued any such order, either during the previous day's briefing or on the date the killings were carried out. Resolution of the conflict between his testimony and that of the accused was for the triers of the facts. United States v Guerra, 13 USCMA 463, 32 CMR 463 (1963).

The general findings of guilty, with exceptions as to the number of persons killed, does not indicate whether the court members found that Captain Medina did not issue the alleged order to kill, or whether, if he did, the court members believed that the accused knew the order was illegal. For the purpose of the legal sufficiency of the evidence, the record supports the findings of guilty.

In the third assignment of error, appellate defense counsel assert gross deficiencies in the military judge's instructions to the court members. Only two assertions merit discussion. One contention is that the judge should have, but did not, advise the court members of the necessity to find the existence of "malice aforethought" in connection with the murder charges; the second allegation is that the defense of compliance with superior orders was not properly submitted to the court members.

The existence *vel non* of malice, say appellate defense counsel, is the factor that distinguishes murder from manslaughter. See United States v Judd, 10 USCMA 113, 27 CMR 187 (1959). They argue that malice is an indispensable element of murder and must be the subject of a specific instruction. In support, they rely upon language in our opinion in United States v Roman, 1 USCMA 244, 2 CMR 150 (1952).

Roman involved a conviction of murder under Article of War 92, which provided for punishment of any person subject to military law "found guilty of murder." As murder was not further defined in the Article, it was necessary to refer to the common law element of malice on the instructions to the court members in order to distinguish murder from manslaughter. . . . In enactment of the Uniform Code of Military Justice, Congress eliminated malice as an element of murder by codifying the common circumstances under which that state of mind was deemed to be present. . . . One of the stated purposes of the Code was the "listing and definition of offenses, redrafted and rephrased in modern legislative language." S Rep No 486, 81st Song, 1st Sess 2 (1949). That purpose was accomplished by defining murder as the unlawful killing of a human being, without justification or excuse. Article 118, Uniform Code of Military Justice, 10 USC § 918. Article 118 also provides that murder is committed if the person, intending to kill or inflict grievous bodily harm, was engaged in an inherently dangerous act, or was engaged in the perpetration or attempted perpetration of certain felonies. In each of these instances before enactment of the Uniform Code, malice was deemed to exist and the homicide was murder. The Code language made it unnecessary that the court members be instructed in the earlier terminology of "malice aforethought." Now, the conditions and states of mind that must be the subject of instructions have been declared by Congress; they do not require reference to malice itself. . . .

The trial judge delineated the elements of premeditated murder for the court members in accordance with the statutory language. He instructed them that to convict Lieutenant Calley, they must be convinced beyond a reasonable doubt that the victims were dead; that their respective deaths resulted from specified acts of the accused; that the killings were unlawful; and that Calley acted with a premeditated design to kill. The judge defined accurately the meaning of an unlawful killing and the meaning of a "premeditated design to kill." These instructions comported fully with requirements of existing law for the offense of premeditated murder, and neither statute nor judicial precedent requires that reference also be made to the pre-Code concept of malice.

We turn to the contention that the judge erred in his submission of the defense of superior orders to the court. After fairly summarizing the evidence, the judge gave the following instructions pertinent to the issue:

> The killing of resisting or fleeing enemy forces is generally recognized as a justifiable act of war, and you may consider any such killings justifiable in this case. The law attempts to protect those persons not actually engaged in warfare, however; and limits the circumstances under which their lives may be taken.
>
> Both combatants captured by and noncombatants detained by the opposing force, regardless of their loyalties, political views, or prior acts, have the right to be treated as prisoners until released, confined, or executed, in accordance with law and established procedures, by competent authority sitting in judgment of such detained or captured individuals. Summary execution of detainees or prisoners is forbidden by law. Further, it's clear under the evidence presented in this case, that hostile acts or support of the enemy North Vietnamese or Viet Cong forces by inhabitants of My Lai (4) at some time prior to 16 March 1968, would not justify the summary execution of all or a part of the occupants of My Lai (4) on 16 March, nor would hostile acts committed that day, if, following the hostility, the belligerents surrendered or were captured by our forces. I therefore instruct you, as a matter of law, that if unresisting human beings were killed at My Lai (4) while within the effective custody and control of our military forces, their deaths cannot be considered justified, and any order to kill such people would be, as a matter of law, an illegal order. Thus, if you find that Lieutenant Calley received an order directing him to kill unresisting Vietnamese within his control or within the control of his troops, *that order would be an illegal order.*
>
> A determination that an order is illegal does not, of itself, assign criminal responsibility to the person following the order for acts done in compliance with it. Soldiers are taught to follow orders, and special attention is given to obedience of orders on the battlefield. Military effectiveness depends upon obedience to orders. On the other hand, the obedience of a soldier is not the obedience of an automaton. A soldier is a reasoning agent, obliged to respond, not as a machine, but as a person. The law takes these factors into account in assessing criminal responsibility for acts done in compliance with illegal orders.

> The acts of a subordinate done in compliance with an unlawful order given him by his superior are excused and impose no criminal liability upon him unless the superior's order is one which a man of *ordinary sense and understanding* would, under the circumstances, know to be unlawful, or if the order in question is actually known to the accused to be unlawful. . . .
>
> . . . In determining what orders, if any, Lieutenant Calley acted under, if you find him to have acted, you should consider all of the matters which he has testified reached him and which you can infer from other evidence that he saw and heard. Then, unless you find beyond a reasonable doubt that he was not acting under orders directing him in substance and effect to kill unresisting occupants of My Lai (4), you must determine whether Lieutenant Calley actually knew those orders to be unlawful.
>
> . . . In determining whether or not Lieutenant Calley had knowledge of the unlawfulness of any order found by you to have been given, you may consider all relevant facts and circumstances, including Lieutenant Calley's rank; educational background; OCS schooling; other training while in the Army, including basic training, and his training in Hawaii and Vietnam; his experience on prior operations involving contact with hostile and friendly Vietnamese; his age; and any other evidence tending to prove or disprove that on 16 March 1968, Lieutenant Calley knew the order was unlawful. If you find beyond a reasonable doubt, on the basis of all the evidence, that *Lieutenant Calley actually knew* the order under which he asserts he operated was unlawful, the fact that the order was given operates as no defense.
>
> Unless you find beyond reasonable doubt that the accused acted with actual knowledge that the order was unlawful, you must proceed to determine whether, under the circumstances, *a man of ordinary sense and understanding would have known the order was unlawful. Your deliberations on this question do not focus on Lieutenant Calley and the manner in which he perceived the legality of the order found to have been given him. The standard is that of a man of ordinary sense and understanding under the circumstances.*
>
> Think back to the events of 15 and 16 March 1968. . . . Then determine, in light of all the surrounding circumstances, whether the order, which to reach this point you will have found him to be operating in accordance with, is one which a man of ordinary sense and understanding would know to be unlawful. Apply this to each charged act which you have found Lieutenant Calley to have committed. Unless you are satisfied from the evidence, beyond a reasonable doubt, that a man of ordinary sense and understanding would have known the order to be unlawful, you must acquit Lieutenant Calley for committing acts done in accordance with the order. [Emphasis added.]

Appellate defense counsel contend that these instructions are prejudicially erroneous in that they require the court members to determine that Lieutenant Calley knew that an order to kill human beings in the circumstances under which he killed was illegal by the standard of whether "a man of ordinary sense and understanding" would know the order was illegal. They urge us to adopt as the governing test whether the order is so palpably or manifestly illegal that a person of "the commonest understanding" would be aware of its illegality. They maintain the standard stated by the judge is too strict and unjust; that it confronts members of the armed forces who are not persons of ordinary sense and understanding with the dilemma of choosing between the penalty of death for disobedience of an order in time of war on the one hand and the equally serious punishment for obedience on the other. Some thoughtful commentators on military law have presented much the same argument.[1]

The "ordinary sense and understanding" standard is set forth in the present Manual for Courts-Martial, United States, 1969 (Rev) and was the standard accepted by this Court in United States v Schultz, 18 USCMA 133, 39 CMR 133 (1969) and United States v Keenan, 18 USCMA 108, 39 CMR 108 (1969). It appeared as early as 1917. Manual for Courts-Martial, U. S. Army, 1917, paragraph 442. Apparently, it originated in a quotation from F. Wharton, Homicide § 485 (3d ed. 1907). Wharton's authority is Riggs v State, 3 Coldwell 85, 91 American Decisions 272, 273 (Tenn 1866), in which the court approved a charge to the jury as follows:

> [I]n its substance being clearly illegal, so that a man of ordinary sense and understanding would know as soon as he heard the order read or given that such order was illegal, would afford a private no protection for a crime committed under such order.

Other courts have used other language to define the substance of the defense. Typical is McCall v McDowell, 15 F Cas 1235, 1240 (CCD Cal 1867), in which the court said:

> But I am not satisfied that Douglas ought to be held liable to the plaintiff at all. He acted not as a volunteer, but as a subordinate in obedience to the order of his superior. Except in a plain case of excess of authority, where at first blush it is apparent and palpable to the commonest understanding that the order is illegal, I cannot but think that the law should excuse the military subordinate when acting in obedience to the orders of his commander. Otherwise he is placed in the dangerous dilemma of being liable in damages to third persons for obedience to an order, or to the loss of his commission and disgrace for disobedience thereto. . . . The first duty of a soldier is obedience, and without this there can be neither discipline nor efficiency

[1] In the words of one author: "If the standard of reasonableness continues to be applied, we run the unacceptable risk of applying serious punishment to one whose only crime is the slowness of his wit or his stupidity. The soldier, who honestly believes that he must obey an order to kill and is punished for it, is convicted not of murder but of simple negligence." Finkelstein, Duty to Obey as a Defense, March 9, 1970 (unpublished essay, Army War College). See also L. Norene, Obedience to Orders as a Defense to a Criminal Act, March 1971 (unpublished thesis presented to The Judge Advocate General's School, U.S. Army)

> in an army. If every subordinate officer and soldier were at liberty to question the legality of the orders of the commander, and obey them or not as they may consider them valid or invalid, the camp would be turned into a debating school, where the precious moment for action would be wasted in wordy conflicts between the advocates of conflicting opinions.

Colonel William Winthrop, the leading American commentator on military law, notes:

> But for the inferior to assume to determine the question of the lawfulness of an order given him by a superior would of itself, as a general rule, amount to insubordination, and such an assumption carried into practice would subvert military discipline. Where the order is apparently regular and *lawful on its face,* he is not to go behind it to satisfy himself that his superior has proceeded with authority, but is to obey it according to its terms, *the only exceptions recognized to the rule of obedience being cases of orders so manifestly beyond the legal power or discretion of the commander as to admit of no rational doubt of their unlawfulness. . . .*
>
> Except in such instances of palpable illegality, which must be of rare occurrence, the inferior should presume that the order was lawful and authorized and obey it accordingly, and in obeying it can scarcely fail to be held justified by a military court.

Winthrop's Military Law and Precedents, 2d ed., 1920 Reprint, at 296–297 (footnotes omitted) (emphasis added).

In the stress of combat, a member of the armed forces cannot reasonably be expected to make a refined legal judgment and be held criminally responsible if he guesses wrong on a question as to which there may be considerable disagreement. But there is no disagreement as to the illegality of the order to kill in this case. For 100 years, it has been a settled rule of American law that even in war the summary killing of an enemy, who has submitted to, and is under, effective physical control, is murder. Appellate defense counsel acknowledge that rule of law and its continued viability, but they say that Lieutenant Calley should not be held accountable for the men, women and children he killed because the court-martial could have found that he was a person of "commonest understanding" and such a person might not know what our law provides; that his captain had ordered him to kill these unarmed and submissive people and he only carried out that order as a good disciplined soldier should.

Whether Lieutenant Calley was the most ignorant person in the United States Army in Vietnam, or the most intelligent, he must be presumed to know that he could not kill the people involved here. The United States Supreme Court has pointed out that "[t]he rule that 'ignorance of the law will not excuse' [a positive act that constitutes a crime] . . . is deep in our law." Lambert v California, 355 US 225, 228 (1957). An order to kill infants and unarmed civilians who were so demonstrably incapable of resistance to the armed might of a military force as were those killed by Lieutenant Calley is, in my opinion, so palpably illegal that whatever conceptional difference there may be between a person of "commonest understanding" and a person of "common understanding," that difference could not have had any "impact on a court of lay members receiving the respective wordings in instructions," as appellate defense counsel contend. In my judgment, there is no possibility of prejudice to Lieutenant Calley in the trial judge's reliance upon the established standard of excuse of criminal conduct, rather than the standard of "commonest understanding" presented by the defense, or by the new variable test postulated in the dissent, which, with the inclusion of such factors for consideration as grade and experience, would appear to exact a higher standard of understanding from Lieutenant Calley than that of the person of ordinary understanding.

In summary, as reflected in the record, the judge was capable and fair, and dedicated to assuring the accused a trial on the merits as provided by law; his instructions on all issues were comprehensive and correct. Lieutenant Calley was given every consideration to which he was entitled, and perhaps more. We are impressed with the absence of bias or prejudice on the part of the court members. They were instructed to determine the *truth* according to the law and this they did with due deliberation and full consideration of the evidence. Their findings of guilty represent the truth of the facts as they determined them to be and there is substantial evidence to support those findings. No mistakes of procedure can cast doubt upon them.

Consequently, the decision of the Court of Military Review is affirmed.

DUNCAN, JUDGE (concurring in the result):

My difference of opinion from Judge Quinn's view of the defense of obedience to orders is narrow. The issue of obedience to orders was raised in defense by the evidence. Contrary to Judge Quinn, I do not consider that a presumption arose that the appellant knew he could not kill the people involved. The Government, as I see it, is not entitled to a presumption of what the appellant knew of the illegality of an order. It is a matter for the factfinders under proper instructions.

Paragraph 216, Manual for Courts-Martial, United States, 1969 (Rev), provides for special defenses: excuse because of accident or misadventure; self-defense; entrapment; coercion or duress; physical or financial inability; and obedience to apparently lawful orders. Subparagraph *d* of paragraph 216 is as follows:

> An order requiring the performance of a military duty may be inferred to be legal. An act performed manifestly beyond the scope of authority, or pursuant to an order that a man of ordinary sense and understanding would know to be illegal, or in a wanton manner in the discharge of a lawful duty, is not excusable.

The military judge clearly instructed the members pursuant to this provision of the Manual. The heart of the issue is whether, under the circumstances of this case, he should have abandoned the Manual standard and fashioned another. The defense urges a purely subjective standard; the dissent herein yet another. I suggest that there are important general as well as certain specific considerations which convince me that the standard should not be abandoned. The process of promulgating Manual provisions is geared to produce requirements for the system only after most serious reflection by knowledgeable and concerned personnel. These persons have full regard for the needs of the armed forces and genuine concern for the plight of one accused. Those who prepared the Manual provision and the President of the United States, the Commander-in-Chief, who approved and made the provision a part of our law, were aware that disobedience to orders is the anathema to an efficient military force. Judge Quinn points out that this Court has established as precedent the applicability of the special defense upon proof adduced pursuant to the Manual standard. These are important general reasons for not aborting a standard that has been long in existence and often used.

It is urged that in using the Manual test of "a man of ordinary sense and understanding" those persons at the lowest end of the scale of intelligence and experience in the services may suffer conviction while those more intelligent and experienced would possess faculties which would cause them to adjure the order with impunity. Such an argument has some attraction but in my view falls short of that which should impel a court to replace that which is provided to us as law.

It appears to me that all tests which measure an accused's conduct by an objective standard—whether it is the test of "palpable illegality to the commonest understanding" or whether the test establishes a set of profile considerations by which to measure the accused's ability to assess the legality of the order—are less than perfect, and they have a certain potential for injustice to the member having the slowest wit and quickest obedience. Obviously the higher the standard, the likelihood is that fewer persons will be able to measure up to it. Knowledge of the fact that there are other standards that are arguably more fair does not convince me that the standard used herein is unfair, on its face, or as applied to Lieutenant Calley.

Perhaps a new standard, such as the dissent suggests, has merit; however, I would leave that for the legislative authority or for the cause where the record demonstrates harm from the instructions given. I perceive none in this case. The general verdict in this case implies that the jury believed a man of ordinary sense and understanding would have known the order in question to be illegal. Even conceding arguendo that this issue should have been resolved under instructions requiring a finding that almost every member of the armed forces would have immediately recognized that the order was unlawful, as well as a finding that as a consequence of his age, grade, intelligence, experience, and training, Lieutenant Calley should have recognized the order's illegality, I do not believe the result in this case would have been different.

I believe the trial judge to have been correct in his denial of the motion to dismiss the charges for the reason that pretrial publicity made it impossible for the Government to accord the accused a fair trial.

Both the principal opinion and the analysis of the Court of Military Review state that in the enactment of the Uniform Code of Military Justice Congress has, in effect, codified the requirement of malice aforethought by defining murder as the unlawful killing of a human being, without justification or excuse. Article 118, UCMJ, 10 USC § 918. It should also be noted that in the case at bar the members of the panel were charged that a finding that the homicides were without justification or excuse was necessary to convict for premeditated murder. Furthermore, I cannot say that the evidence lacks sufficiency to convict in respect to any of the charges.

DARDEN, CHIEF JUDGE (dissenting):

Although the charge the military judge gave on the defense of superior orders was not inconsistent with the Manual treatment of this subject, I believe the Manual provision is too strict in a combat environment. Among other things, this standard permits serious punishment of persons whose training and attitude incline them either to be enthusiastic about compliance with orders or not to challenge the authority of their superiors. The standard also permits conviction of members who are not persons of ordinary sense and understanding.

The principal opinion has accurately traced the history of the current standard. Since this Manual provision is one of substantive law rather than one relating to procedure or modes of proof, the Manual rule is not binding on this Court, which has the responsibility for determining the principles that govern justification in the law of homicide. United States v Smith, 13 USCMA 105, 32 CMR 105 (1962). My impression is that the weight of authority, including the commentators whose articles are mentioned in the principal opinion, supports a more liberal approach to the defense of superior orders. Under this approach, superior orders should constitute a defense except "in a plain case of excess of authority, where at first blush it is apparent and palpable to the commonest understanding that the order is illegal." McCall v McDowell, 15 F Cas 1235, 1240 (No. 8,673) (CCD Cal 1867); *In re* Fair, 100 F 149, 155 (CCD Neb 1900); Winthrop's Military Law and Precedents, 2d ed., 1920 Reprint, at 296–97.

While this test is phrased in language that now seems "somewhat archaic and ungrammatical," the test recognizes that the essential ingredient of discipline in any armed force is obedience to orders and that this obedience is so important it should not be penalized unless the order would be recognized as illegal, not by what some hypothetical reasonable soldier would have known, but also by "those persons at the lowest end of the scale of intelligence and experience in the services." This is the real purpose in permitting superior orders to be a defense, and it ought not to be restricted by the concept of a fictional reasonable man so that, regardless of his personal characteristics, an accused judged after the fact may find himself punished for either obedience or disobedience, depending on whether the evidence will support the finding of simple negligence on his part.

It is true that the standard of a "reasonable man" is used in other areas of military criminal law, *e.g.,* in connection with the provocation necessary to reduce murder to voluntary manslaughter; what constitutes an honest and reasonable mistake; and, indirectly, in connection with involuntary manslaughter. But in none of these instances do we have the coutervailing consideration of avoiding the subversion of obedience to discipline in combat by encouraging a member to weigh the legality of an order or whether the superior had the authority to issue it. See Martin v Mott, 25 US 19, 30 (1827).

The preservation of human life is, of course, of surpassing importance. To accomplish such preservation, members of the armed forces must be held to standards of conduct that will permit punishment of atrocities and enable this nation to follow civilized concepts of warfare. In defending the current standard, the Army Court of military Review expressed the view that:

> Heed must be given not only to the subjective innocence-through-ignorance in the soldier, but to the consequences for his victims. Also, barbarism tends to invite reprisal to the detriment of our own force or disrepute which interferes with the achievement of war aims, even though the barbaric acts were preceded by orders for their commission. Casting the defense of obedience to orders solely in subjective terms of *mens rea* would operate practically to abrogate those objective restraints which are essential to functioning rules of war.

United States v Calley, 46 CMR 1131, 1184 (ACMR 1973).

I do not disagree with these comments. But while humanitarian considerations compel us to consider the impact of actions by members of our armed forces on citizens of other nations, I am also convinced that the phrasing of the defense of superior orders should have as its principal objective fairness to the unsophisticated soldier and those of somewhat limited intellect who nonetheless are doing their best to perform their duty.

The test of palpable illegality to the commonest understanding properly balances punishment for the obedience of an obviously illegal order against protection to an accused for following his elementary duty of obeying his superiors. Such a test reinforces the need for obedience as an essential element of military discipline by broadly protecting the soldier who has been effectively trained to look to his superiors for direction. It also promotes fairness by permitting the military jury to consider the particular accused's intelligence, grade, training, and other elements directly related to the issue of whether he should have known an order was illegal. Finally, that test imputes such knowledge to an accused not as a result of simple negligence but on the much stronger circumstantial concept that almost anyone in the armed forces would have immediately recognized that the order was palpably illegal.

I would adopt this standard as the correct instruction for the jury when the defense of superior orders is in issue. Because the original case language is archaic and somewhat ungrammatical, I would rephrase it to require that the military jury be instructed that, despite his asserted defense of superior orders, an accused may be held criminally accountable for his acts, allegedly committed pursuant to such orders, if the court members are convinced beyond a reasonable doubt (1) that almost every member of the armed forces would have immediately recognized that the order was unlawful, and (2) that the accused should have recognized the order's illegality as a consequence of his age, grade, intelligence, experience, and training.

The temptation is to say that even under this new formulation Lieutenant Calley would have been found guilty. No matter how such a position is phrased, essentially it means that the appellate judge rather than the military jury is functioning as a fact finder. My reaction to this has been expressed by the former chief justice of the California Supreme Court in these words:

> If an erroneous instruction or an erroneous failure to give an instruction relates to a substantial element of the appellant's case, an appellate court would not find it highly probable that the error did not influence the verdict.

R. Traynor, The Riddle of Harmless Error 74 (1970).

The same authority also expressed this thought:

> The concept of fairness extends to reconsideration of the merits when a judgment has been or might have been influenced by error. In that event there should be a retrial in the trial court, time consuming or costly though it may be. The short-cut alternative of reconsidering the merits in the appellate court, because it is familiar with the evidence and aware of the error, has the appeal of saving time and money. Unfortunately it does not measure up to accepted standards of fairness.

Id. at 20.

In the instant case, Lieutenant Calley's testimony placed the defense of superior orders in issue, even though he conceded that he knew prisoners were normally to be treated with respect and that the unit's normal practice was to interrogate Vietnamese villagers, release those who could account for themselves, and evacuate those suspected of being a part of the enemy forces. Although crucial parts of his testimony were sharply contested, according to Lieutenant Calley, (1) he had received a briefing before the assault in which he was instructed that every living thing in the village was to be killed, including women and children; (2) he was informed that speed was important in securing the village and moving forward; (3) he was ordered that under no circumstances were any Vietnamese to be allowed to stay behind the lines of his forces; (4) the residents of the village who were taken into custody were hindering the progress of his platoon in taking up the position it was to occupy; and (5) when he informed Captain Medina of this hindrance, he was ordered to kill the villagers and to move his platoon to a proper position.

In addition to the briefing, Lieutenant Calley's experience in the Pinkville area caused him to know that, in the past, when villagers had been left behind his unit, the unit had immediately received sniper fire from the rear as it pressed forward. Faulty intelligence apparently led him also to believe that those persons in the village were not innocent civilians but were either enemies or enemy sympathizers. For a participant in the My Lai operation, the circumstances that could have obtained there may have caused the illegality of alleged orders to kill civilians to be much less clear than they are in a hindsight review.[8]

Since the defense of superior orders was not submitted to the military jury under what I consider to be the proper standard, I would grant Lieutenant Calley a rehearing.

I concur in Judge Quinn's opinion on the other granted issues.

[8] A New York Times Book Reviewer has noted, "One cannot locate the exact moment in his [Calley's] narrative when one can be absolutely certain that one would have acted differently given the same circumstances." See Paris ed., New York Herald Tribune, September 13, 1971.

13. *Calley* v. *Callaway,* 382 F. Supp. 650 (1974)

Opinion, Elliott, Chief Judge.

. . .

Having exhausted the appeal procedures provided in the military system, the Petitioner on February 11, 1974 filed a petition for writ of habeas corpus in this court praying that he be discharged from custody on the ground that his conviction is constitutionally invalid

. . .

When he enlisted in the Army he was given the usual basic training and he later asked for and received a recommendation for Officer Candidate School and was accepted for a class starting in March, 1967. After he finished OCS he was assigned to the 11th Infantry Brigade in Hawaii where he was taught the usual infantry subjects and was specifically informed that he was required to give strict obedience to orders.

The Petitioner's first assignment in Vietnam was at Duc Pho. He had a short series of classes there and most of the instruction was given by ARVN instructors. This was his first indoctrination about the character of the potential enemy. He was told that women were as dangerous as men and that children were even more dangerous because they were unsuspected. He was also informed that the women were frequently better shots than the men and that the children were used to plant mines and booby traps. The first military operations in Vietnam in which he was engaged were those in which his unit was used for reconnaissance along trails and in seeking out and seizing enemy materials. During these missions the unit was continually subject to fire from unknown and unseen individuals. A number of men in the company had been killed or wounded and prior to the operation at My Lai Four they had never seen the persons responsible for the death or injury of their buddies. Consequently, they formed the opinion that civilians were in part responsible.

. . .

[J]ust one day before Petitioner was due to be discharged from the Army at Fort Benning, Georgia, charges were preferred against him. He later went to trial on four specifications which charged him with the murder of more than 100 occupants of the village of My Lai, the alleged victims not being identified by name, age or sex. By the time charges were brought against Calley most of the members of the company who participated in the assault at My Lai were no longer in the Army and, therefore, not subject to court-martial. The Army subsequently brought charges against some additional individuals who still remained in the Army, but all of these other cases were either later dismissed or the defendants were promptly acquitted. Of all those present at My Lai on March 16, 1968, only the Petitioner was convicted.

The Petitioner contests the validity of his conviction . . . the Court considers only three of these contentions . . . dimension and, therefore, appropriate for consideration by this Court on review. These contentions, . . . in the order listed. . . . as follows:

1. The contention that the Petitioner was denied a fair and impartial trial because of massive adverse pre-trial publicity.
2. The contention that the Petitioner was denied his right of confrontation with witnesses and was denied compulsory process for obtaining witnesses in his favor.
3. The contention that the Petitioner was denied due process by being convicted on charges and specifications which were improperly drawn and illegally used by the prosecution.

. . .

The Pre-trial Publicity Issue

Never in the history of the military justice system, and perhaps in the history of American courts, has any accused ever encountered such intense and continuous prejudicial publicity as did the Petitioner herein. Virtually every newspaper, periodical, magazine, television station, radio station, and every other news medium carried continuous and extensive interviews, reports, pictures, articles, statements, quotes, and editorial comments concerning the Petitioner's role in the so-called My Lai incident.

An examination of the publicity itself, the actions taken (and not taken) to protect the Petitioner's individual right to a fair trial, the lack of power inherent in the military judge and in the military system itself to protect that right, the lack of cooperation on the part of the United States Department of Justice in enforcing the judge's orders, the inherently prejudicial nature of the publicity itself, and the ineffective nature of the protective restraints placed on witnesses and jurors prior to the court-martial lead me to the inescapable conclusion that the Petitioner was denied a fair trial as required by our nation's Constitution. Stated otherwise, I find that the Petitioner was denied a fair hearing at his court-martial, not only because of the inherently prejudicial nature of the publicity to which the triers of fact were exposed, but because certain inherent defects in the military system which tried him existed, making it impotent to protect the Petitioner from the prejudicial publications.

On September 5, 1969 the Petitioner was charged with the murder of civilians as a result of the My Lai incident. There was a short initial period during which there was little or no media coverage of the charges against the Petitioner. However, on November 13, 1969 an article by Seymour Hersh triggered an avalanche of publicity concerning the incident and the Petitioner's role therein.

In the military justice system there is no continuously sitting judicial officer who may act to protect the rights of the individual accused. Unlike the civilian system, in the military system there is no judge with the judicial powers to protect the individual until the case is *referred to trial* by court-martial. Under the Uniform Code of Military Justice there is *no court* until a convening authority convenes the court-martial and details a military judge. Before an accused's case is *referred* to trial there must be a *preferral* of charges and an investigation. The investigating officer makes a recommendation as to the disposition of the case. Only after this recommendation and review by the convening authority's legal officer does the convening authority *refer* the case to a general court-martial and *only then* is a court of special jurisdiction created. The convening authority refers the case to a court-martial convened by a "court-martial convening order" in which he has selected the court members, the triers of fact, the prosecutor, the detailed defense counsel, and the military judge. Thus a situation is created where an individual stands accused of a crime but there exists no judicial officer to whom he may turn for protection of his right to a fair trial until a later time when the charges are referred to trial by court-martial. In Petitioner's case, during this period of time between preferral of the charges against him and the referral of the case with the concomitant appointment of a military judge, much of the highly prejudicial matters were first broadcast and published by the media. During this time Petitioner was without the means to protect himself, through no fault of his own, but because the military system did not provide a judicial officer to protect him. The impact of the publicity released during this period when there was no military judge cannot be doubted.

Calley was originally painted as a "mass murderer" involved in the unlawful killing of some 567 Orientals which number included men, women and children. The newspaper articles and television interviews quoted prospective witnesses and stated factual and legal conclusions. Some of the more common phrases used by the news media in describing the My Lai incident included the following: "massacre", "atrocity", "slaughter of non-combatants", "dozens of women and children shot down in cold blood", "wanton killing", "an act of brutality that cannot have been exceeded in Hitler's time", "unjustified killing of innocent civilians", "a barbaric act". Calley himself was described as everything from a "mass murderer" to a "ghoul".

. . .

On November 17, 1969 the Columbia Broadcasting System TV evening news interviewed ex-GI Ronald Ridenhour, the individual whose letters containing hearsay allegations led to the Army investigation into the My Lai incident, and in response to the news correspondent's question concerning what he had charged in his letters to members of the Government, Ridenhour responded:

> As specifically as I can tell you, the charges were that an American line company had swept through this village and that there were a great, great number of inhabitants of the village who were murdered, who were slaughtered or massacred or killed, whatever, without provocation.

Of course, the daily newspapers also interviewed Ridenhour and in the newspaper interviews Ridenhour actually named Lt. Calley as being one who was involved in the incident which Mr. Ridenhour characterized in the same breath as being "murder", "slaughter" and "massacre".

The desire of news representatives to publish statements of prospective witnesses took them to Vietnam, where they interviewed "survivors of the assault on My Lai Four". On November 18, 1969, the American Broadcasting Company TV evening news reported that inhabitants of the hamlet near My Lai had been interviewed by their representative and that they had stated that 567 civilians were killed without provocation, and the newscaster stated that statements from these survivors had been taken live from the inhabitants on the scene. These interviews, in which Calley's name was freely bandied about, were conducted by the TV anchorman in front of a large map of Vietnam on which blotches of blood appeared, obviously for the purpose of accentuating the horror of the story.

. . .

By mid-November, 1969 Ronald Haeberle, a former Army photographer, had copyrighted and sold for $19,500 some pictures to Life Magazine which were alleged to represent views of the "dead bodies" at My Lai. Mr. Haeberle made an additional $35,000 by sales of his pictures to Time Magazine and certain newspapers and overseas publications. These horrifying full-page color pictures were published in gruesome detail by Life and later by many newspapers and other periodicals both in this country and throughout the world, and Calley's name and the fact that he was facing court-martial was frequently mentioned in connection with them. On November 20, 1969 these pictures were displayed by CBS-TV news along with comments by Newscaster Harry Reasoner. Each photograph was displayed in close-up detail, and to increase the shock effect of the display there was absolute silence while the pictures were on the TV screen. On that same date NBC-TV likewise dealt with the Haeberle photographs. *Some of these pictures were the very exhibits which were later used by the prosecution in the prosecution in the Calley trial and constituted some of the most damaging evidence presented by the prosecution.*

Thus, we have a situation where the prosecution's evidence is being broadcast, published and displayed to the world (including all prospective jurors) before there is even a court constituted for the trial.

. . .

On November 26, 1969 Secretary of the Army Resor appeared before a Congressional committee and it is interesting to observe that in his remarks to them he started out by saying:

> As you know, it is not *normally* the policy of the Executive Branch to disclose information pertaining to ongoing criminal investigations . . . especially when, as in the case here, new and perhaps conflicting evidence may come to light as the investigation continues. In addition, there has already been far too much comment in the press on matters of an evidentiary nature, and we are very concerned that prejudicial pre-trial publicity may make it difficult to accord the accused in any prosecution a fair trial. (Emphasis added.)

But having so said, the Secretary then proceeded to tell the committee all about the details of the alleged incident and even exhibited picture slides, etc., for the edification of the committee and told the committee that the Army intended to prosecute. This was on the day after the Army court-martial was first convened for the consideration of the Calley case and, of course, his recital received wide publicity at the same time the first convening of the court was being publicized.

. . .

On the same date, November 26, 1969, in a news conference at the White House Press Secretary Ziegler in a press interview, specifically stating that he was speaking for the President of the United States, made the following pronouncement:

> An incident such as that alleged in this case is in direct violation, not only of U. S. military policy, but is also abhorrent to the conscience of all the American people. . . . Appropriate action is and will be taken to assure that illegal and immoral conduct as alleged be dealt with in accordance with the strict rules of military justice.

Also on that date Mr. William P. Rogers, Secretary of State, was interviewed on a national television network and when asked about "the alleged massacre of Vietnamese civilians" made this comment:

> I think that if the allegations are true it is a shocking, shocking incident and all we can do is to court-martial any responsible persons and to show the world that we don't condone this. Obviously, if anything of this kind happened, it is in direct contradiction of the orders. . . . It is a tragic event, if it is true. And certainly there is indication of some truth at least. So we are highly concerned; it is a shocking thing.

Obviously, since Calley was already being court-martialed Rogers was saying that he considered Calley a person responsible. And then he accentuates that by expressing his opinion that there is truth in the allegations made against Calley.

The first date on which the military judge had authority to sit and take any action in the Calley case was November 25, 1969, and although it is fundamental in our American system of justice that a defendant is to be presumed innocent until proven guilty by competent evidence in a valid court proceeding, there were many representatives of the news media who were by that time telling the American public (including all prospective jurors) that the "facts" as developed by the news media and published by them had overcome that presumption, and indeed, that they would be justified in presuming that Calley was guilty, some even insinuating that to give the man a trial would be sort of a superfluous act.

. . .

In summary, the American public (including all prospective jurors), and indeed the entire world, had by that time been so impregnated with the thought of Calley's guilt that it could well have been assumed that all that would be necessary would be for the court-martial to convene and for the Judge to announce: "Bring the guilty rascal in and we will give him a fair trial."

The avalanche of prejudicial pre-trial publicity in this case and the dangers inherent therein were recognized by the military judge on the first day on which the court was empowered to sit, November 25, 1969, and he made a finding on that date that the news media had so widely publicized the alleged events and the statements of witnesses that there was a "clear and present danger" to the constitutional right of the Petitioner to a fair trial and due process of law, and on that date, in an unusual motion, both the prosecution and the defense joined in asking for the issuance of a show cause order to segments of the news media prohibiting further disclosure of statements made by any individual allegedly connected with the My Lai incident. This joint motion recited that:

> This motion is based upon the repeated and unprecedented newspaper, television, radio and periodical accounts and pictures purporting to represent evidentiary accounts of alleged witnesses to the case now pending before this court and representing a clear and present danger to the constitutional and inherent rights of 1st Lt. William Calley, Jr. to a fair trial under the Fifth and Sixth Amendments to the United States Constitution, and to his right to restrict prejudicial news reporting under the Ninth Amendment of the United States Constitution, to the rights of the United States Government to a fair trial and to the rights of both parties to enjoy military due process of law.

Numerous newspaper clippings, summaries of television broadcasts, and other evidentiary items, were submitted in support of the motion. The military judge denied the motion and stated:

> I frankly believe that the responsible news media are capable of policing their own activities.

During this hearing on November 25 the military judge in a futile attempt to protect the Petitioner from prejudicial publicity did order all prospective witnesses not to discuss their testimony or to disclose any other evidence to anyone except counsel in the case or in related proceedings. However, he did this fully realizing that he did not have the power to enforce those orders. In fact, his orders were repeatedly violated. He also issued an order to the prospective court members (jurors) instructing them to avoid contact with media reports of the My Lai incident and to refrain from discussing the case. Unfortunately, only one of the six members who eventually sat on the courts as jurors was subject to this order since the other five members were detailed one year later by the convening authority.

Three days later in another pre-trial hearing the military judge took note of the fact that he had evidence before him of wilful violations of the order which the court had issued to witnesses not to allow themselves to be interviewed and of the fact that representatives of the news media were enticing witnesses to do so, but he then proceeded to say that:

> 1. The possibility of prejudice to this defendant's constitutional rights to a fair trial is real and apparent.
>
> 2. It is recognized . . . that the courts-martial system is a federal jurisdiction, but it is not a part of the federal judiciary system.
>
> 3. Thus as a matter of law this court does not possess the pre-trial power of contempt or any other judicial remedy to enforce the mandates of the United States Supreme Court as that court provided in Sheppard v. Maxwell, 384 U.S. 333. [86 S.Ct. 1507, 16 L.Ed.2d 600]

He then observed that he thought he had done everything within his power to safeguard the rights of the defendant and he concluded his findings by saying that in view of the alarming situation:

> . . . counsel are directed to seek appropriate relief from a court within the federal judicial system or elsewhere as deemed necessary.

A joint petition was filed by the prosecution and defense counsel with the United States Court of Military Appeals, but the relief prayed for was denied by that court on the basis that the trial judge "could protect the petitioner".

On December 8, 1969 the military judge, over defense counsel's objection, ruled that the publicity surrounding the Petitioner's case had subsided and he thought the danger to a fair trial was past. This determination was made in spite of the fact that defense counsel presented evidence showing further interviews with witnesses on television, on radio and in the newspapers. . . . [T]here was in fact *no* relaxation of the news coverage or of the danger and prejudice it brought to bear on the Petitioner's case. When defense counsel introduced exhibits showing recent public statements made by the President and other members of the Defense Department the military judge stated "But I couldn't stop that". It is made obvious by the military judge's own admission and by everything else in the record that his efforts to control witnesses and media between the dates of November 25, 1969 and December 8, 1969 availed nothing and is a perfect demonstration of the impotence of a military judge in the military system when civilian outsiders and authorities senior to the military judge within the military system decide to publicize matters which are prejudicial to an accused.[7]

On December 16, 1969 the military judge again determined that some

[7] The Petitioner has not questioned nor does this Court question the sincerity of the military judge. However, these efforts were ineffective; his orders were all bark and no bite, and necessarily so, because by law his orders had no teeth. The contempt power of the court-martial judge is limited to punishment of an act of contempt occurring in the presence of the Court. For example, even though process may issue to compel civilian witnesses to testify and to compel the production of other evidence as in the federal civilian courts, any violation of such a subpoena or order must be prosecuted by the Justice Department in the Federal Courts. See Articles 47 and 48 of the Uniform Code of Military Justice.

potential prosecution witnesses were violating his orders by granting interviews, and again he proclaimed that he was helpless to protect the Petitioner as could be done by courts in the federal judicial system under the *Sheppard* mandate. But he did direct trial counsel to notify the Justice Department of the violations and ask the assistance of the Justice Department in enforcing his orders to prospective witnesses. Trial counsel did, on December 17, 1969, follow the direction of the military judge and wrote to then Attorney General Mitchell, calling the Attorney General's attention to the orders which had been issued by the trial judge concerning disclosure of evidence and calling his attention to the fact that it was clear that the judge's orders were being violated by certain witnesses and by certain segments of the news media, and enclosing with the letter matters in support of the allegation that the violations were occurring. The letter stated that these matters were being called to the Attorney General's attention because of the military judge's lack of authority over civilians and with the request that the Attorney General initiate possible prosecutions by the Department of Justice in order that Calley's rights to a fair trial would not be jeopardized, etc.

Not only did the Attorney General fail to take any action whatever, *he even neglected to acknowledge receipt of the communication from the military court.*[8]

. . .

Although the military judge had on November 25, 1969 ordered all prospective witnesses in the Calley case not to make any public statements concerning the matter, and although it was well known that one of the contentions which would be made by Calley in his defense would be that the company was carrying out orders given to it by the company commander, the military judge on December 3, 1969 made an exception to this rule and permitted Captain Medina to hold a news conference in the Pentagon the next day. On December 4 Captain Medina, accompanied by his lawyer, put on an impressive performance for all the news media and repeated his statements in subsequent television appearances and newspaper interviews that took up the next four or five days, in all of which he denied issuing orders to kill civilians. No immediate attempt was made by the military judge to bar Medina from speaking out even after he repeatedly denied issuing orders to destroy the village, although as hereto-

[8] But when a civilian witness who had been subpoenaed to testify *against* Calley failed to comply, as the prosecution thought he should, the Justice Department *promptly* initiated criminal proceedings in aid of the military court. See United States v. John Sack, U.S.D.C. for the Middle District of Georgia, Columbus Division, Cr.No.5514 (1971). So, it would appear that with the Department of Justice "justice" was a one-way street where Calley was concerned.

fore noted, this was a question which bore heavily on the defense of Lt. Calley. Calley's lawyers were greatly disturbed by the development and the military judge explained that he had excepted Medina from his order "because I didn't think he would grant an interview". He then—after Calley's defense had been effectively torpedoed—ordered Medina to stop talking.

This development is highly important in our consideration of this case because it later appeared that one of the jurors who sat in judgment on Calley witnessed these interviews of Medina and said that he *was impressed and thought that Medina was a credible witness.* Since Medina later appeared as a witness in the Calley trial, what this means is that one of the jurors had already concluded that Medina was credible and that in consequence Calley could not be credible on this vital point.

Although Medina was finally barred from talking, his attorney, F. Lee Bailey, continued to take Medina's case to the public and point the finger at Calley. Within a period of two days in mid-January, 1970 Bailey appeared on two Washington television shows and on one of these broadcasts he said that he didn't think that anyone "of any higher rank than Lt. Calley is going to be put on trial because right above him is Captain Medina. . . . it wouldn't make it more fair to charge Medina if he had nothing to do with it. If Calley shot some people he shouldn't have shot . . . Medina didn't know about it, didn't tell him to and had no opportunity to stop him."

So, here was the lawyer for Medina instructing the public (and all prospective jurors) that Calley's defense was a sham. Of course, the newspapers gave "ample" pre-trial coverage to Medina's damaging "testimony".

. . .

As if enough damage had not already been done to Calley's chances to obtain a fair trial, the President of the United States, who was also the Commander in Chief of the Armed Forces and therefore the Commander in Chief of each of the military board members who would decide Calley's case, on December 9, 1969 held a nationally televised news conference in which he discussed the My Lai incident, during the course of which he made the following startling statement:

> What appears was certainly a massacre, and under no circumstances was it justified. . . .
>
> Now this record of generosity, of decency, must not be allowed to be smeared and slurred because of this kind of an incident. That's why I'm going to do everything I possibly can to see that all the facts in this incident are brought to light, and that those who are charged, if they are found guilty, are punished, because if it is isolated it is against our policy and we shall see

> to it that what these men did—if they did it—does not smear the decent men that have gone to Vietnam in a very, in my opinion, important cause.

Then to further compound the damage General William C. Westmoreland, the Chief of Staff of the Army and therefore the highest ranking Army officer to whom all of the later court members were subordinate, held a press conference in Charlotte, North Carolina, during the course of which he said:

> I would say there is no justification for it whatsoever, and it is contrary to the rules of land warfare which has always governed the conduct of our troops on the battlefield. And strictly contrary to regulations and contrary to the instructions that were issued to the troops in Viet Nam. . . .
>
> . . . [t]he individuals who have committed offenses, after appropriate investigation has been made of course, will be charged and if the charges are supported by further investigation known as a Form 32 investigation, . . . they will be court-martialled. . . . In other words, the law of the land which pertains in this case, now the Uniform Code of Military Justice, will be followed and the individuals will be given justice.

Three days earlier General Westmoreland appeared at Fort Campbell, Kentucky and was reported by the press as having declared "that an unlawful order from a superior does not excuse or justify one of our soldiers in killing an innocent civilian".

Thus did the President and the highest ranking Army officer instruct all prospective jurors in advance of trial (1) that Calley had no defense, and (2) that the Army's good name was at stake.

It has heretofore been noted that when these statements by the President and General Westmoreland were brought to the attention of the military judge, along with those made by the Secretary of State, Secretary of Defense, and the Secretary of the Army, the military judge candidly admitted "I can't stop that".

. . .

From late November, 1969 until Calley's trial began and continuing while the trial was in progress various persons prominent in the Government (including the President and the Secretary of Defense) and high ranking officers in the Army granted interviews and made statements to the effect that My Lai was to be regarded as an "isolated incident", "not typical" and "to be condemned"; that the Army's image had been "besmirched", and that the "guilty" should be convicted, thereby "clearing the air" and restoring the Army's good name. The clear implication was that unless "somebody" was convicted by court-martial the Army would suffer, and there wasn't much doubt about who that "somebody" was.

. . .

By mid-1970 the question whether Calley could obtain a fair trial was a subject widely discussed in legal circles and the concern of the profession was, in this Court's opinion, wholly justified because by the time Calley's trial began he had already been crucified.

. . .

Petitioner does not claim that the press was not entitled to report the news concerning the litigation in which he was involved, rather he asserts, and rightfully so, that he is entitled to relief if the court in which he is being tried and the government which tried him are unable to prevent the adverse effect of the free dissemination of the material. No system of justice can rightfully call itself just if it operates in an atmosphere where the courts are unable to protect the accused who appears before them. Such a requirement is surely fundamental to due process of law.

. . .

The published and televised statements of Ridenhour, Meadlo, Terry, Thompson, Medina, Westmoreland, the President and others were of such nature to clearly convict the Petitioner. Meadlo said that Calley not only ordered him to shoot "innocent civilians" but shot them himself. Medina denied giving Calley any order to act as he did. The statements of the President and Westmoreland ruled out any justification or excuse for his actions. The total effect was to convict the Petitioner just as surely as if he had confessed on the television screen.

Yet the due process clause of the Constitution guarantees to every accused, whether civilian or military, that the evidence against him shall come in open court, from the witness stand, admitted according to law, with the full judicial protection of the accused's right to confrontation and cross-examination.

. . .

Petitioner's counsel at the beginning of his trial placed before the military judge a two-part motion requesting dismissal of the charges because of prejudicial pre-trial publicity. The first portion of the motion contended that the prejudice from publicity precluded Calley from *ever* receiving a fair trial. This motion was denied before *voir dire*. The second portion contended that the publicity had so tainted the prospective jurors that he could not receive a fair trial. The judge withheld his ruling on this motion until after *voir dire* with the express purpose of determining the effect of the publicity on the jurors. During *voir dire* only two of the six members eventually impanelled on the court were expressly challenged for cause on the ground of pre-trial publicity and it might have been better procedure for defense counsel to have reiterated the "publicity" challenge after *voir dire* of each member, but in view of the judge's procedure in holding his decision in abeyance, it can be fairly concluded this defense motion was, in effect, a challenge to each member on the basis of pre-trial publicity. The second portion of the defense motion was denied upon completion of the *voir dire* procedures, the judge accepting as valid the protestations of the prospective jurors that their judgment would not be affected by the publicity.

. . .

The *voir dire* showed that each of these court members who ultimately sat in judgment on the Petitioner had in-depth prior knowledge of the alleged facts, circumstances and participants involved, some even being able to recall the names of witnesses whose accounts they had seen on television or read in publications.

Colonel Ford, the President of the court-martial, was the only member of the court who was under the military judge's order of November, 1969 to refrain from exposure to the case. He stated that prior to receipt of the order he had read news articles concerning the case and he remembered the names of Meadlo, Ridenhour, Medina, Mitchell and Calley. He had seen Calley's picture in a magazine. He had read articles in which the hearsay statements of Ridenhour had appeared. He had seen pictures of alleged killings at My Lai on the front page of a Cleveland newspaper. After receiving the order he tried to avoid exposure to the case but did see some newspaper headlines and did see and hear some news broadcasts.

. . .

It is not required that jurors be totally ignorant of the facts and issues involved in the case to be tried, and the mere existence of a preconceived notion as to the guilt or innocence of the accused is not, in itself, sufficient to rebut the presumption of impartiality *if* the juror can lay aside his impression and render a verdict based only on the evidence presented in court.

But this general rule does not foreclose inquiry whether, in a given case, the application of the rule works as a deprivation of liberty without due process.

In a number of cases in recent years the federal courts have moved away from the earlier doctrine that a denial by a juror on *voir dire* that he has been affected by damaging publications must be accepted as true, these later cases establishing the principle that adverse and inflammatory publicity has an *inherently* prejudicial impact on jurors and that it is not necessary that the prejudice be "isolated" and "demonstrated" as a prerequisite to reversal.

. . .

The United States Supreme Court has on a number of occasions looked beyond the *voir dire* statements of impartiality by jurors to determine the effect of prejudicial publicity. In Marshall v. United States, 360 U.S. 310, 79 S.Ct. 1171, 3 L.Ed.2d 1250 (1959), newspapers published evidence which had been ruled inadmissible during the trial. Seven of the jurors were exposed to the articles but *all seven swore that they would not be influenced by them,* that they could decide the case only upon the evidence of record, and that they felt no prejudice against the defendant as a result of the articles. The trial court accepted their statements at face value but on appeal the Supreme Court reversed and granted the Defendant a new trial, holding that the exposure to this inadmissible evidence (i.e. accused had previously practiced medicine without a license) was so prejudicial to the accused, who was on trial for unlawfully dispensing drugs, that reversal was required, *despite the assertions of the jurors.*

In Irvin v. Dowd, 366 U.S. 717, 81 S.Ct. 1639, 6 L.Ed.2d 751 (1961), the Defendant was charged with a number of murders and shortly after his arrest police officers made statements that he had confessed, these statements being widely publicized. Because of the publicity a considerable number of the jury panel stated that they had formed an opinion that the Defendant was guilty. A jury was selected from among those who stated that they would not be influenced by the publicity. On appeal the Supreme Court recited the ancient rule that it is sufficient if the juror states that he can lay aside his impressions and render a verdict based only on the evidence, but then went on to say that the rule does not close inquiry to determine whether in a given case the application of the rule deprives a defendant of due process. The Court then found prejudice established despite the jurors' statements that they would be fair and impartial.

In *Marshall* and *Irvin* the Court made an examination of the facts to determine whether prejudice resulted and based upon such examination determined that the jurors were probably incapable of laying aside their opinions in view of the prejudicial pre-trial publicity. In four later cases the Supreme Court broke away from the requirement that *actual* prejudice must be shown.

. . .

The record in this case shows that the Petitioner's trial was affected by isolatable demonstrated prejudice and by inherent prejudice to such an extent that the Petitioner was denied due process. Judged by every standard established by the decided cases, his conviction should be set aside. Stated otherwise, if there has ever been a case in which a conviction should be set aside because of prejudicial publicity, *this is it.*

This opinion of the Court should not be construed as holding that if an individual who is charged with offenses achieves sufficient notoriety as a result of his alleged acts the charges should be dismissed. The guidelines enunciated by the Supreme Court in the *Sheppard* case contain the remedies for pre-trial publicity problems created by the great majority of cases. Unfortunately, the court-martial system could not and cannot effectively invoke some of these guidelines. What the Court holds is that an individual should not be required to stand trial by his government without protection from the publication of prosecution "testimony" against him in advance of trial and the sale of evidence to the highest bidder to be used against him; that every citizen of this nation, no matter how notorious, has the right to be tried in a court, whether military or civilian, that can protect him against prejudicial coverage by the news media; that an accused should not be tried by a court which must announce that it is powerless to enforce its own orders; that a court or a system within the constitutional framework of our nation that is so sterile that it cannot protect the accused from such publicity denies him due process; that the accused should not be tried by jurors who are members of an organization which is in some respects itself on trial; that if investigation by the press and public comment by government officials is accorded such high value that it must prevail, then the exercise of those rights should not be enjoyed at the expense of the accused's right to a fair trial.

. . .

II. The Denial of Compulsory Process and Confrontation Issue

. . .

There is perhaps no right under our nation's Constitution more fundamental to the concept of fair trial than is this right of the accused to confront witnesses and to have process issue to compel attendance of witnesses. This right to offer testimony of witnesses and to compel their attendance is, in essence, the right to present a defense, and a fundamental element of due process of law.

. . .

One standing accused of criminal acts may not be denied those witnesses whom it is believed would aid in his defense. The fundamental rights of confrontation and compulsory process inherent in the due process clause of the Fifth Amendment and embodied specifically in the Sixth were, in the Court's opinion, denied Petitioner during his trial.

. . .

During the hearing of his case Petitioner asserted that he had been deprived of due process of law as a result.

The military judge ruled that the defense had made a *prima facie* showing of command control and placed the burden on the prosecution to dispute this showing. It was the Petitioner's position that those entrusted with the fair administration of justice in the pre-trial processing of his case had been wrongfully influenced by their superiors; that the decision to prosecute him was made by the President of the United States and that this information was passed down the chain of command to those who preferred, investigated, and referred the charges to trial.

To rebut the *prima facie* case the prosecution subpoenaed Major General Talbott, Brigadier General Oscar E. Davis, Colonel Robert M. Lathrop, Lieutenant Colonel Henry E. Vincent, Lieutenant Colonel Dwayne C. Cameron, and Lieutenant Colonel Frank L. Garrison, all as witnesses for the prosecution. They testified in essence that they had not been influenced by their superiors. In order to rebut their testimony and to prove the Petitioner's case concerning command influence, Petitioner's counsel requested that the trial counsel, the prosecutor, subpoena certain witnesses including Secretary of Defense Melvin R. Laird, Secretary of the Army Stanley R. Resor and Chief of Staff of the Army General William C. Westmoreland. When the trial counsel refused to subpoena these witnesses, the defense counsel presented a written petition to the military judge.

. . .

The military judge denied the Petitioner's subpoena. . . .

The Court is constrained to hold that even if there was some technical non-compliance with procedure here the Petitioner was nevertheless entitled to the presence of these witnesses.

The issue of command control and influence improperly imposed on those who determined Petitioner's fate was a live issue at Petitioner's trial. After development of a *prima facie* case demonstrating such control, it is necessary that the Petitioner be given an opportunity to rebut the prosecution's evidence to the contrary. A cursory glance at the statements of the President of the United States and General Westmoreland set out in

Section I of this Opinion, indicating their intention to fully prosecute those involved in the My Lai incident pursuant to the Uniform Code of Military Justice and to punish those found guilty indicates great interest on the part of these individuals. The shock and dismay expressed in the statements by Secretary Laird and Secretary Resor, similar to those of the President and General Westmoreland, indicate their intense interest in the Petitioner's case. There can be little question that the requested testimony was both relevant and material on the issues of command control and pre-trial publicity.

. . .

Petitioner . . . argued strenuously that there was sufficient reason for the exercise of improper influence in his case by *his superiors* because of the very nature of the charges against *him*. He argued that under the laws of war his superiors could be charged themselves for not prohibiting his act under the precedents set at Nuremburg and in the case of In re Yamashita, 327 U.S. 1, 66 S. Ct. 340, 90 L.Ed. 499 (1945). Indeed, the press drew the same conclusions in many of their reports concerning the incident in which the Petitioner was alleged to have participated. As was pointed out by the Petitioner in his brief on the merits herein, the chief United States prosecutor at the Nuremburg trials stated that Petitioner's superiors, in particular General Westmoreland, stood "a very strong possibility that [he] would come to the same end that [Yamashita] did." Certainly these precedents set the stage for an argument that the Petitioner's superiors could well have been worried about their own possible criminal responsibility as a result of the My Lai incident.

. . .

While this Court does not conclude, as a matter of fact, that the Petitioner proved his case of improper influence, yet we cannot conclude that it was so clearly disproved that the witnesses requested should not have been called. Certainly their testimony was relevant. A judge of the highest military court has said:

> As members of a hierarchical system, with promotion and type of duty largely dependent upon the rating of superiors, military personnel would naturally tend to regard all policy as mandatory.[37]

Everybody from the Commander in Chief on down had certainly made it clear to everybody at Fort Benning what the "policy" was in the Calley case. In such a situation the Sixth Amendment required that those witnesses sought to be subpoenaed by the Petitioner should have been called, and the military judge's refusal to subpoena them violated the Petitioner's right to due process of law.

. . .

The Court finds, therefore, that the refusal by the military judge to issue the defense subpoenas requested amounted to a violation of the Petitioner's rights under the Fifth and Sixth Amendments to the Constitution and requires the grant of the relief which the Petitioner seeks. It clearly appears that these constitutional issues were not fully and fairly considered in the military judicial system. In fact, neither of the reviewing courts, the Army Court of Military Review and the United States Court of Military Appeals, so much as mentioned this issue.

. . .

III. The Notice Issue

The Petitioner alleges that he was denied due process of law by being convicted on charges and specifications which were improperly drawn and illegally used by the government. He also contends that he was denied due process by the failure of the United States to adequately train and prepare him to disobey the order of his superior which he alleges brought about his conviction herein. Both of these allegations are essentially contentions that he was deprived of the requisite notice required by the due process clause of the Constitution before conviction may be had.

The evidence of record in the case does not clearly indicate, one way or the other, whether Petitioner received adequate training concerning his duties. There is some evidence that he did not receive full benefit of the training necessary before being sent to a war zone. There is also indication that he did not receive instructions concerning the handling of prisoners or the requirement of the laws of war. The testimony of the Petitioner is ambiguous in this regard and there was no evidence presented by the government covering Petitioner's training. Neither the Court of Military Review nor the Court of Military Appeals addressed this issue. Had they done so they might have appropriately ordered a remand of the case for enlargement of the record.

If indeed the Army did fail in its responsibility to adequately instruct and prepare the Petitioner for action or nonaction pursuant to an illegal order, it appears to me that a question of due process would certainly be raised. The Petitioner's superior officer acted with the full authority of the United States in his relations with the Petitioner. The acts of such an officer are the acts of the government where such acts lead to a deprivation of due process. . . . For the government to compel one to commit an act at his peril without any warning of the peril is certainly violative of due process of law. . . . The Constitution of the United States guarantees to our citizens certain rights that the laws of other nations do not guarantee to their citizens. There is validity in the Petitioner's argument that "just as governmental power is circumscribed by the laws of war embodied in the Geneva Convention and as understood in the law of nations, the individual nation has the duty to circumscribe the actions of its own individual soldiers. This circumscription places on the government a dual obligation: (1) Not to order the individual to act illegally and (2) To train the individual as to what action may be considered illegal even in the face of orders from his government." If the United States failed, through Captain Medina, in the first of its obligations, it would seem to be a requisite of fairness that the United States not fail in the second. Absent an adequate record, this Court makes no determination with regard to this question.

. . .

Obiter

It is appropriate to remember that the Petitioner was sent to participate in a war where the enemy was as frequently clothed as civilians as in military uniform.

It is also appropriate to keep in mind that war is war and it is not at all unusual for innocent civilians to be numbered among its victims. It has been so throughout recorded history. It was so when Joshua took Jericho in ancient Biblical times.

> And they utterly destroyed all that was in the city, both man and woman, young and old . . . with the edge of the sword.[52]

Now Joshua did not have charges brought against him for the slaughter of the civilian population of Jericho. But then "the Lord was with Joshua," we are told.

> So the Lord was with Joshua; and his fame was noised throughout all the country.[53]

When Russian troops occupied the Polish border city of Polotsk in

[52] The Holy Bible, Joshua 6:21 (King James Version).
[53] Ibid., 6:27.

1565 Ivan the Terrible ordered the entire Jewish civilian population drowned.

In World War II Churchill ordered the RAF night-time saturation bombing of German cities, and Eisenhower had his bomber armada carry on the slaughter by day. Approximately a half million Germans were killed and a large percentage of this number were women and children. Yet Churchill was acclaimed as the great man of the Twentieth century and Eisenhower was twice elected President. Then Truman bombed Hiroshima, leaving 80,000 dead, most of whom were women and children, but he was later elected President. The airmen who dropped the bombs got medals and honorable discharges.

General Sherman said "War is Hell" and as he marched through Georgia to Union sainthood he proved it by explicitly and sardonically mocking the West Point canons that condemn atrocities, calling the canons "old notions." He said, "War is cruelty, and you cannot refine it." In his view the mission of the Army was to kill, burn, mangle and destroy, and in a memorandum to President Lincoln he urged a policy of ruthlessness, contending that the war must go on until "enough" southern landowners (innocent civilians) were killed off. He did not hesitate to invoke terror. He wrote, "To secure the navigation of the Mississippi River I would slay millions; on that point I am not only insane, but mad." [54]

When the Mayor of Atlanta pleaded with Sherman that if he forced the evacuation of the city hundreds of innocent women and children would starve in the woods Sherman readily agreed, saying:

> I give full credit to your statements of the distress that will be occasioned. [But] my orders are not designed to meet the humanities in the case.

He put the torch to Atlanta and burned it to the ground, then ordered his troops to scorch a corridor 30 miles wide to the sea. Referring to this operation Carl Sandburg asks:

> What was it other than a human conflagration, a wide-moving cyclone, a plague of locusts, a cloud of giant biped grasshoppers, an Old Testament visitation of the vengeance of Jehovah or the raucous laughter of hell-hounds spawned from the cesspools of demoniac nether regions?

Then with regard to Sherman (who he described as "The Terrible") he poses this question:

> Was Sherman a modern impersonator of Attila the Hun, a manner of sadist, a wanton and a monster who took pleasure in seeing an enemy people suffer? Or was he a soldier doing a necessary job?

[54] On November 28, 1969 the CBS network news commentator, in talking about Calley and My Lai, made this unctuous pronouncement: "Deliberate terrorization of civilians is against, not part of, our national policy of war."

Sherman was a barbarian and he was proud of it. Of the Georgia campaign he later said:

> No doubt many acts of pillage, robbery and violence were committed.

And when he reached Savannah he wrote his wife:

> They (the Georgians) regard us just as the Romans did the Goths and the parallel is not unjust.

He refused to set up a military police unit to watch and discipline his own men because to have done so would have "delayed the operation" and he excused the atrocities committed by his troops with this comment:

> This may not be good morality, but is war.

Sherman waged war with admitted calculated cruelty and he did so with the grateful blessings of his commander in chief, who did not suggest that he be court-martialled, but instead sent him the following message when he reached Savannah:

> God bless you and the army under your command.

And he was not condemned from the podium and the pulpit, but he was instead glorified, idolized, beatified and sanctified. In 1884 he barely escaped being nominated for President.

The point is that Sherman was absolutely right; not about what he did, but about the nature of war; war *is* hell, and when we take a young man into the Army and train him to kill and train him to take orders and send him into a strange foreign land to follow the flag, and he then in the wild confusion of combat commits an act which, long after the event, is made the basis of a capital criminal charge, simple justice demands that he be treated fairly by the press, by his government and by the branch of the service in which he served. Sadly, it must be admitted that Calley was not accorded such consideration. Quite the contrary.

He was pummelled and pilloried by the press.

He was taunted and tainted by television.

He was reproached and ridiculed by radio.

He was criticized and condemned by commentators.

His commander in chief publicly aligned himself with the prosecution.

His government denied him access to evidence.

His pleas to the Department of Justice went unanswered.

His conviction was to be a cathartic to cleanse the national conscience and the impellent to improve the Army's image.

His country not only denied him a fair trial—it even denied him a fair chance for a fair trial.

14. *Calley* v. *Callaway*, U.S. Court of Appeals for Fifth Circuit, 10 September 1975

. . .

AINSWORTH, CIRCUIT JUDGE:

In this habeas corpus proceeding we review the conviction by military court-martial of Lieutenant William L. Calley, Jr., the principal accused in the My Lai incident in South Vietnam, where a large number of defenseless old men, women and children were systematically shot and killed by Calley and other American soldiers in what must be regarded as one of the most tragic chapters in this history of this nation's armed forces.

. . .

We reverse the district court's order granting a writ of habeas corpus and reinstate the judgment of the court-martial.[5]

I. Summary of the Facts

On March 16, 1968, in the small hamlet of My Lai, in South Vietnam, scores of unarmed, unresisting Vietnamese civilians were summarily ex-

[5] The Army has granted Calley's application for parole and he has been released from confinement. This fact, however, does not deprive the federal courts of habeas corpus jurisdiction, for a person on parole is "in custody" for purposes of habeas corpus jurisdiction. *Jones v. Cunningham,* 371 U.S. 236, 83 S.Ct. 373, 9 L.Ed.2d 285 (1963). See also 28 U.S.C. § 2253, which grants this court jurisdiction to review on appeal the final order in a habeas corpus proceeding before a district judge.

ecuted by American soldiers. A number of American soldiers were charged [6] but only First Lieutenant William Calley was convicted of murder in what has been called the My Lai Incident and also the My Lai Incident and also the My Lai Massacre.

. . .

. . . District Judge Elliott's extensive written opinion concluded that Calley was entitled to a writ of habeas corpus for four principal reasons: (1) prejudicial pretrial publicity concerning the My Lai incident and Calley's participation therein deprived him of an opportunity to receive a fair and impartial trial; (2) the military judge's failure to subpoena certain witnesses requested by the defense deprived Calley of his right of confrontation and compulsory process and deprived him of due process; (3) the refusal of the House of Representatives to release testimony to the defense taken in executive session in its My Lai investigation deprived Calley of due process; and (4) the Charges, Specifications and Bill of Particulars under which Calley was tried did not adequately notify him of the charges against him nor fully protect him against possible double jeopardy.

. . .

To summarize, the scope of review may be stated as follows:

> Military court-martial convictions are subject to collateral review by federal civil courts on petitions for writs of habeas corpus where it is asserted that the court-martial acted without jurisdiction, or that substantial constitutional rights have been violated, or that exceptional circumstances have been presented which are so fundamentally defective as to result in a miscarriage of justice. Consideration by the military of such issues will not preclude judicial review for the military must accord to its personnel the protections of basic constitutional rights essential to a fair trial and the guarantee of due process of law. The scope of review for violations of constitutional rights, however, is more narrow than in civil cases. Thus federal courts should differentiate between questions of fact and law and review only questions of law which present substantial constitutional issues. Accordingly, they may not retry the facts or reevaluate the evidence, their function in this regard being

6 Information in the record, particularly in the volumes containing newspaper clippings and magazine articles, shows that a total of 12 infantrymen were formally charged with violations of the U.C.M.J. for their part in the My Lai incident. Some of these individuals went to trial and were acquitted, while the charges against others were dropped. A number of soldiers participating in the My Lai incident (as many as 22) could not be charged by the Army as they were civilians and no longer amenable to trial by court-martial for their acts while in uniform, under *Toth v. Quarles*, 350 U.S. 11, 76 S.Ct. 1, 100 L.Ed. 8 (1955).

> limited to determining whether the military has fully and fairly considered contested factual issues. Moreover, military law is a jurisprudence which exists separate and apart from the law governing civilian society so that what is permissible within the military may be constitutionally impermissible outside it. Therefore, when the military courts have determined that factors peculiar to the military require a different application of constitutional standards, federal courts are reluctant to set aside such decisions.

With these principles in mind, we consider the . . . issues raised by this appeal.

III. Pretrial Publicity

Neither side disputes the magnitude of the publicity which surrounded this case: the original record contains volumes of clippings, reports and extracts from written reports on the case, as well as video tapes of certain televised broadcasts and programs. No factors peculiar to military life or important military considerations have been asserted to justify a departure from the standards and requisites established by Supreme Court decisions.

In the past two and one-half decades, the Supreme Court has handed down a number of decisions discussing and balancing the conflicts created when there exists the possibility that the press may have jeopardized the important right of a defendant to a fair trial. The primary problem here is that a court member who has had substantial contact with reports and stories concerning the defendant whose fate he will decide, may make his decision based on information gathered outside the courtroom. An important prerequisite of a fair and impartial trial "is the requirement that the jury's verdict be based on evidence received in open court, not from outside sources." *Sheppard v. Maxwell,* 384 U.S. 333, 351 . . . (1966). . . . The general rule is that a defendant has the burden on appeal of proving actual jury prejudice if a conviction is to be reversed on grounds of prejudicial publicity. *Irvin v. Dowd,* 366 U.S. 717, 723 . . . (1961). . . . Other Supreme Court decisions have reversed convictions and dispensed with the requirement of showing actual prejudice in the jury box in extreme circumstances where there has been inherently prejudicial publicity such as to make the possibility of prejudice highly likely or almost unavoidable. See *Estes v. Texas,* 381 U.S. 532, 542–543, 85 S.Ct. 1628, 1632, 14 L.Ed.2d 543 (1966).

The Supreme Court has noted that generalizations are not helpful, and that "each case must turn on its special facts." *Marshall v. United States,* 360 U.S. 310, 312 . . . (1959), . . . F2d 1399, 1401, cert. denied, 397 U.S.

THE MERITS OF THE PRETRIAL PUBLICITY ISSUE

There is no contention here that publicity has been a driving force behind the securing of an indictment—that publicity has initiated the prosecution.[34] As the district court noted, though Calley was charged on September 5, 1969, for the murder of civilians at My Lai, there was little or no publicity surrounding the charges or the My Lai incident until mid-November of the same year. Moreover, Calley's trial was conducted with restraint and dignity, and there is no assertion that the court members, though not sequestered, had any contact with the massive publicity spawned by the trial itself. Thus, our focus is on the post-indictment, pretrial publicity and its impact on petitioner's trial.

A. The District Court's View

The district judge concluded that Calley had been persecuted and pilloried by news media so intent on making prejudicial revelations about the incident that Calley's right to a fair and unbiased hearing was impossible. The court's review led it to conclude that the publicity was clearly improper, largely biased and undoubtedly prejudicial. The district judge concluded that "it was not humanly possible for the jurors not to be improperly influenced by prior exposure," that "[n]o person, however honest minded he might try to be, could avoid the lasting emotional impact" of some of the publicity, and that, with all the publicity given the incident, "it would be sheer fantasy to believe that the jurors did not see, hear and read [the publicity] or that they were not influenced by it." 382 F.Supp. at 685, 672, 686. These findings led the court to hold the publicity inherently prejudicial to Calley's Sixth Amendment rights. The court also found "isolatable prejudice" in the fact that one court member stated during *voir dire* that he had seen Captain Medina on television at one time, and that Medina had appeared credible and straightforward. 382 F.Supp. at 690. We hold that the trial court's findings of inherent and actual prejudice are erroneous, and conclude that pretrial publicity did not deprive Calley of a fair trial.

B. Inherent Prejudice

The district court emphasized that the case involved "massive" and "intense" publicity. Yet this court has noted previously that "[w]e cannot accept the position that 'prominence brings prejudice.' " *Hale v. United*

34 Compare *Sheppard v. Maxwell, supra,* where newspaper headlines asked "Why Isn't Sam Sheppard in Jail?" and urged "Quit Stalling—Bring Him In" until Sheppard was later arrested and indicted.

States, supra, 435 F.2d at 747. Moreover, no court has held that the only impartial juror is an uninformed one. We cannot expect jurors to live in isolation from the events and news of concern to the community in which they live.

> It is not required, however, that the jurors be totally ignorant of the facts and issues involved. In these days of swift, widespread and diverse methods of communication, an important case can be expected to arouse the interest of the public in the vicinity, and scarcely any of those best qualified to serve as jurors will not have formed some impression or opinion as to the merits of the case. This is particularly true in criminal cases. To hold that the mere existence of any preconceived notion as to the guilt or innocence of an accused, without more, is sufficient to rebut the presumption of a prospective juror's impartiality would be to establish an impossible standard. It is sufficient if the juror can lay aside his impression or opinion and render a verdict based on the evidence presented in court.

Irvin v. Dowd, supra, 366 U.S. at 722–723.

. . .

The effect of the publicity on the American public in general is of course uncertain, but material contained in the record belies the district court's conclusion that anyone familiar with the news reports surrounding the My Lai massacre would automatically convict Calley. *Time* magazine was severely castigated by him for its role in the publicity. But a survey conducted for and published by *Time* in the first week of January 1970 (when the publicity was at its peak) reached the conclusion that there was "considerable sympathy" for Lieutenant Calley among the people interviewed. "By a margin of 55 percent to 23 percent, they believe Calley is being made a scapegoat by the Government"; also, that most people were disturbed over the publicity given the alleged massacre. Sixty-seven percent of those polled "believe that the press and TV should not have reported statements by soldiers involved prior to a trial." The results of a Harris Poll published January 8, 1970 showed that 66 percent of the public felt that soldiers killing even civilians should not be court-martialed if they did so under orders. These polls and figures are, of course, not directly relevant to a determination of whether the panel which ultimately convicted Calley was influenced by such publicity. We mention the above material only to emphasize that the district judge overlooked important aspects of the record in reaching his conclusions, and to note that there appears to have been no single sentiment regarding the case held by a vast segment of the American public.

The critical issue is the actual or probable effect of the pretrial publicity on the trial itself and, more precisely, on those who sat in judgment of Calley. A careful review of the exhaustive *voir dire* conducted at trial indicates that there is no likelihood that pretrial publicity prejudiced Lieutenant Calley such as to deny him a fair trial. An important concern in all prejudicial publicity cases is whether the publicity has led prospective jurors to hold preconceived notions of the defendant's guilt. Two prospective court members felt that the charges against Calley had some substance. Captain Cooch stated that his initial reaction to the charges was that "somebody was getting railroaded." But since the Army had adhered to its charges after the Peers Commission report, he believed there was substance to the charges and did not believe Calley was innocent. A defense challenge for cause was granted. Captain Cox also stated he believed there was some truth to the charges against Calley or the Army would not have pursued the prosecution. A defense challenge for cause was also granted.

On the other hand, four prospective court members were dismissed from the panel because they held views so sympathetic to Lieutenant Calley that they could not objectively judge the case.

. . .

Of the court members selected, none stated that he had formed an opinion as to the guilt or innocence of Calley. All court members stated that their decision would not be influenced by any of the publicity with which they had been in contact. The district judge dismissed these statements, made under oath and after extensive questioning by all parties, as being largely meaningless. . . .

Two factors in particular give support to the credibility of the court members' claims that they would reach a verdict unimpressed by pretrial publicity. The first is the long period of time between the peak of the publicity and the beginning of the trial. The publicity surrounding My Lai and Calley's trial was at its peak during November and December of 1969 and January of 1970. Very little new information was thereafter brought to light, and the publicity subsided substantially. The court members were not selected and the trial begun until November 1970. The military judge had delayed the trial in part to aid in empanelling an impartial court; he felt that the publicity had dissipated and that the court members selected were impartial and untainted by publicity.[41]

[41] The military judge stated:

> The voir dire has now been completed, and I'm satisfied that any potential adverse effect of the pretrial publicity has been dissipated by the very delay in this case, and, of course, that is the reason I delayed the trial of this case as long as I did, that is, to let the effect of any pretrial publicity dissipate, and I am satisfied that the selected jurors aren't tainted by the publicity and will decide this case solely on the evidence that they hear presented in open court, and follow the law that I will give them following the presentation of the evidence.

Tr. at 918.

Sheppard v. Maxwell states that "where there is a reasonable likelihood that prejudicial news prior to trial will prevent a fair trial," "continu[ing] the case until the threat abates" is one means of assuring a fair trial. 384 U.S. at 363, . . .

. . .

The second reason to credit the court members' statements is that they were the product of searching and sensitively conducted *voir dire*. The military judge conducted the *voir dire* in accordance with the recommendations of the American Bar Association Project on Standards for Criminal Justice, Standards Relating to Fair Trial and Free Press 3.4(a) (Approved Draft, 1968).[42] The examination of each court member was held out of the presence of other prospective jurors. Judge Kennedy, the military judge, himself inquired into the prospective court members' exposure to publicity and ability to render a fair and impartial verdict. But more importantly, both defense counsel and the prosecution were allowed almost unlimited freedom to inquire into the court members' attitudes, perceptions, backgrounds and the nature and extent of their exposure to pretrial publicity. Counsel were provided with the Army's personnel files on the prospective court members. The result was that the record fully reflects the possible biases of all potential court members. The fact that after meticulous questioning none of the prospective court members was shown to hold preconceived notions of guilt or innocence or to be unable to adjudge Calley free of outside influences requires great deference to the military judge's conclusion that a fair and impartial jury had been empaneled. Our own review of the *voir dire* (which consumed five days and created almost 400 single-spaced, legal-sized pages of record to select six court members) convinces us that there was no substantial likelihood that the court members selected were other than fair and impartial individuals who would determine Calley's guilt or innocence based solely on the evidence developed before the court. The district

[42] 3.4 Selecting the jury.

It is recommended that the following standards be adopted in each jurisdiction to govern the selection of a jury in those criminal cases in which questions of possible prejudice are raised.

(2) Method of examination.

Whenever there is believed to be a significant possibility that individual talesmen will be ineligible to serve because of exposure to potentially prejudicial material, the examination of each juror with respect to his exposure shall take place outside the presence of other chosen and prospective jurors. An accurate record of this examination shall be kept, by court reporter or tape recording whenever possible. The questioning shall be conducted for the purpose of determining what the prospective juror has read and heard about the case and how his exposure has affected his attitude towards the trial, not to convince him that he would be derelict in his duty if he could not cast aside any preconceptions he might have.

judge assumed that exposure to publicity alone made it impossible for the court members not to be improperly influenced.

. . .

There are other reasons why this is not a case that has close parallels in previous free press-fair trial litigation. The district judge was concerned that any court member who had any knowledge of the facts surrounding this case or any familiarity with the principal figures in the case would be unable to render a fair decision. Yet a concerted effort was made by the defense to have placed on the panel officers who had knowledge of many aspects of this case. The defense at one time objected to the *voir dire* panel, claiming inadequate representation of officers who had served as platoon leaders in combat in Vietnam. The apparent goal was to have as court members officers who had been in combat, who knew the stresses of the "dirty little war" in Vietnam, who understood the need for unquestioning obedience to orders, who understood that there was no clear distinction between friend and foe in Southeast Asia, and who were aware of the horrors of any war. All six court members in Calley's trial had combat experience, and five had served in Vietnam. Some court members knew or had heard of atrocities in Vietnam committed by the Viet Cong or others. Captain Salem, like Calley, had served in Vietnam as a platoon leader after obtaining his commission through Officer's Candidate School. He had operated in a free fire zone, and stated that it was his impression that a person would have to be berserk to kill over 100 people even in a combat situation; Salem was seated on the jury over prosecution objection. Major McIntosh had combat experience, and had been subjected to terrorist attacks. McIntosh had received two Silver Stars, and had been wounded four times; he said he felt it was the duty of a soldier to obey any and all orders. Major Bierbaum had been fired on in combat during his two tours in Vietnam; his belief was that all orders are presumed to be legal. Captain Brown had served two tours in Vietnam; he had received his commission through O.C.S. after seven years as an enlisted man. He had combat experience, had captured enemy suspects, and had heard of Viet Cong atrocities. Major Kinard also had received an O.C.S. commission, after nine years' service as an enlisted man. In his two tours of Vietnam he had received a Bronze Star and a Silver Star. Major Kinard had combat experience, and had heard of hostile acts by women, old men and children. He stated he would treat the Viet Cong and their sympathizers in the same way. In short, a major goal of the defense was to have on the court-martial officers familiar with the killing, the stress, and the inhumanity of ground combat in Vietnam, and this goal was achieved. To contend that these same men, whose familiarity with circumstances relevant to the case was desired by the defense, should be disqualified merely because they had heard or read news reports regarding this incident is to ignore the reality of Calley's trial. The district court's conclusion that mere exposure to publicity necessarily prevented any person from serving as a juror has an extremely unsettling sidelight. If, in this age of instant, mass communication, we were to automatically disqualify persons who have heard about an alleged crime from serving as a juror, the inevitable result would be that truly heinous or notorious acts will go unpunished. The law does not prohibit the informed citizen from participating in the affairs of justice. In prominent cases of national concern, we cannot allow widespread publicity concerning these matters to paralyze our system of justice. . . .

D. Control of the Media by the Military Court

. . .

It is not disputed that the military court used most of the means suggested by *Sheppard v. Maxwell* to ameliorate potential prejudice stemming from publicity. The court delayed the proceedings to allow publicity to abate, it allowed extensive *voir dire* examination to probe for any possible influence on the court members by the publicity. The court successfully took great pains to insure that no publicity reached the court members during the trial.[48] Moreover, the court issued an order to all prospective witnesses, civilian and military, prohibiting disclosure of their prospective testimony. The military court refused, however, the defense request

> to restrain the three major television networks, certain named daily newspapers, news magazines and wire services, as well as "all radio and television networks and stations, newswire services, newspapers, and magazines operating or otherwise doing business in the United States of America, or any territory thereof", from publishing the statements of any witness to the events giving rise to the charges against Lieutenant Calley, or any photographs, sketches, or other pictorial reproductions purporting to represent the bodies of persons allegedly killed in the village of My Lai 4, Republic of Vietnam on March 16, 1968, . . . until the first witness testifies on the merits, at the contemplated trial.

United States v. Calley, 19 U.S.C.M.A. 96, 41 C.M.R. 96 (Memorandum opinion December 2, 1969).

In all likelihood it would have been unconstitutional for the court to grant the defense request. . . .

. . .

[48] The trial court offered to sequester the court members throughout the trial, but the defense said this was unnecessary. The members were sequestered, however, throughout the almost two weeks of deliberation.

IV. Compulsory Process

Prior to trial, defense counsel sought unsuccessfully to have subpoenaed the following persons: Secretary of Defense Melvin R. Laird, Secretary of the Army Stanley R. Resor, and Chief of Staff of the Army William Westmoreland. The defense stated that these individuals were essential to establish Calley's defense that all charges against him should be dismissed because "command influence and control had permeated the processing of the charges against the Petitioner." The military judge declined to require the appearance of these witnesses. The district court held that the failure to compel the attendance of these witnesses deprived petitioner of his Sixth Amendment right "to have compulsory process for obtaining witnesses in his favor . . . ." We conclude, however, that the district court's holding was erroneous and exceeded the proper scope of review for reasons we shall articulate.

. . .

Most charges of command influence relate to attempts by superior officers to influence the court's decision as to the guilt or innocence and punishment of the accused. This is not, however, the contention raised here. Rather, it is that Calley was charged "in order to insulate higher-ups . . . ." If, as counsel alleged, the charges were coerced, or unauthorized influence was utilized in having the allegations against Calley brought to trial, such activity would, in all likelihood, have violated Art. 37 of the U.C.M.J., 10 U.S.C. § 837, which makes unlawful the use of any influence on the action of the convening authority. But even if Calley had been unable to establish a violation of Art. 37, should he have been able to persuade the military court that there was a reasonable possibility that command influence had triggered the accusations against him, the charges could have been dismissed by the court pursuant to its supervisory obligation to do everything possible to eliminate command influence from the court-martial system. Cf. *United States v. Gordon,* 1 U.S.C.M.A. 255, 2 C.M.R. 161 (1952).

Calley's accusations that command influence was involved in bringing charges against him, and that he was being singled out as the Army's scapegoat, were based on speculations to this effect in news articles. The military prosecutor objected that such unconfirmed reports were an insufficient basis either for issuing subpoenas or for requiring the Government to come forward with proof rebutting the allegations. The military judge ruled, however, that since the issued of command influence had been raised, the prosecution was required to meet the issue. The military judge further indicated that he would accept defense counsel's allegations as fact unless the prosecution showed otherwise.

The Government subsequently called a number of witnesses: Colonel Lathrop, the staff judge advocate; Lieutenant Colonel Vincent and Captain Hill, who formally accused Calley of the charges subsequently lodged against him; Lieutenant Colonel Garrison, who had forwarded the charges with a recommendation of general court-martial; Lieutenant Colonel Cameron, who was directed to conduct an impartial Art. 32 investigation into the charges against Calley and submit his independent recommendations to the court-martial convening authority, the commanding officer of Fort Benning; and Generals Oscar Davis and Orwin Talbott, who together commanded Fort Benning (where Calley was accused, tried and convicted) from August 1969 until the completion of Calley's trial. The testimony of these individuals is discussed fairly and at length in the opinion of the Court of Military Review. 46 C.M.R. at 1151–1157. In substance, each person testified that his aspect of the charging process was unimpeded and uninfluenced by "higher-ups." Captain Hill testified that some of the younger Army attorneys in his legal office feared that Presidential or command interest, together with the political repercussions of bringing charges against Calley, would lead to a cover-up. But the young officers vowed that at least one of them would prefer charges against Calley regardless of any such pressure or cover-up attempt. Captain Hill himself later accused Calley and preferred a charge against him. Lieutenant Colonel Cameron was brought in to establish that his investigation of the charges was unbiased and uninfluenced. The defense interrupted the testimony of Lieutenant Colonel Cameron, and conceded and stipulated on the record that Cameron's investigation was impartial and not improperly influenced. General Talbott, who was the final arbiter of the decision to convene the court-martial and try Calley, testified that he referred the charges to trial "solely on my judgment, on the principles of law, and the Article 32 investigation." The defense called Colonel Kiersey to substantiate their allegations of superior influence, but the record shows that even Kiersey's actions were unaffected by command pressure.

In sum, the military courts' findings conclusively demonstrate that there was no colorable showing that any of the officers involved in processing charges against Calley were influenced either directly or indirectly by command pressure in their disposition of the case. At the conclusion of the testimony on this issue, Judge Kennedy stated, "[A]t this point there is absolutely no evidence that these people [Secretary Laird, Secretary Resor, General Westmoreland] communicatd with any of the commanders down here." The Court of Military Review exhaustively reviewed this question, and concluded:

> All of the officers required to make a decision or recommendation in the processing of the charges against Lieutenant Calley testified that they did

> not receive, directly or indirectly, any instructions as to the appropriate disposition of the case.

46 C.M.R. at 1154.

The rule governing the issuance of subpoenas under military law, paragraph 115a of the Manual for Courts-Martial (Rev. ed. 1969), makes materiality and relevance important factors in the discretionary decision to issue a subpoena, and is very similar to Fed.R.Crim.P. 17(b). Rule 17(b) vests broad discretion in the district judge to grant subpoenas on behalf of indigent defendants where it is claimed that "the presence of the witness is necessary to an adequate defense." But we have consistently held that the discretion vested in the trial court is circumscribed by the requirements of the Sixth Amendment. We have also adhered to the rule that

> "if the accused avers facts which, if true, would be relevant to any issue in the case, the requests for subpoenas must be granted, unless the averments are inherently incredible on their face, or *unless the Government shows, either by introducing evidence or from matters already of record, that the averments are untrue* or that the request is otherwise frivolous." . . . That test places the burden of showing frivolity or abuse of process on the Government, where it properly belongs.

Under our previous cases, it is clear that if the prosecution successfully shows to be untrue the allegations upon which a request for the subpoenaing of a witness is based, there is no statutory or constitutional infirmity in the refusal to subpoena such witnesses. The military judge conducted an extensive hearing on Calley's contentions. He found there was no evidence to support the accusations of command influence. The defense was then forced to take the position that, although no one at Fort Benning was pressured into bringing charges as a result of command influence, General Westmoreland, the Secretary of Defense and the Secretary of the Army might nonetheless state, if called as witnesses, that they had in fact wielded such pressure. We hold that the conclusions of the military judge, which were fully and fairly considered and reaffirmed by the Court of Military Review, amply support the decision not to subpoena the witnesses in question.

In holding to the contrary, the district court exceeded the proper scope of review, and completely disregarded the finding of the military judge and the Court of Military Review that there was no factual basis for the allegations upon which the subpoena requests were premised. The district judge instead conducted his own review of the testimony presented to the military court, and concluded that there was improper influence and that the requested witnesses were necessary to Calley's defense. See 382 F.Supp. at 695 & n. 31, 696, 697 & nn. 35 and 36, 699. In our previous discussion of the scope of review, we have shown that it is erroneous for federal courts to "reweigh[] each item of relevant evidence in the trial record . . . ." *Burns v. Wilson,* 346 U.S. at 146, 73 S.Ct. at 1051. *Burns* and its progeny require at a minimum that findings on disputed factual issues be adhered to where, as here, the issues have been "fully and fairly considered." See, e. g., *Parker v. Levy, supra,* where the Court stated that factual determinations adverse to a petitioner could not be relitigated in habeas corpus proceedings and thus were beyond the proper scope of review. 417 U.S. at 760–761. . . . As we held, *supra,* where a particular claim is inextricably interwoven with or dependent on factual disputes and determinations appropriately considered by the military, federal courts may not intervene further by way of habeas corpus. It was therefore improper for the district judge to reweigh and reevaluate the factual disputes previously resolved and considered within the military courts.

There is another important factor. After denying the request to subpoena Laird, Resor and Westmoreland, the military judge left open the possibility of granting the defense request. The military judge suggested that defense counsel attempt to obtain information from those persons about what their testimony might be, because defense counsel had conceded that he knew of no instance in which the individuals had been contacted personally regarding this matter. Defense counsel stipulated that he would make personal inquiries to the three individuals, and return subsequently with an offer of additional proof to justify granting the subpoenas should he develop any new information. Counsel failed to offer to the court any further evidence on the subject. Accordingly, petitioner may not now successfully claim that the military court's procedures were so grossly improper that there exists an error of constitutional magnitude. Cf. *United States v. Smith, supra,* 436 F.2d at 790.

. . .

V. Discovery of Congressional Testimony

After the charges had been made against Calley and others, and national attention had been directed to the Army's handling of the case, Chairman L. Mendel Rivers of the House Armed Services Committee appointed an investigating subcommittee to make "a completely independent assessment of the case," to be in charge of Congressman F. Edward Herbert. During its investigation, the subcommittee interviewed 152 witnesses, held 16 days of hearings, took 1,812 pages of sworn testimony, and examined hundreds of documents. In addition, the subcommittee took 3,045 pages of statements from witnesses, and conducted its own field investigation in Vietnam. . . .

. . .

After the publication of the subcommittee report, the defense moved to obtain production of "[a]ll witness testimony and documentary evidence in the custody and control of the House of Representatives of the United States." The Army prosecutor made an informal inquiry of Congressman Hebert whether the material might be furnished. Hebert replied that it was the subcommittee's position that the documents requested were neither within the purview of *Brady v. Maryland,* 373 U.S. 83, 83 S.Ct. 1194, 10 L.Ed.2d 215 (1963) nor subject to the requirements of the Jencks Act, 18 U.S.C. § 3500. However, a list of persons who had testified before the subcommittee was provided counsel. On October 13, 1970, Judge Kennedy denied the general discovery request pertaining to all material in possession of the subcommittee. . . . The district judge held that Congress acted wrongly in declining to provide the materials, notwithstanding Rule XI, paragraph 26(m), of Rules of the House of Representatives, and Article I of the Constitution, which provides that each House of Congress need not publish in a journal of proceedings "such Parts as may in their Judgment require secrecy." The district court further held that the inability of the defense to obtain the prior testimony before the Hebert Subcommittee of those witnesses who also testified for the prosecution at trial denied Calley due process. The district court concluded that the inability to obtain this privileged congressional testimony violated the Jencks Act. We disagree, and conclude that there was no denial of due process in the failure to supply the prior testimony, and that even if a Jencks Act violation occurred, it does not rise to a level warranting habeas corpus relief.

. . .

VI. Notice and Double Jeopardy

The district court also held that the Charges, Specifications and Bill of Particulars under which Calley was tried did not adequately notify him of the charges against him nor fully protect him against the possibility of double jeopardy. The court apparently found fair notice problems in the fact that the first and second Specifications of the Original Charge against Calley (the killings at the trail in the southern part of the hamlet and at the ditch in the eastern portion) covered multiple unnamed victims in a single specification. The double jeopardy problem discerned by the court was two-fold. First, quoting a hypothetical situation posed by Calley's counsel, the district court found that there was a risk that Calley might have been twice convicted for killing the same individual within the same trial. See 382 F.Supp. at 710. Second, the district court speculated that Calley might again be charged for other killings in Vietnam and might not be able accurately to plead former conviction. We find no merit in these conclusions.

Fair notice and double jeopardy issues involve requirements of both the Fifth and Sixth Amendments. See *United States v. Sanchez,* 5 Cir., 1975, 508 F.2d 388, 395. The Constitution requires that criminal charges be sufficiently specific (1) to apprise the defendant of what he must be prepared to meet at trial, and (2) to enable the defendant to show with accuracy the extent to which he may plead former acquittal or conviction in other proceedings brought against him for a similar offense. *Russell v. United States,* 369 U.S. 749, 763–764 . . . (1962) and cases cited. We are satisfied that the charges against Calley, as amplified in the Bill of Particulars, met these requirements.

The charges set forth the time and place of the alleged offense. Under the Bill of Particulars, the prosecution set forth the chronological sequence of the separate charges: the killings at the trail occurred first, followed by the killings at the ditch, and next followed by the murder of the monk and then the child. The Bill of Particulars specified the actual physical location: the killings at the trail were in the southern portion of the village, those at the ditch occurred in the eastern part of My Lai (4). The instructions of the military judge were detailed and thorough, and required the prosecution's proof to conform to these allegations in the Bill of Particulars. The killings of the monk and the child, for example, were required to be proven as occurring in sequence after the mass killings at the ditch. The effect of Judge Kennedy's instructions is most evident with regard to the alleged killings at the trail. While there was substantial evidence of extensive participation by Calley in the slaying of the estimated 30–40 persons at this location, the court members returned a verdict of guilty for "not less than one" murder. This was no doubt due to the instructions and the testimony of a pathologist that he could point to only one wound on one body which he was certain to have been instantly fatal. Also, in considering the fair notice requirement, we mention again that Calley did not deny his involvement and participation in the mass killings at the ditch and the trail. It is difficult to understand how a defendant is deprived of fair notice of the charges against him when he confirms that the alleged incidents happened and that he participated in them. We are convinced that there was no failure to provide Calley fair notice of the charges against him, nor is there any likelihood that there will be any double jeopardy problems.

VII. Petitioner Calley's Cross-Appeal

. . . We have carefully considered Calley's other contentions and, in light of our discussion of the proper scope of review in part II, *supra,* conclude that the additional issues presented for review are beyond the scope of review of the federal courts.[68]

VIII. Conclusion

This Court is convinced that Lieutenant Calley received a fair trial from the military court-martial which convicted him for the premeditated murder of numerous Vietnamese civilians at My Lai. The military courts have fully and fairly considered all of the defenses made by him and have affirmed that he is guilty. We are satisfied after a careful and painstaking review of this case that no violation of Calley's constitutional or fundamental rights has occurred, and that the findings of guilty were returned by impartial members based on the evidence presented at a fairly conducted trial.

There is no valid reason then for the federal courts to interfere with the military judgment, for Calley has been afforded every right under our American system of criminal justice to which he is entitled.

Accordingly, the order of the district court granting a writ of habeas corpus to Calley is

Reversed.

Bell, Circuit Judge, with whom Gewin, Thornberry, Morgan and Clark, Circuit Judges, join (dissenting).

Justice Holmes once observed that:

> Great cases, like hard cases, make bad law. For great cases are called great, not by reason of their real importance in shaping the law of the future, but because of some accident of immediate overwhelming interest which appeals to the feelings and distorts the judgment. These immediate interests exercise a kind of hydraulic pressure which makes what previously was clear seem doubtful, and before which even well settled principles of law will bend.

This is such a case. It was tried in the midst of the unusual emotion of the Nation's Vietnam Era. It was an emotion generated by a people

68 The other issues presented in the cross-appeal are as follows: (1) whether Calley was denied due process of law because he received inadequate training and preparation on when to disobey an order; (2) whether the members of the Army Court of Military Review panel which reviewed Calley's case should have disqualified themselves; (3) whether command influence prevented Calley from obtaining a fair trial; (4) whether the court-martial was without jurisdiction to try Calley because Army Chief of Staff General Westmoreland had an alleged personal interest in the proceeding, see note 50, *supra;* (5) whether the application of the "ordinary sense and understanding" standard to the defense of superior orders deprived Calley of due process or subjected him to cruel and unusual punishment; (6) whether Calley was denied due process by being prosecuted for the crime of murder under the U.C.M.J. rather than for a war crime; and (7) whether Calley's sentence by the court members was unconstitutional under the Eighth Amendment.

sharply divided over the unprecedented and extraordinary use of our military resources in diplomacy; an emotion fueled by the print and electronic media in shaping public opinion without the impediment of censorship in what for all intent, purpose, and result was a war. The issues presented in this case, with the exception of the contention respecting the charges and their specificity, are all permeated to some extent with this atmosphere. In the view we take of the case, the withholding of evidence by the Congress (a Committee of the House), requires a new trial, or further proceedings in the district court.

. . .

Lt. Calley was in the army at the behest of his government; he was sent to Vietnam by his government; he was sent into combat at My Lai by his government. He was at My Lai with the consent and implied approval of the Congress. The government court-martialed him through the army and withheld evidence from him through the Congress. It is said that this is not a denial of due process. We disagree.

. . .

In *United States v. Nixon,* the President challenged a subpoena served on him as a third party requiring the production of materials for use in a criminal prosecution on the ground of privilege. The Supreme Court, rejecting the claim of privilege, held:

> We conclude that when the ground for asserting privilege as to subpoenaed materials sought for use in a criminal trial is based only on the generalized interest in confidentiality, it cannot prevail over the fundamental demands of due process of law in the fair administration of criminal justice. The generalized assertion of privilege must yield to the demonstrated, specific need for evidence in a pending criminal trial. 418 U.S. at 713. . . .

The Nixon holding is applicable to this case. Congress has no greater privilege than the President in the circumstances presented. There was no claim of privilege or of confidentiality except for the letter referred to in the majority opinion stating that testimony would be taken in executive session to avoid prejudicing the rights of any defendant in the My Lai prosecution. There is no general claim of secrecy under Art. I, § 5, Cl. 3, of the Constitution.

We would hold that the government, through Congress, caused the army, *prima facie,* to deny Lt. Calley due process of law in withholding the testimony of the witnesses who testified against Calley. We say *prima facie* because the testimony has never been examined for its materiality on mitigation, culpability or impeachment.

This brings us to the remedy we would afford. The district court should be directed to examine the testimony of the witnesses before Congress for materiality. Should it prove to be material, the writ should issue conditioned on the retrial of Lt. Calley within a reasonable time. If not material, the writ should be denied. In the event Congress refuses to produce the testimony or refuses to claim constitutional secrecy within a reasonable time, the district court should grant the writ conditioned upon the retrial of Lt. Calley, but with the stipulation that those witnesses whose testimony before the subcommittee is sought and not obtained shall not be allowed to testify. These directions are without prejudice to the district court considering the testimony *in camera* for materiality should congress so request.

One underlying principle of American jurisprudence is that no man or institution is above the law. Congress is not exempt from this principle. The military judge sustained this principle in the Sgt. Mitchell My Lai trial, n. 5 *supra*. The military judge failed to uphold this principle in the Calley trial. The majority of this court now condones that breach.

15. *DaCosta* v. *Laird*, 471 F.2d 1146 (2d. Cir. 1973)

Before Kaufman, Anderson and Oakes, Circuit Judges.

Irving R. Kaufman, Circuit Judge:

We are called upon to decide the very specific question whether the Secretary of Defense, the Secretaries of the Army, Navy and Air Force, and the Commander of American military forces in Vietnam,[1] may implement the directive of the President of the United States, announced on May 8, 1972, ordering the mining of the ports and harbors of North Vietnam and the continuation of air and naval strikes against military targets located in that battle-scarred land. The appellant seeks a declaratory judgment[2] that the military operations undertaken pursuant to that directive are unlawful in the absence of explicit Congressional authorization, and asks for what he terms "appropriate equitable relief." Like any American with the most rudimentary knowledge of the political history of this Nation, we are aware of the familiar adage that "[s]carcely any political question arises in the United States that is not resolved, sooner or later, into a judicial question."[3] We fear, however, that deTocqueville's apothegm loses some of its force with age and over-use and, like all generalizations, is of interest as much for the situations it fails to describe

[1] The President of the United States was initially named as a defendant in this action. The district court dismissed as against the President, seemingly without objection from the appellant. In any event, DaCosta here does not argue the propriety of dismissal with regard to the President and we do not address that question.

[2] 28 U.S.C. § 2201 provides:

In a case of actual controversy within its jurisdiction, except with respect to Federal taxes, any court of the United States, upon the filing of an appropriate pleading, may declare the rights and other legal relations of any interested party seeking such declaration, whether or not further relief is or could be sought. Any such declaration shall have the force and effect of a final judgment or decree and shall be reviewable as such.

[3] DeTocqueville, 1 Democracy in America 280 (1945).

as for those it accurately characterizes. Unless deTocqueville believed that "judicial resolution" embraced a determination by the courts that they lack the power to resolve a political question, we are of the view that this case would prove an exception to his observation.

On another occasion, this Court acting within its powers and duties under the Constitution, has been obliged to rule on the legality of the war in Vietnam, Orlando v. Laird, 443 F.2d 1039 (2nd Cir.), cert. denied 404 U.S. 869, 92 S.Ct. 94, 30 L.Ed.2d 113 (1971). Here, however, the appellant invites us to extend the reach of judicial inquiry with respect to the Vietnam war into the domain of tactical and strategic military decisions ordered by the President in his capacity as Commander-in-Chief of the Armed Services. The district court denied DaCosta's motion for summary judgment and for injunctive relief under Rules 56 and 65, F.R.Civ.P. In our view, the matter pressed by DaCosta in this case is a nonjusticiable political question. Accordingly, we remand to the district with instructions that the complaint be dismissed.

I.

Ordinarily, we preface our discussion of the legal issues in a case with a recitation of the underlying facts. Even that threshold task is made difficult in a matter such as this, where the "facts" concerning the methods employed in waging war are difficult to sift, *sui generis* in nature and not of a kind ordinarily involved in framing a question for judicial resolution. Indeed, the difficulty encountered by a domestic judicial tribunal in ascertaining the "facts" of military decisions exercised thousands of miles from the forum, lies at the heart of the determination whether the question is a "political" one, *see* United States v. Sisson, 294 F.Supp. 515 (D. Mass.1968); where there are serious doubts concerning a court's power or fitness to decide the question raised, the political question doctrine may come into play.

The following, however, may be stated with relative certainty. The appellant, Ernest DaCosta, is a United States citizen, and was, at the time he commenced his action on May 11, 1972, a Specialist Fourth Class in the United States Army, stationed in Vietnam as a machine gunner, and assigned to combat duty. His complaint focuses upon military operations undertaken by the United States government pursuant to an executive directive announced to the public by the President in a television and radio address on May 8, 1972. The "record" in this case, to the extent it provides us with a factual context in which to set the dispute presently before us, consists of DaCosta's complaint, the government's answer, supporting affidavits submitted by each side, and the text of two addresses delivered by the President in the spring of 1972. From this skimpy fare, although the events were matters of great public moment, and hence wide-spread coverage, we have attempted to reconstruct the following narrative.

In early April, 1972, apparently at the start of a new "spring offensive," three North Vietnamese divisions crossed the demilitarized zone into South Vietnam. Shortly thereafter, three additional divisions of communist troops crossed the South Vietnamese border at points further south. On April 25, it was announced that an agreement had been reached to resume plenary sessions of the Paris "peace talks," wtih the first meeting of the negotiations scheduled to be held on April 27, 1972. The evening before these negotiating sessions were to resume, President Nixon addressed the Nation over radio and television from his office in the White House. The President's stated purpose was to give "a firsthand report on the military situation in Vietnam, the decisions I have made with regard to the role of the United States in the conflict and the efforts we are making to bring peace at the negotiating table." The President began by noting that American troop strength, numbering 549,000 men in January 1969, had been sharply reduced over a period of three and one-half years to 69,000 men and that casualty rates had been cut by 95%. He noted what he described as the administration's most recent proposals for a negotiated peace—including a cease fire, exchange of prisoners of war, withdrawal of forces and internationally supervised elections in South Vietnam—terms he said he believed were "generous." The President then commented on the presence of more than 120,000 North Vietnamese troops in South Vietnam; that presence, he said, marked "a clear case of naked and unprovoked aggression across an international border." The President reviewed an evaluation of the military situation in Indochina submitted by General Creighton Abrams, commander of American Troops in South Vietnam, which predicted that the enemy offensive would ultimately prove unsuccessful. Based upon his assessment of the military situation, President Nixon anounced that the policy of "Vietnamization" was proceeding according to schedule and that an additional 20,000 American troops would be recalled within two months, lowering the troop ceiling to 49,000 men by July 1. Among other announcements, the President noted that air and naval attacks against military installations in the North would be continued. He stated:

> We are not trying to conquer North Vietnam or any other country in this world. We want no territory. We seek no bases. We have offered the most generous peace terms—peace with honor for both sides—with South Vietnam and North Vietnam each respecting the other's independence.

The President said he could see the day when no more Americans would be involved in Vietnam, and urged the Nation to remain "steadfast" as "we come to the end of this long and difficult struggle."

Less than two weeks later, on May 8, 1972, the President again addressed the Nation in a television and radio broadcast. He began by discussing the "massive invasion" launched by the North Vietnamese in early April, "an invasion," he said "that was made possible by tanks, artillery and other advanced offensive weapons supplied to Hanoi by the Soviet Union and other Communist nations." The President commented on the mounting number of casualties, and noted that America's response had nonetheless been restrained. He pointed out that the United States had resumed negotiations at Paris, and that Dr. Henry Kissinger, in meetings with Soviet leaders for four days beginning on April 20, 1972, had learned of a new Russian interest in bringing the war to a speedy close. The President outlined the content of peace offers made to the North Vietnamese, and stated that "North Vietnam has met each of these offers with insolence and insult. They have flatly and arrogantly refused to negotiate an end to the war and bring peace. Their answer to every peace offer we have made has been to escalate the war." The President then said:

> There are only two issues left for us in this war. First, in the face of a massive invasion do we stand by, jeopardize the lives of 60,000 Americans, and leave the South Vietnamese to a long night of terror? This will not happen. We shall do whatever is required to safeguard American lives and American honor.
>
> Second, in the face of complete intransigence at the conference table do we join with our enemy to install a communist government in South Vietnam. We will not cross the line from generosity to treachery.
>
> We have now a clear, hard choice among three courses of action: Immediate withdrawal of all American forces, continued attempts at negotiation, or decisive military action to end the war.

The President rejected the first alternative—immediate withdrawal—because in his view it would leave world peace in "grave jeopardy." He stated that the second course—negotiations—was preferred, and that America would continue to seek a negotiated settlement; but he claimed that North Vietnam's "arrogant" refusal to negotiate in good faith made this course unavailing. In addition, sole reliance on negotiations, he said, would give the enemy "the time he needs to press his aggression on the battlefield." Therefore, the President concluded that the only way "to stop the killing" was to interdict the supply of weapons flowing into the hands of the North Vietnamese. He went on to say:

> In these circumstances, with 60,000 Americans threatened, any President who failed to act decisively would have betrayed the trust of his country and betrayed the cause of world peace.
>
> I therefore concluded Hanoi must be denied the weapons and supplies it needs to continue the aggression. In full coordination with the Republic of Vietnam I have ordered the following measures which are being implemented as I am speaking to you.

> All entrances to North Vietnamese ports will be mined to prevent access to these ports and North Vietnamese naval operations from these ports. United States forces have been directed to take appropriate measures within the internal and claimed territorial waters of North Vietnam to interdict the delivery of any supplies. Rail and all other communications will be cut off to the maximum extent possible. Air and naval strikes against military targets in North Vietnam will continue.

The President said that all neutral nations had been given notice and that the military operations just announced would cease upon release of American prisoners of war and upon commencement of an internationally supervised cease-fire. He gave notice to the world that the military operations on which the United States was embarking were aimed solely at North Vietnam, and no other nation. He stated:

> Their sole purpose is to protect the lives of 60,000 Americans who would be gravely endangered in the event the Communist offensive continues to roll forward and to prevent the imposition of a Communist government by brutal aggression upon 17 million people.

II.

A preliminary dispute concerning DaCosta's standing to sue has been raised in this case, and since the Government asks us to dismiss this appeal and the underlying action for lack of subject-matter jurisdiction, we believe it appropriate to address that question at the threshold.

Judge Dooling concluded that DaCosta met the necessary standing conditions required by Article III, Section 2 of the Constitution, which provides that the judicial power shall extend only to "cases" and "controversies." The district judge was of the view that DaCosta's standing did not depend on his military status but rather that "plaintiff, any member of the military, *and any citizen,* all alike exposed to mortal risk in war, has standing to challenge the validity of action by which large scale international combat or a new departure in belligerency is initiated." [Emphasis added.] Wholly apart from the difficulty, if not the impossibility, of reaching agreement as to the meaning of phrases such as "large scale international combat" or "new departure is belligerency," we believe that the general rule announced below is without support in law. In Pietsch v. President of the United States, 434 F.2d 861 (2nd Cir. 1970), cert. denied 403 US. 920, . . . (1971), we held that a citizen-taxpayer was without standing to challenge the constitutionality of the Vietnam war and that the necessary nexus announced as the test for standing in Flast v. Cohen, 392 U.S. 83, 88 S.Ct. 1942, . . . (1968), a case relied upon by the district judge in this action, had not been established.[6] The Tenth Circuit, in Velvel v. Nixon, 415 F.2d 236 (10 Cir. 1969), cert. denied, 396 U.S. 1042, 90 S.Ct. 684, . . . (1970), reached a similar result with respect to an attack upon the validity of the war raised by a professor of constitutional law in his capacity as a citizen and taxpayer. Massachusetts v. Laird, 451 F.2d 26 (1st Cir. 1971), also relied upon by the district court, is, in our view, inconclusive. There the Court noted that in addition to the Commonwealth of Massachusetts, "[t]he individual plaintiffs are residents of Massachusetts and members of the United States forces who are either serving in Southeast Asia or are subject to such service." 451 F.2d at 28. After noting its own doubt whether the Commonwealth of Massachusetts had standing to sue, the court declined to decide that question, since it believed in any event, that "some of the plaintiffs are properly before us." *Id.* at 29. Exactly which plaintiffs were "properly before the Court," was not clarified, but the panel did shed some light when it found no merit "in the claim that the individual plaintiffs, particularly those serving in Southeast Asia, lack standing." To the extent the standing issue in Massachusetts v. Laird, *supra,* may have been resolved on the ground that persons ordered to duty in Vietnam may properly challenge the constitutionality of the war effort there, this Court is in full agreement, and has said so in the past. . . . In any event, Massachusetts v. Laird, *supra,* like Orlando v. Laird, *supra,* hardly sustains the citizen-wide view of standing adopted by the district court. Those cases support the proposition that a soldier with orders to report for duty in a war-zone has standing to challenge the constitutionality of the war. But, that question is not now before the Court—as appellant concedes. DaCosta, instead, presses the more limited question whether within the context of a lawful war, the President's order to mine the harbors of North Vietnam was properly authorized. Since we have stated, in *Pietsch,* that a citizen-taxpayer does not have standing to challenge the constitutionality of the

[6] In *Flast,* Chief Justice Warren, speaking for the Court, noted:

> [T]he nexus demanded of federal taxpayers has two aspects to it. First, the taxpayer must establish a logical link between that status and the type of legislative enactment attacked. Thus, a taxpayer will be a proper party to allege the unconstitutionality only of exercises of congressional power under the taxing and spending clause of Art. I, § 8, of the Constitution. It will not be sufficient to allege an incidental expenditure of tax funds in the administration of an essentially regulatory statute. . . . Secondly, the taxpayer must establish a nexus between that status and the precise nature of the constitutional infringement alleged. Under this requirement, the taxpayer must show that the challenged enactment exceeds specific constitutional limitations imposed upon the exercise of the congressional taxing and spending power and not simply that the enactment is generally beyond the powers delegated to Congress by Art. I, § 8. When both nexuses are established, the litigant will have shown a taxpayer's stake in the outcome of the controversy and will be a proper and appropriate party to invoke a federal court's jurisdiction."

392 U.S. at 102–103, 88 S.Ct. at 1954.

Vietnam war, it is difficult for us to understand how such a citizen-taxpayer would have standing to challenge specific military orders issued in furtherance of the war effort. . . .

We are left then without any authority that either directly or inferentially substantiates the district judge's conclusion that any citizen has standing to challenge the legality of military decisions ordered by the President in his capacity as Commander-in-Chief. We are, on the contrary, confronted with a number of cases that have decided that even where the challenge is to the legality of a war, rather than specific tactical military decisions, something other than taxpayer status must be alleged.

Yet, although the district court may have erred in its broad statement of the law on standing, since at the time this action was commenced DaCosta was actually in combat duty in Vietnam, it is argued that the narrower principles of standing announced in our decisions in Berk v. Laird, *supra,* and Orlando v. Laird, *supra,* might be applicable. But since we are of the view that the substantive issue presented to us is a non-justiciable political question, we need not address any further the issue of this plaintiff's standing to present the question. The Supreme Court instructed us recently in Sierra Club v. Morton, 405 U.S. 727, . . . (1972) that what has been traditionally referred to as the question of standing, necessarily involves analysis of "whether a party has a sufficient stake in an *otherwise justiciable controversy* to obtain judicial resolution of that controversy . . . ." 405 U.S. at 731–732, . . . (emphasis supplied). In sum, the standing of a party need not come into question if a court determines that for other reasons the issue raised before the bench is non-justiciable. The district court, it appears, believed that the issue raised by *DaCosta* was a justiciable question. Accordingly, it felt compelled to resolve the question of standing. We, however, are of the view that the issue raised in these proceedings is a political question which the court is without power to hear. Thus, the non-justiciable nature of the dispute not merely obviates, but logically precludes, resolution of the question of plaintiff's standing to sue, and we must decline the government's request that we both address and decide that issue.[10]

[10] Standing is an aspect of justiciability, *see* Flast v. Cohen, *supra,* 392 U.S. at 98. . . . Unlike the political question doctrine, which focuses on the nature of the *issue* presented to the court, questions of standing focus on the nature of the *party* seeking a judgment. The two doctrines are thus, at once, analytically separable and, in certain circumstances, closely linked. Thus, "a party may have standing in a particular case, but the federal court may nevertheless decline to pass on the merits of the case because, for example, it presents a political question." Id. at 100, . . . Such occasion might arise if the dismissal on the political question grounds is discretionary. But if, for example, no judicially discoverable and manageable standards exist for resolution of the question presented to the court, it may very well be that no one has standing to sue. In such a case, the nonjusticiability of the question requires dismissal of the action wholly apart from any consideration of the question of standing.

III.

Scholars have written extensively about the political question doctrine.[11] Those who have explored and analyzed the doctrine divide themselves into a variety of schools of thought on the subject.[12] One student comment has boldly stated that "the [political question] doctrine has defied formulation despite numerous attempts to systematize it." Note, The Supreme Court, 1968 Term, 83 Harv.L.Rev. 7, 63 (1969). We receive our guidance, nevertheless, from the Supreme Court. Although each case clearly must turn on its own facts, certain general principles emerge from the relevant cases, *see, e. g.,* Baker v. Carr, 369 U.S. 186, . . . (1962); Powell v. McCormack, 395 U.S. 486, . . . (1969). Of primary significance is the principle that "[t]he nonjusticiability of a political question is primarily a function of the separation of powers." Baker v. Carr, *supra,* 369 U.S. at 210, . . . Thus, "in 'political question' cases, it is the relationship between the judiciary and the coordinate branches of the Federal Government, and not the federal judiciary's relationship to the States, which gives rise to the 'political question.'" *Ibid.* In Baker v. Carr, *supra,* after reviewing previous cases involving consideration of the political question doctrine the Court synthesized its decisions in the following language:

> It is apparent that several formulations which vary slightly according to the settings in which the questions arise may describe a political question,

11 *See, e. g.,* Tigar, Judicial Power, the "Political Question Doctrine" and Foreign Relations, 17 U.C.L.A.L.Rev. 1135 (1970); Note, The Supreme Court, 1968 Term, 83 Harv.L.Rev. 7, 62–77 (1969). An interesting debate over different interpretations of the doctrine may be traced in Wechsler, Toward Nutral Principles of Constitutional Law, 73 Harv.L.Rev. 1 (1959); Bickel, The Least Dangerous Branch (1962); and Scharpf, Judicial Review and the Political Question: A Functional Analysis, 75 Yale L.J. 517 (1966).

12 Some are of the view that the Court must decide all cases which are properly before it, and that discretion in the exercise of jurisdiction is forbidden by the Constitution. The only circumstance in which a court may decline to hear a matter is when constitutional jurisdictional requisites have not been met, or when the "Constitution has committed to another agency of government the autonomous determination of the issue raised . . . ." Wechsler, *supra* n. 10, at 8. Others view application of the political question doctrine as a matter of judicial discretion, not of constitutional compulsion, and argue that there are matters so controversial and inappropriate for judicial resolution that courts follow a wiser course by abstaining, *see* Bickel, *supra,* n. 10. This approach, as Baker v. Carr, 369 U.S. 186, . . . (1962) and Powell v. McCormack, 395 U.S. 486, . . . (1969) attest, has not been favored by the Supreme Court. Still others, *see* Scharpf, *supra,* note 10, seek to establish categories of cases or concerns which have previously invoked application of the political question doctrine, and indicate that when the objective achieved by a court in refraining from deciding a case is important, the political question doctrine will be a means of achieving that objective.

> although each has one or more elements which identify it as essentially a function of the separation of powers. Prominent on the surface of any case held to involve a political question is found [1] a textually demonstrable constitutional commitment of the issue to a coordinate political department; [2] or a lack of judicially discoverable and manageable standards for resolving it; [3] or the impossibility of deciding without an initial policy determination of a kind clearly for nonjudicial discretion; [4] or the impossibility of a court's undertaking independent resolution without expressing lack of the respect due coordinate branches of government; [5] or an unusual need for unquestioning adherence to a political decision already made; [6] or the potentiality of embarrassment from multifarious pronouncements by various departments on one question. *Id.* at 217, . . .

Clearly, some of the principles enumerated call for discretionary judgments that will not always require a court to refrain from action. Nevertheless, we are at a loss to understand how a court may decide a question when there are no judicially discoverable or manageable standards for resolving it. While in certain instances there may be a dispute among judges whether such standards exist, where all agree that standards are presently unavailable, the court has no alternative but to dismiss for lack of jurisdiction. This conclusion is not reached by the exercise of discretion, but rather of necessity.

We have set forth the legal framework of the issue *in extenso* in order that the problem presented to us may be viewed in the proper perspective. We inquire at the outset, therefore: what is the question we are asked to decide? On the one hand, DaCosta concedes that "this appeal does not —and should not—question the wisdom, propriety or morality of Executive acts of war against North Vietnam. Such questions must be resolved, not by the courts, but by the political branch of government entrusted by the Constitution with the awful responsibility to act upon such matters." Furthermore, we are told that the appeal does not challenge the constitutionality of the war as it was prosecuted prior to the mining of North Vietnam's harbors. Indeed, such a claim would clearly prove fruitless in light of the Court's earlier decision in Orlando v. Laird, *supra,* holding that there has been participation by Congress sufficient to authorize and ratify American military activity in Vietnam, 443 F.2d at 1042–1044 and our decision in the first *DaCosta* case, 448 F.2d 1368 (2nd Cir. 1971), cert. denied 405 U.S. 979, . . . (1972), which held that repeal of the Tonkin Gulf Resolution did not nullify Congressional support for the war. The gravamen of this appeal must be, therefore, that the President's conduct has so altered the course of hostilities in Vietnam as to make the war as it is currently pursued different from the war which we held in *Orlando* and *DaCosta* to have been constitutionally ratified and authorized by the Congress, or that Congressional ratification and authorization has terminated.

Appellant argues that the President's unilateral order to mine the harbors of North Vietnam lacked the "mutual participation" of which we spoke in *Orlando*. We do not understand appellant to argue that every tactical decision made by the President is subject to challenge under the theory advanced in this case. Any such contention would necessarily be unpersuasive in light of the Constitution's specific textual commitment of decision-making responsibility in the area of military operations in a theatre of war to the President, in his capacity as Commander in Chief.[13] What is unique about the President's action presently under consideration, according to DaCosta, is the "unilateral escalation" involved in the decision. With this characterization in hand, the appellant draws on language in DaCosta v. Laird, 448 F.2d 1368 (2nd Cir. 1971), where we said, "[i]f the Executive were now escalating the prolonged struggle instead of decreasing it, additional supporting action by the Legislative Branch over what is presently afforded, might well be required." *Id.* at 1370, and argues that the "escalation" represented by the order to mine North Vietnam's harbors is illegal because unsupported by additional Congressional authorization.

The district court approached this problem by asking whether the actions taken by the President were "an expectable part of the continued waging of the Vietnamese war," assuming the facts as asserted by the President in his May 8th address were true. If so, no further Congressional authorization would have been necessary. Thus the court was of the belief that judicial review of the President's order was proper but that inquiry into whether or not the facts as found by the President were based upon errors of judgment or lacked the support of adequate evidence, was impermissible. In our view, even the district court's limited inquiry was improper. As a general rule, we see no reason why Executive fact-finding must be totally insulated from judicial review. We have always demanded that there be, at the very least, some reasonable or rational basis for a

[13] Article II, § 2, of the Constitution provides, in part:

> The President shall be Commander in Chief of the Army and Navy of the United States, and of the Militia of the several States, when called into the actual Service of the United States . . .

The clause, at least with respect to the President's function as Commander-in-Chief of the Army and Navy, seemed self-explanatory to the Framers and required little discussion at the Convention. What little debate there was, centered on the question whether the President would have the authority to take personal command of troops in the field, a question that was answered in the affirmative. *See,* Luther Martin, The Genuine Information, Delivered to the Legislature of the State of Maryland, Relative to the Proceedings of the General Convention, Held at Philadelphia, in 1787 (1787), printed in 3 Farrand, The Records of the Federal Convention of 1787 at 172, 217–18. ("Objections were made to that part of this article, by which the President is appointed Commander-in-Chief of the army and navy of the United States and the militia of the several states, and it was wished to be so far restrained, that he should not command in person; but this could not be obtained.") *See also,* 1 Farrand, *supra,* at 244.

finding of fact, whether made by an administrative agency, the Congress, or the Executive.[14] There are occasions, however, as the district court sensed, when judicial review of the Executive fact-finding process on even this limited basis is inappropriate. The proper response in such situations is not to "assume" the truth of the facts, but candidly to recognize that the court is incapable of assessing the facts and that the issue presented is therefore non-justiciable. Such a course has the advantage of avoiding the appearance that courts act as rubber-stamps for policies developed by a coordinate branch of government which fall without the realm of judicial consideration.

The difficulty we face in attempting to decide this case is compounded by a lack of discoverable and manageable judicial standards. Judge Dooling believed that the case could be resolved by simply inquiring whether the actions taken by the President were a foreseeable part of the continued prosecution of the war. That test, it seems to us, is superficially appealing but overly simplistic. Judges, deficient in military knowledge, lacking vital information upon which to assess the nature of battlefield decisions, and sitting thousands of miles from the field of action, cannot reasonably or appropriately determine whether a specific military operation constitutes an "escalation" of the war or is merely a new tactical approach within a continuing strategic plan. What if, for example, the war "de-escalates" so that it is waged as it was prior to the mining of North Vietnam's harbors, and then "escalates" again? Are the courts required to oversee the conduct of the war on a daily basis, away from the scene of action? In this instance, it was the President's view that the mining of North Vietnam's harbors was necessary to preserve the lives of American soldiers in South Vietnam and to bring the war to a close. History will tell whether or not that assessment was correct, but without the benefit of such extended hindsight we are powerless to know.

When we said in DaCosta v. Laird, *supra,* that "[i]f the Executive were now escalating the prolonged struggle instead of decreasing it, additional supporting action by the Legislative Branch over what is presently afforded, might well be required," we implied, of course, that litigants raising such a claim had a responsibility to present to the court a manageable standard which would allow for proper judicial resolution of the

[14] Even when Congressional findings concerning as serious a matter as the scope of Communist Party activities in America came before the Court in Communist Party v. Control Board, 367 U.S. 1 . . . (1961)—after "extensive investigation by Committees of Congress over more than a decade and a half," *Id.* at 94 . . . —Mr. Justice Frankfurter's majority opinion indicated that these findings, while entitled to great respect, were not entirely immune from review. In that case, the findings were accepted because "[w]e certainly cannot dismiss them as unfounded or irrational imaginings." *Id.* at 95. . . . There, of course, the record of public hearings and Congressional proceedings from which the Congress had drawn in making specific legislative findings of fact were matters of public record. Nothing of a comparable nature, in the way of fact-finding proceedings, is presented in the instant case.

issue. No such standards have been forthcoming from the appellant in this case. In so stating, however, we specifically do not pass on the point urged by appellant whether a radical change in the character of war operations—as by an intentional policy of indiscriminate bombing of civilians without any military objective—might be sufficiently measurable judicially to warrant a court's consideration, i.e., might contain a standard which we seek in this record and do not find. Appellant does suggest that a blockade such as the one imposed by the President is an "unambiguous" act of war under the canons of international law. We fail to understand what this argument proves. None would deny that the United States, like its North Vietnamese enemy, has engaged in acts of war in Indochina. Yet it is the thrust of this Court's decisions in *Orlando* and *DaCosta I*, that the war in Vietnam is a constitutional war. Thus appellant's argument that a blockade is an act of war takes us no further than to state the obvious fact that the Nation is at war: it says nothing of any moment about escalation, or whether one course of conduct is "expectable" within the framework of the war as previously prosecuted.

Appellant invokes the so-called "Mansfield Amendment," P.L. 92–156, 85 Stat. 423, Section 601(a) which provides:

> Sec. 601. (a) It is hereby declared to be the policy of the United States to terminate at the earliest practicable date all military operations of the United States in Indochina, and to provide for the prompt and orderly withdrawal of all United States military forces at a date certain, subject to the release of all American prisoners of war held by the Government of North Vietnam and forces allied with such Government and an accounting for all Americans missing in action who have been held by or known to such Government or such forces. The Congress hereby urges and requests the President to implement the above-expressed policy by initiating immediately the following actions:
>
> 1. Establishing a final date for withdrawal from Indochina of all military forces of the United States contingent upon the release of all American prisoners of war held by the Government of North Vietnam and forces allied with such Government and an accounting for all Americans missing in action who have been held by or known to such Government or such forces.
> 2. Negotiate with the Government of North Vietnam for an immediate cease-fire by all parties to the hostilities in Indochina.
> 3. Negotiate with the Government of North Vietnam for an agreement which would provide for a series of phased and rapid withdrawals of United States military forces from Indochina in exchange for a corresponding series of phased releases of American prisoners of war, and for the release of any remaining American prisoners of war concurrently with the withdrawal of all remaining military forces of the United States by not later than the date established by the President pursuant to paragraph

(1) hereof or by such earlier date as may be agreed upon by the negotiating parties.

Judge Dooling held that the first sentence of Sec. 601 was binding on the President, but that the second sentence and sections (1), (2) and (3) were merely precatory. Although we neither address nor decide the question, we note that weighty constitutional considerations which support the President in his duties as Commander-in-Chief preclude too hasty an adoption of the view taken by the district court. Furthermore, it is arguable whether the legislative history of the Mansfield Amendment supports the position of the district judge. In any event, even assuming, *arguendo,* that the first sentence of Sec. 601 is binding national policy, we see nothing in the language of the amendment which in any way prohibits the President's action challenged here. We have no way of knowing whether the military operations in question further or hinder the goals expressed in the Mansfield Amendment, or whether they have any bearing on those goals at all.

Thus it is our judgment that this Court is without power to resolve the issue narrowly presented in this case. Having previously determined, in accordance with our duty, that the Vietnamese war has been constitutionally authorized by the mutual participation of Congress and the President, we must recognize that those two coordinate branches of government—the Executive by military action and the Congress, by not cutting off the appropriations that are the wherewithal for such action—have taken a position that is not within our power, even if it were our wish, to alter by judicial decree.

Remanded with instructions that the complaint be dismissed. . . .